SLAVERY, COLONIALISM AND ECONOMIC
GROWTH IN DAHOMEY,
1640 – 1960

AFRICAN STUDIES SERIES   30

The African Studies Series is a collection of monographs and general
studies that reflect the interdisciplinary interests of the African Studies
Centre at Cambridge. Volumes to date have combined historical, anthropological, economic, political and other perspectives. Each contribution
has assumed that such broad approaches can contribute much to our
understanding of Africa, and that this may in turn be of advantage to
specific disciplines.

AFRICAN STUDIES SERIES

SLAVERY, COLONIALISM AND ECONOMIC GROWTH IN DAHOMEY, 1640–1960

PATRICK MANNING

CAMBRIDGE UNIVERSITY PRESS

CAMBRIDGE
LONDON   NEW YORK   NEW ROCHELLE
MELBOURNE   SYDNEY

Published by the Press Syndicate of the University of Cambridge
The Pitt Building, Trumpington Street, Cambridge CB2 1RP
32 East 57th Street, New York, NY 10022, USA
296 Beaconsfield Parade, Middle Park, Melbourne 3206, Australia

© Cambridge University Press 1982

First published 1982

Printed in the United States of America

Library of Congress catalogue card number: 81–7684

British Library Cataloguing in Publication Data

Manning, Patrick
Slavery, colonialism and economic growth in
Dahomey, 1640–1960 – (African studies series; 30).
1. Dahomey – History
I. Title II. Series
966′.83 DT541

ISBN 0 521 23544 8

à Damien d'Almeida, Guillaume da Silva
et Clément da Cruz, qui ont travaillé
pour garder le passé du Dahomey, et qui
ont ainsi consacré leurs vies à
l'avenir du Bénin

Contents

Maps

viii

Tables

List of Tables

Figures

List of Figures

Preface

This is a study of long-term and short-term economic change in a West African region, based on analysis of foreign trade statistics, colonial finances, and descriptions of the domestic economy. Of the many economic conflicts considered in this survey, two stand out: the export of roughly two million slaves in the years 1640–1865, which depopulated the region for part of that time, and the export of tax revenues by the French government in the years 1905–60, averaging over twenty percent of the value of exports each year. Nevertheless, despite such negative external influences, the economy grew over this three-century period. The apparent contradiction between negative external influences and positive domestic growth is resolved through the elucidation of a mechanism of accumulation: based on a detailed analysis, for the years 1890–1914, of short-run economic dynamics and the economic significance of social, political and legal disputes, I attribute the distillation of long-run growth out of short-run activities to specific causes, of which population growth and producer investments were most fundamental. The analytical framework of the mechanism of accumulation and the modes of production through which it operated provided the structure for my analysis of long-run economic change.

The study is centered on Dahomey, as I will call the southern portion of the modern People's Republic of Bénin, a rectangle of one hundred kilometers from east to west and two hundred kilometers from north to south, which includes the eastern Aja–Ewe peoples and the most westerly Yoruba peoples. Dahomey, thus defined, occupies a central position in the Bight of Benin, and encompasses the bulk of modern Bénin's population and economic activity. The kingdom of Danhomè, which dominated this area in the eighteenth and nineteenth centuries, accounted for forty percent of the region's population and twenty percent of its area: Danhomè and the Fon people are thus set in the context of Dahomey. Aspects of the study extend beyond Dahomey to a wider area: the analysis of slave exports covers the whole Bight of Benin, extending along the coast from Keta in

Togo to Lagos in Nigeria and inland to include the Oyo empire; and several statistical series for the twentieth century refer to the whole of colonial Dahomey rather than to just its southern portion.

During the past three centuries' contact with the world economy, what is now Bénin became a poor country. The level of material economic welfare for the population has improved in that time, but in relative terms the area has fallen behind much of the world, and has become relatively stagnant and dependent on outside economic forces. The solution to the economic problems of a small country like Bénin cannot lie wholly within its boundaries. At the same time, the consistency and stability of the domestic economy during three such tumultuous centuries demonstrates that domestic realities cannot be ignored in planning for the future. This long history of interaction between the local and world economies, with its strong elements of both continuity and change, indicates the necessity of viewing this West African economy in a wider context. It also indicates that no picture of the world economy is complete without including Africa: the significance of two million slave exports from the Bight of Benin is a clear case in point. It is fortunate, therefore, that steps are now being taken to integrate the literature on African economic history with the literature on economic history of other regions, particularly Europe and the Americas.

Almost until the 1970s, the main authorities on West African economic history were studies from the colonial viewpoint such as those by McPhee and Hancock. The viewpoint represented by such studies indicated that precolonial economic history consisted of trade along the littoral, while colonial economic history was oriented around government policy on export commodities. The postwar atmosphere of rising African nationalism, however, helped to stimulate new studies of history, geography, agricultural economics, economic development, and economic anthropology, out of which the economic history of West Africa emerged as a distinct field of study by the late 1960s.

Two major works have had particular influence in broadening the outlook of West African economic history and in tying it to the economic history of other regions. Philip D. Curtin's *The Atlantic Slave Trade: a Census* laid out the quantitative dimensions of the slave trade, and thus provided the basis for comparison of regions and time periods in Africa. Curtin's work tied into the developing quantitative work on American slavery, and has had a catalytic effect in getting American historians of slavery to set their studies in the context of the West Indies, Brazil and, ultimately, Africa. Similarly, the response to Curtin's work has brought the more rigorous and relevant questions of New World studies of slavery to the attention of students of Africa. A. G. Hopkins's *An Economic History of West Africa*, the first comprehensive economic history of the region, interprets West Africa since AD 1000 through a single framework – the expansion of the market. Hopkins's thorough and imaginative summary of findings and theses has facilitated comparisons within West Africa, and enables West Africa to be conveniently related to the rest of the world economy, particularly for the nineteenth and twentieth centuries. A third corpus of analysis, the works of Samir Amin, is serving to concentrate wide attention on problems of twentieth-century economic change in West Africa. In a sense Amin is developing, in an African context, a rationale for the arguments of the South in the current North–South discussions on international trade.

Dahomey is the subject of substantial documentation for the period beginning in the seventeenth century. With the rise of the Fon kingdom, narratives tended to center on Ouidah and Abomey: the most influential narrative has been that of Dalzel, which pictured Danhomè as a rapacious state based on slave trade. The narratives touch on every decade from the 1660s to 1800 and, after lacunae up to 1840, become even more numerous for the nineteenth century. The period of French conquest brought a great outpouring of narratives, novels on the conquest, and descriptions of the new colony and its resources. Outstanding among the latter are the works of Foà, who wrote a broad description of Dahomey in the 1890s, Savariau, who wrote a thorough study of agriculture, and Le Herissé, who wrote an historical and anthropological study of the Fon kingdom. In 1938 M. J. Herskovits published a two-volume anthropological study of the Fon kingdom. This work fit into his larger project of documenting the continuity in the diaspora from Africa to the New World. No major studies relating to economic history appeared until after 1960. Nonetheless, many small articles, by French and Dahomean writers, provide valuable documentation.

In the 1960s works appeared relating to economic history in the eighteenth, nineteenth and twentieth centuries, though they were unrelated to each other. Karl Polanyi's study of the eighteenth-century slave trade attracted much attention because of the author's reputation as an innovative scholar in economic anthropology. I. A. Akinjogbin's study covering the same time period is far more soundly based on documents, though it has the normal weaknesses of trade-and-politics history. Catherine Coquery-Vidrovitch published essays on the nineteenth-century crisis of the Fon regime. C. W. Newbury did a remarkably wide-ranging review of politics and trade in the Bight of Benin, 1600–1914, including a comparison of colonial Togo, Dahomey and Nigeria. Claude Tardits published several sociological studies of the Porto-Novo area. More recently, work has broadened. Pierre Verger capped his years of work with a monumental study of ties between the Bight of Benin and Bahia in

Brazil. Maurice Glélé has written on the political history of Dahomey over three centuries. David Ross's important thesis on nineteenth-century Dahomey awaits publication. And many American, French and Béninois theses are now being completed.

Government records are more uneven. Data on the slave trade were pieced together from a wide range of usually fragmentary sources. Estimates of nineteenth-century commerce are scattered among consular reports, though records in Lagos provide more systematic help beginning in 1863. French commercial statistics on Dahomey, while relatively well ordered for the years 1897–1914, are in general abysmal: nine separate series of publications are required to collect all published commercial statistics for the years 1887–1960, and appalling lacunae remain even after an immense labor of compilation, interpolation, and estimating missing data. Colonial budgets and financial reports are far more systematic and more readily available. Nevertheless, no single library or archive has a complete set for Afrique Occidentale Française (AOF) or any of its territories, and the documents themselves include major reorganizations of categories every few years, performed in order to employ bureaucrats and confuse auditors, or perhaps in order to bedevil future researchers. The archival holdings of the former AOF archives in Senegal are ample and well classified. The archives of Bénin are ample but are only partially classified, and suffered the misfortune of being moved twice in the 1960s. Archives in Nigeria, France, Britain, Bahia and elsewhere are useful for the nineteenth century and before, and continue to yield evidence on Dahomey to scholars who investigate them.

In the course of my study of this economy, I have come to have steadily greater regard for the people of Bénin and their response to their economic problems. A small country, now as in the past, its inhabitants have seen themselves as part of a larger world, and seem often to have concluded that they could change their own conditions only by changing the wider world. This is not to romanticize the Béninois, for they have many conflicts among themselves and have too often been willing to destroy each other. But they are always thinking, always active. Their history of participation in world affairs goes back to the embassies sent to Europe by the kings of Ardra and Danhomè, the embassies sent to Brazil by the kings of Danhomè, and the early contributions to African nationalism by Louis Hunkanrin and Marc Tovalou Houénou. Ironically, the Dahomeans were passive and ineffectual in the key era of the re-establishment of independence, but such passivity came about only as the product of an extreme combination of economic and political deprivation. This small country and its people are down, but should not be counted out.

I wish to acknowledge the support of the Foreign Area Fellowship

xvi

Program for support of my research in France and Dahomey in 1966 and 1967, and the support of the Ford Foundation for research in Senegal and Dahomey in 1973 and for participation in the African Economic History Workshop in Madison in 1974. I was the beneficiary of kind and efficient service from the staffs of several libraries: the IRAD library in Porto-Novo, the Bibliothèque Nationale, the Archives nationales, Section Outre-mer and the Musée de l'Homme in Paris, the British Museum and, in the United States, the Library of Congress, the Hoover Institution, the University of Wisconsin, the University of Chicago, the College of San Mateo, Stanford University and the University of California at Berkeley. Two dedicated archivists gained my deepest gratitude and highest respect: Damien d'Almeida of the Archives nationales du Bénin, and Jean-François Maurel, then of the Archives nationales du Sénégal; I wish also to thank the staffs of the Archives nationales, Section Outre-mer in Paris, the Public Record Office in London (now Kew), and the Nigerian National Archives, with thanks to Dr Obaro Ikimẹ for his introduction there. The following authors have kindly given permission to use copyrighted material: Phyllis Deane and W. A. Cole, John Coatsworth, Werner Peukert, Richard Bean and E. Phillip LeVeen.

My greatest scholarly debt is to Philip D. Curtin, who has provided a fine example, solid training, and invaluable personal support. Jeffrey Williamson has provided essential support and valuable criticism of portions of the manuscript. Marjorie Murphy has graced the work with her inexhaustible store of ideas, and has inspired and cajoled the author into completing it. A. G. Hopkins has provided encouragement, valuable insights, and a demanding standard of scholarship. Hélène d'Almeida, whose important work on the early colonial Dahomean economy was being completed at the same time as this study, has generously pointed out statistical publications which had escaped my notice. In addition, I have benefitted from the assistance and commentary of Elizabeth Wetton of Cambridge University Press, and of Myron Echenberg, Allen Howard, Margaret Jean Hay, Guillaume da Silva, Clément da Cruz, Ivan Livingstone, Catherine Coquery-Vidrovitch, Claude Tardits, Tony Judt, Sylvain Anignikin, Joseph Adrien Djivo, Richard Bean, James Spiegler, Marvin Miracle, Jan Vansina, Jan Hogendorn, Henry Gemery, Joseph La Torre, Karen Fung, Morton Rothstein and Richard Sutch.

Paris, June 1980

Note: the quotations from French original sources have been translated by the author.

1

Slavery, colonialism and economic growth, 1640–1960

The Bight of Benin came to the attention of the wider world in the late seventeenth century as it became the leading supplier of slaves for the plantations of the New World.[1] The accumulation of wealth and power in the hands of rulers and merchants proceeded in the eighteenth century with the consolidation of control over the coast by the kingdom of Danhomè, and with the establishment of the broader hegemony over much of the Bight of Benin by the empire of Oyo. Throughout the nineteenth century the impression of wealth and power in the Bight of Benin continued as Danhomè kept European powers at bay. Even at the beginning of the twentieth century, colonial Dahomey was wealthier in commerce and tax revenue than all of France's West African colonies but Senegal. Yet the People's Republic of Bénin is now listed among the world's poorest nations, with a 1974 per capita income of $120.[2]

Historians of Dahomey have tended to see a long-term decline in the region's wealth and power, certainly in relative terms, and perhaps in absolute terms.[3] In contrast, however, the quantitative evidence tends to contradict the thesis of long-term decline and to substitute for it a thesis of long-term growth: the economy has grown at a modest rate, with periodic interruptions, over the course of its modern history. Data presenting more than three centuries of trans-Atlantic commerce are summarized, in Figure 1.1, through three related time series. These are (I) annual average value of exports by decade in current pounds sterling, (II) real export revenue or import purchasing power in 1913 pounds, and (III) per capita import purchasing power in 1913 pounds.[4] The region to which these figures refer is the southern portion of the modern People's Republic of Bénin, which encompasses the bulk of modern Bénin's population and economic activity, and which lies centrally located in the Bight of Benin as a whole. I shall use the term Dahomey to refer to this geographic region: while place names and political structures have changed repeatedly over the past three centuries, the region itself has retained its identity.

1

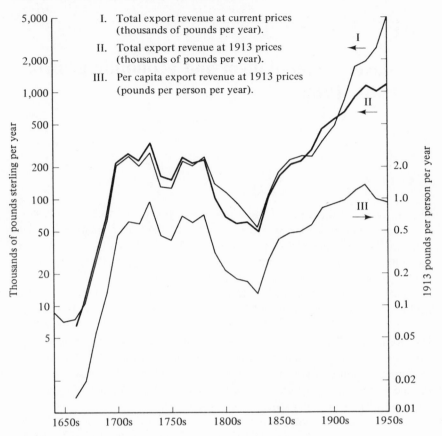

Figure 1.1 Export revenue from Dahomey, 1640–1960.
Source: Table A1.1.

By any measure, Dahomey has been deeply involved in trans-Atlantic trade throughout this period, and its level of participation has grown: from the 1670s through the 1950s, the average annual rate of growth in important purchasing power was 0.9%, or 0.7% per year on a per capita basis.[5] The nineteenth century, for example, brought no sudden impact of Europeans nor of the world market, but only the modification of a long-standing relationship.[6] Average real export revenue (or import purchasing power) in the nineteenth century fell by 10% from that of the eighteenth century in aggregate terms, and declined by 25% in per capita terms. But while export revenue in the eighteenth century fluctuated around a declining trend, in the nineteenth century it grew steadily. In the twentieth century, average real export revenue has been over four times that of the

2

Table 1.1. *Average annual growth rates (percent) for total exports, at constant (1913) prices*

	Dahomey	Great Britain	USA
A. Short term			
1690s–1730s	4.2	1.5	
1730s–1760s	− 1.0	1.3	
1760s–1790s	− 2.9	0.8	
1790s–1830s	− 1.9	2.8	3.1
1830s–1870s	3.8	4.9	3.6
1870s–1900s	3.0	2.3	4.7
1900s–1930s	2.4	0.4	1.1
1930s–1950s	0.1	1.6	3.4
B. Long term			
1700s–1950s	0.7	2.5	
1790s–1950s	2.1	3.0	3.4

Table 1.2. *Per capita export revenue, in 1913 pounds*

	Dahomey	Great Britain	USA
1700s	0.47	0.69	
1730s	0.95	1.03	
1760s	0.70	1.37	
1790s	0.31	1.42	0.61
1830s	0.13	2.53	0.64
1870s	0.49	11.1	0.86
1900s	0.90	15.7	1.88
1930s	1.36	14.5	1.61
1950s	0.93	18.2	2.60

Sources for Tables 1.1 and 1.2: Appendix 1; Deane and Cole, *British Economic Growth*, 6, 8, 29, 319–21; United States Bureau of the Census, *Historical Statistics*, 8, 537–8. Details of calculations available on request from the author.

nineteenth century, or more than twice that of the nineteenth century in per capita terms. The rate of growth has been slower in the twentieth century than in the late nineteenth century, and per capita growth has recently been negative.

These estimates of growth in external trade are compared in Tables 1.1 and 1.2 with equivalent estimates for Great Britain and the United States. The relatively high level of per capita exports from Dahomey in the eighteenth century may come as something of a surprise. This results

3

partly from my restricting the population considered to that within Dahomey as I have defined it, while a minority of slaves exported were taken from beyond that region. But any variant of this calculation throws into relief the active participation of Dahomey in world commerce, especially through slave exports.

These same estimates of import purchasing power may be treated as a proxy for the total domestic product of Dahomey; on this assumption, overall economic growth for Dahomey may be compared with growth rates for other economies. This step requires the rather stringent assumption of a long-run correlation between the value of exports and the value of total output. The first defense of this approach is that trans-Atlantic commerce provides the only systematic data we will ever have on this economy before 1890. In addition, the assumption has intuitive plausibility in this case, though only for the long run. For periods of less than four or five decades, the correlation between growth in domestic product and foreign trade can be extremely weak, since increased exports could stem from a mere transferral of effort from the domestic economy. In the extreme case, the astonishing quantity of slave exports from 1690 through 1740 increased export revenue but decreased domestic product because of depopulation. Yet in the longer run the correlation shows up again, as the smaller population led to a reduction of slave exports. Over the last three centuries, exports have been a substantial portion of total output (usually ranging from 10% to 20%, judging from data since 1950), and exports have generally been more than a transfer of effort from the domestic economy. As long as we restrict consideration to the period after Dahomey began heavy participation in trans-Atlantic commerce–after 1670–export revenue can be taken as a proxy for domestic product which, if not precise, is quite instructive.[7] Tables 1.3 and 1.4 show comparisons of this proxy for domestic product with growth rates and per capita levels of domestic product for Great Britain, the United States, Brazil and Mexico.

Table 1.3. *Comparative growth rates (percent) of real national income (with growth of import purchasing power for Dahomey)*

	Mexico	Brazil	Great Britain	USA	Dahomey
1800s–1840s	−0.1	2.1	2.4	4.1	1.1
1840s–1860s	−0.4	2.8	2.0	4.6	3.4
1860s–1890s	3.0	2.1	3.4	4.4	2.7
1890s–1910s	3.7	1.8	1.8	4.2	1.7
1910s–1930s			1.0	2.7	2.8
1930s–1950s			2.0	3.4	0.1

Table 1.4. *Per capita domestic product, in 1913 pounds (with Dahomey per capita export revenue, in 1913 pounds, multiplied by 7)*

	Mexico	Brazil	Great Britain	USA	Dahomey
1800s	4.7	4.0	13	11	1.5
1840s	3.6	4.6	21	18	1.9
1860s	3.2	5.0	24	23	3.4
1870s	4.0	5.4	32	28	3.4
1890s	5.9	5.7	48	47	5.8
1910s	8.5	6.1	52	71	6.7
1930s			60	84	9.5
1950s			81	154	6.5

Note: The final column in Table 1.4 is calculated on the assumption that domestic product averages seven times the level of exports for Dahomey.
Sources for Tables 1.3 and 1.4: Appendix 1; Coatsworth, 'Obstacles to Economic Growth,' 82; Deane and Cole, *British Economic Growth*, 6, 8, 284; US Bureau of Census, *Historical Statistics*, 8, 139.

The rate of growth for Dahomey in the nineteenth century seems not to have been greatly different from those of Mexico or Brazil, nor greatly inferior to that of Great Britain; the level of per capita income for Dahomey may have been roughly on a par with those of Mexico and Brazil. The extreme relative poverty of Dahomey is thus a phenomenon of the twentieth century.

The resolution of the contradiction between theses of growth and decline is, in short, that the economy suffered relative decline when compared with economies outside Africa or with other African regions, yet it experienced absolute growth over the long run. This growth took place because of both domestic and trans-Atlantic factors which were sufficient to overcome the substantial negative influences of slave exports (from 1670 to 1860) and French fiscal policy (from 1900 to 1960).

The fundamental issue under study in the twelve chapters of this book is the elucidation of a dialectic between the forces of growth and the forces of decline. Chapter 1 summarizes the argument. Chapter 2 presents the analysis of long-run economic change up to the beginning of colonial rule in 1890. Chapter 3, in contrast, is cross-sectional: the economic structure revealed there for the 1880s may, to a degree, be projected backwards in time; it also provides a base line against which to measure the analysis of succeeding chapters. Chapters 4 through 8 concentrate on the years 1890–1914 and treat, in succession, production, demand, exchange, the state, and socio-political conflicts. These 25 comprehensively documented years – strategically located at the juncture of the precolonial and colonial eras – permit clarification of the structure and short-run dynamics of the economy, and at the same time throw light on its long-run developments. Chapter 9 draws together the preceding analyses of short-run and long-run change to propose a mechanism of accumulation – a thesis explaining how the forces of domestic growth overcame external constraints – and an historical interpretation posed in terms of counterfactual alternatives. Chapters 10 and 11 extend the analysis of economic changes from 1915 to 1960. Chapter 12, after a brief recapitulation, links developments of the early national period to those of the years before 1960.

Foreign trade provides the most systematic data on Dahomey available to the economic historian, but this study gives primary emphasis to the domestic economy rather than to foreign trade: I have treated foreign trade as a 'window' on the domestic economy, using patterns of foreign trade to imply the structure and changes of the domestic economy. This method is analogous to the work of the archaeologist who, working from the analysis of durable remains of past civilization, seeks to reconstruct an image of the whole society. Further, and again as with the archaeologist, the integration of all other available source material with the basic source is indispensable to the success of the analysis: I have relied on descriptions of the domestic economy, political histories drawn from oral and written sources, data on money and government finance, and anthropological studies.

The method of analysis draws on both Marxian and Neoclassical traditions of economic history. While readers trained in one or the other tradition may experience some discomfort in perusing a work which utilizes both, they may also find advantages in a comprehensive approach which analyzes growth, in Neoclassical terms, and transformation, in Marxian terms. The Neoclassical framework, abstracting from social data, is useful in short-run analysis of economic structure and dynamics, and in analysis of long-run growth; the Marxian framework, by including social data in an analysis couched in terms of modes of production, is appropriate for analysis of long-run economic transformation, and for study of short-run interactions of social, political and economic factors. While the Neoclassical approach is, ultimately, subordinated to the Marxian perspective, both have been important in analyzing such aspects of Dahomey's economic history as its periodization.

Establishing a periodization is important in African economic history, if only to emphasize that the conventional periods of political history, however important in their own right, do not necessarily mark significant economic transitions. The criteria for periodization include not only governments, policies and statesmen, but also modes of production,

6

international economic ties, and levels of economic activity. The periods I
have identified include the 'mythic era,' to 1660; the 'era of slave exports,'
1640–1860; the 'era of agricultural exports,' 1840–1960; and the 'capitalist
era,' since 1930.[8] As a summary of the results to be developed in detail in
succeeding chapters, the remainder of the present chapter is devoted to a
chronological review, within this periodization, of the major themes in the
economic history of Dahomey.

THE MYTHIC ERA, TO 1660

Although neither written documents nor oral traditions have yet provided
detailed evidence on this period, the outlines of Dahomey's early economic
conditions are visible.[9] By the fifteenth century, Dahomey had a relatively
dense population and a monetized economy based on the cultivation of
African yams, on fishing and on manufactures; a network of markets tied
the region together under the supervision of small states and enabled it to
participate in commerce with neighboring regions. Socio-economic
changes from the fifteenth to the mid-seventeenth century took place
through the evolution of this system, rather than through migration or
other abrupt changes. States were prepared to enter into commercial
relations with the earliest Europeans to arrive; although the volume of
trans-Atlantic commerce was small, it is conceivable that exports of
agricultural produce and manufactures were greater than is now known.
Dahomey's Atlantic commerce was oriented toward the Gold Coast
and perhaps also toward the kingdom of Benin: Ardra cloth was exported,
while cowries were eagerly purchased to supplement the money supply. The
agricultural economy shifted in this period to make maize the dominant
crop, ahead of yams, and also saw the adoption of other American and
Asian crops. The new crops diversified Dahomey's economy, and may also
have led to significant population growth.

Stated in terms of modes of production, the economy of the Bight of
Benin was dominated in this early period – as, indeed, for all eras since – by
the commodity exchange mode of production.[10] In this mode of production or sector of the economy, individuals and family units produced
goods for sale, sold them in the local market, and purchased a large portion
of the goods they consumed, including food, manufactures, raw materials
and luxuries. The familial mode of production, in which families produced
goods for their own consumption, probably accounted for a greater
volume of goods than that passing through the domestic market.[11]
Nevertheless the commodity exchange sector was then and has since
remained the leading sector, providing the adjustment mechanism in which
the gamut of local, West African and eventually trans-Atlantic influences

7

interacted to determine prices and the allocation of resources. The continuous increase in the circulation of money reflects the historic expansion of this sector.

The commodity exchange mode of production created one social class, and sometimes two. Where land and tools were all owned by producers, the producers formed a single class. Conflicts among members of this class naturally took place, as over access to productive resources such as land, and as with conflicts between buyers and sellers. In cases where some individuals or families owned land while others worked it, two social classes, landlord and tenant, emerged. In such cases, class conflict centered around the portion of the tenant's produce which was taken by the landlord. Surplus over immediate needs in the familial sector could only be held from year to year, or was in part collected as tribute by states. Surplus in the commodity exchange sector, however, was marketed locally or in other regions, and thus gave support to the development of merchants, states and landowners, who in turn appropriated a portion of this surplus.

Long-distance caravans and shipping throughout West Africa and beyond composed the mercantile system: this articulative structure linked the local economies with each other and with economies outside the region. Merchants who performed this function profited from it, which made them both allies and antagonists of the producers and purchasers. In part, those who owned the merchandise and those who carried it were identical, but more generally the owners formed one social class specialized to long-distance trade, with a second class being formed of porters, be they wage-earners, slaves, or junior members of a lineage.

Slavery, while not unknown in the Bight of Benin, was not yet the basis of a separate mode of production: slaves were a part of the familial, commodity exchange or mercantile sectors.

The state, in its economic functions, existed primarily to provide order in the commodity exchange sector, by resolving disputes over land and local exchange. But the state also provided important regulatory and protective functions to the mercantile sector. In large or powerful states – Ardra, the Hueda kingdom, Oyo and perhaps others – taxation of agricultural produce, local and long-distance trade permitted the development of a strong aristocracy, wealthy in land, commerce and slaves. Other states, even including Tado, the ancestral kingdom of many of the Aja states, continued to operate at a minimal level: kings were mediators among lineages and merchants, rather than members and servants of a ruling class. The distinction between large states and small states – with the small states governing half or more of the region's population – was to remain a constant factor in Dahomey's economic history.

This early regional economy – in which coexisted two modes of pro-

8

duction, links to other economies and a variety of state structures – may be characterized as a social formation dominated by the commodity exchange mode of production.[12] Even before the major impact of the world market, Dahomey had grown beyond mere subsistence and self-sufficiency. It seems likely that this regional economy grew at a modest pace from the fifteenth to the seventeenth centuries, as a result of new crops, population growth, producer investments in clearing fields, waterways and roads, and perhaps as a result of an expanded money supply and new West African market opportunities.

These were the economic conditions into which the slave trade intruded.

THE ERA OF SLAVE EXPORTS, 1640–1860

In the course of two centuries roughly two million slaves were exported from the Bight of Benin, comprising one fifth of the total Atlantic slave trade. The level of slave exports was remarkably steady – from 7,000 to 15,000 annually, after the 1670s – and most of the slaves came from Dahomey, and hence from within two hundred kilometers of the coast.[13] Through the export of slaves, the Bight of Benin participated in what may be termed the world mercantile economy: in exports, it was linked to the plantation economies of the New World, which in turn were linked to the growing European market from agricultural produce. In imports, the Bight of Benin received tobacco from Brazil and rum from the plantations of Brazil and the Caribbean. But it also received cotton cloth from India, cowries from the Maldives, and manufactures from Europe.

The effective New World demand for slaves began with the expansion of Brazilian plantations in the 1630s. Portuguese and Dutch slave merchants were followed by English and French merchants in the 1650s. The years 1640–70 must therefore be seen as years of decision for Dahomey, for it was at this time that the institutions from exporting slaves were developed. The West African price of slaves declined in this period, while the quantity exported grew sharply beginning in the 1670s, suggesting that a system was developed in those years which could provide a large number of slaves at low cost to slave exporters. In other terms, the slave-catching system was developed in the years 1640–70: this set of institutions corresponded to a mode of reproduction, for it served to reproduce the labor force of New World plantations and later of African plantations, and it further served to expand the families of African slave owners. The institutions, in general, included warfare, raiding, kidnapping, judicial procedures, tribute, and sale of persons by destitute families; these structures further reinforced a willingness to tolerate or justify the enslavement of one's enemies or even one's own.

9

State power played a crucial role in the collection and delivery of slaves: Danhomè and some other states became quite devoted to the slave-catching sector. The mercantile sector throughout the region became heavily, if not dominantly, oriented toward collaboration with slave-catching activities. While sale of slaves was governed by the state, and while many slaves were exported by the state, the mercantile sector exported the majority of the slaves on private account. The commodity exchange sector also participated in the slave trade, by selling slaves and by buying slaves for integration into families.

The beginnings of a slave-labor mode of production took form in the eighteenth century, as slaves were used in growing numbers to support royal retinues. This did not spread far beyond royalty because the comparison of prices in the trans-Atlantic market with the value of slave produce in either the West African or trans-Atlantic markets favored the export of slaves until roughly the 1830s. Nonetheless, many female slaves were placed in new West African families, slaves were used as porters in commerce and as laborers in coastal factories, and slaves became officials in Oyo and in states drawing on the tradition of Oyo, such as Porto-Novo.

Comparison of the prices and quantities of slave exports over time reveals several distinct periods in the history of slave exports, corresponding to changing political, demographic and market conditions. In most of these periods, the price elasticity of supply of slaves was over 1.5, indicating that an increase in slave prices brought an even larger increase in the quantity of slaves supplied. Slave exporting, hence, was a business – more a cause of war than an effect of it. The exception proves the rule: from the 1700s through the 1730s, the price of slaves skyrocketed, but the quantity of slave exports declined somewhat. The reason, however, was that the slave exporters were running out of people to send.

For the Aja peoples in particular, the heavy drain on population actually led to population decline in the eighteenth century: an average of over 8,500 Aja slaves per year ($\pm 40\%$) were exported for fifty years from 1690 to 1740, which amounted to some three percent of the total population per year. No birth rate would have been high enough to prevent depopulation under these conditions. For the balance of the eighteenth century, Aja slave exports averaged from one to two percent of the population per year. The exports of Eastern Voltaic peoples (mostly Bariba) came to about one percent of population per year all during the eighteenth century. The losses of the Yoruba peoples to the slave trade are better known because they occurred later: Oyo played a modest role in slave exports until late in the eighteenth century, and the Yoruba only became the dominant ethnic group among slave exports in the 1820s with the collapse of Oyo, after which their exports reached 0.6% of the population per year. Two-thirds of

10

the slaves exported were Aja peoples enslaved most commonly through wars among themselves, notably through raids by Danhome on its neighbors. In the Bight of Benin, therefore, the notion of coastal peoples selling slaves obtained from the distant interior is exaggerated.

Figures on slave exports alone underestimate the dislocation caused by slave raiding. Enslaved women tended to be kept by their captors rather than be exported. Weaker peoples tended to suffer preferentially, although military reverses were not uncommon for even the strongest states. And with the nineteenth-century decline in the trans-Atlantic trade, slaves captured in the wars of the Sokoto Caliphate, the Yoruba wars and other battles tended to become domestic slaves.

The loss and dislocation of population because of slave trade were thus a clear detriment to the economy of Dahomey, more so than for most other areas of Africa because of the particular intensity and consistency of slave exports. The exports, on the other hand, provided revenues which were used for the purchase of imports. Nevertheless, while it is sometimes argued that these imports provided access to new goods, new technology, and that they engendered collateral commerce, the cost of foregoing most imports would probably not have been large. Domestic substitutes existed for most imports, a smaller volume of commerce would not have impeded the spread of improved technology to Dahomey, and necessities such as iron could have been imported with the more modest proceeds for agricultural exports. Thus, accounting for exports and imports together, Dahomey would have been better off if it had not participated in the export of slaves.

Growth of Dahomey's economy was arrested and reversed by the export of slaves, and the distribution of the region's wealth was skewed. Population growth was reversed, and wars cut the level of production and producer investment. Refugee groups formed, subsisting at reduced levels of living while the victors enjoyed the spoils of war, harems, and windfall profits from sale of slaves – if only until the next war.

The overall characterization of Dahomey's economy in the era of slave exports – that is, the issue of its social formation – is a complex and controversial issue. Observers have attempted variously to demonstrate that the key element of the economy was state policy, slave exports, tribute, or peasant production; some have argued that Dahomey was isolated from the world economy, and others that its development was determined by the world economy.[14] In fact, none of these factors can be ignored, and no one of them was clearly dominant. The economy of the slave-exporting era remained based on the commodity exchange mode of production which, in intimate association with the familial sector, produced goods and services, reproduced the labor force, and sustained the states and the mercantile system. At the same time, the procuring of slaves and the exporting of most

11

male slaves constituted major economic activities. From a local viewpoint slave exports could be considered as a factor superimposed on the substratum of the commodity exchange economy. Viewed from the outside, in contrast, the region served as a source of slave labor, in which the commodity exchange sector gave support to the reproduction of slaves for export. The commercial value of slave exports was far inferior to the value of all other domestic production, and was presumably less than the value of other domestic production for the market, yet the slave-export sector was important in its own right and did much to shape the whole economy. Slave commerce constricted the commodity exchange system because of war and the export of slaves; on the other hand it expanded the commodity exchange system through the circulation of imported manufactures and imported money. Strong states and governing classes, as in Ardra and Danhomè, facilitated the collection and export of slaves; yet continued political fragmentation of the Bight of Benin as a whole perpetuated the wars which yielded slaves.

The depopulation of Dahomey at the turn of the eighteenth century brought a search for political solutions to the strains of slave exporting. According to I. A. Akinjogbin, Danhomè's rapid expansion in the 1720s was an attempt by King Agaja to put an end to slave exports. This result was achieved in practice at much the same time on the Gold Coast, where the establishment of Asante control over the Akan heartland virtually ended the export of Akan slaves. Whatever Agaja's intentions, the expansion of Danhomè was immediately cut short by the invasions from Oyo which rendered the region tributary; Dahomey remained politically fragmented for another century, during which massive exports of Aja slaves ontinued. Exports of Yoruba slaves, in turn, grew only as Oyo weakened and then collapsed.

THE ERA OF AGRICULTURAL EXPORTS, 1840–1960

With the industrial revolution, the Bight of Benin became linked directly to the industrial economies of Europe.[15] Trade relations with Brazil, which was the major trading partner of the Bight of Benin until the mid-nineteenth century, were gradually reduced to insignificance: palm product exports to Brazil fell off while those to France, Britain and Germany grew; Brazilian tobacco was replaced by US tobacco; European cloth replaced that of India; European distilled liquors competed with New World rum; and the money system saw Maldive cowries successively supplemented and challenged by dollars of varying origins, East African cowries, British sterling, and finally by French francs. Europeans came to dominate Dahomey's nineteenth-century trans-Atlantic commerce in large part because of their increasing military power and technical advances such as steamships. Also significant, however, was the fact that the European market for Dahomean produce was growing faster than that of Brazil. Europeans monopolized the trade connections to Europe, which helped them to crowd out Brazilian and African merchants and shippers, and suppress the trade to Brazil. By the mid-twentieth century, the foreign trade of colonial Dahomey was directed almost exclusively toward France. Despite the change in orientation of trans-Atlantic commerce, however, the composition of goods imported and exported changed very little until late in the era of agricultural exports – exports of palm products were exchanged against textiles, beverages, tobacco, money, and a wide variety of other local needs.

Dahomey began exporting palm oil to France and Britain in the 1830s. While exports of palm oil and other foodstuffs had obviously taken place for the whole duration of the slave trade, the rise in European demand for palm products brought a new era in foreign trade. Export of slaves and palm products coexisted from the late 1830s to the mid-1860s; revenue from slaves and palm products were roughly equal in the 1840s, after which palm products dominated. This substitution of agricultural exports for slave exports has been analyzed extensively as a policy question for the leading states of the Bight of Benin. The most basic factors in the substitution, however, were the declining trans-Atlantic demand for slaves and the growing demand for palm products. The production of agricultural exports took place wherever oil palms grew, inside and outside of major kingdoms. Most of the new demand was met by a growth and reorientation of the commodity exchange sector, as small farmers harvested and marketed more palm products. The value of land rose with the value of its produce, thus providing as incentive for wealthy individuals or families to buy or otherwise obtain land.

At the same time, the shrinking and eventual abolition of the slave-labor sector of the New World economy further conditioned the diversion of slaves gathered by the slave-catching sector into a domestic slave-labor sector. Slaves now produced palm products for the trans-Atlantic market in addition to supplying the palaces and producing for the West African market. Slave plantations were set up in Danhomè by the kings, by a range of notables and officials within the kingdom, by chiefs in the states of the Egba and the Ijebu, and perhaps in areas outside these states. The growth of slave-labor production provided further encouragement for the establishment of large land holdings. But the constitution of a large class of slaves led, not surprisingly, to slave revolts: the abortive revolt of 1855 on the Abomey plateau served to check the enthusiasm of slave owners for unlimited expansion of plantations.

13

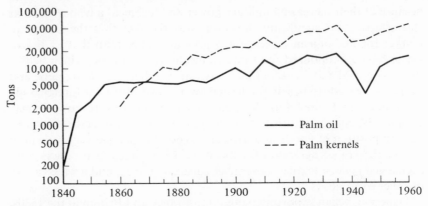

Figure 1.2. Palm oil and palm kernel exports, 1840–1960, in tons (five-year averages).
Source: Figure 2.4; Tables A4.2, A4.4, A4.6.

The era of agricultural exports opened a sustained period of economic growth for Dahomey. Capture of slaves continued much as before, with its attendant destruction, but the slaves remained in Dahomey and population growth resumed. The commodity exchange sector expanded throughout the region, while the slave-labor sector expanded in the larger states: the steady investment in increased production is reflected in the regular growth in exports from the 1840s to the 1930s, as shown in Figure 1.2. Parallel to changes in production, the mercantile sector was reorganized: the network for physical distribution of imports remained much the same as in previous years, but the financing changed somewhat and a network had to be developed for bulking and transporting palm oil and kernels. While the value of imports did not expand much if at all over the preceding era, purchasing imports with palm oil rather than with slaves lowered their real cost. The era of agricultural imports, in sum, brought steady if not spectacular growth to Dahomey, and made the control of the region's destiny a timely issue.

Under the impact of this economic growth and transformation, the social formation of Dahomey began to undergo redefinition in the mid-nineteenth century. The issue came to be posed in terms of the nature of political power, as three types of parties pursued solutions to their own advantage. The princely class, especially in Danhomè, pursued an 'Ethiopian' solution, in which the monarchy would gain European recognition and maintain dominion over a largely precapitalist domestic economy. The second party to emerge was the landed and commercial elite, with representatives from Brazilian, Fon and other Dahomean backgrounds. This group, anchored in the commercial tradition of the region,

14

but also expanding its holdings of land and slaves with the growth of oil palm commerce, gradually assumed the identity of a Dahomean bourgeoisie: it pursued a 'Liberian' solution, in which it would dominate the state and lead in the development of a capitalist economic organization. European merchants and consuls, finally, came more and more to support a colonial solution, in which capitalist development would take place under European rule.

The struggle among these groups was played out across the latter half of the nineteenth century. In the Egba state and in Porto-Novo, princely and mercantile interests allied with each other and with Europeans in the course of contesting Danhomè's bid for regional hegemony. In Danhomè the aristocracy, itself divided into parties as its expansionism was frustrated, resisted granting concessions and eventually led a bitter and memorable fight against the French conquest. The landed and commercial elite in Danhomè, after failing in an attempt to establish a Portuguese protectorate over the kingdom, threw its lot in with the French during the war of colonial conquest, in hopes of achieving a privileged position under the new regime. European merchants – French, German and British – had each to content themselves with political power over only a portion of the coast; even that soon escaped them, for the colonial state was to become a formidable power in its own right.

With the French conquest (1890–3) of what became the Colony of Dahomey, and with conquests by Britain and Germany in adjoining areas, the issue of political power was resolved. Colonial conquest failed, however, to bring about the immediate opening of a new economic era. Despite certain changes, the organization of the economy continued to be that established after the end of slave exports, and it would remain so for another half-century.[16] The importance of the colonial conquest was that now the French state, rather than African states, would govern the disposal of wealth produced in the economy.

The colonial state, far from being based on or allied to social classes in Dahomey, was a foreign government, responsible only to foreign influences. It sought to benefit Dahomey and its economy only to the degree that doing so would benefit France or leading French interests. But Dahomey never attracted European capital, as it appeared to lack agricultural or mineral resources susceptible to large-scale capitalist development. In effect, therefore, the French regime treated Dahomey as a sort of preserve, a hedge against the day when it might turn out to have resources worth developing. That day never came for the French. In the meantime, for the seventy years of colonial rule, the people of Dahomey were almost powerless to use the state for their own economic ends.

The French government immediately outlawed the capture and sale of

15

slaves, and moved rapidly to undercut slavery itself: by 1900 many slaves had been freed, and those remaining were dispersed as wives, as tenants, or as members of lineages. The slave-owning class suffered accordingly. The French dismembered Danhomè in 1893, thus breaking any remaining power and unity of its aristocracy, and in 1900 they dismissed or demoted virtually all the protected sovereigns in southern Dahomey. This nearly eliminated the aristocracy, and indicated to the aristocrats that their only hope for advance lay through the ranks of the French state.

The impact of French conquest provoked a struggle among Dahomeans, concentrated in the period from 1895 to 1920, for the redistribution of control over land and labor.[17] Slaveowners sought to redefine their control over slaves as control over land, over tenants, and over lineage members. Villages sought to redefine boundaries of lands and fishing preserves. Religious disputes scarcely veiled the factional struggles over control of land and commerce which underlay them. Factions struggled for the leadership of great families. Many of these disputes ended up in the courts, usually in 'customary' courts under the aegis of the administration, but sometimes under French law. The protagonists, seeking administrative support, issued frequent and at times ingenious professions of loyalty to France. But the state was a fickle ally at best, so all of the litigants had to be prepared to resist the state as well as to curry its favor.

Meanwhile the commodity exchange sector continued to grow without interruption, both in domestic and trans-Atlantic activities. It absorbed the impact of successive changes in the monetary system, as British sterling coin was adopted by producers and merchants in the 1880s, and as French currency was imposed on them after 1900, demonetizing other currencies without compensation. The commodity exchange sector continued in efforts to export crops other than palm oil and kernels: the most successful such exports were maize, occasionally in large quantities, and cotton, which yielded a small but steady export revenue.

The capitalist mode of production, which made its appearance in transport and commerce during the nineteenth century, expanded at the turn of the twentieth century. It now consisted of a portion of regional commerce and transport, a small amount of private construction and manufacturing, and state production – construction, railroads, electric power and printing. The old mercantile system of caravans was steadily pushed to the fringes of the country, as an aggressive group of European and Dahomean commercial firms set up small retail outlets and bulking centers throughout the country. Dahomean merchants and transporters, though almost driven out of the trans-Atlantic trade, maintained a large share of the commerce and transport of the countryside, especially with the improvement in motor transport after World War I.

16

The initial impact of French policy on Dahomey's economic organization was modest.[18] The maintenance and reinforcement of French policy, however, became influential in setting the conditions for the capitalist economic transformation to come. Primary emphasis in fiscal affairs went to capital investment in transportion infrastructure and social services, to creation of budgetary surpluses which tended to be transferred to the government of Afrique Occidentale Française (AOF) in Dakar, and to orientation of the domestic economy toward France. In social policy the prime emphases were the maintenance of strict law and order and the creation of a docile wage-labor force. The cost of each of these, borne entirely by the population of Dahomey, was paid through taxes, forced labor, prison terms, and the cost of opportunities foregone because of state interference. The greatest source of revenue was customs duties, followed by the head tax (*impôt de capitation*) and by many other fees and levies. The use of forced labor, unpaid or underpaid, helped the state to undertake public works and still maintain a budgetary surplus. An immense administrative effort went each year into collecting the *impôt* and into requiring people to construct and repair roads: the rationale underlying this approach was apparently that, through continuing administrative pressure, Dahomeans could eventually be convinced to pay taxes unquestioningly, and to accept wage employment readily, regardless of the level of pay.

Dahomeans of all social groups responded orally and in print to French social and fiscal policy: the resultant ideological dispute between the rulers and the ruled is one of the more fascinating aspects of the country's colonial history. In many cases the rural population came forth only tardily to pay taxes or to work, and in some cases they simply refused, which led to revolts and confrontations, as in Awansouri in 1911, Grand Popo in 1913, among the Holli in 1914–15, and in the Mono in 1917–18. Landed and commercial families found their attempts at self-aggrandizement frustrated at every step, and they began to criticize the state for failing to provide them with support. Another strand of protest came from what might be termed the intelligentsia: its outstanding figure, the teacher and journalist Louis Hunkanrin, drew widely on ideas of republicanism, nationalism and socialism to criticize the administration.

As a result, what had begun in the early colonial years as the disparate complaints of peasants, merchants, civil servants, wage workers and traditional aristocrats became a veritable national movement.[19] Shifting coalitions of Dahomeans formed to demand an end to fiscal stringency and administrative abuses, through petitions, demonstrations, legal battles, the press, and through efforts to rally support among other colonized peoples and sympathetic Europeans. The most consistent and powerful group in this national movement was the landed and commercial bourgeoisie; the leading organ of the movement was its newspaper, *La Voix du Dahomey*.

The crucial periods for the movement were its formation during the resistance to recruitment during World War I, the Porto-Novo events of 1923, and the Administrative Council elections of 1934. At each of these points the administration made concessions to the movement, but also carried out a repression against its leaders and reaffirmed its basic policy: after the 1923 events, for instance, the state lowered taxes and expanded the franchise, but exiled Hunkanrin.

The bourgeoisie's economic base, which had never been strong, was undermined by state fiscal policies and by the competition of European firms. In the political arena, further, the state set up its *chefs de canton* and certain civil servants as an alternative faction of the bourgeoisie, encouraging them to enrich themselves at the same time it frustrated the ambitions of its critics. This approach helped to bring about the split in the movement in the 1930s. One faction of the bourgeoisie now argued that the interests of the state were primary and that private capital and national development must remain subordinate, while the leaders of the national movement argued the opposite: the state and its allies won the 1934 election. The administration failed in its subsequent prosecution of the directors of *La Voix du Dahomey*, but the electoral results had already confirmed the pattern of Dahomey's development and had sealed the doom of the national movement.

The state intended to have ultimate control, rather than answer to the population. It extended its influence over the economy by extracting an ever-increasing portion of the economic surplus: it expanded the absolute and relative level of its taxation in several stages, and it also required the donation of labor by its subjects. This large portion of the national product collected by the state was spent for the financing of an expensive administration, for the support of a state capitalist sector which precluded much private capitalist development and, most painfully, as tributary payments to the AOF government in Dakar. That is, the governments of AOF and Dahomey collected revenues in Dahomey which greatly exceeded the expenditures by those governments in Dahomey: from 1910 to 1950, the annual value of this fiscal surplus from Dahomey averaged 21% of the value of exports. Assuming that exports averaged 15% of the level of domestic product, the fiscal drain averaged 3% of domestic product per year.

Domestic product grew from the mid-nineteenth century to the 1930s at an annual rate well over two percent per year.[20] But French economic and social policies ultimately took their toll, and the effects of the Depression and World War II completed the processes of taming the bourgeoisie, bleeding the peasantry, and undermining economic growth.

THE CAPITALIST ERA, SINCE 1930

The capitalist era in Dahomey thus opened not with robust growth, but in an atmosphere of restrictions, calamity and ambiguity. The terms of the transformation were so disadvantageous to the domestic economy that, although the commitment to capitalism was economically rational and perhaps inevitable, it also corresponded to the end of an era of growth and the beginning of decades of stagnation.[21] A change in the structure of imports, beginning in the 1930s, marked the new era: the declining relative prices of imported capital goods induced Dahomeans to devote a large portion of export revenue to purchasing intermediate goods used in transportation and in some aspects of production. Capital goods thus grew sharply in importance in the domestic economy, beyond state and European-owned enterprises. From the 1920s to the 1950s, for example, the quantity of motor vehicle imports rose by a factor of eight and gasoline imports rose by a factor of fifteen; calculated at 1927 prices, the value of gasoline imports rose from 5% of cotton cloth imports in the 1920s to 100% in the 1950s. In that same time period the quantity of staple imports – such as cotton cloth, alcoholic beverages, tobacco and kerosene – remained almost unchanged.

The expansion of capitalist influence did not, however, entail the flourishing of capitalist enterprise. The level of private domestic investment grew sharply after World War II, most conspicuously in transportation. But the full-time urban wage-labor force remained tiny: in the 1950s it reached only two percent of the total population, or five percent of the economically active population. The Depression added to other hindrances to the growth of capitalism: the level of French money in circulation was driven for a time to such a low level that Dahomeans resorted to Nigerian currency, cowries and even barter. And during World War II, with gasoline impossible to obtain, head transport and other elements of the old mercantile system were revived.

The commodity exchange sector, still in many ways the most important sector of the economy, now found itself compressed by a growing capitalist sector. To a degree, the state's negative approach furthered the encroachment of the capitalist sector: forced labor, conscription and taxation pushed labor and resources from the commodity exchange sector to the capitalist sector, at considerable cost to the producers. But the changing structure of costs and demand in the market served the same end. For instance, the rising consumption of imported food and the growth of local bakeries and bottleries cut into the food-processing activities of the commodity exchange sector. The establishment of mills to extract palm oil (in 1950) and to crush palm kernels (in 1964) soon took away a major productive activity from the commodity exchange sector, and left women in particular with less work and less income.

The state continued its expansion, financing public investment, as always, out of current tax revenue. The net benefit of such public investment depended on the cost to the economy of removing investable funds from the taxpayers, a cost which was not negligible. For, despite common impressions to the contrary, the colonial system did not lead to substantial metropolitan investment in most of Africa. The French are known to have invested less than the British, but are widely thought to have made substantial investments after World War II with the FIDES (Fonds d' Investissement pour le Développement économique et social) program. Yet for Dahomey, and perhaps for other colonies, there was no net French investment in the colony. What passed for investment funds was in fact a partial rebate of tax moneys collected. In the FIDES period, 1946–52, the rebate was larger than in other periods, but was never as large as a full rebate.

Real per capita income declined from its peak in the 1930s, and population growth rose to an annual two percent; imports grew even more rapidly, while exports foundered after the war. The resultant balance of payments deficit was covered only as workers began to leave Dahomey in growing numbers, repatriating salaries after finding employment in both public and private sectors in Ivory Coast, Gold Coast and elsewhere.

Politics in the capitalist era were marked by disillusionment and division. The merchants and landowners lost their crusading zeal after the primacy of the state over the private sector was reaffirmed in the 1930s: indeed, when Dahomeans began to gain political power in the 1950s, they opted for expanding state activities rather than lowering taxes. The major change with independence was that the Dahomeans reversed the historic fiscal surplus maintained by the French – a fiscal deficit replaced it as state expenditures shot up again. No other groups, however, were able to replace the leadership of the defeated merchants and planters. Successful strikes by Cotonou dockers and railroad workers in 1923 and 1929 had established wage workers as a significant economic force, but the slow growth in capitalist production limited the influence of trade unions: they flexed their muscles during the 1947 railroad strike and the 1958 general strike, but they could not lead the country. Nor was Dahomey's remarkable cadre of intellectuals able to develop a clear program around which to organize. The producers of the countryside, whose political pressure was effective in their own villages and cantons, were quite lacking in impact at the territorial level. The alliances among Dahomey's social groups, so frightening to the administration in the 1920s and 1930s, could not be reconstructed after the war and the Vichy interlude.

Prewar political leaders made one last attempt. When the time came to choose Dahomey's first delegates to the Constituent Assembly in 1946, the selection committee – which represented a remarkably broadly based and single-minded group – selected the French missionary, Fr Aupiais, to run for one seat, and accepted his recommendation of an unknown young technocrat, Sourou Migan Apithy, for the second seat. Both were elected, but Aupiais died before he could attend the first session, and political leadership fell unexpectedly into the hands of Apithy. The subsequent political meanderings of Dahomey, including the reorganization of its politics along ethnic lines in the 1950s, were reflective of its exhausted economic conditions.

Throughout modern history, domestic and external political and economic conditions have interacted to influence Dahomey's development to such a degree that all must be considered together. The periods of economic history are distinct from the periods of political history, but each can give fuller meaning to the other. The conquests by Danhomè in the 1720s may be seen as the achievement by the Fon monarchy of control over many of the benefits of an economic system developed decades previously, which collected and exported slaves. In a very close parallel, the French conquest of the 1890s may be seen as the achievement by an alien and generally non-resident French capitalist class, through the colonial state, of control over many of the benefits of the economic system which produced and exported palm products. Similarly, the accession to independence in 1960 and the declaration of the People's Republic of Bénin in 1975 correspond to a reorganization of the benefits of an economy which was increasingly centered on capitalist production.

2

The Dahomean economy, 1640–1890

By the late seventeenth century Dahomey had become populous, had developed sizeable states, and had an economic organization which can be characterized as including familial and commodity exchange modes of production, with a mercantile system linking it to other economies.[1] In Dahomey and throughout the Bight of Benin, the major ethnic groups were well established in their present positions: such migrations of families and ethnic groups as took place subsequently have done little to change the geographical distribution of Aja–Ewe, Yoruba, Voltaic and other groups.[2] The patrilineal social structure of the seventeenth century was that of succeeding centuries. The kingdoms of Hueda, Ardra and Oyo were the largest and best known, but European observers knew many smaller kingdoms and noted that all the Aja peoples had a common political structure, though with variations in scale.[3] The agricultural economy relied on fairly intensive land use, with yams and maize as staples. Millet, sorghum, beans and sweet potatoes were also cultivated, along with oil palms, coconuts, oranges, pineapples and other fruits. Fishing occupied a significant minority of the population, and domestic animals included poultry, goats, sheep and cattle.[4] The producers were tied together through a network of local markets, and used cowries as currency. The local markets were tied to more distant regions through caravans on the land and through large canoes on the lagoons and along the coast.[5] In sum, seventeenth-century society resembled nineteenth- or even twentieth-century society in many details.

How did the economy and its institutions come to be as they were in the late seventeenth century? Available evidence suggests that the population and institutions of Dahomey at that time were similar to those encountered by the first Europeans in the fifteenth century, and that the basic patterns had developed still earlier. This 'early growth' thesis contrasts with the 'late growth' thesis which is still advanced occasionally by those who suggest

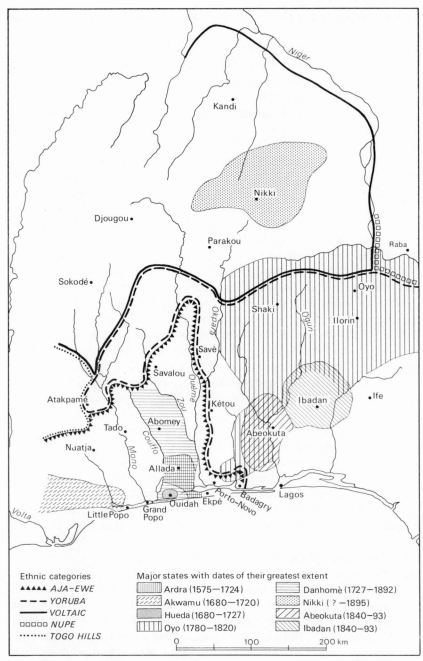

Map 1 The Bight of Benin, 1640–1890

that the society of Dahomey took shape in the years after European contact.[6]

Linguistic evidence suggests that the geographic location of the population has been extremely stable. One must count in thousands of years the distinctions among major language groups such as the Kwa languages of the West African coast and the Voltaic languages which lie to the north of them. Within the Kwa language group, the Aja–Ewe languages are in quite a different subgroup from Yoruba. This linguistic evidence shows it to be impossible for the coastal peoples to have migrated from the far interior or for the Aja–Ewe peoples to have descended from the Yoruba at any time within the past millennium.[7] Movements of smaller groups of people, dynastic movements in particular, have taken place within that time, but these movements of small groups are not to be confused with the migration of whole populations. Even within the Aja–Ewe- and Yoruba-speaking areas, the fairly regular spatial distribution of dialects suggests that neither has experienced a rapid territorial expansion in recent centuries.

The magnitude of population prior to the seventeenth century has been little studied. Presumably the size and growth of population depended on the level of agricultural technology. The 'early growth' thesis implies that the West African yam, millet and the oil palm were intensively cultivated before the Portuguese. D. G. Coursey has argued convincingly that the generalization of the West African yam took place in antiquity, and even suggests that it was developed in the Bight of Benin. The 'late growth' thesis implies, in contrast, that rapid population growth began with trans-oceanic contacts and new crops: yams from Southeast Asia, maize and sweet potatoes from the Americas.[8]

The existence of local markets and money before Portuguese times has yet to be documented directly. Cowries were the money of the Bight of Benin by the mid-seventeenth century, and Portuguese imports of cowries to the region had gone on for some time before that. But it is unlikely that the region could have obtained cowries in any quantity before the opening of maritime contact with the Indian Ocean. The 'early growth' thesis would postulate that another currency, perhaps another shell or cloth, preceded cowries.[9]

Oral traditions of the Aja–Ewe peoples have been interpreted to imply that their states rose during the sixteenth century, and Portuguese documents confirm the existence of Ardra and Grand Popo in this era.[10] This was well after European contact, and also well after the twelfth- or thirteenth-century origins assigned to the myths of origin of the Yoruba and Akan peoples.[11] But it may be argued on two separate grounds that the Aja–Ewe peoples had also developed states before European contact. First, the ancestral kingdom of Tado, from which all Aja–Ewe states

24

claim descent, was formed at least a century before Ardra and Grand Popo became large enough to trade with the Portuguese in the sixteenth century. Second, myths of origin such as that of Tado refer in general to the origin of particular dynasties rather than to the institution of the state: the idea and the institution of the state came earlier, though earlier states were doubtless smaller and more rudimentary.[12]

Assuming the 'early growth' thesis to be correct, it remains to explain the evolution of the economic system in the absence of trans-Atlantic contacts: what follows, then, is a hypothetical reconstruction of the development of an economy consisting of familial and commodity exchange modes of production, a mercantile system, and states. The reconstruction begins by postulating, at some earlier time, an isolated familial mode of production consisting of self-sufficient family units with neither markets nor states, for whom exchange among families was of little significance. Pierre-Philippe Rey's model for a 'lineage mode of production' applies to this situation. His model, it may be noted, is devoid of neither exploitation nor slavery; he even argues that it includes the essence of class conflict, though not actual classes.[13] But such an economic system does not require a state.

The commodity exchange mode of production developed out of the familial mode of production: growing agricultural productivity led to a larger population and to a larger economic surplus over bare subsistence, which in turn permitted specialization and the development of local commerce. The growth of commerce eventually required the invention of money to facilitate transactions, and the growth of markets led to greater concentration of population and to an increased value of land. The familial mode of production, now no longer isolated, interacted with the commodity exchange mode of production. It continued to produce the majority of goods and services, but it underwent some changes as families found themselves able to purchase commodities in the market. The commodity exchange sector gradually grew at the expense of the familial sector as changes in techniques of production or perhaps even changes in social structure made the market more convenient than self-sufficiency.

Long-distance trade may have existed before the development of local markets, but the creation of specialized long-distance traders came about only once they could link local markets. The mercantile system thus grew out of the commodity exchange sector. The extent of the mercantile sector depended on transportation costs, on the level of surplus available for exchange, and on the availability and usefulness of commodities for trade.[14]

The commodity exchange mode of production, though well known in abstract theories of economic history, is not included in most of the statements on African modes of production.[15] Yet it corresponds to a

25

significant reality: a level of production which was definitely beyond bare subsistence, a substantial reliance on local markets, the absence (for most producers at least) of a feudal landowning class which extracted large tithes, the absence of capitalism, and a state which collected only modest taxes. It is largely equivalent to what is known as the 'peasant economy' in contemporary Africa.[16] The very simple institutional structure I have set out for it could be modified to account for landowning and tenant classes or for a stronger state: the essence of the commodity exchange mode of production is independent producers or families relying significantly on a domestic commodity market. As such, it is neither subsistence nor capitalism.

The commodity exchange mode of production led to the development of states. The growth of population and its concentration in towns and near markets gave birth to land disputes between families which, along with disputes in the market, required an authority to mediate them.[17] The authority, perhaps initially rotated among lineage leaders, became that of a king once it was provided with lands, taxing power and judicial authority, each of these being provided to strengthen the authority of the mediator. The state, in addition to its functions in the commodity exchange system, then performed valuable protective and regulatory functions for long-distance trade. Once a state was formed in a given region, it led to formation of nearby states, as neighbors with similar economic systems felt pressure either to join the first state or create one of their own. State formation, according to this model, did not require an exploiting class as a precondition, though the process created a privileged governing stratum. Alternative models which assume states to have been stimulated by the commodity exchange mode of production include the control of a scarce resource, such as salt or metal ore, by an authority who is then able to gain wider recognition, or the development of state authority out of the need for organization of labor to perform public works such as clearing fields or waterways.[18]

The tension between the state as authority and the state as provider of services set up a policy choice for the kings: emphasize social service or emphasize self-aggrandizement. Kings who began as mediators could, through fortune or manipulation, become rulers and oppressors rather than peers and mediators. But the dichotomy of the policy choice became clouded with ambiguity. Were the services of the state to be provided uniformly to the whole economy, or to the commodity exchange sector, or to the mercantile sector, or to smaller groups within those sectors such as landowners and merchants? At what point did wealth and power in the hands of the monarchy become unjustified? While states commonly oppressed slaves, some lineages and even whole regions, the ability of small

26

but determined peoples to resist conquest and escape oppression placed a real check on the temptation of kings to rule by plunder alone. In the larger states of Dahomey, kings and an aristocracy accumulated great wealth through control of land, persons, commercial profit and tax revenue, while in the smaller states the kings and aristocracy were less separated from the cultivators. An ideology of growth and hierarchy pervaded the former, while an ideology of independence and self-sufficiency held on in the latter. All, however, participated in the same economic system, and all drew on a common political tradition.

In these ways Dahomey developed its economic and social system, independent of European contact. Even under this 'early growth' thesis, however, the established commodity exchange economy was affected by trans-Atlantic factors from the late fifteenth to late seventeenth centuries. The interaction of domestic and trans-Atlantic factors, seen here for the first time, presents a dialectic which returned in a new form with every succeeding era. This time the resultant changes included the adoption of new crops, the opening of new markets along the coast, the adoption of new currency and the expansion of states. But the dialectic suggests that while the arrival of new crops and the opening of new markets accelerated the development of the domestic market and of the state during this period, the prior existence of state and market served to speed the adoption of the new currency, commerce and crops.

THE ERA OF SLAVE EXPORTS, 1640–1860: DEMOGRAPHY

The level of demand for slaves rose sharply in about 1640 as both Dutch and Portuguese interests in Brazil sought labor for sugar production.[19] By 1660 English and French interests had begun purchasing slaves from Ardra, and before the trade was over Danish, Brandenburger, Spanish and American merchants had purchased slaves in the region. Slave exports doubtless preceded 1640, and exports of foodstuffs and manufactures and continued throughout the slave trade, but slaves were the dominant export from 1640 until 1850.[20]

The quantities of slave exports shown in Figure 2.1 and Table 2.1 refer to the entire Bight of Benin – that is, Dahomey plus Badagry and Lagos. They were estimated primarily from shipping data, but also from New World census data, consular reports and commercial returns, and can be considered to be accurate to within $\pm 20\%$, but no more. The export of slaves was most intensive in the late seventeenth and early eighteenth centuries, but it reached peaks again in the late eighteenth and in the early nineteenth centuries. Overall, however, the export of slaves was remarkably stable, averaging from 70,000 to 150,000 per decade from 1690 to

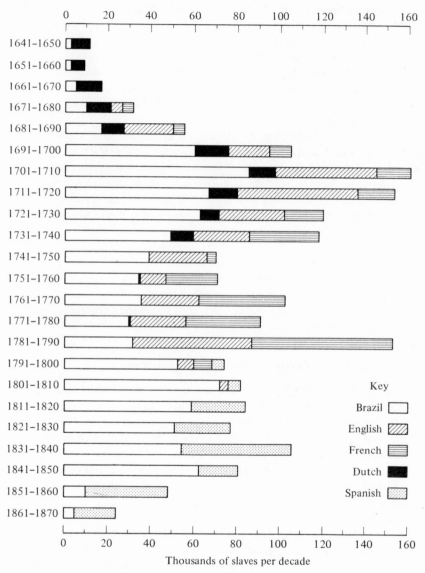

Figure 2.1. Bight of Benin slave exports by purchaser.
Source: Manning, 'Slave Trade,' 117.

Table 2.1. *Slave exports from the Bight of Benin, by purchaser*

Years	Brazil	English	French	Dutch	Spanish and American	Total
1641–1700	99,000	46,300	20,000	64,800		230,100
1701–1800	491,400	313,000	259,300	45,300	5,000	1,114,000
1801–1890	316,000	3,900			181,700	506,600*
1641–1890	906,400	363,200	279,300	110,100	186,700	1,850,700*

* Includes 5,000 slaves exported during the 1880s, mostly to colonies in Africa.
Source: Manning, 'Slave Trade,' 117.

1850. This steady export of slaves yielded a total of nearly two million slaves, or roughly one-fifth of the volume of the Atlantic slave trade.

The Bight of Benin thus shared with the Congo–Angola coast the unhappy distinction of being the most dependable source of supply for slaves. In contrast to other regions which supplied slaves on an intermittent basis, the Bight of Benin provided a large and stable supply of slaves for over two centuries, and the Congo–Angola coast exported roughly two and a half million slaves over the course of three centuries.[21] The Bight of Benin drew its slaves from a much smaller though more densely populated area than the Congo–Angola coast. Taken together, the two regions supplied almost fifty percent of the slaves in the trans-Atlantic trade. The relative intensity of the slave trade in these areas is emphasized by the fact that they account for only twenty percent of the African area from which slaves were drawn.[22]

The majority of Bight of Benin slaves went to Brazil, both overall and in each century. Almost all of these went to Bahia to work on sugar and tobacco plantations and in gold mines. Merchants of Bahia exported large quantities of tobacco to the Bight of Benin in exchange for slaves; the trade was thus carried by Brazilians rather than Portuguese.[23] In the seventeenth century the Dutch followed the Brazilians in numbers of slaves exported: these went first to Dutch sugar plantations in Pernambuco, and later were sold mainly to Spain under the *asiento*.[24] In the eighteenth century the English followed the Brazilians in volume of slaves purchased, and landed slaves primarily in Jamaica but also in North America, Barbados and the Leeward Islands. The French were a close third in the eighteenth century, sending most of their slaves to Saint-Domingue, but sending many to Martinique early in the century. In the nineteenth century, the trade to Brazil was followed by the trade to Cuba, as that island finally entered into large-scale slave production of sugar. The slave trade to Brazil

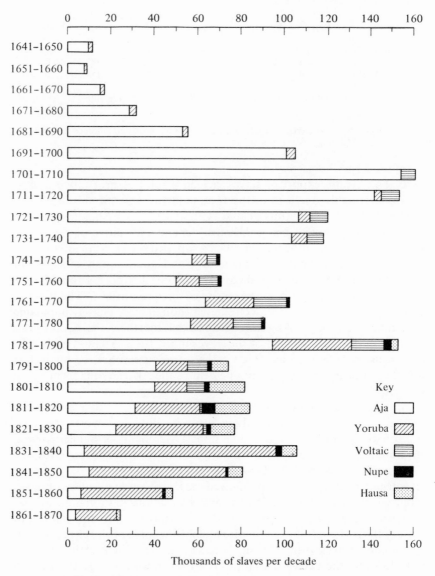

Figure 2.2. Bight of Benin slave exports by ethnic origin.
Source: Table A2.1.

Table 2.2. *Slave exports by ethnic origin*

Years	Aja	Yoruba	Voltaic	Nupe	Hausa	Total
1641–1700	217,900	11,800				229,700
1701–1800	873,500	127,400	95,800	7,900	10,500	1,115,100
1801–1870	124,300	298,500	10,600	12,800	55,200	501,400
	1,215,700	437,700	106,400	20,700	65,700	1,846,200

Source: Table A2.1.

ended shortly after the legal abolition of slavery in 1851, and the trade to Cuba ended with the conclusion of the American Civil War. Even after 1865 it was still possible for the Bight of Benin to export slaves to other areas of the African coast through French, German and Portuguese merchants.[25]

The same quantities of slave exports may be broken down according to the ethnic origins of the slaves. This is done by assuming that the distribution of slaves exported from the Bight of Benin is reflected in the ethnic identities noted in various New World documents.[26] Figure 2.2 shows the ethnic origins of slave exports by decade, while Table 2.2 summarizes the results by century. A substantial error factor of $\pm 40\%$ must be attached to these figures because of the indirect method of their calculation. The ethnic groups identified are broad categories, and they do not account for the proportions of slaves from the well-defined subgroups within these categories because of the lack of specificity in most New World records.

The Aja peoples provided the great majority of the slaves until the nineteenth century. Virtually no other ethnic groups were represented until the 1740s, and only in the 1820s did the Aja peoples cease to be the major ethnic group exported.[27] Yoruba slaves provided the second largest group in exports. They may have been exported in relatively large numbers in the mid-seventeenth century, but their numbers fell to a low level until the mid-eighteenth century, after which they grew until Yoruba peoples became the largest source of exports after 1820.[28] The proportions of the Yoruba peoples in this total are not known, although it is likely that the peoples of the south and west were more heavily represented than those of the north and east. The third largest contributors of slave exports were the Eastern Voltaic peoples, especially the Bariba of modern Bénin and Nigeria and the peoples of the Atacora mountains of northern Togo and Bénin. The Eastern Voltaic slaves came almost entirely in the eighteenth century. The fourth largest ethnic group in slave exports was the Hausa, who came from

31

the far interior mostly at the time of the formation of the Sokoto Caliphate in the early nineteenth century. Nupe slaves came from the area between the Yoruba and the Hausa at roughly the same time as the Hausa.

Ninety percent of the slaves exported came from the Aja and Yoruba peoples, and hence from within 200 km of the coast. Probably most of the slaves came from the southern portion of this coastal area, for that is where population is densest, reflecting the productivity of the land. The Bight of Benin thus differed from the Senegambia and Angola, where many slaves came from far inland, and was similar to the Bight of Biafra, where slaves came from near the coast.[29]

By assuming rates of population growth, it is possible to estimate the rate of population loss due to slave exports for each ethnic group with time. John D. Fage performed similar calculations for West Africa as a whole, and concluded that the rate of population loss averaged 0.16% during the eighteenth century.[30] My population estimates for each ethnic group were based on 1931 estimates, and were projected backward at an annual growth rate of 1% until the 1870s, and at a growth rate of 0.5% per year before that, though special assumptions had to be applied to account for the depopulation of the Aja.[31] Dividing the slave exports in each decade by the relevant population gives the estimated annual rate of population loss due to slave exports, as shown in Table 2.3. Assuming that a loss of 0.2% of the population a year to slave exports was significant, in that it was of the order of magnitude of the natural growth rate, the Hausa never had a significant loss, the Nupe had a significant loss in the 1780s and again in the 1810s, and the Eastern Voltaic peoples suffered significant losses from 1700 to 1810. The Yoruba lost 0.2% per year or more from the 1760s to the 1780s, and from the 1810s through the 1850s. For the Eastern Voltaic peoples in the eighteenth century and for the Yoruba in the nineteenth century, the export of slaves was of clear demographic significance, and probably caused depopulation at least in those sub-regions where enslavement was most serious, if not for the ethnic group as a whole.

But for the Aja peoples, the rate of population loss was of a completely different order, exceeding 3% per year for five full decades. This is six times the estimated normal rate of net growth, and is greater than the rate of natural increase could ever have been. The impact of slave exports on the Aja peoples was, therefore, a general and terrible depopulation. Assuming, for example, that a 3% annual loss of population through slave exports led to no more than a 1% annual population decrease, the Aja population fell from an estimated peak of 511,000 in the 1680s to a low of 280,000 at the turn of the nineteenth century.[32] The Aja population did not again reach its earlier peak until World War I, as compared with neighboring ethnic groups which more than tripled in population in the same time period,

32

Table 2.3. *Average annual population loss rates (percent) due to slave exports, by ethnic origin*

Decade	Aja	Yoruba	Voltaic	Nupe	Hausa	Total
1640s	0.2					
1650s	0.2					
1660s	0.3					0.1
1670s	0.6					0.2
1680s	1.1					0.4
1690s	2.2					0.7
1700s	3.7		0.5			1.0
1710s	3.8		0.5			1.0
1720s	3.2	0.1	0.4			0.8
1730s	3.3	0.1	0.4			0.7
1740s	1.9	0.1	0.3	0.1		0.4
1750s	1.6	0.1	0.5	0.1		0.4
1760s	2.2	0.2	0.8	0.1		0.6
1770s	1.9	0.2	0.7	0.1		0.5
1780s	3.6	0.3	0.7	0.2		0.8
1790s	1.5	0.1	0.4	0.1		0.4
1800s	1.5	0.1	0.4	0.1	0.1	0.4
1810s	1.1	0.2		0.4	0.1	0.4
1820s	0.8	0.3	0.1	0.1	0.1	0.3
1830s	0.3	0.6		0.1		0.5
1840s	0.3	0.4				0.3
1850s	0.3	0.2				0.2
1860s	0.1	0.1				0.1

Note: Total is based on ratio of all slave exports to population for all areas except Hausa.
Source: Appendix 3.

assuming uninterrupted growth. By these same assumptions, in the 1690s the Aja peoples accounted for 33% of the population of the Bight of Benin, the Yoruba for 51%, the Eastern Voltaic peoples for 9% and the Nupe for 7%. Another century of slave trade had, by the 1820s, reduced the Aja peoples to 12% of the Bight of Benin's population, while the Yoruba rose to 67% of the total, the Eastern Voltaic peoples accounted for 12% and the Nupe for 9%.

The enormity of the demographic impact of the slave trade on the Aja peoples has been forgotten with the passage of time. Far better known is the slave heritage of the Yoruba, whose numbers were greater in the last years of the trade, who gained recognition as returning ex-slaves from Brazil and Sierra Leone, and whose culture has left such a clear imprint in Brazil and in Cuba.[33] But the Aja impact in Haiti is well known, particularly in religion, and other examples of the Aja heritage in the New World can perhaps be pieced together to reveal a general pattern.[34]

The last column in Table 2.3 gives the rate of population loss for the Aja,

Yoruba, Eastern Voltaic and Nupe combined. It shows loss rates of 0.2% or more per year for the whole period of the slave trade, and loss rates of 0.5% or more per year for nine decades. Thus, even if the estimated proportion of Aja slaves should prove to be exaggerated, the export of slaves was demographically significant for the region as a whole and its two million inhabitants.

The volume of the slave trade estimated here is based on the number of slaves landed in the Americas. The full demographic effect of the slave trade included additional factors: mortality on the trans-Atlantic voyage (generally estimated at about ten per cent), mortality on the African coast and on the way to coastal trading points, and the number of people enslaved but retained in Africa. The retention of slaves was particularly significant in inland areas such as Nupe and Hausa, and it also grew with the passage of time.[35] If one considered the total incidence of slave exports, the mortality of slaves and the retention of slaves within Africa, the proportion of the population affected would rise from the figures given in Table 2.3, which range up to 1% per year for the whole region, to figures perhaps twice that large. The slave trade unquestionably had a major demographic impact on the Bight of Benin.

It is sometimes suggested that those who lost family members to slave raids adjusted for this by increasing their birth rate, thus offsetting any tendency toward depopulation. This thesis is reinforced by the observation that most slaves exported were men – the conventional ratio was two male slave exports for each female – so that the women left behind could still raise children.[36] The increase in birth rate following famine and epidemic is a well-documented phenomenon. The loss of population through slave raiding, however, was less similar in its effects to famine than to warfare and emigration: the prime targets of slave raids were young men and women from adolescence through their twenties. These were precisely the people who would be called upon to provide new children. Further, the decision to have another child to replace an infant lost to disease is easier to implement than the equivalent decision for an adolescent lost to slavers, as the parents' fertility declines with age. The only way to compensate for the loss of family through slave raids was therefore to have more children in advance of the raids, and this approach put a larger family at risk. Finally, for the women who were enslaved but retained in Africa, many of them ended up in harems, where they had smaller families than they would have had as a sole wife or with one or two co-wives. In sum, the notion of a compensating rise in birth rate to offset losses to slave raiding, while conceivable, entails some difficulties. Perhaps more significant was the change in relative size of ethnic groups, as those groups who captured women grew at the expense of those who did not.

Table 2.4. *Manning and Peukert estimates of slave exports, 1740–97*

	Manning	Peukert						
Decade	Total	Total	Ouidah	Popos	Ekpé	Porto-Novo	Badagry	Lagos
1741–50	70,100	140,500	40,500	15,000	70,000		15,000	
1751–60	70,500	129,000	29,000	15,000	42,500	17,500	25,000	
1761–70	102,700	149,500	54,500	14,500	14,500	33,000	33,000	
1771–80	90,700	175,500	38,500	8,000	8,000	68,500	53,500	
1781–90	153,100	164,000	47,000	5,000		85,500	21,500	5,000
1791–97	74,000[a]	130,000	31,000	3,500		25,500	35,000	35,000

Note: [a] 1791–1800
Source: Appendix 2; Peukert, *Sklavenhandel*, 305–6.

Werner Peukert has performed an independent estimate of eighteenth-century slave exports from the Bight of Benin.[37] Table 2.4 compares his estimates, based primarily on records from the English and French forts in Ouidah, with mine, which are based primarily on shipping data collected in the Americas. While the totals of the estimates vary by as much as a factor of two, they rise and fall in a similar pattern with time, with the exception of the 1770s and 1780s. On the latter point, it is quite possible that my estimates are, relatively, too low for the 1770s and too high for the 1780s.[38]

Several factors may account for the difference in absolute magnitude of the two estimates. My calculations omitted the trans-Atlantic mortality factor of roughly ten percent. On the other hand, sources on the West African coast seem generally to have overestimated the volume of slave exports, especially for ports and for nations other than their own. Sometimes this resulted from their calculating a volume of trade based on a 'normal year' which was overly optimistic.[39] In particular, while Peukert's figures for slave exports from Ouidah confirm my own, his estimates for the other ports seem to be too large, especially for the years before 1770.[40] It is likely, therefore, that the actual number of slaves exported lies somewhere between my estimates and Peukert's. To the degree that my estimates are low, the demographic consequences of the slave trade were greater than those outlined above.

Peukert's figures indicate the eastward trend in slave exports during the course of the eighteenth century. The entry of Oyo into direct exports of slaves in the 1760s and 1770s through Porto-Novo and Badagry is shown clearly. The opening of the port of Lagos – which Peukert shows as being delayed until the 1790s – might correspond to the eastward deflection of trade from Porto-Novo and Badagry, or it might reflect the entry of the Ijebu into the Atlantic slave trade.[41]

THE ERA OF SLAVE EXPORTS: POLITICAL ECONOMY

Slaves were a commodity. Once enslaved their humanity was subordinated to the laws governing commodities – to prices, productivities and profits. The demand for African slaves, for example, depended on their productivity in sugar and other commodities in the New World. The willingness and ability of Africans to supply slaves depended on factors such as the cost of obtaining and delivering slaves, the population available for enslaving, alternative uses for slaves, and legal and moral limits on enslavement. The results of the interaction of these factors are shown in Figure 2.3 which displays, for each decade, the prices and quantities of slave exports from Dahomey. The changing pattern of prices and quantities defines six chronological periods in the history of the slave trade.

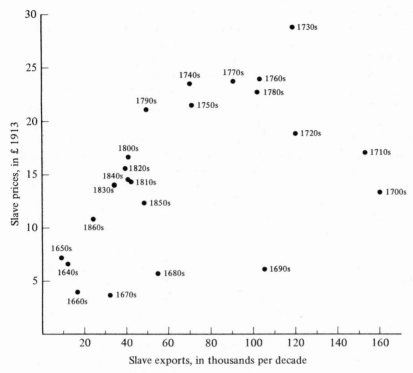

Figure 2.3. Prices and quantities of slave exports from Dahomey.
Source: Table A1.1.

During the first period, from the 1640s through the 1660s, slave prices fell but the quantity of exports grew. These were the years of decision, in which the slave-catching system was developed. With the rise in New World demand for slaves accompanying the rapid growth of sugar plantations in the mid-seventeenth century, slave merchants scoured the African coast in search of supplies. Given this new level of demand, some African regions – Dahomey in particular – responded by setting up efficient, inexpensive systems for delivering slaves. As they supplied more and more slaves, prices fell, and other areas less committed to slave exports tended to drop out of the trade.

The details of the slave-catching system – that is, the institutions which I have lumped together behind that term – remain elusive. As is well known, the system involved a combination of captives from wars, small-scale raiding for slaves, judicial condemnations, and the selling of persons in times of disaster. But to list these categories provides no explanation of the increase in slave supply in the late seventeenth century. Perhaps a change in

37

social values took place or was induced, for the coming century would see not only wars with distant enemies but internecine war and mutual raiding as the Aja peoples steadily depopulated themselves. Beyond any change in social values, a state and mercantile apparatus had to be set up to deliver slaves efficiently. European merchants described those parts of it in which they participated, but not the rest of it: Dutch, Brazilian, English and French merchants set up trading stations along the Bight of Benin, eclipsing the Portuguese from São Thomé who had traded there during the previous century. Ardra sent diplomatic missions to Europe, received delegations of missionaries, and became the center of the slave trade. By 1670 the system for slave trading was set up, including the places of trade, the system of inland collection and delivery, and the customs and fees of exchange between Africans and Europeans.[42]

For the people of the Bight of Benin, this must have been a time of serious discussion about the implications of the commitments and the decisions to which their future was being tied. The Yoruba peoples, after an apparent initial spate of slave exporting, withdrew from the trade for almost a century. But for the Aja peoples, once they were committed to slave exports, it seemed there was no going back.

From the 1670s through the 1700s the price of slaves rose almost fourfold and the quantity exported grew fivefold. Assuming that these decades saw the expansion of an established slave-delivery system, rather than changing conditions or techniques of supply, the relevant points in Figure 2.3 may be taken as a long-run supply curve. The price elasticity of supply was then 1.5, which is greater than the elasticity of 0.75 calculated for all of West Africa by Richard Bean. The Bight of Benin was a very price-responsive supplier of slaves in these years, which demonstrates almost irrefutably that the price of slaves figured in decisions on the intensity of slave raiding.[43] In this and later periods, the Bight of Benin was known as an area where prices of slaves were low.[44] This was probably not so much a reflection of the quality of these slaves in the eyes of the planters as it was a reflection of the low cost of collecting and delivering slaves. This low cost, of course, included only the cost to the slave catchers and merchants – the cost to the slaves, their families and the whole society was, unhappily, left out of the calculation.

The geographic focus of slave exports shifted following the sack of Offra in the mid-1670s by an army from Grand Popo. The Dutch, French and English moved their main factories from this inland Ardra town to Savi, capital of the neighboring Hueda kingdom, and its port of Glehwe (now Ouidah) became the main slave port of the coast. But wars raged among all the Aja states, including the inland Fon kingdom, and slaves were to be purchased at every point of the coast from Little Popo to Ekpé.[45]

In return for slaves, the Europeans sold cowries, Brazilian tobacco, cloth, and a wide variety of other goods, including guns and powder. The total revenue from sale of slaves rose from £11,000 per year in the 1670s to £205,000 per year in the 1700s. This certainly enriched the states and enriched the merchants. It must also, given the amount of money and consumer goods imported, have restructured the commodity exchange sector.[46] Perhaps the imported goods were simply added to those domestically produced; more likely they replaced goods produced in the domestic commodity exchange and familial sectors. On the other hand, the growing export trade required food and other goods and services for the care and handling of slaves, and thus stimulated more market production.

The categories of slaves, which were to become more fully documented in later years, were probably established by the late seventeenth century.[47] The children of slaves remained slaves, but those born within the families or the states of their masters could not normally be sold. Those enslaved through capture or condemnation, however, were disposed of in several ways. Most of the men and many of the women were exported. The remainder of the men and most of the women were allocated among royalty, notables such as state officials and merchants, and the common people. Slaves of royalty included those who worked the fields to supply the palaces, those executed in human sacrifice, household servants, wives and concubines, and state officials. Merchants and officials with large land holdings used slaves to produce for and serve their families, as concubines, and in their commercial operations. The slave-labor mode of production in this era was probably limited to the use of slave workers in the mercantile system and slave production of goods for royalty and large families – the market for slave produce was not yet well developed, except to the degree that slave produce was sold to supply slave caravans. The slaves, mostly women, who were sold or allocated to the common people were absorbed into the familial and commodity exchange sectors.

Before the turn of the eighteenth century the situation had run out of control, even by the distorted logic of the slave trade. Wholesale depopulation had begun. Goods and money flowed into the country while its people left in chains. Yet, so far as contemporary European observers cared to indicate, this state of affairs was accepted by everyone in the Bight of Benin. Instinctively, today's observer cries out at the immorality of the system which induced neighbors to enslave neighbors, and one seeks to assign responsibility for this inhuman trade. But to condemn its immorality, to stigmatize the Europeans who initiated it and the Africans who adopted it, is not to explain how it continued. In recent years, several economic models have been developed, based on microeconomic theory, which clarify the rationale of the slave trade in terms of market forces.[48]

39

But the individual calculus of profits and losses in the short term is not intended to account for the contradictions in treating humans as commodities, nor to explain the origins of institutions such as those of the slave trade, nor to calculate the long-term costs and benefits of slave trade to society. These broader tasks will be the burden of the study of the political economy of African slavery in the years to come – to explain how such an extraordinary system of exploitation and mutual destruction could have been maintained for so long.

The first four decades of the eighteenth century, the 1700s to 1730s, spanned a time of sharply rising prices and slightly declining quantities of slave exports. The price increases stemmed from the ever-growing New World demand for slave labor. While Africa as a whole continued to supply more slaves as prices rose, for Dahomey the supply schedule shifted steadily to the left because there remained fewer people to enslave.[49] For almost half a century, an average of more than three percent of the Aja population was sent each year across the Atlantic. For those who remained, the alternatives were flight or absorption by the Fon kingdom, which emerged from the fray of competing states to dominate the Aja peoples in the 1720s. Many chose to flee: the Gbaguidi dynasty, who moved north to Savalou (in an earlier period, but reflecting a similar sentiment); the Weme, who were defeated by the Fon shortly after 1700, and who left the Abomey plateau for the safety of the marshes along the river to which they gave their name; the Tofin, who formed by fleeing the Allada plateau and building or expanding villages on Lake Nokoué; the Gun people who moved east to set up the states of Porto-Novo and Badagry; and the Hueda, who after the destruction of their kingdom in 1727 formed refugee groups to the east and especially to the west of Ouidah, from which they fought the Fon for the rest of the eighteenth century.[50]

Akinjogbin and others have described the diplomatic and military events that led to the sudden supremacy of the Fon kingdom of Danhomè. Akinjogbin hypothesized that Danhomè – King Agaja in particular – sought to conquer the coast in order to end the slave trade.[51] The thesis remains attractive despite the buffeting it has received, for it clearly represents what *ought* to have been done, given the demographic toll the Aja peoples were inflicting on each other. But slave raids among Aja peoples – or in Dahomey generally – could only have been brought under control if the whole region had been drawn into a single polity so that no one was left to raid. Perhaps Agaja had this goal in mind. But just as Danhomè emerged as the leading Aja power, the Oyo empire undertook repeated invasions and by 1748 had rendered it firmly tributary. The Oyo incursions made it impossible for Danhomè to extend its conquests – the kingdom expanded very little after 1734 – so that most of the Aja peoples remained outside of Danhomè, able to raid Danhomè and open to raiding in return.

As for whether Agaja or any other ruler of Danhomè attempted in fact to stop the slave trade, the evidence gives little support to Akinjogbin's thesis. Even for the 1720s, the only real opportunity for Danhomè to stop the slave trade because the suzerainty of Oyo was not yet established, David Henige and Marion Johnson have argued that Agaja made no such attempt.[52] Over the longer run, David Ross argues, the Fon rulers had been little more than a band of slave raiders until the time when conquests and new responsibilities of state tempered their piratical approach.[53] The Fon rulers, viewed from this angle, were probably little different from other leaders of the region except as measured by their success.

The rising prices for slave exports provided Dahomey with steadily growing export revenue in the early eighteenth century. Whether the profits of slave trade grew, however, is a more speculative matter. The cost of supplying slaves grew as the population declined, and as social values came to oppose or limit enslavement. If the costs of supply rose more slowly in Dahomey than in other areas, then exporters in Dahomey benefitted from economic rents. Slave exporters may also have gained monopoly profits. The states of Dahomey had no monopoly on commerce, though they collected taxes and maintained special commercial privileges.[54] But private slave exporters could have maintained a broad front, led or supported by the state, thus forcing prices upward. Tests for monopoly power can be performed, once enough prices become available, by a comparison of prices in Dahomey and elsewhere with the passage of time. Regardless of the level of profit for slave exporters, however, the social cost of exporting slaves remained very high, as the depopulation of the coastal region continued.

Karl Polanyi and Rosemary Arnold, representing the substantivist school of economic anthropology, have suggested that Ouidah under the Fon regime became a 'port of trade', isolated from the domestic economy and its trade controlled completely by the king. While there is no question but that the Fon attempted restrictive practices in Ouidah and succeeded in part, almost all of the substantivist case is faulty. Arnold, in her attempt to support the 'port of trade' thesis, ignored the period before 1727 and exaggerated any hint of the isolation of slave trade from other commerce.[55] Ouidah was as free a port as existed prior to the Fon conquest of 1727, and the interactions of the slave trade and the domestic market were intimate. Private merchants continued to trade alongside the king after 1727 and import goods, in the majority, circulated generally.[56] How then could an act of the state have made the port into an isolated enclave, protecting the

41

domestic economy from the evils of price fluctuations? Polanyi, going over the ground of his associate some years later, recognized the need to discuss the earlier period, and to back away from Arnold's most simplistic assertions on the economic isolation of Ouidah. The product of his review of the issue, while still offered under the title 'port of trade', is not so much an interpretaion as a narrative of politics and commerce from 1680 to 1730, though he ascribes a special significance to Danhomè's status as an 'inland' kingdom.[57] Both Arnold and Polanyi erred in assuming that Danhomè exported mainly slaves obtained from far inland, and in assuming that the Fon monarchy carried on slave trade as a state monopoly. Each erred as well in confounding evidence from three quite different centuries to develop a composite image of Danhomè.[58] The substantivist interpretation of slave trade in the Bight of Benin is thus distorted and ahistorical, perhaps as a result of too great a determination to demonstrate that social institutions have primacy over economic forces.

By the 1730s the Dahomean slave-supply schedule ceased moving inward, and remained stable until the 1790s: the decade of lowest export quantity in this period was also the decade of the lowest real selling prices.[59] The sharp decline in the Aja population was muted, while exports of Eastern Voltaic, Yoruba and Nupe slaves grew in importance.

If ever there were a time when Dahomey could be described as having had a slave-export economy – a social formation dominated by the export of slaves – it would have been this period. The price elasticity of supply averaged 2.2, reflecting a very high price responsiveness for slave exports and indicating clearly economic behavior. The smaller quantities of slaves sold at any given price in this period suggest that Dahomean suppliers were earning monopoly profits in comparison to previous periods in the same region, and that they were earning economic rents or monopoly profits in comparison to other regions in the same period. Slave-export revenue was a higher percentage of Dahomean domestic product from 1730 to 1800 than in any other era. One is tempted, therefore, to treat the export of slaves in this period as a rationalized system through which Danhomè harvested the surrounding population for sale. In contrast, the period 1660–1700 appears as the initial expansion of slave exports, and the years 1700–30 appear as an anarchic time when war and enslavement raged out of control.

From the viewpoint of slave purchasers in the New World and Europe, eighteenth-century Dahomey – the Slave Coast – certainly appeared as a slave-export economy. The relationship between Danhomè and Oyo stabilized, and Danhomè relinquished its annual tribute of slaves and imported goods to Oyo. Wars between Danhomè and the Hueda continued on the coast, and from the interior flowed a steady supply of Voltaic slaves, probably resulting from raids by the Bariba principalities on each other:

slave exports through the ports of Grand Popo, Ouidah and Ekpé stemmed from these sources. Further, Oyo began a deliberate expansion toward the coast and into slave trade, with colonization first among the Anago and then the Egbado, resulting at the end of this period in a close relationship between Oyo and Porto-Novo. The exports of Porto-Novo and Badagry thus included, in addition to Aja and Voltaic slaves, slaves of Yoruba, Nupe and perhaps Voltaic origin sent down by Oyo merchants.

Nevertheless, despite the importance of slave exports in the eighteenth century, it is too extreme – or at least too simple – to say that the export of slaves dominated Dahomey's economy. Instead, the commodity exchange mode of production dominated the economy in this period, as in previous and subsequent eras.[60] To explore this issue more fully, however, one must turn to the interactions among all the sectors of the economy.

The mercantile sector is seen a bit more clearly than before in the late eighteenth century, thanks to records from the forts and from slave-trading voyages. In a sample of two voyages to Ouidah, roughly ten percent of the slaves exported were sold by the Fon state, twenty to thirty percent were sold by big merchants, thirty to fifty percent were sold by small merchants selling three to ten slaves each, and twenty percent were sold in ones and twos by individuals. The state thus had a surprisingly small share of the export trade: even the addition of European fees and duties brought the state's share of export revenue to no more than twenty percent of the total.[61] The state regulated Atlantic commerce and was one of many participants in that commerce, but did not monopolize it.[62] For ports other than Ouidah, where the states were smaller, weaker or more distant, the state's share in export commerce was presumably smaller.

The twenty percent of slaves sold by ones and twos probably indicates the sale of slaves out of the commodity exchange sector: the trade in slaves was so pervasive that every level of society was drawn into it. The core of mercantile involvement in slave exports, however, consisted of big and small private merchants, who together provided sixty to seventy percent of slaves exported. The big merchants were perhaps best able to organize long-distance trade in slaves from the interior, while slaves in the hands of small merchants may have been sold several times on their way to the coast. The details of the inland organization of slave catching and slave trade, however, remain elusive. One cannot yet say to what degree the state was content to regulate and protect the slave trade, and to what degree it actually conducted the collection and merchandizing of slaves. For example, if most slaves were captured in war, a mechanism must have existed to transfer slaves from the state, who presumably claimed them upon capture, to the merchants who exported them. On this and other key details, contemporary European observers pleaded ignorance.[63]

The structure of late eighteenth-century imports seems to have been much the same as in earlier and later eras: cotton, linen and other textiles accounted for over one-third of the value of imports, followed by cowries, alcoholic beverages, tobacco, and small quantities of many other goods.[64] Most imports went to the mercantile and commodity exchange sectors rather than to the state. In Ouidah, records of the English fort from 1752 to 1811 show that purchases of imports by the state were consistently less than one-third of the total. The Fon state's share of imports was, however, larger than its share of exports, which implies that the state also used revenue from taxes on the mercantile and commodity exchange sectors to buy imports.

Cowries continued to represent 20-35% of the value of imports, which implies an average value of £50,000 to £75,000 per year in cowrie imports to the Bight of Benin throughout the eighteenth century. Assuming a constant annual cowrie import and an annual loss of two percent of the current cowrie stock, the money supply would reach a limit at one hundred times the annual import: hence an aggregate money supply of up to £4 million.[65] Assuming that cowrie imports fed a zone including the Aja, Yoruba, Eastern Voltaic, Nupe and Hausa peoples, a population of 4 million persons would yield a stock of money averaging up to one pound sterling per capita. That would indicate a thoroughly monetized economy and, indeed, a per capita money supply close to that of the early twentieth century.

Estimates of the total level of domestic output, while they cannot be precise in this era, are important to attempt because of their significance in interregional and intercontinental comparisons. I have assumed that the proportion of trans-Atlantic trade to domestic product for Dahomey has averaged about 15% since the late seventeenth century. The proportion varied with time, of course: it rose from a very low level before the slave trade to a level much higher than the average (for the Aja at least) during the worst years of depopulation and during the high-price years of the eighteenth century. But in the longer run the relationship stabilized, as slave exports declined and domestic production recovered. Werner Peukert has estimated that export trade was only one-fortieth of domestic product in the eighteenth century. Given an average per capita export revenue of £0.5 in the years 1740–1800, Peukert would then project an average per capita output of £20 in those years. Since this would have been substantially greater than per capita output in Great Britain and the United States, where per capita output in 1800 reached £13 and £11, respectively, Peukert's estimate of the proportion of export revenue to domestic product is too low. On the other hand, the ratio of 15% yields a per capita output averaging £3.9 for the eighteenth century, which is more plausible on the face of it, and is slightly lower than the £4 and £5 per capita output for Brazil and Mexico in 1800.[66]

Thus the export of slaves can neither be dismissed as lacking real impact nor can it be taken as Dahomey's primary economic activity. The monarchy in Danhomè supported and relied on the slave trade, but by no means monopolized it, as large and small merchants and competing states each carried large segments of the trade. The bulk of wealth, output and perhaps even state revenue was assured by the familial and commodity exchange modes of production. At the same time, the familial and commodity exchange sectors reproduced the population from which the slaves were drawn, and the sale of slaves permitted the immense imports of cowrie currency which, *ceteris paribus*, facilitated the expansion of the domestic market. In sum, while Dahomean slave exports and domestic production had important interaction, the only sense in which the export of slaves dominated the economy is that in which a parasite is said to dominate its host. In the case of Dahomey, the effect of the parasite was grave but not fatal.

From the 1780s through the 1840s, large numbers of slaves were exported not only from Dahomey, but from the western and northern portions of present-day Nigeria.[67] The Nigerian contribution to Bight of Benin slave exports was shorter-lived and of smaller magnitude than that of Dahomey, and it obeyed a more erratic dynamic. The great expansion of Yoruba slave exports in the 1780s coincides with the reign of the Alafin Abiodun, a monarch reputed to have been an active supporter of the slave trade. Then the wars of the nascent Sokoto Caliphate provided large numbers of Hausa slave exports in the first two decades of the nineteenth century. These were only a tiny portion of the Hausa population, however, and almost all were male – indicating that most Hausa enslaved during the wars remained on the continent. The Nupe, who were also swept up in the formation of the Caliphate, were well represented among slave exports at this time. On the other hand, exports of Eastern Voltaic slaves virtually ceased in the nineteenth century, perhaps as a result of reduced pressure from Oyo. Further increases in Yoruba slave exports coincided with the decline and fall of Oyo: with the Owu war and the Muslim revolt in Ilorin during the 1820s, Yoruba slaves first became the dominant ethnic group among Bight of Benin exports. The collapse of Oyo in the 1830s, followed by the southward flight of the Oyo Yoruba and the establishment of Abeokuta and Ibadan, led to the largest export of Yoruba slaves ever. The Ijebu became slave merchants at the turn of the nineteenth century, selling slaves from the Yoruba heartland to Lagos, which became the main slave port of the region from the 1820s through the 1840s. If there was ever depopulation among the Yoruba, this is when it occurred: the wholesale displacements and the tragic histories of Yoruba families have been recorded in some detail.[68]

Despite the flourishing of slave trade in nineteenth-century Nigeria and its continuation in Dahomey, the turn of the century had seen the beginning of the end for slavery in the world economy. Among the signs of the times – all interrelated – were the successful slave revolt in Haiti, the rise of industry based on wage labor, declining purchases of African slaves, the formation of vocal anti-slavery organizations, and the outlawing of the Atlantic slave trade.[69] The demise of slavery would require more than a century to complete, however, and the process ironically brought about an expansion of slavery in Africa during most of the nineteenth century.

For Dahomey, slave exports continued to flow systematically, in contrast to the more irregular Nigerian exports. But the pattern was new, as a result of the secular decline in slave demand and the independence of Danhomè from Oyo. Treating the exports of slaves from Dahomey from the 1790s to the 1860s as points on a long-run supply schedule, one finds that the schedule has become much more steeply inclined than before, with a price elasticity of demand of 0.7. This figure suggests that the leaders of Dahomey were now less dedicated to the export of slaves as a means of earning revenue than they had been in earlier times – or that they were less able to control the number of slaves exported. In fact this period, which begins with over two decades of commercial disruption accompanying the French Revolution and the Napoleonic wars, saw changes in the structure of politics in the Dahomean interior and changes in the organization of commerce on the coast. The decline of Oyo permitted Danhomè to declare its independence in the 1820s and to renew its territorial expansion: the wars of Danhomè were henceforth against Yoruba peoples more often than Aja peoples, and the export of Aja slaves declined. But from the 1830s, Danhomè had to contend with the new and populous Egba state centered on Abeokuta: four decades of hostilities between the two powers left the stalemate unbroken.[70]

The European powers ended their official presence in Dahomey, abandoning their forts: the French in 1797, the Portuguese in 1805 and the English in 1812.[71] But the slave trade to Brazil continued unabated, and a new trade to Cuba sprang up. African merchants and states continued to handle much of the factoring in the export of slaves, as they had in the past. The niche left by the departed Europeans, however, was soon filled by immigrant Brazilian merchants, led by Francisco Felix de Souza, who came to be the wealthiest and most powerful of West African merchants in the nineteenth century. De Souza built up a network of factories from Little Popo to Lagos early in the century and, after helping Ghezo to seize the throne of Danhomè in 1818, became an official in the Fon regime and

46

presided over his commercial empire from the Portuguese fort in Ouidah until his death in 1849.[72] In addition to de Souza and later Brazilians, however, Dahomean merchants and factors held a significant portion of the export market. For the 1780s, Peukert lists Grand Boucaud, Tineou, Becun, Ayaponou, Zoppé, Zerobou and Pierre; the latter is the same as Monsieur Pierre or Tammata, of Hausa origin, described by Adams. In the 1840s, Forbes lists Ahjovee (Adjovi), Quenung (Quénum or Houénou) and Narwhey (Nasali) in addition to the Yovogan, Dagba.[73]

A further change in the organization of slave exports came after 1830, as the illegal status of Atlantic slave trade became more firmly established, and as the British navy began serious attempts to suppress the export of slaves from the West African coast. Slave ships captured by the British were generally escorted to Sierra Leone and the liberated slaves, mostly Yoruba, became part of the creole community in Freetown. The export of slaves now became clandestine: elaborate stratagems were devised for notifying those on land of the approach of slave ships, and for hurrying the slave cargoes to isolated points for rapid embarkation. Once the export of slaves from the Gold Coast was closed off by the presence of the British beginning about 1820, Akan and Voltaic slaves were moved from Accra across the Volta and exported from Little Popo, Agoué and Grand Popo.[74] As the complexity and the intrigue of the clandestine export trade grew, the costs, profits and influence of the exporters rose accordingly.

Since imports in the early nineteenth century are not well described, it is unclear whether the demands of the Dahomean market were met as before, now that shipping patterns had changed. Of particular interest is whether the Brazilian, Spanish and American merchants were able to supply cowries in the quantity to which importers had become accustomed. One change is well documented: the growth in imports of silver dollars of varying origins. These coins, being of much higher denomination than cowries, were more convenient for the rapid exchange required in the clandestine trade; they also came to circulate in the interior.[75]

The bulk of slave exports went to Brazil until 1850. A sizeable countercurrent of freed slaves began to move in the opposite direction, especially after the abortive slave revolt of January 1835 in Bahia. This revolt so frightened the authorities in Bahia that they began to urge free blacks to emigrate to Africa. Over the next forty years some three thousand people left Bahia for the Bight of Benin – some returning home, others going for the first time.[76] They settled at every point along the coast, but particularly at Lagos and Agoué. The 'Brazilian' community in the Bight of Benin thus emerged, in effect, as an ethnic group. It included mulatto and white merchants from Brazil, Portugal and even Spain, returned ex-slaves, Brazilian-born creoles, and the descendants, slaves and relatives by

47

marriage of the immigrants. The community had in common the Portuguese language and, most often, the Catholic religion, although some of the Brazilians were Muslims. They tended to specialize in commerce, maintaining their ties to Brazil: they exported slaves, palm oil, cloth and kola, and imported tobacco and rum.

Later in the 1840s, a similar group of liberated slaves began to come to the Bight of Benin from Sierra Leone. Known as 'Aku' or 'Saros,' these Sierra Leonians were English-speaking, Protestant, mostly Yoruba, and closely tied to British missionary and diplomatic interests.[77] They also returned as merchants, particularly to Lagos and Badagry, but some of them returned to spread the gospel to the peoples of the interior.

The British, meanwhile, added diplomatic initiatives to their naval efforts to end slave exports in the 1840s, and sent a series of missions to the various states in the Bight of Benin. They were rapidly drawn into the conflict between Abeokuta and Abomey – the Sierra Leonian and missionary interests drew the British close to the Egba and made close relations between Britain and Danhomè almost impossible. Brodie Cruickshank, following a mission to Abomey in 1848, reported the king's revenue from duties and sale of slaves to be £60,000 per year, and thus concluded that Britain could not afford to pay Dahomey to cease exporting slaves. In fact the king's gross revenue from export of slaves was more like £8,000, and his profit after costs was below that.[78]

In 1851, eight months after the failure of a Fon assault on Abeokuta, the British occupied Lagos, replacing King Kosoko with their candidate Akitoye and ending the export of slaves. The sphere of influence formed by the British and the Egba, in opposition to that of Danhomè, in effect determined what would later become the colonial frontier. The diplomacy of the period thus tended to isolate Danhomè from the growing European influence on the coast, and to inflate its reputation among Europeans as a barbaric and tyrannical center of slave trade. This impression was reinforced during one final decade of large-scale slave exports. Most of the slaves were destined for Cuba, and the leading exporter was Domingo Martins, a Brazilian immigrant who had been prominent as a landowner and merchant, and whose chief factory was at Sèmè.[79]

A new period in Dahomey's economic history opened up in the 1840s with the expansion of the slave-labor mode of production. This development, moreover, was a response throughout West Africa to declining trans-Atlantic slave prices, and to rising demand – in both West African and trans-Atlantic markets – for goods which could be produced by slaves. Price theory suggests some propositions on the behavior of slave prices over time which should clarify the timing, the extent, and the regional variations in African slave production. Since the amount of data so far assembled is limited, these propositions must now be stated as hypotheses, in the expectation that future work will confirm them. To begin with, African coastal prices for both male and female slave exports declined, in real terms, beginning in the late eighteenth century. Further, the excess of New World prices for male slaves over females declined in the nineteenth century, as slave owners saw that abolition of slave trade meant their slaves would have to become self-reproducing.[80] In Africa, therefore, where the relative price of male slaves was already low, it would have become even lower. On the other hand, the availability of cheap male slaves encouraged their utilization in market production in Africa. The growth of the domestic market in the West African savanna increased the demand for slave produce, which in turn led to a derived demand for male slaves, thus limiting the decline of male slave prices.[81] Closer to the coast, as among the Aja and Yoruba peoples, similar growth in slave plantations took place, although here it was more in response to growth in European than in domestic demand. The price elasticity of slave export supply, finally, rose in this period: a decline of export prices encouraged the diversion of slaves into remunerative domestic production, while a rise in export prices had the reverse effect.

Dahomey and its inhabitants would have been better off if the region had never participated in the export of slaves.[82] The individual and social advantages secured in the course of more than two centuries of slave exports were more than outweighed by the economic and human costs. Slave trade drew Dahomey early, tightly and permanently into the world economy, but the usual benefits of international commerce were eliminated by the terms and the commodity of this trade. Autarky, not normally an attractive alternative to interregional economic ties, might here have been preferable. Best of all would have been trans-Atlantic commerce restricted to the produce of human labor, rather than sale of human labor itself: its volume would then have been smaller, but its impact more positive.

The export of slaves did not, however, cause the destruction of society. The population of Dahomey was somewhat smaller in 1850 than in 1650, but the level of per capita output had grown, and the market economy had expanded. Slave trade was not sufficient to suffocate the economy: rather, it slowed the rate of growth. Yet the judgment on the slave trade is not thereby rendered less harsh. If the slave trade slowed the growth of domestic product by as little as 0.1% per year, the result after two hundred years was a domestic product twenty percent lower than would otherwise have been the case. With that additional wealth, Dahomey would have been much better prepared to withstand the onslaught of capitalist expansion during the subsequent century.

Supposing that Dahomey had avoided the export of slaves, its import purchasing power would have been greatly reduced until the nineteenth century rise of demand for palm products. Imports of textiles, cowries, alcoholic beverages, tobacco and other goods such as iron would have been cut far back. Higher-cost domestic industries would have expanded to substitute for the imports. The money supply would have been much smaller without the huge imports of cowries, unless alternative currency could have been adopted. Slave prices would have been lower for male slaves if not for females, and the incentive to raid for slaves would have been much reduced. Technical and economic innovations would still have diffused to the region, as long as some trans-Atlantic commerce continued. The larger population and the greater certainty in life would have allowed the domestic economy to grow more rapidly.

Could Dahomey have refused to sell slaves? The pressures forcing Africans into the sale of slaves were formidable: the domestic market for slaves – already tied to the trans-Saharan slave market – provided a structure that European slave merchants could buy into and expand. Even if one segment of the coast refused to sell slaves, surrounding areas could begin exporting slaves and, through raids, draw the reluctant region into warfare and slaving. Yet the process was not inevitable. In some regions and some periods of time, the peoples of Africa were able to refuse to export slaves: the cases of Yoruba before 1750 and the kingdom of Benin after 1550 may be cited. Perhaps Dahomey could not have altogether avoided exporting slaves, given the level of European demand. But, given different political conditions and perhaps different social values, it could have reduced the number of slaves exported.

If Africa as a whole had refused to export slaves, the history of four continents would have been different. One would have to imagine the Americas without African slaves, Europe without slave merchants, lesser profits on sugar and tobacco because of higher labor costs, and Africa as a source of commodities rather than slaves. In the ongoing discussion of the development of the modern world economy, therefore, a more explicit treatment needs to be given to the African contribution to the growth of capitalism through the provision of slave labor.[83]

THE ERA OF AGRICULTURAL EXPORTS

The rise of English industrial production of soap brought about a demand for palm oil at the beginning of the nineteenth century; other uses for palm oil followed as the growing industrial system developed a demand for many sorts of oils and fats. English demand for palm oil was initially satisfied by producers of the Niger Delta and Cross River hinterlands, probably the lowest-cost producing area in Africa, as oil palms grew abundantly in the rain forest and canoe transport to the coast was cheap. But demand grew with the passage of time, prices rose, and industrialization spread to France and other areas of Europe.[84] So it was that in the 1830s the Marseille merchant Victor Régis and the Gold Coast merchant Thomas Hutton came to the Bight of Benin to purchase palm oil. By 1841, Régis had arranged to take possession of the old French fort in Ouidah, and made it his commercial headquarters. During the 1840s Régis, Hutton and the Hamburg firm of O'Swald purchased palm oil at many points along the coast; after the establishment of British consular authority at Lagos in 1852, additional European firms came to the coast.[85]

The export of palm oil to Europe, while it prefigured the state of things to come, was not the beginning of agricultural exports. Quite aside from the sale of ships' provisions for the slave trade, the Bight of Benin was already exporting palm oil, kola and cloth to Brazil; the Brazilian market continued to provide a viable alternative to the European market until late in the nineteenth century.[86] Nor did European merchants easily gain control of the export of palm oil, even to Europe: Thomas Hutton himself was born of an African mother, and Brazilian, Sierra Leonian, Yoruba and Aja merchants transported and exported palm products alongside the European firms.

Export quantities of palm oil and palm kernels between 1840 and 1900 are shown in Figure 2.4 for Dahomey and for Lagos.[87] Consular estimates put palm oil exports for Dahomey at 7,000 metric tons by the 1850s, a figure which equalled the quantity exported in the 1890s. Even assuming export volume estimates of the 1850s to have been high, it remains clear that a large supply of palm products awaited only shipping capacity and a remunerative price to be exported. For palm kernels, the slower development of export quantities reflected initially lower prices. The relative price of palm kernels grew steadily, however, and the relative proportion of palm kernels grew in response: the demand for palm kernels came especially from Germany and the Netherlands, where they were used in margarine and cattle feed.[88]

Cyclical fluctuations in Bight of Benin palm products, with a period of about nine years, may be observed from the 1860s up to the present day. These cycles, which result from some combination of climatological factors, fluctuating prices and perhaps planting cycles, are projected back to 1840 in Figure 2.4. The projections are by no means precise, but they may serve as a reminder that exports fluctuated primarily in response to weather and price conditions, and only secondarily in response to the influences of slave trade or government policies.

The policy dilemma facing the kingdom of Danhomè – whether to emphasize exports of slaves or palm products – has become a famous case

51

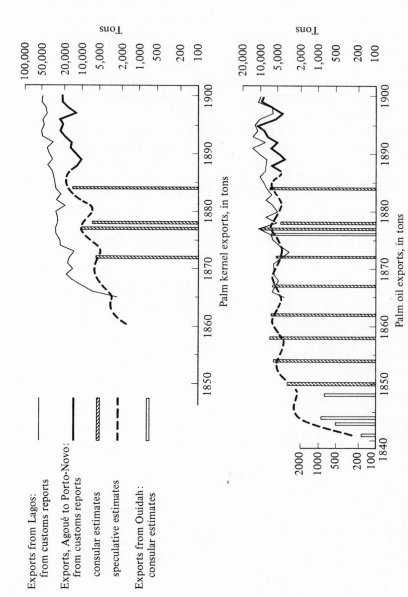

Figure 2.4. Palm oil and palm kernel exports, 1840–1900.
Sources: Table A4.4; Statistical Abstract for Lagos, United Kingdom Parliamentary Papers; Allioza, 'Le Commerce entre Marseille et le Dahomey,' 52; Argyle, *The Fon*, 48–9; Coquery, 'Le Blocus,' 391; Coquery–Vidrovitch. 'De la traite,' 118; Newbury, *Western Slave Coast*, 58, 123–5; Ross, 'Autonomous Kingdom,' 181–98; Ross, 'Domingo Martinez,' 85; Schnapper, *La Politique*, 172.

52

in the nineteenth-century contest between slave trade and 'legitimate' trade.[89] As significant as this policy issue may have been, its import was limited by the significance of commerce in surrounding portions of the Bight of Benin, and by the limits on any state's power to change its economic system. During the 1840s palm oil was exported from almost every port on the Bight, and its value exceeded that of slave exports before 1850. Any attempts by merchants and kings to prevent the export of palm oil were therefore short-lived. David Ross dates the Fon state's active encouragement of palm oil exports to Thomas B. Freeman's 1842 visit to Abomey, which is a plausible timing although, with the general expansion of exports from the region, it is hard to see how the Fon could have missed the point regardless of Freeman's visit.[90]

The continuation of slave trade was another matter, tied not only to New World demand for slaves, but to complicated internal politics and to diplomatic contacts with the British and French who ruled the seas. For a time in the late 1840s, Domingo Martins was the greatest exporter of both palm oil and slaves. Every state had a faction devoted to continuing slave exports, and a faction willing to end slave exports in order to achieve an alliance with the British. When Anglo-Fon negotiations for a treaty to end the slave trade broke down in 1850, the partisans of war with the Egba gained the upper hand in Abomey. The Fon attack of March 1851 on Abeokuta failed, however, and in turn contributed to the British decision to occupy Lagos, ally with the Egba, and blockade the coast of Danhomè from January to June of 1852.

In this situation, with the dangers of continuing slave exports clear to see, King Ghezo of Danhomè attempted to halt the export of slaves and establish a royal monopoly on the commerce of palm products. The policy choice, therefore, was not whether to begin palm-product exports, but whether to impose a royal monopoly on existing commerce. In practice the export of palm produce was impossible to monopolize because of the dispersed nature of its production and commerce, and by 1854 the failure of Ghezo's monopoly was evident.[91] Instead, the state settled for a share in production and commerce in palm products, special prices for royal trade, and a tax on the trade of others: a solution not unlike that for the eighteenth-century slave trade. Meanwhile the slave trade to Cuba recovered and entered its final boom.

In sum, the policies of Danhomè and other states, while important in influencing the distribution of earnings from export of palm products, probably did little to determine the volume of exports. Ample groves of oil palms were in production, and the decision to harvest and export them depended on the level of price and demand, and on weather conditions. The kingdom of Danhomè, further, produced only about one-fourth of the

53

volume of palm products exported from the coast between Agoué and Porto-Novo, or half that if Lagos and its hinterland are included.

Most of the palm products exported came from the commodity exchange sector – that is, from family farms. Oil palms throughout the country were cleared and harvested more intensively, and new trees were planted. Some of the palm oil exported may have been diverted from the domestic market, thus forcing domestic prices up, but European demand for palm kernels presented the producers with a brand new market, as domestic demand was almost nil. The export of palm products represented a substantial new opportunity for small producers, providing a more dependable income than slave trade, and providing a major addition to the revenue available from sales on the domestic market. Real export income rose from the 1840s through the 1880s, as the quantity of exports rose and the terms of trade improved. A sharp decline in export prices in the late 1880s, however, stirred unrest among European merchants and contributed to the European conquest of the Bight of Benin.[92]

The slave-labor sector also expanded to meet the demand for palm products, probably at a greater rate than the commodity exchange sector. The Fon monarchy set up plantations on the Abomey plateau, warlords set up plantations around the major Yoruba cities, Fon officials and merchants established plantations near Ouidah, and Brazilian merchants set up plantations along the coast from Sèmè to Little Popo. No clear descriptions of the operation of these plantations have been advanced, but the economies achieved probably had more to do with working the slaves long hours than with any increased technical efficiency. The revolt of Yoruba slaves on the Abomey plateau in 1855 – nipped in the bud by Fon authorities – provides an indication of the scale of slavery and the severity of exploitation at that time.[93]

The mercantile sector made certain adjustments to the new export commerce. Since the composition of imports did not change greatly, they could be handled in much the same way as before. But the export of bulky agricultural produce presented a different problem than the commerce in slaves, whose activities were now limited to the domestic market, including the growing demand from slave plantations. The well-developed domestic market for foodstuffs, however, provided a model of institutions for the export of palm products. Factors on the coast now received produce collected by itinerant merchants, bulked it and delivered it to the shippers. In some cases, an individual or firm was able to participate at once in the production, collection, factoring and shipping of palm produce: Domingo Martins was able to do so for a time. More generally, competition raged in each portion of the mercantile system: firms often participated in collection and factoring or in factoring and shipping. The entry of steamships into

West African commerce in the 1850s helped Europeans to dominate shipping almost entirely, but they had to share factoring with Brazilian, Sierra Leonian, and a few Aja and Yoruba merchants. Almost all collection and all production was accomplished by Africans, including those of Brazilian and Sierra Leonian background.

The import of cowries began again on a large scale as German merchants shipped cowries – now from Zanzibar rather than the Maldives – to Ouidah and Lagos beginning in about 1847. The quantities were large enough now, however, that a steady devaluation of cowrie values proceeded until cowries virtually ceased to function as money in the early twentieth century. Imports of dollars dropped off following the end of the slave trade, but British sterling coin, circulated on a small scale in Lagos in the 1860s, grew rapidly to become the major currency used in palm-product commerce all along the coast.[94]

Imports continued to be dominated by textiles, alcoholic beverages, currency and tobacco, but other imports grew in significance as new industrial products appeared and as import purchasing power grew. Kerosene, first imported in the 1870s, began to replace palm oil in lamps, and the lamps were now lit with matches. Building materials imported from Europe were used increasingly.

Not only did the new orientation of commerce toward Europe require changes in the productive and mercantile systems, but it required new social values and political orientation. In the days before it became obvious that Europe would conquer Africa, the economic and political leaders of the Bight of Benin prepared themselves for the new burdens and opportunities of leadership. Missions and schools sprouted all along the coast. The de Souza family had operated its own school in Ouidah since the 1830s, but the Brazilian community as a whole clamored for Catholic churches and schools. In 1861 the Société des Missions africaines de Lyon opened a mission and school in Ouidah, and in subsequent years opened missions and schools in Lagos, Porto-Novo and Agoué. The priests of the French order were dismayed to find that they would have to teach in Portuguese, but they acquiesced to the demands of the community. Sierra Leonians set up schools and missions in Lagos, Badagry and Abeokuta in the 1850s, instructing in both English and Yoruba.[95] Literacy, previously limited to a tiny group of merchants and officials, now became widespread among the elite: by the 1880s literacy in English, Portuguese, French or Yoruba had become common to the commercial leaders of the coast, to some of the major landowners, and to officials in all the major states of the region.

Rulers of states–notably in Abomey, Porto-Novo and Abeokuta– sought alliances with the European powers which would guarantee close commercial ties yet preserve their economic and political independence. While the kingdoms sought to retain recognition from the European states, leading merchants and landowners saw the possibility of becoming the arbiters of new European protectorates in the region. Francisco Chico de Souza convinced the Portuguese to reoccupy their fort in Ouidah in 1865. His successor as *chacha*, Julio F. de Souza, brought in Portuguese missionaries in 1884, and in 1885 he signed treaties with the governor of São Thomé placing Dahomey under the protection of Portugal. The gambit was ill-fated, however, and de Souza paid for his adventurousness with his life as Glele, apparently seeing little advantage in a Portuguese tie, imprisoned the *chacha* in 1887. Many other prominent figures of the Bight of Benin, though in less spectacular fashion, acted out the expectation that they would continue to be leaders in independent African states, though perhaps under European protection, participating actively in international trade.

In a rapid adjustment to new demand for agricultural exports, the Bight of Benin had by 1860 established the institutions for this commerce, and was exporting large though still growing quantities of palm produce. African merchants, landowners and officials made plans for expanding their role in the growing world economy. These plans, however, would have to be put on the shelf for some seventy years, as the aggressive efforts of some European merchants and officials combined with growing national rivalry in Europe to cause the partition of Africa. The British colony of Lagos expanded bit by bit along the lagoons, the French established their protectorate of Porto-Novo in 1882, and the Germans laid claim to Togo in 1885. The hinterland was occupied in the early 1890s after a major war in Dahomey, and through signing of treaties elsewhere.[96] This colonial conquest marks an important turning point, though its economic importance has been greatly exaggerated by the implicit assumption, too widely and easily adopted, that a change in governments means a change in economic life. In the short term, the imposition of colonial government led simply to a redistribution of control over the revenues and produce of the domestic economy, and, with the important exception of the abolition of slavery, only over a longer period of time did colonial rule lead to changes in the modes of production.

3

Struggles with the gods: economic life in the 1880s

The preceding chapters, in their emphasis on long-range developments, have perhaps encouraged the reader to view those changes as smooth and gradual transitions. But if the transformations of centuries appear to have been smooth, the fluctuations of individual years were jarring. The 'normal year' never takes place: one always places it in either the future or the past. Nor is the sweep of human history independent of the events of any year. Rather it is the result, over the passage of centuries, of innumerable tiny events, conflicts and processes, each insignificant in itself and unrelated, apparently, to most others – yet in the aggregate these many events lead to occasional periods of rapid change. The importance of the short run in history, further, is seen perhaps more clearly from the perspective of the individual than from that of the society: man, unlike the societies he constructs, does not live in the long run. He cannot be content to take the long view of society when faced with the pressing needs of subsistence and the desires for economic and social advance. Each year's changes in many arenas are of vital importance to his well-being, and they are of concern as well to the historian who would know the structure of society and the processes of its change. This is as true for Africa, where the documentation on daily life is often meagre, as it is for Europe and North America, where such documentation is at times overwhelming.

The present chapter prepares the ground for short-run analysis with a cross-sectional view of the economy of the 1880s; Chapters 4 through 8 consider short-range economic changes in a subsequent period (1890–1914); and these in turn are followed by a synthesis in Chapter 9, relating short-range changes to long-range changes.

The cross-sectional description of this chapter is intended to provide a sort of base line – a comprehensive review of the various sectors and activities of the regional economy. The decade of the 1880s provides a convenient period for this presentation for various reasons. It is relatively well documented, both in contemporary sources and in sources from subsequent periods which may reasonably be used to describe that time.[1] Further, since it precedes the period of colonial rule, it enables the observer to abstract from the impact of colonial government, and thus obtain a view of the economic system which may be projected with some confidence both forward and backward in time. Finally, it is adjacent to the succeeding period in which short-run changes are analyzed. During these years no fundamental changes took place in the technology of production, in the goods and services exchanged, nor in the orientation of commerce, though such changes had occurred in the mid-nineteenth century and would occur again in the mid-twentieth century. Stability, however, should not be mistaken for a stagnant steady state. Indeed, the economy in this period exhibited considerable activity, tension, fluctuation, innovation, and redistribution. Even in a period of stability, the economy should be viewed in dynamic terms.

The people of the Bight of Benin certainly viewed it in such terms. Though perhaps innocent of the notion of 'progress' now implanted into the minds of most of the world's population by a century-long technological revolution, they did view change as inevitable, and they viewed themselves as active participants in changes. They consulted Fate regularly – through the diviners of *Ifa* and *Fa* – yet they often challenged their fates as foretold by the oracle.[2] And while a lavish funeral was sometimes the highest objective toward which a man might strive, the energies and imagination of a lifetime went into achieving that goal. In the meantime the gods might send floods, disease, tax collectors, lazy and faithless relatives or bad prices with which to test him and perhaps destroy him. He, in turn, by relying on his own resources and acting in accord with the wishes of the gods, would be able to overcome the resistance of natural and human spirits, and go on to extend his fields, increase the size of his family, and profit commercially.[3]

Turning, then, to the cross-sectional, general equilibrium view of the economy, emphasis will naturally concentrate on the leading role of agriculture. The significant non-agricultural aspects of the economy (craft industries, fishing, commerce, consumption of manufactured goods, and production for psychic benefits, as for religion and prestige) were most often linked to agricultural pursuits. I have followed a qualitative equivalent to input–output analysis in describing the economy, by dividing the economy into a set of industries – defining an industry for the production of each agricultural good, each craft good, and for services such as transportation, including categories for foreign trade and government – and considering the input to each industry and the output from each industry. The result is a description of the structure of the economy including, for several industries, a regional breakdown. In the

58

concluding pages of the chapter 1 propose some analytical results of the input–output approach.[4] While the nature of the input–output approach tends to blur distinctions among the familial, commodity exchange and slave-labor modes of production, it throws the mercantile sector into clear relief.

The input–output analysis of the economy in the 1880s shows it to have been a working system, composed of identifiable subsystems defined by region, by product and by mode of production. Given the economic constraints on resources and the technical constraints on production and transportation, the system was quite well developed. Local differences were, however, pronounced: the differences depended on ecology (soil quality and other natural resources), on location, and on the political and social peculiarities of each area. This multitude of factors, playing upon an area which was basically uniform in its environment and population, gave a real richness and variety to economic life. The economic interactions within regions and between regions became so rich and complex only after a long period of development; in this sense, it is possible to characterize the economy as mature. It used with reasonable efficiency the technology at its disposal, it was well attuned to its social and political realities, it was flexible, and showed itself able to adjust to economic and non-economic changes.

The economic system was articulated on one hand with the geography of the country, and on the other hand with the social and political systems of the people. In terms of input–output analysis, these articulations may be treated as boundary conditions to the operation of the economy – that is, they are not the subject of the analysis, but they must be known and taken as given in order to complete the analysis. Each of these areas is therefore investigated briefly before proceeding to the details of the economic structure.

THE GEOGRAPHIC CONTEXT

The sandy soil of the coastline extends inland some three or four kilometers to the lagoon, and in some cases slightly beyond the lagoon. While coconut palms and manioc grow well on this soil, other crops do not fare so well. From there, a heavy lateritic soil known as *terre de barre* extends inland to slightly beyond the latitude of Abomey and Kétou, except where it is broken by rivers, lagoons and marshes. This generally rich soil supported the bulk of the population of southern Dahomey. Further inland lies very porous soil so that, despite a rainfall level at least equal to that of coastal areas, agricultural productivity and hence population density were far lower.

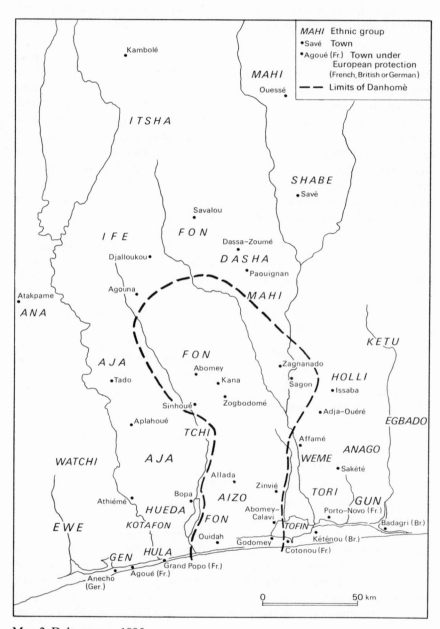

MAHI	Ethnic group
•Savè	Town
•Agoué (Fr.)	Town under European protection (French, British or German)
– – –	Limits of Danhomè

Map 2 Dahomey, c. 1885

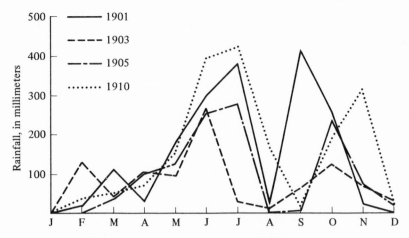

Figure 3.1. Monthly rainfall for selected years, in millimeters.
Source: Table A6.1.

The lagoon system has been built up along the entire Bight of Benin as a result of the transport of sand by the eastward-moving coastal current. Three rivers – the Mono, the Couffo and the Ouémé – flow into the lagoons: the Couffo empties into Lake Ahémé, and the Ouémé empties into the wide Porto-Novo lagoon, which connects to Lake Nokoué. During the floods of the late summer, a large proportion of the country is inundated: not only the lagoons, but the lower Mono valley, the lower Ouémé valley, and the flood plain of the Sô, which drains the Lama and is also fed by overflow from the Ouémé. Further inland are two great depressions: the Lama (or Ko), and the marshes in which the Holli live. The latter include some rich, black soil which is farmed actively.

Average rainfall ranges from a low of 900mm per year in the southwest at Grand Popo to a high of 1,400mm per year in the southeast at Sakété; for most of the rest of the country, rainfall averages from 1,000 to 1,200mm per year. But rainfall fluctuated sharply from year to year, and the monthly pattern of rainfall within years fluctuated equally, as is indicated in Figure 3.1.

Population density tended to reflect the relative fertility of the land and the productivity of fishing. The relatively dense population in the area of Porto-Novo tended to develop more intensive techniques of production; the same may be said for Abomey. Other areas of the country, however, could have supported greater populations at the same level of technology. Map 3B, showing population density as of 1954, may be taken as an indication of the relative population density of the 1880s, since internal

Map 3 Dahomey: population, rainfall, oil palm density
A Average rainfall, in millimeters per year
B Population density per square kilometer, 1954
C Oil palm density, 1910

Sources: Cornevin, *Histoire du Dahomey*; Mercier, *Cartes ethno-démographique de l'Ouest africain*, feuille 205; Adam, *Le Palmier à huile*

migration in the interim was minimal. The total population of the 1950s was something over twice that of the 1880s.

Three economic regions may be discerned for Dahomey, including the 'Coast,' running from the coastline through the plateaux centered on Sakété, Allada and Athiémé; the 'Plateau,' including the plateaux centered on Kétou, Abomey and Aplahoué; and the 'Center,' of which the two main towns were Savalou and Savè. (This leaves the 'North' to refer to the area from Parakou north.) These three regions are useful for discussing crops, agricultural techniques, transportation and marketing.

In addition to these north–south divisions, the region may also be divided up from east to west in a pattern reflective of its ethnic and political history: in the center of southern Dahomey lay the kingdom of Dahomey, running from Ouidah through Allada, Abomey and Savalou. To the east lay predominantly Yoruba areas – Savè, Kétou, the Nago – and the areas of Porto-Novo and the Weme. To the west lay the Aja, Gen and Ewe groups, as well as the Yoruba Ife and Ana. Further, southern Dahomey was divided into *cercles* under French administration. These *cercles* were revised from time to time, but they generally numbered from seven to ten, and were known by the name of the town from which they were administered. The *cercles* reflected a combination of pre-existing regions and French administrative outlook, but they are often useful in describing the economy.

THE SOCIAL CONTEXT

Both the Yoruba and the Aja peoples were organized into a system of non-segmentary lineages.[5] The central social unit was the major patrilineage, known as *henu* among the Aja and *agbole* among the Yoruba. Its chief (Aja *henugan*, Yoruba *bale*) was the oldest man of the lineage. The council, consisting of the old men and women of the group, had to give its assent on all major decisions. Among the Yoruba, members of an *agbole* were preferred to live in a single area; among the Aja, the *henu* was usually divided into several local sections in different towns.

Each *henu* or *agbole* consisted of several minor patrilineages or extended patrilineal families, called *hueta* by the Aja and *ile* by the Yoruba; the chief (Aja *huetagan*, Yoruba *bale*) was again the oldest male of the group, aided by a council. Each of these extended families was in turn composed of a set of minimal patrilineal families consisting, for instance, of a man, his wives and children, and perhaps an unmarried younger brother and his widowed mother. Among the Aja, the *hueta* was generally the unit of economic activity, under the direction of the *huetagan*, while among the Yoruba the economic unit was more often the minimal patrilineal family.

Among the Aja, several *henu* were combined to form a maximal

63

patrilineage or clan, the *ako*, of which all the members were descendants of the founder, the *tohwio*. This group had little social importance, but was the focus of occasional religious celebrations. Among the Yoruba, several *agbole* were grouped together to form an *idile*, which was comparable in some respects to the Aja *henu*, and in other respects to the *ako*.

The depth of the lineage structure varied widely, depending on individual circumstances and on the particular ethnic group. The system was at its most elaborate among certain of the Fon, while for some Yoruba groups *idile*, *agbole* and *ile* were in practice coterminous. Fission of lineage groups took place after a family quarrel or following a migration of part of the group; the new lineage then formally inaugurated its ancestors.

At every level, the chief of the lineage collectivity was responsible for the ancestral ceremonies, and for the settling of disputes, the disposition of lands, and the making or approval of marital and political alliances. The men stayed fixed to the land where they were born, and the women moved from family to family at marriage. The lineages were generally, but apparently not strictly, exogamous. Women were not integrated into the lineage of their husband: among the Aja, an old woman returned to the compound of her birth, and took her place on the council.

Land belonged to the first man to occupy it, to a person receiving a gift of land from its original occupant, or to its purchaser. With the passage of time, the land came to belong to the lineage or descendants of the original owner. The lineage chief supervised the use of lineage lands, which were divided into collective lineage lands and plots used by individuals and small families. Lineage land could be sold, given the approval of chief and council. It was only at the lower levels of the lineage structure that the chief paid any real attention to the use of individually farmed lands. The collective lands, administered directly by the chief, consisted of his own personal lands, those of the office of chief, and those of the lineage – the lands of the founder, the ancestral shrines, and other lands which had been allocated to the collectivity. Each level of a lineage held collective lands of this sort, but the lands of a whole *ako*, for instance, might consist only of a sacred grove and a few fields, while at the *hueta* level the majority of the land was frequently collective. This system too met with local variation – the Yoruba did not emphasize collective work or ownership as much as the Aja, and some Aja peoples tended to be quite individualistic. Land used by a man would be passed on to his direct descendants. Control of land, wives and personal belongings passed from a man to his younger brothers and to his sons, the elder sons receiving larger portions. In certain circumstances women inherited goods and land. Where disputes could not be resolved or where there was no descendant, the land became collective land.

Two other types of social structure cut across the descent system: voluntary associations and social strata. Cooperative work associations and mutual aid or savings societies were two economically important types of associations. The *donkpe* of the Fon consisted of all the young men of a village, under a special chief. The group could be called forth at any time to perform tasks such as preparing fields or building houses either for individuals or for a collectivity. Other cooperative work societies of less elaborate nature were noted among the Fon, the Weme and the Yoruba. In mutual aid societies or *tontines*, members made regular payments into a common treasury, administered by a set of officers. Each member in turn received the contributions of the group, and most often used the funds for funeral expenses, purchase of ritual cloth, and other ceremonies. Other voluntary associations were recreational societies, cult groups involving worship of a special pantheon of deities, and secret societies of various sorts.

The lowest social stratum was that of slaves, of which there were several sorts: chattel slaves of the fields of great nobles, those exported or sold to other peoples, those executed as religious sacrifices, household slaves, soldiers, artisans, porters and, the largest group, those who were bought to increase family size, as wives and concubines. The stratum of 'second-class citizens' was composed of second-generation slaves (who could not be sold, but were required to stay on the land they worked), children of slave parents or slave and free parents, pawns being held as security for loans, and those who had lost their liberty and rights for whatever reasons. The commoners, the next and largest stratum, were mostly free farmers, fishers and artisans, but also included chiefs and holders of local offices, and further included the priests, who everywhere led a life more or less apart. The great officials, where they existed, formed the next stratum – ministers of state, provincial chiefs, generals and great priests. The peak of the social structure was the royal family, consisting of the families and descendants of present and past kings.

The basic political institution was the office of village chief or king, whose holder, aided by a council, was responsible for direction of the affairs of the territory of his village. The concepts behind this institution were elaborated to a greater or lesser degree among different peoples: among some of the refugee groups, social chiefs (*henugan, huetagan, bale*) were also the political chiefs; yet the same basic concept may be seen at work in the elaborate organization of the Fon kingdom. Village chiefs were chosen from among the leaders of lineages, though chieftainship often became hereditary in one family. The chiefs dealt with relations among groups within the village, and represented the village in its relations with the outside. In some cases, as among the Watchi and the Itsha, these were the highest political offices in the land. In other cases, village chiefs formed themselves into confederations and had vague tributary relationships with one of their number or with outside powers, as among the Shabe, the northern Mahi, and the Nago. Other village chiefs were regarded as local leaders in loosely grouped kingdoms – the Hula, Ketu and Gun. Finally, the chiefs in the kingdom of Danhomè were seen as cogs in a broad yet tightly organized social machine. 'Chiefs of the land,' descendants of the local chiefly families who had been conquered by the Fon, had been given titles by their conquerors to integrate them into the larger state; the political chiefs appointed from Abomey to work alongside them handled the bulk of administrative duties.[6]

ECONOMIC LIFE

As in farming communities all over the world, the rains guided and dominated the economic life of Dahomey. Dahomean farmers prayed for rains, called upon diviners to predict rains, cursed the rains when they were ill-timed, and labored unremittingly to keep their farms attuned to the weather. Every aspect of the weather had its impact on production: the amount of sunshine, the temperature, the total rainfall, its interannual variations, its distribution between the two rainy seasons, the timing of the initial rains, and (in riverain and lagoon areas) the timing of the floods.

The long rains came in the spring, from March to July, followed by a season of fine, light rains through August. The short rainy season ran from September into November, and the dry season, from November to March, was punctuated by the cool, dry harmattan in December and January. The month of August was often crucial. It had to be dry enough to permit the completion of the first harvest, and wet enough to get the second crop off to a good start.

Preparing land for sowing could not begin until the first rains had fallen. Farmers had to decide how much land to clear and what to plant, based on their conjectures on the rains for the year. If rains halted after crops had been sown, then the seedlings died and the fields had to be resown. When the rains continued through the growing season, crops grew well. But if the rains continued too long, the harvest of grains was ruined. If the rains began late and a farmer responded by planting fast-growing varieties of his crops, the harvests might be ruined if the rains continued longer than usual.

The rains determined the height of the flood on the rivers, the degree of inundation of the Lama and the marshes of the Holli, the level of water in the coastal lagoons, and whether the lagoons broke open to the sea. For those who farmed in the flood plains, a high flood was advantageous. A high flood also made water transport easier, and more palm products and maize could be moved from the upper regions of the Mono and the Ouémé; low water prevented the movement of canoes to many parts of the country. Exceptional floods, however, washed away crops and bridges, and made it difficult to catch fish in the lakes and lagoons, where fishing devices were designed to operate at normal flood level. The rains helped determine prices – most obviously of agricultural goods, but also of artisanal and manufactured goods. Dry years drove the prices of staple foods to levels four and five times normal; but the appearance of early rains, with a promise of relief to the food shortage, would bring the price down sharply. Demand for agricultural implements rose in years of heavy rainfall, when fields were expanded. The volume of production and exports of palm products, maize and other goods rose and fell with the rains. Military expeditions, too, were timed by the rains: the French, for example, timed their invasion of Dahomey to coincide with the Ouémé flood, and succeeded in landing their army deep in Fon territory. In sum, while the rains cannot explain long-run changes in the economy, they were the most important factor in the dynamics of any given year or even any given series of years.

Farmers selected their most fertile fields and cleared them in the dry season, in February and March. The family chief usually chose the fields; through experience, he recognized the fertile soils by their physical consistency, their color, their taste, and by the vegetation covering them. Around Porto-Novo, black soil, the richest, was reserved for maize, while red soil was used for beans and sweet potatoes, and white soils for peanuts; the color changes were the result of the extraction of humus from the soil.

Groups of four to ten men of the family generally did the clearing. They cut weeds and shrubs, killed large trees with annular incisions, and burned the fields. They protected useful trees (oil palms, shea butter trees, and the African locust bean) by such means as removing the brush from the field before burning it; in any case, these trees were noted as being more resistant to brush fires than others. Farmers rarely removed stumps, for they would abandon the field in a few years. They hoed the fields, again by group labor, beginning about two weeks after the first rains, after allowing the soil to become workable. In the Center and for certain crops, notably yams, the fields were worked into mounds, which consisted of piles of surface soil covered with soil containing vegetable material, which averaged 1.2 m in diameter and 60 cm in height. The people of the Coast and the Plateau worked their fields into rows, which they traced in the direction of the greatest slope. The rows were smaller for plants with their useful part in the air (maize and millet), and larger for tubers and pulses. Some fields were not hoed: the Aja proper tended simply to clear and plant their fields, while the Weme prepared fields on the flood plain by overturning the soil in little squares.

Most of the major field crops – maize, manioc, yams, millet, sweet potatoes, beans – grew throughout the country, but were better adapted to certain areas. On the Coast, maize predominated, followed by manioc, sweet potatoes, beans, yams and peas. The variety of crops was greatest on the Plateau: maize, yams, manioc, millet, sweet potatoes, beans, peas, cotton and peanuts. The main crops in the Center were yams and sorghum, but maize, manioc, millet, peanuts, beans, tobacco, cotton and other crops were grown.

Southern Dahomean farmers generally grew two crops of maize per year, and sometimes two crops of beans, millet and sweet potatoes. They planted the first maize crop in late March and early April, and harvested it at the end of the rains in June and July; they planted the second crop in September and October, and harvested it in December and January. Yams were planted in late March, and required roughly seven months to mature. Millet was planted in April, and harvested in late July. Sorghum was planted in May, and harvested in December. Manioc could be preserved in the ground over a period of up to eighteen months, so farmers planted it indifferently between March and July, and harvested it as needed over the next year, until the July harvest of maize. Sweet potatoes were difficult to preserve, especially after harvesting, so farmers planted them gradually over a period from July to November, and harvested them some three months after planting. Peanuts, planted in April and May, were harvested in October and November; earth peas, planted in May and June, were harvested in October and November; pigeon peas were planted in May and June; okra was planted in June and harvested in the dry season; tobacco was planted in March.[7]

Farmers used a more or less regular system of crop rotation, but always kept it empirical, and never reduced it to hard and fast rules. A wide variety of factors determined the exact rotation followed: different crops, soil quality, field size, food needs, and individual preferences. In the Plateau and the Center, yams occupied a field first, sometimes followed by or associated with cotton; maize and millet were next, often grown in association; manioc might follow; and the pulses (peanuts, beans, peas) were last. Maize was first on the Coast, followed by manioc and sweet potatoes, and finally by beans.

Maize, manioc and yams were grown for as many years as possible on a given field, often three to five years, while millet, beans, and sweet potatoes tended to occupy fields only a year at a time. Farmers around Abomey grew crops in association more frequently than those near Porto-Novo. They often grew yams with cotton or maize, and maize with millet, manioc or beans, although they generally cultivated the pulses alone. If fields were worked with sufficient care, they could remain productive even for fifteen or twenty years, or they might be worked as few as two years. The fallow period often rose to twenty years, but it too could be cut as low as two years, depending on the richness and position of the field, the crops grown on it, population density, and the needs of the village and the individual owner.

Land use varied from farmer to farmer. In response, for instance, to a bad year for maize, some might sow more the next year to make up the deficit, while others would sow less for fear of another disaster; farmers usually tended to plant more beans when a bad maize harvest was expected. In the Porto-Novo area, some farmers restricted their horizon to production of maize for home consumption, while others thought in terms of production of a surplus for sale, and still others in terms of getting more output for their effort by planting more manioc. Consumers preferred maize, and it was limited in expansion mostly by the availability of land; consumers favored manioc rather less, but producers found it easy to grow and highly productive, so that it became more important as population pressure grew; consumers regarded sweet potatoes highly, but sweet potato cultivation was limited by the difficulty of preserving them.

Tree crops were important throughout Dahomey, and unquestionably the most important tree was the oil palm. Oil palms abounded in the coastal portion of the country, were relatively numerous on the Plateau, and were found in small numbers in populated areas of the Center. Palm fruit could be harvested year round, but the main harvests were from December through March, and in August. The oil from the pericarp of the fruit was used for cooking, the nuts and kernels could be used us fuel, and large amounts of palm oil and kernels were sold to exporting merchants at the coast. In the Center, cooking fat was obtained from the fruit of the semi-domesticated shea butter tree, whose fruits were collected as they fell. The African locust bean, which grew spontaneously in the Plateau and the Center, was also protected, and during the dry season it yielded seeds which were made into a paste, *makari*. Kola trees grew on the coast, especially in low, humid areas, notably around Abomey-Calavi. The single variety found in southern Dahomey was that with four or five cotyledons (*Cola acuminata*), rather than the two-cotyledon variety (*Cola nitida*) grown notably in the Gold Coast forest, which was the object of a wide commerce. Therefore the kola from Dahomey and its substitute, *Garcinia kola*, were produced mostly for local consumption; there was no commerce in kola to the north, although there was some export of kola to Lagos and to Brazil. Coconut palms were found near most villages, and especially in low, sandy areas. They were regarded far more as a source of fruit for consumption

69

than for commerce. As the nuts fell, they were opened, the copra was eaten and the oil was sometimes pressed out for cooking. By the 1880s, exports of coconuts to Europe had begun on a small scale. Two other trees of importance were the silk-cotton tree and the raphia palm. Both of these trees yielded useful fibers, the raphia palm from its leaves, and the silk-cotton tree from its fruit (the fiber is known as kapok). In addition, the silk-cotton tree was at times used as the hull of dugout canoes, and the ribs of raphia palm leaves, generally called bamboo, had wide use in building, in furniture and as poles for canoes.

Dahomean homes tended commonly to be surrounded by fruit trees. The portion of an average diet furnished by fruit is difficult to gauge, but the available variety was impressive: bananas, pineapples, oranges, lemons, mangoes, papayas, avocados, guavas, sugar cane and breadfruit trees all grew in the region, with bananas most numerous along the Ouémé and oranges most plentiful around Abomey. Cashews and pistachio nuts were also grown, and the cashew apple was a favorite fruit. Pepper was gathered, and red peppers were grown to provide spice for sauces. For convenience, daily fruits and vegetables, or crops harvested on consumption such as manioc, were grown near the houses. Since manioc and sweet potatoes do not require as much sunlight as maize, oil palms could be allowed to grow densely around houses, where it was easier to harvest them. Maize fields were generally more distant, and were purposely thinned of excess oil palms.

Chickens were universal, ducks and guinea fowl were fairly common, and even turkeys were kept by a few of the rich. Of the larger domestic animals, pigs were the most common, followed by goats and sheep in about equal numbers. These animals were most numerous in the areas of Porto-Novo, Sakété, Athiémé, Aplahoué and Abomey. Every family in the Center had a certain number of sheep, goats and poultry, and many owned cattle. Along the coast to the east of Cotonou, in the *banlieue* of Porto-Novo and along the Ouémé, there were a significant number of the small tsetse-resistant lagoon cattle. Animals were allowed to run free following harvests, but while crops were in the fields they were restricted to fallow fields or were kept around the houses. In any case, the pigs, goats and sheep were left to forage for themselves. Along the Ouémé, the cattle were kept in small elevated pens during high water, and had to be brought food every day. Disease was a great danger for all domestic animals: every few years, an epidemic swept through the country and killed sometimes half of one species or another.

Men did the work in the fields. Women helped occasionally with lighter tasks such as planting and weeding, or with harvesting, but they were occupied mostly with household duties and marketing. The typical

70

cultivator left for his fields at daybreak, ate two or three *akansan* (boiled maize meal wrapped in a leaf) for breakfast, worked for three or four hours, rested, ate and slept during the heat from 11:30 to 2:30, worked through the afternoon and returned home by nightfall. Most Yoruba farmers worked individually or in small family groups on their own plots, while cooperative or collective work was more frequent among the Aja. The family chiefs and men of stature in general were exempt from work in the fields. In areas such as Ouidah where slaves were plentiful, a situation arose where a good portion of the men were exempt from agricultural labor, and among this group at least, agriculture came to be despised.[8] On the other hand, in Abomey, an area where slaves were if anything more important in production, a saying held that 'Every Dahomean must know three things well: how to cut a field, how to build a wall, and how to roof a house.'[9]

The communal system of labor, under the direction of family or other chiefs, was competitive, task-oriented and flexible. Members of the *hueta* worked first on the fields of the chief, then on parcels of land allotted to them individually. At least in the area of Abomey, the *donkpe* was of importance in farming. Headed by a chief (*donkpegan*) under whom worked three other officials, the group rendered aid to its members, to those who were ill or old, to those whose fields were very extensive and were able to pay a sum to the *donkpegan*, and to young men who had to fulfill marriage obligations to their wives' families (a man often had to do a major piece of work for his father-in-law). Men asked the *donkpegan* to summon a *donkpe* for work, and paid for its services if possible or agreed to work when called. At the appointed time, the whole group arrived and got on the job–often preparing a field or roofing a house.

The royalty and nobility of the Fon kingdom owned great estates, and Porto-Novo too had its wealthy merchant and landowning families, as did other regions of the country. In addition the balance of the population, instead of forming a uniform peasantry, owned widely distributed quantities of land. Some men owned more land than they and their families could work, and paid for cooperative work groups or hired laborers individually. Others, whose fields were too small to occupy them completely, hired themselves out several days a year, or even full time.

Fishing was the main occupation of the people who lived along the lakes, lagoons and rivers of southern Dahomey. The salty waters of the lagoons and lakes supported large populations of oysters, shrimp and fish. All of these were of marine origin, belonging to species able to adapt to seasonal variations in salinity. Fishermen used a wide variety of techniques for catching fish, which varied with the season and with the objective. Most commonly, they used casting nets, thrown from two-man canoes. They used a wide range of lines, with single or multiple hooks. Weirs, traps and shelters were far more productive means of fishing. Weirs were set across lagoons, streams, and specially prepared trenches. The Tofin built shelters for fish by forcing large numbers of branches into the mud of the shallow Lake Nokoué. Fish gathered in the shelters, and the fishermen captured them periodically after surrounding the shelter with a net.

Much of the handicraft work necessary to sustain fishing, agriculture or other aspects of the economy was done by men when they were free from work in the fields. All men took part in the building and repair of houses and walls, in basketry and in various small tasks. Other handicraft work was performed by specialists, who tended to spend little time with agriculture. But even the busiest blacksmith or weaver, as well as other specialists such as priests, drummers and merchants, found some time to practice agriculture, or at least owned fields. Virtually every village had a smith, whose prime activity was the fashioning of hoes, knives and other implements from imported iron. Weaving remained an important handicraft despite the long competition from cheap European imports: Yoruba weavers used a certain amount of imported thread in their cloth.

People of the lagoons prepared salt, notably at Kéténou, Ouidah and Grand Popo, either by evaporation or by filtering through sand and boiling; this industry too faced stiff competition from European imports. Chalk for whitening houses was made from the oysters of Ouidah lagoon. Alcoholic beverages were prepared: palm wine, raphia wine, maize and millet beer. There were butchers (mostly Muslim), and tanners (only the Yoruba were tanners, for the Aja simply dried and pounded hides). Makers of bamboo furniture, canoe-makers and artists were other specialists. Abomey was a great artisanal center, since the king brought to Abomey any famed artist in copper, gold, silver, wood, calabashes or pottery, plus weavers of umbrellas and clothes for royalty and chiefs. The artisans stayed at the palace and worked solely on the account of the king.

Women, to a greater extent than men, had special occupations – dyeing, making pottery, or transforming and selling some good on the market – and women of the same family tended to have the same occupation. Preparation of food was an important activity for women, whether the food was to be eaten at home or sold on the market. Women ground such grains as maize, millet and sorghum into flour, they made flour and *gari* (meal) from manioc, they pounded yams and sweet potatoes and made them into paste, and prepared sauce from red peppers, fish, and various herbs and leaves. The wives of fishermen dried and smoked fish, then marketed them. Women dominated the preparation of shea butter from the collected fruit, they made palm oil by mashing and cooking the oil palm fruit, and they later cracked open the nuts to obtain palm kernels. Kola nuts were packed and preserved. The fibers from raphia, kapok and cotton were spun into thread. Younger women took the more strenuous occupations, such as the preparation of *akansan*, while older women tended to concentrate on such activities as gathering medicinal herbs. Women were thus occupied with preparation for market on those days when they did not actually attend one.

The familial and commodity exchange modes of production shared the same system of production. The distinction between the two lay instead in the destination of the goods and the institutions of exchange: in the familial mode of production, goods were exchanged within the family unit under the supervision of the family chief, while in the commodity exchange mode of production goods were bought and sold for money in the local market. In areas where a large amount of the land was owned in common, family chiefs controlled the granaries and other stores of common goods, while individual families kept the stores from their own fields at home. As the need for common stores arose, the chief doled them out to members of the community. Portions of the produce of the collectivity could be sold on the market, and the chief then held in common trust the excess of income over the expenses of the collectivity. In cases where the economic unit was not a lineage segment but was a minimal patrilineal family, an analagous type of family exchange took place on a more restricted level. Within the collectivity, individuals or families specialized in producing a certain good, say red peppers or firewood, and received in turn from the collectivity an appropriate amount of final consumption goods.

The technology of production in the slave-labor mode of production differed little if any from that of the familial and commodity exchange modes of production, though it tended to be on a larger scale. The essence of the slave-labor mode of production was that slaves were required to produce a sizeable surplus for their masters, and received virtually nothing in return for it. Slaves, in providing for their own subsistence, maintained a sort of familial exchange among themselves, and they participated in the local market system to the extent that time and their minimal wealth permitted. Slave owners, on appropriating the produce of their slaves, consumed it themselves – as was often the case for royalty – or sold it, perhaps on the local market, but more likely to the mercantile sector.

Local markets formed the basic institution of exchange in the commodity exchange mode of production. Since the finances of husbands and wives were accounted for separately, however, market relations reached beyond marketplaces and even into the home. Farmers sold their crops to their wives or to other women, who sold the produce on the local market. If men sold their crops to their wives in advance of the harvest, they became their spouses' debtors.

Most local markets were integrated into an interlocking network based

73

on a four-day market week.[10] Each market was known by its own name and by the day of the four-day week on which it was held. (The Dahomeans said that a market was held every fifth day, counting the market day as both first and fifth.) A few major markets were held more often: that at Abomey-Calavi was held every second day, and the great market at Ouidah was held every day. If the market were distant, women might leave home the day before and walk all night to get there. They preferred not to walk more than ten kilometers to market, but they might go as far as twenty to thirty kilometers. Some women spent two or three days preparing their goods, and one day at the market (where each had her own stall); others followed the circuit for several days. Market activity began early in the morning, hit its peak in the late morning and early afternoon, and continued on to late afternoon. Markets were divided up into areas according to the product marketed, the age and ethnic group of the market women.

The goods sold on the market consisted, first, of prepared food: women who were marketing did not cook for themselves, and wives at market did not cook for their husbands, so that a fairly large portion of all food consumed was purchased daily at local stands. Primary agricultural products were sold on one hand to housewives who used them to prepare meals at home, and on the other hand to itinerant traders who took larger lots of produce either to other villages for sale, or for export. Handicraft products were most often marketed by the men and women who fabricated them. Goods imported from Europe were also on sale, in larger quantities and at lower prices in areas with greater access to the coast: liquors, cottons, tobacco, salt, soap, matches, firearms, gunpowder, knives, sugar, kerosene, beads and other jewelry and luxuries.

Price arrangements varied according to the market and the good involved. Very often, prices were set for each good by the first woman to begin selling the good in the morning, and they did not change that day; for staples, prices were often quite uniform. In other cases, prices were maintained by trade societies, organizations of the vendors which set prices and saw to it that members did not undercut each other. Seasonal price fluctuations were, however, inevitable. In Porto-Novo, the Zangbeto secret society was required to approve any changes in the price of maize and *akansan*, and to announce these changes to the whole town just before they went into effect, in order to minimize the unpleasant effects of price fluctuations. Prices also fluctuated during the course of the day, especially for perishable goods, but also in response to varying crowds and the desires of vendors to sell their quota of goods. Even with prices normally unchanging, bonuses and credit were offered to induce people to buy, or the quantity given at the nominal price was raised or lowered. Prices of manioc and maize ran inversely: manioc was most consumed from June to August, when maize was scarce and its price high. Manioc was least consumed and most expensive from December to February when the tubers were hardest to remove from the ground, and when maize was plentiful. The prices of imported cotton goods were subject to rather sudden fluctuations in response to changes in taste: if a given pattern suddenly became popular, its price shot up, while the price of the formerly preferred pattern fell.

The market was a sacred place, under the protection of certain divinities; it was a meeting place for individuals and groups, a place where news and rumours were passed on, and where new children were presented. In the words of Bastide and Verger, the market was a counterweight to the compartmentalization of society, enabling women to break out of their family constraints, and allowing different and even warring ethnic groups to meet and feel the complementarity of their economic order, which resulted from the division of labor along ethnic lines.

Virtually all market transactions were against money, primarily cowries. The standard units of cowrie currency included the string or 'toque' of forty cowries (40K), a 'galline' of five strings (200K), a 'head' or 'cabess' of ten gallines (2,000K), and a sack of ten heads (20,000K). Cowries had been undergoing a devaluation since mid-century, in response to continuing cowrie imports by German merchants, and as silver dollars and British sterling coin increased in circulation. In the 1880s cowries circulated at the rate of one shilling per head (£0.05 per 2,000 K); dollars exchanged at the rate of four shillings (£0.2) each.[11] The annual circulation of money rose to its height just after harvests and with the marketing of palm products; at other times of year currency was stored away.

Land entered the market only infrequently, but mechanisms outside inheritance enabled land to change hands in response to immediate needs, so that land tenure was not as isolated from other workings of the economic system as might first appear. The basic principle was that land was owned by the lineage, was inalienable, and was allocated to individuals by the chief for their use, but not for their disposition. A number of contractual arrangements were available, however, which enabled people to gain control of more land, or to obtain money or services in return for relinquishing control of land. How frequently these arrangements were made cannot be said. Land and the trees on it could be owned separately: a man could loan a field to another, who could grow and harvest crops, but the borrower could not plant or fell trees. Land (and less frequently trees) could simply be given away, with all rights to them, except that the land could not be alienated by the new owner. Both land and trees could be pawned in return for a sum of money. There was no interest on the loan, but the creditor had the usufruct of the property as long as the loan was not repaid. If the borrower were unable to make the payments, the transaction

75

could quietly be transformed into a sale of the land. Finally, land could be sold outright, but it had to be sold by the chief, and the council had to give its approval.[12]

The mercantile system tied local markets to each other and to other West African and trans-Atlantic markets. To a certain degree, local markets interacted through diffusion, as market women moved small amounts of goods from one market to another. Most ties among markets, however, consisted of transit and wholesale marketing handled by specialized merchants organized as families or as firms, and employing porters, boatmen, clerks and guards. Wealthy market women sometimes came to control large numbers of porters. Other specialists in regional commerce included Muslim merchants among the Yoruba, the *ahisinon* or great merchants of the kingdom of Danhomè, canoe-transport specialists of the rivers and lagoons, surf-boat crews, Brazilian merchants, and Hausa merchants, both resident and itinerant. Trans-Atlantic merchants and shippers – almost all European by the 1880s – completed the mercantile network. The middlemen, operating with the aid of credit granted them by coastal merchants, brought European imports from the coast – tobacco, salt, fabrics, alcoholic beverages, novelties – and returned to the coast with palm oil in puncheons, palm kernels in sacks, and smaller amounts of such goods as kola nuts, ivory, coconuts and shea butter. In the Mono area, short-distance middlemen carried goods back and forth from Athiémé to the coast, and Muslim merchants came from the North to sell 'arrows, quivers, fabrics, amulets, little Korans and sometimes little children' in return for salt manufactured on the coast.[13]

The coastal regions were accessible to each other by river and lagoon. Elsewhere, accessibility was a question of political security and proximity to major trade routes. Allada and Abomey saw a great deal of regional trade; Athiémé, Aplahoué, Zagnanado, Savalou and Savè had regular external contacts; but the region of Kétou had few such contacts, particularly after the Fon destruction of Kétou in 1886. The roads, which were well-worn footpaths, were arranged in a conventional network followed by caravans, with clear stopping points, provisions and markets along the way. Major trade routes went north and south – basically one each in the east, the west, and in the Fon kingdom.[14] The most heavily travelled route, however, was the east–west route of the coastal lagoons. Goods moving by land over long distances tended to be light and valuable – cotton, cloth, salt, and expensive imports in general. A major exception to this rule was the considerable quantity of palm oil and kernels carried from Abomey to the coast–the produce of the king's plantations, carried by the king's slaves for sale on his account. Interregional exchange of food along land routes was restricted to short distances or to expensive food such as kola and *makari*. Along the water routes, however, exchange of food was important. Fishermen took their catch to market and brought back food for their villages. But they also brought firewood, palm oil and pottery to urban markets, returned imported goods to local markets, and carried staples, fruit, fish and animals from one market to the next.

Trans-oceanic trade was carried on through factories on or near the coast. Two Marseille firms, Cyprien Fabre and Mante frères & Borelli (agents of Victor Régis), each had factories at Porto-Novo, Cotonou, Abomey-Calavi, Godomey, Ouidah and Grand Popo. German firms carried as much trade as the French: G. L. Gaiser, Witt & Busch, and Voigt had factories at Porto-Novo, Gödelt had factories at Ouidah and Grand Popo; Volber and Bröhm had factories at Grand Popo, Agomé-Séva and Agoué. Brazilian merchants had factories at each port, though they now worked through European shippers: among the leading Brazilian merchant families were Médeiros, Sastre, Angélo, Monteiro, Paraiso and Sant'Anna.[15] Porto-Novo was the greatest port of the coast west of Lagos, though it had no direct access to the sea. German firms in Porto-Novo did all their trade via Lagos, using a regular lagoon steamer service they set up, while the French firms transshipped their goods at Cotonou, which was also the seaport for Godomey and Abomey-Calavi. Ouidah was the main port of the Abomey kingdom. Grand Popo served the area of the Mono, and also that part of the Abomey kingdom to the west of Ouidah. At each port, ships had to anchor more than a kilometer offshore and transfer their goods to lighters piloted by Gen and Hula boatmen, which then crossed the surf to land the goods. The bar was particularly difficult at both Ouidah and Cotonou: the average loss of goods was estimated at five percent of the cargo, sharks were plentiful, and occasionally a man was lost.

The participation of the state in the economy of the 1880s centered about its role as a regulator of economic activity, though the wide range in size and power of Dahomean states had led inexorably to an uneven state impact on economic life. Only the Fon kingdom had a full-blown territorial organization. Other kings administered their capitals and left surrounding areas autonomous except for payment of taxes and tribute: such were the arrangements in Grand Popo, Porto-Novo, Kétou, Savalou, Savè and Tado. In still other areas, the functions of the state were decentralized among local chiefs, as among the Tofin and Watchi.

Each state, in addition to the basic task of provisioning the palace, had to address several economically important policy arenas: landholding, usually regulated through the courts with the king as final authority; commerce, including the provision of stability in local markets and protection for long-distance commerce; public works such as the maintenance of roads and waterways; and labor, centering on the state's policy toward slave labor.

The social and diplomatic policies of states – for example, maintaining established families in power or attempting to attract foreign merchants – also carried economic implications. To support their regulatory and other activities, states collected taxes, particularly on trade and, to a lesser degree, on production.

Beyond regulation and taxation, states acted as producers, consumers and merchants. Whether to supplement or to utilize their tax receipts, kings and their families purchased goods and services on the local market. As landowners, kings produced not only for the palace but for the market, and thereby became merchants as well, often obtaining advantages in trade because of their royal status. The complications of being both ruler and merchant did not, however, always work to the advantage of kings: Kpohizon, king of Tado, was exiled by the French in 1900 on a pretext related to an old commercial dispute between him and King Gbaguidi of Savalou.[16]

The institutions of the Gun kingdom of Porto-Novo provide an indication of the economic impact of the smaller kingdoms. The king of Porto-Novo was absolute in theory, but in practice he had to contend with an entrenched aristocracy consisting of his ministers, numerous princes, and the rich merchants. The ministers, or *mito*, formed his council. Several members of the council dealt with economic affairs, but they were not powerful, and they dealt mostly with the operation of the palace: the *yovogan* presented Europeans to the king, the *adoklunon* directed the provisioning of the palace, and the *ahisigan* supervised markets and collected customs duties. The *lari* were subaltern officials (slaves or political refugees in origin) who served the king and the major ministers as personal servants, policemen, customs officials and messengers. They were identified by their black clothing and elaborately dressed hair. At night the young men of the Zangbeto society acted as police. Outside the capital, each village of the kingdom had its own chief who governed it, paid taxes, and maintained relations with the king.[17]

The Gun king collected taxes in kind from all adults, but his taxes on commerce were far more important: he collected import and export duties, as well as tolls on canoes and caravans coming to market. In 1883, the French paid King Toffa (1872–1907) 10,000 francs a year for the privilege of collecting customs on imports. When the French extended their protectorate over the lower Ouémé, they forced Toffa to cease collecting tolls on market canoes coming downriver. The French did, however, allow him to continue to collect a duty of five francs per ton on all palm product exports, which brought him a total of about 100,000 francs per year.[18]

The Fon kingdom of Danhomè, which included one-third of the

population of southern Dahomey, was far more centrally administered than the surrounding states. The powers of Fon kings had almost no constitutional limits, and were limited in practice only by popular opinion and the techniques of government available. The ministers, the *gbonugan daho*, were a group of high-level bureaucrats rather than an independent source of power (as had been the case for the *Oyo mesi* in Oyo). The *gbonugan daho* included the prime minister, the top generals, palace officials, priests, a treasurer and an agriculture minister. Many other officials in the palace kept elaborate records, and checked on each other regularly.[19]

The Fon conventionally listed seven provinces for their state: Abomey, Allada, Ouidah, Zagnanado, Aja, Mahi and Atakpamé; in practice only the first four were administered fully. Each province had an administration based on that of Abomey. Provincial officials, known as *gbonugan*, were in regular contact with the capital. Villages had hereditary chiefs, the *tohosu*, who were 'chiefs of the land' descended from the dynasties conquered by the Fon. In many areas, Abomey set a political chief (*togan*) beside or above the *tohosu*. Lineage chiefs and ward chiefs also became links in the Fon governmental system.

All the inhabitants of the kingdom were organized by occupation into groups, and the chief of each group was responsible for the group and for paying that group's taxes at the annual ceremonies at Abomey or at the provincial capital. Hunters, smiths, and merchants organized themselves into corporate groups with chiefs; farmers (*gletanu*) in each village were grouped under a *glegan*; and the *glesi* or slaves on the great plantations formed a corporation and chose a chief.

The ceremonies for the ancestors of the royal family lasted for three months. They were the focal point of the year in the Fon kingdom: thousands of people came to Abomey to be present as the political and judicial acts of the preceding year were sanctioned. The subjects reaffirmed their loyalty to the king, and the king demonstrated his fealty to his ancestors. The religious rituals included numerous human sacrifices. The chiefs of each group presented their taxes to the king, and he in turn made a great show of generosity by distributing portions of his wealth among the soldiers, officials, priests and dancers present. The climax of the ceremonies came with a great parade and display of the king's wealth.[20]

The responsibilities of three of the *gbonugan daho* were mainly economic. The *binazon* or treasurer received all the taxes, and made a careful accounting to ensure that the required amounts had been paid. The *sogan* was responsible for provisioning the palace, where several thousand people lived. He therefore directed the royal plantations near Abomey, which produced much of the provisions. The *tokpo* or minister of agriculture directed the survey of all fields in the kingdom, including the great plantations, in order to assess them for taxation, and to maintain a balance among the crops grown. He had power to order farmers or whole areas to change the crops they grew. He was aided by a crew of official surveyors, the *humekponto*, whose job was to survey each field, delineate it, and note the probable yield. They marked the fields with fast-growing plants, and then planted oil palms and African locust beans to demonstrate the king's interest in those trees.

In theory, whole districts were devoted to the production of a single crop, on the orders of the king through his agent to *tokpo*. This was in fact possible only to a certain extent, for people needed a variety of foods to live, and the usual crop rotation could only be ignored at the cost of a rapid exhaustion of the soil. Clearly, however, the Fon regime attempted to organize production rationally and to plan a balance of crops.[21]

A further Fon official of importance to the economy was the *yovogan*, who handled relations with the Europeans at Ouidah. He collected anchorage and customs duties, and handled any sort of negotiations between Europeans and the court. Europeans tended to overestimate his importance in the Fon hierarchy because of their frequent dealings with him: although Europeans often wrote as if he were one of the king's closest advisors, he seems not even to have been a *gbonugan daho* (member of the council). Other officials competed with the *yovogan* for importance in the Ouidah region, and it is not entirely clear that he was even governor of the province. For most of the nineteenth century the *yovogan* was over-shadowed by the *chacha*, a similar office created by Ghezo on his accession in 1818. The *yovogan* regained his influence in the 1880s, however, and the last *chacha* was disgraced and arrested in 1887 for plotting to make Dahomey a Portuguese protectorate. Whatever the importance of the *yovogan* in the kingdom as a whole, he held great power over European merchants in Ouidah: merchants had to pay him fees in order to begin trade, and they had to leave their factories on the beach at dusk and remain indoors in Ouidah until the next day. The young men of the Zangbeto secret society acted as police at the factories and in town at night.[22]

The Fon regime restricted the production and consumption of certain goods for social and political reasons. One objective was to make clear the distinction between commoners and nobles by restricting to the king and his favorites certain local and imported luxuries, or the profits from lucrative ventures. Certain farmers in the area of Abomey were required to produce two pots of honey each year, which the army used in the annual campaign. The same farmers grew pepper and ginger and were required to send it all to the palace. Farmers were permitted to grow a single raphia sack full of pepper for their own use, but they were required to buy whatever other pepper they needed from the produce of the seven villages near Allada where pepper was grown in large quantities.

From time to time, Fon policy prohibited the export of certain goods. Glele is supposed to have forbidden the cultivation of peanuts near Cotonou in 1884, out of fear that people would abandon their food crops, and he is reported to have forbidden any cultivation of coffee, sugar cane, rice, or tobacco around Ouidah.[23] These economic decisions may have been politically motivated – for example, by the desire to prevent a lower social group from finding a significant source of income. If, however, Glele really believed that exporting peanuts would lead to the neglect of food crops then he was in error and was guilty of the same sort of economic misperception as later governments – no amount of encouragement would make peanuts important in the Fon kingdom, and no amount of discouragement would make them disappear; similarly for shea butter, sugar cane, and tobacco.

The Fon government unquestionably encouraged the planting and care of oil palms. The kings planted many palms of their own around Abomey and in other areas. They gave oil palm plantations as gifts to favorites, and they encouraged commoners to plant them. The king exported the palm oil and kernels he collected in taxes, as well as the produce of his own plantations.

The major source of royal revenue was the *kuzu*, a tax in kind. It was originally levied on such crops as maize and millet in order to supply the army and palace, and was extended to palm oil during the nineteenth century. The *humekponto* determined the amount to be assessed from each farmer – it ran up to one-third of the amount produced. The palm oil and kernels collected by the king's agents were sold at the coast through the *ahisinon*. An analogous tax in kind was collected on every good produced – all crops, animals, fish, and handicrafts – by methods which were sometimes direct, sometimes devious.

Fon officials collected a variety of other taxes, including fees paid by market women, inheritance taxes paid by the rich, payments for the investiture of new *tohosu*, judicial fees, and a sort of taxation whereby the king arranged for the robbery of people who had become too rich and powerful.

Customs duties were a significant source of revenue, but their collection also had important political functions. In addition to the customs posts at points on the frontiers of the kingdom, there were numerous posts within the kingdom: as the Fon conquered the smaller states that preceded them, they left the old customs posts intact. The king was thus able to collect more revenue – four separate toll gates separated Ouidah from Abomey. More importantly, the roads could be closed at any time for reasons political or commercial. Escaped slaves found it difficult to evade capture at these posts, and merchants who were out of favor could be barred from trading. The customs posts were operated by tax farmers, who held their positions for relatively short periods of time, and who made the best of the position while they held it. Le Herissé stated that they collected a standard fee of eighty cowries on each passing load, while Skertchly noted that pottery from Agrimé on its way to Ouidah was charged at ten cowries a piece at Allada.

Vessels in the roadstead off Ouidah paid an anchorage fee based on the number of masts or the size of the cargo. At Cotonou in the 1880s, the Fon charged 2.50 francs per puncheon of rum (450 liters), or 15 centimes per case of gin – far lower than the duties subsequently charged by the French. At the customs post of Aroh near the west end of the Ouidah lagoon, Europeans paid a bottle of rum and a head of cowries to pass, while the Fon paid some rum and one-tenth of the produce they carried.[24]

Le Herissé estimated that the annual revenues of Behanzin (1889–94) reached 2.5 million francs, of which 1 million francs came from the slave trade. Such a figure is surely exaggerated – the visibility of the state, as with that of exports, leads to exaggerations of its importance – though it correctly emphasizes the king's wealth and the impact of government throughout the kingdom.[25] The state – big states and small states together – accounted for perhaps five percent of the domestic product of Dahomey in the 1880s.

THE ECONOMIC SYSTEM

The economy of Dahomey was led by a commodity exchange mode of production with particular concentration on maize, yams, palm products and fishing, which was, on one side, tied intimately to a familial mode of production, and which was tied on another side to a mercantile network oriented both toward West African and European markets, and which was dependent to a significant and growing degree on imported goods. A slave-labor mode of production was expanding in response to growing demand in both domestic and trans-Atlantic markets, and changes in the world market were stimulating the beginnings of a capitalist mode of production. The term 'peasant' economy provides a fairly satisfactory characterization of this system. It presents, however, at least two basic problems. The first is the question of whether the term 'peasant' necessarily implies the ubiquity of landlords: the realities of landholding in Dahomey included a mixture of individual land ownership, lineage land ownership, tenancy and slavery.[26] The second problem is that, while the notion of a peasant economy seems readily to invoke an image of family production and the commodity exchange mode of production, it does not necessarily make clear the additional but important elements of the slave-labor sector, of commercial, fishing and manufacturing activities, nor of the ties to the capitalist world economy. Alternative terms, however, present even greater difficulties. For instance, the economy could be labelled 'traditional' in the sense that its technology and its social organization were of long standing and operated under limits set by custom.[27] But it was neither static, isolated nor unwilling to respond to changing economic circumstances. Further, the term 'traditional' – as well as such similarly conceived terms as 'modern' and 'pre-modern' – is basically a cultural label rather than an economic designation. The economy could be labelled 'capitalist' in the sense used by Polly Hill – that of an economy characterized by market production for profit.[28] Yet the economy, despite the duration and intensity of its ties to the world economy, was not capitalist in the sense of being primarily organized around wage labor and with a high level of invested capital. The alternative, 'pre-capitalist,' is a vague residual category. No author has yet labelled this economy 'feudal,' and I do not propose to begin now.[29] Nor does it add much, if the economy cannot be fit easily into other categories, to wedge it between them by labelling it 'transitional.' 'Peasant' economy, therefore, is the best shorthand description of Dahomey's economy.

This peasant economy has been described above in cross-sectional terms, in accord with the limits of existing documents. Some of the short-term dynamics of the 1880s can be reconstructed, however, even without direct documentation. To this end I have estimated a hypothetical input–output model for the economy and, after calculating its solution, have applied it by considering possible changes in final demand and their impact on the quantities and directions of input.[30] Three examples follow.

The first type of change was failure of the rains and of crops. The shortages in output of field crops and tree crops were rapidly translated into price increases, shortages of real and money income and, hence, a decline in final demand. Domestic demand thus fell for field crops, for tree crops, and for fish. As demand fell, the amount of employment in each of those areas declined accordingly. More serious declines were felt in the areas of transport, marketing and especially manufactures, as each of these was linked to other areas of production: with agricultural production declining, the need for manufactured inputs such as hoes, matchets and canoes might fall to nil. Production of palm products for export was hurt less seriously since, even though the level of supply had fallen as with field crops, the level of external demand continued as before. Finally, government demand for labor, supplies and taxes was not greatly affected by these

83

changes. Where government paid for the labor and supplies, it was a boon in time of hardship; where these were simply requisitioned, as for war or corvée labor, it provided an additional burden.

A second change in demand was provided by growing demand for exports, which manifested itself through prices and more intensive purchasing by export merchants. The primary impact of this demand, all other things being equal, was to require the provision of an equivalent increase in labor applied to export crops. Manufacturing and transport activities also had to expand to service the growth in exports, and these caused additional demand for labor and other inputs. Similarly, additional imports of packaging materials – casks and jute sacks – were induced. The expansion of palm product exports tended to draw labor away from field crops, but the opening of new palm groves tended also to support the clearing of new fields.

The expansion of government demand for labor and transport services provides the third example. Such demands came in time of war or, as in the colonial period to come, with a new and more demanding government. This direct demand for labor and demand for the labor-intensive service of head transport brought less interaction among the sectors of the economy than the previous cases. In the case where government paid little or nothing for the labor provided, negative effects of this action on production and income were preponderant. Nevertheless, expansion in transportation brought with its higher demand for canoes, road repairs and provisions. And any expansion in transport or any forced movement of people by government brought an increase in marketing, as porters carried a small private trade in addition to their official business.

The interdependence of productive activities meant that changes in one area of the economy had repercussions throughout the system. Transport was expensive and limiting, except along Dahomey's fortunate network of waterways. Water and firewood were in chronically short supply, in part because of the cost of transporting them: they were used not only for household purposes, but in production and processing, as with palm products, smoking of fish, pottery-making and smithing. Overall, however, production was direct rather than indirect in southern Dahomey. Production was small-scale and relatively simple in technology, and labor was everywhere the greatest input into production, far exceeding the value of produced inputs. As the above examples indicate, changes in the level of final demand were met above all by increases and decreases in the amount of labor applied to production. The fundamental problem in production, therefore, was the allocation of labor among a variety of tasks. In times of expansion a further problem was how to obtain sufficient labor; in times of contraction the problem was where to find work.

84

4

Production, 1890–1914

The production of agricultural and craft goods may be represented as a continuing struggle, pitting the energies and inventiveness of man against the forces of nature. The struggle was not so much for basic subsistence and survival – for the economy produced a significant surplus in all except the infrequent years of serious drought – but for the best allocation of effort among the crops, animals and household chores competing for the producer's attention. Pursued by nagging fears of drought, flood, pestilence or glut, the producer strove to anticipate the developments of each year.

The struggle for production may be seen, first, at the level of maximizing the output of individual goods. For agricultural goods, this amounts to the choice among different varieties of a given crop, the methods of planting, care during growth, harvesting, processing and storing. Equivalent choices had to be made in methods of fishing and in techniques of breeding animal stock.[1]

Each producer had, second, to decide on the effort to devote to each of a wide range of productive activities. A farmer's objective was not simply to produce a maximum amount of maize or palm oil, but to balance the efforts he applied to food crops, tree crops, domestic animals, handicrafts, perhaps fishing, and social responsibilities. The time he spent harvesting distant oil palms might prevent him from planting or tending a field of sweet potatoes. Dahomean farmers grew several different food crops in order to stagger the harvests, spread their risks, and vary their diet. Fishers had to choose where and when to fish, plus allocate time for repair and construction of fishing equipment. Weavers and smiths had to anticipate demand for their goods, and decide how much time to allocate to their own fields. Women, whether in families concentrating on farming, fishing or manufactures, had to decide on allocation of their effort among family care

85

and household production, artisanal production, assisting the men in their work, and marketing.

Third, production may be seen in terms of the struggle for access to the two basic productive factors, land and labor. Even when granted by lineage chiefs, land was never free: the effort of clearing, by burning or with hoe and matchet, was considerable. Land – very little of which was without an owner – was owned by individuals, lineages, and by the state. Similarly, lineages and villages owned fishing grounds on the lakes, lagoons and rivers. Within lineages, the allocation of land and labor tended to favor older men and those with large families. Among lineages, land was distributed in holdings of widely varying size, and could be transferred by purchase or pawning. Those who owned insufficient land to employ themselves had to assume an obligation in order to produce: either hire themselves out to a person with land, or rent land on which to farm. Cooperative labor, widely used within lineages, was extended to interlineage cooperation on major tasks at the village level. Thus, in the commodity exchange sector, not only finished goods but land and labor moved among the producers in response to economic pressures. Large landholders, who had obtained their lands and slaves through previous fortunes and through their access to the state, found themselves on the defensive under French rule. They lost much of their hold over their slaves, and they held on to their lands only after major disputes and some redistribution. Their role as employers of labor remained nonetheless significant. The state too sought access to land and labor, although where precolonial states had emphasized holdings of agricultural land, the colonial state was more concerned with lands for commercial use and for the railroad. Requirements for military service declined with the installation of the French regime, but total state demand for labor increased as the colonial government added its own requirements for porterage and public works to those continued within the precolonial polities.[2]

Fourth, the struggle for production may be seen through the stages of the agricultural calendar. The dry season was the time of craft production, of home repairs, of social affairs, and of clearing fields for the next year. It was, in essence, a time of investment. With the onset of the rains came the preparation of fields, which were generally hoed in their entirety. Yams were planted first, then maize, then manioc, and so forth for the full range of crops. If the rains failed, producers could resow, sow different crops, draw on their reserves, or turn to neighboring regions for supplies. In dry years farmers tended to plant more peanuts; in wet years they tended to plant more beans. The harvesting period entailed very intensive work, and it could be made more difficult if rains continued through the harvest. Producers of cotton in the Center lost much of the quality of their crop

86

because they left it on the plant too long. But this was unavoidable, as their sorghum crop matured at the same time and it, as a food crop, had a higher priority than cotton. The second and shorter rainy season entailed all the problems of the first, amplified by a greater irregularity in the rains. Throughout the year Dahomeans were faced with the steady effort required to secure adequate supplies of water and firewood. And the threat of disaster was never absent: great floods might occur in the summer, drought was occasionally severe, brush fires escaped control from time to time and damaged towns, and epidemics ravaged animal populations especially, but also crops and the human population.

Finally, the struggle for production may be illustrated through examples of specific productive systems. Two are offered here: those of the Weme agriculturalists of the Ouémé valley, and the Tofin fishers of Lake Nokoué. The Weme lived in villages on the raised embankments overlooking the river.[3] With the annual flood, from July through October, the river spilled over its banks and into a broad flood plain, leaving the embankments as islands until the flood plain gradually drained. The Weme developed a system for intensive exploitation of this environment. The embankments were cultivated with a variety of crops, including manioc planted in November and harvested beginning in June. Further down the embankment toward the flood plain, beans were planted in November and harvested in February and March. The same fields were then sown with maize which was harvested in July. The flood plain was sown with maize as the flood retired, generally in January and February, and harvested in June just before the next flood. The humidity of the flood plain nurtured the maize even before the rains began to fall. In addition, some Weme villages had fields on the nearby plateau, where farming was done according to the normal Dahomean technique and timing. Farming the flood plain meant, however, that whole villages had to work to clear channels draining water from the flood plain back to the river bed. Earth from the ditches was piled into mounds on which peppers and other condiments were grown. The practice of digging ditches was also applied to digging ditches for fish – small fish trapped on the flood plain grew during the year, but were restricted to the ditches as the waters receded. Shortly before the flood, families chased the fish to the end of each ditch and scooped them out with baskets. Several other fishing techniques were practiced. When the flood came, little agricultural work could be done, so most men fished from canoes. The Weme also kept cattle, which grazed on certain portions of the embankment and which, during the flood, were placed in raised pens and had to be brought fodder every day.

The Tofin of Lake Nokoué were another refugee population who developed an intensive system of production.[4] They lived in homes built on

87

stilts at the edge of the lake or in the lake. Underneath the main floor of the houses were one or often two sub-floors: on the bottom level were kept goats and pigs, and on the next level up were kept chickens. During the flood the animals moved to the top level. The Tofin concentrated heavily on fishing, though they did have fields and oil palms at the edge of the lake. The two main fishing seasons were from late December to May and from July to September (both are times of little rain and low water), and the Tofin were thus able to cultivate some fields during the rains. Most fishing was done from two-man canoes, with one man propelling the canoe and the other casting the net. Groups of canoes often combined to drive fish to the center of a circle, so that more could be caught with nets. But fish were caught by a variety of other techniques, notably through the use of traps and through refuges known as *akadja* consisting of branches forced into the mud, which were harvested from time to time by surrounding them with nets, pulling out the branches, and capturing the fish. Tofin women dried and smoked the fish, using salt from the edge of the lagoon and firewood purchased in the interior. The dried fish went to nearby markets and the smoked fish went to more distant markets. Large Tofin canoes were used for carrying goods to market; the Tofin thus provided transportation services for all the populations of the lagoons.

EXPORTS AS A WINDOW ON DOMESTIC PRODUCTION

Foreign trade can be studied (1) as a sector in and of itself, (2) for its influence on other aspects of the economy, and (3) as it reflects changes in other sectors of the economy. If it were assumed that production for export represented an independent activity for Dahomean producers, involving separate technology, separate ideas and separate families, then information on export would provide few insights into the remainder of the economy. Or if export production had just begun, one would study the influence of this new factor on other elements of the regional economy. For colonial Dahomey, however, export production was well integrated into the economy, both in terms of its long history and in terms of its considerable overlap with domestic production.

This situation allows for the treatment of exports as a 'window' on domestic production. Since information on exports is relatively plentiful, and assuming that export production is one aspect of an economy which is in some sort of equilibrium among its sectors, foreign-trade data may be used to infer trends and dynamics in domestic production. The resulting inferences on domestic production are necessarily limited, but they have the merit of moving the focus of analysis away from exports, the main focus of contemporary European observers, and toward production for domestic consumption, which was far more significant in terms of aggregate output and priority of the producers. Continued application and elaboration of this technique should provide a useful avenue for analyzing African economies in days prior to surveys of production. The two major examples followed in this chapter are maize and palm products, where export statistics and qualitative descriptions of production and commerce are combined in attempt to give a picture of the functioning of the productive system as a whole.

This approach conflicts sharply with the notion of the 'dual economy.'[5] According to this notion, a traditional local economy provides for the nourishment and basic needs of the population. Superimposed on the local economy is a 'modern' sector in which transactions take place in cash, where the profit motive rather than subsistence rules, and where the world market dominates. Links between these two sectors of the economy are assumed to be weak. Only the need for cash to pay taxes or the desire for goods which must be bought with cash motivate producers to cross the barrier into the modern sector.

In the Bight of Benin, however, no such frontier between traditional and modern sectors was discernible.[6] The whole economy was monetized, and exchange rates between local and world-wide currencies meant that any good was susceptible to exchange. European, American, and Asian goods had flowed into the region for centuries; slaves, palm products and other goods had flowed out. The colonial period brought alien rule to Dahomey, but the impact of the world market had long preceded conquest.

As an example of the relation between production for domestic and foreign markets, consider the interior region of Savè, which had been too far inland to sell its agricultural products abroad. As the railroad neared in 1909, the farmers of the area expanded their output of palm products, maize and yams, in anticipation of being able to export them. They were disappointed, because railroad rates were too high. But they did sell food crops to those working on the railroad, and they were soon able to send yams to the coastal cities.[7] The decision on whether to produce for export or for long-distance trade had primarily to do with the question of costs, and little to do with crossing a frontier between sectors.

Figure 4.1 provides a framework for analyzing short-run interactions between world and local supply and demand in the case of agricultural exports: it is, in effect, the vent-for-surplus model for exports.[8] The right side of the figure shows local supply and demand, while the left side shows world supply and demand. Local exports are shown as AB on the right, and also as CD on the left. (It is assumed, therefore, that local demand is satisfied first, and any surplus is exported if prices are high enough.) VW is the cost of transportation from the local market to the world market. AW

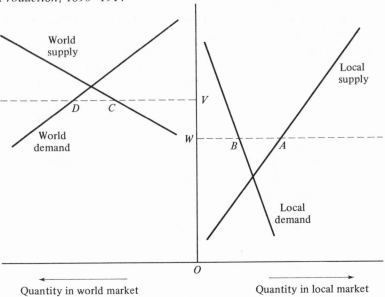

Figure 4.1. World and local markets for primary products.

represents local consumption, and *AB* represents exports as a portion of local production *BW*; *CD* represents local exports as a portion of world trade *DV*. The mechanism for determination of the equilibrium price and output is, theoretically, as follows: for each set of supply and demand curves, and for a given transport cost, the world price *OV* (and hence the local price *OW*) adjusts to a level where *AB = CD*, thus determining the volume of local exports.

Changes in levels of world supply or demand cause change in the world price, and hence in the local price. World demand may be expected to increase along with industrial demand, but would decrease if substitutes became cheaper (whale oil and tallow, for example, were substitutes for palm oil). World supply fluctuates with weather conditions, but tends to grow over time with increasing agricultural productivity. Any decreases in transport costs would lead to higher local prices – and to higher exports and lower consumption, *ceteris paribus*, The level of local demand depends on the size of the population, the relative priority placed on the product, the level of consumer income, the availability of substitutes and – as shown in Figure 4.1 – the level of price. Local supply depends on weather and other conditions of production, on price and on the relative priority of this product as compared to other activities of the producer.

For commodities which are traded heavily, the world price (less transportation cost) will reign in the local market, although a great shortage of supply might at times send the local price higher than the world price, thus ending exports. For commodities marketed with less intensity, or for commodities whose quality is not uniform, local prices may diverge significantly from world prices.

The analysis to follow includes estimation of the price elasticity of supply of maize and palm product exports, along with estimation of the influence of rainfall conditions on the supply curve. In addition, for maize, a more informal analysis considers the impact on production of changing trans-portation costs, short-term price fluctuations, and marketing activities. Brief analyses follow for other exports. Thus revealed, the dynamics of export production indicate changing allocations of labor in the domestic economy, fluctuations in output for the domestic market running both parallel and inversely with export fluctuations, and changing producer income. The performance of analagous exercises for consumption and for exchange in Chapters 5 and 6 gives a fuller picture of the domestic economy in the short run, as seen through its interaction with the world economy.

The basic data for the analysis of production are French foreign-trade statistics. These were recorded on a systematic basis beginning in 1887 for Porto-Novo, Cotonou, Grand Popo and Agoué, and in Ouidah beginning in 1893; they are listed separately by port until 1895, and then for the whole of Dahomey beginning in 1896. Later on, smaller customs stations were set up along the southern parts of the Togolese and Nigerian borders. The quantity of each good exported was recorded, and the recorded value was the quantity multiplied by the *mercuriale*, which was an approximation to the price of the good set each year by a commission; sometimes only the value figure was published. Goods of interest to the administration (palm oil and kernels, rubber, cotton) were given greatest attention in the returns, while goods of only local interest (fish, kola, livestock) were poorly presented, especially in the early years.[9] The commercial returns are supplemented by abundant qualitative commentary and scattered figures drawn from published and archival sources.

MAIZE

Maize was cultivated perhaps more intensively in southern Dahomey than in any other area of the continent. In addition to being the primary food crop, maize was occasionally exported in large amounts. The first recorded export of maize was in the seventeenth century, and maize was presumably exported as ships' provisions for the duration of the slave trade.[10] But the great pulse of maize exports from 1905 to 1916, and the even greater pulse in maize exports from 1934 to 1945, raise questions as to why such dramatic increases should take place and why the exports, once begun, should not be continued. Among the possible explanations of the pattern of exports are that maize exports were a compensatory response to the loss of other export income, that they were a response to world price changes, that they resulted from special marketing conditions (as distinguished from price conditions), that they were related to changes in prices and quantities of substitute domestic staples, or that they resulted from bumper crops caused by weather conditions. A subsidiary question is whether, as was alleged by some French administrators, the expansion of maize production in the years 1904–15 was damaging to the land and thus counterproductive.

These possibilities are sorted out in the discussion below, which concentrates on the period 1904–14: description of the technology of production is based on thorough cross-sectional studies by contemporary French agronomists, and longitudinal data come from the monthly reports from the *cercles*, written beginning in 1905, which provide considerable description of fluctuations in maize production and commerce. In sum, I conclude that southern Dahomey has consistently had the capacity to produce large quantities of maize for export and that, in periodic times of world shortage, Dahomey was drawn into the world maize market through aggressive buying campaigns by European merchants. Fluctuating output, caused by undependable weather conditions, provides a partial explanation for subsequent departure of Dahomey from the world market. But more important was the failure to develop adequate storage and transportation facilities, which were needed to promote a dependable level of quality for Dahomean maize sold on the world market. The additional labor required to export maize in such quantities also placed a strain on the energies of the domestic economy.

The technology of maize production has been described by several authors.[11] Eight varieties were grown, each with different color, size, hardness, growing time and taste. Their characteristics follow. Early white – a variety with small, hard kernels, which ripened in two to two and a half months, required little water, was cultivated in the short rains, and was eaten boiled or grilled. Ordinary white – had hard kernels, ripened in three and a half months, was tall and of average productivity; it furnished the majority of maize exported, and was made into *akansan*. Late white – the most highly regarded for taste, it had tender kernels, was grown only in the long rains, and was made into flour. Hard yellow–very hard kernels, little cultivated. Early yellow–similar to early white, had small kernels, ripened in three months, and was eaten boiled or grilled. Late yellow–the usual yellow maize, ripened in three and a half months, and was ground into flour. Late red – very tall and productive, ripened in four to five months, required much water, and was therefore little used.

The success of a maize crop depended on the weather. A long dry period just after planting would kill the seedlings, so successive plantings were sometimes necessary. Late varieties were generally sown in the longer first rainy season, and early varieties were sown for the short rains. Most farmers sowed maize in rows (or mounds in the Center), in pockets with two or three seeds each, placed one-third of the way down the side of the row. They performed one or two weedings and perhaps a hoeing while the plants were young. The first crop, sown in March and April, came to maturity in August, when it was important to have as little rain as possible so that the seeds would not germinate, and so that the harvest could be dried properly. Poorly dried maize was invaded by molds and weevils. (Some maize matured in July, and some varieties were harvested before maturity in June and July, grilled, and eaten on the cob.) The second crop was planted as soon as the first was harvested, and if for any reason the sowing were missed, the second rainy season was too short to permit replanting. Plenty of rain in September helped the new crop, while a dry December aided in its collection and preservation. If the harmattan began to blow early, the development of the second crop was arrested. The yield of the second crop was roughly two-thirds the size of the first.

Dried ears of maize were kept in their husks for a certain time but, once stripped, the tender varieties especially were easy prey for rats and weevils. For this reason, only the harder varieties were exported, but they characteristically suffered in warehouses awaiting export. To avoid these attacks, farmers often suspended maize from ceilings, where the smoky atmosphere protected it, or stored it in granaries elevated to keep out termites and other pests: they removed the kernels from the ears and put them in large covered jars in the granaries, under which they often kept a fire burning. In some areas, as among the Dasha, the maize was sealed in the vessels, so the carbon dioxide generated prevented pests from breathing.

Maize was mostly consumed as *akansan*: women mashed and soaked the kernels to separate out the envelopes, they ground and boiled the starch until it was pasty, and then wrapped portions of about 400g in two large leaves. They made a number of other maize dishes, involving cooking maize paste with vegetables, or with salt, red peppers and fish; they prepared certain varieties of maize simply by boiling or grilling. Southern Dahomeans made a good deal of maize beer and some liquor distilled from maize. Leftover stalks and other refuse went to the pigs and chickens.

While maize was grown throughout the country, certain areas normally grew surpluses over their own needs. The area north of Agoué and Grand Popo sent maize to the Fon kingdom in the 1880s, and exported small amounts by sea in the early 1890s. Allada, Sakété, Zagnanado and the Holli sent maize to nearby regions. Abomey did not export maize, but produced it intensively, especially in low-lying regions. In the Center, especially above Savè, only one crop of maize was grown a year, and it was usually grown in association with other crops, as in half-harvested yam fields, or with cotton.

Early colonial estimates of maize yields are, unfortunately, of little value. Yves Henry, in an otherwise careful study, gave wildly optimistic estimates of 15 to 30 quintals per hectare in 1908. In contrast, a 1954 survey estimated maize yields at an average 5 quintals per hectare.[12]

The involvement of Dahomey in large-scale maize exports resulted from an increase in world maize prices: for example, British prices for the quinquennium 1906–10 averaged over 40% higher than for 1896–1900.[13] The aggressive buying campaigns by European merchants, particularly Germans, found Dahomean farmers willing and able to supply maize. The quantities supplied were large in absolute and relative terms: the peak volume of 20,000 tons exported in 1908 was two-thirds of the total volume of palm oil and kernel exports for that year, and was equal to over 1% of the volume of British maize imports. Dahomean maize exports, normally less than 5% of domestic production, rose to higher levels, reaching 25% or perhaps even 40% of output in the peak year, assuming an annual domestic output of from 50,000 to 80,000 tons.[14] Local maize prices were driven up in the same proportion as world prices or more, and these prices affected the domestic and West African maize markets, as well as the relative cost of staple foods. Higher maize prices tended to stimulate local demand and production of manioc and yams.

In addition to the influence of external demand, two other factors determined the volume of maize production and exports. The first of these was the level of rainfall, which determined the yield of maize. The second was the volume of palm produce exports. In years when the volume of palm oil and kernel exports fell to low levels because of low prices or low rainfall, producers turned to maize exports in attempt to limit the decline in their income.

The significance of these determinance of exports is confirmed in a regression study of the years 1898–1912. As no dependable series of local prices has been constructed, British import prices were used in the regression. Palm product export quantities were based on an index including both palm oil and palm kernels. Growing-season rains (March through July and September through November) were measured at Porto-Novo.[15] The regression equation is as follows:

$$M = -4.19 + 20.34\,P - 7.09\,Q + 3.58\,R \quad (R^2 = 0.72)$$
$$(4.95) \quad (2.23) \quad (1.63)$$

where $M = \log(\text{maize exports in metric tons})$
   $P = \log(\text{British price in shillings/cwt})$
   $Q = \log(\text{palm-product export volume index})$
   $R = \log(\text{Porto-Novo growing season rain in mm}).$

Each of the variables is significant at the 99% level and has the expected sign: increases in price and growing season rain brought sharp increases in exports; increased palm-product exports reduced the exports of maize.[16] Interestingly, rainfall during the harvest season did not show the expected negative correlation with exports.

The regression equation thus shows that a strong pattern underlies the seemingly erratic swings in maize exports seen in Figure 4.2. The same causal factors attended maize exports in both earlier and later years.[17] Nevertheless, the great magnitude of the fluctuations in maize exports begs further explanation, and for such explanation one must turn to the qualitative accounts of maize exports. The following narrative summarizes, step by step, the developments and the issues in the great boom of maize exports, at least as they were perceived by the local French administrators on whose reports it is based.

Maize exports underwent a remarkable expansion from 207 tons in 1904 to 20,000 tons in 1908.[18] Not only were the rains relatively favorable in these years, but German merchant firms began scouring the countryside for all the maize they could buy. In addition, the newly opened railroad held out the possibility of facilitating maize exports. As a result, each year farmers planted more maize, and undertook an immense effort of clearing which, given that both clearing and cultivation were performed by hoe, meant that labor was drawn away from other activities. The network for exporting maize intensified: maize was brought in from steadily more distant areas, as Dahomean merchants, French exporters and even the administration took an interest in this booming new commerce. Most exports continued to come from areas near water transport – the Mono, Ouidah, the Sô and the Ouémé. Producers in the area of Allada were disappointed in 1905 and 1906 as merchants had urged them to grow maize for export by railroad, and had then refused to buy the maize because the high cost of railroad transport prevented them from profiting on the world market. Instead, Allada producers sent their maize to Zinvié by head, and then down the Sô and by lagoon to Cotonou. Prices continued to rise, and in 1907 and 1908 it was in Abomey that high railroad rates prohibited the export of otherwise profitable maize. Finally in August, 1908 railroad rates were reduced, and with immediate effect: the railroad suddenly found that all its available cars had been reserved by merchants for the transport of maize, and the merchants themselves began to run out of sacks for the maize. This was the high point of maize exports.[19]

Subsequently, the problems of maize exporting became increasingly prominent. Merchants in Abomey claimed the railroad did not have a satisfactory installation to protect maize from humidity. And complaints began to return from Europe of maize being harvested before maturity, and rotting en route. The boom appeared to continue in 1909, though exports reached only half the level of 1908, or 9,334 tons. The second harvest of 1908 had not met expectations: many farmers, having sold most of their first harvest, had found themselves short. In 1909, therefore, they resolved to hold on to their first harvest until the success of the second was assured. This step, while obviously wise in one sense, nevertheless brought with it the problem that storage of the maize for three months was an invitation to moisture damage and infestation by insects. It also meant that, because of fluctuations in the world market, they got a lower price.

The extension of maize culture brought other changes to Dahomean farming. New maize fields were not heavily populated with producing oil palms, so concentration on maize production tended to cut into production of oil palm products because of the factors of distance and time. Nevertheless, oil palms were planted in virtually every new maize field. The extension of maize planting also brought an extension of manioc planting. If the maize was to be sold abroad, manioc, which requires far less care, could be used for home consumption.

In 1910 the first harvest was fairly good, though the rains had begun late and had lasted too long, tending to harm some of the maize. But the second harvest was a disappointment: the rains ended very early, and the crop did not mature. At the same time, world market prices fell somewhat from the level of the two previous years. The shortage of maize during the spring of 1911 drove the local price up until it exceeded the world price by a large margin. A dry spring also served to keep prices and anxieties at a high level. The common practice of harvesting immature maize in June and roasting the cobs took place to an unusual degree this year. Sizeable amounts of rice and maize were imported, and the first harvest went entirely to local consumption and to reserves. Exports in 1911 reached only 65 tons. In the second season, many producers cut back on maize fields and planted manioc, peanuts, or other crops. Merchants attempting to buy maize for export met with little success, and complained of the weevil-eaten maize they bought.

The years 1909–12 were also peak years for oil palm exports, which cut into maize exports. But both producers and merchants remained committed to maize exports, as 1913 brought another bumper crop. While the year was called a dry year by most observers, maize exports reached the second-highest total ever to that date: 13,256 tons. Imports of manioc and maize from nearby colonies fell sharply. Great amounts of maize were sold in August and September. But then European prices fell in October, and merchants stopped buying. Exports continued in the beginning of 1914, and the first crop appears to have been successful. The war, however, cut Dahomey off from the German market, and maize exports did not return to their prewar level for over two decades.

Each year seemed to bring a new experience in maize production and commerce. Each major factor in exports – prices, rainfall and palm produce volume – varied from year to year, and different factors dominated in different years. Hence the great fluctuations in maize export volume. It is clear, however, that the potential levels of maize production and export were high, measured in terms of technical feasibility. Variations in rainfall caused the technically feasible levels of output to fluctuate, as indicated, for example, by the failure of the second harvest in 1910. More often, however, southern Dahomey produced less than the technically feasible output of maize.

The most fundamental factor in maize exports was demand, in the sense that when European merchants failed to seek out Dahomean maize, it was not exported, except to its West African neighbors. Dahomean maize was apparently regarded as of uneven quality, and came at a higher cost than that from major exporting areas.[20] The limits on satisfying trans-Atlantic demand, in the years when it was felt, were provided by the productivity of maize, as determined by rainfall conditions, and by the availability of labor for maize production. The availability of labor was determined as a residual of the alternative demand for labor in the care and harvesting of oil palms and other crops. In sum, Dahomey faced fluctuating export prices, its export price elasticity was high because exports were a residual after satisfaction of domestic demand, rainfall fluctuations led to sharp variations in yield, and the low price of maize relative to palm products meant that great quantities had to be exported in years when maize export revenue was sought to make up for lost oil palm export revenue. Each of these factors help make the fluctuations in maize exports understandable and, to a surprising degree, predictable.

Additional factors were changes in transportation costs (for example, the increased maize production enabled by the railroad in the areas of Allada, Sakété and Abomey) and the erratic short-term fluctuations in world maize prices. In some years, selling the August harvest immediately would bring the best price; in other years, prices were higher in December and January.[21] Inadequate storage facilities were a constant hindrance to production and exports. Farmers preferred to withhold a portion of their first crop from the market until the success of the second crop was assured, but the work of rats, weevils and moisture ensured that the first crop would fetch a lower price after months of storage.[22]

Typically, the French government, while willing to streamline the commerce in maize, showed no interest in improving conditions of storage nor of experimenting seriously with new varieties of seed. Improvements in these areas would not only have advanced domestic welfare, but might have made the export market for maize a more reliable resource for Dahomean producers. Instead, the region remained a reserve, to be called upon in times of world shortage and otherwise to be left untouched.

PALM OIL AND PALM KERNELS

The oil palm dominated southern Dahomey's export economy. Virtually all of the palm kernels and about half of the palm oil produced in the country were exported to Europe, and they consistently provided some 90% of the country's export earnings. The level of exports grew steadily, despite short-term fluctuations: between 1850 and World War I, palm oil exports grew at an average annual rate of 1.5%, while palm kernel exports grew by an average 4% per year from 1870 to 1914. The qualitative and quantitative analysis which follows is intended to show, first, the methods of production of palm oil and palm kernels; second, the elasticity of supply – that is, the degree to which exports varied with changing conditions of price and rainfall; and third, the manner in which production of palm oil and palm kernels was constrained by the other activities to which farmers had to devote their time, by the rudimentary transportation network, by the shortage of such factors of production as water and wood, and by such elements of the social organization of production as unequal distribution of land.

The oil palm, like the kola tree and shea butter tree, is semi-domesticated: it is native to Dahomey and grows there spontaneously, but is numerous only where it has received human care. Dahomeans frequently planted or transplanted oil palms. The trees produce fruit in bunches year-round, but the main harvests are in the two dry seasons. Oil palms begin to yield fruit at four or five years of age, and yield in large quantity from about eight to forty or fifty years, after which the yields decline until the tree dies at sixty to seventy-five years. Harvesting the fruit consisted of climbing the tree and cutting off all the bunches of fruit which were ripe or near-ripe, as well as any dead branches. An able man might climb over fifty trees a day; a well-tended tree was harvested three times a year. Rancoule's careful estimates of oil palm yield indicate that an average palm receiving regular care yielded seven bunches of fruit per year, yielding 3.3 kg oil and 4.8 kg kernels with normal methods of extraction.[23]

98

Preparation of palm oil required time and effort. The fruit was usually left a few days to ferment, to make easier its removal from the stem. Fermentation was the most important aspect of quality variation: the esterified oils broke down into their constituent free fatty acids if treated too roughly or too slowly, and this gave the oil a bad taste and smell. Women usually did the work of boiling the fruit with about double its volume of water for a few hours, and then poured it into a rectangular basin of clay or into a canoe, where they trampled it or beat it with a stick to remove the oily pericarp from the nut. In some regions they did no heating, and simply allowed the fruit to ferment in the sun under some leaves or rocks – with a resultant high fatty acid content. They separated out the nuts, mashed the pulp to squeeze out the oil, and pulled the fiber into a pile at the corner of the basin. They then skimmed the oil off the top of the water with a calabash. They collected the pulp and extracted more oil and the rest of the nuts from it. In most areas they boiled the oil thus collected, first to separate out organic impurities, and then to evaporate the water. In a dry period or in dry regions, the washing of nuts and pulp was done until the water was very viscous, so the oil no longer surfaced – the water was used so intensively that the yield of oil was low, acid content was high, and the taste unpleasant. Finally, the palm nuts were dried, and were cracked open by women, children and the elderly at their leisure. This method collected from forty to sixty percent of the oil.[24] To get a ton of palm oil, the requirements were 17 tons on bunches (or 10 tons of fruit), 140 work days to harvest and transport the fruit, 90 work days for removing it from the bunches, 85 work days for cooking the fruit, preparing and purifying the oil (including carrying the necessary 20 m³ of water and 15 m³ of wood) – for a total of 315 work days. For preparing palm kernels, a woman could break 3–6 kg of nuts per hour with a rock. If she sorted the kernels at the same time, she cracked 2–3 kg of nuts. In a day she could crack 25 kg of nuts and gather 6 kg of kernels – for an additional 167 work days per ton of kernels.[25]

The use of the oil palm was not limited to its oil and kernels: dried leaves, nut shells and even kernels were used as fuel; portions of the trunk, when burned, yielded potassium salts which were boiled with palm oil to make soap; the fibers of the fruit were fashioned into little balls and used as kindling; the leaves were used in construction; and the refuse from preparation of palm oil was fed to domestic animals.[26]

Dahomeans kept palms around the house well cleared, pulled off vines, and cut off dead leaves on harvesting the trees. They treated similarly the palms along paths, near sources of water and in cultivated fields; those not in cultivated fields but which were regularly visited had circles of two to three meters cleared around them. Trees in secondary bush were visited when the land was cleared or when the owners needed money. Every palm had an owner, and disputes over ownership and inheritance were similar to those over land, which was owned separately. Oil palms were unequally distributed in the same way land was, perhaps even more so, since many of them were pawned. Those families who owned few palms often found their men hiring themselves out to harvest the trees of others.

As the palms grew old, they became too tall to climb conveniently and they began to yield less. Ultimately they might be cut down. Smaller trees were removed from fields when they interrupted the cultivation of food crops. The Aja peoples prepared palm wine by felling trees, but they were usually careful to pick unproductive trees for felling. People were reluctant to cut down trees which required so long to grow, and which would take years to replace; there was a tendency in the early twentieth century for the average age of palms to increase, as many palms had been planted in the last half of the nineteenth century. Observers in the early twentieth century noted groves throughout the country of from ten to forty years of age; the most famous of these were those of Sinhoué, south of Abomey, planted and maintained by the slaves of the Fon king.[27]

The whole area from Porto-Novo to Sakété was covered with oil palms, virtually all of which were exploited every year. Of the numerous plantations in the Ouidah area, some continued to be operated on the same scale as before the conquest, and most were turned over to the people who had worked them as slaves, who now paid rents or tithes to their former masters. The area of Athiémé had a very dense oil palm population, but the trees were not regularly cleared or exploited because of transportation difficulties and because of the relative shortage of rain and ground water, so a large amount of palm wine was made instead. Palms were dense again around Zagnanado, and they were especially dense around Abomey.

The French hoped that Dahomey's exports of palm oil and kernels would grow sharply in the colonial era, and made calculations showing that even at the same level of technology, a great deal more oil and kernels could be grown. Export growth continued at the precolonial rate, however, and the reason lay not so much in the insensitivity of Dahomean farmers to their own interests as in the set of economic constraints in which oil palm cultivation was fixed. The basic constraint was on time: the primary responsibility of any farmer was the cultivation of staple food crops, and oil palms were exploited only after that responsibility had been seen to. A second constraint was price and transportation. Especially in more distant regions, the cost of collecting fruit or of transporting oil and kernels to the coast soon exceeded the return. Another constraint was on resources – production of palm oil ceased as soon as the amount of wood and water consumed began to interfere with other needs. A final factor became

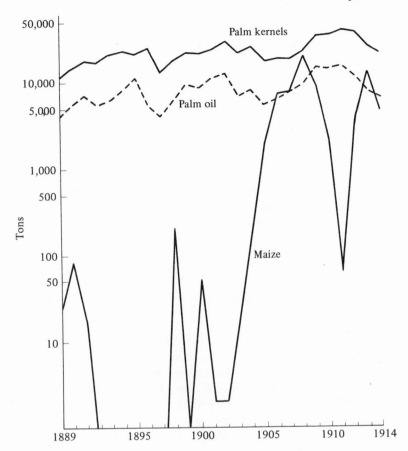

Figure 4.2. Exports of maize, palm oil and palm kernels, in tons.
Source: Table A4.4.

more important in the interwar period when the government began more intensive programs of planting oil palms – the unwillingness of Dahomeans to submit to the regimentation of government schemes.

The pattern of moderate growth in export volume is evident in Figure 4.2.[28] Equally evident is the cyclical fluctuation in exports: such cycles, with a periodicity of eight to nine years, have been characteristic of West African palm product exports from the mid-nineteenth century to the present.[29] A substantial portion of the variation in palm oil and palm kernel exports can be explained by changes in world prices and variation in rainfall. Each year's harvest depended on the rainfall of the preceding year.[30] World prices were taken as given, since Dahomey produced less

101

than five percent of the volume of world trade in both palm oil and palm kernels. The relevant prices were current rather than lagged prices, since Dahomean producers faced a decision on how much to harvest, not how much to plant. Further, since palm oil and palm kernels were joint products – each being a by-product of the other – the price of both products was relevant to the output of either. The two products differed in one important respect, however: roughly half the palm oil produced in Dahomey was consumed domestically, while virtually all palm kernels were exported.[31]

A regression analysis of exports for the years 1898–1913 confirms the significance of prices and rainfall in determining palm oil and palm kernel export volume. In addition, the regression for palm oil confirms that the increasing imports of kerosene, which gradually replaced palm oil in lamps, liberated additional quantities of palm oil for export. The clearest regression equation for each product follows:[32]

$$XO = 0.53 + 13.52\,PO^{**} - 9.77\,PK + 2.64\,R^* + 0.31\,L^* \quad (R^2 = 0.40)$$
$$(7.44)\quad(6.00)\qquad(8.03)\qquad(1.94)\qquad(0.18)$$

$$XK = -9.07 + 16.33\,PK^* + 6.08\,R^* \qquad\qquad\qquad (R^2 = 0.41)$$
$$(14.29)\ (10.33)\qquad(3.41)$$

where: XO = palm oil exports, in thousands of tons
XK = palm kernel exports, in thousands of tons
PO = palm oil price, deflated by import prices
PK = palm kernel price, deflated by import prices
R = previous year's rainfall, in meters
L = lamp oil (kerosene) imports, in hundreds of tons
** indicates coefficient is significant at 95% confidence level
* indicates coefficient is significant at 90% confidence level.

These results suggest that, while exports of each product did not depend heavily on the price of the other, palm oil prices had the greater total impact on producers.[33]

Over the long run, world prices for palm kernels rose at a greater rate than palm oil prices, and the ratio of palm kernel exports to palm oil exports grew with time. Palm kernels, which were once discarded or used as fuel, and which were only incompletely processed in the nineteenth century, came to be processed intensively in the twentieth century. On the other hand, even the growth of population and domestic palm oil consumption failed to prevent the expansion of palm oil exports: output grew at a greater rate than consumption, in part because of rising kerosene imports.

Dahomey's export of palm products was a deep and long-term commitment, rather than a short-term, marginal participation in exports such as maize turned out to be. The steady growth in output, while hardly apparent in the short run, becomes clear with the passage of decades. Palm oil and palm kernel prices, as well as the prices of imported goods purchased out of export revenue, determined the variations in output both in the long run and in the short run, while rainfall variations determined output changes from year to year. These clear correlations should act as a counterweight to the common tendency to attribute changes in palm product output to political factors. Political factors – changes in governments and in the policies of governments – may have had some influence on the volume of palm product exports, but they were subordinate to the influence of prices, rainfall, and domestic palm oil demand.[34]

The labor utilized in production of palm oil and kernels included, in various stages, that of men, women and children. If, as has been assumed, exports comprised some 15% of domestic product, then palm products required roughly 15% of the economy's labor.[35] To a considerable extent, the heavy work in palm products fell outside the seasons of clearing, planting and harvesting, but conflicts were inevitable. In part, these conflicts were resolved by specialization – some farmers concentrated in staples, others in oil palms. But for many farmers, the task was to produce both field crops and palm products, and to try each year to make the best allocation of effort among them.

OTHER PRODUCTS

The production of goods other than maize and palm products is observed with somewhat more difficulty through the window of exports, since the quantities exported were smaller, and export statistics are often less reliable. Some major commodities are lost almost entirely from view through this optic because they were not traded in significant quantity across the frontier, despite active local markets: these include yams, manioc, sweet potatoes, millet, sorghum, pepper, and most local manufactures, as well as construction activities.

Yam production is the most important unknown, followed by manioc: neither qualitative nor quantitative data on these important staples are adequate, as agronomists showed little interest in the tubers, and commerce across the Nigerian and Togolese borders was minimal or was ignored by officials. Yams were important not only historically but in current consumption, and the importance of manioc grew in both the nineteenth and twentieth centuries.[36] Surveys in the 1950s indicated that the outputs of yams and manioc each exceeded that of maize, and that the yield of the

103

tubers per acre was several times higher than that of maize.[37] While the surveys are of limited reliability, they confirm that yam cultivation was concentrated among the Yoruba peoples of Dahomey, and they further raise the possibility that yam and manioc production may have approached or exceeded that of maize at the turn of the century.

With these important exceptions, a wide range of significant products can be analyzed through the method of inferring patterns of domestic production from exports. Dahomean producers demonstrated a consistent willingness to sell any local product on West African or trans-Atlantic markets, as permitted by conditions of supply, price, and marketing. In the West African market they exported sizeable quantities of fish, poultry, livestock, kola and maize. Trans-Atlantic demand for agricultural products led to exports of copra, cotton, rubber, peanuts, and shea butter. And while most local manufactures were limited to the domestic market, high-quality cotton cloth continued to be exported to Nigeria and to Bahia in Brazil. Tiny quantities of many other goods were exported from time to time.

For many commodities, a significant portion of total output was exported – that is, greater than five to ten percent. This was certainly true for palm oil and palm kernels, and it was true for maize in many years. It was also true for fish, copra, rubber, cotton, beef, poultry, sheep, kola, pigs and perhaps textiles. Most export goods, therefore, represented a significant portion of domestic output, and variations in export quantity are likely to have mirrored variations in total domestic output.

The accompanying figures show the relative significance of export commodities, calculated in terms of average annual value of exports for the years 1899–1914, at 1908 prices. Figure 4.3 shows the average value of the four major exports as compared with the aggregate of minor exports; Figure 4.4 shows the average value of several minor exports.

Roughly ten percent of the population of southern Dahomey specialized in the production of fish. The Hueda, Gen, Hula, Tofin and Weme specialized most heavily in fishing the lagoons and rivers, but every area of the country had people who depended primarily on fishing for their living. Fishing peoples were naturally drawn into active trade with the agriculturists surrounding them, though Dahomey's export trade in fish was almost entirely from the Ouémé and Lake Nokoué to Lagos, with smaller amounts of fish being exported to Togo. Fish exports, shown in Figure 4.5, rose and fell in long, gradual cycles, and showed no long-term tendency either to rise or to fall.[38] The rise and fall of exports was influenced by the rains and by the periodic opening of the lagoon to the sea at Cotonou. Pélissier has argued, from oral tradition, that Lake Nokoué was formerly a freshwater lake, and that it rather abruptly became salty as the isthmus at

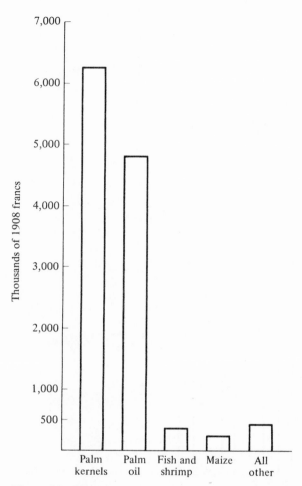

Figure 4.3. Major exports: average annual value, 1899–1914, at 1908 prices. *Source:* Table A4.4.

Cotonou began to rupture every few years in response to unusual floods from the Ouémé, after which the fish population became similar to that of the lagoons to the west.[39] In fact, French consular officials pierced the isthmus during a high flood in 1885, thus inhibiting Abomey's troops from reaching Porto-Novo. This was the first breach in the nineteenth century, though breaches are implied in reports of earlier centuries; subsequent openings of the isthmus took place in 1887, 1893, 1900 and 1911.[40] Fish exports increased in years of breaches of the isthmus and the years following. The periodic irruption of the ocean, a fish population acclima-

105

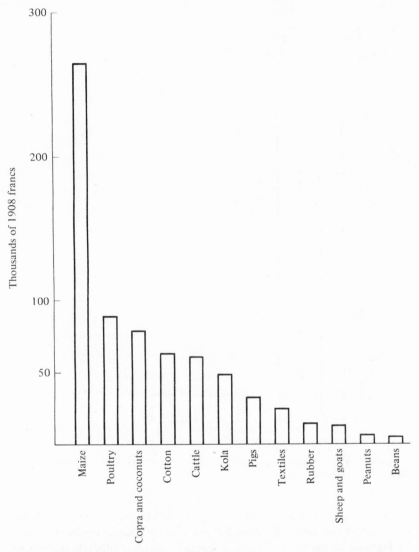

Figure 4.4. Minor exports: average annual value, 1899–1914, at 1908 prices. *Source:* Table A4.4.

tized to salt water, and the accompanying *akadja* (fish shelter) technique of fishing can therefore be traced as far back as the late nineteenth century. It may be that periodic breaches of the isthmus have occurred for an even longer time, and that the oral traditions recorded by Pélissier refer to the end of a time when the lagoon had remained cut off from the ocean for an unusually long time.

After fish, the largest West African export from Dahomey consisted of chickens, which were of course the most numerous of domestic animals. Export figures are reported as poultry, because a few ducks, guinea fowl and pigeons were included. Most of those exported went to Lagos, but some went to Togo, to other French colonies, as ships' provisions, and even to Europe. As with other domestic animals, chickens were periodically decimated by disease: an epidemic of spirillosis in 1909–10 took a heavy toll of ducks and chickens, and the decline in exports after 1910 may reflect the smaller population.[41]

Cattle were the next most important domestic animal in value of exports from Dahomey. Most of those exported were lagoon cattle sent live to Lagos, to be butchered there. After 1900 the price received for these cattle was high enough to attract cattle from northern Dahomey, which were now driven to the coastal cities of Dahomey and to Lagos. Pécaud was of the

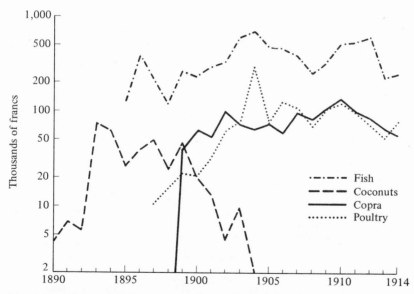

Figure 4.5. Exports of fish and poultry (in thousands of current francs), and of coconuts and copra (thousands of 1908 francs).
Source: Table A4.4.

107

opinion that cattle had earlier been important among the Mahi and Shabe, but that Fon raids during the nineteenth century had cut down their number, and that the great rinderpest epidemic finished them off in 1892. (Lagoon cattle, however, were not affected by the rinderpest epidemic.) Some 1,200 cattle were counted in 1908 in the Savè area just before pneumonia cut their number seriously; the 500 cattle around Ouessé were reduced to 100. Export statistics show a great drop in cattle exports beginning in 1908, with recovery only in 1913 and 1914.[42]

Pig exports were about half the value of cattle exports. Again, the factor of disease affected production and export. In October of 1907, an epidemic of hog cholera began in Togo, following the import of some American pigs. In March 1908 it had reached the Mono, by April it was in Allada, and by June it had reached Porto-Novo. Pig populations were extremely difficult to estimate, but Pécaud estimated that there had been about 150,000 head of pigs in Dahomey before the epidemic, that of these about 40–50,000 survived, and that the number was back up to about 70,000 in 1912.[43]

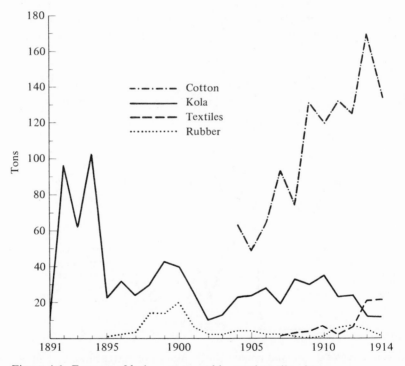

Figure 4.6. Exports of kola, cotton, rubber and textiles, in tons.
Source: Table A4.4.

108

Goats and sheep were produced in roughly equal numbers. Sheep, however, were exported in significant numbers, while goats were hardly exported at all. Sheep were regarded as providing better tasting meat, while goats were used heavily in sacrifices, and thus had a lively domestic market.[44]

Kola nuts exported to Lagos amounted to five or ten percent of the 500 tons which Chevalier estimated to be the annual production of Dahomey.[45] Exports of *Cola acuminata* had gone to Lagos and to Bahia from Dahomey at least since the mid-nineteenth century. In fact, much of the exports shown in Figure 4.6 was probably sent from Lagos on to Bahia, as the direct tie between Dahomey and Brazil had been broken in the 1880s.

Turning to agricultural commodities which were exported primarily to Europe rather than to West Africa, the coconut palm enjoyed a period of expansion in the nineteenth century. While coconut palms had been known in the Bight of Benin for centuries, they were planted much more densely along the littoral during the nineteenth century at the hands of the Brazilians, notably the *Chacha* de Souza; further encouragement of plantations came from the Catholic missions, and finally from the French administration. Aside from the sandy coastline where coconuts thrived, coconut palms spread in smaller numbers to the villages of the interior in the late nineteenth and early twentieth centuries.[46] Coconut palms in the villages were treated as fruit trees, and the albumen was eaten fresh. Along the coast, merchants and heads of large families established large plantations of several hundred trees. They sold most of their produce on the local market, but gradually began to export.

The expansion of coconut palm groves appears to have brought changes to the economic life of fishermen around Grand Popo: their fishing life gave them time to devote to agricultural pursuits, but there had not previously been a crop which grew well on the sandy coastline. Whether they owned their trees or worked on the plantations of others, coconut palms provided them with additional income, with firewood, and with palm fronds used in construction.[47]

Dahomean coconut producers faced the choice of exporting whole coconuts or of preparing and exporting copra. They exported small quantities of copra from 1890 to 1892, then exported only coconuts until 1899, after which they turned almost entirely to exports of copra. The value of coconut and copra exports combined showed mild fluctuations similar to those of palm oil and kernels, with peaks and troughs in the same years. Actually, a large portion (sometimes a majority) of coconut products exported from Dahomey came from the plantations of the Missions de Lyon in Nigeria, and were exported via Cotonou.[48] Most of the increase in copra exports, however, can be attributed to the growing plantations near Porto-Novo and Grand Popo.

The French had mild success in encouraging an export trade in cotton. The semi-official Association cotonnière engaged an agronomist, Eugène Poisson, to work in Dahomey: he attempted to revise the low priority which farmers accorded to cotton by encouraging yam cultivation and marketing, in the expectation that cotton would be grown in the new yam fields. With the opening of the railroad, cotton gins were built at Savalou, Bohicon and Cotonou, and exports of cotton and cottonseed began on a regular basis.[49] Cotton exports showed growth and mild cyclical fluctuations; cottonseed, a by-product of the ginning process, was sold abroad at whatever price it would fetch. The stability of cotton exports suggests that certain farmers in the Center devoted themselves regularly to cultivation of cotton for export. Meanwhile, cultivation of the hardier, more drought-resistant domestic varieties continued, supplying the needs of local weavers.

The world-wide rubber boom of the 1890s and early 1900s came to Dahomey in the form of a largely futile attempt to find and tap wild rubber plants, and then to establish rubber plantations. The few rubber and latex plants which existed were tapped intensively by Dahomeans at the behest of coastal merchants, and by traders from Togo and Lagos who carried rubber back with them. The administration began restricting the bleeding of rubber plants, fearing that they would be killed off. Meanwhile, Europeans and Dahomeans experimented with numerous varieties of rubber throughout the colony. Chevalier in 1910 noted fields aged five to twelve years around Ouidah, Porto-Novo, Adja-Ouéré, Zagnanado, Savalou, Savè and Kambolé.[50] But in no case was the collection of rubber very successful, and it tended to drop off with time. The plantations remained, uncared for, a testimonial to the unresponsiveness of the environment. The boom reached its peak in 1900, several years before officials expressed much concern for rubber exports. Exports fluctuated quite sharply, correlating in a fairly obvious way with changes in price.

Despite continued experimentation, neither coffee nor cocoa were to be successful in Dahomey. Plantations were established in the 1890s at Ouidah, Allada, Porto-Novo and Zagnanado. Tiny quantities of coffee and cocoa were exported, and many different varieties were tried, but most of these ventures died quickly for lack of productivity. The Catholic Mission at Zagnanado was perhaps the most tenacious in its attempt to make coffee and especially cocoa production work, while the Dahomeans, with the exception of a few farmers on very good land near Allada, returned to the cultivation of staples and oil palms.

Peanuts were grown throughout the country, but grew best in the Center, on the Plateau, and in the sandy area around Cotonou. Small quantities were exported from time to time: Ghezo forbade exports of peanuts in the

1840s. In 1897 French merchants imported great quantities of peanut seed and gave the seeds free to Dahomean farmers in return for a promise to buy their harvests.[51] The farmers responded, especially in the area of Abomey. The harvest was plentiful, but the price was too low to encourage much export trade, as Senegal had a particularly large crop that year. The response of Dahomean farmers to the encouragement of merchants is reflected in the rise of exports to sixty tons in 1898, and the decline to seven tons in 1901. Again producers invested in peanuts – intensive planting was noted around Cotonou – and exports climbed to their peak of 464 tons in 1907. But Northern Nigeria then entered the market, forced down the price, and eliminated Dahomey as a serious exporter of peanuts for several decades.[52]

Shea butter provided most cooking oil and lamp oil in the Center and in northern Dahomey, and was widely traded in that region. A small boom in exports ran from 1909 through 1914, reaching a peak of some 200 tons, but shea butter was not produced nor transported cheaply enough to be sustained as an export crop.

While most clothing worn in Dahomey was of European textiles, the export statistics show that the Dahomean weaving industry still functioned actively in the early twentieth century.[53] Three categories of clothing exports were significant: 'pagnes,' a term of Portuguese origin meaning cloths made by sewing together strips of locally made cloth; 'cotton print,' meaning indigo-dyed cloth; and 'men's clothing,' meaning the products of tailors. These textiles and garments went to Lagos and from there, in part, to Bahia. They were produced primarily by Yoruba weavers and tailors, and sent to Afro-Brazilians of Yoruba descent. Both imported and domestic thread were used by weavers. The spread of the occupation of tailor required the continued import of sewing machines.

THE PRODUCTIVE SYSTEM

By drawing on cross-sectional descriptions, on the analysis of exports and on the insights of the input–output approach, it is now possible to propose an explicit summary of the structure and short-term dynamics of Dahomey's productive system.[54] In economic structure, the various sectors of productive and service activity during the early colonial years ranked roughly as follows, in order of the value of their output:

staple agriculture
tree crops
fishing
state activities
manufacturing

    marketing
    domestic animals
    non-staple agriculture
    transport
    construction

In its short-term dynamics, the changes in this labor-intensive economy were dominated by the reallocation of labor from one productive activity of another, under the pressure of changing final demand.

Final demand, in turn, was composed of domestic monetary and non-monetary demand and of foreign demand. Total domestic demand reflected total domestic income: the value of familial production, money income from the sale of commodities on local and world markets, and wage income. Also influencing domestic demand, however, were changing levels of taxes and changes in consumer preferences; non-monetary demand, further, was conditioned at the lower level by the basic requirements of subsistence. Foreign demand was felt through the rise and fall of world prices, but also through the relative aggressiveness of European purchasers, as in the case of maize exports. In sum, however, of all the factors conditioning the level of income and hence of demand, the amount of rainfall stands out as the single greatest determinant in any given year.

While the reallocation of labor was the primary means by which the productive system adjusted to changes in demand, the reallocation took place under important technical and institutional constraints. The institutional constraints are conveniently summarized in the modes of production. Since family production units were the rule, family size established the scale of production, regardless of whether it was technically optimal. Within the familial mode of production, each family sought self-sufficiency; in the commodity exchange mode of production, each family depended on commodities purchased in the market, and thus had to sell marketable commodities in exchange: virtually all families had one foot in each of these modes of production. Some large-scale productive units existed, under the leadership of landowners – what had previously been the slave-labor mode of production now survived as the wealthiest element of the commodity exchange mode of production. Further institutional constraints were the large effort that had to be devoted to local marketing, the heavy state reliance on forced labor, the lack of organized capital markets, and the rarity of wage labor except in transportation, large-scale commerce and government.

Technical constraints on labor allocation included the cost and physical limits of transportation, the contemporary techniques for manufacturing and fishing, the crops and varieties available for growing, and the limits of

112

hoe agriculture, in which labor very rapidly becomes a limiting factor. Similarly, work was limited by resource endowments: the soils and climate, for instance, were simply inadequate at existing prices for crops such as cocoa, coffee and rubber, which thrived in neighboring colonies. The most important short-run technical constraint on labor, however, was the variation in labor productivity with weather conditions. The usual input–output assumption of constant productivity must therefore be relaxed for this agricultural economy: a given input of labor simply could not produce as much output in a dry year as in a year of adequate rains.

If the past year's rains were poor and the current year's were good, oil palm productivity would be low and that of maize would be high, so farmers gave extra effort to maize production for foreign exchange. Production of yams and manioc varied inversely with that of maize, both in the short term and in the long term. Bean and peanut production also varied inversely with maize production. Fish production varied inversely with the rains because fishing was easier in low water, although periodic high floods were necessary to sustain the fish populations of the lagoons. Manufacturing and construction activities varied positively with the demand for output, but varied inversely with alternative demands for labor. Further, the total amount of labor performed varied from year to year. In years of exceptional price or rainfall, an extra effort was put forth, as in the clearing of maize fields in 1907–8. But if domestic or foreign demand fell, or if productivity were low because of failure of the rains, less labor would be applied. While the notion of 'unemployment' is less clear-cut in an economy with family production units than in a wage-labor economy where workers are laid off, sometimes there was simply no more work to do in Dahomey.

The value of all productive activities in Dahomey, summed up for each year, gave total output for each family and gross domestic product for the economy as a whole. The level of domestic product fluctuated in response to the range of influences indicated above, including weather, disease environment, taxes, world and local prices.[55] But since the level of rainfall was the principal determinant both of domestic demand and of changes in labor productivity, to a first approximation the magnitude of domestic product varied with the level of rainfall.

5

Demand, 1890–1914

THE ELEMENTS OF DEMAND

The need for goods and services, backed up by the ability to produce or purchase them, constitutes demand. For early colonial Dahomey, demand may be broken into two basic components: final demand, stemming from the needs and desires of consumers, and intermediate demand, stemming from the input requirements of producers and of the state.[1] While consumer demand was the dominant component, intermediate demand was growing, and it varied according to a different dynamic. The two components of demand are therefore treated separately.

The level of final demand for any good, expressed by individuals or family units, depends in the short run on the purchase price of the good in question, on prices of other goods, on the level of consumer income, and on the relative consumer preference for the good. Yams, for example, were consumed out of home production and were also purchased on the market: whether a family grew its own yams depended not only on how well its members liked yams, but on how well yams grew on their land in comparison with other crops. The purchase of yams in the market, meanwhile, depended on family income, the level of yam production at home, the price of yams on the market, and the price and availability of such substitutes as maize, manioc or rice. While the composition of consuming units ranged widely, from slaves and isolated individuals to great landowning and royal families, the typical consuming unit was a minor lineage composed of from five to twenty persons. The family chief guided the family's decisions on consumption of self-produced goods and of goods purchased on the market; family members also had individual incomes, which allowed them some discretion in consumption. For any family, its total demand for goods and services was limited at the lower end by the minimal requirements for subsistence, and was limited at the upper end by the family's productivity and money income.

Intermediate goods went into the production of final goods and services.

114

They are taken here to include intermediate goods used in production of current output, such as casks used as palm oil containers, and capital goods used in production of future output, such as rails and locomotives. The units expressing demand for intermediate goods were the producers, whose demand was derived from their level of output. Thus, producers of field crops, of tree crops, fishers, manufacturers, merchants and transporters each had specific requirements for inputs. In addition, state purchases of materials are classified here with intermediate goods, as they went into state production and into the provision of government service. Beyond the level of producer output, intermediate-good demand was influenced by the price of the intermediate good, the prices of other inputs into production, and the levels of selling price and producer revenue from the final good. The fluctuations of capital-good purchases were typically much greater than the variations in purchases of intermediate goods used in current output.

IMPORTS AS A WINDOW ON DEMAND

Just as exports can be used as window on production in Dahomey, imports can be used as a window on demand. In fact, imports should shed relatively more light on the patterns of demand, in that the variety of imported goods was far wider than that of exports, and more representative of the total of all goods consumed. Imports act as substitutes and complements for local goods, and the changes in volumes of imports can be used to imply changes in volumes of domestic goods consumed. Demand for several major consumer-good imports is analyzed below through estimates of the income and price elasticity of demand. These estimates are calculated through linear regressions performed on series of price, quantity and income statistics for years from 1896 to 1914. The analysis is based on the following equation, which states that the volume of imports of any consumer good depends on the level of consumer income, the price of the good, and the prices of any closely related goods:

$$M = a_0 P_1^{a_1} P_2^{a_2} P_3^{a_3} Y^{a_4}$$

where M = volume of imports of the consumer good
P_1 = price of the consumer good
P_2, P_3 = prices of closely related goods
Y = value of income from exports
$a_0, \ldots, a_4$ = constant parameters.

This equation may be made into a linear equation by taking logarithms of each side:

$$\log M = a'_0 + a_1 \log P_1 + a_2 \log P_2 + a_3 \log P_3 + a_4 \log Y.$$

115

In this form, the elasticities $a_1, \ldots, a_4$ may be estimated by linear regression when imports, income, and prices are known. Normally, a_4 should be positive, indicating that higher income leads to purchase of more imports. Similarly, a_1 should be negative, indicating that a higher price leads to purchase of less imports. If the closely related goods are substitutes, a_2 and a_3 should be positive, as higher price of a substitute good leads to more purchases of the good in question. But if the related goods are complements, a_2 and a_3 should be negative, as higher price of the complement leads to smaller purchases of the good in question.

It is assumed, for these calculations, that imports were purchased only with the income obtained from sale of imports: Figure 5.1 shows the rise and fall of export earnings from 1890 to 1914. As exports consisted almost entirely of palm products, export earnings depended on the price and yield of palm products. Export income should, however, be considered as a proxy for aggregate cash income of Dahomeans, for it was one of several overlapping categories of income. These also included income in cowries, income in francs and sterling in the domestic economy, and income in good not marketed. Consumers could, for example, use income in cowries to purchase imported goods. Much export income went for intermediate goods and to pay taxes; the government did not necessarily spend the money as its subjects would have. Virtually all imports were financed by Dahomeans, through their domestic income, export income, through customs duties or through other taxes.

The demand for intermediate-good imports is analyzed through a process analogous to that for consumer goods. Demand is taken to depend

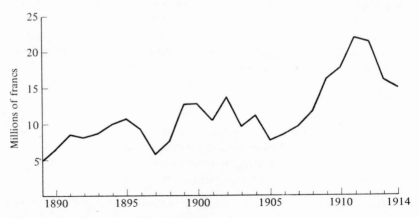

Figure 5.1. Exports, in millions of francs.
Source: Table A4.4.

116

on the level of exports of final goods for which the intermediate good is used (exports serving as a proxy for total output), and on the price of the intermediate good. Thus:

$$M = b_0 Q_1^{b_1} Q_2^{b_2} P^{b_3}$$

where M = volume of imports of the intermediate good
Q_1, Q_2 = export volume of final goods

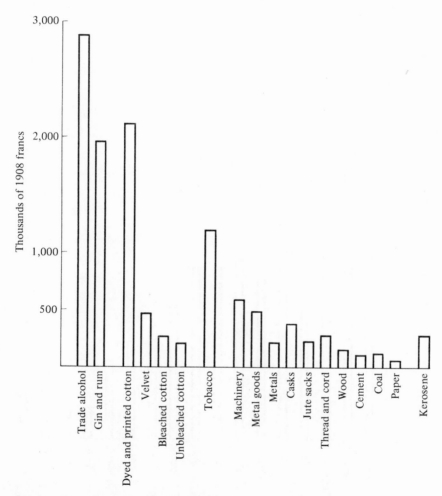

Figure 5.2. Imports of major consumer goods and intermediate goods: Average annual value, 1897–1914, at 1908 prices. Compare with Figure 5.3. in which kerosene is also shown to indicate the relative scale.
Source: Table A4.5.

P = price of the intermediate good
$b_0, \ldots, b_3$ = constant parameters.

This equation may also be expressed in linear terms:

$$\log M = b'_0 + b_1 \log Q_1 + b_2 \log Q_2 + b_3 \log P.$$

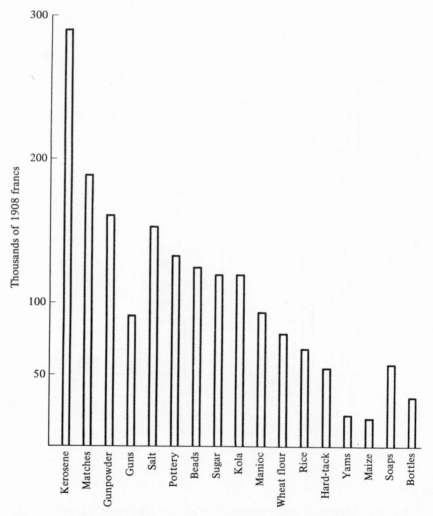

Figure 5.3. Imports of minor consumer goods: average annual value, 1897–1914, at 1908 prices.
Source: Table A4.5.

118

The sign of b_3 is expected to be negative, indicating that higher intermediate-good prices would decrease their usage, while the signs of b_1 and b_2 should be positive, as larger output requires larger input. Two additional factors influenced imports of intermediate goods: the prices of other intermediate goods used in the production of the same final goods, and the level of producer revenue available for purchasing or financing intermediate-good imports.[2]

In the regression calculations for both consumer goods and intermediate goods, the recorded quantity of imports is assumed to be correct, but the recorded value (and hence the price) cannot be depended upon because of erratic French recording practices. The prices used in the regressions are proxies for Dahomean selling prices, constructed out of British export prices which are adjusted to include the full amount of import duties in Dahomey, on the assumption that these were passed on to the consumer.[3]

Imports to Dahomey are displayed in Figures 5.2 and 5.3 as average annual values of imports, 1899–1914, calculated at 1908 prices. Major consumer goods, consisting of alcoholic beverages, cloth, and tobacco, accounted for roughly 60% of the value of imports. Minor consumer goods, including food, household needs and luxuries accounted for roughly 15% of the value of imports, and intermediate goods accounted for another 20% of the value of imports. The remaining 5% of imports consisted of many minor consumer goods, often not identified specifically in the returns. The quantitative analysis of these imports is integrated, in the remaining sections of this chapter, with qualitative analysis of domestic goods to propose to picture of the structure and short-term dynamics of demand in Dahomey.

CONSUMER GOODS

A survey of the typical family's consumption patterns begins naturally with the consumption of staple goods. The same staples were consumed throughout the country, except that sorghums and millet were neither produced nor consumed on the Coast. Maize, manioc, yams, sweet potatoes, beans, peas and peanuts were consumed everywhere, though the relative quantities consumed varied from region to region, as well as the preferred means of preparing foods. Consumers also prepared for the eventuality of famine with manioc (they simply left some in the ground) and with the African locust bean tree. Markets carried local staples as well as those brought from nearby regions and from overseas via the waterways, overland and, after 1905, by rail.

Maize was the favorite staple on the Coast, and perhaps also on the Plateau. The consumer could choose from several varieties, which were

119

usually consumed in different fashions: the early varieties tended to be boiled or grilled and eaten on the cob, while later varieties were made into flour. Tender varieties were preferred to the hard, but were more difficult to preserve. Maize was in shortest supply just before the July harvest, and its price was then at a peak – manioc was consumed as a substitute when maize was scarce and expensive.[4]

The consumption of imported foods, which had been restricted to a small number of the elite in earlier times, grew steadily beginning in the mid-nineteenth century.[5] Staple imports, growing at an annual average rate of six percent, had become a significant portion of total food consumption in the early twentieth century. In the peak year of 1912, trans-Atlantic staple imports (rice, wheat, and hard-tack) reached 2,300 tons, while West African staple imports (maize, manioc and yams) reached 3,000 tons.[6] High food imports in that year resulted from the shortage of staples after a poor harvest, combined with the purchasing power resulting from a large palm product harvest. Manioc, the cheapest staple, was used as a substitute when crops failed; the prices of yams and especially maize were somewhat higher. Staples brought by sea cost somewhat more than twice those produced in West Africa: hard-tack was most expensive, wheat flour was intermediate, and rice was cheapest, corresponding to the degree of processing of each.[7]

Fish and poultry provided high-protein foodstuffs. The fishers themselves consumed a large amount of fish – raw or cooked in palm oil, and sometimes dried and smoked. The non-fishing population ate mostly smoked fish. Those closer to the rivers and lagoons ate more fish than the

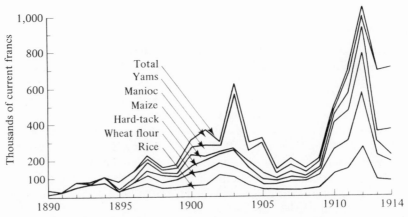

Figure 5.4. Imports of staple foods, in thousands of current francs.
Source: Table A4.5.

rest, but almost everyone in southern Dahomey consumed some fish, usually mixed into sauces. Most families raised their own chickens, and an active poultry market provided a supply for those who did not. Smaller quantities of goats, pigs, sheep and cattle were consumed, while wild game provided an occasional treat.

Okra, greens, peppers, cooking oil, and a variety of fruits and nuts filled out the Dahomean diet. In sum, Dahomeans appear to have been relatively well nourished. Their caloric intake was adequate, thanks to the volume of staples produced, and their protein consumption was sufficient and well-balanced, not only because of their fish and meat consumption, but because of the protein complementarity among maize, yams, beans and peanuts.[8]

The largest single use of palm oil was for cooking, but it was also used for lamp oil, as a lubricant and as a balm for the skin. Average palm oil consumption may be estimated at 7,000 tons per year, or somewhat over 10 kg per person per year; consumption varied considerably from year to year, however.[9] Coconut oil, shea butter and peanut oil were potential substitutes for palm oil as cooking oil. Consumption of coconut oil grew slowly in coastal areas, while the use of shea butter remained restricted to areas where palm oil was rare. Peanut oil became popular for cooking later in the colonial period.

Kola nuts, which were consumed as a stimulant, were presented to people as a gesture of hospitality, and they had a clear religious association. Yoruba and Aja religion were associated with the four- or five-lobed *Cola*

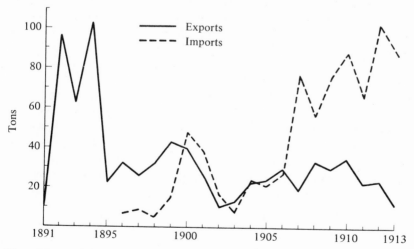

Figure 5.5. Kola imports and exports, in tons.
Source: Tables A4.4, A4.5.

121

acuminata, while Islam was associated with the two-lobed *Cola nitida*: this explains why kola nuts were imported to Dahomey from Lagos at the same time they were exported in the opposite direction. Dahomey had exported *Cola acuminata* to celebrants of Yoruba religion in Brazil during much of the nineteenth century; exports had first gone directly to Brazil, then by way of Lagos, and finally the trade died out. But Dahomeans continued to sell *Cola acuminata* and perhaps *Garcinia kola* to Nigerians. The imports, meanwhile, consisted of *Cola nitida* which was first imported to Lagos from the Gold Coast, and then grown in Lagos. The large increase in kola imports beginning in 1907 corresponds to the entering into production of the new kola trees in Nigeria, and the development of a market for the new crop among Dahomey's Muslim population.[10]

Beverages, in addition to water, included palm wine tapped from trees and allowed to ferment briefly before drinking, beer made from the fermentation of maize, millet and sorghum, and imported beverages. Palm wine consumption rose when imported liquors became scarce or expensive, but Dahomeans did not have an adequate local substitute for imports until the development of *sodabi*, distilled palm wine, during World War I.[11]

Alcoholic beverages were consistently the greatest Dahomean import, in terms of cost to the consumers: per capita consumption ranged from four to seven liters per year. Trade alcohol, gin and rum accounted for roughly 70% of the value of all alcoholic beverage imports. Merchants imported puncheons of trade alcohol, distilled until it was almost pure, and sold it in bulk or diluted it before sale; they imported rum in puncheons, gin and geneva in cases of several bottles, and smaller amounts of many other types of alcoholic beverages, including wine, beer and liqueurs. Dahomean consumers used imported liquors (properly diluted, in the case of trade alcohol) for general consumption, as gifts, and for consumption and libations at religious ceremonies. But the imports became increasingly dear: selling prices, as shown in Figure 5.6, rose dramatically because of customs duties. When the tax rates were roughly doubled in 1899, the purchase price of trade alcohol rose by more than thirty percent, and the amount imported in 1899 fell to one-third the amount imported in 1898 – and this in a year in which export income had risen. In the same year, imports of gin and rum rose sharply, as the tax increase hit concentrated alcohol more severely than those already diluted.[12]

Regression equations estimating the price and income elasticities of demand, calculated for the years 1897–1914, are as follows:

Trade alcohol

$$M = 5.56 - 3.18\,P(TA)^* + 0.61\,P(R) + 1.04\,Y^*\ (R^2 = 0.68)$$
$$(0.72) (0.30) (0.31)$$

Gin and rum:

$$M = 0.95 - 1.41\,P(R)^* + 1.64\,P(TA) + 2.20\,Y^* \quad (R^2 = 0.78)$$
$$(0.48) \qquad\quad (1.16) \qquad\quad (0.49)$$

where $M = \log$ (volume of imports, in thousands of liters)
$P(TA) = \log$ (price of trade alcohol, in francs per liter)
$P(R) = \log$ (price of rum, in francs per liter)
$Y = \log$ (export revenue, in millions of francs)
* indicates coefficient is significant at 95% confidence level.

The income elasticity for gin and rum, relative luxuries, is far higher than that for trade alcohol. The price elasticities of demand, -3.18 and -1.41 respectively, have the expected negative sign. The two types of beverages are shown to be substitutes for each other, in that the cross-elasticities of demand, 0.61 and 1.64, respectively, are both positive.[13] Overall, these calculations confirm that the decline of alcoholic beverage imports after 1900 resulted from the increased purchase price caused by higher duties. The rebound of alcoholic beverage imports in the years 1910–13 resulted from higher income in an era of stable prices.

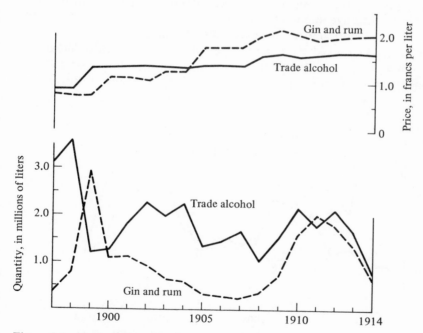

Figure 5.6. Alcoholic beverage imports and prices.
Source: Table A4.5.

Purchases of clothing comprised an important portion of the consumer's budget: textiles, shoes, hats, and such accoutrements as imported beads. Clothing was needed not only for everyday wear, but had to be purchased for occasions such as weddings and funerals. Both imported and domestically-made clothing spanned the range from very expensive to very cheap; the poorest Dahomeans wore locally-made cloth, in part because of its greater durability. Tailors worked increasingly by sewing machine, and a market for ready-made clothes sprung up. The majority of textiles consumed were imported – textile imports were 8–20m (or 1.0–2.5 kg) per person per year – but domestic production was far negligible. Weavers on the Coast produced cloth made partly of imported thread, in inland areas they made cloth of local cotton or of cotton mixed with other fiber. Local standards of dress varied – some Fon were white or bleached cloth, and others dyed local or imported cloth with indigo. Imported cotton print, however, in a wide variety of patterns, dominated the market.[14]

Because the taxes on textiles were relatively stable, Dahomeans tended to substitute textile imports for imports of alcoholic beverages as taxes on the latter rose. Figure 5.7, which shows the value of imports (at 1908 prices) of the three major types of alcoholic beverages as compared with the four major groups of cloth imports, indicates this tendency toward substitution: alcoholic beverage imports fell at a two percent annual rate, 1897–1914, while cotton cloth imports rose at a rate of four percent.

Consumers ranked the several types of cloth into a clear hierarchy, according to cost and preference. Cotton print, including dyed cottons, constituted the major import and was relatively inexpensive. Regression

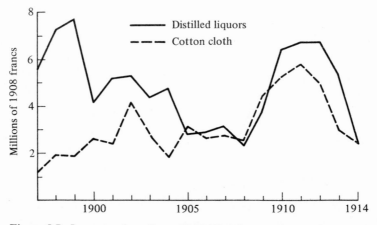

Figure 5.7. Imports of textiles and distilled liquors, in millions of 1908 francs. *Source:* Table A4.5.

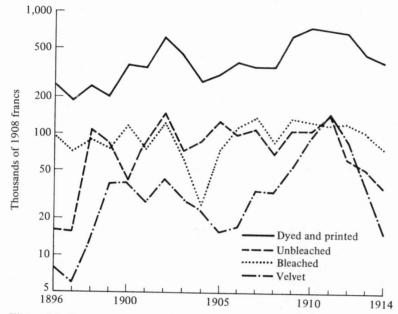

Figure 5.8. Imports of cotton cloth, in thousands of 1908 francs. (Note: 1907 unit values used for 1906; bleached and unbleached figures for 1908–9 are estimates.)
Source: Table A4.5.

calculations on its imports, which showed a remarkably high level of significance, are as follows:
Dyed and printed cotton cloth:

$$M = 0.19 - 2.26\,P(DP) + 13.67\,P(BL)* - 8.40\,P(UN)* + 0.98\,Y* \quad (R^2 = 0.82)$$
$$\quad\quad\quad (3.18) \quad\quad\quad (4.13) \quad\quad\quad (3.62) \quad\quad\quad (0.26)$$

where $M = \log$ (volume of imports in metric tons)

$\quad$ $P(DP) = \log$ (price of dyed and printed cotton cloth in francs per kilogram)

$\quad$ $P(BL) = \log$ (price of bleached cotton cloth in francs per kilogram)

$\quad$ $P(UN) = \log$ (price of unbleached cotton cloth in francs per kilogram)

$\quad\quad\quad$ $Y = \log$ (export revenue in millions of francs)

$\quad\quad$ * indicates coefficient is significant at 95% confidence level.

Income elasticities calculated for the range of imported cottons reflect their hierarchy clearly: unbleached cottons (0.44) were at the bottom, followed

125

by cotton print (a neutral 0.98), then by bleached cottons (1.65), and finally by velvet, the most income-sensitive import (2.32).[15] Further confirming the hierarchy, the cross-elasticities in the regression equation for dyed and printed cottons show bleached cottons to have been a substitute and unbleached cottons a complement for cotton print. The full hierarchy of textiles included both domestic and imported components: domestic textiles dominated at the least expensive level, though unbleached imports were added to this category; imported cotton print dominated the market for medium-priced textiles; and high-priced textiles, while dominated by domestic production, also included such imports as velvet.

Tobacco was another import of long standing. Tobacco had been imported to Dahomey from Bahia since the beginnings of the plantations there in the seventeenth century; American tobacco, which first arrived in the course of the nineteenth-century slave trade, dominated imports during the colonial era. Most tobacco was imported in leaf form, and Dahomeans smoked it in clay pipes of both local and foreign manufacture.

The pattern of imports of tobacco, as shown in Figure 5.7 and in the regression equation below, is one of an ingrained habit: the income elasticity of import was significant, but was a very low 0.37–that is,

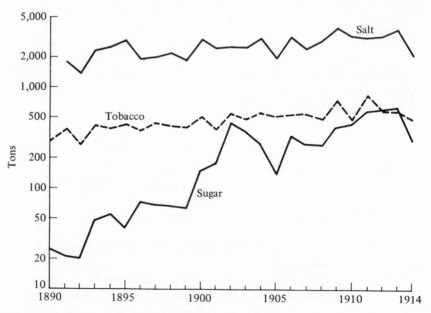

Figure 5.9. Imports of pipe tobacco, salt and sugar, in tons.
Source: Table A4.5.

smoking continued almost unabated if income dropped. The calculated price elasticity is insignificant. Tobacco imports averaged 1 kg per person per year, or over 2 kg per smoker. Domestic tobacco, grown in the region of Savè, was mostly consumed in that area.
Tobacco imports:

$$M = 5.27 + 0.03 \, P(T) + 0.37 \, Y* \quad (R^2 = 0.23)$$
$$(0.15) \qquad (0.19)$$

where $M = \log$ (tobacco imports, in metric tons)
$P(T) = \log$ (price of tobacco, in francs per kilogram)
$Y = \log$ (export revenue, in millions of francs)
* indicates coefficient is significant at 95% confidence level.

The wide range of household needs included building materials, salt, soap, firewood, water, matches, kerosene, knives, other hardware, and containers of basketry, pottery, metal, calabashes, wood and glass. Imported soaps and dishware provided a substantial portion of domestic consumption. The soaps ranged from expensive perfumed soaps to brown soaps little different from those made domestically. The dishware included pottery, tin and pewter plates. Imports of salt, divided between French marine salt and German-supplied rock salt, grew steadily at a 2.5% annual rate: about half the increase can be attributed to rising population; the remainder resulted from increased per capita consumption, substitution for domestically-produced salt, or expansion of the salt market in the interior.[16] Sugar imports grew at a faster rate of 8% per year, as refined sugar was adopted into domestic consumption: imports rose from some 200 g per capita before 1900 to 1 kg per capita after 1910. At this stage sugar was a luxury, as its income elasticity of demand was quite high.

Kerosene and matches were the leading household goods imported into Dahomey, and their value exceeded that of food imports after about 1905. Imports of matches, which began as soon as matches became available in the 1870s, grew at the rate of ten percent per year from the mid-1890s to 1914, and grew at a slower rate thereafter.[17] The first reported import of kerosene was in 1891: as its price declined, it came to be widely adopted as lamp oil, replacing palm oil. Imports rose from a scant 0.1 kg per person per year before 1900 to over 4 kg after 1910. The latter figure compares favorably with the level of palm oil consumption, estimated above at 10 kg per person per year, indicating that the adoption of kerosene not only improved the quality of illumination in Dahomey, but also led to increased exports of palm oil.[18]

Completing this survey of consumer demand, a small portion of total expenditure went toward luxury goods. For the very poor, of course, a few meters of cotton print could be a luxury. At the other extreme, jewellers fabricated ornaments of silver and gold, and the great families of the towns, relying on mail-order catalogs and parcel-post service, ordered the latest in clothing, shoes and hats from the *grands magasins* of Paris.[19] More generally, however, purchases such as guns and gunpowder, used for firing on ceremonial occasions, constituted luxuries. Several thousand flintlock guns

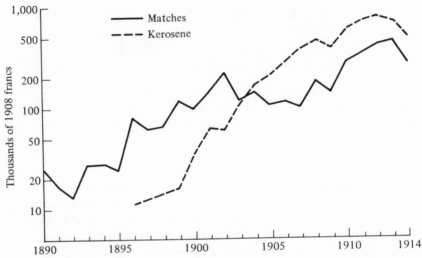

Figure 5.10. Imports of kerosene and matches, in thousands of 1908 francs. (Note: Matches at current prices, 1890–1904.)
Source: Table A4.5.

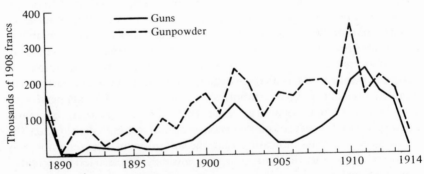

Figure 5.11. Imports of guns and gunpowder, in thousands of 1908 francs. (Note: Estimates for guns, 1890–1, 1893, 1896–8.)
Source: Table A4.5.

128

were imported a year, along with powder to fire them. Regression equations show the income elasticity of demand for guns to be significant and quite high:

Guns:

$$M = -1.33 + 1.26\,P(G) + 0.86\,P(P) + 2.48\,Y^* \quad (R^2 = 0.64)$$
$$ (1.06) \qquad (3.25) \qquad (0.55)$$

Gunpowder:

$$N = 7.35 - 1.91\,P(P) - 1.01\,P(G) + 0.56\,Y \qquad (R^2 = 0.25)$$
$$ (2.53) \qquad (0.83) \qquad (0.43)$$

where $M = \log$ (gun imports, in pieces)
$\quad\;\; N = \log$ (gunpowder imports, in tons)
$\;\; P(G) = \log$ (gun price, in francs per piece)
$\;\; P(P) = \log$ (gunpowder price, in francs per ton)
$\qquad Y = \log$ (export revenue, in millions of francs)
$\quad\;$ * indicates coefficient is significant at 95% confidence level.

The positive price elasticity of demand for guns indicates that consumers bought more expensive guns in high-income years. The levels of significance calculated for gunpowder are low, but the signs are as expected: the negative cross-elasticity of demand for gunpowder, for example, shows it to be a complement for guns.

INTERMEDIATE GOODS

Every sector of the economy required intermediate goods, and those of trans-Atlantic origin were of marked significance. Ten percent of total Dahomean imports consisted of intermediate goods destined for the commodity exchange and mercantile sectors: these purchases, which came to between one and two percent of domestic product, were led by casks, sacks, thread and cord, then followed by metal goods, metals, machinery and wood. Another ten percent of Dahomean imports, and hence another one to two percent of domestic product, consisted of intermediate goods utilized in the state and capitalist sectors. These imports were led by machines and rails, then followed by metal goods, wood, cement, coal, metals and paper. Adding to these imports the amount of domestically-produced intermediate goods, most of which went to the commodity exchange sector, one may conclude that intermediate goods totalled a minimum of five percent of domestic product, and perhaps as much as twice that amount.

The dynamics of Dahomean demand for intermediate goods are shown

129

most clearly for the case of casks and jute sacks, imported as packing materials. As the marketing and export of maize and palm kernels grew in the late nineteenth century, the demand for containers strained and then exceeded the capacity of domestic artisans to produce raphia sacks. At the same time, decreasing costs of ocean transport reduced the price of imported jute sacks, with the result that these imported sacks became a regular input into the production of palm kernels and maize. The casks in which trade alcohol was imported were sold separately from their contents, and were filled with palm oil for export. A larger number of casks was imported in pieces and assembled by coopers, either at coastal factories where much palm oil was bulked, or in the interior so that casks full of palm oil could be rolled to the coast. Regression analysis confirms that demand for these containers was derived from the level of output of the final goods:[20]

Wooden casks:

$$M = 1.30 + 1.38\,X(O)^* - 2.06\,P(C)^* + 1.19\,Y\ (R^2 = 0.83)$$
$$\quad\quad\quad (0.58) \quad\quad\quad (1.08) \quad\quad\quad (0.93)$$

Jute sacks:

$$N = -5.75 + 1.13\,X(K)^* + 0.05\,X(M)^* - 0.07\,P(J)\,(R^2 = 0.70)$$
$$\quad\quad\quad (0.23) \quad\quad\quad (0.02) \quad\quad\quad (0.35)$$

where $M = \log$ (volume of cask imports, in arbitrary units)
   $N = \log$ (jute sack imports, in thousands of sacks)
   $P(C) = \log$ (cask price, in arbitrary units)
   $P(J) = \log$ (jute fiber price, in arbitrary units)
   $X(O) = \log$ (palm oil exports, in tons)
   $X(K) = \log$ (palm kernel exports, in tons)
   $X(M) = \log$ (maize exports, in tons)
   * indicates coefficient is significant at 95% confidence level.

Cask imports depended not only on the level of palm oil exports, but on cask prices and on the level of export revenue: the value of cask imports averaged a substantial ten percent of the value of palm oil exports. Demand for jute sacks depended primarily on the level of palm kernel export, which accounted for 55% of the variance in sack imports, while maize exports accounted for another 15% of the variance.[21]

Imported thread and cord went to the commodity exchange sector, where weavers used thread in the production of textiles, while fishers used cord in the manufacture of nets. Regression analysis of these intermediate goods shows the expected reactions of imports to changes in price and purchasing power: the price elasticity of demand is negative, and the

relatively low income elasticity of demand for thread and cord indicates
that these imports were seen as necessities:
Thread and cord:

$$M = 2.93 - 0.74\,P(T)^* + 0.90\,Y^* \quad (R^2 = 0.51)$$
$$\quad\quad\quad (0.38) \quad\quad\quad (0.25)$$

where $M = $ log (thread and cord imports, in arbitrary units)
$P(T) = $ log (average thread and cord price, in
  arbitrary units)
$Y = $ log (export revenue, in millions of francs)
*indicates coefficient significant at 95% confidence level.

Attempts to show significant ties between thread imports and textile or fish
production did not, however, meet with success.[22]

Producers of field crops and tree crops required tools with which to do
their work and containers in which to store their produce. Kola nuts, for
example, required special packing material. Fishing peoples required not
only cord but hooks, canoes, firewood for smoking fish, and materials for
construction of weirs, traps and shelters for fish. Weavers required looms as
well as thread, soap-makers required potash and oil, and smiths required
iron, bellows and charcoal. Building materials for residential and commercial construction included domestic wood, earth, thatch and chalk, as
well as imported cement, wood, chalk, galvanized iron and nails. Imported
tools and machinery grew steadily in importance as new products became
available: bicycles, sewing machines and mills for grinding maize were to
be among the most important of these. Most of this machinery, along with
building materials, canoes and looms, can be considered as capital goods
rather than as inputs into current output.

State and capitalist demand for intermediate goods fluctuated sharply:
these were primarily used as capital goods rather than in current output.
The period 1902–12 spanned a long construction boom, during which the
physical structures of the colonial regime were set up: the railroads, the
pier, and public buildings. At the same time, merchant firms imported
boats and built new warehouses and boutiques, and several small
industries were set up: bakeries, a brick factory, a lemonade works, and the
government printshop and electric power plant. Automobile purchases by
state and private buyers began as the construction boom died down.

Imports of metals, metallic goods and machinery were divided fairly
equally between the commodity exchange sector and the state and
capitalist sectors. Metals – in sheets, bars and wire – included tin, steel,
copper bars, laminated zinc sheets for roofs, and 30–60 tons of iron bars
imported each year for use by smiths. Metallic goods included tools,

131

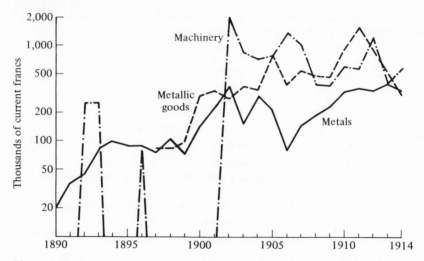

Figure 5.12. Imports of metals, metallic goods and machinery, in thousands of current francs.
Source: Table A4.5.

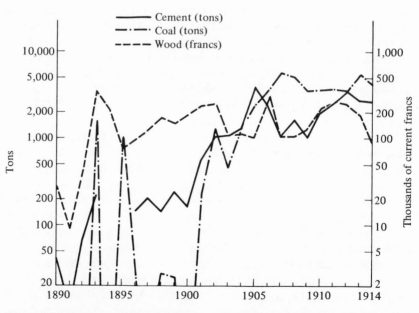

Figure 5.13. Imports of wood (in thousands of current francs), cement and coal (in tons). (Note: Cement estimated for 1890 and 1892.)
Source: Table A4.5.

knives, wrought iron, scales, needles, pins, nails, and building materials. Machinery imports were dominated by imports of rails, but included steam shovels, electrical machinery and bicycles.

Imports of wood, used as building material, were divided among the commodity exchange sector, which imported wood from adjoining territories (*rôniers* or African fan palms from Lagos, for instance), and the state and large merchant firms, which imported wood from Europe – the latter being the larger portion. The level of wood imports fluctuated with the level of export revenue, and also in response to state construction projects.[23] Cement imports fluctuated similarly, though they grew more with the passage of time. State construction accounted for most cement imports – it went into public buildings, streets, wells and bridges – but merchants and other city-dwellers used cement as well.

Two final imported intermediate goods suggest important but quite different changes in the economy of Dahomey. Coal imports reflect the level of activity in railroad construction and utilization, and thus reflect state-dominated, capital-intensive economic activity. Imports of paper and books, meanwhile, provide an index of the level of bureaucratization in the colonial state. While coal imports fluctuated according to the level of state investment and the demand for transportation services, paper imports climbed steadily upward, at an annual rate approaching fifteen percent.

THE STRUCTURE OF FINAL DEMAND

The dominant aspect of final demand was that in the familial and commodity exchange sectors for domestic goods – or, to go a step further, demand in those sectors for staple foods. The full range of consumer goods, however, presented a diverse array of objectives among which Dahomeans allocated their energies and incomes. As a summary in terms of input–output analysis, the elements of consumer final demand are ranked below in rough order of the magnitude of their value. Asterisks mark those categories in which imports played an important role.

   staple foods
*alcoholic beverages and tobacco
*clothing
   fish
   tree crops
*household goods
   meats
   non-staple foods
   construction
*artistic and ceremonial purchases

This ranking may be compared with that given above for productive activities to obtain an impression of the problems of allocating labor, resources and income in this economy.[24] While the evidence available does not permit a fully quantitative approach, it is possible that further analysis of materials on Dahomean production and consumption, using a semi-quantitative input–output approach, may produce new hypotheses and new insights on the structure and functioning of this agricultural economy.

Fluctuations in consumer income were the main cause of short-range changes in the level of consumer demand. The after-tax income out of which consumers made their purchases depended on several factors: domestic income (both from non-market and market production), export revenue, income from wages and from property, and the level of taxes. Total output tended to grow along with the population and the labor force, at a rate above two percent per year in the early twentieth century. For field crops, production varied in proportion to the current year's rainfall, while for oil palms, output varied with the previous year's rainfall. The level of consumer income was, then, the level of production multiplied by the appropriate price: implicit prices in the case of familial production, market prices in the case of production for the domestic market, and export prices for export production. Wage and property income were added to this total, and taxes were subtracted from it. Most taxes were indirect, being added to the prices of imports, but head taxes and market fees were collected directly; taxes grew steadily during the early colonial years. Forced labor, while not a monetary tax, nonetheless decreased the incomes of those who were taken away from their normal work.

Price changes caused changes in the level of consumer demand in the short run and the long run. When prices of food crops rose because of shortages, or prices of imported goods rose because of higher customs duties, consumers cut their consumption of the goods affected. When the terms of trade improved, as they did after 1910, it was easier for Dahomeans to buy a wide range of imported goods. Some prices declined as a result of fundamental improvements in technology: improved maritime technology made imports generally more attractive, and the rapid growth in imports of matches and kerosene followed on the innovations which made them available. These changes in prices tended to stimulate more permanent changes in Dahomean demand, as well as changes in the technology of production.

Changes in preference also affected the level of demand, but their importance is easy to exaggerate. The best example of changes in preference was the continual variation in the preferred style and design of imported cottons, which kept the merchants continually on their toes. French observers, meanwhile, were forever seizing on Dahomean consumption of imported goods as confirmation of the beneficial impact of colonial rule on

134

the economic outlook of Dahomeans. But their reasoning was generally specious: the arrival of many such imports had preceded colonial rule, the growth rate of imports was uninflected by colonial conquest, and importing of many such goods – matches, salt, and tools, for example – had to do with simple economic realities rather than the cultural benefits of colonialism. The cultural and political atmosphere of colonialism was not, however, without its effect. In the towns especially, it became important to the economic and political leaders of Dahomean society to remain in touch with the tastes and prejudices of their colonial masters, as an aspect of their effort to advance themselves under colonialism. Hence French education and the accoutrements of French culture came into increasing demand: purchases of wines, liqueurs and French clothing, for instance, increased at the expense of other spirits and clothing.

In schematic terms, one may reduce the basic approaches of consumers to a 'subsistence target' and a 'satisfaction target'. The satisfaction target was most commonly pursued and the most easily observable consumer behavior. Here more labor was forthcoming as producer prices rose, and higher consumer prices tended to reduce purchases. In 1900, for instance, a year in which the rains brought a good harvest of staples and an average palm product harvest, total producer income rose from the previous year. As a result, purchases of domestic and imported consumer goods rose, and purchases of luxuries rose disproportionately. At the same time, however, the sharp tax increases of 1900 took away much of the increased income and raised the relative prices of certain imports: thus, imports of expensive imported alcoholic beverages suffered as consumer expenditures were diverted to domestic alcoholic beverages and imported textiles. All of this reflects the normal behavior of consumers unconstrained by special conditions.

In the year 1912, however, the subsistence target became visible in Dahomey at the territorial level for the case of staple foods. The harvests had failed, and many farmers had been called away to perform labor for the state, so that resources had to be drawn from wherever available to purchase food, even high-priced imported foods. This was achieved without starvation because the harvest of palm products had been large, thus providing ample revenue for those who had palm products to sell. Imports of tobacco, alcoholic beverages and clothing were foregone to purchase foodstuffs. The subsistence target, therefore, need not operate in all areas of consumption at once: more likely, it operates in a particular area of privation, while the satisfaction target continues to operate for other areas.

The subsistence target thus corresponds to the special conditions brought by poverty and privation. This target set minimum required levels

135

of consumption – as for food, clothing and shelter – for which cash income or home production had to be achieved at all costs. These minimum required levels of consumption were determined not only by physical needs, but by social needs as well: effective participation in the society required, for example, large expenditures at weddings and funerals. Subsistence needs had first call on consumer income, but they were met out of both familial and market production, according to which was most remunerative. In the cases of skilled artisans or land-poor agriculturists, for example, the best route to subsistence lay not in familial production but in market production for the artisan and in tenancy or wage labor for the farmer. Subsistence, in short, was quite a different matter from self-sufficiency: subsistence defines minimum required levels of consumption, while self-sufficiency describes a way of meeting consumer needs at or beyond the requirements of subsistence.

Those who were poverty-stricken had to pursue the subsistence target, working long hours to get by, and reducing their hours only when their compensation improved. Such behavior corresponds to the 'backward-bending labor supply curve' so often discussed for colonial Africa. But colonial taxation, by increasing required expenditures, had the effect of increasing subsistence levels: much of the colonial economic strategy consisted, therefore, of reducing Africans to a level where the subsistence target took effect, so that they could be induced to do more work for a lower rate of return. Apologists for colonial economic policy argued that this behavior was inherent in Africans, whereas in fact it is a behavior specifically characteristic of low income levels or of particular constraints on consumer expenditure.[25]

Studies of African economies have generally given too little attention to the role of demand, both for consumer goods and for intermediate goods. This neglect is part and parcel of the extractive mentality which has dominated writings on African economies – Africa has been seen more as a source of labor and raw materials than as a market for domestic or imported goods. But the influence of demand is powerful, and the level of demand in Dahomey was influenced systematically by consumer income, prices and preferences: the customer, in the short run, was king. It is true, of course, that consumer sovereignty fades away in the long run, as technology, the organization of production and income distribution act to constrain the consumer's choices, so that production tends to determine consumption, and supply tends to determine demand. Yet in the long run as well, the remarkable stability of Dahomey's demand for both domestic and imported goods, even as many economic conditions were greatly transformed, speaks to the significance of Dahomean consumption patterns in themselves.

136

6

Exchange, 1890–1914

THE LOCAL EXCHANGE SYSTEM

Moving a marketplace, the French found, was an expeditious way of punishing an insubordinate town. After the 'one-gun-shot war' of April 1911 in Kétou, in which an interpreter was assassinated in the market by opponents of labor recruitment, the French moved the market from its place one kilometer outside the northern gate to a point within the old city wall. Similarly, the French in 1913 moved the market from Yévié, in the Sô valley, three kilometers northwest to Zinvié, at the request of merchant firms, and after the chiefs of Yévié had led a hold-up of palm oil in 1909. In each case the aggrieved town took advantage of the outbreak of war in 1914 to seek redress. In Kétou the townspeople began immediately to clear the old marketplace, but were halted by the administration.[1] In Yévié two hundred armed men, led by 'féticheurs et marabouts,' rose in rebellion in September to re-establish the market. They laid their hopes for liberation on the arrival of the Germans, and had begun work on a German flag when their revolt was suppressed.[2]

The combination of local market exchange (in and out of the marketplace) and non-market, familial exchange formed the local exchange system. The needs of this system sometimes conflicted with the concerns of the state, as the case of Kétou indicates, and at times conflicted with the needs of the interregional exchange system as well. The French administration, as the Yévié–Zinvié example suggests, showed more interest in exports than in local commerce.

The marketplace served as the rallying point for local society, and as the keystone of the local exchange system. Solidarity among the participants was less than complete, however, as the market was also the place for expressing the tensions between producer and consumer. These were at times expressed as ethnic tensions. Thus at Bopa, on the west shore of Lake Ahémé, Aja farmers came to market in February 1905 brandishing arms, professing fear of kidnapping by the Hueda fishers.[3] And in 1912 a fight broke out in the Holli market at Issaba, as Ketu vendors refused to accept payment offered by the Holli, since the 5- and 10-centime coins which they offered in payment bore the unfamiliar face of Louis Napoléon, having been minted in the years 1853–7.[4] Such occasional outbursts notwithstanding, the system of local market and non-market exchange worked efficiently to equilibrate local supply and demand.

An act of exchange logically intervenes between an act of production and one of consumption. In the case of the familial or non-market sector, exchange was virtually from right hand to left, as each family unit consumed its own produce. The institutions of family exchange worked on two levels: first, many goods were placed under the care of the family chief (*huetagan, bale,* or chief of the extended patrilineal family), and he doled them out as necessary. Second, individuals within the family unit produced and consumed goods on their own – in addition to, or in place of, communal goods. Exchange within family units was even monetary at times, as with the husband's sale of maize or fish to his wife for processing and resale. Familial exchange, though non-monetary, was subject to all the regular pressures of an exchange system – shortages, gluts, changes in taste and demand – and the implicit prices of goods exchanged within the family unit rose and fell in response to these pressures. The same goods were exchanged at explicit prices in the adjoining commodity exchange system, so that if yams, for example, were undervalued or overproduced in a given family, the producer would attempt to get a better return on his yams in the local market.

The interlocking network of alternating village markets, based on a four-day week, formed the central institution of the commodity exchange sector. Local markets linked all the individual and family producing units in Dahomey, serving to collect from them their marketable produce, to remunerate them according to current prices, and to provide the full range of consumer and intermediate goods. Women dominated the local markets, both as buyers and sellers: most men who sold in the market were craftsmen selling their own wares. Perhaps half the adult women in Dahomey were market women at least part time. When not attending the market, they worked in the fields, did household chores, or prepared for the next market. Girls learned the methods of trade from their mothers, but they did not participate on their own until menstruation or until marriage, when husbands commonly provided their brides with the small amount of capital necessary to begin trade.[5] Women who sold prepared food had to buy the ingredients, while those who sold domestic manufactures or imported goods had to buy an attractive stock from producers or regional merchants.

The primary function of local markets was to facilitate local exchange, as producers and consumers met to exchange among each other the produce of the region. A second function, the diffusion of goods from market to market, took place simply through purchase and resale of small lots of domestic goods, imports and exports, which sometimes moved great distances by this process. Most interregional movement of goods, however, took place not through the mechanism of diffusion but through the interaction of the local exchange system with the mercantile system. This interaction yielded three additional functions of the local markets: they were bulking stations, as agricultural and other produce was transferred to regional merchants; they were stations for breaking bulk, as goods brought to the area by regional merchants were distributed to market women for sale to final consumers; finally, they were entrepôts, at which goods were transferred from one group of regional merchants to another. Kéténou, for example, was an important bulking point in the palm oil and palm kernel trade, Djalloukou was an entrepôt in the salt commerce, and Agoué acted as both an entrepôt and a bulking point between Keta (in Togo) and Ouidah for poultry, fruits and cereals.[6] Breaking bulk took place at every market, but the markets at Ouidah, Abomey and Adjarra (outside Porto-Novo) were outstanding for the quantity of goods on sale imported from overseas and from distant West African points.

Markets were concentrated in the areas of densest population and along major transportation routes, as may be seen in Map 4. (The indications on maize and palm kernel exports given on the map are relevant to a later discussion of transport costs.)[7] In the Center, where villages were relatively isolated, periodic markets were less important than to the south. Many of the markets had been founded hundreds of years earlier, but their relative importance changed with time. Some of the openings, closings and displacements of markets took place on the initiative of participants, while others were imposed by the authorities. In the area of Abomey, where the four days of the market week were *Mionhi, Adokwi, Zogodu* and *Adjahi*, the early twentieth century found five major *Mionhi* markets, three major *Zogodu* markets, and no major *Adokwi* or *Adjahi* markets. (The *Mionhi* markets were Cana, Abomey, Ounbégamé, Boguila and Dainho-Dénou; the *Zogodu* markets were Bohicon, Agbagnizon and Tindji.) The administration attempted to regularize this system by holding two of these markets on each of the four days. The chiefs opposed the plan and defeated it for a while, but when the French opened the new market at Ouansougon on the rail line to replace Dainho-Dénou, they changed the day from *Mionhi* to *Adjahi*.[8] The succession of markets surrounding Porto-Novo was Adjarra, Porto-Novo, Djégan, and Dangbo, while the great Zobe market at Ouidah was held daily. The government moved the Abomey-Calavi market, which was held every second day, from the lagoon to the

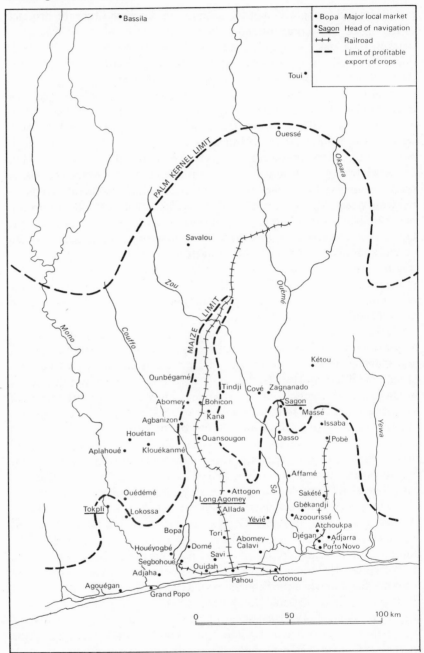

Map 4 Major local markets, 1905–14; export transit limits

town, and moved several markets to the rail line: from Tori-ville to Tori-gare, from Desso to Attogon, and from Dainho-Dénou to Ouansougon. Major markets grew up at rail termini at Segbohoué, Pobè, Bohicon and, as the railroad moved north from 1903 to 1911, at Dan, Paouignan, Agouagon and finally Savè. Sagon, important as a terminus for river traffic on the Ouémé, lost importance as a market with the coming of the colonial period, and its decline was furthered by the opening of the railroad to Bohicon; Togodo on the Mono suffered a similar fate. Zogbodomé, a flourishing market under the Fon regime, died out as slaves quartered in the area escaped after the French conquest.[9]

In principle, all market exchange took place in the marketplace, but in fact exceptions were required. Every village had isolated vendors and a small market every day to meet the immediate needs of the villagers, and local traders, acting as agents for regional merchants, bought up palm products, yams, maize and other goods from producers and delivered them to market. Other developments, however, tended to draw additional commerce outside the marketplace. Beginning in 1907, the French set up a system of patents, licenses and market fees, and as the fees grew year by year, smaller traders increased the portion of their sales outside the marketplace in attempt to avoid the fees.[10] Meanwhile Dahomean and expatriate firms set up a network of boutiques at or near marketplaces, which represented a new and competing element of commerce.

THE DEMISE OF THE MERCANTILE SYSTEM

The activities of merchants and transporters, linking local markets with the wider world, made up the mercantile system. This sector of the economy relied on transport by head, by canoe and by sailing ship, and it was financed through credit arrangements dependent on personal contacts. While elements of this venerable system survived into the mid-twentieth century, it was first challenged nearly a century earlier by capitalist methods of economic organization, themselves reliant on industrial technology. By 1930 the mercantile sector was to be largely absorbed into the capitalist mode of production.

The relatively plentiful data of the early twentieth century allow for a description of the mercantile sector and its operation, and permit the tracing of its progressive displacement and absorption by capitalist methods. The main determinants of the pace of change were changing costs of transport, marketing and finance. The conflict between the mercantile and capitalist organizations of transport and commerce, fundamentally, was economic rather than cultural. Although Europeans dominated capitalist commerce and transport at the turn of the century, and Dahomeans dominated the mercantile system, Europeans and Dahomeans were leaders in both systems. The conflict of cultures was far more evident in the activities of the state which, now in European hands, used its economic and political power to deflect in a new direction the pace and the terms of the transformation in commerce and transport.

Description of the mercantile system must encompass its routes, its merchandise, its personnel and its methods. In the interior, beyond the lands of the Yoruba and Aja–Ewe peoples, a great east–west commercial route tied such towns as Kano and Sokoto in the Sokoto Caliphate with Salaga in Asante. This interior network had long been tied to the Bight of Benin by two routes, coinciding roughly with the eastern and western frontiers of modern Bénin. Meanwhile the populous heartlands of the Aja–Ewe and Yoruba peoples were tied to the coast by shorter routes, and tied to each other by routes leading along the lagoons and across the plateaux. Merchants specialized according to the trade routes they followed, and their varying ethnic groups reflect this specialization.[11]

Hausa, Dendi and other northern merchants, known as *gambari* in Dahomey, carried trade on north–south routes. Skertchly met a Hausa slave caravan north of Abomey in 1873, and Hausa merchants continued to grow in numbers until the 1890s. Some of them were itinerant, while others lived in small, closed colonies in the towns. Yoruba-speaking Muslims, the largest group of regional merchants, included Muslims among the Nago, Ketu and Shabe, and returned slaves from Brazil who became leading merchants in such coastal towns as Agoué, Ouidah and Porto-Novo. (The Muslims among the Brazilians tended to specialize in commerce on the continent, while Catholic Brazilians were more specialized in coastal or trans-Atlantic commerce.) With the establishment of French power in the 1880s and 1890s, many Muslim merchants moved to Porto-Novo and Cotonou. Some three thousand Yoruba Muslims lived in Porto-Novo in 1904, and about a hundred Yoruba were in commerce in each of Cotonou, Ouidah and Grand Popo, with a larger number in Agoué.[12] In the days of the Fon kingdom a group of notables, the *ahisinon*, traded on the account of the king, but also traded on their own. They left the kingdom to buy grindstones from the Mahi, or salt, fish and shrimp from the Hueda and Hula. They thus participated in both north–south and east–west commerce. The *ahisinon* dealt with the importers at Ouidah, where they obtained goods on credit. The European merchants were forbidden to alter the price paid for local produce, under penalty of fine; they had to get permission to import or export any new goods; and they were forbidden to sell certain goods in retail quantities. These restrictions began to fall into disuse even before the conquest of the Fon state, but the families of the *ahisinon* remained wealthy, and merchants continued to perform the same services in regional exchange under the new system.[13]

142

Goods moving north along the routes to the interior, according to records kept at Savalou, included large amounts of salt, and smaller amounts of textiles, guns and powder, dyes, alcoholic beverages, beads, matches, copper and tobacco. Goods moving south included makari, shea butter, cattle, sheep, goats, hides, pepper, mats, kola, soap, potash, calabashes, horses, donkeys, turkeys, beans, yams, and occasionally ostriches and ivory.[14] East–west commerce was of little significance in the Center, but regular caravans linked the towns of the Plateau – for example, from Abeokuta to Abomey to Atakpamé. In the commerce recorded between Kétou and Meko in Nigeria during 1912, eastward-moving goods were led by gunpowder and followed by kola, cattle, guns, pepper, textiles and sheep. Larger numbers of sheep and goats were sent from Abomey to Abeokuta by nearby routes. Westward-moving goods included beads, potash, Nigerian-made clothing and silk.[15]

The transport workers on land were porters who carried merchandise by head. In days before the French conquest, many of them were slaves of the merchants. But porters also included wage workers and members of the family carrying the trade. Later the French government and coastal merchant houses demanded a great deal of labor for porterage: porters were now almost universally paid wages, though they were often recruited under duress. Wages ranged from one to one-and-a-half francs per day, and the porters bore loads of 25–30 kg for 25–35 km per day. Another important group of transport workers was the rollers of puncheons, who pushed puncheons loaded with palm oil along paths to waterways or to the coast: these too included both slaves and wage workers.[16]

The greatest highways for transport of goods were the lagoons and rivers; the east–west route along the lagoons was the most heavily travelled. Fish and staple foods, as well as fruits, local and imported manufactures of every description moved in both directions along the lagoons, in response to fluctuating market conditions. The canoes which plied the waterways were propelled by poles except when the water was more than three meters deep, when they were paddled. Along major thoroughfares the canoe men, mostly Gen and Hula on the lagoons, formed corporate groups with chiefs, who negotiated with those wishing to hire canoes and acted as dispatchers. Between Porto-Novo and Cotonou or other points on Lake Nokoué, the rate was about six francs per ton for a thirty-kilometer journey of some six hours, with similar rates on the Mono, along the Ouémé, and on the lagoon stretching west from Ouidah.[17]

A fleet of surf-boats was necessary to move goods between the beach and ships, which had to anchor more than a kilometer offshore. Crews of Gen and Hula boatmen, as well as boatmen from Accra and Cape Coast, transported goods across the difficult surf. For a wage of thirty francs a

143

month, meals and a bottle of rum each day, plus a bottle of rum for the crew after each trip, the boatmen made up to sixteen trips per day. Merchandise was often lost or damaged in the surf: merchants estimated their losses at five percent. As with the lagoon canoemen, boatmen were organized into crews under a chief, and contracted with the shippers.[18]

The last link in the old mercantile system was provided by the sailing ships of the French, Brazilian, English and German merchants. These ships, owned by the merchant firms which hired captains and crews, took some thirty-five days to make the trip to Europe, or twenty-five days to Brazil.

This was the first link of the mercantile system to feel the impact of capitalist technology and methods. The African Steam Ship Company began service from England to Lagos in the 1850s, and thus carried some of the trade of Porto-Novo. By the 1880s steamships had come to dominate West African navigation: the British lines (soon to be united as Elder–Dempster) and the German Woermann Line dominated the trade of Lagos, and made regular stops at Cotonou, Ouidah and Grand Popo. G. L. Gaiser, the leading Hamburg merchant firm in Lagos and Porto-Novo, had three small steamers making regular trips on the lagoon between the two towns. The Brazilians, financially unable to make the transition to steam navigation, had reoriented most of their commerce toward Europe by 1890. The French firm of Cyprien Fabre began sending steamers to Dahomey in the 1890s, though sailing ships still carried salt from Port-de-Bouc to Grand Popo. By 1900 two French steamer lines, Fraissinet and Chargeurs Réunis, subsidized with postal contracts, made regular calls at Dahomean ports.[19] Meanwhile the Woermann Line, which had entered into the British-led agreement known as the Shipping Ring, had become the dominant shipper for the Dahomean ports. The steamer lines had regular schedules, and merchant firms contracted with them. Crew sizes decreased with each new development in steam transport.

If the growth of steam navigation came about primarily through efforts of private capital, most other changes in transportation and communication at the turn of the century were financed by the state. Following the war with the Fon, the French built a wooden pier at Cotonou in 1893. It extended 300 m into the ocean, beyond the surf, and goods were transferred between the pier and ships anchored offshore by lighters, occasionally aided by motorized tugs. With the advantage of the pier, Cotonou extended its domination of the international trade of Dahomey over Ouidah, Porto-Novo and Grand Popo, and the demand for surf-boat crews declined. By 1910, the wooden pier had been replaced by a longer steel pier on which tracks had been laid, and it was operated in conjunction with the railroad. The government granted concessions for a similar pier at Grand Popo in

1893 and 1896, but it was never built. The French postal system was extended to all the main towns of Dahomey following the conquest, and telegraphic communication was opened up to Cotonou and to northern Dahomey. No longer did merchants have to wait weeks for price quotes from Europe or to change orders for imports.

The railroads were the largest capital investment of the early colonial years. Originally conceived to be a partnership of private and public capital, the railroads ended up being constructed entirely out of public funds raised from taxes in Dahomey. In 1899 the government of Dahomey decided to build a railroad from Cotonou to Carnotville (north of Ouessé), and gave a concession for that purpose to the Compagnie des Chemins de Fer du Dahomey, led by Georges Borelli of the Marseille mercantile firm of Mante frères & Borelli.[20] The colony agreed to build the roadbed, and the company contracted to lay the rails and operate the railroad. The company formally established itself in 1901, and the colony began work on the roadbed in 1902. In 1904 the convention was modified: the colony assumed the full expense of building the railroad, and the company would simply operate it.

By July 1905, 143 km of 1-m gauge track linked Cotonou and Dan, just north of Abomey. The main line reached Paouignan in 1906, and construction stopped at Savè in 1911, at kilometer 261. A branch line to Ouidah opened in 1903, and it was extended in 1906 to Segbohoué, on Lake Ahémé. Two trains ran daily from Cotonou to Ouidah. One train a day went north from Cotonou, and it was restricted to passengers on Sunday. The trip from Cotonou to Dan required seven hours. Traffic in the north and especially beyond Abomey proved to be light – in 1909 the schedule was reduced to four trains a week on the main line, two of which stopped to Bohicon. Bohicon, 9 km east of Abomey, became the rail and commercial center of the Abomey plateau. A second railway was built between 1904 and 1908 from Porto-Novo to Sakété, and it was extended in 1913 to Pobè. It was also of 1-m gauge, and was built and operated entirely by the government of the colony.

To the east, the Nigerian railroad opened from Lagos to Abeokuta and Ibadan in 1900, and to Jebba on the Niger in 1909. In Togo, the Lomé–Anécho line opened in 1905, and the line from Lomé to Atakpamé was constructed between 1908 and 1913. The Dahomean lines carried somewhat less traffic than those in Togo, and far less than the Nigerian line. On the Cotonou–Savè line the company received a subsidy each year to cover its losses, while the Porto-Novo–Pobè line ran at a tiny profit. The Dahomean railroads, in the years before 1914, brought in the lowest freight receipts per kilometer of any West African railroad.[21]

The railroads diverted and truncated the long-distance caravan routes

145

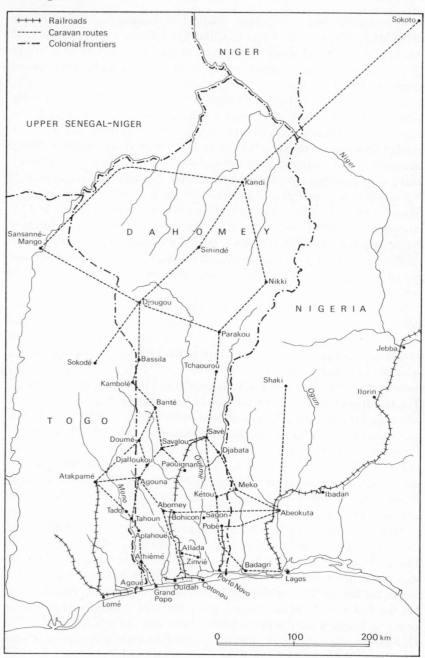

Map 5 Commercial routes, c. 1912

leading to the interior. In the west, the route had begun at Grand Popo, had gone up the Mono to Togodo, and then via Tado and sometimes via Savalou to its terminus at Djougou. Togodo, in the nineteenth century, became a major slave market; Djalloukou, Adjaha and Agouna were entrepôts for the large quantities of salt moving northward. *Gambari* merchants carried much of the trade for the full length of the route, and had colonies in each of its towns, but the royal families of Tado and Savalou also played a role in this trade.[22]

As soon as the railroad opened to Dan in 1905, traffic from Grand Popo to Djalloukou declined, and the entrepôt for salt moved to the end of the rail line. The people of Agouna claimed that the lack of water had driven the merchants away, and induced the administration to dig a well there in 1905. The area had always been short on water, however, and the main change was that an alternative had developed. The *gambari* population of Grand Popo began to decline: some of the Hausa left southwest Dahomey for Cotonou or other points, while others moved inland a little or tried slightly different commercial activities, such as the new contraband trade across the Togo border.[23] In 1907 the administrator in Savalou reported that trade was concentrated almost entirely on the route Djougou–Kambolè–Savalou–Paouignan, with Paouignan being the entrepôt for salt. The impact of the railroad was not, however, absolute: later in 1907, when salt was in short supply at the rail head, trade threatened to shift west to a route through Togo, where no railroad had yet been built.[24]

What the railroad began, the state pursued, though more by accident than by design. Four major points of commerce along the western route were nudged into obscurity by changes in the Togo–Dahomey frontier. In 1897 France ceded its territory west of the Mono and north of the lagoon to Germany: as a result, Agoué was cut off from its hinterland, and Togodo found itself on the German side of the border. In 1912 Tado and Kambolè were ceded to Togo in a further frontier adjustment: Tado declined somewhat and Kambolè, having lost its role as a major way-station to nearby Bassila, declined into a minor village.[25]

The eastern route to the interior, which was also to be diverted in the twentieth century by railroads, had been diverted earlier by political conditions. Parakou remained its northern terminus from the eighteenth century. Its southern terminus, which may have been Ouidah or Ekpé in the mid-eighteenth century, became Porto-Novo in the late eighteenth century as the power and commerce of Oyo in that region grew. The Ouémé River served as an important avenue to the interior, as did the Ogun further east. Then as Oyo's influence waned, the main southern terminus moved to Badagry in the early nineteenth century and to Lagos in the mid-nineteenth century.[26] Lagos, which emerged as the regional commercial metropolis, exerted a steadily growing attractive power throughout the Bight of Benin.

When the railroad reached Agouagon in 1907 and Savè in 1911, the trade of Parakou began to be reoriented toward Cotonou. Shaki, which had become the predominant entrepôt for salt on its way to Nikki and the north, now lost its place to Savè. Cattle-drivers, while they did not often use the railroad, also began to shift west. In 1910 some people of Tchaourou and Kilibo took cattle to Lagos and lost money in a glut. They decided henceforth to market their cattle in Porto-Novo and Cotonou. Later the same year, merchants brought back reports of poor sales in Cotonou, so herds at Savè and even Paouignan turned again toward Lagos. The establishment of low rail rates for moving cattle from Northern Nigeria to Lagos in 1914, however, undercut the cattle merchants of northern Dahomey, and tended to restrict them to the markets of Cotonou and Porto-Novo.[27]

In the Yoruba and Aja–Ewe areas of southern Dahomey, the mercantile network connected all markets large and small, and focused particularly large volumes of trade on the ports of Grand Popo, Ouidah, Cotonou, Porto-Novo and Lagos, and on such interior towns as Lokossa, Abomey and Sakété. The railroad, even when its rates were unreasonably high, as was often the case, was cheaper than head transport, and thus replaced head transport in its immediate vicinity. Imports, exports and domestic commerce all benefitted from the railroad, and transport by head and by canoe reoriented themselves about the railroad stations. While the railroad did not bring new oil-palm producing areas within reach of the coast, it increased the profitability of palm groves already in production. The export of maize, however, could not have taken place on such a large scale without the railroad, particularly for maize grown in the vicinities of Allada, Sakété and Abomey. Once the railroad reached Bohicon, Aja traders from Aplahoué brought maize to Abomey–which was further inland – in exchange for imported goods. Sagon on the Ouémé, long an entrepôt for trade to the plateaux of Abomey and Zagnanado, lost its prominence to Bohicon. But Affamé, further down the Ouémé and out of reach of the railroad, remained an important river port, as did Zinvié on the Sô.[28]

French plans to bring new infrastructure to the Mono region came to nought. The pier was never built, the railroad was postponed for decades, and an improved road lay incomplete. To assuage its fear that the region might fall into the commercial orbit of Togo, the colonial administration bought a small steamer in 1904, the *Mono*, which was intended to carry the trade of the Mono River and Lake Ahémé to Grand Popo. The steamer never functioned, however. It sat steadily lower in the water at Grand Popo until it was towed off to Cotonou for repairs in 1909, never to return. The

Table 6.1. *Estimated transport rates, c. 1910*

Head	1.0 franc per ton-km
Canoe	0.2 franc per ton-km
Railroad	0.1 franc per ton-km
Pier	10 francs per ton
Shipping to Europe	35 francs per ton

Source: see n. 31.

mercantile organization of transport, therefore, retained its place in the Mono valley.[29]

In another modest administrative move toward capital-intensive transport, 60-cm gauge Décauville railways were constructed from Bohicon to Abomey and over the four kilometers from Ouidah to the beach. Each tended, on a small scale, to displace the workers who had previously performed the same functions, though the Décauvilles broke down on occasion.

On the lagoon between Lagos and Porto-Novo, steamers and canoes coexisted, each carrying much of the trade, and neither able to establish clear supremacy over the other. Between Porto-Novo and Cotonou, however, where channels were too shallow for steamers, a great flotilla of canoes shuttled between the two towns, carrying the cargoes of a growing commerce and a more rapidly growing administration.

The quantity and quality of roads improved in early colonial Dahomey, but they were not constructed by capitalist methods, nor did their existence provide much impetus to the spread of capitalist commercial organization. Instead they were built by corvée labor and, for the most part, the only wheeled vehicles on their surfaces were the bicycles and then the automobiles of the administration.[30] The colonial administration, indeed, became a major supporter of the mercantile system of transport, as it requisitioned porters to bear its supplies. Similarly, as capitalist commercial firms expanded to the interior they, too, were required to hire porters to assure the delivery of their merchandise.

A rough comparison of the relative cost of the various modes of transport is presented in Table 6.1. Actual rates varied, of course, according to the time, the place, and the nature of the cargo.[31]

Head transport, because of its high cost, brought a serious limitation to West African commerce. How serious a limitation it was can be gauged, for imported goods, through estimation of prices in the interior by adding the cost of head transport to coastal prices. Table 6.2 shows estimates for four major imports at three points in the interior.

High value-per-weight goods are generally expected to be best suited to long-distance trade. But salt, while relatively heavy, provided a large

149

Table 6.2. *Estimated interior prices of imports, c. 1910, in francs per ton*

Good	Coastal price	Price after 50 km porterage	Price after 200 km porterage	Price after 500 km porterage
Salt	100	150	300	600
Textiles	5000	5050	5200	5500
Spirits	2000	2050	2200	2500
Tobacco	2000	2050	2200	2500

Source: Tables 6.1, A4, 5.

portion of the volume of trade to the Niger valley and, on its arrival if not at its departure, a large portion of the value. After two hundred kilometers the price of salt tripled, while that of textiles rose by four percent. Porterage, while expensive, was not prohibitive in cost for high value-per-weight goods.

In the case of export goods, a slightly different estimate of the limits of head transport may be calculated, using an approximate cost of production and the price of the good on the coast: once all the profits separating the two have been eaten up by the cost of porterage, the producer will cease to export. Based on calculations for palm oil and palm kernels, I have assumed that the cost of production for all exports from Dahomey was two-thirds of the coastal price.[32] The difference between coastal price and production cost, when divided by the cost of head transport, is shown in Table 6.3 as the estimated maximum porterage distance for each good.

Table 6.3. *Estimated porterage limits for exports, c. 1910*

Good	Coastal price, francs per ton	Estimated cost of production, francs per ton	Estimated porterage limit, km
Palm oil	450	315	135
Palm kernels	250	165	85
Maize	60	40	20
Coconuts	50	35	15
Copra	300	200	100
Peanuts	250	170	80
Shea butter	450	300	150
Fish	500	330	170
Cotton	1000	670	330
Kola	2000	1300	700
Rubber	3000	2000	1000
Textiles	4000	2700	1300

Source: Tables 6.1, A4.4.

An additional characterization of the limits of the transport system is shown in Map 4. The first dotted line indicates the maximum distance inland from which, in a normal year, maize could be profitably exported to Europe – by head, canoe, railroad, or a combination. The second dotted line, further inland, indicates the maximum distance inland from which, in a normal year, palm kernels could be exported.[33] The map indicates the positive effect of the railroad on maize exports, but it also indicates that the railroad did little to call forth new exports of palm products.[34] Thus, at least with regard to the tapping of new exports from the interior, the configuration of the rivers and the population of southern Dahomey left the railroad doomed to relative failure.

While the changing nature of transport and communications was the primary avenue through which the capitalist mode of production absorbed the mercantile mode, the organization of commerce itself also underwent important changes. The first hint of such change came in the 1850s as German firms in Lagos and Porto-Novo, emphasizing trade in cash rather than exchange of import for export goods, began to separate the import trade from the export trade. This led them to increase imports of cowries and, beginning in the 1880s, British sterling coin. The changing monetary system is thus associated in part – though only in part – with the entry of capitalism into the Bight of Benin.

The greatest change in the organization of commerce was the entry of capitalist firms into retail trade. Rather than rely further on granting goods on credit to regional merchants, and on allowing the domestic mercantile firms to handle the distribution of imported goods and the bulking of exports, coastal firms began setting up boutiques, first along the coast, and then in all the main towns of the interior. The firms, both European and Dahomean, invested in the construction of the boutique, in a stock of goods to be maintained there, and in wages for the employees. The scale of this capitalist enterprise was small, but it represented a clear challenge to the mercantile system.

The expansion of this new organization of the commercial system may be followed through the colonial state's grants of concessions. The government attempted to stimulate economic growth by giving land grants or concessions to Europeans and to Dahomeans who wanted to develop them.[35] Concessions were first awarded provisionally, becoming definitive if they had been developed within three years. The first concessions were granted in 1895 to European firms which established boutiques in coastal towns, and to missions which established stations in major inland towns. In 1896 wealthy families in Ouidah began taking out urban lots and agricultural concessions of up to 25 hectares. The pattern was thus established: concessions in southern Dahomey enabled merchants to

151

obtain free lots for their boutiques, and enabled influential families to obtain farm land controlled by the government.[36] At least half the commercial concessions were always in towns along the littoral, reflecting the continual turnover of small firms entering and leaving commerce. The first concession for a commercial house beyond the coast was for a lot in Zagnanado in 1900. From 1902 to 1904 the number of new concessions granted rose sharply to more than twenty per year, as the railroad began to open and merchants, European and Dahomean, began to establish outposts along its route. Of these concessions, about half were given up in two or three years, and the number of new concessions fell gradually from 1906 to 1909. Concessions ceased to be important from 1910 until after World War I.

The typical pattern, repeated yearly from 1897 to 1910 in regions steadily deeper into the hinterland, was that European and Dahomean firms first applied for commercial lots, then some of the European firms withdrew, and others came to be represented by Dahomean agents. At least one Dahomean–European partnership existed (Angélo and Haag, who represented Walkden in Porto-Novo), and Dahomean firms continued to compete successfully with European firms: d'Almeida Brothers in Ouidah, for example, were on a par with five major European firms. But even within the space of the years before 1914, European firms secured a growing portion of the market. Dahomean merchants were forced to become employees of their former competitors, though here they played an important role: the German firms owed some of their success to their reliance on Dahomean agents, while the boutiques of French firms were more often headed by Europeans.[37] The overall trend, nevertheless, was the removal of Dahomeans from the most powerful positions in commerce.

The mercantile sector remained alive and well as the early colonial period drew to a close, but it was now circumscribed within limits set by the growing capitalist sector. The long-distance caravans had been pushed north, their routes changed and their goods carried by the railroad. Even beyond the railroad, the opening of boutiques in such northern towns as Savalou, Bassila and Djougou cut into the caravan trade. Maritime transport had converted fully to steam, Cotonou grew at the expense of Grand Popo on the coast, and Bohicon grew at the expense of Sagon in the interior. Still, the mercantile system was left an ample field in which to function. If canoe transport had lost influence on the rivers, it had grown in volume on the lagoons; if the railroads had replaced head transport on two main routes, porterage was still required on the collateral routes; and if the boutiques had grown in influence in the main towns, all the market places of southern Dahomey – including those of the main towns – still had to be supplied with goods.

The growth in the capitalist mode of production, while unmistakably real, was deceptive. Steamers, railroads, European money, and the movement of markets to suit the needs of expatriate firms did, in fact, tie southern Dahomey more tightly to the world economy. But those who celebrated closer ties were often too quick to forget how ancient and deep were the ties of Dahomey to the world economy. Much of the growth of capitalism was extensive rather than intensive – taking over the transport and commercial functions of the previous system rather than achieving net economic growth. (Even intensive capitalist growth only contributed to the overall growth rate to the degree that it exceeded growth in competing modes of production.) The dominant element of the capitalist sector, further, was neither commerce nor industry but the state, which financed most of the construction and paid most of the wages in the colony. Again, however, the state achieved its growth at the expense of other sectors, by collecting revenue and labor from the commodity exchange, mercantile and private capitalist sectors. Thus the replacement of the mercantile system, which appeared as a spectacular change to anyone who walked through Cotonou from the rail yards past the warehouses to the pier, appeared as no more than a modest inflection to the clerks who drew up the annual trade returns.

PRICE INDICES AND TERMS OF TRADE

Figure 6.1 presents an array of indices summarizing early colonial Dahomey's foreign trade.[38] Since earnings from palm oil and palm kernels accounted for between 80% and 95% of the value of exports, it is reasonable to treat them as an approximation of the totality of the foreign-exchange earnings of Dahomey, and to use them to estimate the changes in prices received by Dahomean farmers. Export prices, which had fallen sharply in the 1880s, recovered somewhat in the early 1890s and were generally stable until they began a rather sharp rise in 1910. This rise in Dahomean prices was a direct consequence of the rise in European prices, and reflected the increasing world demand for primary products.

The figure shows two indices of import prices: the first represents the viewpoint of the consumers, under the assumption that the full amount of customs duties was passed on to them; the second index, neglecting customs duties, represents the viewpoint of the local economy as a whole – or, perhaps more precisely, the viewpoint of the state. Comparison of these two indices helps explain the divergent views of producers and officials about the trends in Dahomey's economic welfare. Underlying this distinction is the question of whether the state or the private sector is seen as the basic source of productivity and growth, and whether one or the other

153

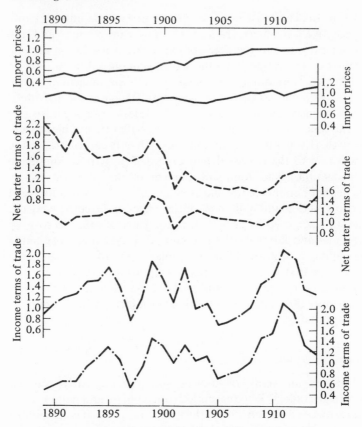

Figure 6.1. Foreign trade indices, 1889–1914. Left-hand scale: including customs duties in import prices. Right-hand scale: neglecting customs duties. *Source:* Table A5.1, A5.2.

should have greater access to resources. French officials assumed that the state, rather than the private sector, was the source of growth and productivity; the only question for the analyst is whether they exaggerated their case or were flat wrong. They implemented their view by using the tax system to transfer resources from the commodity exchange and familial sectors to the state, and undermined the ability of producers to invest in expanded production.

The net barter terms of trade, defined as the quantity of imports which may be purchased through sale of a given quantity of exports, reflect this same distinction. From the producers' viewpoint the terms of trade worsened, and the decline was concentrated in the years 1900–1, when the

154

sharpest rise in customs duties occurred; 1901 was an especially bad year because of the brief collapse in palm product prices. The decline in purchasing power ranged from 50% to over 100%, depending on which years are chosen for comparison. From the viewpoint of the state, however, net barter terms of trade underwent a modest improvement from 1889 to 1914.

Income terms of trade represent the net barter terms of trade adjusted for changes in the quantity of exports: this index thus reflects total real import purchasing power. From the producers' viewpoint, income terms of trade fluctuated greatly from 1890 to 1914, and neither improved nor worsened over the whole period. On a per capita basis, income terms of trade declined somewhat. For the state, however, income terms of trade improved unambiguously.

The overall impression conveyed by these terms of trade calculations is that Dahomeans had to struggle to stay even in international trade. Net barter terms of trade turned sharply against them because of colonial tax increases. The vagaries of the world market as well as local weather conditions could lead to boom or bust in export earnings. But Dahomeans were able to break even in income terms of trade by exporting larger amounts of palm products, and thus continued to buy the same quantity of imports – in fact, they achieved a modest increase in import quantity. Figure 6.2, which shows a comparison of volume indices for imports and exports, indicates that export volume did indeed increase faster than import volume after 1907, thus causing a recovery in income terms of trade during 1909–12.

Dahomean producers responded to two contradictory sorts of economic

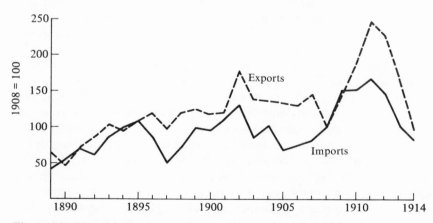

Figure 6.2. Import and export volume indices, 1889–1914 (1908 = 100).
Source: Table A5.1., A5.2.

155

signals: in years of high export prices they produced large amounts for export, because of greater profitability. But as import prices rose, they also increased output of palm products in order to meet tax assessments and to buy necessary imports. Thus, both positive and negative motivations are seen to have had an economic effect.[39] Dahomeans surely preferred positive stimuli; the colonial government, however, intervened regularly with negative stimuli – high taxes and forced labor in the lead. The stick of colonialism came to be as important as the carrot of the world market.

MONEY

In the colonial period as in precolonial years, any currency which gained wide acceptance was, *ipso facto*, money. Thus cowries, dollars, sterling, francs and other currencies all circulated at once. The demand for money – that is, the aggregate value of money demanded, as well as the relative demand for specific currencies or denominations – depended on the type of transactions and the volume of transactions completed, as well as the level of prices. As transactions changed, so did the demand for specific types of money. The supply of money, all of which was imported, depended on its cost of production and delivery, and on its exchange rates for goods or other currencies.

Three types of change in the southern Dahomean money supply took place in the years from 1880 to 1914. First, the quantity of money in circulation fluctuated with the seasons of each year, and with the rise and fall of the volume of trans-Atlantic trade in the nine-year cycle. Within each year, demand for money peaked at harvest season, especially during the harvest of palm oil, and merchants who supplied coin were able to charge a premium of about five percent at such times.[40] A similar annual variation in demand for cowries existed in local commerce. Over the longer run, the money supply varied with the volume of trade, since all money was imported, and an increase in the money supply could only be achieved with an export surplus.[41]

The second change in the money supply was its secular growth. The levels of population and domestic product grew at rates of between one and two percent annually, while the level of foreign trade grew at somewhat over two percent annually. This in itself would have led to a near-doubling of the money supply between 1880 and 1914. In addition, the increase after 1850 in the proportion of foreign-trade transaction which took place against cash, rather than simply as the exchange of goods, caused merchants and producers in southern Dahomey to want higher cash balances. The demand for money – that is, the total value of all currencies in circulation – therefore grew at a rate of over two percent per year.

The third and most spectacular change in the money supply was the repeated substitution of dominant currencies, from cowries to sterling to francs. The change to sterling as the main currency for overseas commerce (and for much local commerce as well) was accomplished through the market mechanism, without government intervention. The devaluation of cowrie currency because of its cheap supply and its continued imports by merchants who preferred to trade in cash – especially German firms – led these same firms to begin large-scale imports of British sterling coin after 1880, and this currency was widely adopted.[42] The change from sterling to francs after 1900, however, was accomplished only through the imposition of extreme measures by the French government, notably the physical destruction of cowries and heavy taxation of sterling imports. In each case the cost of the transition was borne by the Dahomeans: twice within three decades they had to purchase a new money supply with a surplus of exports and, particularly for the case of cowries, they received no compensation for their holdings of the previous currency. In the end, the imposition of francs served to tie Dahomey more closely to France, but in other respects the monetary system of 1914 remained quite similar to the cowrie system of a century earlier.

Government had no direct control over the money supply: it could influence money supply and demand indirectly through taxation and regulation, but even the French colonial government did not obtain direct control over the money supply through a central bank until after 1945. The kings of Danhomè had collected taxes in cowries and had obtained discounts by using heads of cowries containing less than the normal number of shells, but otherwise the precolonial governments undertook little monetary regulation. The French worried not about the quantity of money nor about its value, but only about its point of origin. From the early 1890s, the government attempted to circulate francs by paying its salaries in francs, requiring taxes to be paid in francs, and declaring all other currencies to be demonetized. But at various times it rescinded these orders for lack of cooperation by Dahomeans and Europeans alike.[43] In 1895 the government levied a 5% duty on imports of foreign money, and in 1898 agencies other than Customs began refusing sterling. But sterling was still the preferred currency: in 1896, imports of francs were 2% of total recorded currency imports. The portion of francs imported rose to 10% in 1898 and 24% in 1900, but in 1901, of the 221,275 francs of head taxes collected in Porto-Novo, only 500 were actually in francs. Finally, the government laid a prohibitive duty of 25% on the value of foreign currency imports in 1902, and francs rose to 66% of imported money in that year. Within a few years francs had become the dominant currency, and the 25% duty was abolished in 1907.[44]

157

Even then, francs were not adopted uniformly. Areas beyond the commercial orbit of the coastal towns were the last to adopt francs. Kétou, Zagnanado and the Holli traded with Lagos, and continued to use British sterling for commerce and paying taxes as late as 1911. Sterling also came to southern Dahomey from the north, as merchants bringing cattle from Togo and northern Dahomey to Savalou brought sterling – which might have come both from the Gold Coast and Nigeria – and which was taken by the Yoruba of Paouignan to Lagos for their purchases. German coin was used to some degree in the area near the Togo frontier, and its circulation was aided by German merchants as far from the border as Abomey. Cowries, finally, remained the main currency in areas such as Aplahoué. There in 1908 the administration, while requiring payment of the *impôt* in francs, still had to give taxpayers a few extra weeks to go to Grand Popo, Lokossa or Ouédémé to exchange cowries for francs.[45]

Recorded quantities of imports and exports of sterling and francs are displayed in Figure 6.3, along with estimates for years in which no data are available. The movement of currency correlated clearly with the value of exports: money imports rose and fell in nearly the same pattern as export values, and averaged ten percent of the value of exports.[46] Money exports fluctuated inversely with the value of total exports, and averaged less than one percent of total exports, or about eight percent of money imports. Through 1901, most recorded money imports were in sterling; francs predominated beginning in 1902.

Government estimates of the money supply, available for the years 1907–9, averaged just over 9 million francs. These estimates are low of the mark, however, because they exclude the value of cowries in circulation and they underestimate holdings of British coin.[47] French estimates of currency held by the Dahomean public were blind guesses and were, on the

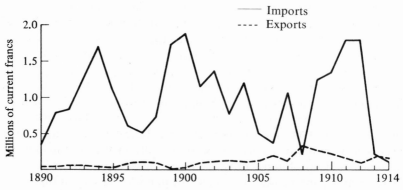

Figure 6.3. Money imports and exports, 1890–1914, in millions of current francs. *Source:* Table A8.1.

Table 6.4. *Official money supply estimates, in millions of francs*

Year	British coin	French coin	French paper	Total
1907	1.0	8.0	1.5	9.5
1908	0.8	5.9	2.0	8.7
1909	0.7	6.4	2.4	9.6

Sources: Banque de l'Afrique Occidentale, *Rapport*, 1907–10; Afrique Occidentale Française, Gouvernement Général, *Situation générale*, 1907–9.

face of it, far too low for an economy in which money was used for most domestic transactions as well as for overseas trade.[48]

An alternative estimate of the money supply can be derived from net imports of currency from 1890, which are shown in Figure 6.4. Since money was imported to build up a stock of cash, this series can be considered, for the period after 1900, as an estimate of the money supply. This measure reflects both the growth and the fluctuation of the money supply. For the year 1909, the estimated money supply is 15 million francs, sixty percent higher than the official estimate.

Net recorded imports, while providing an improved estimate of the

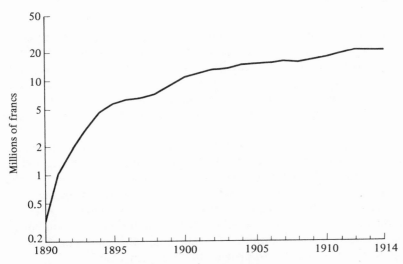

Figure 6.4. Net recorded money imports, 1890 – 1914, in millions of francs. *Source:* Table A8.1.

money supply, remain a crude measure. Figure 6.4 exaggerates the actual rate of growth in the money supply, though less so with the passage of time. It does not explicitly account for cowries, and it may exaggerate the holdings of sterling, as British coin may have been melted down or may have left the country unrecorded – though these two factors tend to cancel out. Nevertheless, I believe, it gives an adequate but not excessive estimate of the money supply.[49]

An aggregate money supply of 15 million francs in 1909 corresponds to 25 francs per capita, or one pound sterling per capita at 1913 prices – roughly the same level of real per capita money holdings as was estimated above for the late eighteenth century.[50] For all the tumultuous change which took place in the intervening years, this suggests a remarkable continuity.

Ironically, despite the continual imports of money, the twentieth century brought to Dahomey the chronic money shortage which it has yet to overcome. In particularly short supply were the small copper and lead coins in which most domestic transactions were carried out – 10-, 5- and 2-centime pieces.[51] As the small-denomination coins were in extremely short supply in comparison to demand, it became common practice to place a premium on these small coins and a discount on coins of 50 centimes and larger. The discounts ranged from 5% to over 25%, depending on the rarity of small coins, and were generally higher in more isolated areas. The discount on 50-centime silver pieces against bronze pieces of 5 and 10 centimes was commonly 5% to 10% in Ouidah and Abomey; among the Holli the equivalent discount was 20% or more. Pieces of 2 centimes often received an additional premium of 25%, as when two 2-centime coins were exchanged for one 5-centime coin. In contrast, demand for 1-centime pieces was not great, and an excess existed in some parts of Dahomey. Dahomeans attempted to pay the *impôt* in franc pieces or in paper money, to prevent the government from retiring small coins from circulation even temporarily.[52]

European commercial houses, being in the same network of exchange, often gave the same discounts as the Dahomean merchants, while administrators expressed anger and consternation at this disrespect for the face value of coinage. Some such administrators responded by jailing those who discounted silver coins, or by attempting to block circulation of the offending bronze coins. More sensible officials sent repeated pleas to Porto-Novo to send large quantities of small coin. But the capital, while sympathetic, was not able to provide the necessary coin.[53]

Neither the government nor the Banque de l'Afrique Occidentale had direct control over the money supply. The BAO, founded in Senegal in 1901, opened a branch in Porto-Novo in 1902. It was a private bank, though it came increasingly under government influence. It was the bank of issue for AOF, and provided paper money (backed by 100% reserves in francs) estimated at 2.4 million francs in 1909, or some 15% of the money supply. The major activity of the BAO was discounting bills of exchange for the larger import–export firms; its activities and revenues thus fluctuated with the volume of overseas trade.[54] To obtain additional supplies of small coin, the bank or the administration had to make arrangements with banks in France. Such arrangements were rarely made, apparently because of insufficient profit incentive for the French banks.

7

The alien state, 1890–1914

The colonial state of Dahomey differed from the states which the French had conquered and absorbed. It was greater in scale and more modern in its techniques of administration, though it adopted many policies and institutions from the prior system. Most fundamentally, however, the new government was alien: the colony of Dahomey was a distant province in a far-flung empire, ruled by authorities who looked to Paris for direction, inspiration, and recognition. Government by consent of the governed was a thing of the past and, perhaps, of the future. The people of Dahomey maintained the power to threaten revolt – a threat made good often enough to remain credible – and the power to slow down those processes of government which could not work without them. Some could act as favored collaborators, building their illusory power on the real threats and pressures of their countrymen. But no Dahomeans, not even the most autocratic and unrepresentative faction, nor the most loyal and Westernized servants, had any constitutional power. The French governed in Dahomey by a political theory in conflict with that of the French Republic, and in conflict as well with the political outlook of their Dahomean subjects. The ideological dispute between the rulers and the ruled was an important dimension of the colonial experience – bit by bit, Dahomeans were able to gain real constitutional authority and to win concessions in political theory. But in the beginning of the colonial era and for many years thereafter, they were conquered peoples.

In whose interests did the French state rule? In the interest of humanity, claimed those who celebrated the new limits on capital punishment and slavery under the French; yet the *indigénat* continued. In the interest of economic development, read the government tracts; but a third of the taxes were collected only to be sent out of the country. The question becomes more specific, however, if it is rephrased to refer to the constituency of the state rather than to its ideals. At whose command did the colonial state act? Certainly not at the command of its Dahomean subjects. At the command of the French merchants, perhaps? Victor Régis would sadly reply in the negative: his firm had sought French control of Dahomey beginning in the 1840s, but collapsed after a decade of colonial rule. Three possibilities remain. First, the state in Paris and Dakar was an obvious reference point. Yet to have one state act as sole constituency for another state seems incomplete. Second, the French bourgeoisie: that the leading class in France should set policy for its colonies is a sound premise, yet it remains to be shown what specific requests it would have of Dahomey. Third, if these avenues fail, one must conclude that the colonial state had no principal constituency, and acted on its own in response to the interests of individual officials, or in an eclectic reaction to varying pressures from many sources.

CONQUEST AND CONSOLIDATION

From the raising of the tricolor at Porto-Novo in 1883 to the pacification of the Holli and the Aja during World War I, the development of the colonial regime in Dahomey underwent several stages. From 1882 through 1889, the French established their presence along the coast. Between 1890 and 1893 they defeated the Fon and established control throughout southern Dahomey. From 1894 to 1900 they ruled most of the country through a set of protected sovereigns until, in actions which coincided with major tax increases, they replaced most of the sovereigns with direct French administration. With the integration of Dahomey into Afrique Occidentale Française in 1905 as one of its constituent territories, the administration had achieved a structure that was to remain little changed until the last days of colonial rule.

King Toffa of Porto-Novo, in order to fend off his enemies, the Fon and Egba, and in hopes of establishing his lineage as the sole royal lineage in Porto-Novo, signed a treaty of protection with the French in 1882 and welcomed their officials in 1883. In the short run, his gambit succeeded: the French chose to define his kingdom as including all of southeastern Dahomey. But by his death in 1908, Toffa's authority was again reduced to the town of Porto-Novo, and his successor was not even recognized as king. As the French set up their protectorate in Porto-Novo, they also began collecting customs duties in Cotonou, citing an 1878 agreement by which the Fon had allegedly ceded the port to France. King Glele never recognized the cession, and so for part of the 1880s both the Fon and the French collected taxes in Cotonou. In the west, the French decreed a protectorate over Grand Popo and Agoué in 1883 and landed a resident at Grand Popo in 1885. They entered a customs entente with the Germans to their west, and dismantled the Fon customs posts just east of Grand Popo. In 1885 they signed a treaty of protection over the Gen and Watchi who lived west of the Mono in the area north of Agoué and Grand Popo, but

163

they never administered more than the lagoon fringe of the area, and in 1897 they ceded it to Togo.[1]

The strength and diplomatic skill of Danhomè and the Egba state were responsible for delaying the European scramble for territory in the Bight of Benin. But the array of conflicts among African and European parties eventually narrowed down to an armed clash between France and Danhomè. After a brief and inconclusive war in 1890, both sides retired to prepare for the final test. The pretext arose when, in March 1892, the Fon fired on a French gunboat in Fon territory on the Ouémé: Colonel Dodds mounted a carefully planned offensive which went up the Ouémé and fought its way from south of Zagnanado to Cana and Abomey, facing vigorous opposition all the way. Behanzin burned Abomey November 16, 1892 and retreated to the north with the remnants of his army and retainers. The French occupied Ouidah in December 1892. Throughout the kingdom, people took to the bush and hid as the French arrived. People in the south of the kingdom were quicker to acknowledge French rule than those further north. Ouidah appeared to be nearly normal a few weeks after its occupation, and such towns as Allada and Abomey-Calavi were at least partly inhabited in the months after the conquest, but Abomey remained deserted all through 1893.[2] The French mounted a second expedition late in 1893 which fought a war of ambushes north of Abomey, but failed to capture Behanzin. He surrendered in January 1894, shortly after the French had proclaimed his brother king under the name Agoli-Agbo, and was exiled first to Martinique and then to Algeria, where he died in 1906. The army left Dahomey in July 1894.

Before leaving, Dodds (now General) dismembered Danhomè, shattering its unity and its institutions by setting up separate administrations in each province. Although several branches of the royal family remained influential, neither the Fon as an ethnic group nor the kingdom as a political unit were to achieve unity from that day forth.[3] Cotonou and Ouidah were administered directly by the French. Gi-Gla was appointed king in Allada, as the French attempted to revive the old Allada kingdom. Abomey-Calavi was governed at various times from Cotonou, Ouidah and Allada. Savalou was separated from Abomey and its king Gbaguidi recognized as a protected sovereign. Kpohizon, king of Tado, was recognized as king of the Aja. Agoli-Agbo's fragment of the old kingdom was reduced even further to the limits of the Abomey plateau when, in 1894, Yoruba slaves and the people of Agony (the region surrounding Zagnanado) each rebelled against his authority. Dosso-Yédéo was then made *chef supérieur* for Agony.[4]

Aside from direct rule in the coastal areas of Ouidah, Cotonou and Grand Popo, the French attempted initially to rule all southern Dahomey through protected sovereigns. Toffa in Porto-Novo had been the first such case, most of the Fon kingdom was divided into protectorates, and the French in 1894 re-established the Ketu kingdom, which had been destroyed and its people dispersed by the Fon in 1886. The Ketu signed a treaty with the French and returned to rebuild their capital; *Alaketu* Oyengen received the beaded crown.[5]

In 1899 and 1900, however, the French tightened their administrative control and dismissed three protected sovereigns: Agoli-Agbo, Dosso-Yédéo and Kpohizon. As Agoli-Agbo was exiled, the Abomey plateau was made into a *cercle* composed of twelve *cantons* plus the town of Abomey. Princes of the royal family gained most of the positions of *chef de canton* (and of *chef de quartier* in Abomey town) and had themselves installed with the ceremonies of kings. As Maurice Glélé has shown, however, this 'proconsulate' of *chefs de canton,* far from being a continuation of the old order, represented a substantial constitutional change and a further fragmentation of the Fon political heritage. The replacement of protected sovereigns by direct rule was one aspect of a general strengthening of the French state at the turn of the century: in 1899 customs duties rose sharply, the number of administrative personnel grew, and the *impôt* or head tax was collected after it had been collected on an experimental basis early in the year in Savalou *cercle* – a region presumably chosen because it included elements both of northern and southern Dahomey, and because the French had a dependable ally there in Gbaguidi.

By 1908 the last traces of the regime of protected sovereigns were gone. Toffa died in 1908 and Gi-Gla in 1909; their successors were not allowed to take the title of king, but were called *chefs supérieurs.* The king of Kétou saw himself demoted to *chef supérieur* in 1908, and effective power in Kétou passed into the hands of those who would work closely with the French. Gbaguidi remained in power in Savalou, but had to accept a similar diminution of his title. Most of the dynasties of Dahomey continued to exist in fact, though recognized only by the people of the kingdom. Abomey has had no king since 1899, but the role of king was played in fact by seven succeeding sons of Glele, who from the deposition of Agoli-Agbo until 1978 led the ceremonies for the royal ancestors.[6]

The administration of colonial Dahomey, while peaceful in a sense, was punctuated by an unending series of arrests, protests, minor military confrontations and occasional assassinations. Major revolts flared up in Sakété in 1905, among the Holli in 1914 and again in 1915, and among the Aja in 1917.[7] French governors, who crushed the revolts and punished the rebels with fines, prison and high taxes, sought nevertheless to restrain their most zealous administrators from precipitating revolts. In the informal system of resolving disputes which evolved out of this crucible, the village

165

chiefs and especially the French-appointed canton chiefs played a role which was central yet so fraught with ambiguities that Dahomey suffered a continuing 'crisis of chieftaincy.'[8]

The establishment of firm frontiers was another element in the consolidation of French power in Dahomey. By 1889 the French, Germans and British had agreed on the borders of French influence on the coast, and it was only a matter of extending the lines inland and getting the West African population to accept their new destiny. During the 1890s several border commissions worked out the details of the eastern and western frontiers of Dahomey. As the borders were delineated, the customs inspectors were not far behind. By the beginning of 1893, the entire seacoast was patrolled and subject to customs duties. All later customs posts were established in attempt to tax trade to Togo and Nigeria.[9] Dahomean merchants began smuggling as soon as the inland customs posts were established, at first simply to avoid taxes on short-distance trade in locally produced goods. But, because the duties were different in Togo, Dahomey, and Nigeria, imported goods came to have different relative prices in the three colonies, which offered an opportunity for profiteering to anyone who could smuggle goods across the border. The borders also came to mark differences in tax and labor policies. By 1910, for example, the head tax was 7.5 francs in Togo at a time when it was 2.5 francs in Dahomey, so those families who had homes on the Dahomey side and fields on the Togo side came to be reluctant to go to their fields. Some people in the area of Savè moved to Nigeria to avoid the *impôt* and forced labor on the roads, but returned to their old homes for commerce. In times of drought, governments sometimes prevented food from crossing colonial boundaries and, during epidemics, colonies were quarantined from each other.[10]

The colonial powers occasionally handed pieces of territory back and forth: the British gave up their claim to the lagoon town of Kéténou in 1889, and in 1897 the French ceded to Germany the area north of Agoué and west of the Mono. The impact of the latter change was devastating for Agoué. In 1885 when the French first arrived, Agoué had a population of several thousand. It was the center of Brazilian settlement west of Lagos, and drew on a productive hinterland for an active commerce. In 1897, sixteen commercial firms were represented. But the establishment of the frontier across the lagoon meant that customs duties would have to be paid on any goods coming from the hinterland to Agoué, and within three months the commercial houses and most of the people had left town. Agoué was trapped between the frontier and the sea, for at this same time the coastal current was physically carrying away the beach and portions of the town. The value of exports from the town fell from 143,000 francs in 1897 to 18,000 francs in 1898 to nil in 1899. It took the Germans until 1899 to occupy the market of Agouégan, across the lagoon from Agoué, but at that point they expelled inhabitants of Agoué from the market and denied them permission to buy food. Poiret, administrator in Grand Popo, proposed in 1900 that Agoué be made into a free port: the proposal was discussed until 1906, as far up as the Ministry of Colonies, but was dropped on grounds that it would complicate relations with the Germans. Agoué, now populated mostly by the old, lapsed into obscurity. Later the French made further territorial concessions to Togo, in an atmosphere conditioned by the Franco-German conflict over Morocco. In January of 1913 they ceded the cantons of Tahoun and Tado, along the Mono, and in March they also ceded the important northern entrepôt of Kambolè.[11]

The establishment of strong, well-patrolled frontiers served to cut down the economic contacts of Dahomey to the west and to the east, and served equally to efface the memory of previous east–west contacts. The attractive power of the metropolis of Lagos could not be denied, nor could the markets of Nigeria and Togo. But the commerce of Porto-Novo with Lagos, for example, declined sharply in the early colonial years. The new frontiers oriented the southern Dahomean economy toward the sea and, more gradually, reinforced ties between the northern and southern parts of colonial Dahomey.

COLONIAL FISCAL POLICY

The clearest economic change colonialism brought to Dahomey was a sharp increase in the level of taxes – an increase which exceeded any accompanying increase in government service to the population. The level of taxes paid by Dahomeans rose by a factor of eight from 1893 to 1910, while state expenditures rose by a smaller factor of four in the same period: in 1910 only forty percent of government revenue was spent inside the colony, and the rest was sent to Dakar and to France. This overall development in fiscal policy breaks into three periods: the small, autonomous administration through 1898, the growing autonomous state from 1899 through 1904, and the period of integration into AOF, beginning in 1905. Figures 7.1 and 7.2 summarize the changing levels of taxation and expenditure in the early colonial years.[12]

The French set customs duties in the 1880s to cover the costs of a very small administration, and tried to set them lower than duties in nearby Lagos, in attempt to attract trade. From the beginning, import duties on alcoholic beverages were the main source of revenue, ostensibly to reduce African alcoholic intake, but in fact because they were remunerative and easily collected. In customs accords signed with Germany and Britain, the French agreed not to levy duties discriminating according to the origin of

167

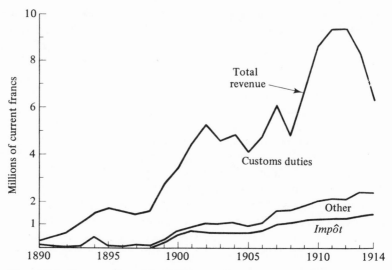

Figure 7.1. Taxes collected in Dahomey, in millions of current francs.
Source: Table A7.1.

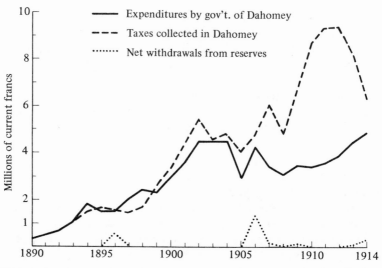

Figure 7.2 Colonial expenditures in Dahomey, 1890–1914, in millions of current francs.
Source: Table A7.1.

168

imports, but they taxed German-imported gin and geneva (Dutch gin) more heavily than French-imported rum, and later taxed German rock salt more heavily than French marine salt.[13]

While each colony was expected to pay for its own administration, the metropolitan government was willing to pay for military adventures. The Chamber of Deputies allocated 20 million francs for the conquest of Dahomey, and the cost of the war to the colonial administration was little or none. After the war, however, the administration had a larger territory to govern, so it increased taxes for that purpose and to meet customs duties in Lagos, which were also rising. A small grant from France in 1894 to cover additional military costs enabled the colony to set aside a modest surplus.[14] The colony thus covered its costs until 1897, when the combination of a bad commercial year and unexpectedly determined opposition to the occupation of northern Dahomey caused the government to use up all its reserves. Since it was a military matter, however, the metropolitan government provided a grant of 740,000 francs in 1898.

In 1899 the colonial government raised taxes sharply. It nearly doubled duties on alcoholic beverages, as may be seen in Table 7.1, causing selling prices to rise by fifty percent. At the same time the administration began to levy the *impôt de capitation:* the rate was 1.25 francs per person over ten years of age everywhere in the colony except in the coastal towns, where the rate was 2.25 francs. All persons over ten were defined as 'adults' for this purpose. The village chiefs collected the tax, and they were paid 10 centimes for each tax collected, or 25 centimes in the coastal towns.[15] The main utilizations of the new revenues were the expanded system of local administration, reserves, and railroad construction: direct administration had largely replaced the regime of protected sovereigns before the end of 1900, and a total of 3 million francs was saved out of current revenue from 1899 to 1904 to be placed in a Caisse de Réserve, from which some of the funds were invested in French securities. Most significantly, from 1899 to 1904 the colony spent some 6 million francs out of current revenue on bridges and roadbed for the railroad.

The Government General of AOF, although formally established in 1899, only became a reality in 1905. In that year it gained a revenue source by confiscating customs revenues from its constituent colonies.[16] The colonies thus lost their main source of revenue with little diminution in their administrative responsibilities; the Government General, on the other hand, now had substantial revenue and vague responsibilities. The efforts of the Government General were concentrated in three areas: establishing a central bureaucracy in Dakar, directing the military occupation of the inland territories, and accumulating and allocating funds for capital investment. In the latter area, the Government General assumed

169

Table 7.1. *Customs duties, 1887–1908*

Year	Gin 60°, francs per liter	Rum 80°, francs per liter	Tobacco, francs per kilogram	Powder, francs per kilogram	Guns, francs per piece	Cotton, francs, per kilogram	Rock salt, francs per ton	Marine salt, francs per ton
1887	0.125	0.05	0.125	0.07	0.625	–	10	10
1890	0.25	0.10	0.25	0.14	1.25	–	10	10
1893	0.45	0.25	0.35	0.50	2.00	–	10	10
1894	0.45	0.40	0.35	0.50	2.00	10%	10	10
1895	0.45	0.40	0.35	0.50	2.00	10%	14	6
1897	0.45	0.40	0.35	0.50	2.00	0.50	14	6
1899	0.90	0.72	0.50	0.50	2.00	0.50	14	6
1903	0.90	0.96	0.50	0.50	2.00	0.50	14	6
1905	0.96	1.44	0.50	0.50	20%	0.50	15	10
1908	1.20	1.60	0.50	0.50	20%	0.50	15	10

Note: for goods not shown, duties were 10% ad valorem on the amount of the bill plus 25%.
Source: Journal officiel du Dahomey.

the debts of the colonies (Dahomey had virtually none) and borrowed large sums through bond issues: 65 million francs in 1903, 100 million francs in 1907, and 14 million francs in 1910.[17] With its new-found wealth, the Government General bought out the Dahomean railroad company in 1904, bought out the pier company in 1909, spent 2 million francs each on the extension of the main railroad line to Savè and the extension of the Porto-Novo railroad from Sakété to Pobè, and undertook such other construction as the improvement of the pier. Further, the Government General allocated an annual grant averaging just under 2 million francs to the government of Dahomey.

The total of these expenditures by AOF in Dahomey fell far short, however, of the flow of customs duties from Dahomey to Dakar. Only in the first year of AOF did Dahomey receive as much from the Government General as it sent to Dakar. After 1905, the administration in Porto-Novo found itself facing a fiscal crunch which was met in 1906 by the consumption of reserves, and in years thereafter by higher tax rates and the imposition of new taxes. In 1906 the *impôt* rate of 2.25 francs was extended from the coastal towns to the whole of the *cercles* of Cotonou and Ouidah, and in 1907 it was extended to everyone over ten in Dahomey south of the *cercles* of Savalou and Savè. In 1910 the *impôt* was raised again to 2.50 francs for everyone over eight years of age. New sources of revenue were sought at every turn: miscellaneous local revenues (i.e., other than customs duties and the *impôt*) rose from 0.2 million francs in 1901 to 0.5 million francs in 1907, and then to 1.1 million francs in 1913.

The evolution of colonial government expenditures in Dahomey is shown in Table 7.2, which displays total expenditures, by category, for selected years from 1899 to 1913. AOF grants to Dahomey after 1904 were general-purpose revenue to the colony, and their expenditure cannot be distinguished from other expenditures; direct AOF expenditures in Dahomey, however, are listed separately.

The net fiscal impact of colonial rule in Dahomey was to bleed the country, especially with the establishment of AOF in 1905. Immense amounts of wealth were removed from Dahomeans through taxation and, even by the most conservative calculation, one-fourth of those revenues were simply transferred out of the country. By other calculations two-fifths of the taxes collected were withdrawn from the Dahomean economy, and much of the rest was spent wastefully.[18] This, then, is the real basis for the feeling of so many modern Béninois that AOF simply bled Dahomey, and thus encouraged its economic stagnation. The verification of popular sentiment is to be seen in Figure 7.3, which displays the wide and growing gap between exports and imports of revenue across the Dahomean frontier. Dahomean customs revenue provided between 20% and 30% of AOF

171

Table 7.2. *Colonial expenditures in Dahomey, in thousands of francs*

	1899	1903	1908	1913
Government of Dahomey				
Administration	293	452	852	1074
Treasury	325	184	160	248
Police	188	404	458	547
Public works	329	310	305	491
Public health	106	140	192	267
Railroad	189	1300	149	234
Post and telegraph	n.a.	280	257	374
Education	—	35	84	135
Transportation	n.a.	396	237	384
Other	710	674	412	782
Total	2144	4519	3070	4542
Government General				
Construction	—	—	99	595
Salaries	—	—	200[a]	200[a]
Total	—	—	299	795

[a] estimate

Source: Colonie du Dahomey, *Rapport d'Ensemble*, 1900; France, Agence générale des Colonies, *Statistiques des Finances des Colonies Françaises pour les années 1902–1911*; Colonie du Dahomey, *Compte définitif, 1913*; Afrique Occidentale Française, Gouvernement Général, *Compte définitif, 1913*.

customs receipts in the years after 1904, and stood second in magnitude behind Senegal. A smaller but persistent type of revenue export took the form of remittances to France of travel expenses and salaries of French officials paid by the government of Dahomey. Part of the price of colonial rule was that Dahomeans had to pay to bring in aliens to rule them, had to pay for their holidays, and could not hope even for a trickle-down effect from the large portion of bureaucratic salaries which were remitted directly to savings and families in France.[19] Revenue imports to Dahomey, as may be seen in Figure 7.3, were dominated by AOF grants to the Porto-Novo government and by AOF expenditures on construction in Dahomey.[20]

The export of revenue was modest in the years up to 1898, totalling roughly 1 million francs.[21] From 1899 to 1904 the revenue export reached 2 million francs, though the government also withheld funds from current expenditure sufficient to build up reserves of 3 million francs.[22] The accumulation of reserves was interrupted in 1905 when the Government General appropriated the largest source of local revenue, and began instead to build up reserves in Dakar. The Porto-Novo government consumed 1.5 million francs in reserves in 1906 and 1907, after which reserves grew slightly. Meanwhile, a net total of 23 million francs flowed from Dahomey to Dakar from 1905 to 1914; in those same years an additional 4 million

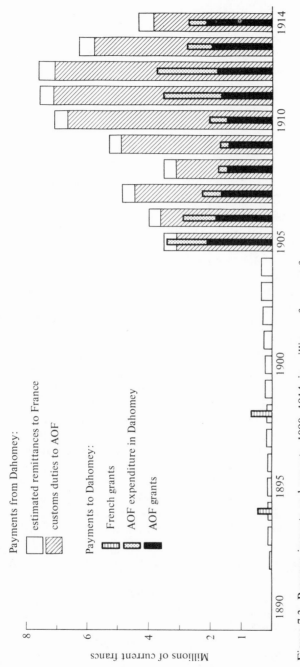

Figure 7.3. Revenue imports and exports, 1890–1914, in millions of current francs.
Source: Table A7.1.

173

francs in salaries and travel expenses left Dahomey for France. The outflow of revenues from Dahomey averaged roughly one-third of the value of revenue annually, over 16% of the value of exports, or 2–3% of Dahomey's gross domestic product each year. This steady drain of tax revenue, which was to continue relentlessly until the end of the colonial period, could not fail to provoke economic stagnation.

REGULATORY POLICY

The colonial state in Dahomey, stronger than the previous governments yet small and weak by twentieth-century standards, attempted to regulate in those areas where it could not command: in land, commerce and production. Even there, results of the state's initiatives demonstrated that its efforts would have to remain modest until its powers grew. For a brief time, for example, it appeared as if colonial land policy in Dahomey might involve the granting of large agricultural concessions to European individuals and firms. Three sizeable concessions were granted in 1898 and 1899: 364 hectares to M. Saudemont and his Compagnie agricole du Dahomey near Allada, 136,000 hectares to the Société Ouémé–Dahomey near Adja-Ouéré, northwest of Sakété, and 295,000 hectares to the railroad company along the railroad line from the coast to Tchaourou.[23]

Every trace of these concessions, however, had disappeared by 1905. Saudemont attempted to set up a palm oil press, and later experimented with other crops on other lands, without success: he complained of Dahomean farmers encroaching on his lands. He took over the Adja-Ouéré concession following the failure of the Société Ouémé–Dahomey, but soon gave it up and restricted his efforts to commerce. By the time another merchant, Armandon, took over the Adja-Ouéré concession, it had been whittled down to 1,200 hectares in three separate lots. The experience of the railroad company was similar: of its huge land grant, only 15,000 hectares were in the densely populated coastal area, 80,000 hectares were on the Plateau south of Paouignan, and 200,000 hectares were to be north of Paouignan. The company immediately ran into strong opposition to its concessions, both from Dahomeans and from European merchants, and never attempted to use the land. The concessions were formally relinquished as the company was bought out in 1904.[24] Land grants, henceforth, consisted only of concessions of up to 200 hectares approved by the governor, given primarily as commercial lots in towns and at railroad stations, to both European and Dahomean merchants. Land policy extended little further than that, except for government policy on who should be awarded land in the wave of disputes among Dahomeans from 1905 to 1915. The large land grants had failed because of Dahomey's dense population, the absence of a new and highly remunerative crop and, most importantly, because the concessionnaires in Dahomey were never granted the political powers of concessionnaires in Central Africa, which became independent administrations.[25]

The government's commercial policy included an attempt to support the extension of European and particularly French commerce. French merchants, for instance, were appointed to most of the available seats on the government's advisory councils, and they usually headed the chambers of commerce. But the government, prevented by treaty from setting extra duties against non-French imports, had to accept the fact that the Germans and the British dominated the expatriate merchant community, and had also to respect the position of Dahomean merchants. Government movement of key marketplaces and taxation at marketplaces and along caravan routes, meanwhile, helped to divert commerce from the mercantile sector into the capitalist sector.

Beyond the taxation of commerce, government made some attempts to regulate it. In response to the adulteration of palm oil and palm kernels by producers and regional merchants, a common West African problem, the administration set up an inspection system, beginning in 1892, and extended it in subsequent years. (Meanwhile the government ignored the equivalent problem of merchants selling imported cloth weighted down with clay, which disappeared on washing to reveal a lighter fabric.) In other regulatory efforts, the government issued periodic decrees forbidding the destruction of forests and encouraging reforestation, or requiring permission from provincial officials before farmers could fell oil palms, or fixing the minimum size of holes in fish nets and weirs, or preventing the bleeding of rubber plants.[26] Enforcing the decrees was another matter.

AGRICULTURAL POLICY

Government agricultural policy in the early colonial years, while it made some original contributions, served mostly to supplement the ongoing process of agricultural experimentation in the domestic economy. The experiments of earlier centuries, which added American maize, Asian yams and other exotic fruits and staples to the crops of the Bight of Benin, were followed by a new but less fruitful wave of experimentation in the nineteenth century. Catholic missionaries sowed wheat, grapes and potatoes on the coast in the 1870s, with the inevitable results. More serious experiments with coffee, peanuts and other crops as early as the 1840s led to results which were not much more encouraging. Still the experiments continued.[27]

The colonial state, in 1899, set up a botanical garden of 250 hectares in

175

Porto-Novo at which to carry on its own experiments. In 1902 agriculture and zootechnology services were established, though with a combined budget of only 16,000 francs.[28] In 1907 the agricultural service opened a station at Niaouli in Allada *cercle*, and attempted to open another at Sinhoué, the site of the Fon royal oil palm plantations.[29] Some of the most useful work of the agricultural service consisted of the agronomic and botanical descriptions by Norbert Savariau, head of the agricultural service, and by visiting agronomists in the service of AOF, including Jean Adam, Yves Henry and Auguste Chevalier; other French technicians published equivalent descriptions of Dahomean animal husbandry and fishing.[30] The government was therefore not unmindful of local agriculture, and devoted a portion of its efforts to improving local crops and, especially in the case of domestic animals, to halting the spread of disease. Primary emphasis in agricultural policy, however, went to developing export crops, and in this effort the administration cooperated with European commercial interests. Yet the small size of the agricultural budget restricted government to more of the same: to plant – or rather to induce Dahomeans to plant – every conceivably successful variety of crops, domestic or imported, and see what happened. For some crops, such as cotton and coconuts, the planting campaign continued over many years. In other cases, as with soybeans and sisal, one-year planting campaigns were followed by long periods of disinterest. The timing of the planting campaigns was influenced by such factors as world market conditions for each crop, the availability of new varieties, the passage through Dahomey of an agronomist studying a given crop, or the arrival of new administrators.

For such major crops as oil palms and maize, French agronomists were able to do little more than observe production and commerce. They were occasionally able to offer useful advice, as in recommending a reduction in railroad rates to facilitate maize exports in 1907 and 1908. Through a semi-official effort, however, the French did succeed in establishing a cotton export industry in Dahomey. The campaign began in 1905, when the semi-official Association cotonnière employed Eugène Poisson in Dahomey in what became a cooperative effort of the association and the government. Poisson toured the country until his death in 1910, distributed cottonseed, encouraged planting, and bought as much of the crop as Dahomeans would sell at the price he could offer.[31]

Not surprisingly, the campaign began badly: in 1905 the administration grew six fields of cotton near Savè and Savalou, and discovered that it grew poorly in comparison to local cotton. Late planting and insufficient rains had hurt the crop. Twenty-five sacks of seed were distributed in Zagnanado *cercle* in July 1905. But the Holli, who grew most of the local cotton in the *cercle*, refused to accept any seed, noting that it was too late to plant more cotton: in succeeding years, however, they accepted seed and sold cotton on the market in Cové and Pobè. In 1906, administrative cotton experiments expanded to Allada and Abomey *cercles*. Rumors had spread, and chiefs in cotton-growing regions of Mono *cercle* asked for seeds of the European variety. Further experiments in Ouidah during 1907 led to uniform failure. Indeed, rains during harvest in late 1907 contributed to a decline in Dahomey's 1908 exports as compared with 1907.[32]

The Association cotonnière came to rely on working with chiefs: Poisson gave them seed (new seed had to be provided every year), the harvests belonged to the chiefs, and the chiefs received in additional twenty francs per hectare if the land were planted as the association wished. Laborers were requisitioned to plant the government fields. The association constructed cotton gins in Savalou, Bohicon and Cotonou during 1908, and by 1910 French efforts were concentrated on maintaining production in the Center, rather than on seeking new areas in which to grow cotton. Nine tons of cotton seed were distributed in Savè and Savalou in 1910 and again in 1911, with 120 tons of export in 1911 and 170 tons in 1912, mostly from those areas. Still, the Association cotonnière occasionally withdrew from carrying seeds to the producers: producers from Cové had to go to Savalou to get seed in 1911 and again in 1914.[33]

While French efforts to develop cotton exports led to some success, a parallel effort put into rubber experiments met with complete failure. At the time of the great rubber boom, 1897–1901, the Catholic Mission at Zagnanado, the French merchant and planter Saudemont at Allada and Dahomean planters experimented with both vine and tree varieties of rubber. These experiments had only minimal success, and virtually the entirety of rubber exported came from collection of wild rubber. During a second, smaller rubber boom in 1904–6, the administration directed the planting of as many as several hundred thousand shoots of several different rubber species throughout southern Dahomey.[34] Following the failure of this effort, further attempts to develop rubber plantations ceased for some time.

The administration undertook a similar planting campaign for coconuts, and at the same time experimented with methods to defeat insect pests. From 1906 to 1915, some five to ten thousand coconut seedlings were given out in the area from Grand Popo to Agoué. In 1912, the campaign was accelerated, as land concessions were given out in the coastal area from Ouidah to the Nigerian frontier, stipulating that they were to be planted with coconuts.[35] The results of this campaign did not lead to the expected growth in copra exports for two reasons: the local market for coconuts as fruit was developed enough to consume virtually all the coconuts produced, and the Dahomeans who registered for the concessions did so to

177

a large degree as land speculation in an era of high land prices and many legal disputes over land ownership.

In 1907 the administration conducted a campaign to plant *Cola nitida* seedlings, imported from Guinée, throughout the area in which *Cola acuminata* was grown. This was a reasonable idea, in that the administration was facilitating a change already taking place in the West African economy, as Dahomean demand for *Cola nitida* from Lagos was growing rapidly. It also corresponds, however, to the passage through Dahomey of Auguste Chevalier who was then studying kola. A group of planters in Porto-Novo *cercle* refused to accept free seedlings because of a rumor that the administration would extend to agricultural fields the license fees that had just been imposed on traders. Little more is heard of this project in succeeding years, except an occasional request for seedlings noted as coming from villages. In 1914 an administrator asserted that 'some agents of Behanzin' had monopolized production of *Cola acuminata* around Godomey, and that the agricultural station at Niaouli could not meet the demand for seedlings of *Cola nitida*.[36]

Too often, experiments were carried out haphazardly: in May of 1909 the agricultural service sent a sack of La Plata maize to Abomey to plant. Only 62 kg of the 92 kg in the sack were in good enough state to plant, and it was planted late, in June, by a *chef de quartier* of Abomey. By July the administrator announced that it gave terrible results, and in August the remains were being eaten by red monkeys.[37] This sort of disheartening result led, paradoxically, both to discontinuation of experiments and to their endless repetition. In a sense, the administration left no stone unturned in its search for agricultural innovation: it experimented with coffee, vanilla, rubber, cocoa, bananas, cotton, shea butter, coconuts, sisal, kola, maize, millet, yams, oil palm, manioc, pineapple, avocado, breadfruit, mango, peanuts, *rônier*, rice, soybeans, castor bean, indigo and sesame. But with limited administrative resources, and with an environment whose limits had already been probed by Dahomean farmers, the colonial state could do little more than turn the stones.

INVESTMENT POLICY

Colonial investment policy, while dominated by government investment in infrastructure, included other elements of government investment, and also included a significant component of policy on private sector investment. Investments carried out by Dakar and Porto-Novo differed substantially from those carried out by *commandants de cercle*, and the requirements of forced labor constituted yet another element of state investment. Beyond explicit state policies, the actions of government left an impact, often unintended, on levels of private investment, by transferring resources from the commodity exchange and mercantile sectors to the state and capitalist sectors.

The state launched an ambitious program of support for private capitalist investment in 1898–9, with the railroad concession and large land grants.[38] The failure of such gestures to bring more than a trickle of private French capital to Dahomey was soon, evident, however, and state policy toward private capital was trimmed to more modest dimensions. Only in ocean shipping and in commerce was private capital forthcoming: the state supported French shipping with postal contracts, and supported the expansion of capitalist commerce with land grants for boutiques.

Very soon, therefore, the state shifted its emphasis to public capital formation. The efforts of early colonial governments in building a network of transport and communication facilities in Africa before World War I are well known. Three aspects of this construction program, however, have received insufficient attention: the high proportion of domestic rather than foreign funding of construction, the opportunities for profiteering by private firms involved in the construction, and the large proportion of direct African investment in the form of unpaid and underpaid labor. Railroad construction in Dahomey provides examples of each of these phenomena.

According to the terms of the 1899 agreement, the Compagnie des Chemins de Fer du Dahomey, led by Georges Borelli of the Marseille merchant firm of Mante frères & Borelli, was to issue stock, lay the rails, construct stations, and operate the railroad. The colony of Dahomey, meanwhile, undertook to construct the roadbed, including earthwork and bridges, it paid the cost of the land survey, and it agreed to grant 300,000 hectares in land to the company. From 1900 to 1904 the colony completed the roadbed at a cost of just over 6-million francs. This expenditure, which consisted dominantly of imported materials and salaries for French supervisors, was financed virtually entirely out of current local tax revenue. The balance of the 6 million francs went, aside from local materials, to salaries for Dahomean workers and to fees for the chiefs who recruited them.[39] In the aggregate, however, the workers received less than the 'normal' wage of one franc per day plus subsistence: that is, the government paid the recruits less than the opportunity cost of their absence from home. The effect of foregoing home production by virtue of working on the railroad was that the workers themselves made a substantial investment in the railroad.[40]

In contrast to the energetic performance of the colony, the railroad company failed to raise the capital it anticipated, and failed to maintain its schedule in laying rails and building stations. Its land grants had become

179

the object of complaints by those who feared to lose their land, and, one suspects, it was involved in further difficulties which the authors of official reports found it indelicate to specify. The Government General of AOF, meanwhile, had begun to take shape as an agency for centralizing the financing and direction of large-scale capital investment. In a 1904 revision of the concession agreement, AOF and Dahomey took over full responsibility for construction, while the company's responsibilities were reduced to simply operating the railroad. The company was guaranteed that any operating losses it sustained would be reimbursed by AOF up to a level of 400,000 francs per year. In fact even this generous allowance was exceeded in 1908.[41] To establish its title to the railroad, AOF purchased stock in the amount of 8.5 million francs – a figure which, given the low level of company expenditure in Dahomey, leaves both parties open to the charge of using public funds for the purchase of watered stock. AOF financed the stock purchase through a 12-million-franc loan from Crédit algérien, and consolidated this debt with its bonded indebtedness. The bonds in turn were redeemed with AOF revenues, which consisted mostly of customs duties.[42]

Beginning in 1904, railway construction in Dahomey took place under two regimes. The Porto-Novo government built a second railway from Porto-Novo to Sakété between 1904 and 1907, at a cost of 1.9 million francs, paid as before entirely out of current local tax revenue. The Government General financed and directed the construction of the Cotonou line until it reached Savè in 1911, and also undertook the extension of the Porto-Novo line to Pobè. In each case substantial amounts of direct Dahomean investment were required, consisting of unpaid or underpaid labor.

Investment in early colonial Dahomey meant, therefore, not the injection of wealth into the colony from foreign private or public sources, but the determination by colonial authorities of what allocations should be made of Dahomean resources, accompanied by a transfer of wealth outside the colony. Beyond the expectation of individual gain which French participants in this sort of forced investment may have held – and which some of them realized – the only basis for expecting the investment to be profitable was the hope that the new technology was efficient enough to compensate for the cost to the workers and taxpayers. In this case it was not. Even AOF's use of a French loan to purchase the railroad was, rather than foreign investment, more a case of requiring colonial subjects to pay principal and interest for shady dealings in the metropole.

While the railroad represents the grandest level of state investment in Dahomey, the colonial government also participated in investment projects of small magnitude and purely local interest. One instructive example was the attempt by local administrators to improve water supplies through wells and cisterns. While a few areas of Dahomey were spared serious water shortages, most rural areas were limited in the dry season to streams and pools, often distant from residences. In 1905 and 1906 the administrators in Abomey and in the northern end of Mono *cercle* directed the digging of a few wells. In 1910 a major campaign of well-digging began, again both in Abomey and in Savalou, stimulated by the dry year. Work on the wells continued until 1911, and their depths passed sixty meters, without substantial results – only the well at the hospital in Abomey was successful. But by that time the administrator recognized that the campaign to dig wells had not been a success, in part because no survey had been done on where to dig them. Then, recognizing the merit of the existing system of cisterns on the Plateau, administrators turned to suggesting covering them so that animals and people would not fall into them. Nevertheless, work continued on wells in Abomey during 1913, and by that time work on wells had begun in Ouidah and Allada *cercles*.[43] The project as a whole was inconclusive, and the colonial administration had again failed, despite a modest but sincere effort, to bring significant technical change to Dahomey.

The most perplexing and yet revealing aspect of colonial investment policy was its policy on road construction. At the turn of the century, as French ambitions expanded, the government undertook not simply to maintain the precolonial road network but to extend it. Henceforth road work, along with collection of the *impôt,* became the main focus of local administrators. This aggressive campaign of road work was continually hindered, however, by technical and economic problems. The technical problems can be summed up in the impermanence of the roads: each year the roads were overgrown with brush, and the rains washed out much of the earthwork. The next year, therefore, the administrator again called upon the chiefs to provide hundreds of workers in each area to clear the roads again, and to perform the necessary terracing, filling and bridge construction.[44] Yet this chronic disrepair of roads was not inevitable: the railroad roadbed had been built quite permanently beginning in 1900, and needed only minor maintenance thereafter.

The economic problems were the high cost of building and rebuilding the roads, and the limited usefulness of the roads once built. Despite the esthetic appeal of smooth, broad roads, they cannot have cut transport costs by much in a country were most transport was by head. Of course good roads, once constructed, were at least marginally preferable to bad roads: the railroad line immediately became a major footpath, while road and bridge construction brought an increase in commerce between Abomey and Aplahoué in 1905. But at other times the only advance noted

181

with the construction of a new road was that the administrator or merchants could now ride to outlying areas on their bicycles.[45]

In recognition of the high cost to Dahomeans of this manner of road building, as measured by their unwillingness to do the work, the colonial administration announced a reform in 1907. Henceforth all road construction would take place under the Service des Travaux publics. This service, which had previously been charged with public works in the towns – administrative buildings and street work – was now to provide funds for all road construction in the colony. But the project was doomed. If all the road work done in Dahomey was now to be paid at the rate of roughly one franc per day, the resultant cost would have been many times the budget of Travaux publics. As a result, the administrators in the *cercles* complained for months that they had received no credits for building roads, and they finally resorted to the old system of forced labor with small payments to the chiefs. By 1909 the distinction was as sharp as ever: public works in the towns were part of a special budget, Travaux publics, the workers were paid regularly (except for prison laborers, who were often used), and the expenditures on materials, European and Dahomean labor are recorded with some care.[46] Road construction in the countryside was done through forced labor on very skimpy budgets, and the records on the number of workers involved and the amounts paid them are very scarce.

The heavy French emphasis on the difficult, conflict-ridden and unrewarding task of road construction is difficult to explain in terms of its contribution to local or international commerce. Some of the perplexity of the issue is resolved, however, if the campaign is treated as an effort in socialization rather than in investment. Administrators were trying to teach Dahomeans to be ready to work for the state on whatever they were asked to do, with enthusiasm, and regardless of compensation. Dahomeans remained unconvinced by repeated explanations of the benefits of road work. This only showed, from the perspective of their mentors and rulers, that they did not yet understand the modern economy: the colonial mission was to assign road work until the Dahomeans could discipline themselves to pay for it.

THE STATE AND ECONOMIC SURPLUS

To rephrase the argument advanced in the pages above, the French colonial state appropriated for itself a large and growing portion of the economic surplus of Dahomey, and then allocated it in a manner which, while tending to provide support for the capitalist sector at the expense of other sectors, was detrimental to the cause of economic growth. This shortsighted policy held sway because the government of Dahomey saw its interest as the satisfaction of short-term needs of the Government General; the latter, in turn, felt neither pressure from nor responsibility toward Dahomey.

In its appropriation of surplus, the state withdrew resources from every sector of the economy, but especially from the commodity exchange sector. Customs duties, the largest source of revenue, laid a burden on all who participated in commerce – on buyers and sellers in the capitalist, mercantile and commodity exchange sectors, but particularly the latter. Market fees, patents and licenses also fell on all levels of commerce. The *impôt* fell on every colonial subject and hence on every sector of the economy, but mainly on the commodity exchange and familial sectors. These along with other fees and taxes comprised the monetary portion of government surplus appropriation, whose aggregate level rose at nearly 20% per year in the 1890s and at 5% per year after 1900. Further, through its requirement of forced labor the state extracted an additional non-monetary surplus from the commodity exchange, familial and mercantile sectors in the amount of perhaps 20% of the value of monetary revenue.[47] The surplus accumulated by the state each year thus rose from some 2% of gross domestic product in 1893 to 9% in 1903, after which it remained roughly stable for some years. (An estimate of domestic product based on labor time rather than on export value tends to confirm this ratio.)[48] Thus the state, though small and weak in comparison to other contemporary states, came rapidly to control a significant portion of the economy's total resources.

Some of the state's allocations of the funds and labor it controlled had positive effects on the economy, though not enough to counterbalance the negative effects of taxation. The cost of maintaining police and administrative control over Dahomey, while hardly regarded with favor by the conquered population, must be seen as an inevitable and acceptable state expense. Investment in the railroad yielded benefits for the economy, as did smaller investments in public health, public utilities, roads and agriculture. State purchases of imported goods were no more harmful than the equivalent import purchases by private consumers, except in cases where the state failed to buy available local goods. And salaries paid to Dahomeans for whatever reason, or that portion of European salaries which was spent within the colony, served to recirculate wealth to the area from which it was taken.

Other state expenditures were of no benefit or were positively harmful to the domestic economy. Large portions of salaries paid to French civil servants were repatriated to France. The nationalization of the railroad and pier firms on terms highly favorable to the owners led to a further export of resources from Dahomey. The accumulation of substantial government reserves, while it may be seen as prudent financing from the state's viewpoint, led to the withdrawal of further resources from current use. Finally and by far most seriously, large sums of revenue were exported, systematically, from Dahomey to Dakar after 1905, amounting to 2–3% of GDP annually.

The AOF regime thus set Dahomey on the road to economic stagnation. Stagnation took hold, however, not with a bang but with a whimper. The contractive effect of state policy, while undeniable, was able to negate the forces of domestic economic growth only after the passage of decades. By the end of the colonial era, when Dahomey had become poor, stagnant and deficit-ridden, few could remember the days of its relative prosperity and none could agree on the point at which poverty had taken hold.

While the negative impact of state policy on the economy is the most important point to emphasize, the relative impact of the state on various sectors of the economy is of interest. The French state annihilated the slave-catching sector and greatly weakened the slave-labor sector, both out of moral conviction and to ensure the defeat and destruction of the Fon ruling elite. The master's right to extract labor and produce from slaves on farms or in villages was ended, though slave wives and concubines saw little change in their position. The resources which had been utilized in these sectors then moved into other sectors, especially the familial and commodity exchange sectors. For the familial mode of production, the surplus of the family over the cost of maintaining itself took the form either of leisure or of storing its produce for future consumption. The state did little to add to the level of output or surplus in the familial sector, but taxation and forced labor each influenced the quantity of output, the time for leisure and the level of surplus retained by producers.

In the commodity exchange sector, the economic surplus consisted of the difference between the value of marketed output and the cost of reproducing the productive system. The cost of reproduction was defined in social as well as in technical terms, and was thus subject to modification. For example, not only food but social life were necessary to maintain production and, under the influence of severe privation, producers might find that large funerals and weddings were no longer socially necessary. The surplus in the commodity exchange sector took such forms as money savings, rent and tithes paid to landlords, consumption of surplus as luxury goods, and taxes. If the cost of maintenance was reduced, *ceteris paribus*, the surplus was increased.

Stated government policy toward the commodity exchange sector was that it should increase its production of export crops. This change was to be achieved through the state's agricultural experiments, fiscal incentives, regulations, moral exhortation, support of merchants, and investment in networks of transportation and communication. The magnitude of state contribution was minuscule in all but the last two of these, and led to marginal increases in output. The colonial administration, in replacing the previous states, made commerce easier than before within the frontiers of Dahomey, and more difficult across colonial frontiers. Forced labor and taxes had an impact similar to that for the familial sector: the impact of the state was to reduce the cost of reproduction slightly, to increase the level of output in the short run though not in the long run, and to reduce the level of surplus retained by producers.

The mercantile sector, already circumscribed by the rise of private capitalist commerce and transport, found its opportunities for growth further narrowed by the state. It absorbed the higher cost of porterage after the end of slavery, and accomodated to the railroad. Surf-boatmen benefitted as commerce continued its steady though cyclical growth, but they were hurt by the pier at Cotonou. Similarly lagoon boatmen and porters benefitted from state demand for their services, but they paid the *impôt* and import taxes.

In the capitalist sector the surplus was taxed through customs duties and license fees.[49] Private capitalist enterprise benefitted from such subsidies as postal contracts for steamer lines, from the pier and railroad concessions, and from political support such as that given to merchant firms on the location of markets. State enterprise in construction, transport and utilities, which was organized along capitalist lines even if it was not run to maximize profits, received subsidies and other assistance from the government. Further, state policies of taxation and recruitment expanded the labor force available at cheap wages, and thus helped expand the capitalist sector at the expense of others. As a result of these state activities, transport costs declined, and private enterprise grew in transport, commerce, and in such industrial efforts as bakeries and cotton gins. State enterprise itself expanded more rapidly.

The government of Dahomey defined its constituency in the course of the initial two decades of colonial rule. Les Etablissements français du Golfe de Bénin, as the colony was known until 1893, formally and practically depended on the Ministry of Colonies, though it was also reliant on allies within the colony: King Toffa and the interpreter Xavier Béraud, for instance, preserved substantial influence well into the 1890s. But as French rule became more entrenched, the government lost interest in such allies. Beginning in 1898 the colonial government reached out to French businessmen as a new constituency, attempting to reorient its policy to serve their interests. That constituency provided only a weak response, however, and was unable to maintain the allegiance of the government which had sought it out. So it was that when the structure of AOF was set up in 1904, the government of Dahomey accepted the Government General

185

as the constituency to which it was responsible. The acquiescence of the Dahomean government in a steady export of revenue from that time is perhaps the strongest possible evidence that its constituency lay outside the colony, in Dakar. The influence of Paris lay behind that of Dakar, but Porto-Novo treated the two as a monolith, not even daring to play one against the other.

While the government's flirtation with large-scale private capital ended rapidly for want of a response, there remained two senses in which the state served the cause of capitalism. The first was through the expansion and subsidization of state-owned and -operated capitalist enterprise in Dahomey. Secondly, and more generally, government policies helped to build a docile wage-labor force, ensured the supply of raw materials to the world market (though not particularly to France), and held the colony as a reserve which might be of future use to France. And, to the extent that these two theories – allegiance to Dakar and allegiance to capitalism in general – fail to explain the behavior of the Dahomean government, one is left with a pluralist model of state responsibility: the state almost never sought the opinions of its subjects, but it did accomodate to pressures from Dahomeans (organized as they were into towns, economic interests, families and ethnic groups), and to pressures from foreign and French merchants, from adjoining colonies and, most certainly, from the personal interests of the state officials.

8

Social struggles for economic ends, 1890–1914

Giscard, the administrator of Abomey *cercle*, had been chided by the governor in Porto-Novo for writing inadequate reports. So in May of 1910 he wrote a long and flowery report, in the course of which he announced that in order to reduce the amount of labor necessary to clear the roads each year, he had instructed the people of the *cercle* to walk abreast of each other, across the full width of the roads, rather than in single file.[1] Three years later at the same post another administrator, first complaining of the 'grumblings of students,' soon realized that he faced a broad movement in reaction to the zealous labor recruitment of an appointed chief.[2] In neither of these cases was the sequel recorded: they were added to the long list of unresolved disputes reflecting the social strains brought by French rule in southern Dahomey.

Since the French state itself was the biggest change in the economy and society, it brought the most strains and the most complaints. In its role as arbiter, the state also entered into conflicts it did not initiate – often redefining them as it did so. Further, since the state kept most of the records, its role in social conflicts is highlighted and exaggerated. Available documents thus tend to impose an anlysis of 'the government' *vs.* 'the people' which, while unquestionably the major element of the colonial situation in Africa, was only part of a wider network of social interaction.[3]

Economic conflicts led to social conflicts. Without going so far as to treat social conflict as a mechanical reflection of economic issues, one can nevertheless investigate social conflicts in search of insights into the interests, the alliances and the relative power of participants in the economic order. In simplified terms, social groups, as defined by the economic structure, perform economic functions. Modes of production and ethnic groups, in this perspective, are analytical constructs providing a map of the economic structure: thus, Hausa merchants, Hueda fishers, and Gun agriculturists. To each of the social groups may be attributed objectives, or at least outcomes by which they would benefit. Thus slaves

187

stood to benefit from freedom and land, while slave owners, given the end to the legal status of slavery, might hope at least to maintain title to their land and informal control over the slaves. Wage workers benefitted from higher wages, while their merchant employers benefitted from lower wages and higher selling prices for their wares. The interests and objectives of social groups gave rise to policies for each group, and consequently to a set of alliances and actions in the social and political arena intended to advance their economic interests.

Some participants in the economic order could hope for state support of their interests: those who had ethnic or economic ties to the French state, and those who had enjoyed access to precolonial states. The Fon, Gun and other royal families sought support of the French state, as did leading Dahomean merchants and landowners. European merchants and investors did likewise. Most Dahomeans, however, did not aspire to gaining support of the state and sought instead to avoid it. The colonial state, far more so than states based on representative government, was an independent actor on the social scene, especially as its political strength grew and as it gained control over nearly one-tenth of the colony's domestic product. Its motives in the short term were to assert French authority and, after 1904, to do the bidding of Dakar.

The manner and the vigor with which social groups pursued their objectives depended on the means at their disposal. In the 1890s the French state acted as final authority but otherwise intervened little in local affairs, with the exception of the nearly two-year military occupation of the Fon kingdom. From 1894 the Fon kingdom was dominated by local leaders on an *ad hoc* basis, while outside the Fon kingdom the pre-colonial political structures functioned much as before. In the regime of *cercles* under French administrators set up in 1900, chiefs lost their independent status and became appointed functionaries of the French state, receiving salaries and rebates on revenue they collected. A Conseil général composed mainly of administrators acted as the deliberative body of the colony; it included at least one appointed Dahomean. The court system, formalized in 1903, distinguished French law from 'customary' law, though the administrators of the *cercles* stood at the pinnacle of the customary court system. The *indigénat*, adopted by AOF in 1904, provided administrators with power to impose fines, jail and forced labor on colonial subjects with no recourse.[4] As such, it gave formal standing to a system already in practice.

CONFLICTS IN THE DOMESTIC ECONOMY

Two groups – large landowners, who also acted as merchants, and independent lineages – stand out in the recorded conflicts within the

188

domestic economy.[5] To a lesser degree, conflicts involving slaves and wage laborers came into the open as well. The objectives of landowners were to gain title to productive land and to register it with the state. As a result of their social standing they sought to maintain direct relations with the government: their wide network of political and commercial ties gave them hope of influencing administrative decisions and, if they lost there, they could appeal to the courts. Gaining title to land was also an objective for independent lineages, as well as obtaining good terms for their commerce and, since the state provided little service for them, the minimization of state interference in their lives. They acted through their appointed chiefs or through the *notables* – the French term for all leading figures who did not have a French title. While the involvement of the state in disputes among these groups often led to new conflicts and to a complex redefinition of the issues, the complexity of the conflicts stemmed at base from their origin within the domestic economy.

When state support for slavery ended, the institution withered away. The French, after destroying the Fon state and halting the slave trade, took little more direct action against slavery, but nonetheless gained the reputation of having abolished slavery. The actual abolition of slave status depended, however, on the station of the slaves. For these purposes, the slaves of southern Dahomey may be placed in four categories: (1) palace slaves, mostly in the Fon kingdom but also in the Gun and other kingdoms, (2) state slaves placed in villages as agricultural laborers, almost all within the Fon kingdom, (3) slaves of large and wealthy lineages inside the Fon kingdom but outside it as well, and (4) slaves in lesser lineages, mostly outside the Fon kingdom.[6] In the lesser lineages slaves were functionally part of the lineage: some slaves of the larger lineages were functionally part of them, while others lived a life apart. The condition and distribution of slaves in these categories, further, varied by sex. Female palace slaves included royal wives and concubines, some with positions of authority, and domestics. Women in slave villages were agricultural laborers like the men. The female slaves of large and small lineages were mostly wives and concubines, though some were stationed in slave villages controlled by the lineages. The male palace slaves acted as officials. Men in slave villages outnumbered the women, while female slaves outnumbered the males in lineages. Male slaves in large lineages ranged from domestics to agricultural laborers and artisans, while in the lesser lineages they functioned much the same as other family members. While male slaves could marry, and at times married daughters of the family head, it is likely that they often remained unmarried: if slave owners took slave women for themselves, male slaves must often have remained with no opportunity to marry.

189

In proclaiming the French protectorate over Dahomey, Dodds decreed that slave trade would end. Though he did not abolish the institution of slavery, it came to be understood that he had done so. More precisely, the immediate effect of the conquest and of Dodds's subsequent proclamations was to free the slaves of the royal family and the leading officers of the Fon state.[7] Further, since slavery lost its legal sanction under the new regime, the French occupation led to a rapid change in the conditions of servitude both inside and outside the Fon kingdom. Finally, those slaves who wished formal release from their servitude could gain it by appealing to the state, though the state would provide compensation neither to former masters nor to former slaves.

The sharpest change came among the Fon, particularly in the inland areas. In Abomey, Allada, Zagnanado and in closely allied Savalou, Fon officials simply departed with the invasion, leaving their slaves to fend for themselves; Fon leaders eventually returned to Abomey, but not to the other areas. In Ouidah some of the leading families rallied to the French quickly, and thus remained to hold an influence over their slaves they might otherwise have lost. Overall, most of those in slave villages escaped; many lineage slaves left, and most stayed; men were more likely to leave and women were more likely to stay. Most Fon palace slaves left, but Agoli-Agbo had six hundred women slaves at the time of his exile in 1900, and the *laris*, the Gun palace slaves, acted as state officials into the twentieth century.

The change in condition of servitude had begun in Porto-Novo under the French protectorate in the 1880s, and was extended to all of southern Dahomey in 1893. With the slave trade abolished, all first-generation slaves were advanced to the status of second-generation slaves, who could not be sold. Further, slaves now had the same civil rights as other colonial subjects: in the Fon kingdom, the master had no right to punish a slave, but could bring charges against a slave before the state; under the French the master gained no new rights, and the state which would hear any charges against slaves no longer recognized a separate code for slaves. Within families, male slaves were assimilated to the status of younger sons, except that they did not generally inherit. Finally, the slaves who were functionally outside the families of their masters formed new contracts which amounted to peonage: they gained control of the land they worked in return for regular contributions of labor or produce to their former masters.

The slaves faced several choices under the new regime. At first many of the slaves on the Abomey plateau flocked to the French military posts. Many hoped to stay on the land they worked, on their own conditions: the villages of Aoundonon and Evedji were founded by ex-slaves in 1893 near Agrimé. But in 1894, as the French reached an understanding with the Fon, set Agoli-Agbo on the throne and prepared to withdraw the army, they advised the villagers that the Fon landowners would be back to claim their lands, and that the freed slaves would do best to seek out their original homes.[8] Although thousands of slaves returned home, to do so was a mixed blessing – homes and families had been destroyed in the slave raids, years had passed, and few freed slaves could be sure that land and a family awaited them at home. In the case of Kétou, however, the French actively assisted in the re-establishment of the old kingdom, destroyed in a Fon attack of 1886.

Another possibility, which became more realistic in later years as French rule became more established, was for slaves to leave and go to the French towns – new towns such as Cotonou and Bohicon – in search of wage work. A more attractive urban safety valve, for those who could make the distance, was Lagos.

Most slaves, however, stayed where they were. There were two aspects to this decision: staying on the land, and staying in the family – the first typically male, the second typically female. Slaves renegotiated the terms of their servitude and the masters, recognizing the changed conditions, revised their terms. Village slaves and lineage slaves made the lands they worked into their own lands, though they continued to make payments in produce and in labor to the former masters. The labor contribution, which constituted a form of peonage, also became similar to the *donkpe*, except that it was not reciprocal: the master provided a feast for the slaves after the work party had completed its construction or its work in the fields. In return the slaves made no move to register an official end to their slave status. Their reasoning, then, was that the security of their economic condition was as important as their formal status. In cases where this informal arrangement did not provide enough of a living, the slaves took their leave or asked the state for a certification of their free status. In such cases, the former master ended any further obligation for support of the slave and regained – or attempted to regain – control of the land, but made no attempt to regain control over the slave.[9]

For the women, who were generally tied to the master's family with the bonds of children, the inhibitions to leaving or to declaring free status were great. The condition of slave wives was not sharply different from that of free wives, except that slaves had no family to fall back on in times of need or in case of family disputes. This sexual distinction in mobility was not, however, absolute: men too were bound by family ties, and women who were unmarried or married to men in slave villages could view the problem in terms of land rather than family. Women who did not wish to accept impending marriages fled to the French administration. One administrator in Ouidah responded by determining whether the refugees were of free or

191

slave status: if they were slave he granted them asylum, but if they were free he returned them to their family and their fate.

Observers at the turn of the century concluded that to be a slave in the Bight of Benin was to be in an economic relationship and to have suffered a personal misfortune, but that it did not carry the racial and social stigma of slavery among Europeans. Yet three decades later, when Herskovits visited villages of slave descendants, he found them to be frightened and respectful in the presence of the Fon aristocrats with whom he was travelling. The heritage of slavery, in this region where slavery and slave trade were so much a part of life for centuries, is deeply and subtly ingrained.[10]

The proportion of slaves in the population can be gauged only with difficulty. Administrators in the Fon kingdom thought that in 1904 one-sixth to one-fifth of the population was of servile origin.[11] Taking account of the departure of some slaves and the probable undercounting of female slaves, the preconquest proportion might have been one-fourth to one-third of the population, including both first- and second-generation slaves. Outside of the Fon kingdom the proportion of slaves is even harder to judge, but it was undoubtedly smaller. The work they did was the same – construction, manufactures, field crops, tending oil palms and domestic service – and their conditions had changed similarly under colonial rule.[12]

The attempts by slaves to redress their position depended on their political strength. In Ouidah the administrator was surprised to find the chief of Brazil *quartier* sending large numbers of laborers to help the de Souza family rebuild its house, particularly since the same chief had recently been induced only with difficulty to provide two workers to the administration for street work. It turned out that all, chief included, were ex-slaves of the de Souza family, and were fulfilling the yearly obligation of labor in return for a feast, in accord with the new understanding. The administrator urged that the laborers demand wages for any such work and, backed by this authority, workers did indeed demand wages for their work. The de Souza family responded by attempting to eject those ex-slaves from the lands they held, which had indeed been those of the family. The administration acted to support the ex-slaves, ruling that anyone who had occupied land for ten years (it was now just ten years since the French occupation) held title to it. The slaves had thus used a political opportunity to improve their status – though it is likely that the old relations were re-established in some cases once the administration's attention was drawn elsewhere.

The state and the slaves each desired a change in slavery; the masters acquiesced. Few of the changes, however, were registered by the state: master and slave preferred to handle the delicate balance of the relationship informally; the French feared involvement in the issue of compensation.[13] (On the other hand, the changes in land titles which accompanied this change in status were fought out in public and with considerable state involvement.) The recorded cases of legal liberations of slaves are, therefore, interesting exceptions. In Allada, a slave woman wished to obtain free status yet remain with her husband. She paid her purchase price to her husband, who in turn gave it to her family as the bride price.[14] The four requests for freedom in Porto-Novo during 1903 included a woman sold twelve years earlier by the Fon to a Sakété woman, whose marriage had failed and who wanted to find her father; a Nupe woman of thirty who had been mistreated by the son of her former master, a Gun prince, and who wished to settle down in Porto-Novo with another man; and two Fon men sold at Adjohon by Glele, who wished to return to Abomey. Their masters agreed, but thought they should have a certification of their freedom to identify them.

The refugee peoples saw in the colonial period an opportunity to broaden their social and economic life with less fear of reprisal than in former times. Mansell Prothero has characterized as 'downhill' movements the spontaneous resettlement, following the establishment of colonial rule, of refugee peoples in more fertile, open lowlands throughout Africa. The Dasha had built villages on rocky hills to hold off the Fon, but they gradually moved them to lower levels in the colonial period. The Aja proper, who preferred isolation in precolonial years, eventually moved as far as the shores of Lake Ahémé, where they took up shrimp fishing.[15]

The Weme furnish an example of a 'downhill' movement which was actually uphill. Having fled from the Fon to the marshes of the Ouémé, and fearing attacks from the Nago to the east as well, the Weme lived only along the river, where their dense population and intensive exploitation of the area required a tightly knit and cooperative social structure. The only sizeable village on the plateau before the twentieth century was Gbékandji, founded after a succession dispute in Dangbo, on the river. But with the end of any danger of incursions from the east, the Weme began to cut fields on the empty plateau above the river. The process was the same from Dangbo in the south to Bonou in the north: first they established seasonal camps in the forest at the edge of the plateau, then they built paths through the forest to transport their harvests to the villages, then the young men established permanent farms on the plateau. Finally, villages began to be established: the first recorded movement, a distance of about four kilometers, led to the founding of the village of Zounta in 1902. Further north, the expansion to the east began later and went more slowly. The colonization of the plateau took almost the whole colonial period to complete, but it was well under way by 1914.[16]

Social changes accompanied the population movement, since the farms on the plateau were operated by small groups who had plenty of room and were no longer dependent on the elaborate organization necessary for life in the flood plain. A pioneering spirit grew among the migrants: they became individualistic, independent, and contentious, and their elders in the valley chastised them for their scorn of the old ways. The migration itself and other factors brought a change in Weme land tenure.[17] The authority of Weme lineage leaders was diminished simply by the establishment of the French administration above them. In addition, head taxes were to be paid by each adult male for himself, his wives, and his children over eight or ten. The family chief, who held most of the money, paid only for himself, his wives and children. The younger men, who had to find cash for their *impôt* elsewhere, began to resent working to add to the communal stores. Further, the gradually increasing availability of goods on the market nurtured a desire of the young men to break out of the family exchange system.

As a result, at the death of a family chief, his sons tended to divide the family lands into individual holdings rather than pass control of all the land to the eldest son. Often, younger sons simply migrated to the plateau, leaving the eldest in the valley alone. The process was gradual, and varied according to the family, the size and quality of its holding, and the region; but the breakup of Weme lands was an irreversible tendency beginning in the early twentieth century.

After the partition of lineage lands, the lineage (*henu* or *hueta*) lost much of its social and economic importance, and the minimal patrilineal family became the unit of economic activity. With a man and his sons now alone on each farm, farmers had to restrict the size of their fields because of the intensive labor required in peak seasons. As a result, agricultural output fell on individual farms and even for the region as a whole. In the flood plain, where cooperative labor was necessary to maintain the channels which drained the floods from the fields, the end of the cooperative system eventually meant that those fields were abandoned. Paradoxically, because of a social change, the Weme found themselves with a growing population but with an increasingly severe labor shortage.

The case of the Weme is extreme, in that it fits the old stereotype of a communal African landholding system transformed to individual tenure at the hands of colonialism.[18] In fact the land tenure system was more varied, more flexible, and more stable than this case would suggest. Both individual and communal holdings existed throughout southern Dahomey, on both large and small scale. Inheritance remained the leading means of land transfer, but it coexisted with gifts, state intervention, court action and purchase. States expropriated land from their enemies, kept it for

194

themselves, and gave it to their supporters. The French state assumed this role from precolonial states; it even exaggerated precolonial powers of eminent domain in order to justify its own actions.[19] The role of the courts in resolving disputes over land was put to a serious test when, after 1900, the reformed court system had to handle an immense number of disputes occasioned by the political and social changes of colonial rule. Land sales accelerated with the growing value of agricultural exports in the nineteenth century, and the land market had become quite lively by the early twentieth century, as indicated by rising prices, by instances of land speculation, and by the legal and other disputes over land.[20] In addition to agricultural land, fishing grounds were important properties, over which contentions could lead to unexpected results.

For the Lake Nokoué fishing village of Awansouri, what began as a 'downhill' movement came to be complicated by land disputes, and ended up in a disastrous confrontation with the state. The people of Awansouri had come there over a period of centuries, mostly as refugees from the Fon, and assumed the identity of the Tofin people. The last major group of refugees arrived at the time of the French conquest. The town had a population of three thousand, divided into six quarters, all built on stilts in the late. The lake people were primarily fishermen, but they also grew some crops on the land, and they exploited the palm groves along the adjoining southern shore of the lake, surrounding Awansouri–Agué. These palms were not owned individually or even by families: anyone in the village had rights to cut fruit.

The end of the threat from the Fon made settling on the land appear more attractive, and a segment of Awansouri began moving to Awansouri-Agué. Led by Tossé, who was a religious chief for the whole area, a group of people from Awansouri gained authorization from Governor Liotard in December 1900 to establish a village at Awansouri-Agué. This move was accompanied by considerable dispute in the community about whether it was better to live on the lake or on the shore.

As settlers at Awansouri-Agué became more involved in cultivation, they sought to make the most out of the oil palms. This led to their forming a demand for division of the palm grove into two sections, one for each village. In 1908 they made several requests to the administration for such a division. The lake people, however, were not at all interested – they wanted to maintain the old system of free and open harvest of the palms.[21]

This simple dispute was complicated by a number of factors. First, Awansouri, being on the lake, was part of Porto-Novo *cercle*, while Awansouri-Agué was part of Cotonou *cercle*, which was under French law. A further complication was presented by Lawani Kossoko, the son of the deposed king of Lagos, and chief of the western part of Porto-Novo *cercle*,

195

who was influential in Awansouri. The final complication, of course, was that the inhabitants of Awansouri were there because they did not want to pay taxes–to the Fon, the French, or anyone else. Other people of like mind tended to move to the village.

The people of Awansouri demonstrated forcefully their claim to free harvest of the palms by sending a group of 150 people who fired shots and collected some fifty palm fruit one night in March 1908. In May they tried to get out of paying the *impôt*, saying that the people from Awansouri-Agué had harvested all the oil palms. Actually, they had harvested at least a portion of the palm grove, and had sold it to the French merchant Saudemont. Lawani Kossoko had arranged the sale and had collected a fee, and he may well have supported the March demonstration.

The people of Awansouri-Agé expressed the fear that their chief Tossé might be replaced by Kossoko, and they claimed to be under French law. In June of 1908 they made another attempt to obtain a division of palms, this time through a complaint drawn up and presented to the inspector of administrative affairs. The complaint had been drawn up for Tossé by Hampaty, former hammock-bearer, and by Taylor, a Senegalese *originaire* who worked for the telegraph in Cotonou. The administration responded fiercely: five inhabitants of the village were given a week in prison for 'inexact claims,' and Hampaty was given two weeks in prison for making the complaint. But nothing could be done to Taylor because he was a French citizen.

The administration decided that the dispute could be resolved by transferring Awansouri from Porto-Novo to Cotonou *cercle*, and the transfer was implemented in June. Rather than solve the dispute, the transfer aggravated it. For now the *impôt* from Awansouri was to be collected by Cotonou *cercle*, and it was collected more assiduously than it had been by Porto-Novo. The chiefs, led by village chief Hounkarin, asked for military help in collecting the *impôt*.[22] Such a situation so close to the port of Cotonou was very embarrassing to the French, and it turned the administration against the lake village. By 1909, administrator Dreyfus looked more favorably on the complaints from Awansouri-Agé that the lake people were stealing their palm fruit, and he labelled the lake village 'un vaste repaire de bandits.'

Dreyfus proposed a two-part plan of action: first, force the lake people to move to the shore and, second, remove Awansouri-Agué from French law so that the palm disputes could be settled under customary law, and to avoid placing the three thousand inhabitants of Awansouri under French law. The lake village was to be given three months in which to move to the shore, and Dreyfus magnanimously suggested an indemnity of 2,000 francs be paid the villagers for the cost of moving. The removal of Awansouri-

Agué from French law called for some real legal legerdemain, but Dreyfus was backed by his superiors, and the people of Awansouri-Agué lost their appeal of his decision.

From the middle of 1909, the administration tried steadily to induce or force the lake people to move to the shore. They would not move, and disputes over palm harvesting continued. The governor visited Awansouri in August, the Awansouri chiefs were convened in Cotonou in September, and finally in November 1909 the administration could report that 67 houses had been built and more were under construction. The division of the village was clear – three quarters would move to Thémé and live under Kossoko, and three quarters would move to Awansouri-Agué with chief Hounkarin. But still they did not move. Finally on August 2, 1910, a meeting was held at Awansouri. The villagers were given a final deadline of September 2, and were told the governor would act after that date.

The threat was carried out: on September 4, the village was destroyed completely.[23] Little is heard from the people of Awansouri-Agué following the destruction of the lake village. In 1912 they became embroiled in a dispute over control of fisheries with people from the nearby village of Afotonou. Aside from that, they turned to more intensive exploitation of palm kernels, only now with no recourse to government to settle disputes. They were also induced, in order to pay their *impôt*, to do work on roads in the *cercle*, and even to ask to perform such work.

The problem of over-fishing in Lake Ahémé presents another case in which the attempt to resolve an issue in the domestic economy led to a confrontation with the state. After twenty years of colonialism, and partly because of the removal of old authorities, the fishing people of Lake Ahémé had ceased to conform to restrictions, and the lake began to be over-fished. Some of the chiefs brought the problem to the administrator, and asked for authorization to return to the old customs of regulation of fishing.[24] The administrator and the government of Dahomey decided on a different approach – to require the purchase of a fishing permit, which would cost one franc per year, and for which the fisherman would be given a token to hold. The principle, therefore, was to regulate fishing by using the market mechanism: to raise the cost of fishing, and keep some of the smaller fishermen out of the business.

The new tax was most unpopular. Some two hundred fishermen came over twenty kilometers to demonstrate against it. The administrator said the tax would protect them: 'Ce jeton leur permettraient de pêcher sans être tracassés.' They responded that it had always been their lake and they needed no interference. The administrator sent them away with a promise to visit them. By September of 1913 a coordinated campaign of protest had been set up by fishermen at Grand Popo and on the lake. The administrator

197

finally went to the lake for his visit, where he held an afternoon meeting with about twenty chiefs. But the surrounding crowd, not convinced by his explanations, got more and more angry, and continued browbeating him for four hours. The administrator and ten policemen were forced to spend the night besieged in an enclosure. The next day they were relieved by the army from Grand Popo. Once reinforced, the administrator captured all the canoes on the lake, and refused to release them until the owners paid their tax.[25] They had no choice but to pay. But the fishermen ultimately won their point, for in another year the administration gave up trying to collect this tax.

Most disputes in the domestic economy had to do not with declining output, as on Lake Ahémé, but with expanding production. This was particularly true for oil palm groves. The Fon royal family, in its attempt to preserve and extend its palm groves, ran into trouble with the French administration in Abomey in 1905. Mévo, the chief of Djegbé quarter and a former minister in the Fon state, had attempted to dispossess a cultivator of a palm grove in order to give it to a son of King Ghezo. Under Fon law the king had been able to select any land for his use or that of his family, sometimes after a judicial proceeding. The French, however, responded with an order from the governor dismissing Mévo from office.

Following this decision, at least one cultivator responded by attempting to regain control of a palm grove taken from his father sixty years earlier by Ghezo and given to one of his sons, Sossou-Ouèta. The administration ruled, however, that since Sossou-Ouèta had cultivated the palm grove since then, it would remain his.[26]

The palm groves of the former kings themselves presented another problem. According to Fon law, half the palm oil had gone to the king (or for his ceremonies and the upkeep of his palace after his death), while the other half of the oil and all the kernels had gone to the producers. The question arose as to how this division was being implemented, and whether it should be changed. The administrator Le Herissé favored bringing the whole harvest to the Residence where he would divide it, half to the producers, and half to pay the palace guardian and to cover costs of ceremonies for the kings. Chief Houdohouè argued differently – and apparently in favor of an arrangement that would give more to the chiefs. He was imprisoned for two days for taking that position, and shortly thereafter he was imprisoned for a longer term on charges of sequestering a woman for several months.[27]

At the same time as the land disputes began in Abomey, a more spectacular set of disputes over control of land and family goods began in Ouidah. The greatest disputes and most of the legal actions centered on the great families of Quénum and Adjovi, but other families were drawn into these disputes and had similar disputes of their own. The dispute in the Quénum family came into the open in 1905 when one segment of the family began legal proceedings seeking to break up the family or to overthrow the leadership of the other segment. Tovalou Quénum, who was chief of the family variously estimated at from 300 to 2,000 members, was the central figure. His father, Kpadonou Quénum, held the title *ahisigan* in the Fon kingdom, and hence acted as commercial counselor to the king.[28] Tovalou succeeded his father as family chief in 1894, and in 1896 went so far as to draw up and sign a notarized act, in the presence of French officials, merchants, and family members. This document confirmed his appointment as family chief and defined his rights and obligations, which included making all family goods his personal goods.[29]

Tovalou had been most active in both agricultural and commercial pursuits. Much of the family land had been uncultivated. With the part of family close to him, and with a large number of former slaves whom he settled down as farmers and made part of the family, he began expanding agricultural production. He drove a hard bargain, though – not half but all the palm oil produced went to Tovalou, while the family members and ex-slaves on the land got the palm kernels and food crops. Tovalou, meanwhile, moved from Ouidah to Porto-Novo and directed his business as a merchant from that point.

Tovalou's uncles Possy Berry and Koudessi led the other faction. They may well have fallen into debt with German merchants in Ouidah. In any case they filed suit against Tovalou in 1905, and the case ended up mixed up in both French and customary courts. They accused Tovalou of fabricating the notarized act of 1896, they sought to remove his title as family chief, and they asked for partition of family goods according to the *code civil*.[30] In addition to their court cases, Possy Berry and Koudessi also took direct action – they began confiscating palm oil puncheons from the fields in some cases, and preventing the rolling of puncheons to market in other cases.

In the meantime the Adjovi family, another old and wealthy family, had initiated a set of disputes over possession of palm groves. Akanwanou Adjovi had been family chief for some years, and he was an energetic businessman. He began to use the courts to establish control over Adjovi family land which had long since fallen into the hands of others, or which was otherwise disputed. He first gained a favorable judgment in Porto-Novo in 1903, giving him control over the Cotonou side of a palm grove spanning the border of Cotonou and Ouidah *cercles*. As he pursued his advantage and attempted to establish legal control over more palm groves in Ouidah *cercle*, the administration was put into the position of having to make long inquiries into the facts for each palm grove concerned. The administration tried to give support to Kenné, who cultivated the grove in

199

Cotonou *cercle*, and who had contested Adjovi's right to it.[31]

To handle their legal affairs, both Tovalou Quénum and Adjovi turned to Germain Crespin. Crespin, a Senegalese mulatto, had been both a lawyer and a judge in Senegal; his brother Georges Crespin continued to practice law there. Crespin came to Dahomey apparently at the request of Quénum and Adjovi, and he successfully represented these and other clients for years. The administration treated him as a thorn in the side. Crespin could only handle cases in the French courts. So when his clients lost cases in the customary courts, it was necessary to find grounds to appeal them to the French courts. For inhabitants of Ouidah and Cotonou this was generally easy to do, for they had been placed under French law in 1904. But Crespin lost the case of one palm grove when the French were able to make stick the accusation that his client had falsely listed his residence as Ouidah, and that he lived just outside town.[32]

But for Tovalou Quénum and Adjovi, Crespin was able to get the cases into French court, and to win at least partial victories. Possy Berry and Koudessi Quénum were rebuffed repeatedly in 1905 and 1906 in their attempts either to split the family or remove Tovalou, and they spent the next two years regrouping themselves. Adjovi won the legal right to the contested palm grove in Cotonou *cercle*. The French were, however, able to give some satisfaction to Kenné – the governor general issued an order that Kenné should be able to farm the grove for an additional ten years before it was turned over to Adjovi.[33]

The administration began to see over more ominous implications in the activities of Tovalou and Adjovi, and attempted stronger measures. Following a hearing in the customary court in December of 1908, administrator Cuvillier arrested Adjovi for 'tenue malhonnête' during the hearing and refused to release him for some time. Cuvillier put heavy pressures on chiefs in Ouidah and on judges in the customary courts to make sure they gave no support to Adjovi and Tovalou, and he encouraged their enemies to take the offensive, saying he would imprison Tovalou if his enemies would come up with appropriate charges. Possy Berry Quénum returned to the customary court in late 1908, and obtained a favorable ruling.

Tovalou and Adjovi responded to this challenge by adding a political organization to their legal efforts in 1909 and 1910, including public demonstrations, secret meetings of leading figures and *chefs de quartier* in Ouidah, pressures on judges in the customary courts, marshalling public support from leading Ouidah families, and even seeking out support in the Government General in Dakar.

In January, 1909 the lieutenant-governor came from Porto-Novo to Ouidah to hear both factions of the Quénum family. The issue was now whether Tovalou could be removed from his position as family chief. Before his visit, the governor received a letter from Crespin giving details on Cuvillier's biased and underhanded methods in dealing with Tovalou, and an emotional and self-justifying response to Crespin from Cuvillier. Following the hearing, Possy Berry and his followers wrote their summary of the proceedings to the governor, asserting that a family had the right to remove a family chief when he misbehaved, and that Tovalou had kept the family goods for himself. Tovalou did not write the governor. Instead, he arranged for the other main family leaders of Ouidah to write as disinterested parties. They pointed out that family heads could be dismissed under customary law, but only for specific crimes. Tovalou had not been accused of any such crimes.[34] The governor took no action, and Tovalou remained family chief and in control of all family goods.

Cuvillier, in his report for March 1909, noted with horror that the governor general had made some indication that French law might be substituted for customary law, and that this only encouraged Dahomeans to try again in French law every case they lost under customary law. The leading families wanted French law, he observed, not only because they would then have a better chance of winning the lands they wanted, but also because they would escape the *indigénat*. He predicted that if the likes of Tovalou and Adjovi gained French legal status, they would then ask for further assimilation, such as to become part of the electorate and send a representative to the Conseil supérieur des Colonies.[35]

The campaign of Tovalou Quénum and the Adjovi family to establish economic leadership in Ouidah met another complication in the same year of 1909, as members of the royal family of Abomey made attempts to regain control of palm groves in Ouidah *cercle* which had belonged to the kings. In October they won a judgment in the customary court in Ouidah. Tovalou and Jean Adjovi, son of Akanwanou Adjovi, responded by organizing a public demonstration following the hearing, verbally assaulting the princes and parading in the streets. Soon thereafter, Tovalou won a case in the customary courts, presumably on this same issue, which the administration was sure he would lose – indicating that his influence over judges could be as great as that of the administrators. These and other pressures had their effect: the administration began to announce flatly that the royal family had no intention whatever of taking over palm groves in Ouidah *cercle*, and that it was prevented from doing so by the treaty of 1894.[36]

Despite his remarkable staying power, however, Tovalou Quénum was unable to prevent the division of the family. In May of 1910 a division of the family and of family property was agreed to by Tovalou and Possy Berry, and it was registered with the government.[37] Nevertheless, Tovalou

201

continued to have great influence in Ouidah, in Porto-Novo, and throughout southern Dahomey. Administrative records after 1910 show a continuing series of skirmishes related to Tovalou's efforts to protect and expand his properties.

The Adjovi family faced a major crisis in 1913 with the death of Akanwanou Adjovi on November 16, of cancer of the larynx. Before his death, Adjovi had drawn up a proposed convention dealing with the family's lands, but the administration rejected it on the grounds that it was based on a mixture of French and customary law, where it should have been based strictly on customary law. For some months, during the funeral ceremonies, the various parties in the family maneuvered for position. For a brief time in April Outondji, brother of Akanwanou, acted as chief, but he was unable to maintain his position. Finally on June 2, 1914, Jean Adjovi was selected chief of the family. Jean Adjovi was young, mission educated, and a son of Akanwanou. He was close to Tovalou Quénum. During World War I, he volunteered to become a *tirailleur*, and served in Europe. At the conclusion of his service, he obtained letters of support from Blaise Diagne, who had led in the recruitment of soldiers from AOF, and Adjovi used these in support of his request for admission to French citizenship. Though he achieved this goal, family disputes eventually arose, as a result of which the Adjovi family and its goods were officially divided in 1928.[38]

Such figures as Tovalou Quénum and Akanwanou Adjovi worked energetically to control the country's most valuable resource – capitalized, producing palm groves. They sought to mobilize their resources in land and labor to increase output. In the resulting legal conflicts, they had no firm initial preference for French or customary law, and they had victories and defeats under each. Gradually, though, they found that French law offered them more protection, and they embarked upon a concerted campaign to gain status as French citizens. Thus the question of 'assimilation' to French culture may be fruitfully posed in terms of economic calculations as well as in terms of political theory.[39]

They may be seen as aspiring bourgeois, whose success in capitalism depended on their ability to establish an alliance with the French political and economic network. Such a policy was made difficult by the reluctance of French and German merchants to enter into more than short-term alliances, and was made even more difficult by the opposition of the French government to any sort of alliance. Yet the aspiring bourgeoisie pressed on. The selection as chiefs of young and French-educated figures such as Tovalou Quénum and Jean Adjovi and the registration of family contracts with the government both reflect an attempt to gain status in the French system. At the death in 1910 of Lohoué Hodonou, another prominent Ouidah family chief, he too was succeeded by the young, French-educated

Ignacio Hodonou, and the family obtained a recognition of this fact and a commendation from the governor.[40] These leading families were at times able to establish better relations with the French, as the experience of Jean Adjovi shows. But they were never able to obtain the full support of the state. Instead, the state regularly took opportunities to weaken and undermine them, as if that were an objective in itself. This state of affairs was surely one reason for the continued splits in the large families, such as those of the Adjovi and Hodonou families in the 1920s.

Another set of land disputes, which broke out in and around Porto-Novo in 1912, accompanied the purchases of both urban and rural property by Yoruba Muslims. Their approach in rural areas was to make loans of a few hundred francs to farmers at the time of funerals and marriages, and to charge interest at rates which ran from 2.5% to 4% per month, or 45% per year. When the borrower could not pay, he was induced to give the field or palm grove over to the lender. The farmer was then reduced to the position of a tenant. Inland, in the area of Sakété, further land disputes could be traced to grants of land by Toffa to his followers in Porto-Novo. The expansion of fields which came with the growth of maize production after 1905 brought disputes into the open: the followers of Toffa tried to expand their holdings, the Nago farmers of Sakété tried to re-establish control of their lands, and the Muslim moneylenders continued to increase their land holdings.[41]

The growth in importance of Muslim landowners led to a factional dispute within the Muslim community in Porto-Novo. On one side, and largely supported by the government, were the Brazilians, led by Ignacio Paraiso, the Lopez family, and the *imam*. The other party, often called the *alhajis*, was led by Mouteiro Soulé and his brother, and included the younger and wealthier Muslims. The *alhaji* party, despite its growing strength, was unable to win the major issues of the day. First, they were unable to prevent the construction of the grand mosque at a place they regarded as too close to the administration, so they gradually moved to the mosque at Attaké, on the north side of town. Second, their request for the appointment of a chief for all Muslims in Porto-Novo was denied. Third, their request in 1913 to separate from the rest of the Muslims and have their own *imam* was also refused. The objectives of the *alhaji* groups were in many ways similar to those of the Ouidah families, though they operated through a different set of institutions. But they ran into the same problems, as the French refused to give them firm support.

Wage workers, while a small category of people working under quite diverse circumstances, were drawn by their conditions into repeated conflicts. Leaving aside the large number of people who collected wages

203

from the state in casual or forced labor, wage workers included transport workers and employees of merchants in both mercantile and capitalist sectors, domestics, workers in Dahomey's tiny industrial establishments, and salaried employees of the state. In Bohicon, which grew rapidly as the rail and commercial center for the Abomey plateau, a community developed of wage-earners, mostly from Ouidah, who worked for the railroad, the commercial houses, and as domestics. This working-class community began to assert an identity and outlook: disputes broke out in 1911 in which an administrator accused the workers of treating the people of Bohicon as savages.

The French, too, were involved in the dispute, and the domestics of the Europeans joined the side of the workers. The administration labelled them 'arrogant' and asserted that they were 'imbued with ideas too advanced for their mentality.' Part of the conflict led to thefts by the workers, including the theft of a barrel of white wine from the Fabre warehouse.[42]

Another case of theft from merchants occurred at Bonou, on the Ouémé, where a canoe was robbed. The administrator accused the 'Zampétos' of this and other thefts. This is a case of the border-line between conflict among merchants and conflicts between merchants and their employees. The Zangbeto society had the function of ensuring that merchants charged only the prices agreed to by their association, which provides one interpretation of the robbery. But when the administrator responded to the robbery by sentencing fifteen men to three years of prison and an additional two years' prohibition from entering Zagnanado *cercle*, one is led to suspect that they were workers trying to get even with their employer.[43]

In Grand Popo, boatmen had a two-year running dispute with the administration and the commercial houses over wages and other conditions of work. Much of the transport in Grand Popo *cercle* had to be by water, including the landing of goods by surf-boats: the boatmen, mostly Gen, formed a community, though groups of them specialized in different tasks and routes. In May 1910 certain of these groups began a selective slowdown of transport. Canoemen in Athiémé, on the Mono, opposed construction of the new road inland from Grand Popo. The merchants of Athiémé reported frequent thefts, and had to call on canoes from Grand Popo to get any goods moved down the river. The German merchants in Grand Popo were able to find boatmen, but the French had to come to the administration for help in rounding up boatmen. Meanwhile, canoe transportation of goods from Grand Popo to Ouidah, which normally took six or seven hours, was taking up to six days for French houses: the shortage of labor stemmed in part from the administration's cutting its wages to boatmen by fifty percent.[44]

After the interruption of road construction in 1911 the conflict continued, though in a different vein. The focus of the slowdown now shifted to the surf-boats, and to the German houses. When the firm of Althof reported a theft of goods, the administration found some of the goods among boatmen, and sentenced fifty of them to penalties of up to two years in prison. The other boatmen refused to land goods for Althof at any price for several months, and some ships were forced to leave port without loading or unloading their cargoes. The administrator attempted to mediate between the boatmen and the commercial houses, but ended up giving an ultimatum to the canoe chiefs that they would have to end their boycott or they would be arrested and forced to work on the roads, from which they had previously been exempt. To punctuate his threat, he arrested ten boatmen. In the ensuing months he spoke of the 'delicate relations' with the boatmen. Another dispute flared up in December 1911, as canoemen refused to take loads to Ouidah for Cyprien Fabre because it was too late in the day. The administrator rejected Fabre's complaint, but warned the boatmen that they should obey their chiefs and employers. The complaints by commercial houses of thefts by their employees continued, as did the judicial proceedings, but in a lower key.

STATE-INITIATED CONFLICTS

The state, though alien in origin and in its loyalties, participated as a social force in the Dahomean economy. In the conflicts surveyed above, the state was drawn into disputes among other participants. Even beyond its act of conquest, however, the state was bound to initiate economic disputes itself through the policy of increasing its share of the economic surplus. While the merchants and great landowners were able to avoid a confrontation on this issue, the mass of the population could not. Lacking the resources to pay the taxes readily or to pay for substitutes in the corvées, they attempted at some times to avoid the state's requirements, and at other times they demanded that the requirements be reduced.

Customs duties were far and away the majority of taxes paid. But they were less visible than direct taxes and licenses, which is surely one of the reasons they were used so widely. The impact of customs duties was sometimes gradual: the steady increase of duties on alcoholic beverages raised the purchase price enough to drive consumers away from importing them. In the words of a French observer, 'It was not unusual to hear the owners declare that their palms would feel the duties.'[45] That is, people turned from imported alcohol to the local substitute of palm wine (and later to distilled palm wine), and they also turned to using their export revenue more for other imports, such as textiles. Sometimes, however, the impact of higher customs duties was visible and sudden. When duties on alcoholic

205

beverages went up again in 1905 the Dahomeans, though warned about it repeatedly in advance, were angry when it happened. In one village a trader was assailed by a crowd which threw his goods, valued at 1,200 francs, into the river. In the same year the French caused a great uproar in Porto-Novo when they levied an import duty on maize, which came from Lagos. A boycott was declared against all commerce on the lagoon, with King Toffa in full support. The French were able to bring the protest to an end by cutting the duty in half.[46]

The *impôt*, which rose steadily from 1900 to 1910, was the main source of popular complaints about taxation, and its collection was one of the main administrative occupations. An indication of the real cost of the *impôt* was the fact that people would move their residence to avoid it or reduce it. The amount of the *impôt* varied from *cercle* to *cercle*, being higher in the towns and on the coast. Numerous individuals and sometimes whole villages were reported to have moved from Cotonou and Ouidah *cercles* to Allada, Abomey and Mono *cercles* to avoid the *impôt*. On Dahomey's western frontier, the higher German direct tax had caused many people to move into Dahomey, and on the eastern frontier, several villages on the Nigerian side of the Okpara River were formed by people who had moved there from Savè to avoid the *impôt*.[47]

One objective of the *impôt* was to force Dahomeans more deeply into the 'cash economy' – that is, into increased export production and provision of more wage labor to government and European enterprise. This objective was achieved in the short run. In the longer run, however, it was self-defeating: the 'cash economy' properly defined – that is, the commodity exchange, mercantile and capitalist sectors – simply underwent a re-allocation among its sectors, the growth in total output was slowed, and eventually growth in the 'cash economy,' narrowly defined, was slowed as well.

The obverse side of the policy of expanding the 'cash economy' was the requirement of labor for state projects. Paid and unpaid labor, penal or recruited labor, short-term or long-term recruitment, all fit into a grand design to develop a new African work ethic whose emphasis lay firmly on process rather than on goals. In this colonial twist to the Weberian ethic it was work and not works which counted. Voluntarism was to be the essential quality of the worker; the employer would handle any necessary reflection. That personal rewards or social benefits should be negative or unfathomable was of no matter. Except, of course, for the chiefs who collected fees based on the number of their recruits.

In the rural areas, labor recruitment was divided into short-term corvées and longer-term recruitment. The main uses of corvée labor, whether it was paid or not, were for building and repairing roads, and for porterage. Road construction was a major occupation for many French administrators in southern Dahomey, and it became an obsession for some. In the Center, corvées for porterage and road work assumed special importance: the area was sparsely populated, and recruits were called up regularly. The impact of the *impôt* in this area was to force people more deeply into this sort of work. In 1905 a porter received 1.15 francs per day, and the chief who recruited him received 0.10 francs per day. The level of recruitment was staggering, if official figures are to be believed: the total number of recruits listed for Savalou and Savè sectors in 1906 was 14,181. The census report for June 1907 showed those sectors to have a population of 39,822, including 13,682 adult men.[48]

An example of the waste of human labor which was possible in these circumstances is that of the administrator of Savè who conscripted virtually the entire adult male population of the *cercle* from October 1910 to February 1911 to build a road of some 150 km leading to Parakou, at the successful conclusion of which the Governor general was able to ride triumphantly from the coast to Parakou in a motorcar, on his way to the Niger. Little wonder that when army recruiters came to Savè in March of 1912 they found that nobody wanted to join.[49]

The most famous road-builder in southern Dahomey was Antoine Rouhaud. An insight into his approach may be gleaned from the fact that when he took charge of Savalou *cercle* in April 1907, after the departure of the administrator who had recruited the 14,181 men listed above, he denounced his predecessor as weak, saying that the Dahomeans had gained the upper hand. He made his name, however, during his posting at Grand Popo from May 1908 through March 1911. It was during this time that he built his reputation as 'the man of the Grand Popo–Lokossa road.'[50]

His work in Grand Popo began with no more than the usual arguments between the colonizer and the colonized. Rouhaud complained that the chiefs would not command the people, and that they would not bring in the *impôt*. He would tell the population to get to work, and they would reply that they were not slaves. Then he would conclude that the only way to settle the issue was to bring in the police. He expressed great satisfaction that the governor, in his passage through Grand Popo in October 1909, had made public statements of support for Rouhaud, for the chiefs were forced to accept them.

Construction of the road from Grand Popo to Lokossa began in April of 1910. It was a difficult road, having to cross many marshes and streams. By the time of Rouhaud's departure in March 1911, the whole *cercle* was in rebellion. Rouhaud had concealed a great deal from his superiors but, bit by bit, the elements of the story came out.

Rouhaud had envisioned a technically superb road, which would withstand the elements and satisfy any possible needs of commerce and administration. Difficulties arose to compound the paucity of resources at his disposal, but he adamantly held out for completion of the road as planned. He became obsessed with it, and began subordinating all his other activities and, indeed, all activities in the *cercle* to the completion of the road. An exceptionally large flood of the Mono in August 1910 washed out some of the bridges: Rouhaud's spirits were only temporarily dampened, and he took courage from the survival of most of the road to push his workers ahead.

Each *cercle* received a certain amount of credits for road construction, to be used for materials and labor. When Rouhaud ran out of credits for the road, he began dipping into other sources of funds in order to continue the work. Thus it was found, after Rouhaud's departure, that the lagoon canoemen in government employ, who had previously received 3 francs plus subsistence to go from Grand Popo to Segbohoué, had been reduced to 1.50 francs, while the commercial houses paid 3.75 francs for the trip. No official decision could be found reducing the rate. Meanwhile, Rouhaud had piously complained in his reports for months of the shortage of labor, especially in canoemen. Similarly, the men who operated canoes on the Mono had the same complaints. At the same time, a running dispute broke out between the surf-boat crews and the French and German merchant houses in Grand Popo. One is tempted to suggest that Rouhaud may have worked out some sort of deal where the merchants cut wages to boatmen and gave the difference to Rouhaud. In any case, the disputes lasted until the end of 1911.[51]

Another source of money for the road was to increase collection of the *impôt* by overestimating the population: Rouhaud's population report for 1910 showed a sharp increase over 1909. He also kept for the road the rebate on the *impôt* collected which was supposed to go to the chiefs. Beyond the collection of more money, Rouhaud simply collected more labor. He inflicted disciplinary penalties on so many people for real or imagined infractions, that people fled to the bush on seeing an administrator. Beyond prison labor, Rouhaud extracted large amounts of corvée labor. He left a lasting impression on many farmers by forcing them to do road work at the peak agricultural season.

In March of 1911, Rouhaud took a final tour of the *cercle* before his reassignment, taking his replacement along to show him his two favorite projects, the road and the Houéyogbé market. He admonished his successor that the road would take heavy maintenance for the next two years, that the earthwork would have to be shored up, and that more credits would be needed to build bridges. He recommended that all road credits for the *cercle* be used for the Grand Popo–Lokossa road.

Grand Popo *cercle* remained in turmoil for all of 1911, and administrator Maria noted in May 1912 that Governor Merwart specifically urged him to re-establish calm and let the people rest. Rouhaud, meanwhile, was assigned to Savalou *cercle* in June 1912, where another opportunity for road-building turned up. In a border protocol, the French had agreed to move the frontier eastward so that the town of Kambolé would be turned over to the Germans. Rouhaud's job was to improve the road from Savalou to Bassila along the new frontier, and to build an automobile road from Savalou to Dassa-Zoumé. The governor hoped to prevent him from repeating the Grand Popo situation by giving him restricted projects and limited funds.

Rouhaud, of course, was equal to the challenge, and he recruited 3,000 workers to do 74 km of road with 5,000 francs. He violated orders and refused to stop when he ran out of money. The workers deserted, and Rouhaud called for energetic measures against them. The governor refused, and instead sent an additional 2,000 francs to be paid to the workers. He wrote to the governor general, and though remarking how impressed the engineer was with Rouhaud's road, asked that Rouhaud be transferred to another colony.[52]

The recruitment of labor differed from corvées to the extent that the recruits were sent away from home for extended periods of time ranging from weeks on up, and they were almost always paid wages of some sort. Recruitment was especially important for such major projects as railroad-building. Construction of the northern section of the Porto-Novo railway, from Sakété to Pobè, brought out widespread opposition to recruitment policy. In Zagnanado *cercle*, for instance, a major recruitment drive began in November 1910 and continued to mid-1911. On good months the administrator was able to get over 600 workers, mostly for two-month contracts. In order to get recruits, administrator Bertheux had to deal with arguments that Sakété was too far, that the work was too hard, that the previous workers who had gone there had not returned, and that people died while working there. Bertheux's main response was to arrest and fine leading figures in Bonou *canton* and other areas, which had a 'salutary effect' in producing recruits. As he prepared to do the same in Kétou, tensions erupted into the 'one-gun-shot war.' There the king had gone blind, the pro-French *sous-chef* Abimbola had set himself up as the partisan of recruitment, and the opposition to his efforts led to the assassination of an interpreter in April 1911. The French arrested the assassin, placed an administrative post in Kétou, appointed as *chef de canton* the king's senior wife, Ida Alaba, moved the marketplace from outside the town to a point within the town walls, and resumed recruitment. The end of the smallpox outbreak in the rail yards also made it easier to recruit.[53]

Recruitment of workers for Sakété was hardly more popular in Abomey, but the chiefs still sent men to work. The administrator began to feel as if revolt were in the air: 'Is there a need for workers? – Abomey. A corvée? – Abomey. Increase of any kind of taxes: – Abomey is never forgotten! If police or soldiers are needed, it's always Abomey.'[54] Abomey provided, he argued, as many men as all the other *cercles* of southern Dahomey together. It had long been that way but, he felt, French errors and excesses threatened to ruin this precious workforce.

TOWARD A SOCIAL CONTRACT?

French colonial rule perpetuated into the twentieth century some unresolved political issues of earlier years. Conquest and disfranchisement had long been in the heritage of France's Dahomean subjects: for the Fon the shoe was now on the other foot, while for such refugee peoples as the Holli and Dasha, the colonial period brought the replacement of one set of exploiters with another. The French came to Porto-Novo in 1883 as guarantors of independence, but within a decade they ruled the Fon kingdom by right of conquest. In the conflict between the two ideals the latter won handily and, by 1900, it had been extended as the theoretical basis for French rule throughout colonial Dahomey. Opposition in principle to the legitimacy of rule by conquest was not at first the dominant belief among the new colonial subjects, though it was later to become so.

In other respects, however, the political theory of French colonialism clashed immediately with the political experience of Dahomeans. The state was responsible to France, to Dakar, and perhaps to the abstract principle of 'civilization,' but not to its subjects in Dahomey. All loyalties were to be focused toward the top, and there was little room for shifting alliances. Policy was to be carried out, at times, in the interest of the colonial subjects, but these subjects had no power in determining whether their own interest was being served. Councils existed only at the higher levels and were only consultative, not legislative. Government functioned by fiat: decrees, orders and executive actions spilled forth from the capitals and the administrative posts.

Precolonial government had been monarchical, with executive power ranging from the formidable in Abomey to the very weak at the other pole. But councils functioned at every level, with power of approval over legislation and often with power to initiate legislation. Government was not formally democratic but it was often representative, and the state was

210

responsible to a constituency within its frontiers. Politics functioned through a system of factions and countervailing interests: the faction currently out of power remained as a check on those in power, and could hope to gain power in the future.

In a continuation of their old beliefs, and then in an evolution of beliefs as they attempted to grapple with the French system, groups of Dahomeans attempted to establish what may be labelled as a social contract with the French – an informal agreement as to the rights and responsibilities of themselves and of the state. The French resisted the notion of such a contract, but Dahomeans in several different arenas pressed their case. The French, in succession, refused to negotiate openly, held out for very restrictive terms, and ultimately treated the results more as a truce than as a contract.[55] But in fact they did accommodate to pressures from Dahomeans. For Dahomeans to pressure the French into taking the next step, however, proved impossible: the state simply would not make any positive alliances with any elements of Dahomean society. The illustrations which follow highlight three arenas of the Dahomean search for a social contract: the role of the church, the press, and the position of chiefs in the political structure.

In 1861 the Société des Missions africaines de Lyon established the Catholic Church permanently in the Bight of Benin. Father Borghero and his colleagues learned immediately, however, that their function would be less to proselytize than to service the existing Brazilian Catholic community of several thousand, which had been struggling along with chapels, an occasional visit of a priest from São Thomé, and tiny schools in their homes. The Catholic Church and the Brazilian community became largely coterminous, and the former grew mostly as the latter grew through immigration from Brazil and intermarriage in West Africa. The family schools were replaced during the 1860s with mission schools, in which the Brazilians required Portuguese as the language of instruction, although French was taught as a second language along the entire coast, and English was taught in Lagos.[56]

Most of the missionaries were French, and they worked closely with French officials, but two factors served to cause tension between church and state: the anti-clerical tradition of French public service, and the close identification of the church with the Brazilian community. Once France had conquered Dahomey, the state insisted that French become the language of instruction; the Brazilians acquiesced, but only after a stiff fight. The state's attempt to establish a competing set of lay schools in the 1890s failed for want of funds, thus enabling the church to extend its mission into the interior, along with the Brazilians and at the same time beyond them: to Zagnanado in 1895, Kétou in 1897, Abomey-Calavi in

1898, Athiémé in 1899, and Abomey in 1902. After AOF set up its education service in 1903, Dahomey was the only colony in which the missions not only maintained their schools but expanded them. This special status of the church was achieved because the Brazilians and other Catholics defended the mission schools as their own, and because of the active campaign in behalf of the schools by Mgr Steinmetz, Superior at Ouidah, and Fr Francis Aupiais, head of the mission school in Porto-Novo from 1904. The state abandoned its attempt at exclusive control of education, but in 1914 required that church schools follow the same curriculum as the state schools.[57] The church retained this ambiguous role throughout the colonial era: the priests taught loyalty to France and assimilation to Western culture, yet they were leaders in preserving and reconstructing the heritage of precolonial Dahomey. They and the church provided an alternative way of dealing with the problems of the twentieth-century world, without leading their communicants into opposition to the state. For those who were Catholic, therefore, the church became an intermediary in the maintenance of a social contract.

The beginnings of a press in Dahomey provided another means by which Dahomeans could seek to make contact with the state or gain redress from it. The first private newspaper, *L'Echo du Dahomey*, was published from 1905 to 1907 by L. Cressent, a French employee of a small merchant firm in Porto-Novo. Its primary purpose was to criticize the policies of Governor Liotard from the viewpoint of small French merchants: the paper opposed the construction of the railroad, opposed construction of a railroad from Porto-Novo to Cotonou, called for extension of a network of roads, and demanded formation of a chamber of commerce. The newspaper also opposed the extension of state schools, thus putting it in tandem with the church, and called for restrictions on the police. On the other hand, it attempted to change the minds of those Dahomeans who were seeking French citizenship.

Dahomean writers had access to *L'Echo*, and in 1906 Pedro d'Almeida used it to make a set of accusations against Bada, the Yoruba chief of the Fon *canton* of Abomey-Calavi, dealing with his collection of the *impôt* and his judgments in land disputes. The effect was two-fold: this form of attack did put pressure on the French to make some changes (in this case they assigned a European to the post at Abomey-Calavi, but left Bada in office); but it also stiffened the determination of the French to protect Bada no matter how many disputes he got into.[58]

Dahomeans rapidly found that it was advisable to declare their loyalty to France as a preliminary to any serious discussion. Whether they were demanding redress of grievances, as with Pedro d'Almeida's complaints, or requesting an advancement in status such as admission to French citizenship, Dahomeans preceded and surrounded the substance of their discourse with protestations of loyalty and, if possible, examples of past actions demonstrating devotion to France. Within weeks of the outbreak of World War I, for instance, a great demonstration of fealty had been arranged, in which 210 leading Dahomeans published their names in the *Journal officiel*, urging France on to victory and listing the amount of their cash contributions to that cause.[59] Declarations of loyalty to France came from rural areas as well as towns (excepting those areas in revolt or on the verge of revolt). Such declarations, while necessary for dealings with the state, were not sufficient: the French believed only those they wished. In one sense these protestations were sheer flattery and opportunism. In another sense they were a statement of fact: the future of these colonial subjects and citizens was tied to that of France, and advance lay through the French system. In a third sense, given the power of the repetition of words, they were heartfelt expressions of principle, though this last aspect has been overemphasized by subsequent scholars.[60]

The conflicts of the colonial situation put a continuing strain on those called upon to act as intermediaries between the state and the mass of the rural population: the chiefs. The term 'chief' carried a variety of meanings in early colonial Dahomey. The French sometimes applied it to any leading figure from the head of a small family to a chief of state, so the meaning of the term in many documents is ambiguous. Most often, however, it had the specific meaning of a person serving at the lowest level of French administration, having responsibility for collecting taxes and passing out orders, and receiving fees for doing so. In this sense, the term could be contrasted with the term *notable*, which was applied to major figures who were outside the employ of the French. The chiefs, then, had standing among the French, and the *notables* had standing among the Dahomeans. It was difficult for a single person to have both.

In Ouidah the administrator complained that the chiefs, most of whom were ex-slaves, had little power among the Dahomeans, and were simply agents of the French. For example Tao, chief of Tové quarter, had been a slave of the Santos family, and he took the position of chief only when his former masters agreed to it. Echoing this view was the administrator of Porto-Novo, who said that the area had two sets of chiefs: 'the Tônon, chief of the land, and the Yovogan, the white man's chief.' The latter had no authority except with whites. To get any action, the administration would have to know both chiefs and get them to agree to the action.[61]

The French, if they did not consciously intend to create such a situation, in practice did everything possible to create it, by exerting a steady set of pressures on the chiefs. They were to be loyal to the French, to recruit workers and collect taxes, and to build a disciplined workforce. They were

213

to enrich themselves, especially through fees from taxes collected and recruitment, but they were not to become too independently wealthy, nor were they to cause revolts from overly severe exactions. Finally, they were to maintain authority and the respect of the people they governed. That this included many contradictions was obvious, but the French continued to insist on it.

The Dahomeans, for their part, seem to have had a fairly strong, if not well articulated, concept of the functions and the limits of government and of the economic order. The government had to be, in some sense, responsible to the people it ruled. It was expected that taxes and labor would be required of them, it was expected that chiefs would enrich themselves, and even that there would be a certain amount of abuse of power of the state. But there was a limit to these exactions, and the state had the obligation of recognizing the limit by regularly demonstrating its ties to the people.

The chiefs, needless to say, were always in a delicate position, and the people were usually in the delicate position of deciding how much to work through the chiefs, and how much to resist and oppose them. When chiefs got out of hand, their constituents made moves to change their policy or to replace them. In 1905 the *notables* of Djalloukou made a series of accusations against their chief: he had collected the *impôt* in order to get the rebates, he had kept half the price of the cotton field, he had made extra money on the road by keeping the wages to be paid to certain workers, and he had sent men to work on the railroad for a fee. The administrator in Savalou, on learning of these accusations, sent for the *notables*, but they said they were sick. He then sent police to bring them in, but they came before the police did. Administrator Dusser gave the *notables* a point-by-point response: the *impôt* was required by the administration, not by the chiefs; the *impôt* was minimal and was paid by villages poorer than they; they had grown seven cotton fields of one hectare for 62.5 francs per hectare, which was the going price, while in Savalou the cotton fields earned 125 francs for fields of double that size; he had asked the governor for a credit to indemnify Djalloukou for furnishing the extra workers for the road; and the administration had asked the chief to send workers for the railroad so they could earn money, but he now found he had more men than he needed, and they could stay home.[62] In other words, according to Dusser, the *notables* had their facts straight but their interpretation wrong. Nonetheless, the *notables* had gained two concessions: an additional 25 francs, and freedom from railroad work for the moment.

Administrator Samson in Savè found himself faced in March 1914 with a crowd of sixty people who had come to demand the replacement of chief Adido. The petitioners must have been very secure in their conviction, for

214

they expressed it quite frankly to Samson: Adido was wrong to furnish the number of porters requested by the administration, since he could easily have satisfied the administration with a smaller number. Samson exploded with fury: 'Faced with such infantile pretensions, expressed in the most violent tone, we immediately proceeded to arrest the four most fiery orators, including three blindmen.' Recovering his composure, Samson then asked Adido to start a movement asking for the pardon of the imprisoned blind orators. Adido did as he was told, and Samson released the prisoners, announcing that he had given clemency mainly because of Adido's intervention.[63]

Occasionally movements to remove chiefs were successful. One such case, that of Aholoupé in Sagon, also illustrates some of the ambiguities of the position of chief. Before the railroad, the chief commercial route from the Abomey plateau to the coast was through the Ouémé, and Sagon was the terminal point for canoes at high water. Aholoupé, as chief of Sagon, had furnished the canoemen, porters, and hammock-bearers in large numbers, and had collected large sums as his portion of their fees. With the construction of the railroad, he lost all that. In fact, the administrator chided him for refusing to send any men to work on the railroad and collecting his fee, but the refusal was understandable. Aholoupé and his sub-chief Ahijadé thus became poor, and attempted to maintain themselves at their former level at the expense of the people of Sagon. When the village chiefs and the general population protested, the administration allowed complaints to be filed, and the two chiefs were replaced.[64]

When chiefs served their constituents well, on the other hand, the people protected them. In Grand Popo under the regime of Rouhaud, the administration complained bitterly that the chiefs were too closely tied to the people, and would not force them to work. The people agreed, and said that it would take 'foreign chiefs' to get them to work for the French. In order to help the chiefs pay the fines levied against them by the administration, the people set up *tontines*, in which everyone made a contribution for the common cause. The chiefs, therefore, were put in the position of acting as a buffer for people against the administration. It was they who were to lead in asking the administration to justify its position on such matters as taxation and recruitment in the hope of gaining some concessions but, failing that, at least to require the administrator to state openly what he was doing. The administrators, for their part, generally took these arguments seriously. In Savè, for instance:

In various palavers I worked to demonstrate to the chiefs and to the natives that the *impôt* was an insignificant cost by reason of the guarantees of peace and tranquillity they enjoyed because of our

215

presence and our administration. I made them understand the necessity of a tax to pay all the administrative personnel of the *cercle*, and to perform such public works as roads, wells, etc.[65]

These arguments over the uses and the justice of the *impôt* and of other taxes tended to take place shortly after the arrival of a new administrator. Chiefs and *notables* naturally sought to gain the best possible terms from the new man. The very month that administrator Duboscq arrived in Zagnanado, for instance, he was visited by a delegation of chiefs from Adja-Ouéré. This area had been resisting the influence of the French, in particular by resisting the building of roads and by paying as little *impôt* as they dared. Their neighbors the Holli were even more intransigent when it came to recognizing French authority, and they usually refused to talk to the French. Duboscq began the discussion with the Adja-Ouéré chiefs cautiously and solicitously by asking about their health and their fields. Then he moved on to discuss the benefits of vaccination, of maintenance of old roads and creation of new roads – and finally the necessity of helping build the railroad from Sakété on to Pobè. In response to the question which was clearly implied by their silence, he told them that the *impôt* was used partly for works such as roads and bridges aimed at increasing the wealth of the country, and partly for police which guaranteed the security of the inhabitants. He promised to visit their villages and do what he could to improve their welfare. As they left, the chiefs thanked him for his 'good words.'[66]

One may deduce what the chiefs must have thought of these 'good words': in 1914 the Holli staged a major revolt against the French, and they were aided by the Adja-Ouéré. The revolt was provoked by the police, and by an administrator overzealous for complete submission. The revolt was put down by the police who caused it. The roads and railroads, built by Dahomeans, provided the lines of supply necessary to suppress the revolt. The people thus paid for their own subjugation, not only through the fines they paid after the revolt, but also in advance of the revolt through the *impôt* and through labor recruitment.

9

The mechanism of accumulation

To a first approximation, the economy of southern Dahomey did not change in the early colonial years: the methods of production, the types and quantities of goods produced and consumed, and the economic organization of society all remained much the same on the eve of World War I as they had been on the eve of the French conquest. Descriptions of the economy are remarkably similar from the beginning of this period to the end.[1]

To a second approximation, such change as took place consisted mostly of fluctuation and redistribution of output and wealth. Most basic were the fluctuations caused by weather, disease, and conditions in local and world markets; then came the redistribution resulting from the fortunes of inheritance and marriage, and from the uneven quality of decisions on production and investment. The most spectacular redistribution of wealth and resources resulted from the colonial conquest: as the old states were destroyed or subordinated to the new, the privileges held by royalty and its allies were voided, and could only be reaffirmed through ties to the French state. As a result there occurred a partial replacement of one economic elite with another, with European merchants, for example, gaining a new advantage over Dahomeans.

Only at the level of a third approximation does the significance of net change become apparent, for it was relatively small in magnitude and difficult to distinguish unambiguously from short-term fluctuations. But in the early colonial years export volume grew by an average of over 2.5% per year, imports of major consumer goods rose at 3.5% per year, and population grew by an average 1.5% per year. The dominant commodity exchange sector and the economy as a whole grew by roughly 2.5% per year, and per capita gross domestic product grew by as much as 30% from 1890 to 1914. The state, the public capitalist and private capitalist sectors

217

grew even more rapidly than the commodity exchange sector, partly through the diversion of its resources, and also at the expense of the declining mercantile sector and the collapsing slave-labor and slave-catching sectors.

The distillation of net change and transformation out of the fluctuations, cycles and turmoil of a brief period provides the essential link between economic history of the short term and that of the long term. In what follows, analysis of the mechanism of accumulation and the rate of economic growth first yields the results just cited for early colonial Dahomey; then the principles of the analysis, developed for these relatively well documented years, are then applied to the issues of growth and accumulation for the full recorded history of the Bight of Benin. The analysis may be summarized in four steps, through the establishment of: (1) the basic sources of economic growth, (2) the main causes of accumulation of wealth and productive power by forces other than the producers, (3) changes in the modes of production resulting from the process of accumulation, and (4) the estimated rate of net economic growth, after accounting for the preceding factors.

The most basic sources of economic growth from 1890 to 1914 were population growth and private domestic investment in agriculture. Population growth allowed for extensive economic growth in a region which, while densely populated, was not overcrowded at existing levels of resources and technology. Investment in agriculture led to both extensive and intensive growth, particularly through clearing fields and planting trees, but also through investment in packaging materials, and in facilities for processing and storage. Other basic contributions to economic growth, though of lesser magnitude, came from local and imported technical change, from changing market opportunities, from private investment in fishing, manufactures, commerce and transport, and from domestic public investment in transport and communications.

Accumulation of wealth and productive capacity proceeded through several mechanisms.[2] Two were of particular importance: accumulation of land by a landowning class, and accumulation of tax revenue and power over labor by the state. Of measurable but lesser importance were the accumulation of profits by capitalist merchants, and the relative growth in wealth of holders of sterling and then of franc currency. These processes of accumulation tended on one side to suppress growth by withdrawing resources from the producers and final consumers, yet they served on another side to create new and different growth, modifying the overall social organization of production by transforming, expanding and restricting the various modes of production.

The state, by an act of conquest, abolished the slave-catching system and

218

caused a rapid elimination of the slave-labor mode of production. In so doing it displaced thousands of people and brought about an equivalent expansion of the commodity exchange and familial modes of production. Through accumulation of tax revenue and forced labor, the state was able to expand the scope of government and to establish a new public capitalist sector. The commodity exchange sector, while expanding both because of investment and the decline of slavery, experienced considerable turmoil in the fierce contest for land holdings. The private capitalist sector continued to grow, gradually displacing the mercantile sector, and drawing capital in part from expatriate merchants, in part from the fortunes of Dahomean landowners, and in part from the commercial earnings of both. Finally, the devaluation and displacement of cowries and then sterling by francs gave an advantage to the state and capitalist sectors where holdings of sterling and then francs were concentrated.

These judgments, beginning with that on population growth, are reviewed in the passages below in order to provide support for the conclusion on the rate of net economic growth. Population growth, the most basic source of economic growth, lay between one percent and two percent annually, according to estimates derived from French *impôt* records. While by no means a census, the tax collections were based on estimates of 'adult' populations (usually those over ten or even eight years of age) established at the village level.[3] These records may be expected to overestimate the rate of population growth, in that taxpayers might succeed in hiding their true numbers from government for a while, and also in that zealous tax collectors might choose to overestimate the rate of growth. On the other hand, since in a situation of accelerating growth the most rapid growth occurs at the youngest ages, leaving out young children gives a downward bias to the figures. Assuming a constant level of output per capita, this change in population led to an equivalent change in output. This assumption, of course, is modified in practice because of uneven age composition and uneven allocation of additional labor among various modes of production and economic activities. Nonetheless, this growth of population was a fundamental factor whose influence was felt regardless of the impact of other factors of growth.

The commodity exchange mode of production experienced both aggregate and per capita growth. Beyond the growth in population and the diversion of ex-slaves into this sector, the main reason for growth was producer investment: the most spectacular such activity was the clearing of land for maize in the years 1905–9. Other examples of investment were purchase of packing materials, clearing roads and waterways, digging wells and cisterns, residential construction, and planting of trees. Market opportunities led to increased domestic trade in yams, maize and makari,

219

greater exports of fish, livestock and kola to Lagos, and brief booms in exports of rubber and peanuts. Technical change encouraged some growth: imported kerosene, matches and sewing machines increased domestic efficiency. Small-scale technical advances in African production, as in fishing and farming, have been underrated in general, and have perhaps contributed significantly to domestic economic growth.[4] A more artificial growth in the commodity exchange sector came as taxes and forced labor caused people to reduce their degree of self-sufficiency and increase their dependence on the market.

Accumulation in the commodity exchange sector included several countervailing trends. The destruction of the Fon kingdom and the demise of the slave-labor sector meant the disaggregation of land holdings in the mid-1890s. But by accommodating to the transformation of slavery into peonage, ex-slaveholders maintained control over the land, or, failing that, required contributions of produce and labor from the ex-slaves. After 1900 leading Fon families, of which the Quenums and Adjovis are best documented, began expanding their lands. Similar expansion of land holdings took place to the east of the Ouémé, where occasional bad years served to accelerate the concentration of land holdings. Officials of the French state also acquired lands in the course of their service.[5] By 1914, while the largest holdings no longer reached the magnitude of Fon state lands in 1890, a greater total amount of land was now in large holdings. Whether these large farms operated at greater technical efficiency than small farms is doubtful, but they were probably more remunerative to their owners because of a more intensive exploitation of their work force. Currency had a mixed effect: producers holding stocks of cowries suffered losses through devaluation in comparison to those whose currency holdings were in sterling and francs. Meanwhile, the state accumulated large amounts of tax revenue and forced labor at the expense of the commodity exchange sector.

The familial mode of production grew in the aggregate, but remained little changed in per capita terms. Ex-slaves, while they participated in production for the market, also gave emphasis to self-sufficiency; this factor, along with population growth and producer investment, brought the growth of the familial sector. At the same time, this sector underwent contractive influences: both forced labor and the taxation system acted to force people away from self-sufficiency into additional cash earnings, and acted to divide the family chief from others, thus tending to reduce the amount of group labor. Occasional droughts had contradictory effects: lacking cash, families emphasized self-sufficiency, but as their crops failed they turned to cash purchases.

The mercantile sector contracted in both aggregate and per capita terms. While the growth in population and commerce tended to expand the mercantile system, these factors were counteracted by the growth of capitalist commerce and transport, particularly in the coastal regions and along the railways, where the new methods reduced both the volume and the profitability of the old.[6] The devaluation of cowrie currency and displacement of sterling faced the mercantile system with a loss, while labor for porterage became scarce and expensive with the end to slave labor and the extensive recruitment of porters by the state. As with other sectors, the state accumulated tax revenues and forced labor. But the mercantile sector, though doomed to extinction, remained resilient. Investment continued in canoes, roads, and stocks of goods. The caravans survived, if in diminished magnitude, by adapting their activities to the railroad. New market opportunities occasionally arose, as with the livestock trade to the major towns. And even in transport, where capitalist methods made such advances, the canoe transport system of the lagoons enjoyed a remarkable flowering before it was constricted in the interwar years by rail and automobile transport.

Private capitalist transport, commerce and production benefitted from the rising volume of commerce, from technical advances embodied in investment, and from increasing technical and political advantages over the mercantile sector. Steam shipping completed its displacement of sail, with the Woermann Line growing to dominate Atlantic shipping. French foreign private investment contributed to the Cotonou pier and railroad, but the investors received a handsome return only through the rapid nationalization of these facilities. Most domestic and foreign capitalist investment was in commerce, for the construction of boutiques and warehouses, and for creating stocks of merchandise. Here a fierce competition reigned: German firms, already dominant, and British firms tended to grow at the expense of the French, and the expansion of Dahomean firms was largely restricted to small-scale operations. Changes in the money system provided a marginal advantage for capitalist merchants, who avoided the losses from devaluation of large stocks of cowries. Capitalist firms also benefitted from state pressures to keep wage low, and from the redirection of commerce toward the railroad lines; on the other hand, they too had to pay taxes, and expatriate firms and employees remitted profits and salaries to Europe.

The public capitalist sector was entirely new, created by the actions of the French colonial government. At first it restricted itself to the telegraph and construction of government buildings. Then, as the lack of private capital for infrastructure became evident, the public capitalist sector expanded sharply, to include the railroads, the pier, public utilities, and a wider range of urban construction. The sector grew to include expensive French supervisors, several hundred permanent Dahomean workers, and thousands of temporary construction workers, recruited through compulsion and taxation. Investment funds for the rapid expansion of this sector came from current tax revenue and forced labor, both drawn in the majority from the commodity exchange sector.

The state as an instrument of government, as distinguished from state production of goods and services, also grew in the early colonial years. With the destruction of the Fon kingdom and the weakening of other kingdoms, crowds of retainers were dispersed and the number of people supported by the state declined for a time, but in subsequent years the French state added a growing number of employees to its payroll. The state accumulated land by declaring a right of eminent domain, but far more significant was its accumulation of tax revenue through customs duties, the *impôt*, and other taxes, and its requisitioning of labor for porterage and for road work. The state altered the social organization of production by crushing slave trade, by restricting slave labor, and by favoring growth of the private and public capitalist sectors at the expense of the mercantile sector. For the commodity exchange sector, the state enforced the peace, provided public works, and provided some measures for public health and agriculture, but these were insufficient to justify the level of taxation. With the passage of time, however, these redistributive effects of the state came to be dwarfed by its action to drain the economy: the remittances of salaries to France, and especially the uncompensated remittance of tax revenues to Dakar after 1905.

The net rate of economic growth in the early colonial years was roughly 2.5% per years. This figure is chosen because it is the same as the rate of growth of exports in the same period, but additional factors suggest that the choice is realistic.[7] Population was growing at roughly 1.5% annually, and the market opportunities and technical advances of the era make it likely that per capita income grew as well: these figures suggest that per capita income grew by nearly 30% from 1890 to 1914. Exports accounted for some 15% of gross domestic product, and accounted for a larger proportion of the commodity exchange sector. Further, domestic elements of the commodity exchange sector grew at a similar pace: fishing, yams and kola production, for example. Imports of major consumer goods grew even more rapidly, at an annual 3.5%. In comparison with the commodity exchange sector, some elements of the economy grew more rapidly (e.g., the capitalist sector and the state), while others contracted (the mercantile and slave-labor sectors). The sum total of these considerations is to render a growth rate of 2.5% plausible.

This growth rate was most fundamentally conditioned by domestic and international economic factors. But it was modified by colonial state action, especially in two areas: the abolition of slavery and the export of tax

222

revenue. The effect of the first was positive, but the negative effect of the second was even greater. In the initial turmoil of conquest and liberation of slaves, the level of domestic output declined. In the longer run, however, the commodity exchange mode of production led to greater economic growth than the slave-labor mode of production. The latter was doubtless profitable to slave owners, as they squeezed their slaves for extra hours of work and kept their rations at a minimum.[8] But a system of slave villages meant escapes, raids, counter-raids, repeated thwarting of any long-term agricultural plans, and the under-utilization of good lands where farmers were easy targets for raids: those outside Danhomè suffered more from such insecurity than inhabitants of the kingdom. Even beyond this military aspect, slavery led to unsettled family life and uneven sex ratios which lowered the rate of population growth. The end to these conditions under French rule led, therefore, to a relative increase in economic growth.

The most sharply negative aspects of French fiscal policy did not take effect until the practical establishment of AOF in 1905. In the years up to 1905, taxes rose sharply but were largely spent inside the colony, and state action led to a modest export of revenue averaging 0.2% per year of GDP (or 1.3% of export values), mostly through remittances of salaries to France. But from 1906 to 1914, the export of revenue to Dakar averaged 3.3% of GDP (or 22% of export values). For a maximal estimate of the impact of this policy, one may assume that the export of revenue reduced current GDP by the amount of the revenue exported: then, compounding the difference between actual and potential GDP, one would estimate that Dahomey's 1914 GDP was only 70% of what it would have been if tax revenues had not been exported.[9] At the other extreme, if one assumed the level of investment and output to be unaffected by current income, then the reduced level of income after revenue exports would have caused no reduction in economic growth. More plausibly, if current investment were determined in part by current income and by expected future income, the decrease in each of these resulting from the export of tax revenues would have caused a decline in investment and in future output. A variety of calculations can be proposed, but in short one must conclude that the level of GDP in 1914 would have been from 5% to 40% higher if the state had not exported tax revenues.[10]

GROWTH OVER FOUR CENTURIES

Many of the forces leading to economic growth in the early colonial years had been present for centuries. In the 'mythic era,' before the slave trade, the commodity exchange sector was in place and expanding through producer investment and population growth. Yam cultivation had led to a dense population, states, and a mercantile system by the end of the fifteenth century. Occasional contact with Europeans in the next two centuries added somewhat to the rate of growth, as new American and Asian crops were adopted, opportunities arose for agricultural exports, and imports of cowrie currency grew.[11] By the late seventeenth century, the process of accumulation had generated a level of per capita output somewhere between one-fourth and one-half that of England.[12]

Even during the 'era of slave exports,' wherever and whenever a region escaped the corrosive effects of slave raiding, the commodity exchange sector resumed its growth. The slave trade itself provided a great market opportunity – that is, as soon as leading interests in the Bight of Benin were willing to treat it as such and accept the social consequences. From that point, a transformation took place as slave merchants accumulated wealth and as states grew to protect and direct the collection and marketing of slaves. Wealth was not simply concentrated in this process, it was destroyed in the course of war, and it was repeatedly redistributed with the changing fortunes of war. The export of slaves reduced population growth, and led to absolute depopulation among the Aja peoples from the late seventeenth to the mid-eighteenth centuries, among certain of the Voltaic peoples in the eighteenth century, and among some of the Yoruba peoples in the nineteenth century. The imports of goods and money in exchange for slaves led to an expansion of market exchange and to a reorientation of commerce toward the Atlantic, but the rate of economic growth may have been slowed by the heavy reliance on imports.

Despite the destruction wrought by the slave trade, the economy of Dahomey in 1860 showed growth in comparison with that of 1640. The population had rebuilt itself, agriculture and manufactures had expanded. At the same time, the region had undergone great redistribution in wealth and in the composition and location of its population. While Britain had grown rapidly, per capita income in Dahomey had grown little if at all during the slave trade, and by the mid-nineteenth century it was no more than one-sixth that of Britain.

The end to slave exports brought a greater rate of population growth, but the concomitant expansion of the slave-labor sector led to continued displacement of people and restrictions on the growth of population. As the 'era of agricultural exports' opened, accumulation came to be centered on increased holdings of land and slaves and on profits from agricultural output, rather than on profit from slave exports. The mercantile sector underwent a significant transformation, as it moved to export of agricultural produce from the coast, increased West African trade in foodstuffs and manufactures, and continued slave trade in support of each: this transformation was hardly complete when the mercantile sector found itself facing a challenge from capitalist transport and commerce. The domestic market grew along with growing population, continued producer investment, and perhaps technical advances. These in themselves provided market opportunities in addition to the opportunity provided by European demand for palm products. The economic conditions of the time served to strengthen the commodity exchange sector and the small states, while political conditions strengthened the slave-labor sector and the large states. The net result was rapid economic growth during the last half of the nineteenth century: during these years per capita output in Dahomey grew at a rate similar to that of Britain, and remained at a level one-sixth that of Britain, or roughly equal to per capita output in Mexico and Brazil. French conquest brought about the repression of the slave-labor sector, but the other processes of economic change continued much as before, only now under a more extractive state.

Expansion of the capitalist mode of production continued under colonial rule, and led to some increased efficiency, but in the public sector capitalist methods were imposed by the state in a manner detrimental to economic growth. Even in the years to come, when the capitalist mode of production would replace the commodity exchange mode as the leading force in the economy, the economy would retain a clear and strong continuity with previous eras. Ironically, however, it was with the opening of the 'capitalist era' that growth slowed again, and by the mid-twentieth century per capita income in Dahomey was less than one-tenth that of Britain.

THE SEARCH FOR RELEVANT COUNTERFACTUALS

When Archibald Dalzel wrote in 1793 that slaves sent from Ouidah across the Atlantic were fortunate in comparison to their families who remained in Africa, he argued that life in Africa offered little hope, and that slave trade, far from worsening conditions, provided deliverance for those exported. In this case as in most other judgments, the observer's evaluation of what he saw was influenced by what he believed might have been. Later, at the beginning of the colonial era, French colonial apologists wrote confidently that money, European imports and economic growth had come to Dahomey only as a result of French colonial rule, thus implicitly assuming the domestic forces of progress to be so meager that only outside influence could end stagnation.[13] Others have questioned the inevitability of war and stagnation in Dahomey, along with the efficacy of slave trade and colonial rule as means of rescuing the region from its unhappy fate, and have even questioned the inevitability of the present-day poverty and underdevelopment of Bénin.[14] The use of explicit counterfactual comparisons, while it

225

cannot remove all elements of subjectivity from the resolution of these issues, nonetheless clarifies the evaluation of historical hypotheses and can lead to the posing of useful new hypotheses.[15] Four counterfactual situations are proposed here, two for the era of the slave trade and two for the colonial era, to complete this review of long-run developments in the economy of the Bight of Benin.

Let us imagine, first, that there had been no export of slaves across the Atlantic from the Bight of Benin. That such a possibility was not totally out of the question is indicated by the fact that some African peoples avoided participation in the export of slaves for long periods of time.[16] The level of population would certainly have grown at a greater rate in such a case: the region would have avoided the direct loss of population through slave exports, and would have avoided some of the loss of population through warfare and through displacement and domestic enslavement of its people. Slavery was present in the Bight of Benin and might have grown after the sixteenth century even without an Atlantic slave trade, but the horrendous scale of the slave trade could never have been achieved without the steady demand by Europeans which stimulated the establishment of the in-stitutions of slave trade and large-scale slavery. With a freer range for the commodity exchange sector, agricultural development would have been greater in aggregate and per capita terms. Technical change – new crops, techniques and devices – would still have reached the region as long as it maintained some commercial contacts with the Atlantic world.[17] Without the export of slaves, however, export revenue and import purchasing power would have been far lower. The region would thus have been unable to buy such large quantities of import goods and cowrie currency. With lesser quantities of imported textiles, alcoholic beverages and iron, domestic consumers would have had to pay higher prices for smaller quantities of goods. But the economy did have alternative, domestic sources of supply for these needs, and might well have benefitted in the long run if they had been more fully exploited. This West African 'infant industries' argument, a sort of retrospective import substitution, is meant to suggest that, even with shortages for consumers and relatively high-cost production of textiles, tobacco, iron and other manufactures, a greater diversification of the region's economic base in this era would have provided it with a sounder base for long-run growth. (A comparison with Kano, where relative isolation from Atlantic commerce coincided with a remarkable development of manufactures, would be relevant.) If less money had been imported, the restriction in its circulation would have reduced the extent of the market; on the other hand, the existing supply of money might have been revalued to serve a growing market. Alternatively, the region might have changed to another currency, domestically produced, and thus have avoided the cost of exporting goods to purchase money. The political development of Dahomey would have been different without the export of slaves; with fewer wars and slave raids the strongest states might not have grown as strong, but the refugee peoples would have had less need to exercise self-denial as the price of survival. All in all, I believe the counterfactual alternative of no exports of slaves would have been much to the advantage of Dahomey over the actual course of its history, not only for reasons of human decency, but also in terms of the economic growth and welfare of the region. If this view is correct, then attention is centered back on the question of how the region got drawn into the export of slaves, and whether alternative policies might have been followed to prevent the export of slaves.[18]

As a second and more extreme counterfactual, let us imagine that Dahomey had never experienced slavery. The relevance of this alternative is perhaps more difficult to accept than the previous case, because slavery existed in Dahomey before the export trade began. Yet from the perspective of the twentieth century, after the abolition of slavery, this counterfactual has a clear relevance.[19] The existence of slavery in this highly commercialized economy meant that raids were carried on to collect slaves for agricultural production as well as to accumulate women. Thus African slavery led to the displacement of population, and a resultant restriction of the growth in population and agricultural production. One might attempt to label African slavery 'progressive' if it led to some net growth and development, perhaps by accumulating resources and developing new markets and new technology. But it seems in fact that this was not the case, and that African slavery led to neither economies of scale nor technical advance.[20] It did provide wealth for the slave owners: some of these riches were compounded for long times, but others were as short-lived as the fortunes of war. The conclusion, then, is that slavery in Africa was not a forward step in its development but rather a historical dead end. Slavery existed in many other areas of the world – China is an interesting example – without gaining as dominant a role as it did in Africa.[21] Only Africa's peculiar historic situation of deep participation in slave exports led to such a great expansion of slavery on the continent, particularly in the nineteenth century. Finally, to the misfortune and humiliation of Africa, slavery and slave trade were abolished not by Africans but in large part by moralizing European conquerors who, ironically, had raised the banner of anti-slavery only a few decades earlier. This legacy, crystallized into the formula that 'Africans are not ready for self-government,' carries its debilitating effects to this day.

Turning to the colonial era, the simplest counterfactual to suggest is 'benign colonialism,' or a system of colonial rule aimed fully at developing

227

the colony's economy.[22] Let us imagine that the government had exported no tax revenue to Dakar, and that it had paid a free-market wage to all its employees, including temporary workers on roads and rail lines. The government could have used the former to pay for the latter; beyond that, it could have gone into debt to finance its development expenses. A policy of government debt rather than surplus would have worked out very well, given the inflation which was to come beginning with World War I, but the basic question is whether greater expenditure in Dahomey – public or private, on consumption or investment – would have yielded significant growth. I believe the evidence presented in Chapters 4 through 8 clearly indicates that increased investment, both public and private, yielded growth, and that restrictions on both state and private expenditure yielded contraction. If this is so, and if 'benign colonialism' would have been better for Dahomey, why did the French not follow such a policy? The answer must be that their priorities lay elsewhere. The AOF government chose not to develop Dahomey but to bleed it, first to pay for its military occupation of the savanna zone, and then to support its bureaucracy in Dakar and its relatively high levels of expenditure in Senegal, Ivory Coast and French Sudan, to collect African funds for European investments, and in attempt to develop a more servile attitude among Dahomeans.[23] These motives cannot be attributed to all the colonial officials who served in Dahomey, for to do so would be unfair to many or perhaps most of them; it was, nevertheless, the overall and systematic effect of colonial rule.

Thus we come to the final counterfactual alternative: neocolonialism. It may be thought of as a contrast of the African and Latin American experiences: in this counterfactual, the power of European governments and firms would have made itself felt in Dahomey through informal influences rather than through formal colonial rule. Indeed, Dahomean merchants and planters sought a 'Liberian' variant of neocolonialism before accommodating to French rule, and the aristocracy of Danhomè struggled and with greater hope of success to achieve an 'Ethiopian' variant of neocolonialism. Without a European conquest of the great mass of West Africa, but allowing for small European coastal enclaves such as Lagos, the European nations would have recognized the strongest African states – the Fon kingdom and the Bariba kingdom of Nikki in the case of Dahomey, and Asante, the Egba, Ibadan and the Sokoto Caliphate in neighboring areas – and the other states would have been absorbed into these larger states. The price for recognition of these states would have been their abolition of slavery and slave trade, and their extension of commercial privileges and extraterritoriality to European merchants. In this case, the people of the smaller states and the people of slave origin would probably have suffered in their position in comparison to the actual history of colonial rule, but the average level of economic welfare might well have been higher.[24] Private foreign investment would have been little different: European investment in mines, transportation networks and commerce around the world was conditioned far more by where the profits lay than by who the government was. In the case of Dahomey, of course, private foreign investment could hardly have been reduced much. Private domestic investment would also have been little changed without colonial rule, as agricultural development underwent changes mostly in response to the world and local market, rather than in response to government. The African states could conceivably have arranged for foreign construction of railroads, but would not have done so in Dahomey; construction of a railroad to Kano, however, would seem to have been inevitable. Tax revenues of the state would have been used to enrich people within each state rather than to build the city of Dakar. There might even have been less forced labor under independent regimes, as the Europeans watched potential colonies more closely for abuses than they watched each other.[25] The major disadvantages of this counterfactual, then, are that the region would have had smaller political units, thus restricting trade and growth, and Dahomey would not have had its railroads, pier and public utilities at such an early date. It would have had to rely on water and head transport until after World War I, at which point it would have established a network of motor transport.

It can be maintained, therefore, that economic growth in the late nineteenth and early twentieth century would have been greater if the French had not conquered Dahomey. Further, the investigation of this historical might-have-been suggests a way of looking at the function of colonialism in the European-dominated world economy. The level of private investment did not depend on whether a territory was under colonial rule, but the level of public investment did. Colonialism could thus act as a fail-safe mechanism for European economic interests: for a relatively small investment in colonial conquest, the metropole could set up a government which would be supported entirely by local taxes. Further, that colonial government would compel the people of the colony to invest in infrastructure through taxation and forced labor. The benefits, should any appear, could be skimmed off by European firms and states; all the costs were borne by the conquered.

10

Capitalism and colonialism, 1915–60

The issues which had been engaged at the beginning of the twentieth century were played out more fully through the remainder of the colonial period. But if political change overshadowed economic change in Dahomey's early colonial years, the middle and late colonial years brought the reverse. The economic dislocation of the period 1915–60 included two wars, a great depression, three periods of rapid inflation, and the rise to dominance of the capitalist mode of production. The economy continued its growth almost half-way through this tumultuous period, but contracted from the thirties to the fifties; when it began to grow again it did so as a substantially transformed economy, in which the role of the state had become determinant. The florescence of capitalism in Dahomey, therefore, far from ushering in a period of growth and prosperity, coincided instead with an era of stagnation and privation.

The analysis of Dahomey's economic history from 1915 to 1960 begins with a review of available statistical series on foreign trade, public finance and money. Based on this and supplementary information, we shall then turn to exploration of Dahomey's major economic transformations: in the rate of growth, in the role of the state, and in overall social formation.

ECONOMIC INDICATORS, 1915–60

The structure of Dahomey's exports continued its modest evolution after 1914.[1] By the end of the colonial period, peanuts and coffee had joined cotton as significant contributors to export revenue. Recorded fish exports tended to decline with time, and maize, of which large quantities were exported from 1934 to 1945, again disappeared from export trade after World War II. The mainstays of the export trade remained palm oil and palm kernels, whose precolonial pattern of growth with fluctuations and cycles continued until the mid-1930s: 1936 was a peak year for both palm oil and palm kernel exports.

230

Table 10.1. *Exports as percent of current export value*

	1906–8	1927–9	1952–4
Palm kernels	48	57	51
Palm oil	35	29	20
Maize	6	—	—
Peanuts	0.4	0.2	11
Cotton	0.5	5.5	4.5
Coffee	—	0.2	4.0
Fish	3.5	0.4	1.3
Copra	0.8	0.2	1.1
Castor beans	—	0.7	1.1
Total accounted for	94.2	93.2	94.0

Source: Tables A4.4, A4.6.

While this peak has been interpreted as a response to low Depression-era prices, it is best seen as the culmination of a long period of growth in output, and a year of particularly fortunate weather conditions. The terms of trade for palm product exporters hit bottom in the low-export year of 1933 and then improved.[2] A more difficult problem is the explanation of the decade-long decline in palm product exports from 1937 to 1947, and the question of why exports had not reached their 1936 level even by 1960. Substitution of other export activities provides part of the answer, as with maize exports from 1937 to 1945 and the growth in coffee exports from 1935. The war era not only restricted the market, it actually took farmers away from their groves in order to meet the administrative requirements for maize production, thus causing a decline in oil palm productivity. Further, the tapping of oil palms to provide palm wine and *sodabi*, distilled palm wine, increased in these years. Finally, many of the palm groves had become aged and were in need of replacement, but farmers were reluctant to cooperate with the state's urging that they plant oil palm strains developed at the Pobè research station.[3] The complete collapse of palm oil exports in 1945–46 is related to terms of trade and the end of the war, though special postwar factors affected different export crops in different ways.[4]

Maize exports from 1937 to 1945 indicate the maximum maize export capability of Dahomey. Prices subsidized by France in the prewar years and obligatory furnishing of maize for the military in Senegal and North Africa during the war brought exports averaging over 30,000 tons 1937–39 and 20,000 tons 1941–45. While drawing on a productive capacity often left untapped, the wartime quotas were onerous to the producers, and led

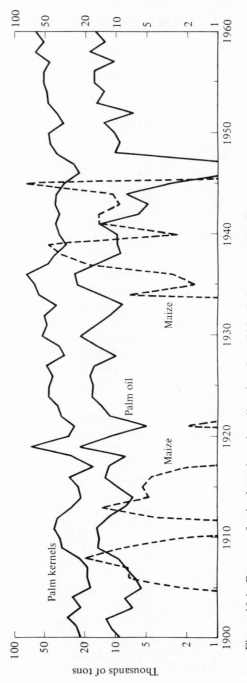

Figure 10.1. Exports of palm kernels, palm oil and maize, 1900–60, in thousands of tons.
Source: Tables A4.4, A4.6.

232

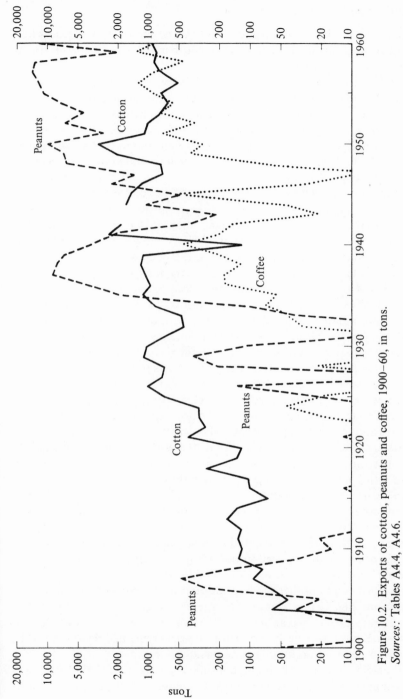

Figure 10.2. Exports of cotton, peanuts and coffee, 1900–60, in tons.
Sources: Tables A4.4, A4.6.

233

to no permanent basis for maize exports. At the end of the war prices fell, American rust invaded, the government banned exports, and trans-Atlantic exports ceased.[5]

Cotton, grown in the Center of Dahomey, grew steadily in export quantity, especially with the high prices of cotton during World War II, until it peaked at 3,000 tons in 1950, after which exports declined to less than 1,000 tons per annum. Beginning in 1935, exports of peanuts, which were grown especially in the region of Abomey and in the North, finally outgrew the pattern of wild fluctuations which indicated that only a small portion of domestic output went to exports, as a result of a rise in peanut prices and the completion of the railroad to Parakou. With the exception of the war years, peanut exports henceforth grew fairly steadily. The year 1935 thus marks the full entry of northern Dahomey into agricultural exports for the trans-Atlantic market. Exports of livestock had gone to the coast since the late nineteenth century if not before, and modest quantities of shea nuts and shea butter had been exported both through Nigeria and by head and railroad to Cotonou, but peanuts now became the main export of the North.[6] Coffee, after a century of experiments, was finally established as a crop of more than peripheral importance, with production centered near Allada and in the Mono valley. The rise in exports resulted partly from improved varieties, but particularly from the rising relative price of coffee.

The great fluctuations in recorded fish exports reflect inconsistencies in the data as well as fluctuations in the West African market. What seems clear, however, is that the capacity to catch fish in the lagoons of Dahomey increased no faster than the growth of the domestic market, so that exports to Lagos and to Togo remained, over the long run, stable. Recorded copra exports underwent a steady decline from 1910 to 1920, and grew thereafter. Several factors combined to yield this pattern: domestic demand continued to rise with population, an insect borer cut down coconut productivity for several years beginning roughly 1910, the railroad fron Anécho to Lomé made it more convenient to export copra from the area of Grand Popo via Togo, plantations of the 1880s and 1890s had become relatively unproductive by 1920, world demand and relative prices rose after World War I, and the opening of the railroad from Cotonou to Porto-Novo in 1930 led to a boom in coconut cultivation along Dahomey's eastern littoral.[7] Castor bean exports were another modest addition to the export revenues of the Plateau and the Center during the interwar years. Encouraged by the agricultural service beginning in 1916, these small trees were easily established, but castor bean and castor oil prices remained relatively stable and output showed no long-term tendency to increase.

Dahomean imports of major consumer goods after 1914 remained surprisingly steady, excepting the great fluctuations of depression and war

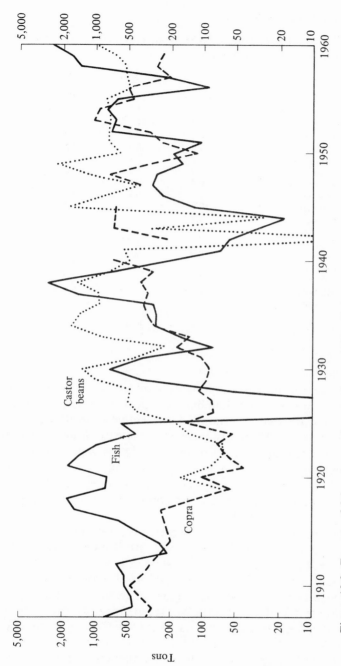

Figure 10.3. Exports of fish, copra and castor beans, 1907–60, in tons.
Source: Tables A4.4, A4.6.

235

Table 10.2. *Imports as percent of current import value, neglecting customs duties*

	1906–8	1927–9	1952–4
Cottons	28.9	24.5	10.0
Beverages	11.1	7.9	4.9
Tobacco	6.6	8.2	2.5
Motor vehicles		1.9	8.0
Sugar	1.0	1.7	3.5
Wheat flour	0.4	0.9	1.6
Rice	0.3	0.7	0.8
Matches	0.8	1.2	0.3
Kerosene	3.4	2.7	1.7
Gasoline		1.3	3.8
Coal	2.2	1.2	0.4
Sacks	2.4	2.9	1.8
Iron and steel	1.3	5.2	4.5
Metallic goods	4.0	7.0	4.7
Machinery	6.9	2.3	5.6
Cement	1.1	1.3	4.0
Total accounted for	70.4	70.9	58.1

Source: Tables A.4.5, A.4.7.

years. Since the population roughly doubled from 1910 to 1950, the absence of an equivalent doubling in imports of textiles, beverages and tobacco indicates that some non-industrial import substitution was taking place. Comparing the mid-twenties with the early fifties, the volume of textiles imported showed no growth, and tobacco imports grew at 1% per year, while motor vehicle imports grew at an average 7.5% per year. Accounting for smuggling only serves to strengthen this differentiation: unrecorded imports from Nigeria were primarily mechanical goods such as bicycles.[8]

Textile imports were affected by a change in customs duties: in 1936 France renounced the 1898 convention with Britain which had required most-favored-nation status for all suppliers of imports, and in 1937 applied the full range of AOF import duties to Dahomey, raising duties on British textiles and cutting the volume of textile imports sharply. The shortage of textiles during World War II put pressure on domestic weavers for a great amount of additional output.[9] Over the longer run, imports of ready-to-wear clothing substituted in part for cotton yardage.

Alcoholic beverage imports, while somewhat erratically recorded, seem to have declined in quantity and value from the 1920s through the 1940s, only to rebound sharply in the 1950s. Relative prices – as compared with

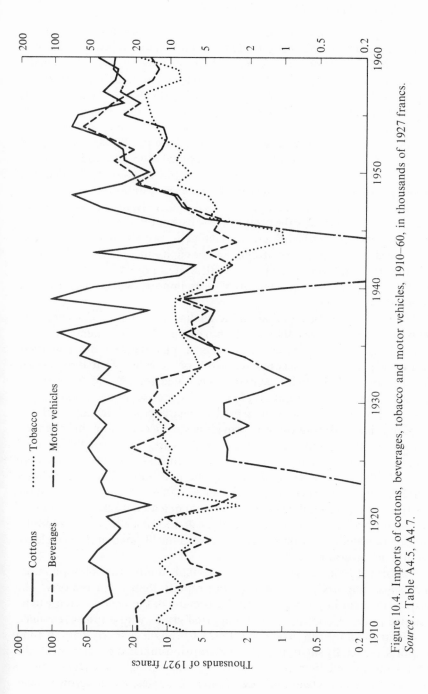

Figure 10.4. Imports of cottons, beverages, tobacco and motor vehicles, 1910–60, in thousands of 1927 francs.
Source: Table A4.5, A4.7.

237

the average of all import prices – rose from the twenties through the fifties, at the same time the terms of trade were quite unfavorable for Dahomey in general. Local substitutes were therefore emphasized, particularly *sodabi*, a beverage developed by an ex-soldier of that name who introduced the technique of distilling palm wine after World War I.[10] Periodic state prohibitions of felling and tapping of palm trees to obtain palm wine and *sodabi* did no more than slow the frequency of tapping, and served to inhibit domestic enterprise rather than facilitate it. The decline in palm product exports after 1936 was, however, related to the increased production of *sodabi*. In the 1950s import purchasing power grew while alcoholic beverage imports became relatively cheaper: purchases of imported alcoholic beverages increased, and oil palm exports grew as well. At the same time, the 1950s saw the progressive substitution of wine and especially beer imports for distilled liquors, a change in taste which was probably reinforced by the long-term decline in per capita income since the 1930s. Finally, the establishment of the SOBRADO brewery just before independence led to the replacement of beer imports with imports of the constituents of beer.

The war years brought about a change in tobacco consumption. Tobacco imported since the seventeenth century had been almost entirely pipe tobacco, though Virginia tobacco had displaced that of Brazil by 1900. But while pipe tobacco accounted for 81% of the value of tobacco imports in 1937 and 87% in 1938, cigarettes accounted for 81% of the value of tobacco imports in 1950 and 71% in 1951. The precise turning point was the year 1941, with the fall in relative price of cigarettes and the unavailability of pipe tobacco during the war providing the incentive for this change.

Automobile purchases – trucks and cars, in roughly equal numbers – jumped sharply in the twenties, thirties, and fifties, and were virtually the greatest single import by the mid-fifties. This change took place despite relative prices which remained stable or even increased. In the postwar years, automobile import firms sold or leased trucks to Dahomean transport firms at attractive rates, and the drivers made their own roads by driving repeatedly over paths, which reduced the lifespan of the vehicles to as little as several months.[11]

Imports of foodstuffs grew at a rate roughly double that of population, and sugar imports grew slightly more rapidly than grain imports. The growth of sugar imports is remarkable because of the steady increase in its relative price, as contrasted with imported grains whose prices remained stable in the long run. The years 1932–4 brought a sharp drop in food imports, especially sugar, because of depression-induced poverty, while the years during and immediately after the war brought a virtual halt to imports of sugar, wheat and rice. Domestic staples, locally grown sugar

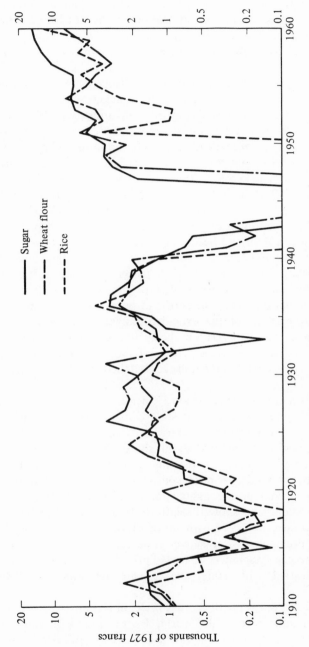

Figure 10.5. Imports of sugar, wheat flour and rice, 1910–60, in thousands of 1927 francs.
Source: Tables A4.5, A4.7.

239

cane and perhaps honey served as substitutes; the production of manioc in particular grew when imported grains became unavailable. Overall, in a gradual and unspectacular fashion, Dahomey was transformed during the colonial era from a net exporter of foodstuffs to a net importer.[12]

Gasoline imports grew at an average 11% annually from the late 1920s to the early 1950s; kerosene imports in the same period grew by less than 5% annually. The growth in gasoline imports reflects the process of transition to motor transport, while the slower growth in kerosene imports indicates that the conversion to imported lamp oil was completed earlier.[13] Gasoline imports, further, declined by far less than kerosene imports in the early thirties, indicating that substitutes existed for imported lamp oil but not for fuel. Relative prices of gasoline and kerosene fell steadily with time, gasoline more so than kerosene. Imports of both fuels were virtually cut off in 1941 and 1942, though the fall in the import of kerosene was again sharper than that of gasoline. The use of wood alcohol, in West Africa as in Germany, was a common response to wartime fuel shortages. The other alternative was a return to head transport.

Coal imports fluctuated far more sharply than gasoline and kerosene imports, as they were tied to yet a third pattern: the railway was the basic source of demand, but the use of coal for construction machinery was a source of fluctuations. Thus the period of railway construction in the late twenties, exploitation of the extended railway 1936–8, and the construction projects under FIDES in the 1950s account for the peaks in coal imports. Coal prices were steady from 1900 to 1940 in relative terms, and fell after World War II, but the railroad switched from coal to diesel fuel in the 1950s.

Imports of cement rose at a steady 5% per year from the beginning of the colonial era, reflecting continued state construction, growing capitalist construction, and substitution of cement for mud in some domestic housing. Cement prices fluctuated, but showed no sharp long-term trend.

Metals, metallic goods and machinery, while in fact including quite different types of goods, are often confounded and listed inconsistently in the returns. Taken in the aggregate, their quantity and value were surprisingly stable and showed relatively little growth.[14] Iron and steel imports fluctuated in accord with varying levels of construction. Metallic goods were dominated by consumer goods, and rose and fell along with consumer income. Machinery consisted primarily of capital goods, whose purchases varied with state and private investment in expanded production.

The instability of twentieth-century prices in Dahomey was shared by all West Africa and most of the world. Export prices provide the most consistent and easily calculable index of prices: a price index based on

240

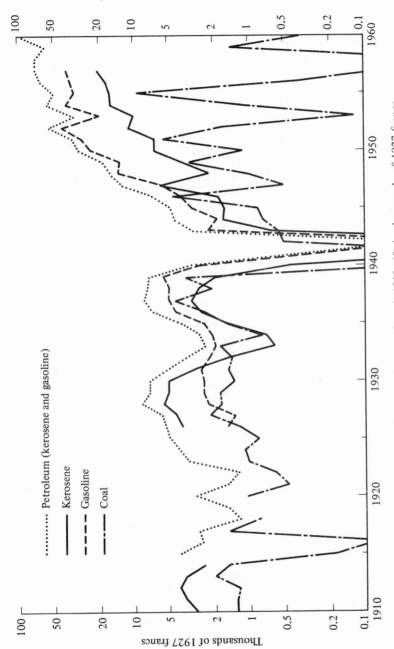

Figure 10.6. Imports of kerosene, gasoline, petroleum and coal, 1910–60, in thousands of 1927 francs.
Source: Tables A4.5, A4.7.

241

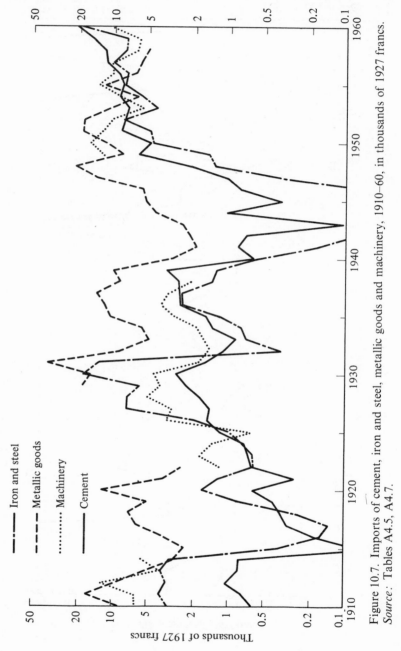

Figure 10.7. Imports of cement, iron and steel, metallic goods and machinery, 1910–60, in thousands of 1927 francs.
Source: Tables A4.5, A4.7.

242

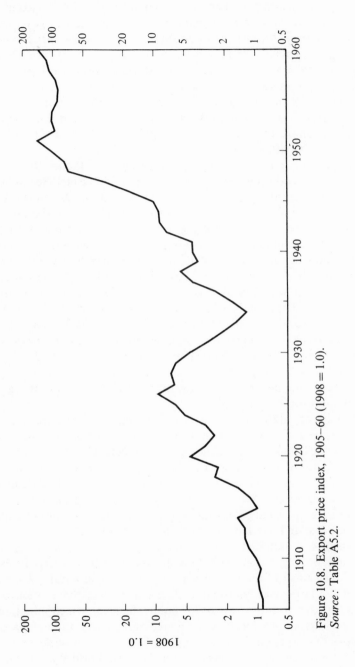

Figure 10.8. Export price index, 1905–60 (1908 = 1.0).
Source: Table A5.2.

243

exports of palm oil and palm kernels, shown in Figure 10.8, is used in this analysis as the deflator for comparisons of foreign trade, government finance and money. Import prices and domestic consumer prices varied according to somewhat different patterns, but export prices are broadly illustrative of the trend in prices. Prices rose during World War I, peaked in 1920, fell sharply in 1922, and rose to a new peak in 1926. Prices then declined until 1929 and then collapsed until in 1934 they had returned to the 1913 level. Prices rose again until World War II, rose again during the war, and then rose more than tenfold from 1945 to 1951, after which price stability held until after 1960.

The terms of trade for Dahomey illustrated in Figure 10.9 were calculated by neglecting customs duties, which should be included in order to present an accurate picture from the viewpoint of Dahomean consumers. If taxes remained the same proportion of imports for the whole of the colonial period, the resultant picture would be unchanged. In fact customs duties continued to rise in comparison to prices, hitting peaks in 1933, 1946 and the early 1950s, thus making Figure 10.9 slightly overoptimistic with the passage of time. The overall picture for net barter terms of trade shows a very negative turn of events in the interwar years, particularly in the depth of the Depression, and a recovery after World War II to a level comparable to that of the years after 1900.[15] For income terms of trade the results are much the same, except that here a tendency to improve with time is more evident. If income terms of trade are divided by an index of population growth, however, it is seen that the per capita import purchasing power out of export revenue declined during the colonial period for Dahomeans.

While Dahomey at the beginning of the colonial period had a substantial surplus in its balance of trade, with the resultant import of large quantities of currency, the balance of trade showed a slight deficit for most years after World War I, followed by the opening up of a huge deficit in the 1950s.[16] In cyclical terms, deficits tended to show up in years of low agricultural exports, and surpluses in years of high exports – that is, up until the 1950s. From that time, the balance of trade was negative despite renewed export growth and despite relatively favorable terms of trade.

Two factors dominated the impact of the colonial state on the Dahomean economy: the growth of the state, and the high level of its fiscal surplus.[17] The effect of the former was redistributive in nature, while the impact of the latter was contractive. These two effects have often been disguised by the structure of AOF public finance, which functioned through the interaction of territorial and federal budgets: this complexity, combined with distortions by government officials, has led some observers mistakenly to conclude that, especially for the post-World War II era, the

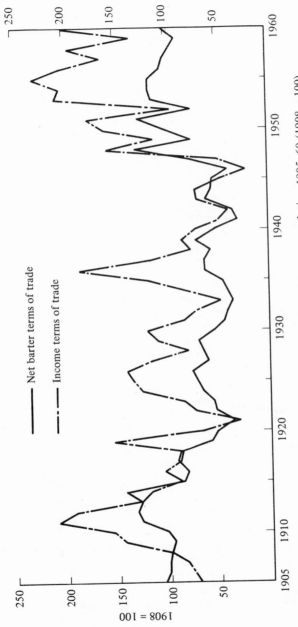

Figure 10.9. Net barter and income terms of trade, neglecting customs duties, 1905–60 (1908 = 100).
Source: Table A5.4.

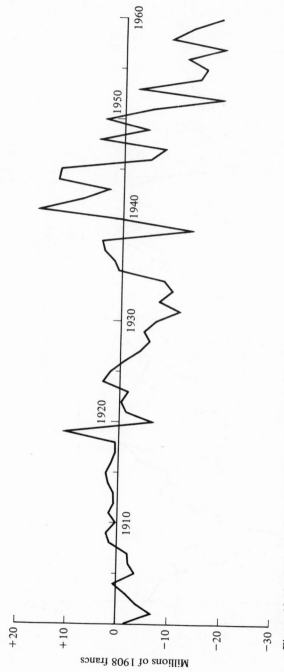

Figure 10.10. Balance of trade, 1900–60, in millions of 1908 francs.
Source: Tables A4.4, A4.5, A4.6, A5.2.

246

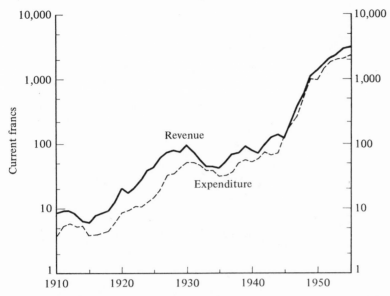

Figure 10.11. Government revenue and expenditure in Dahomey, 1910–55, in current francs.
Source: Tables A7.1, A7.2.

colonial state brought net public investment and a fiscal subsidy to Dahomey from AOF and from France. The illustration of government revenue and expenditure given in Figure 10.11, while exaggerated because of the influence of price increases, nevertheless correctly indicates the continued growth of the state, financed entirely out of local revenue, and the consistent surplus of revenue over expenditure.

In this analysis revenues and expenditures are presented in three formats: in current francs (Figure 10.11), as a percentage of current export value (Figure 10.12), and in constant francs (Figure 10.13).[18] The combination of these three formulations is necessary, given the nature of the data, to account for the influences of price change, the Depression, World War II, and the great investment projects such as FIDES. The graphs show the combined revenue and expenditure of the government of Dahomey and of AOF (more precisely, of that portion of AOF finances dealing with Dahomey). The fiscal surplus, which corresponds to the difference between revenue and expenditure for each year as shown in Figure 10.11, had two main components: the surplus in the local budget, and the export of revenue from Dahomey to Dakar. The latter, by far the largest of the two, is the difference between customs duties sent from Dahomey to Dakar and the level of grants to Dahomey.

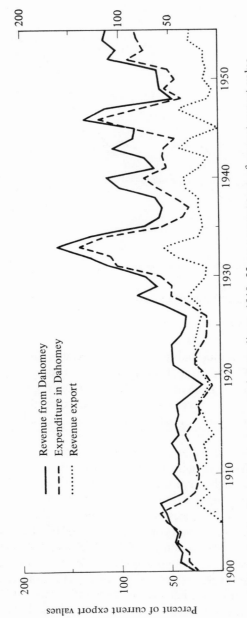

Figure 10.12. Government revenue and expenditure, 1910–55, as a percentage of current export value.
Source: Table A4.4, A4.6, A7.1, A7.2.

248

At the turn of the century the Dahomean colonial state expanded sharply, and by 1906 the regular export of revenue to AOF had begun. This structure of fiscal affairs and this magnitude of the state continued with little change for two decades. World War I and the fluctuations of the twenties brought a modest rise in the level of taxes and revenue exports, but cyclical fluctuations were of greater significance: the burden of taxation on Dahomeans fell in years of export growth and inflation such as 1919 and 1920, and grew in years of export contraction and deflation, such as 1927 and 1928.

In 1929 and 1930 the state, again quite suddenly, doubled its size. This growth, perhaps presaged by the return to railroad construction in 1925, was dominated by a great expansion in railroad construction and an equivalent expansion of the bureaucracy. Where revenues from 1900 to 1929 had averaged 45% of export values, from 1930 to 1952 they averaged twice that amount (see Figure 10.12); the difference in terms of constant prices was even greater (see Figure 10.13). Assuming exports to have represented a constant 15% of gross domestic product throughout the colonial era, taxes would then have risen from 7% of GDP before 1930 to 15% of GDP after 1930.

Even overshadowing this long-run expansion of the state was the short-run crisis of the years 1931–5. The value of exports fell because of lower prices, but the level of state revenue and expenditure did not. The burden of taxation in these years of crisis was astronomical by all previous standards, and denuded the population of money. At the beginning of the crisis, the state drew on reserves to maintain its size, but it soon turned to reliance on gouging its subjects. Not only did it maintain its own absolute magnitude in a contracting economy, it declined to contract debt to finance its activities and further increased the level of revenue export to a peak, in real terms, in 1933.[19] Only the recovery from 1935 to 1938, led by a favorable turn in export prices, brought a relative decline in the level of taxation.

The outbreak of war in 1939 interrupted commerce and brought an increase in taxes. But once France was removed from the war in 1940, prices rose faster than taxes: the effect, as seen in Figures 10.12 and 10.13, was to lower taxes as a proportion of export value and to lower them even more in comparison to export prices. Thus, while wartime constraints on the population were severe, taxes and revenue exports declined, returning to the levels of 1929 and 1930.

The period from 1945 to 1951 was a time of relatively great fiscal support for Dahomey – or, more properly, a time of relatively small fiscal drain. In 1945 state expenditures rose while taxes did not, giving Dahomey its one year of a fiscal deficit since 1905. In succeeding years, grants from Dakar rose more rapidly than local taxes, and came near to equalling the customs

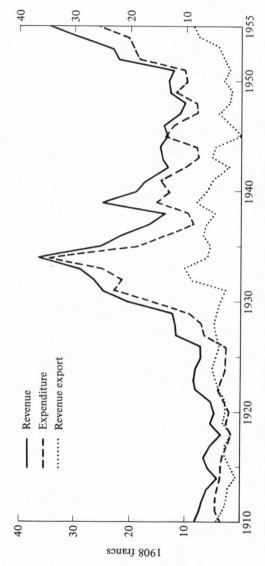

Figure 10.13. Government revenue and expenditure, 1910–55, in 1908 francs.
Source: Table A5.2, A7.1, A7.2.

250

duties sent to Dakar. The low levels of exports in 1946 and 1947 make it appear, in Figure 10.12, as if the state expanded in those years; in constant-price terms, however, as shown in Figure 10.13, it is seen that the change was in the level of exports, not in the size of the state.

These postwar years were the time of the initial economic plan for France's colonies, of which the FIDES program was the leading element.[20] This elaborate public investment program relied on grants and loans from France to the colonies, but it also required the colonies to repay the loans and to make contributions to the fund from which the grants were made. The colonies paid their contributions to AOF and to France quietly, while the disbursements from France to the colonies via AOF were accompanied by great fanfare: the public relations skill with which the plan was carried out led to an exaggerated view of the amount of net investment by France in her colonies.[21] In the years from 1952 through 1956, the second economic plan of AOF led to even higher levels of expenditure and public investment, but was accompanied by a more contractive policy: the export of revenue returned to the levels of the Depression. By the same token, this period was the heyday of the AOF government, the ultimate in its power and its degree of centralization.[22]

Passage in Paris of the 1956 *loi-cadre*, which devolved increasing legislative power from the Government General to the territories, led rapidly to the breakup of AOF and brought a final, abrupt change in the public finance of colonial Dahomey. Customs duties were turned over to the colonies in 1958 and 1959, increasing their revenue sharply. AOF grants to Dahomey, meanwhile, continued at the same level as they had been previously: these grants were now financed out of AOF reserves and grants from France rather than customs duties. Thus the long-standing export of revenue to Dakar was finally reversed. At the same time, however, the territorial government in Dahomey, now with significant Dahomean input, expanded to take over functions previously performed by the Government General, to provide new services, and to invest in state-owned and mixed enterprises. This new expenditure not only consumed the extra income provided by customs duties, but depleted reserves and led to a substantial annual fiscal deficit by 1960. Expansionary fiscal policy, therefore, came to Dahomey only on the eve of independence.

As a postscript to this review of state fiscal policy, a look at reserves may serve to highlight an oft-neglected area of finance. Surpluses in the local budget were deposited in a local reserve account. The revenue exported to Dakar was partly deposited in AOF reserves, and the remainder was allocated by the Government General to its own expenditures or passed on as grants to other AOF territories.[23] Portions of the reserve funds, at both territorial and federal levels, were held as cash in the treasury or in bank

251

deposits, but the rest went to purchase of French securities. One effect of these reserve funds was, therefore, to use West African tax receipts as working capital for French financial institutions. Further, the state policy of accumulating these reserves out of revenue surpluses was not only contractive for the domestic economy, but the reserves were almost vaporized by inflation before they could be used for anything except earning interest: the accumulated reserves of 1914, 1922 and 1945 for both Porto-Novo and Dakar were substantially devalued in the rapid inflations which followed. The depletion of reserves to cover budget deficits – as for Dahomey and AOF in 1929–35 and for Dahomey in 1946–9 – was done in such a fashion as to produce only a minimal positive effect, for the reserves so painfully accumulated were worth little by the time they were spent. Finally, a comparison of the level of reserves for Dahomey and AOF shows a much more rapid and consistent rate of growth for AOF reserves than for Dahomey, and confirms in yet another manner the expansion of the resources of the Government General at the expense of both the economy and the state of Dahomey.

Estimates of the money supply for Dahomey, which are hardly precise for the years before World War I, are even more difficult to establish for the

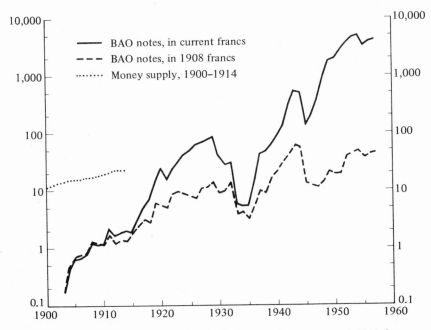

Figure 10.14. BAO notes circulating in Dahomey, in current and 1908 francs. *Source:* Tables A5.2, A8.1, A8.2.

remainder of the colonial period. The main available statistical series is the Banque de l'Afrique Occidentale (BAO) estimate of its notes circulating from the Cotonou BAO office.[24] This series provides a distorted estimate of the money supply because of inflation, because of the deviation in value of paper currency from that of coin, and because paper money was only a portion – and a varying portion – of the money in supply.[25] Figure 10.14 shows the nominal value of BAO notes circulating from the Cotonou office as of December 31 each year, as well as the real value of this paper money supply in 1908 francs. In addition, the estimated total money supply is shown for the years up to 1914. Taken together, these series suggest that paper money was of little significance before World War I, that it rose during the inflation of the twenties to account for nearly half the money supply, and that only during and after World War II did paper money become the dominant element in the money supply. Given this much, it may be concluded that the average annual rate of growth in the money supply for colonial Dahomey was roughly three percent. This was greater than the growth rate of population, of exports and of domestic product, but by a relatively narrow margin. Such a growth rate provides absolutely no support for the caricature of a population moved, through the agency of colonialism, from barter and subsistence to the introduction of cash and marketing. Rather it is consistent with what may be expected of all market

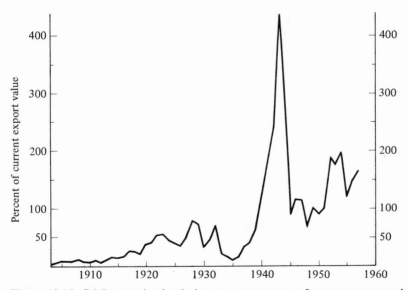

Figure 10.15. BAO notes in circulation as a percentage of current export value. *Source:* Tables A4.4, A8.1, A8.2.

economies in the same period: a growth in cash balances as steadily greater amounts of economic activity take place in the market.[26]

Three periods break up the relatively smooth long-term trend of the money supply: a sharp decrease 1933–6, an unusual increase 1941–4, and another decrease 1945–8. The decline in the money supply of the mid-thirties resulted from the high level of taxation. Here, for the only time in the colonial era, direct taxation exceeded the value of customs duties. The tax moneys were remitted to the state, which in turn deposited them with the BAO: the shortage of currency was desperate. In these straits the population turned to the use of Nigerian currency, the digging out of cowries and any other alternative currencies and, ultimately, barter.

During World War II, the opposite situation obtained – the state required export crops to be furnished and paid for them, but the producers built up huge cash balances since imports were unavailable. Dahomeans were far less likely to deposit these savings in banks than their government was, so the balances remained until consumer goods reappeared.[27] After the war, balance of trade deficits in 1946 and 1947 drew down the size of the money supply, and inflation further reduced the value of the currency that remained.

TRANSFORMATION UNDER COLONIAL RULE

After its independence in 1960, Dahomey became known as a country with declining per capita income, a deficit in its balance of trade, and a deficit in its public finances. These unhappy economic trends took hold, however, in the course of the colonial period rather than after its conclusion: they marked the end of a century of growth, and thus constitute a major economic transformation under colonial rule. In a second transformation, the colonial state grew in relative and absolute magnitude, to assume a pivotal role in the economy at the expense of the commodity exchange and private capitalist sectors. The third and most general transformation was the rise to dominance of the capitalist mode of production in the social formation of Dahomey. These three types of transformation, whose nature and interactions we are now to review, were centered in the years from 1930 to 1960.

The state, once it had expanded with the formation of the Government General in 1905, changed little in its activities and its activities until the mid-twenties, when a new program of public works began, along with an increase in taxes to finance it. The Abomey–Bohicon Décauville railway was extended into a 60–cm gauge steam railroad from Abomey to Zagnanado, completed in 1926. After a causeway had been built in 1921

254

across the Aho, the effluent to Lake Ahémé, a second narrow-gauge railroad was extended from Segbohoué to Hévé, across the lagoon from Grand Popo, and reached Athiémé in 1929. The same year saw the beginning of a more aggressive economic policy in Dahomey, where the arrival of Governor J.–F. Reste marked a sharp increase in capital expenditures, and indeed throughout AOF. Work resumed on the railroad north from Savè: it reached Tchaourou in 1934 and Parakou in 1936. Cotonou and Porto-Novo were finally linked by road and 1-m gauge rail line in 1930, although completion of the bridge across the Porto-Novo lagoon took until 1938. Lagoon transport finally began to contract, though it did not end; in contrast, the Atlantic region along the road and rail lines underwent a boom, especially with the expansion of coconut plantations.[28]

The expansion of state activities was financed by an effective doubling of tax rates. But the full impact of the Depression, beginning in 1931, led to a pitiless gouging of taxpayers, as prices and incomes tumbled drastically while tax rates remained unaltered. Money almost disappeared from circulation from 1931 to 1935 because it all went to tax collectors. Meanwhile the government of Dahomey, under Reste, had established the Sociétés indigènes de Prévoyance (SIPs) in 1929. These local savings societies, one for each *cercle*, directed by the administrator, were to collect savings and invest them in agricultural equipment and local infrastructure. On the assumption that the domestic economy produced no savings, therefore, those savings not already expropriated by taxation were to be collected through state-operated savings associations. During the thirties, Dahomean membership in SIPs was nominally voluntary and was, according to published reports, very restricted; during World War II membership was made obligatory, and the administration set the level of contribution.[29]

Trans-Atlantic commerce in the interwar years became more concentrated in its orientation toward France, and more concentrated in the hands of large expatriate firms. The proportion of Dahomean exports destined for France rose from 29% in 1909 to 48% in 1934, mostly as a result of the expropriation of German merchants in World War I, leaving two French firms (CFAO and SCOA) and two British firms (Holt and Walkden) to dominate Dahomey's foreign commerce.[30] These companies continued an existence in which high profits were gained with relatively little investment, and fared reasonably well through the depth of the Depression: they reported profits each year, though SCOA did not pay dividends for several years. The volume of exports declined little, though import volume declined somewhat more along with Dahomean purchasing power; state programs to subsidize exports helped support the profitability of the expatriate firms. The expatriate firms did increase their level of investment during the thirties, to take advantage of the concurrent increases in state investment expenditures.

The same was true for the Dahomean bourgeoisie. In 1928 a group of Dahomeans led in formation of the Banque du Dahomey, though it closed in 1932. At the Paris Colonial Exposition of 1931 Joseph Santos and Georges Tovalou Quénum set up a private exhibit on oil palm production in Dahomey, independently of the official exhibit: the state was not amused. In 1933 Santos and two West Indian partners, René Maran and Albert Satineau, set up a commercial credit company – their response to the SIPs.[31] The expansion of the Dahomean fleet of trucks during the twenties and thirties resulted mostly from private domestic investment.

Thus, even as the state expanded its activities, and even in the worst moment of the Depression, large and small firms, European and Dahomean, took advantage of improvements in technology and changes in prices to invest in expansion of the private capitalist sector. In consequence, the mercantile sector now expired, and the commodity exchange and familial sectors were restricted on one side by the high level of taxation and on another side by increasing dependence on capitalist technology. The Dahomean wage-labor force, which expanded along with the public and private capitalist sectors, retained its division into distinct segments. In the public sector these included full-time railroad and port workers (the best organized group), postal and other clerical workers, and higher level public positions such as police, teachers and functionaries. The private sector included commercial employees, transport workers, artisans and rural agricultural laborers. Finally, the government recruited short-term wage labor for its construction projects and required virtually the whole adult population to do road work or its equivalent each year.

The processes of economic transformation drew northern Dahomey more fully into the colonial economic system during the 1930s: higher peanut prices and extension of the railroad to Parakou gave the region an export crop, while trucks and tighter state control each served to integrate it with the dominant southern portion of the colony. The entry of the North into Dahomey's political scene, however, was delayed until well after World War II.

The war brought an era of economic confusion different from that of the Depression. The level of taxes was not as high as in the Depression, and the level of exports was lower, despite government requisitioning of maize and palm products. The wartime unavailability of imported goods meant hardship for Dahomey: shortages of such consumer goods as textiles, beverages, tobacco and kerosene interrupted the Dahomean style of life and caused the accumulation of large balances of cash. Perhaps more seriously, the lack of gasoline, trucks, and spare parts for machinery meant that this economy, which was just undergoing a decisive transformation to reliance on industrially produced capital goods, was forced for a time to return to the old ways. Head porterage, hand weaving and the like were now expensive and inefficient by contrast. At the conclusion of the war, however, the trend of Dahomey's economic transformation reasserted itself: the public sector grew, the capitalist mode of production extended its influence, and the economy as a whole stagnated.

After the war the peasants – freed in 1946 from export quotas, forced labor, the *indigénat* and the customary court system – produced for domestic consumption rather than for export because of disastrously low export prices, and spent their accumulated savings on imports, though a drastic inflation rapidly devalued their savings. Even in the fifties, however, exports of palm products remained well below the levels of the thirties, suggesting that a substantial disinvestment in palm groves had taken place during the war years. Administrative attempts to encourage planting of high-yield oil palms met with the usual cautious response from farmers.[32] The commodity exchange mode of production was increasingly constricted and transformed by the influence of the state and the growing capitalist sector. Markets were now all connected by trucks, entailing social and economic changes in marketing, and fragmentation of land holdings was documented for the Porto-Novo *banlieue*, under the impact of the tax system.[33] Gasoline-powered maize mills had diffused to every market in the thirties, and had been followed by tools for the artisanal extraction of palm oil and kernels. The expansion of palm oil mills after the war not only reduced the available amount of work in artisanal processing, but also tended to change the timing and the distribution of oil palm revenues: the year's income now came within a shorter period, and more of it went to men.

France and her colonies underwent staggering political and economic changes in the years of recovery from World War II. The results of these changes for Dahomey, however, were essentially more of the same thing, as its economic interests were sacrificed to those of Dakar and Paris. The postwar economic policies of AOF, centered on monetary reform and economic plans, are best understood not simply as colonial development plans but also as part of the program for the economic recovery of France herself. At the end of 1945, wartime inflation having been greater in France than in Africa, the CFA (Colonies françaises d'Afrique) franc was created as a separate monetary unit. This new unit, while tightly tied to the metropolitan franc, was the first step toward the creation of a West African central bank.[34] Initially, however, the main impact of the CFA franc was to establish an overvalued currency, thus making imports cheaper for

257

Africans and making their exports more expensive to purchasers. This policy, combined with subsidies for exports from the colonies to France, reinforced the effect of the war in concentrating AOF trade in the hands of France: the portion of Dahomey's exports going to France rose from 48% in 1934 to 81% in 1951, while for imports the French portion rose from 30% in 1934 to 71% in 1951.

The first economic plan for the French colonies, 1946–51, was in one sense an expanded version of the *grands travaux* of the thirties, which brought expanded port and rail facilities to Dahomey, but in another sense it was the beginning of real economic planning for AOF. Despite the unmistakable benefits of the plan, its disadvantages are not to be ignored. First, it was based firmly on the ideology that the private domestic sector had little capacity to generate savings and little capacity to invest its savings productively. Second, a great deal of the funds expended, whether of French or African origin, went to French salaries and purchase of French materials. It was in this sense that the plan acted to speed French development as much as African development. On the other hand, African officials, elected and appointed, began to have some power to determine how the funds would be spent, and salaries received by African workers were a benefit of the plan. The third problem, however, was that for Dahomey FIDES did not even bring about net public investment from France. For the first plan, less than eight percent of the funds allocated to AOF went to Dahomey; the second plan, 1952–6, required larger local contributions and allocated them equally unevenly.[35]

Capitalism continued its expansion and its transformation in Dahomey. The state continued to lead and dominate through investment in infrastructure and, increasingly, through creation of government or mixed firms, as in primary product processing. By 1950, four palm oil mills were operated by the mixed Société des Huileries modernes du Dahomey: such mills had become practicable once a network of trucks could bring the palm fruit for processing immediately after harvest.[36] Foreign private capital remained concentrated in import–export firms rather than in production. Import–export firms, which had maintained their profitability during the war, experienced record profits in the immediate postwar years, benefitting from the expansion of commerce, from the economic plans and, in the case of CFAO and SCOA, from the concentration of commerce in the direction of France. As the market for imported goods broadened, these firms invested in reorganized management and in staff training, and gave added emphasis to automobile imports and maintenance. Profits declined in the fifties, in part as African wages were bargained up. But the capital then began to go in new directions: into mixed government-private enterprises in Africa, and into retail merchandising in France. The expansion of

258

private domestic capital was both stimulated and restricted by these developments. Small businesses, particularly transport and other service industries, bakeries and light construction, continued to grow. Meanwhile tax structures, the long history of revenue exports, requirements of scale and government hostility kept Dahomeans from establishing large enterprises.[37] Paradoxically, therefore, while the capitalist sector as a whole had grown markedly since the interwar years, private Dahomean capital was now less visible and less independent than it had been earlier, as it had become more tied to the state and to expatriate firms.

Wage employment continued to grow at a moderate pace. The rural wage-labor force, always neglected in official statistics, was steadily increased by the parcellization of farms under population pressure: in a 1956 survey of the region north of Porto-Novo, over one-third of the respondents used wage labor in the cultivation of their oil palms.[38] The urban wage-labor force in Porto-Novo was heavily concentrated in government service, while that in Cotonou included a wider range of employment. The majority of the workforce, especially in the public sector, joined unions as restrictions against unionization declined, and trade union newspapers began to appear. In addition to the major trade unions, smaller unions served the members of artisanal groups, acting primarily as mutual aid societies.[39] The long-standing distinction and tension between white-collar government employees and those in industrial occupations and in the private sector led first to competition and raiding, and then to unification within a single central.[40]

The Dahomean wage-labor force grew not only within the colony, but outside of it. The large-scale export of labor from Dahomey began in the fifties, coinciding with the development of a gaping deficit in the balance of trade which, in turn, resulted from the combination of such factors as the slow growth in exports, the overvaluation of the CFA franc, and the rapid rise in demand for imports both in the domestic economy and from the state. Dahomey, with its traditionally high level of education and its active merchant class, had been exporting state officials and clerks for commercial firms in small numbers since early in the colonial period. But in postwar years, with the expansion of the state and with the growth of production and commerce in other territories, this trickle turned into a sizeable flow. The emigration of skilled workers from southern Dahomey has received wide notice, but unskilled emigrants were greater in number: many northerners went to Ghana and to a lesser degree to Nigeria; workers from the south went to Ivory Coast, Niger, Nigeria and all along the coast.[41] The remittances sent back by these workers to their families were an important element in the balancing of the trade deficit.

For an economy as market-oriented as that of Dahomey, with such a long tradition of ties to the world economy, the rise of the capitalist mode of production to a dominant role in the social formation was inevitable. The impetus and the timing of this transformation in Dahomey was governed by changes in technology and in relative prices of goods important for that economy and by local levels of investment. This development was more than the imposition of a new phase on the economy from outside, for it also grew out of the previous conditions of the domestic economy. The extraordinary growth in the economic role of the state, in contrast, was a decision of the French government. While expansion of the economic role of the state is a general twentieth-century phenomenon, one must distinguish that, as in France, which acted to serve the needs of domestic enterprise from that, as in Dahomey, which served to displace domestic enterprise. The state did not bring capitalism to Dahomey: rather, it governed the terms on which capitalism developed and on which its rewards were distributed.

Dahomey's remaining colonial economic transformation, the passage into dependency and stagnation in the era when capitalism comes to dominate the domestic economy, is widely known as 'underdevelopment'. In the case of Dahomey, the replacement of growth with stagnation must be attributed primarily to the policies of the colonial state, rather than to the workings of the capitalist-led world economy in general. It may be that, in the absence of these colonial policies, other forces would have restricted Dahomey's growth and would have rendered it nearly equally dependent and underdeveloped. The record is clear, nevertheless, that for virtually all of Dahomey's economic woes in 1960, the colonial government had been the proximate cause.

11

The Dahomean national movement

The opposition of the Dahomean bourgeoisie to the state's extractive and contractive economic policy engendered the major conflict of the colonial era. This polarization – in which the issue was *how* rather than *whether* Dahomey would enter the capitalist world – structured the full range of political conflicts induced by Dahomey's economic transformation. The movement was reformist rather than revolutionary, and it never challenged the right of France to rule Dahomey. Nevertheless it was an authentic, powerful – and, from the state's viewpoint, fearsome – movement seeking to bring economic and political benefits to the entire territory of Dahomey, though particularly to its merchant and planter leaders. From the time of World War I, the national movement maintained constant pressure on the state, and successfully tied virtually all of southern Dahomey into a single political system, extending its influence on a more limited basis into the North. It included among its allies some European entrepreneurs willing to join in the critique of the state, as they stood to benefit from the economic policy of the national movement. Even high state officials surreptitiously provided information and support to those who combatted official colonial policy. The national movement also relied significantly on support and developments in the wider world, particularly on Pan-African, revolutionary and anti-colonial movements centered in Paris. It was defeated and dismantled, however, under the pressure of the state's counterattack and as a result of the effects of World War II. Independence, by the time it was granted in 1960, came on terms closer to those of the colonial state than to those proposed earlier by the bourgeoisie.

RISE OF THE MOVEMENT

Two examples from the turn of the twentieth century may serve as reminders of the breadth of Dahomean experience and imagination in

261

political affairs, which gave such substance to later developments. In the first case, since human rights were to become a rallying cry for Dahomeans seeking relaxation of French restrictions, it is of interest that the first Dahomean appeal to the French Ligue des Droits de l'Homme came from Behanzin himself when in 1902, through the agency of his son Wanilo, he appealed from exile in Martinique for permission to return to Dahomey. Secondly, in the same year a remarkable mobilization in Dahomey produced three petitions calling for revocation of the land grants to the railroad company: they were presented to René Le Herissé, Dahomey's deputy in the Superior Council of the Colonies, on his visit to Dahomey, and did in fact contribute to the retraction of the grants in 1904. All three petitions were headed by signatures of leading French merchants, thus ensuring a positive political effect, but one of the petitions included a total of nine thousand signatures gathered throughout southern Dahomey. There can be little doubt that the petitions represented a substantial point of unity among merchants, large and small farmers, nor can there be doubt that the mobilizing force behind this alliance was provided by the landowning families of Ouidah.

The elements of the Dahomean national movement existed before the colonial period: it required only the experience of the early colonial years and the pressures of World War I to cause them to coalesce into a single movement. The rural farmers, fishers, artisans and traders who may collectively be labelled the peasantry were ready from the first to criticize and resist exactions by the colonial administration and, in extreme cases, to revolt. Wage workers had shown, in embryonic form, the capacity to organize and press their demands. The aristocracy, while defeated militarily in the Fon kingdom and undermined politically elsewhere, nevertheless maintained for some time the capacity for independent thinking and action. The Catholic Church had an ambiguous role to play, for it sought at once to pursue its mission, to support the interests and aims of its communicants, and to remain on good terms with the administration. Two further elements emerged in the early colonial years: Dahomean functionaries of the French regime – chiefs, teachers, interpreters and bureaucrats – ranged in their outlook from unquestioning loyalty to searching criticism of the government; and the tiny but influential intelligentsia provided wider social analysis and political contacts which served to strengthen – and at times to lead – the developing movement.

The national movement thus had several strands, but the most systematic and influential strand was that of the bourgeoisie. The leading merchant and planter families of twentieth-century Dahomey were, in large measure, those of the nineteenth century: such names as Quénum, Adjovi, Johnson, de Souza, Santos, d'Almeida, Paraîso, and Soulé have significance in both centuries. Even before the French conquest these economic leaders of Dahomey, despite their dependence on slave labor, were actively developing their commitment to a capitalist future. They emphasized education and European languages, and they were politically sophisticated in both the European and African networks in which they operated. Once under French rule, this nascent bourgeoisie expected the state to give support to capitalist development, as by providing merchants and planters with land, control over labor, internal improvements, tax breaks, and support in legal disputes. The state, however, on racist and French nationalist grounds, decided instinctively against such a policy: any capitalism would be European capitalism.

In response, the merchant and planter class set about convincing the state to change its mind and give support to domestic capitalism. To carry out this campaign, it became a speaker for the rights of all Dahomeans and thus assumed leadership of a Dahomean national movement. In the resultant polarization between the bourgeoise and the state, every economic and social grouping in Dahomey was broken into factions supporting one side or the other: the state, the expatriate firms, the bourgeoisie itself, the wage workers, the intelligentsia, the chiefs and the peasantry.

Louis Hunkanrin, who along with Pierre Johnson was Dahomey's most outstanding political figure of the colonial era, commented at the end of his life on the beginning of the Dahomean national movement:

> The political awakening of Dahomey was the work of notables who were from fifty to sixty-five years of age at the end of the First World War. The young people, for the most part functionaries and commercial employees, feared for their positions since, for a 'yes' or a 'no', it was dismissal, prison and inhuman punishment.[1]

Among the men to whom he referred were Sognigbé Mekpon and Mouteiro Soulé, but such figures as Joseph Tovalou Quénum and Akanwanou Adjovi were equally well characterized by his words. These fathers of the national movement were formed in the precolonial economy and society of Dahomey, and maintained objectives and judgment independent of that of the colonial state.

The actual leaders of the national movement, however, came from the succeeding generation. Among them were Hunkanrin; Jean Adjovi, who was to succeed his father as family chief in 1914; Pierre Johnson, who took over his family's commercial and agricultural holdings in the Mono region at roughly the same time; and Paul Hazoumé, who became a teacher in 1910 and who worked closely with the Catholic Church.[2] Adjovi and Johnson, therefore, were representatives of the landed and commercial bourgeoisie; Hunkanrin and Hazoumé did not have such clear economic interests, and may be seen as leaders of a Dahomean intelligentsia because of their intellectual, political and educational work. Hunkanrin began his work as a teacher in the highly politicized atmosphere of Ouidah in 1907. He was dismissed in 1910 for 'insubordination.' He worked briefly for CFAO in Cotonou, was convicted of theft at CFAO and served a year of prison in Dakar, was released in 1914 in time to help elect Blaise Diagne as deputy from the Four Communes of Senegal to the National Assembly, and returned to Dahomey where he founded a chapter of the Ligue des Droits de l'Homme.[3]

The outbreak of World War I brought an initial wave of enthusiasm from urban and rural Dahomeans which led to the conquest of Togo by August 23, 1914. Immediately thereafter, however, the increased prices and taxes, the forced contributions of crops, and particularly the recruitment of porters and soldiers brought an end to popular support of the war. Hunkanrin criticized the state's recruitment campaign openly and then, fearing arrest under the *indigénat*, went into hiding in Nigeria. In 1915 he collaborated with Paul Hazoumé and Emile Zinsou Bodé in producing *Le Récadère de Béhanzin*, a clandestine newsletter which for six issues carried on a critique of the abuses of the recruitment campaign and a range of other issues.[4]

The recruitment of 4,500 *Tirailleurs sénégalais* in 1915–16 brought profound unrest to Dahomey, set off two major revolts in the North, and brought about the dismissal of Governor Noufflard in early 1917.[5] The published attacks by Hunkanrin and Hazoumé, combined with the requests for inquiries by Tovalou Quénum and Germain Crespin, caused Dakar ultimately to dismiss two administrators and transfer Noufflard.[6] Most of the *akawé*, the literate Dahomeans, demanded to be allowed to enlist in the *Infanterie coloniale*, the citizen army in which the inhabitants of the Four Communes of Senegal enlisted, rather than the *Tirailleurs sénégalais* to which all subjects were restricted. Their reasoning was that they might thus escape jurisdiction of the administration-controlled customary courts, and become citizens rather than subjects. This demand was refused flatly to all but those few who had otherwise achieved citizenship. Jean Adjovi, on the other hand, took a different tack: he joined the *Tirailleurs* in hopes of thereby becoming a citizen, an objective he achieved in 1920.[7]

In 1918, as Blaise Diagne took leadership of the campaign to recruit 50,000 troops in AOF, he came to Dahomey, accompanied by Adjovi, to help raise the territorial quota of 3,500. Diagne received a cool welcome in Porto-Novo, where most *akawé* still held out for enlistment in the citizen army. He did, however, meet secretly with the fugitive Hunkanrin and arranged for him to enlist, also arranging for the return of Hunkanrin's ally Sognigbé from Nigeria to Dahomey. The unrest stirred by recruitment continued, however, and in September 1918 the Aja peoples of the Mono rose in the last great rebellion against colonial rule.

Hunkanrin, after demobilization in 1920 and despite a subsequent arrest, managed to stay on in Paris where he made contacts with the Pan-African and communist movements which had burst onto the world scene at the close of the war.[8] He broke with Diagne as he returned to opposing recruitment, and in 1921 he was arrested a second time, returned to Porto-Novo and sentenced to three years' prison there for falsifying papers enabling him to remain in France. The Paris newspaper he had founded in 1920, *Le Messager dahoméen*, continued to appear and give him support for a time after his return to Dahomey.

Adjovi, meanwhile, was finally granted citizenship, only to have the administration sieze on that as a reason to remove him from the office of *chef de quartier* in Ouidah, which he had assumed upon becoming family chief. At this, Adjovi joined with Dorothée Lima in the editing of the Cotonou newspaper *Le Guide du Dahomey,* which appeared from 1920 to 1922 and continued the critique of the autocracy and favoritism of the administration and its *chefs de canton* which had developed during the war.

Pierre Johnson had by 1921 been elected to one of the three seats reserved for subjects on the Chamber of Commerce governing board of twelve. Subjects were in fact a majority of the Chamber of Commerce membership, and came to have increasing voice in its governance as a result of reforms in 1916 and 1924.[9] The Chamber of Commerce board, in turn, selected representatives to the Administrative Council of the colony.

The Dahomean national movement thus not only survived World War I, which engendered it, but remained remarkably broad, especially considering the narrowness of the formal and informal institutions on which it had to rely to sustain itself. The consultative Administrative Council of Dahomey, over which the governor presided, included one appointed Dahomean. In Dakar, the analogous Superior Council for AOF included an appointed citizen to represent Dahomey. The Chamber of Commerce was also represented on the Administrative Council. The number of representatives in these bodies and the franchise for their selection were expanded somewhat with time, and all these appointed and elected officials received regular representations from the bourgeoisie.[10]

Since no explicitly political organizations were permitted, three sorts of alternatives served to support informal political parties: social clubs, civil rights and fraternal associations, and newspapers. The first major social club, 'Club de l'Etoile noire,' was founded in Porto-Novo in 1912, and continued until 1927.[11] Hunkanrin's prewar chapter of the Ligue des

Droits de l'Homme disbanded under administrative pressure, but another chapter formed in Porto-Novo in 1921, along with a chapter of the Association franco-musulman established to support activities of the *alhaji* party. After the suspension of *Le Guide* in 1922, Dahomey was without a newspaper until 1927. But taking into account the full range of newspapers, of social, civil rights and fraternal associations in Dahomey, ties to the Church and allies and countrymen in Paris, postwar Dahomey was never lacking in informal structures to give support to the political program of its bourgeoisie and allies.

After two successive bad years in the domestic economy, a 1923 increase in the *impôt* for Porto-Novo and Cotonou *cercles* brought the national movement into confrontation with the administration. At the same time Porto-Novo *chef supérieur* Houdji lay ill, and contending parties jostled for position on the issue of his succession. Houdji had been chosen by the state in 1913 as politically reliable, though his selection violated the succession rules for the Porto-Novo kingdom.[12] Sognigbé, who had been passed over in the successions of 1908 and 1913, was allied to the *alhaji* party and to Hazoumé and Hunkanrin. Hunkanrin, though in prison, was able to provide leadership for the movement which was triggered by the visit to Porto-Novo of Henri Michel, the Cotonou merchant who was Dahomey's representative in the AOF Superior Council. Michel was met by a large delegation detailing grievances on the new taxes and on the policies of administrators. When this was followed by meetings at which the leaders called for withholding taxes, and then by the arrest of the leaders, markets closed, *impôt* payment almost ceased, and Porto-Novo workers went on strike. The government sent troops throughout the *cercle* to force collection of the *impôt*, in the course of which the lake village of Afotonou, east of Awansouri, was burned and its inhabitants ordered to build on land.[13] Before the six-week conflict was over there had been several rural riots, a successful strike by port workers in Cotonou, wide publicity among European and African critics of colonial rule, and a reduction in taxes. The leaders were punished, however, with exile in Mauritania, which only Hunkanrin and Etienne Tété survived.[14]

The Porto-Novo incidents, though eliciting a severe government re-action, also brought new concessions. Municipal councils were established in Porto-Novo, Cotonou and Ouidah, though all members were appointive. Dahomean representation on the Administrative Council was increased to three, and the positions became elective, with an electorate composed of roughly five hundred citizens, civil servants, merchants, school-certificate holders and medal winners. The electoral districts, covering the Coast and the Plateau, were centered on Porto-Novo, Ouidah and Abomey. The representative to the Superior Council became elective, though with a narrower franchise. In addition, the scope of the *indigénat* was narrowed slightly.[15] Meanwhile Fr Francis Aupiais, leader of the Catholic Church's active educational efforts in Dahomey, began publishing a local journal, *La Reconnaissance africaine*, for which writers such as Hazoumé wrote studies of Dahomean culture.[16] In effect, the church thus provided support for the development of Dahomean national culture while maintaining its distance from the revolutionary aspects of the 1923 events.

The net result was to affirm bourgeois leadership of the national movement. Pierre Johnson was re-elected to the board of the Chamber of Commerce in 1924, along with his allies Georges Tovalou Quénum and Fernand d'Almeida. In the first Administrative Council elections in 1925, Johnson became a candidate in the second district (Ouidah) despite administrative discouragement, and was elected; the other two seats went to candidates supported by the administration.

Dahomey's bourgeois political activists in 1927 founded *La Voix du Dahomey,* the newspaper which was to provide support for their candidates and their program for a decade. *La Voix* was edited by Jean da Matha Sant'Anna, and was governed by a large board which oversaw its policy and its finances.[17] This organ of the landed and commercial elite was circulated systematically through the south of Dahomey, and drew on correspondents in town and country. It called for an end to Dahomey's subsidy of AOF, expansion of educational opportunity, and abolition of the *indigénat*; it criticized the regime of canton chiefs and the policies of the colonial administration. In the 1928 Administrative Council elections, *La Voix* supported winning candidates in all three districts: Pierre Johnson was re-elected, and Casimir d'Almeida defeated the pro-administration candidate in Porto-Novo, as did Augustinho Olympio in Abomey.

In 1929 the *Voix* group had a further electoral success as it won a virtual majority on the Chamber of Commerce board, winning two citizen seats as well as the three subject seats; they established a close relationship with the French merchant Delamère, who became president of the Chamber, while Johnson became president *pro tem.* In the same year the *Voix* group successfully supported the French merchant Albert Nègre for re-election to the Superior Council against a challenge by ex-Governor Fourn, who had just retired.

The informal but consistent program of the national movement, especially as enunciated in the pages of *La Voix,* included the support for domestic planters, merchants and other entrepreneurs, an end to the export of tax moneys, the reduction of exactions against the peasantry by *chefs de canton,* the abolition of customary courts, the expansion of educational opportunity, and the provision of basic rights for public and private sector wage workers, including an end to salary discrimination against African

267

civil servants. Such a program, while based on the needs of the bourgeoisie, was constructed so as to maintain alliances with other economic interests and to force the government to seek a compromise with its leaders. The best measure of this proposition, and of the breadth and unity of the national movement, is that as long as the *Voix* group was able to maintain the offensive in its critique of the state, it provided a cover under which other Dahomeans raised their own demands. The peasants unleashed an unprecedented barrage of criticism against the taxation and labor policies of the state-appointed *chefs de canton* in the late twenties. For port workers, following the 1923 strikes, some smaller movements took place in the late 1920s, climaxing in a major Cotonou strike in 1929 in which Gérard Avomassado, who had worked with Gardan Kouyaté's Union des Travailleurs nègres in Paris, played a leading role. In the same year, Fr Aupiais spoke out firmly against the practice of forced labor, though after he had left Dahomey.[18] The Dahomean movement was mentioned frequently in revolutionary and Pan-African as well as more mildly socialist and humanitarian circles.

CRISIS AND DEFEAT, 1929–45

The bourgeois political campaign of the 1920s established two major points: that the colonial regime's economic policy was detrimental to the development of the country, and that the *chefs de canton,* the pivotal element in the colonial administration, followed an aggressive and self-aggrandizing policy. While this political challenge to the state's policies was to be sustained for some time, the movement was unable to gain any of its objectives. The government, maintaining its steadfast opposition to compromise, ultimately provoked an open split in the movement and achieved its defeat.

Even before the critical struggles, the pressures of continuing conflict with the government began to reveal weaknesses and divisions within the *Voix* group. In April of 1929 *La Voix* announced the candidacy of its editor, Sant'Anna, for election to Dahomey's seat in the Superior Council of the Colonies, along with Victor Ballanan, an ally in France. But ex-Governor Fourn, who had been forced to retire the previous year under pressure from Sant'Anna's crusading journalism, declared himself a candidate for the same seat. The *Voix* group chose to sidestep the challenge: Sant'Anna stepped out of the race and, instead, signed the article in *La Voix* presenting the critique of Fourn's candidacy and giving support to the French merchant Albert Nègre. Nègre won the May election easily, and *La Voix* celebrated the victory with its lone descent to vitriol in attacking 'the sixty-four imbeciles' who had voted for Fourn. But the

268

reluctance to run Sant'Anna against Fourn may have been a miscalculation for the *Voix* group, for there was not to be another opportunity to elect a Dahomean to Paris until 1945. Later in 1929 a factional dispute emerged within *La Voix:* Sant'Anna left the paper in November, along with Benjamin Adjovi and Hilaire de Souza, and was replaced as editor in December by Jean Adjovi. This, in turn, followed by one year the division of the Adjovi family. Sant'Anna had just founded another newspaper when he was shot to death in March of 1930 by two men hired by the embittered Fourn.[19] Meanwhile a second newspaper, *Le Phare du Dahomey*, had been founded during 1929 in Cotonou by the printer Augustin Nicoué, who was also one of the founders of *La Voix*. *Le Phare* – edited, significantly, by Paul Hazoumé – took an ostensibly apolitical line, but gave support to Nicoué's unsuccessful candidacy for the Administrative Council in 1930, against Casimir d'Almeida.

The state responded explicitly to the critique of its policies under the leadership of Governor Reste, whose brief tenure in 1929–30 marked a major watershed in colonial administration. The state's response, beneath Reste's conciliatory veneer, was to set up new and more formidable obstacles to bourgeois economic leadership in the colony, in order to induce Dahomean capitalists to subordinate their own needs to those of an alien and capricious state. The expansion of state enterprise, the increase of taxes, and the mobilization of savings by the state to the exclusion of the private sector have been discussed above.[20] The explicitly political aspect of Reste's response was centered on the *chefs de canton*.

Under pressure of critics in town and countryside, the chiefs had become reluctant to do the bidding of the government: Reste therefore moved, through a 1930 ordinance, to provide them with revised status and more support. Village chiefs were still to be paid on the basis of the taxes they collected, but many of them came to be elected: they were thus tied closer to the villages. Canton chiefs were no longer to be paid on the basis of taxes collected, thus insulating them from some of the charges of gouging. They were given flat salaries which included substantial raises, and which varied according to the importance of their canton (or, in the towns, their ward or *quartier*). In addition, they were given supplementary stipends based on a variety of criteria – which were, in effect, merit pay or loyalty pay.[21] Finally, they were given secretaries. Justin Aho, first appointed by Reste as a *chef de canton* in Abomey *cercle*, became the greatest and most controversial of these chiefs: a leading descendant of Glélé, educated, fluent in French, and with military service, he was the archetype of the new look in canton chiefs and the key figure in the state's campaign to combat the bourgeoisie. With his office and with administrative support, he took on several administrative titles, gained control of much of the remaining machinery of the Fon royal family (later claiming to be, in effect, king), and established title to large land holdings, including lands confiscated from the Fon state at the time of the French conquest.[22] In effect, therefore, the state subsidized the advance of its canton chiefs in private capitalist sector, at the same time reinforcing their dependence on and subordination to the state. Chiefs, under these conditions, moved toward monopolizing educational opportunity for their families, restricting the opportunities of others within their cantons.

The worst years of the Depression were 1931 to 1935, as export prices collapsed, import prices fell more slowly, and the real rate of taxation skyrocketed to a level that literally drew most money out of circulation. Soon the *impôt* could hardly be collected: a series of demonstrations broke out in 1932 in Athiémé, Grand Popo, Ouidah and smaller towns, the protesters demanding suspension of the *impôt*, but ultimately obtaining the governor's agreement to a delayed schedule of payment. Following a major confrontation over taxes in neighboring Lomé late in 1932, Dahomean newspapers picked up the issue of excessive taxation and demanded reductions.[23] The administration, predictably, concluded that failure to pay the *impôt* in full was simply a matter of the ill will of its Dahomean subjects. By 1933 the government had managed to obtain 370 troops from Dakar, but they were never deployed to collect taxes or trigger a revolt, largely because of press publicity and the questions raised in Paris by National Assembly members critical of colonial policy and kept informed by Dahomean activists. This avoidance of revolts, while it showed increasing sophistication and coordination in the national movement, did nothing to solve the problem of excessive taxation. The peasants, overwhelmed with falling terms of trade and mounting taxes, were perhaps not entirely surprised to find themselves repeatedly overrun by locusts in the years 1930–2.[24]

The combination of the Depression and the growth of the state brought both good and bad fortune to state employees: salaries and employment were more stable than in the private sector, and state employment expanded almost irreversibly. Some layoffs did occur in the early thirties, however, and urban unemployment became severe. For state employees, usually politically quiescent in order to maintain their jobs, a wave of organization and radical activity characterized this period. The immense difference between salaries of Dahomeans and of French bureaucrats performing similar duties was a particularly sore point.

The national movement, after avoiding open disunity of its varying elements through the twenties, split in the highly charged atmosphere of the early thirties. The unrest among the peasantry and wage workers, the unemployment and threatened layoffs among bureaucrats, the world-wide range of popular movements against the crisis of the Depression, and the rise of fascism brought a new alignment in Dahomean politics.[25] In the 1932 Administrative Council elections Augustin Nicoué, previously close to the administration, now became a critic of the inability of incumbent Casimir d'Almeida and others of the *Voix* group to mitigate the effects of the Depression. He took up the cry of Cotonou parents against restrictions in school enrollment – a key issue in an era when the state was the major source of new urban employment. Though he lost the election, Nicoué was in a position to hammer at d'Almeida for the next two years, calling him a tool of the administration. Several new papers were founded at this time, most of them critical in varying degrees not only of the administration but of the *Voix* group.[26]

Louis Hunkanrin, nearing the end of his exile in Mauritania, sent some articles to *La Voix* in 1932. On his return to Porto-Novo in 1933, he was offered and accepted a government position, working to codify customary law. He therefore avoided open political activity, but he worked behind the scenes to build a coalition which successfully challenged the *Voix* group in the 1934 Administrative Council elections. His closest associate was his nephew Blaise Kuassi, editor of the newly founded *Courrier du golfe de Bénin*, and a man with radical connections overseas like Hunkanrin. The intelligentsia thus returned to the political scene in Dahomey.

Kuassi and Hunkanrin drew support from bureaucrats, workers and peasants, and allied with Nicoué and the formerly conservative merchant Ambroise Dossou-Yovo to stigmatize the *Voix* group as 'capitalist,' 'hypocritical denunciator,' and 'neither politician nor socialist.'[27] The distinctions between this coalition and the *Voix* group included those between Porto-Novo and Ouidah, between state employees and merchant – planters, between a younger and an older group, between those involved in the Porto-Novo incidents of 1923 and those not involved – and, one is tempted to suggest, between the intelligentsia allied with the petty bourgeoisie on one hand, and the bourgeoisie on the other hand.

In the 1934 elections Casimir d'Almeida and Pierre Johnson were defeated handily by Nicoué and Dossou-Yovo; Olympio refused to run for re-election in Abomey, and the seat went to Richard Johnson, the younger brother of Pierre, who ran in opposition to the *Voix* group.

The election results combined with the beginnings of improvement in economic conditions and a changing political scene in France to bring about a crucial political reversal: the victorious Nicoué, along with Dossou-Yovo, almost immediately established a close relationship with the administration, shifting back to a critique of the *Voix* group from the right rather than the left.

The *Voix* suspended publication from February through May 1934, but

271

recovered from its defeat to return to print. The state demanded retraction of a July article alluding to a bribe of 14,000 francs from canton chiefs to a French administrator. As no retraction was forthcoming, in September police raided the *Voix* offices, confiscating piles of allegedly illegally-obtained documents.[28] Hunkanrin, by this time, was willing to join with the administration in order to pursue his differences with the *Voix* group. What resulted, for the next two years, was a relentless administrative campaign to prosecute members of the *Voix* group and any who came to their support.

The split in the bourgeoisie had been achieved. In the twenties, merchants, planters and civil servants had either supported the national movement or had remained silent, and only the canton chiefs had given open support to the state. From 1930 to 1934 two parties had appeared in the national movement, each claiming to be its authentic and most effective leader. But from 1934 the national movement was on the defensive. The bourgeoisie – which now included the ever-wealthier canton chiefs – was split into those who maintained the critique of state policy and of the chiefs, and those who opposed the demands of the national movement and gave full support to the state and the chiefs. As an indication of the speed and the magnitude of this realignment, Paul Hazoumé joined with Justin Aho to give the 1935 Bastille Day elocutions, while Pierre Johnson stood indicted on charges ranging from fomenting revolt to slavery; Hunkanrin began to edit a newspaper publishing articles prepared by the administration.[29]

After Casimir d'Almeida had unsuccessfully sued his critics for defamation following the 1934 election, the administration and its allies turned the tables and obtained prison sentences on defamation charges against Pierre Johnson and several other figures including Blaise Kuassi, who with Richard Johnson was one of the few members of the victorious coalition to maintain his critique of the state. Pierre Johnson, meanwhile, remained president *pro tem.* of the Chamber of Commerce. With the departure of President Delamère for France, Johnson continued to preside over the Chamber and declined to call new elections. His Dahomean allies apparently remained solid, but his European allies folded under administrative pressure, and all the Europeans withdrew in 1935 to establish their own informal chamber. In the same year, Johnson was fined 20,000 francs as a result of an accident involving one of his trucks in Athiémé *cercle* and was further sentenced to four years in prison on a charge of slavery after he had accepted a girl as a pawn; finally, in 1936, he was convicted of organizing the women's tax demonstration of 1932.[30]

This reaction, though severe, failed to sweep all before it. *La Voix* continued to appear, and was joined in 1935 by *Les Rayons solaires* in Abomey, where Victorin Féliho took up the campaign against the excessive power of Justin Aho in Ounbégamé canton, and supported a suit against him. Another suit was filed against canton chief Djibodé Aplogan in Allada, and chief Godonou Houekpe was dismissed as a result of similar accusations. Richard Johnson moved closer to the *Voix* group after his brother Pierre had been removed from the scene.

In the meantime, the state's allegations against *La Voix* were not accepted by the court: of all the documents confiscated by police from *La Voix*, only possession of a 1932 draft budget of Togo was seen by the court as admissible for prosecution. The state therefore presented new charges in May 1935, listing eighty articles which had appeared in the paper and claiming that they violated the 1928 press law, and further charging 28 directors of *La Voix* with illegal association. The trial finally began in January 1936. Hunkanrin, ironically, was a defendant along with Adjovi and the other leaders of *La Voix* despite his current support of the administration, he was charged in 1935 on the basis of articles he had written in 1932, while still in Mauritania. Once charged he was again newsworthy, and support poured in for him and other defendants from France and the West Indies. In June, Judge Mattei rendered his decision: acquittal for some, small fines for Adjovi and several others, and condemnation of the state for prosecuting the case.[31]

The *Voix* group was triumphant – the national movement was rehabilitated, its French and Dahomean opponents having suffered a notable defeat. In the 1936 elections to the Administrative Council, Casimir d'Almeida and Richard Johnson chased Nicoué and Dossou-Yovo from office, while Féliho won election to the Abomey seat which Johnson had held. The Chamber of Commerce, having been reconstituted after negotiations led by the state, had elected Elie Gomez to its board in February, before the court decision, though other candidates of the *Voix* group had not been successful. Germain Crespin challenged Albert Nègre for the position in the AOF Superior Council and lost narrowly. Georges Tovalou Quénum was sent to Paris through subscriptions from his allies, to lobby for the abolition of customary courts, the transfer of acting-Governor Desanti, and an end to the Dahomean subsidy of the AOF budget.[32] By this time, however, the *Voix* group faced an expanded state structure, expatriate firms which had obtained new concessions and greater market power, and canton chiefs whose economic and political positions had been strengthened – so that it was now a question of undoing what had already been done.

The split in the bourgeoisie was not, ultimately, to be healed up, and the administration was to maintain a powerful band of partisans from 1934 to the end of the colonial era. Nevertheless, the results of the *Voix* trial combined with the policy of the Popular Front government (which came to

273

power in France in 1936) to bring a brief period of advance for the national movement. Direct criticism of the administration was now reduced, having apparently become too costly, but attacks on the canton chiefs multiplied. Fifty-one suits had been filed against chiefs by the end of 1937, accusing them of brutality. illegal confiscation of land and taxes, and excessive use of forced labor. The suit against Djibodé Aplogan led to his dismissal; Justin Aho, however, emerged from the suit against him with a promotion, although he had to give up some of his offices.[33] In other administrative concessions, the spy services set up in 1934 were abolished, the *indigénat* was restricted somewhat, and forced labor was sharply restricted. A system of grievance hearings was set up throughout the colony. And, as a result of metropolitan legislation, the right to organize was extended to workers with a primary education certificate: the two main unions to formalize their existence were a civil service association, headed by Richard Johnson, and the railroad union.[34]

The declaration of war in September of 1939 brought a new set of priorities and an end to this period of reform. The state suspended elections, reinstituted forced labor, and began requisitioning export crops. Nevertheless, in a response very different from that of World War I, Dahomeans of all political persuasions expressed solidarity with France against the Nazis.

With the defeat of France in 1940, the AOF government threw in its lot with Marshall Pétain and the Vichy regime. Opposition to this course flickered briefly in Dahomey: several French administrators went over the border to Nigeria, and there was discussion about setting up a Free French committee for Dahomey: Jean Adjovi, Hunkanrin, Pierre Johnson and Féliho were proposed as the executive. But support was lacking and no action was taken. The pro-Vichy government dropped Féliho from the Administrative Council and interned Adjovi in the Sudan. Hunkanrin, working to ferry Free French sympathizers to and from Nigeria, was arrested in Porto-Novo at the beginning of 1941. Three others arrested with him were executed; he managed to avoid execution and was interned in the Sudan.[35]

The population obediently accepted the rigors of war, supplying crops to the state, and adjusting to the absence of imports both by investment in small-scale local industry and by re-establishing the old commodity exchange and mercantile systems. Then at the end of 1942 AOF rallied to the Free French: the photos of Marshall Pétain which had been obligatory were now all to be burned.[36] But the change meant little difference in internal policy, as forced labor, recruitment and requisitioning of crops continued. Nor were those interned on suspicion of complicity with the

Free French released – Hunkanrin was not even released with the end of the war in 1945, but was held until the very end of 1947.

It might have appeared, in 1938, that the Dahomean national movement would survive the impact of the state's attack against it. By the end of the war, however, it was clear that the movement had been a casualty not only of relentless state hostility, but of fascism and of the rigors of war. It is often argued that World War II provided a great democratic impulse and a wide range of experience which fueled the postwar rise of African nationalist movements. While evidence for this trend may be found for Dahomey, the opposite trend was even more significant in this case. Ties among the bourgeoisie, peasantry and workers had been broken, and the state had reimposed effective hegemony over the entire population. When the leaders of Dahomey unanimously gave support to the war effort, they knew what it entailed: men of such experience unquestionably saw that they were subordinating their own national movement, which they had nurtured for decades, to a war against fascism. They cannot have predicted the humiliation of the Vichy regime, but they must have seen that their decision entailed, for the immediate future at least, the dismantling of their movement.

The Dahomean bourgeoisie was not inherently democratic – it was formed out of a slave-owning class which put its needs for land and labor before any rule of law. Yet its experience in the early twentieth century made it into a democratic class: the only way it could hope to pressure the state into a changed policy was by championing the economic welfare of the territory as a whole, and by espousing the causes of merchants, workers, peasants and chiefs who had been wronged by violation of a set of rights which corresponded to those defended in the French Revolution of 1789. The state resisted the movement, discredited its leaders and imprisoned both leaders and supporters. By the mid-thirties, the state had induced some of the main speakers for the national movement to renounce their priorities and claim that the primacy of the French state was the correct path for Dahomean development. The war reinforced this outlook and, as the postwar era opened up, the whole national movement seemed to have been forgotten.

THE LEGACY OF DEFEAT, 1945–60

As the end of the war brought an unprecedented extension of political rights in the French colonies, Dahomey's bourgeois leaders made an energetic attempt to construct a unified party. But the strength and unity of the Dahomean national movement had been extinguished in the course of the war, and the political initiative in AOF now shifted to other colonies; paradoxically, the extension of political rights served as much of weaken as to strengthen Dahomey both internally and in the context of AOF politics.

Newspapers returned to publication in 1945, and Augustin Nicoué of *Le Phare du Dahomey* and Joseph Santos of *La Voix du Dahomey* forgot old differences sufficiently to join in convening Electoral Committees: a call had been issued for the election of deputies to a Constituent Assembly which was to establish the Fourth Republic of France, and Dahomey and Togo together had been allocated two deputies, one for citizens and one for subjects. (A clash between Dahomean and Togolese interests was avoided in this election because Togolese leaders had decided for other reasons to boycott it.) The Electoral Committees called upon Fr Francis Aupiais to come out from France as their candidate for the citizen seat.[37] Aupiais, whose political affiliation was with the MRP led by Georges Bidault, recommended Sourou Migan Apithy for the second seat, and his recommendation was adopted.[38] Apithy had been a student of Aupiais in Porto-Novo, had been in France since the mid-thirties, and had been appointed to the Monnerville Commission which studied postwar colonial reforms. Opposing Aupiais and Apithy were, among others, the lawyer Jean-Louis Bourjac and Casimir d'Almeida. The latter, in his capacity as Administrative Council member, had taken on the task of collecting maize and palm oil quotas during the war. As a result, he was clearly identified with the administration and gained little popular support. Aupiais and Apithy were both elected in October 1945. Aupiais, however, died unexpectedly in December as a result of side-effects from an immunization.

Thus Apithy, the unknown and inexperienced technocrat, was catapulted into the political leadership of Dahomey. It was he who, as Dahomey's deputy to the Constituent Assembly and later the National Assembly, gained credit for the laws abolishing forced labor, the *indigénat*, the customary courts and market fees. His name became not only a symbol of these reforms, but also the synonym for 'député' in some languages.[39] In practice, however, he was a listless legislator and an opportunist without a program. The reforms owed much more to the efforts of Félix Houphouët-Boigny, deputy and leader of a national movement in Ivory Coast which, younger and more powerfully based, had not known the disappointments and defeats of the Dahomean movement.

The Electoral Committees which had approved Apithy's selection went ahead with what seemed like the establishment of a sound political structure: in April of 1946 they established the Union progressiste du Dahomey (UPD), the single political party of the colony, which won 20 of the 30 seats in the first Territorial Council elections of December 1946.[40] From 1946 to 1951 Dahomey maintained an illusory political unity behind Apithy and the UPD. But the party had no strong politico-economic base, nor a clear program, so that the tensions and challenges it faced easily got out of control.

In 1946 Apithy signed the call to the founding convention of the RDA, the AOF-wide political party called together by Gabriel d'Arboussier of Senegal, but soon dominated by Félix Houphouët-Boigny of Ivory Coast. Apithy soon withdrew support from RDA under pressure: the administration and the Catholic Church opposed RDA's ties to the French Communist Party, and Dahomean antipathy toward the Government General reinforced an opposition to federation-wide political action. In the same year, political figures such as Hazoumé and Justin Ahomadegbé began expressing dissatisfaction with Apithy's lack of a clear policy; Ahomadegbé joined with Emile Poisson to offer an opposing candidacy for the National Assembly in 1946, though with meager results.[41] On a different basis Hubert Maga, a teacher and UPD member of the Territorial Council from Natitingou, formed the Groupement ethnique du Nord (GEN) in 1949 to help increase political representation within UPD for the North as that region, now sharing effectively in the economic life of the territory, became anxious to share fully in its political life.

These tensions contributed to the breakup of the UPD and the beginning of regional politics in Dahomey. The final straw came with the timing and the provisions of the law governing the June 1951 National Assembly elections: Dahomeans learned just one month before the election that they were to have two delegates, but that the two were to be the top *one* from each of the *two* leading lists of candidates. The law thus provided an inherent invitation for the UPD to split.[42] The UPD leadership, under Hazoumé's prodding, had now lost confidence in Apithy, and proposed to place him second on its list behind Emile Derlin Zinsou. Apithy indicated that he would not run if he were not first on the list. The GEN, not yet constituted as a party, made clear its desire to have a northerner on the UPD list. The demands were irreconcilable: Zinsou, Apithy and Maga each ended up heading a list of two candidates. To the surprise of many, the personal visibility of Apithy and the regional identification of Maga counted more for votes than the party structure of UPD: Apithy and Maga were elected, Zinsou was badly beaten, and the UPD collapsed. The canton chiefs, who had lost power with the reforms of 1946 and had been bypassed in earlier elections, now became the key to electoral politics: with the greatly expanded franchise, they helped deliver the votes for Apithy in the south and Maga in the north. A new era began as party politics – never firmly established because of UPD's ideological and programmatic indecision – gave way to ward politics, based on region, ethnicity and personality.

Apithy and Maga constituted parties to support them immediately after the 1951 election.[43] Although Apithy remained Dahomey's leading political figure until 1959, from 1951 he no longer held power as the leader of a national movement, but as head of a regional grouping who could maintain power only by establishing an alliance with at least one other party. The parties of the forties and fifties, while numerically stronger and with broader institutions than the movement of the interwar years, lacked the aggressive policy and the economic base – or even the hope of obtaining one – which characterized the earlier years. Dahomean leaders found their weaknesses compounded at every turn, as they were drawn into a vortex of externally-imposed political and economic change. They faced repeated changes in electoral laws, constitutional referenda, and an unending set of elections to an ever-varying array of offices: without too much exaggeration it can be said that the Dahomean electorate went to the polls thirty times from 1945 to 1960, no two times under the same structure.

The political parties of Apithy and Maga were little more than electoral coalitions: once in office they had no firm policy objectives, and accommodated rapidly to the administration's view of reality. The rapid political and economic changes of the fifties, however, caused many Dahomeans to seek more active representation, and a new political party was born of this outlook in 1955. The Union démocratique dahoméenne (UDD) gained support in all regions of the country, came closer to having a national policy than the other parties, and was most critical of an administration whose policy had evolved surprisingly little for the times. At its strongest, the UDD was an alliance of wage workers, peasants, bureaucrats and small capitalists, with the latter two in the lead. It was the only postwar party, except perhaps the early UPD, which paralleled the movement of the twenties and thirties – except that now the workers were stronger, the bourgeois were weaker, and the peasants, though they had the vote, were less influential.

Meanwhile, the AOF Government General had swelled up in size to the point that it burst with the *loi-cadre* reforms of 1956. The intricate structure of federal and local taxes, grants, loans and adjustments of exchange rates left ample room for confusion about who subsidized whom in AOF. As the fifties proceeded, complaints began to be heard that Senegal and Ivory Coast were having to subsidize the poorer colonies, that AOF as a whole was subsidizing France, and the reverse of each: the controversy stirred a series of studies supporting each of these positions.[44] In fact, the Dakar region was the prime beneficiary of AOF expenditures, but this structure had the fatal flaw that, while the government of AOF was increasingly federal, its politics were territorial. Félix Houphouët-Boigny, whose strong base in Ivory Coast and whose leadership of the AOF-wide RDA gave him great power in Paris but little influence in Dakar, gave support to Gaston Deferre's proposal for the 1956 *loi-cadre* which, through decentralization, soon abolished the Government General.[45]

In Dahomey, the new UDD split in 1956 over the issue of affiliation with the RDA. Justin Ahomadegbé assumed leadership of the dominant UDD–RDA, while the initial UDD leaders, Alexandre Adandé and Emile Derlin Zinsou, ended up with the rump UDD-Convention. Ahomadegbé built his party's structure effectively, but he also followed a policy of strict support for Houphouët-Boigny's RDA line, and he began to adopt ethnic and regional politics as well as decry them. He appended the name Tomêtin to his name, to emphasize his descent from the eighteenth-century Fon king Agonglo through the female line. Even so, he was never able to gain full support of the royal family, as Justin Aho and others of the canton chiefs firmly supported Apithy's PRD. The UDD, despite its national aspirations and achievements, was rapidly identified as the party of the Fon, of Abomey and of Cotonou; further, it subordinated its policies to those of Abidjan.[46]

After the 1957 elections, Maga's MDD and the northern independents joined to form a single northern party, the RDD (Rassemblement démocratique dahoméen), after Apithy had attempted to dismiss a northern minister: the regionalization of politics was now complete.

The threatened general strike of 1958 brought a brief collapse in the government, but failed to divert the path of Dahomean politics. The trade unions of Dahomey, previously affiliated with two French centrals, had joined together in the UGTAN, whose all-African founding convention was held in Cotonou in 1957. When a strike for higher wages at the palm oil mill at Avrankou, near Porto-Novo, led to a lockout by the company in late 1957, the UGTAN called a general strike for January 28, 1958. Support strikes broke out in several towns, and a shooting incident in Cotonou on January 24 led to a pitched battle between strikers and troops. Because of the *loi-cadre* reforms, the strikers found themselves face to face not only with the French administration, but with Apithy and his government. In the turmoil, Apithy resigned his position as leader of the Assembly, and his government fell.[47] But because his party had a majority of seats, and because no forceful alternative was provided, Apithy was back in power two months later with a reshuffled cabinet. Ahomadegbé and the UDD, who had been allied to the strikers at the beginning of the conflict, were unable to maintain an alliance between a growing proletariat and a divided bourgeoisie. As a result, ties between UDD and the trade unions weakened, and UDD became steadily more like Apithy's PRD and Maga's RDD, using ethnic organizations to get out votes and participating in any political manipulations which might get the party closer to power.

The legacy of political repression and economic exploitation of the wartime and prewar years had come to its unfortunate fruition: an unprincipled, tripartite political system which responded to difficult choices with passivity and vacillation rather than leadership, and with short-term maneuvers rather than long-term policy. The intricate course of Dahomean politics in the late fifties was of little relevance to its economic future. No matter how much heat was generated by the divisive questions of the era – territorial *vs.* federal political structure, independence *vs.* continued colonial status – they were resolved not in Dahomey but in Paris, Dakar and Abidjan.[48] To compound its problems, Dahomey had to accommodate thousands of its expatriates who, in the narrow economic nationalism which accompanied the breakup of AOF, were expelled from Ivory Coast in 1958.[49] A country in desperate need of an organized economic policy was simply without one. Nevertheless, some positive changes accompanied this unhappy condition of Dahomean society and economy. The level of social services rose sharply, particularly in health and education. Levels of wages rose, albeit unevenly. Positive investment in agriculture began, though it was centered in state enterprise rather than in peasant production. The export of revenue from the country ceased, and was even reversed. And the oppression of the colonial government and of its canton chiefs came to an end. These new and more expansionary policies, though implemented in an era of confusion and demoralization, laid the groundwork for the eventual return of the economy to domestic growth.

12

Epilogue

The commodity exchange mode of production provides the fundamental continuity in the economic history of Dahomey. Estimates of per capita money holdings give a striking illustration to this continuity: money holdings, although showing some growth, were of the same order of magnitude for the late eighteenth, the late nineteenth and the mid-twentieth centuries.[1] This commodity exchange system of peasant agriculture, fishing, manufactures and marketing – closely articulated with non-market familial production and with the West African mercantile structure – developed in relative isolation, evolved and expanded in its interaction with other modes of production once trans-Atlantic commerce began, and remains a sector of major importance to this day.

Economic changes – qualitative transformations in the modes of production and quantitative growth in the economy – unfolded under the influence of four major forces, both internal and external in origin: the domestic mechanism of accumulation, the changing influence of West African and world markets, the development of industrial technology and the capitalist mode of production, and, finally, the state, both precolonial and colonial. The influence of these forces of change, however, was limited by the rate of growth, which has been incremental and evolutionary, rather than rapid or discontinuous. External influences, while they have been a positive stimulus to growth at times, halted and reversed the region's growth in the eighteenth and the twentieth centuries. Slave exports brought a decline in Aja population beginning in the 1690s, but rising prices brought peaks in export revenue in the 1730s and 1780s; exports then declined and the devastated population began to grow again. The French conquest bisected a century of rapid growth based on agricultural exports; it came at the moment when per capita export revenue finally exceeded the level of the 1730s. But on the eve of World War II, thirty years after the establishment of AOF and its revenue drain, aggregate growth came to a halt and per capita economic decline began. The net result, over three centuries, was an

281

unmistakable but inadequate growth rate on the order of one percent per year. The Bight of Benin was unable to approach the growth of the world's economic leaders during the era of the slave trade, and Dahomey failed to grow along with the leading African countries in the twentieth century; only from the 1840s to the 1930s was the growth rate adequate.

This interpretation of growth and transformation reveals the dynamics of long-term change in a West African economy. I have applied static and dynamic, long-term and short-term, general equilibrium and Marxian approaches to a variety of issues, but in each case with the hope of showing how and why the economy changed in the long run. The analysis emphasizes the conflict among classes, among states and in the marketplace which characterized the domestic economy. The conflict between master and slave is classic; that between small peasant and large landowner, while more subtle, became explicit in the early twentieth century.

The most traumatic conflicts, however, were between the domestic economy and external influences, specifically the demand for slaves and the demands of the colonial state. Each of these external influences created additional divisions within the society. In the seventeenth century, leading figures in Dahomey committed themselves to the export of slaves, and the decision was not reversed for two centuries. Whatever the pressures and inducements which led them to this decision, it was an extreme case of the potential gulf between expectations of private gain and the realities of social costs. The colonial state, in its time, at first united Dahomeans in opposition to its exploitative policies, but persevered in those policies until it succeeded in dividing its subjects. Still, Dahomey responded more effectively to the challenge of colonial rule than to that of the slave trade.

Previous writings on Dahomey have not effectively linked the relationships among different historical periods: Karl Polanyi's vision of Danhomè, for instance, with royal commerce in slaves isolated from the domestic economy, was heuristic rather than historical in nature. The seventeenth-century impact of the slave trade, though sudden and extensive, never succeeded in overwhelming the dominant commodity exchange system. Meanwhile the kings, generals, and merchants who led in the slave trade sought to excuse their greed with exaggerated myths of Fon and Oyo national expansion, the inevitability of war, and the distant origin of slaves; these myths found their way into the writings of historians. In fact the slave trade, while influenced by political factors and cultural values, was at base an economic venture: slave exports increased every time prices rose, except as limited by the declining population. And it was the Aja peoples, not the nearby Yoruba nor the inland peoples, who bore the brunt of the loss, displacement, and imbalanced age and sex ratios among those who remained.

282

The nineteenth century, in this review of the relationship among historical periods, must be set in the context of the slave-trading era which preceded it and the colonial era which succeeded it. The transition from slave exports to palm products, although it induced serious policy disputes inside and outside the Fon kingdom, was primarily caused by changing world market conditions rather than by state action. A portion, though a minority, of oil palm exports were produced by slave labor; nineteenth-century exports, including both slaves and palm products, brought lower revenues than in the eighteenth century. The Brazilian immigrants who joined the cosmopolitan community of the coast beginning in the 1830s are best treated, not as an intrusive group, but as an ethnic group of Dahomey, thus emphasizing the evolution of the domestic economy and not simply its clash with Europeans. They took advantage of the commercial opportunities on this frontier of the world capitalist economy to become leaders in a nascent bourgeoisie, along with landowners among the Fon, Gun, Yoruba and Gen.

Colonial Dahomey of the twentieth century was wealthier than in the nineteenth century, but this resulted from the market-induced expansion of the agricultural export sphere rather than from colonially-induced economic change. The relatively rapid growth of the state and of the capitalist sector in the twentieth century stemmed mainly from the transfer of resources to their activities from other sectors, rather than from the creation of new wealth. Dahomey's post-independence stagnation, including deficits in trade and government finance, was a recent development rather than an inherent quality, as the colony had maintained surpluses in both areas into the 1940s.[2]

The politics of the post-1945 area were the weakened remains of a long political tradition. When Dahomean merchants and planters constituted a demand for expansionary economic policy and a more democratic political system, the state stood firm and, under the cover of the Great Depression, split the elements of the national movement arrayed against it, broke its economic backbone, and repeatedly expanded the state sector of the economy. To complete its victory, the state imposed an ideology partly inherent in the outlook of conquerors, and partly developed in the course of the struggle: any advances, wealth, enlightenment, rule of law or participation in the community of nations from which Dahomey benefitted had come as a result of French tutelage. Of their own history, Dahomeans were left their wars, slavery, divination and religion. The Dahomean bourgeoisie began the century trying to obtain state support for the development of private capital; after this economic, political and ideological drubbing, it assumed control in 1960 committed to the expansion of state capital.

The end of such a colonial regime required a period of recovery before growth could resume. Some of the recovery measures began before 1960, as with the return of customs revenues from Dakar to Porto-Novo, and the extension of social services in response to the demands of the widely expanded electorate. A genuine fiscal subsidy, albeit with political strings, came to Dahomey from France for over a decade beginning in 1959.

A deep-water port went into operation at Cotonou in 1964, as industrial expansion continued apace. The opening of palm kernel mills in 1964 brought a virtual end to the artisanal processing of palm kernels, and caused a substantial discontinuity in the income and employment of women. The independent government proceeded with the capitalization of agriculture, especially in the expropriation of land and the constitution of oil palm groves under SONADER.[3] The commodity exchange sector was now restricted to foodstuffs and some manufactures in its productive activities, though it continued in marketing of both domestic and imported goods. Economic ties to France, built to a peak in the 1950s, gradually weakened after independence. Dahomey, as a member of EEC, strengthened ties with West Germany; it also sold growing amounts of palm kernel oil to the United States. In the 1970s the establishment of the Economic Community of West African States helped resolve the dilemma of choosing among Senegal, Ivory Coast and Nigeria as focal points: the country could now build its natural ties to Nigeria without having to break with Senegal and Ivory Coast. Growth, meanwhile, was slow, and per capita income continued to slip downward. Unemployment grew, especially as more Dahomean expatriates were expelled from Ivory Coast, Niger, Congo–Brazzaville, Ghana and Gabon.[4]

The political and economic conditions of Dahomey have interacted closely, and both are rooted in the social structure. The normal pattern has been for the political structure to respond to the economic, rather than the reverse. The kingdom of Danhomè gained control of much of the slave trade in the eighteenth century, thus reaping the benefits of a system already established. In the mid-nineteenth century the same kingdom tried to monopolize oil palm exports; it failed, but did manage to obtain a large and profitable share in the trade. The colonial conquerors did not change the economic system beyond the abolition of slavery, but were determined that European firms should have a larger share of the region's commerce. The state also determined the direction of public investment, but it did not thereby cause the transition to capitalism – industrial technology and changing relative prices did most to stimulate domestic capitalist enterprise in Dahomey. On the other hand, political decisions have brought major economic consequences, as with the Fon maintenance of slave exports and the colonial export of revenue to Dakar. This relationship between political and economic conditions will continue to be important, and if the years to come are to provide an environment in which the forces of growth can function without undue restraint, two main conditions will be required: that world economic forces abstain from draining the economy of its resources, and that the economy be led by an economic policy which rationally encourages growth for the economy as a whole.

Notes

1 Slavery, colonialism and economic growth, 1640–1960

1. The Bight of Benin exported an average of 7,000 slaves a year from 1676 to 1700, and an average of 15,000 slaves a year from 1701 to 1720, in each case roughly one-third of the total export of slaves from Africa. In earlier and later years, Angola was the leading region for slave exports. See Appendix 2 and Philip D. Curtin, *The Atlantic Slave Trade: a Census* (Madison, 1969), 119, 126.

2. International Bank for Reconstruction and Development, *World Bank Atlas*, 11th edn (Washington, 1976).

3. Among the many arguments that the region has suffered with the passage of time, one may cite Dov Ronen's argument that post-colonial Dahomey failed to achieve stable government because its people could not cross the barrier between tradition and modernity; C. W. Newbury's implication that the kingdom of Danhomè became weaker as it gave up exports of slaves for palm products; and I. A. Akinjogbin's argument that King Agaja of Danhomè, after attempting to halt the slave trade in the 1720s, was forced into a tragic dependence on slave exports. Dov Ronen, *Dahomey: between Tradition and Modernity* (Ithaca, 1975); C. W. Newbury, *The Western Slave Coast and its Rulers* (Oxford, 1961), 51–3; I. A. Akinjogbin, *Dahomey and its Neighbours, 1708–1818* (Cambridge, 1967), 73–109.

4. See Appendix 1 for details.

5. These calculations are based on linear regression of the logarithms of import purchasing power with time.

6. The assumption of a sudden impact of Europeans and the world market has been applied by many development economists. The classic statement of this outlook is Allan McPhee, *The Economic Revolution in British West Africa* (London, 1926).

7. In calculations throughout this study, it is assumed that the value of exports from Dahomey remained at roughly 15% of domestic product. In fact, for Great Britain, exports grew by an average 3.0% from the 1790s to the 1950s, as compared with 2.3% in domestic product; for the US, exports grew by an average 3.4% from the 1790s to the 1950s, as compared with 4.0% in GNP. The correspondence in each case is close but not exact. See also Deane and Cole, *British Economic Growth*, 28–9, 33, 309–12.

286

8. Note that I have chosen the convention of allowing the periods to overlap by some twenty years, rather than create 'transitional' periods or attempt to isolate sharp turning points. In political history the period of hegemony by Danhomè, 1727–1892, is usually subdivided according to the reigns of its kings. The French ruled Dahomey from 1892 to 1960.
9. See Chapter 2.
10. The term 'commodity exchange mode of production' is intended to evoke both the 'simple commodity production' of Marx and the general equilibrium exchange model of Walras. In using this term rather than that of 'tributary mode of production' proposed by Samir Amin for the same type of economy, I have chosen to emphasize the aspect of independent producers linked by a market, rather than the aspect of a peasantry subordinate to a state. Karl Marx, *Capital* (3 vols., Moscow, 1971), I: 15–20; Léon Walras, *Eléments d'économie politique pure* (Paris, 1977); Samir Amin, *Le Développement inégal* (Paris, 1972), 4–5.
11. Rey has coined the term 'lineage mode of production.' Pierre-Philippe Rey, *Colonialisme, néo-colonialisme et transition au capitalisme: example de la 'Comilog' au Congo–Brazzaville* (Paris, 1971), 207–15.
12. The term 'social formation' is used here as the overall characterization of the economy, taking account of its modes of production, the state, and its links with other economies. John G. Taylor, *From Modernization to Modes of Production* (London, 1979), 106–7.
13. For details see Chapter 2 and Appendixes 1, 2 and 3.
14. See pp. 40–5, 51–4.
15. The early era of agricultural exports, 1840–90, is considered in Chapters 2 and 3; the period 1890–1914 is investigated in Chapters 4–8; and the later years of this era are considered in Chapters 10 and 11.
16. Economic structures in the early colonial years are analyzed in Chapters 4–6.
17. See Chapter 8.
18. On French policy see Chapters 7 and 10.
19. See Chapter 11.
20. Economic growth is analyzed in Chapter 9.
21. See Chapter 10.

2 The Dahomean economy, 1640–1890

1. Sources for seventeenth century Bight of Benin include Olfert Dapper, *Description de l'Afrique* (Amsterdam, 1686); William Bosman, *A New and Accurate Description of the Coast of Guinea* (London, 1967; first published 1705); John Barbot, *A Description of the Coasts of North and South Guinea*, in A. Churchill, ed., *A Collection of Voyages and Travels* (London, 1732), V: 1–668; Sieur d'Elbée, 'Journal du voyage du Sieur d'Elbée . . . 1669,' in J. Clodoré, *Relation de ce qui s'est passé dans les isles et terre-firme de l'Amérique* . . . (2 vols., Paris, 1671), II: 347–558; Paul Roussier, *L'Etablissement d'Issiny, 1687–1702* (Paris, 1935); Henri Labouret and Paul

Rivet, *Le Royaume d'Arda et son évangélisation au XVIIe siècle* (Paris, 1929).

2. Dapper, *Description*, 303–8; Barbot, *North and South Guinea*, 321–56; Bosman, *Description of Guinea*, 329–37, 395–9; Jean-Baptiste Labat, *Voyage du Chevalier des Marchais en Guinée, isles voisines, et à Cayenne fait en 1725, 1726 et 1727* (4 vols., Paris, 1730), II: 1–5, 273–84. For a careful study of this issue, see P. E. H. Hair, 'Ethnolinguistic Continuity on the Guinea Coast,' *Journal of African History 8*, 2 (1967), 247–68.

3. William Smith, *A New Voyage to Guinea* (London, 1745), 207.

4. Dapper, *Description*, 291, 304; Bosman, *Description of Guinea*, 336, 339, 389; Barbot, *North and South Guinea*, 329.

5. Barbot, *North and South Guinea*, 338–348; Bosman, *Description of Guinea*, 129. See also A. F. C. Ryder, *Benin and the Europeans, 1485–1897* (London, 1969), 60–1.

6. Portuguese ships first sailed along the Bight of Benin at some point between 1471 and 1480. Portuguese documents of the sixteenth and seventeenth centuries make occasional references to the Bight of Benin, as do seventeenth-century Dutch records. Ryder, *Benin*, 24–6, 73–4; John W. Blake, *West Africa: Quest for God and Gold, 1454–1578*, 2nd edn (London, 1977), 222; Pierre Verger, *Flux et reflux de la traite des nègres entre le golfe du Bénin et Bahia de Todos os Santos du dix-septième au dix-neuvième siècle* (The Hague, 1968), 159, n. 1; R. A. Kea, 'Firearms and Warfare on the Gold and Slave Coasts from the Sixteenth to the Nineteenth Centuries,' *Journal of African History 12*, 2 (1971), 191–3.

7. Joseph Greenberg, *The Languages of Africa* (Bloomington, 1966), 8; Robert G. Armstrong, *The Study of West African Languages* (Ibadan, 1964), 12–13.

   Jacques Bertho misinterpreted myths of dynastic origin to mean that the Aja peoples are migrants and lineal descendants from the Yoruba, and he has been followed, for example, by Karl Polanyi and I. A. Akinjogbin. Emmanuel Karl has documented the correction. Jacques Bertho, 'La Parenté des Yoruba aux peuplades de Dahomey et Togo,' *Africa 19*, 2 (1949), 121–32; Karl Polanyi, *Dahomey and the Slave Trade: an Analysis of an Archaic Economy* (Seattle, 1966), 9–16; I. A. Akinjogbin, 'The Expansion of Oyo and the Rise of Dahomey, 1600–1800,' in J. F. A. Ajayi and Michael Crowder, eds., *History of West Africa* (2 vols., London, 1971), I: 305–11; Emmanuel Karl, *Traditions orales du Dahomey–Bénin* (Niamey, 1974), 203.

8. Coursey indicates that African yams (*Dioscorea rotundata*) provide the bulk of yams produced in Ghana and Nigeria, rather than Asian yams (*D. alata*). Asian yams came to West Africa only with the Portuguese, and were never adopted on a large scale. Early European agronomists, however, often mistakenly identified the African *D. rotundata* as the Asian *D. alata*; G. P. Murdock, in his pioneering study on African culture history, erroneously concluded that yams first came to West Africa by diffusion from Asia. D. G. Coursey, *The Yam* (London, 1967), 7–26, 59; Yves Henry and Paul Amman, *Maïs, igname et patate* (Paris, 1913), 55; G. P. Murdock, *Africa, its Peoples and their Culture History* (New York, 1959), 242–59; Marvin P. Miracle, *Maize in Tropical Africa* (Madison, 1966), 82–3, 90.

9. Ryder, however, concludes that shell currency was in use in Benin before the Portuguese, and that these were either local shells or cowries transported overland. Ryder, *Benin*, 60; Dapper, *Description*, 305.

10. For accounts of oral traditions, see Auguste Le Herissé, *L'Ancien Royaume du Dahomey* (Paris, 1911), 274–8; W. J. Argyle, *The Fon of Dahomey* (Oxford, 1966), 4–13; see also Ryder, *Benin*, 73–4.

11. Robert S. Smith, *Kingdoms of the Yoruba*, 2nd edn (London, 1976), 123; Eva Meyerowitz, *The Early History of the Akan States of Ghana* (London, 1974), 71–99; Ivor Wilks, 'The Mossi and Akan States, 1500–1800,' in J. F. A. Ajayi and Michael Crowder, *History of West Africa* (2 vols., London, 1971), I: 364–5.

12. Jan Vansina, 'Traditions of Genesis,' *Journal of African History 15*, 2 (1974), 317–22; Karl, *Traditions orales*, 199–203, 209, 287, 330, 338, 398.

13. Rey, *Colonialisme*, 70–215; Georges Dupré and Pierre-Philippe Rey, 'Reflections on the Pertinence of a Theory of the History of Exchange,' *Economy and Society 2*, 2 (1973), 131–63.

14. Frederic Pryor, *The Origins of the Economy* (New York, 1977).

15. Claude Meillassoux, 'Essai d'interprétation du phénomène économique dans les sociétés traditionnelles d'autosubsistance,' *Cahiers d'Etudes africaines 1*, 4 (1960), 38–67; M. Godelier, *La Notion de mode de production asiatique et les schémas marxistes d'évolution des sociétés* (Paris, 1963); Jean Suret-Canale, 'Les Sociétés traditionnelles en Afrique noire et le concept du mode de production asiatique,' *La Pensée*, 177 (1964), 19–42; Catherine Coquery-Vidrovitch, 'Recherches sur un mode de production africain,' *La Pensée*, 144 (1969), 61–78; Emmanuel Terray, *Le Marxisme devant les sociétés 'primitives'* (Paris, 1968); Rey, *Colonialisme*, 207–15; Amin, *Développement*, 9–48.

16. Lloyd A. Fallers, 'Are African Cultivators to be Called "Peasants"?' *Current Anthropology 2* (1961), 108–11; Alan K. Smith and Claude E. Welch, Jr., eds., 'Peasants in Africa,' special issue of *African Studies Review 20*, 3 (1977).

17. Richard Vengroff's comparative study of 86 African societies shows a correlation between population density and state formation, though only at high levels of population density. States in areas of lower population density are not explained, on a cross-sectional basis, by this factor. Richard Vengroff, 'Population Density and State Formation in Africa,' *African Studies Review 19*, 1 (1976), 67–74. Dahomey was high in population density.

18. Thomas Q. Reefe, 'Traditions of Genesis and the Luba Diaspora,' *History in Africa 4* (1977), 183–206.

19. C. R. Boxer, *The Dutch in Brazil, 1624–54* (Oxford, 1957), 83–4, 137–8; Verger *Flux et reflux*, 667. Gold mines brought an additional demand for slave labor in Brazil beginning in the 1690s. A. J. R. Russell-Wood, 'Technology and Society: the Impact of Gold Mining on the Institution of Slavery in Portuguese America,' *Journal of Economic History 37*, 1 (1977), 64, 68–70.

20. Slaves of Aja origin were noted in Peru as early as 1565, and slaves of Yoruba origin were noted as early as 1605. In Frederick Bowser's sample of Peruvian slaves, drawn from notarial records, three percent of slaves noted from 1600 to

1640 were of Aja origin, and one half percent were of Yoruba origin. F. Bowser, *The African Slave in Colonial Peru, 1524–1650* (Stanford, 1974), pp. 40–1.

21. Other major exporting regions were the Bight of Biafra from the mid-eighteenth to early nineteenth centuries, southeastern Africa in the nineteenth century, and the Gold Coast in the eighteenth century. Curtin, *Slave Trade*.

    On the Congo–Angola coast, see Joseph C. Miller, 'Legal Portuguese Slaving from Angola: some Preliminary Indications of Volume and Direction,' *Revue française d'Histoire d'Outre-mer 62*, 226–7 (1975), 135–76; W. G. L. Randles, 'La Civilisation bantou, son essor et son declin,' *Annales–Economies, Sociétés, Civilisations 29* (1974), 272–4; David Birmingham, *Trade and Conflict in Angola* (Oxford, 1966).

22. The Bight of Benin drew on an area of 350,000 km² (three times the area of modern Bénin), while the Congo–Angola coast drew on 1.3 million km² (the area of modern Angola). The whole area on which the Atlantic slave trade drew, from the Senegal to the Cuanza, reached 8 million km². For somewhat different estimates of the regional impact of slave exports, see Roger Anstey, *The Atlantic Slave Trade and British Abolition, 1760–1810* (Cambridge, 1975), 79–82.

23. Verger, *Flux et reflux*, 28–53.

24. Johannes Postma, 'The Dimension of the Dutch Slave Trade from Western Africa,' *Journal of African History 13*, 2 (1972), 238–9.

25. Jean-Claude Nardin, 'La Reprise des relations franco-dahoméennes au XIXᵉ siècle: la mission d'Auguste Bouët à la cour d'Abomey (1851),' *Cahiers d'Etudes africaines 7*, 25 (1967), 62–6; Newbury, *Western Slave Coast*, 130; Archives nationales de Bénin, Registres de correspondance, 1890–3.

26. See Appendix 2, below. This technique is an extension of the approaches of Debien and Curtin. Gérard Debien and others. 'Les Origines des esclaves des Antilles,' *Bulletin de l'IFAN 23* (1961), 363–87; *29* (1967), 536–58; Curtin, *Slave Trade*. The detailed list of slaving voyages from Nantes drawn up by Jean Mettas tends to confirm the pattern of slave exports suggested here in its total and in its regional, temporal and ethnic distribution. Full assessment of Mettas's extraordinary work must, however, await publication of his equivalent data on other French ports. Jean Mettas, *Répertoire des expéditions négrières françaises au XVIIIᵉ siècle*, edited by Serge Daget (Paris, 1979).

27. The Ewe peoples of modern Togo and Ghana, who form the western portion of the Aja–Ewe peoples, are not accounted for separately here. Those living near the Mono River were, when enslaved, classified among the 'Ardra' and 'Popo'; those living further west were exported in small numbers, and usually via the Gold Coast.

28. Seventeenth-century travellers reported that Yoruba ('Ulkami,' 'Lukumi' and 'Oyeo') slaves provided the majority of exports, but no confirmation can be found in New World data. The easiest resolution to this contradiction is that Yoruba slaves were exported in quantity before 1680, but not after. I have assumed Yoruba slaves to be ten percent of the total before 1680. Dapper, *Description*, 307; Barbot, *North and South Guinea*, 327, 356.

29. Marion Johnson, 'The Atlantic Slave Trade and the Economy of West Africa,' in Roger Anstey and P. E. H. Hair, eds., *Liverpool, the African Slave Trade, and Abolition* (Bristol, 1976), 30–2; Philip D. Curtin, *Economic Change in Precolonial Africa: Senegambia in the Era of the Slave Trade* (2 vols., Madison, 1975), I:177–87; David Northrup, *Trade Without Rulers: Pre-Colonial Economic Development in South-Eastern Nigeria* (Oxford, 1978).

30. J. D. Fage, 'Slavery and the Slave Trade in the Context of West African History,' *Journal of African History 10*, 3 (1969), 393–404; J. D. Fage, *A History of West Africa*, 4th edn (Cambridge, 1969), 81–95; J. D. Fage, 'The Effect of the Export Slave Trade on African Populations,' in R. P. Moss and R. J. A. Rathbone, eds., *The Population Factor in African Studies* (London, 1975), 15–23.

    Caldwell, in contradiction to Fage, has assumed that populations in the forest zone were quite low in AD 1500. J. C. Caldwell, 'Major Questions in African Demographic History,' in University of Edinburgh, Centre of African Studies, *African Historical Demography* (Edinburgh, 1977), 13–15; see also the articles in the same volume by D. Ian Pool, T. H. Hollingsworth, Thurstan Shaw, and H. I. Ajeugbu.

    My results are not contradictory to Professor Fage's conclusion that the population of West Africa was not permanently reduced by slave exports. There is room, however, for a difference of interpretation. In particular, from the perspective of the Aja peoples, one must take exception to Fage's unfortunate remark that 'In the worst affected areas, the effect may have been no more than to cream-off surplus population, i.e. those whom it was more profitable to sell in return for imports than to employ in production at home.' Fage, 'Effect,' 20.

31. See Appendix 3 for details. Assuming a smaller growth rate of 0.2% before 1870 gives substantially the same results.

32. See Appendix 3.

33. Jahnheinz Jahn, *Muntu, an Outline of the New African Culture* (New York, 1961), 62–9 and *passim*; Pierre Verger, *Dieux d'Afrique* (Paris, 1954).

34. Jahn, *Muntu*, 33–9; Pierre Verger, 'Le Culte des Vodoun d'Abomey aurait-il été apporté à St-Louis de Maranhon par la mère du roi Ghézo?' *Etudes dahoméennes 8* (1952), 19–24.

35. Michael Mason, 'Captive and Client Labour and the Economy of Bida Emirate, 1857–1901,' *Journal of African History 14*, 3 (1973), 453–72; David C. Tambo, 'The Sokoto Caliphate Slave Trade in the Nineteenth Century,' *International Journal of African Historical Studies 9*, 2 (1976), 187–217; Jan Hogendorn, 'The Economics of Slave Use on Two "Plantations" in the Zaria Emirate of the Sokoto Caliphate,' *International Journal of African Historical Studies 10*, 3 (1977), 369–83; Paul E. Lovejoy, 'Plantations in the Economy of the Sokoto Caliphate,' *Journal of African History 19*, 3 (1978), 341–68.

36. Fage, *History of West Africa*, 87; Marion Johnson, 'Atlantic Slave Trade,' 30.

37. Werner Peukert, *Der Atlantische Sklavenhandel von Dahomey, 1740–1797* (Wiesbaden, 1978), 305–6.

38. The proportions of ethnic groups in slave exports show no sharp change from

291

the 1770s to 1780s, but it is unlikely that the export of slaves from each ethnic group would have doubled at the same time, especially when price changed little – hence the volumes of the 1770s and 1780s were probably more similar than my estimates show. I used Curtin's estimates for British and French slave exports in the 1770s and 1780s: his estimates of British exports in the 1780s and for French exports were constructed quite indirectly. See Appendix 3; Manning, 'Slave Trade,' 117, 138; Curtin, *Slave Trade*, 177–8; Philip D. Curtin, 'Measuring the Atlantic Slave Trade,' in Stanley L. Engerman and Eugene D. Genovese, eds., *Race and Slavery in the Western Hemisphere: Quantitative Studies* (Princeton, 1975), 110–11.

39. Manning, 'Slave Trade,' 119–21.

40. That Peukert's evidence for the years before 1770 is less detailed than for later years is indicated by the unchanging figures for his annual estimates for ports outside Ouidah. For the whole period, if one adds Peukert's estimate for Ouidah to half his estimate for all other ports, the result is relatively close to my estimate for each decade. Peukert. *Sklavenhandel*, 305–6.

41. Lagos began exporting slaves in the 1750s, but did not become a major port until the 1790s. Verger, *Flux et reflux*, 207–8, 211; Robin Law, *The Oyo Empire, c. 1600-c. 1836* (Oxford, 1977), 222, 224, 226; Manning, 'Slave Trade, 122–3.

42. Richard Nelson Bean. *The British Trans-Atlantic Slave Trade, 1650–1775* (New York, 1975), 69; d'Elbee, 'Journal,' 382; Dapper, *Description*, 305–6; Barbot, *North and South Guinea*, 323–6; Labouret and Rivet, *Royaume d'Arda*, 22, 25. See also Walter Rodney, *How Europe Underdeveloped Africa* (London, 1972), 88–92.

43. Bean, *Trans-Atlantic Slave Trade*, 73, 78; E. Phillip LeVeen, *British Slave Trade Suppression Policies, 1821–1865* (New York, 1977), 122–34.

44. Marion Johnson, 'The Ounce in Eighteenth-Century West African Trade,' *Journal of African History 7*, 2 (1966), 212–13; Bean, *Trans-Atlantic Slave Trade*, 138–47.

45. Barbot, *North and South Guinea*, 326–7, 346, 350; Bosman, *Description of Guinea*, 332, 398.

46. For export revenues, see Appendix 1. For import goods, see Barbot, *North and South Guinea*, 349; K. G. Davies, *The Royal African Company* (London, 1957), 350–7.

47. Descriptions of slavery are given in Labat, *Voyage du Chevalier des Marchais*, II:100–2, 233–9; Auguste Le Herissé, *L'Ancien Royaume*, 50–7; Melville J. Herskovits, *Dahomey; an Ancient West African Kingdom* (2 vols., New York, 1938), I:82–4, 99–101; Law, *The Oyo Empire*, 67–70, 189–90, 205–8.

48. Robert Paul Thomas and Richard Nelson Bean, 'The Fishers of Men: the Profits of the Slave Trade,' *Journal of Economic History 34*, 4 (1974), 885–914; Henry A. Gemery and Jan S. Hogendorn, 'The Atlantic Slave Trade: a Tentative Economic Model,' *Journal of African History 15*, 2 (1974), 223–46; Henry A. Gemery and Jan S. Hogendorn, 'The Economic Costs of West African Participation in the Atlantic Slave Trade: a Preliminary Sampling for the Eighteenth Century,' in Henry A. Gemery and Jan S. Hogendorn, eds., *The*

Uncommon Market (New York, 1979), 143–62; Henry A. Gemery and Jan S. Hogendorn, 'Technological Change, Slavery and the Slave Trade,' in Clive Dewey and A. G. Hopkins, eds., *The Imperial Impact: Studies on the Economic History of Africa and India* (London, 1978), 243–58; LeVeen, *Suppression Policies*; T. C. I. Ryan, 'The Economics of Trading in Slaves' (unpublished PhD dissertation, Massachusetts Institute of Technology, 1975).

49. Bean, *Trans-Atlantic Slave Trade*, 73; LeVeen, *Suppression Policies*, 143.

50. Karl, *Traditions orales*, 175–6, 245; Robert Cornevin, *Histoire du Dahomey* (Paris, 1962), 88–91; Georges Edouard Bourgoignie, *Les Hommes de l'eau: ethno-écologie du Dahomey lacustre* (Paris, 1972), 65–89; Yves Person, 'Chronologie du royaume gun de Hogbonou (Porto-Novo),' *Cahiers d'Etudes africaines 15*, 58 (1975), 232–5.

51. Akinjogbin, *Dahomey*, 74–87.

52. David Henige and Marion Johnson, 'Agaja and the Slave Trade: another Look at the Evidence,' *History in Africa 3* (1976), 57–68.

53. David Ross (personal communication). The contrast with Asante is striking: the consolidation of Asante power over most of the Akan peoples coincided with the end of large-scale exports of Akan slaves and their replacement by exports of Voltaic slaves. On Asante economy and commerce, see Joseph R. La Torre, 'Wealth Surpasses Everything: an Economic History of Asante, 1750–1874' (unpublished PhD dissertation, University of California, Berkeley, 1978).

54. A. G. Hopkins, *An Economic History of West Africa* (London, 1973), 105; Robin Law, 'Royal Monopoly and Private Enterprise in the Atlantic Trade: the Case of Dahomey,' *Journal of African History 18*, 4 (1977), 555–67.

55. Rosemary Arnold, 'A Port of Trade: Whydah on the Guinea Coast,' and 'Separation of Trade and Market: Great Market of Whydah,' in Karl Polanyi and others, eds., *Trade and Market in the Early Empires* (Glencoe, Ill., 1957), 154–76, 177–87.

56. Akinjogbin, *Dahomey*, 31–2; Law, 'Royal Monopoly,' 559–67; Peukert, *Sklavenhandel*, 134–51, 170–8. Peukert provides a detailed refutation of Polanyi's view of Danhomè.

57. The term 'inland' is taken from Dalzel's subtitle: Archibald Dalzel, *The History of Dahomy, an Inland Kingdom of Africa* (London, 1967, first published 1793); Polanyi, *Dahomey*, 3–8, 17, 22, 99–139.

58. Because Danhomè was willing to consider installation of a British consul in Ouidah in 1846, Arnold concluded Danhomè was willing to cede Ouidah to Britain in the 1730s. Polanyi's institutional analyses (of redistribution, reciprocity, householding and exchange) combine sources from the eighteenth to the twentieth century, implicitly assuming that no changes in institutions occurred across three widely different centuries. Arnold, 'Port of Trade,' 160–2; Polanyi, *Dahomey*, 31–95; Pierre-Philippe Rey, *Les Alliances des classes* (Paris, 1973), 29–33. For a comparison of substantivist, world-system and Marxian views of Danhomè, see Katharine P. Moseley, 'The Political Economy of Dahomey', *Research in Economic Anthropology 2* (1979), 69–90.

For a view of Danhomè stressing the role of human sacrifice, see Dov Ronen, 'On the African Role in the Trans-Atlantic Slave Trade in Dahomey,' *Cahiers d'Etudes africaines 11*, 41 (1971), 5–13.

59. Figure 2.3. See also Law, *The Qyǫ Empire*, 92–5; Peukert, *Sklavenhandel*, 305–6.

60. For a view of Danhomè as an economy dominated by slavery and slave trade, see Georg Elwert, *Wirtschaft und Herrschaft von 'Dǎxome' (Dahomey) im 18. Jahrundert: Ökonomie des Sklavenraubs und Gesellschaftsstruktur 1724 bis 1818* (Munich, 1973).

61. These portions of slave exports do not include exports by European factors (that is, I have assumed that European factors bought slaves from big and small merchants and from individuals in the same proportion as each of these groups sold slaves directly to the ships). The French ship *Dahomet* in 1773 purchased 422 slaves in Ouidah, 238 from European factors and the balance from African merchants; the English ship *Swallow* in 1791–2 purchased 142 slaves, 13 from European factors. A larger sample would be preferable. Following Peukert, I have classified big merchants as those selling over ten slaves each (100 oz), and small merchants as those selling three to ten slaves each (30–100 oz). Peukert, *Sklavenhandel*, 333–7.

62. Akinjogbin overestimated the absolute and relative magnitude of state commerce in suggesting that King Tegbesu of Danhomè earned between £216,000 and £280,000 from sale of slaves in 1750 – over twice my estimate of total export revenue for the whole of Dahomey. He accepted high quantity and price estimates, and assumed that all revenue went to the king. Akinjogbin, *Dahomey*, 134; see also Appendix 1.

63. Peukert, *Sklavenhandel*, 289–91.

64. Peukert, taking the French factor Pruneau at his word, concludes that Brazilian slave merchants sold only tobacco, and that tobacco therefore accounted for half the value of imports. But tobacco almost certainly never reached half of total imports. Brazilian merchants presumably exchanged part of their tobacco with English, French and Dutch merchants to obtain the proper variety of imports before purchasing slaves. Brazilian ships stopped at Elmina until 1791, paying ten percent of their cargo to the Dutch for a passport to trade. Peukert, *Sklavenhandel*, 105, 145, 190; Pierre Verger, 'Rôle joué par le tabac de Bahia dans la traite des esclaves au golfe du Bénin,' *Cahiers d'Etudes africaines 4*, 15 (1964), 355–6, 364; Verger, *Flux et reflux*, 44–53; La Torre, 'Wealth Surpasses Everything,' 395–7.

65. Assuming a five percent annual loss of cowries would yield a smaller limit of £1.5 million.

66. Peukert's calculation is for the kingdom of Danhomè only, while mine is for Dahomey as a whole, though that is not the main cause of the difference. The errors in his estimates stem from too high an estimate of population (250,000 – identical to that of the early twentieth century) and too high an estimate of per capita domestic income (4.5 trade ounces or £9 per person). Peukert actually calculates two estimates of the ratio of exports to domestic

product: 20%, which he rejects as unreasonably high, and 2.5%, which he accepts as reasonable. Peukert, *Sklavenhandel*, 195–7, 372; see also Table 1.4, p. 5.

67. For the estimates of Nigerian and Dahomean portions of Bight of Benin slave exports, see Appendix 1.
68. P. E. H. Hair, 'The Enslavement of Koelle's Informants,' *Journal of African History* 6, 2 (1965), 193–203; J. F. Shön and Samuel Crowther, *Journals of the Rev. James Frederick Shön and Mr. Samuel Crowther*, 2nd edn (London, 1970), 371–85; Cyrille Aguessy, 'Esclavage, colonisation et tradition au Dahomey (sud),' *Présence africaine*, n.s. 6 (1956), 58–67.
69. David Brion Davis, *The Problem of Slavery in the Age of Revolution* (New York, 1975).
70. Saburi O. Biobaku, *The Egba and Their Neighbours, 1842–1872* (Oxford, 1957); Edouard Dunglas, 'Contribution a l'histoire du Moyen-Dahomey,' *Etudes dahoméennes*, 20 (1957), 72–125.
71. Akinjogbin, *Dahomey*, 183, 190, 193.
72. Verger, *Flux et reflux*, 460–7, 563–6; Pierre Verger, 'Influence du Brésil au golfe du Bénin,' in Théodore Monod, ed., *Les Afro-Américains* (Dakar, 1953), 26–52; J. Michael Turner, 'Les Bresiliens: the Impact of former Brazilian Slaves upon Dahomey' (unpublished PhD dissertation, Boston University, 1975), 88–98.
73. Peukert, *Sklavenhandel*, 80; Capt. John Adams, *Remarks on the Country Extending from Cape Palmas to the River Congo* (London, 1966 first published 1823), 82–7; Capt. Frederick E. Forbes, *Dahomey and the Dahomans* (2 vols., London, 1851), II:112–13.
74. Newbury, *Western Slave Coast*, 39–41; l'Abbé J. Laffitte, *Le Dahomé: souvenirs de voyage et de mission* (Tours, 1873), 124–5; LeVeen, *Suppression Policies*, 23–32; Edward Reynolds, *Trade and Economic Change on the Gold Coast, 1807–1874* (London, 1974), 89, 141–2.
75. George E. Brooks, Jr., *Yankee Traders, Old Coasters and African Middlemen* (Boston, 1970), 260; Tambo, 'Caliphate Slave Trade,' 191.
76. Turner, 'Les Bresiliens,' 29–78.
77. Jean Herskovits Kopytoff, *A Preface to Modern Nigeria: the 'Sierra Leonians' in Yoruba, 1830–1890* (Madison, 1965).
78. Assuming 5,000 slave exports per year at a price of £15 each yields a gross export revenue of some £75,000 for the Bight of Benin; assuming, as in the eighteenth century, that Ouidah provided half the exports of the coast and that the state sold twenty percent of the slaves at Ouidah, estimated gross royal revenue from slave exports was £8,000 per year. Winniett's 1848 estimate of £10,000 was ignored by the Colonial Office in favor of Cruickshank's. David A. Ross, 'The Autonomous Kingdom of Dahomey, 1818–1894' (unpublished PhD dissertation, University of London, 1967), 86–7; cf. Newbury, *Western Slave Coast*, 51.
79. David A Ross, 'The Career of Domingo Martinez in the Bight of Benin, 1833–1864,' *Journal of African History* 6, 1 (1965), 85–8.

80. LeVeen, *Suppression Policies*, 6–11.
81. For Sokoto Caliphate slave prices, see Tambo, 'Caliphate Slave Trade,' 210–17.
82. The publication of Curtin's *Slave Trade* led to renewed discussion of the impact of slave exports on African society. Fage, 'Slavery and the Slave Trade'; Fage, *History of West Africa*, 81–95; Marion D. de B. Kilson, 'West African Society and the Atlantic Slave Trade, 1441–1865,' in Nathan I. Huggins, Martin Kilson and Daniel M. Fox, eds., *Key issues in the Afro-American Experience* (New York, 1971), 39–53; C. C. Wrigley, 'Historicism in Africa: Slavery and State Formation,' *African Affairs 80*, 279 (1971), 113–24; Hopkins, *Economic History*, 101–23; Albert van Dantzig, 'Effects of the Atlantic Slave Trade on some West African Societies,' *Revue française d'Histoire d'Outre-mer 62*, 226–7 (1975), 252–69; G. N. Uzoigwe, 'The Slave Trade and African Societies,' *Transactions of the Historical Society of Ghana 14*, 2 (1973), 187–212; Marion Johnson, 'The Atlantic Slave Trade'; Gemery and Hogendorn, 'Economic Costs'; P. E. H. Hair, *The Atlantic Slave Trade and Black Africa* (London, 1978). For earlier treatments, see Walter Rodney, 'African Slavery and Other Forms of Social Oppression on the Upper Guinea Coast,' *Journal of African History 7*, 3 (1966), 431–43; Basil Davidson, *Black Mother: the Years of the African Slave Trade* (London, 1961).
83. Eric Williams, *Capitalism and Slavery* (London, 1944); Roger Anstey, 'The Historical Debate on the Abolition of the British Slave Trade,' in Roger Anstey and P. E. H. Hair, eds., *Liverpool, the African Slave Trade, and Abolition* (Bristol, 1976), 157–66; Immanuel Wallerstein, *The Modern World-System: Capitalist Agriculture and the Origins of the European World-Economy in the Sixteenth Century* (New York, 1974).
84. A. J. H. Latham, *Old Calabar, 1600–1891* (Oxford, 1973), 55–7, 66–7; A. J. H. Latham, 'Price Fluctuations in the Early Palm Oil Trade,' *Journal of African History 19*, 2 (1978), 213–18.
85. Newbury, *Western Slave Coast*, 34, 42, 57; Bernard Schnapper, *La Politique et le commerce français dans le golfe de Guinée de 1838 à 1871* (Paris, 1961), 163–7; Henri Brunschwig, *L'Expansion allemande outre-mer* (Paris, 1957), 78–9.
86. For indications on the export of palm oil to Bahia, see Verger, 'Influence,' 88–95; Turner, 'Les Bresiliens,' 61; Newbury, *Western Slave Coast*, 42.
87. Exports from Lagos, shown separately in Figure 2.4, help to indicate the level and fluctuations of exports from Dahomey (though ten to thirty percent of reported Lagos exports were in fact transshipped from Porto-Novo). Exports for the coast from Anécho (Little Popo) to Lomé–the future German Togo–were about one-fifth those of the coast from Agoué to Porto-Novo. See Newbury, *Western Slave Coast*, 125, 147.
88. Comparing Lagos prices for 1865–70 with 1896–1900, the ratio of palm kernel prices to palm oil prices rose by 25% from the former period to the latter. Prices computed from Statistical Abstracts for Lagos Colony, United Kingdom Parliamentary Papers.
89. Recent contributions on the subject include Newbury, *Western Slave Coast*,

37–44, 50–55; Schnapper, *La Politique*, 167–80, 190–4; Coquery-Vidrovitch, 'Mode de production,' 69–78; Catherine Coquery-Vidrovitch, 'De la traite des esclaves à l'exportation de l'huile de palme et des palmistes au Dahomey: XIXe siècle,' in Claude Meillassoux, ed., *The Development of Indigenous Trade and Markets in West Africa* (London, 1971), 107–23; Ross, 'Domingo Martinez'; Ross, 'Autonomous Kingdom,' 55–80; Patrick Manning, 'Slaves, Palm Oil, and Political Power on the West African Coast,' *African Historical Studies 2*, 2 (1969), 279–88; Verger, *Flux et reflux*, 543–97; Honorat Aguessy, 'Le Dan-Homê du XIXe siècle était-il une société esclavagiste?' *Revue française d'Etudes politiques africaines*, 50 (1970), 71–91 Nardin, 'Relations franco-dahoméennes'; Law, 'Royal Monopoly,' 567–76.

90. Ross, 'Autonomous Kingdom,' 70.

91. Ross, 'Autonomous Kingdom,' 123–4, 133–4.

92. Hopkins, *Economic History*, 154–66; A. G. Hopkins, 'Economic Imperialism in West Africa: Lagos, 1880–1892,' *Economic History Review 21* (1968), 580–606.

93. Hopkins, 'Economic Imperialism,' 587–90; Coquery-Vidrovitch, 'De la traite,' 116–17; Ross, 'Domingo Martinez,' 83, 85–6; Ross, 'Autonomous Kingdom,' 142–4. For brief descriptions of plantations, see Forbes, *Dahomey and the Dahomans*, I:115–16, 123–4. J. A. Djivo has recently verified and mapped the location of many plantations in Danhomè. Joseph Adrien Djivo, 'Gbehanzin et Ago-Li-Agbo, le refus de la colonisation dans l'ancien royaume de Danxome; 1875–1900 (fin de la monarchie)' (unpublished thèse d'état, University of Paris I, 1979), 111.

94. Cowrie–sterling exchange rates went from 4 heads of cowries (at 2,000 cowries per head) per pound sterling in 1851, to 10 heads per pound in 1860, to 20 heads per pound in 1880, to 40 heads per pound in 1890. The devaluation was caused not simply by increased imports of cowries, but by their progressive replacement by dollars and especially sterling. Hopkins, 'Economic History of Lagos,' 170–81.

95. Brazilian families set up schools in their homes in Agoué, Grand Popo, Ouidah and Lagos. The de Souza family school was held in the Portuguese fort. Turner, 'Les Bresiliens,' 155–212; Kopytoff, *Preface*, 31–6, 120–1, 236–7.

96. Newbury, *Western Slave Coast*, 111–40; Boniface I. Obichere, *West African States and European Expansion: the Dahomey–Niger Hinterland, 1885–1898* (New Haven, 1971). On the partition in general see J. D. Hargreaves, *Prelude to the Partition of West Africa* (London, 1963), and the same author's *West Africa Partitioned* (Madison, 1974).

3 Struggles with the gods: economic life in the 1880s

1. For a compilation of contemporary descriptions of the technology of production in Dahomey, from which the descriptions in this chapter are taken, see Patrick Manning, 'The Technology of Production in Southern Dahomey, c. 1900,' *African Economic History*, 9 (1980), pp. 49–67. The truly excellent

description of agriculture by Savariau, who served as chief of the Service de l'Agriculture in Dahomey, must be considered the basis of any description of economic life. N. Savariau, *L'Agriculture au Dahomey* (Paris, 1906).

2. On divination and its social role, see Bernard Maupoil, *La Géomancie à l'ancienne Côte des Esclaves* (Paris, 1943); René Trautmann, *La Divination à la Côte des Esclaves et à Madagascar* (Paris, 1940); Julien Alapini, *Les Noix sacrées* (N onte Carlo, c. 1950).

3. Studies of the literature and religion of the Bight of Benin provide insights into the social values underlying the economic activities of its people. See, for example, Paul Hazoumé, *Le Pacte du sang au Dahomey* (Paris, 1937); Paul Hazoumé, *Doguicimi* (Paris, 1938); Melville J. Herskovits and Frances S. Herskovits, *Dahomean Narrative* (Evanston, 1958); René Trautmann, *La Littérature populaire à la Côte des Esclaves* (Paris, 1927); Paul Mercier, 'The Fon of Dahomey,' in Daryll Forde, ed., *African Worlds* (London, 1954), 210–34; Pierre Verger, *Notes sur le culte des Orisa et Vodun* (Dakar, 1957).

4. For a general introduction to input–output analysis, see Hollis B. Chenery and Paul G. Clark, *Interindustry Economics* (New York, 1959).

5. Daryll Forde, *The Yoruba-Speaking Peoples of South-Western Nigeria* (London, 1951); Herskovits, *Dahomey*; Argyle, *The Fon*; Claude Tardits, 'Enquête sociologique sur la population de la palmeraie,' and 'Enquête sur le droit foncier des pays gun et fon,' in J. Clerc, P. Adam and C. Tardits, *Société paysanne et problèmes fonciers de la palmeraie dahoméenne* (Paris, 1956), 9–58, 59–71; Bertho, 'La Parenté des Yorouba,' Geoffrey Parrinder, 'Yoruba-Speaking People in Dahomey,' *Africa 17*, 2 (1947), 122–9; Paul Mercier, 'Notice sur le peuplement yorouba au Dahomey–Togo,' *Etudes dahoméennes*, 4 (1950), 29–40; Cornevin, *Histoire du Dahomey*; Auguste Le Herissé, *L'Ancien Royaume*.

6. Jacques Lombard, 'The Kingdom of Dahomey,' in Daryll Forde and Phyllis M. Kaberry, eds., *West African Kingdoms in the Nineteenth Century* (London, 1967); Adolphe Akindélé and Cyrille Aguessy, *Contribution à l'étude de l'histoire de l'ancien royaume de Porto-Novo* (Dakar, 1953); Geoffrey Parrinder, *The Story of Ketu, an Ancient Yoruba Kingdom* (Ibadan, 1956); Karl, *Traditions orales.*

7. For useful summaries of the agricultural calendar, see Afrique Occidentale Française, Gouvernement Général, *Annuaire du Gouvernement Général de l'AOF, 1909* (Dakar, 1910), 14–37; A. Serpos Tijani, 'Calendrier agraire et réligieux au Bas-Dahomey,' in *Première Conférence internationale des Africanistes de l'Ouest, Comptes rendus* (Dakar, 1951), II:290–8.

8. Richard R. Burton, *A Mission to Gelele, King of Dahome* (2 vols., London, 1864), I:248.

9. Herskovits, *Dahomey*, I:30.

10. Edouard Foà, *Le Dahomey* (Paris, 1895), 144; Herskovits, *Dahomey*, I:52, 58:61; Roger Bastide and Pierre Verger, 'Contribution à l'étude sociologique des marchés nagô du Bas-Dahomey,' *Humanités 1*, 95 (1959), 42–58; Georges Brasseur, *La Palmeraie de Porto-Novo* (Dakar, 1953), 111–12; Claude and

Claudine Tardits, 'Traditional Market Economy in South Dahomey,' in Paul Bohannan and George Dalton, eds., *Markets in Africa* (Evanston, 1962), 92–101.

11. Terms for the currency units were of Portuguese origin. The currency units had been standard for centuries, though the king of Danhomè paid less than 2,000 K per head, and other variations were known. Foà, *Le Dahomey*, 148; E. Courdioux, 'La Côte des Esclaves. XXVI: Monnaies,' *Les Missions catholiques 10* (1878), 538; Marion Johnson, 'The Cowrie Currencies of West Africa,' *Journal of African History 11*, 1 (1970), 17–49, 2 (1970), 331–53; Paul E. Lovejoy, 'Interregional Monetary Flows in the Precolonial Trade of Nigeria,' *Journal of African History 15*, 4 (1974), 563–86.

12. Claude Tardits, 'Développement du régime d'appropriation privée des terres de la palmeraie du Sud-Dahomey,' in Daniel Biebuyck, ed., *African Agrarian Systems* (London, 1963), 304; Tardits, 'Enquête sur le droit foncier,' 65–7; Herskovits, *Dahomey*, I:63–75; Brasseur, *La Palmeraie*, 74–6, 102, 110; Jean Hurault and Jacques Vallet, *Mission d'étude des structures agraires dans le Sud-Dahomey* (Paris, 1963).

13. Alexandre d'Albéca, *La France au Dahomey* (Paris, 1895), 21, 157. See also Alexandre d'Albéca, *Les Etablissements français du golfe du Bénin* (Paris, 1889), 97; J. A. Skertchly, *Dahomey as it is* (London, 1874), 446; Auguste Le Herissé, *L'Ancien Royaume*, 89; Maximilien Quénum, *Au pays des Fons* (Paris, 1938), 134; Paul Marty, *Etudes sur l'Islam au Dahomey* (Paris, 1926), 15–19.

14. E. Lambinet, *Notice géographique, topographique et statistique sur le Dahomey* (Paris, 1893), 16–19; Les Officiers de l'Etat-Major du Corps expéditionnaire du Bénin, *Notice géographique, topographique et statistique sur le Dahomey* (Paris, 1894), 39–42, 57–9; Skertchly, *Dahomey*, 105.

15. Turner, 'Les Bresiliens, 245–7, 270–5; d'Albéca, *Les Etablissements*, 60, 102–5; Foà, *Le Dahomey*, 71; L. Brunet and Louis Giethlen, *Dahomey et dépendances* (Paris, 1900), 42.

16. Archives nationales du Bénin, 1-E-42 (Dossier Pohizoun, 1912).

17. A. Akindélé and C. Aguessy, *Contribution à l'étude de l'histoire de l'ancien royaume de Porto-Novo*, (Dakar, 1953) 43–4; Alfred B. Ellis, *The Ewe-Speaking Peoples of the Slave Coast of West Africa* (London, 1890), 177–8; Montserrat Palau Marti, *Le Roi–dieu au Bénin* (Paris, 1964), 112, 192–3; Foà, *Le Dahomey*, 284–5.

18. Newbury, *Western Slave Coast*, 126–7; d'Albéca, *Les Etablissements*, 108; Foà, *Le Dahomey*, 284.

19. Palau Marti, *Le Roi–dieu*, 139–40, 200; Lombard, 'The Kingdom of Dahomey,' 80–4. The basic sources on the political structure and history of Danhomè in this period are Herskovits, *Dahomey*; Auguste Le Herissé, *l'Ancien Royaume*; Maurice A. Glélé, *Le Danxome, du pouvoir aja à la nation fon* (Paris, 1974); and J.-A. Djivo, 'Gbehanzin et Ago-Li-Agbo.'

20. For a variety of interpretations of the Annual Customs, see Catherine Coquery-Vidrovitch, 'La Fête des coutumes au Dahomey: historique et essai d'interprétation,' *Annales – Economies, Sociétés, Civilisations 19*, 4 (1964),

696–714; Lombard, 'The Kingdom of Dahomey'; Nardin, 'Relations franco-dahoméennes,' 107–19; Ronen, 'African Role,' 5–13. The tendency of these analyses has been to exaggerate the role of the Customs and of state policy generally in economic life. See also Edna Bay, 'On the Trail of the Bush King: a Dahomean lesson in the Use of Evidence,' *History in Africa 6* (1979), 1–15.

21. Herskovits (*Dahomey*, I:113) gives a list of regions around Abomey and Allada and the crops they were expected to grow. René Aho of Abomey (who was Herskovits's informant) gave me a more detailed list which conforms to that of Herskovits (interview, Abomey, Jan. 1967).

22. Palau Marti, *Le Roi–dieu*, 200; Verger, 'Influence, 30–9, 50–2; Foà, *Le Dahomey*, 277.

23. Brunet and Giethlen, *Dahomey*, 382; Burton, *Mission to Gelele*, I:181.

24. Auguste Le Herissé, *L'Ancien Royaume*, 87–9; Skertchly, *Dahomey*, 84–5; Pierre B. Bouche, *Sept ans en Afrique occidentale: la Côte des Esclaves: le Dahomey* (Paris, 1885), 159, 350; Newbury, *Western Slave Coast*, 126; d'Albéca, *Les Etablissements*, 56.

25. Le Herissé's estimate comes to £(1913) 130,000. The French government did not collect this amount in taxes from all of colonial Dahomey until 1899; palm product revenue for the coast from Agoué to Porto-Novo in the 1890s averaged 8 million francs, or three times Le Herissé's estimate of Fon revenue. On both accounts, Le Herissé's estimate seems too high. Djivo, however, has recently made an independent estimate of Fon revenue close to that of Le Herissé. Auguste Le Herissé, *L'Ancien Royaume*, 91; Djivo, 'Gbehanzin et Ago-Li-Agbo,' 194.

26. Eric Wolf, in assigning most of the world's agriculturists to the category of peasant, has argued that landlords are not a necessary ingredient of peasant status. Wolf, *Peasants* (Englewood Cliffs, NJ, 1966). See also Frances Hill, 'Experiments with a Public Sector Peasantry: Agricultural Schemes and Class Formation in Africa,' *African Studies Review 20*, 3 (1977), 25–41.

27. As a nuance to the traditional–modern dichotomy, Karl Polanyi has introduced the term 'archaic,' to refer to economic institutions taken to lie between those of subsistence and the modern market-centered economy. The essence of this term is to suggest that there are two types of 'traditional.' Polanyi, *Dahomey*, xxii–xxiv.

28. Hill centers on land purchase and production for profit as the key elements in determining that Ghana cocoa farmers were capitalists. See her 'Ghanaian Capitalist Cocoa-Farmers,' in Polly Hill, *Studies in Rural Capitalism in West Africa* (Cambridge, 1970), 21–9.

29. Jacques Lombard has used the term 'feudal' to describe the social structures of the Bariba of northern Bénin and Nigeria. His definition, which is carefully constructed and skillfully applied to the Bariba, is not applicable to the structures of the Yoruba and Aja peoples. Lombard, *Structures de type 'féodal' en Afrique noire* (Paris, 1965).

30. In this input–output model I assumed four productive sectors – farming, tree crops, manufactures and transport – and the degree of their interaction. Also

included in the model were inputs of labor, final domestic and export demand, and government demand for labor. I assumed exports to be 15% of domestic product, government to be 5% of domestic product, and total produced inputs to be 25% of the value of labor inputs. Farming was the largest sector. The tree-crops sector was next largest, and over half its produce was exports. Manufacturing was the least labor intensive and transport the most so. Manufacturing and transport were the most linked to other sectors, and tree crops the least so.

4 Production, 1890–1914

1. Manning, 'Technology of Production.'
2. Chapter 8 includes a discussion of the end of slave labor and of the legal disputes stemming from the disposition of former Fon state landholdings and the reallocation of holdings of major Ouidah families.
3. Paul Pélissier, *Les pays du Bas-Ouémé* (Dakar, 1963).
4. Pélissier, *Bas-Ouémé*; A. Gruvel, *L'Industrie des pêches sur la côte occidentale d'Afrique* (Paris, 1913), 81–90; Bourgoignie, *Les Hommes de l'eau*.
5. The classic statement of the notion of dual economy is that of J. H. Boeke for the Dutch East Indies. The key issue is the relationship between dualism and capitalism, and the key question is when capitalism arrives for the economy in question. J. H. Boeke, *Economics and Economic Policy of Dual Societies* (New York, 1953); Benjamin Higgins, *Economic Development* (New York, 1959), 274–93.
6. The opening of the capitalist era in the 1930s, however, may have established new economic barriers. See Catherine Coquery-Vidrovitch, 'L'Afrique coloniale française et la crise de 1930: crise structurelle et genèse du sous-développement: rapport d'ensemble,' *Revue française d'Histoire d'Outre-mer* 63, 232–3 (1976), 386–424.
7. Archives nationales du Bénin, 2-D-88 (Savè, Nov. 1909), 2-D-89 (Savè, Jan. 1914).
8. For a useful view of the limits of the vent-for-surplus model, in the context of an important and detailed study of cocoa farming, see Sara S. Berry, *Cocoa, Custom, and Socio-economic Change in Rural Western Nigeria* (Oxford, 1975), 1–11.
9. See Appendix 4.
10. Verger, *Flux et reflux*, 159, n. 1.
11. Savariau, *L'Agriculture*, 37–8; Yves Henry, *Le Maïs africain, culture et production au Dahomey* (Paris, 1912), 6, 13–14, 18–21, 43; Auguste Chevalier, 'La Culture du maïs en Afrique occidentale et spécialement au Dahomey,' *Journal d'Agriculture tropicale*, 111 (Sept. 1910), 270–1; Colonie du Dahomey, *Notice sur l'Agriculture au Dahomey* (Porto-Novo, 1917), 26, 28.
12. Henry, *Maïs*, 17; Afrique Occidentale Française, Gouvernement Général, *Annuaire statistique de l'AOF, vol. 5 (1950–4)*, I:162. I am indebted to Claude Tardits for pointing out the difficulties with estimates of maize yields; even the

1954 estimates may be too high. (A metric quintal is 100 kg, and a hectare is 10,000 m^2, or a plot 100 meters square.)

13. The concept of a 'world maize price' must be advanced with caution, as maize is a far less homogeneous product than, for example, wheat. I have nevertheless treated average British import unit values as world prices. I am indebted to Morton Rothstein for assistance on this point.

14. Maize output for southern Dahomey was estimated at 165,000 tons in 1954; manioc output was set at 875,000 tons and yam output at 332,000 tons (Afrique Occidentale Française, Gouvernement Général, *Annuaire statistique de l'AOF, vol. 5 (1950–4),* I:161–3). Scaling the maize estimate down by the amount of population growth would give 60,000 tons at the turn of the century. Assuming that manioc had substituted for maize in the intervening years, one might raise the estimated 1900 maize output to 80,000 tons. On the other hand, the 1954 estimates are too high in the aggregate, as they yield a staple output (maize, yams and manioc) of 2.5 kg per person per day, a quantity which only the heartiest eaters could consume. Hence 1900 maize output might have been more like 50,000 tons, which yields (assuming a population of 550,000) an output of 300 g per person per day.

15. Prices calculated from the Statistical Abstract for the United Kingdom, Parliamentary Papers; palm-product quantities from Table A5.2; rainfall from Appendix 6.

16. The coefficient of determination R^2 indicates that 72% of the observed variation in maize exports is explained by variables in the equation; the figures in parentheses are the standard error of each coefficient. This equation is the most straightforward of several possible versions, and also gives the results of the highest significance: using lagged rather than current prices gives poorer results; relative prices (British prices divided by an index of import prices including import duties) showed a very low correlation with exports, and an index of the value of palm product exports showed a lower correlation than the quantity of palm product exports.

17. The export of 17 tons of maize in 1891 came in a year of unusually high maize prices, and maize exports in the 1920s and 1930s correlated inversely with palm product exports.

18. This account is drawn from Archives nationales du Bénin, 2-D (Rapports mensuels des cercles), as follows: Abomey – 1905, 1907–9, 1911; Allada – 1905–6, 1908–10, 1913–14; Cotonou – 1914; Grand Popo – 1910, 1912; Mono – 1905–9, 1912–13; Ouidah – 1905–13; Porto-Novo – 1905–6, 1909–12; Zagnanado – 1908, 1911.

19. Henry (*Maïs,* 32) gives the following regions of origin for 1908 exports:

	Tons
Porto-Novo and Sakété	3,290
Ouémé	1,000
Sô, Nokoué, Porto-Novo lagoon	5,714

Allada (by railroad)	2,300
Abomey (by railroad)	2,600
Ouidah and Ahémé	1,747
Grand Popo and Athiémé	4,090
Total	20,741

This total shows a slight discrepancy from that reported in foreign-trade statistics.

20. The domestic price of maize was below the world price before 1904, but the marginal cost of maize production rose with the great expansion of output and its strain on resources of land and labor, so that Dahomey was a high-cost producer in the world market.
21. Monthly import prices for Britain calculated from the United Kingdom Accounts of Trade and Navigation, Parliamentary Papers.
22. For a discussion of the issue of storage losses of African maize, see Miracle, *Maize*, 241–2.
23. These figures imply that about 5 million oil palms were in production in the early twentieth century. Jean Adam, *Le Palmier à huile* (Paris, 1910), 115–17; A. Rancoule, *Le Palmier à huile au Dahomey* (Porto-Novo, 1943), 16–17. Savariau's estimates (*L'Agriculture*, 68) were only slightly more optimistic.
24. Adam, *Palmier*, 135–9, 151; Savariau, *L'Agriculture*, 64–6; Rancoule, *Palmier*, 18.
25. Rancoule, *Palmier*, 18, 22.
26. Brasseur, *La Palmeraie*, 98–9.
27. Adam, *Palmier*, 3, 95–6; Dahomey, *Notice*, 15; J.-F. Reste, *Le Dahomey, réalisations et perspectives d'avenir* (Paris, 1934), 86, 92.
28. From 1887 to 1914, palm oil exports grew at an average of 1.5% per year, and palm kernel exports grew at an average of 2.5% per year.
29. The cycles may be related to cycles in rainfall or to lags in production. For evidence of this cycle in Togo, Dahomey, Lagos and the Niger Delta, see Figure 2.4; Appendix 4; Newbury, *Western Slave Coast*, 147; and Patrick Manning, 'Some Export Statistics for Nigeria, 1880–1905,' *Nigerian Journal of Economic and Social Studies 9*, 2 (1967), 229–34.
30. The fruit formed in one rainy season and developed during the next. Most fruit formed during the first rainy season; the more humid the second rainy season, the more oil. These fruit were harvested in December and January, and marketed in the first half of the year. Bunches formed during the short rainy season were harvested and marketed from August through October. Adam, *Palmier*, 79–83, 183.
31. For estimates of domestic palm oil consumption, see Chapter 5.
32. Quantity figures are taken from Tables A4.4 and A4.5, and rainfall figures from Table A6.1. Prices were calculated from British imports from French West Africa, as reported in the Annual Statements of Trade, United Kingdom Parliamentary Papers. These prices were deflated by the import price index in

Table A5.1 (including customs duties) to give the relative export prices which were used in the regressions. Regression results showed lower levels of significance when calculated with current rather than lagged rainfall, and when calculated with prices obtained from Table A4.4.

33. Of the several formulations of the regressions calculated, those shown in the text were selected as being most justifiable theoretically and most logical in their results. Calculations with prices deflated by the import index in Table A5.2 (neglecting customs duties) explained a higher portion of the variance (i.e., gave a larger R^2), but showed the price of palm kernels to be insignificant in determining palm kernel exports. The regressions giving the highest R^2 were those using undeflated prices:

$$XO = -11.99 + 28.13\,PO^{**} - 13.12\,PK^{**} + 3.90\,R^{**}\ (R^2 = 0.50)$$
$$\quad\ (6.07)\ (10.19)\qquad\ (6.10)\qquad\ (1.71)$$

$$XK = -29.38 + 62.26\,PO^{**} - 21.35\,PK^{**} + 6.08\,R^{**}\ (R^2 = 0.72)$$
$$\quad\ (9.92)\ (16.65)\qquad\ (9.96)\qquad\ (2.80)$$

The negative coefficient for palm kernel prices in each case is difficult to accept, but it reinforces the conclusion suggested by the other regressions: changes in palm oil prices, rather than in palm kernel prices, were the leading determinant of total palm product output.

34. Babatunde Agiri makes the plausible suggestion that the escape of slaves in Lagos Colony, following British intervention in 1893, cut the volume of palm product exports. But to suggest that this factor explains the low level of exports in 1897 and 1898 is incorrect, since the same decline was felt all along the West African coast. Babatunde Aremu Agiri, 'Kola in Western Nigeria, 1850–1950' (unpublished PhD dissertation, University of Wisconsin–Madison, 1972), 46.

35. Palm product labor requirements cited above (p. 99) are consistent with this estimate: assuming 250 work days per year, production of 25,000 tons of kernels and 18,000 tons of oil would require 40,000 work years; assuming half the population of 550,000 to be economically active, the labor requirement for palm products comes to 18% of the total work years performed.

36. Manioc cultivation expanded in the nineteenth century at the hands of returning Brazilians and the Fon monarchy, and expanded again in the twentieth century in response to pressures on the land.

37. Afrique Occidentale Française, Gouvernement Général, *Annuaire statistique de l'AOF, vol. 5 (1950–4)*, I:161–3.

38. It is probable that shrimp, which were recorded separately beginning 1908, were recorded with fish before that date. I have shown the two combined.

39. Pélissier, *Bas-Ouémé*, 149.

40. Fr. Guilcher, 'Dahomey,' S. M. A. Fathers Archives, Tenafly, New Jersey; Djivo, 'Gbehanzin et Ago-Li-Agbo,' 325; Pierre B. Bouche, *Sept ans*, 295; d'Albéca, *La France au Dahomey*, 12; Henry Hubert, *Contribution à l'étude de la géographie physique du Dahomey* (Paris, 1908), 189; Jean Baptiste Fonssagrives, *Notice sur le Dahomey* (Paris, 1900), 324; Gruvel, *L'Industrie des pêches*, 87. Since the mid-1960s the port of Cotonou and its breakwater have

interrupted the eastward transport of sand, and the isthmus is now permanently open, resulting in a sharp decline in fish population.
41. M. G. Pécaud, *L'Elévage et les animaux domestiques au Dahomey* (Gorée, 1912), 132.
42. Pécaud, *L'Elévage*, 9. See Appendix 4 for export figures.
43. Pécaud, *L'Elévage*, 42, 97–8.
44. The results of the animal census of 1908, although considered to have been highly conservative, give an idea of the regional distribution of goats and sheep (see Pécaud, *L'Elévage*, 61):

	Goats	Sheep
Porto-Novo, Sakété and Ouémé	13,000	10,000
Cotonou	200	100
Ouidah	5,000	4,000
Allada	4,000	3,000
Grand Popo, Athiémé and Aplahoué	16,000	13,000
Abomey	17,000	10,000
Zagnanado and Kétou	8,000	8,000
Savalou and Savè	5,000	6,000

45. N. Savariau, 'Le Kolatier au Dahomey,' *Journal officiel du Dahomey* 15 (1906), 346–50; Auguste Chevalier, *Les Kolatiers et les noix de kola* (Paris, 1909), 358.
46. The northward progression may be noted in Laffitte, *Le Dahomé*, 147–8; Edouard Foà, *Le Dahomey* 140; Savariau, *L'Agriculture*, 69–70. See also M. Bernard, 'Le Cocotier dans le golfe du Bénin,' *Etudes dahoméennes*, 1 (1948), 20–46; Jean Adam, *Le Cocotier* (Paris, 1915), 22–5.
47. R. Grivot, 'L'Industrie du sel dans la subdivision de Grand-Popo,' *Notes africaines*, 21 (1944), 24.
48. Emile Baillaud, *La Situation économique de l'Afrique occidentale anglaise et française* (Paris, 1907), 63. In Figure 4.5, the sum of coconut and copra exports gives total export of coconut products.
49. Dahomey, *Notice*, 41; Savariau, *L'Agriculture*, 74–6; Chevalier, 'Maïs,' 271. See also Chapter 7, pp. 176–7.
50. Auguste Chevalier, *L'Exploitation du caoutchouc et la culture des plantes productrices au Dahomey* (Paris, 1910), 3–4, 10; Yves Henry, *Le Caoutchouc dans l'Afrique occidentale française* (Paris, 1907), 75–8.
51. Burton, *Mission to Gelele*, 1:181; Savariau, *L'Agriculture*, 44; Archives nationales du Bénin, 2-D-28 (Cotonou, Oct. 1908).
52. Jan S. Hogendorn, *Nigerian Groundnut Exports: Origins and Early Development* (Oxford, 1977).
53. Foà, *Le Dahomey*, 129; Savariau, *L'Agriculture*, 79; Marion Johnson, 'Technology, Competition, and African Crafts,' in Clive Dewey and A. G. Hopkins, eds., *The Imperial Impact: Studies in the Economic History of Africa and India* (London, 1978), 259–69.
54. See also the concluding sections of Chapter 3 and 5.

55. The analysis of variations in output makes clear how unrealistic is the assumption of unchanging annual per capita output employed, for example, by Szereszewski in his projection of national income estimates for early colonial Gold Coast. This oversimplification does not, however, invalidate his study. R. Szereszewski, *Structural Changes in the Economy of Ghana, 1891–1911* (London, 1965), 128–250; see also the review by Polly Hill in *Economic Development and Cultural Changes 16*, 1 (1967), 131–7.

5 Demand, 1890–1914

1. Demand for exports and for labor are discussed in Chapter 4.
2. Neglecting the prices of other inputs into production amounts, essentially, to the assumption of fixed proportions of inputs in production.
3. See Appendix 4 for recorded imports, the proxy prices, and a discussion of each.
4. Savariau, *L'Agriculture*, 49; Foà, *Le Dahomey*, 155; Reste, *Le Dahomey*, 129. For further descriptions of maize and other food preparation and consumption, see Manning, 'Technology of Production,' 50–62.
5. The Brazilians helped expand a demand which had previously been restricted to Europeans and nobility. The Fon kings, beginning early in the eighteenth century, served meals to their European guests in the European style; the school which trained the cooks remains in operation in Ouidah, where it turns out some highly skilled chefs.
6. Assuming a population of 600,000, these imports provided 10 g per person per day of trans-Atlantic imports, and 14 g per day of West African imports. These would total 10% of a daily diet of 250 g.
7. Staple consumption by Europeans accounted for a small portion of imports: 200 Europeans would have consumed 18 tons of staples a year, at the rate of 250 g per person per day.
8. Economic historical studies of nutrition in Africa could fill an important need. For pathbreaking work by agronomists and agricultural economists, see Coursey, *The Yam*; Bruce F. Johnston, *The Staple Food Economies of Western Tropical Africa* (Stanford, 1958); William O. Jones, *Manioc in Africa* (Stanford, 1959); Miracle, *Maize*.
9. Assuming palm oil *production* to have been 70% of palm kernel *exports* by weight, estimated consumption is then estimated production less recorded exports: annual consumption estimates ranged from 4,000 to 13,000 tons, and averaged 7,000 tons for the period 1890–1914. These estimates reflect the significant annual variations in palm oil consumption. Daniel in 1902 gave estimates of daily palm oil consumption (80 g for food, 50 g for greasing the body, 50 g for other uses) which Adam used to estimate yearly Dahomean consumption at 36,000 tons, assuming a population of 600,000: projecting adult consumption rates onto a population which was mostly children caused this estimate to be too high. See p. 99; Savariau, *L'Agriculture*, 63; Dahomey, *Notice*, 16; Adam, *Palmier*, 261.

10. Dahomey, *Notice*, 51; Agiri, 'Kola,' 48–115, 215–22.
11. G. Hervet, *Le Commerce extérieur de l'Afrique Occidentale Française* (Paris, 1911), 73; B. Segurola, *Dictionnaire fɔ̀-français* (2 vols., Cotonou, 1963), II:483.
12. The following comparison of landed prices and customs duties shows why imported alcoholic beverages suffered a decrease in demand. Figures shown are a composite of imported gin, rum and trade alcohol; approximations to prices and customs rates are in francs per one hundred liters.

Year	Landed price	Customs duty	Selling price
1890	40	10	50
1895	40	40	80
1899	40	80	120
1905	50	140	190
1908	50	160	210

13. The coefficient of $P(R)$ in the first equation is significant at the 90% confidence level; the coefficient of $P(TA)$ in the second equation is significant only at the 80% level.
14. For a good analysis of the market for domestically produced textiles, see Marion Johnson, 'Technology,' 266–8.
15. Regressions for velvet, bleached and unbleached cottons showed significant income elasticities, as given in the text, but did not show significant price or cross-elasticities.
16. Salt imports averaged 5 kg per person when divided by the population of southern Dahomey, but in fact the salt was divided among a wider population, as it was carried to Djougou, Parakou and beyond. Salt imports were relatively insensitive to changes in price and palm product revenue.
17. Eighteen pounds' worth of matches were sent to Porto-Novo via Lagos in 1878 (see Table A4.1). A decrease in the price of matches after 1908 helped fuel the growing Dahomean demand.
18. See p. 102 above. Kerosene containers and other tins were made into lamps, replacing the earthen lamps used to burn palm oil. France, Agence générale des Colonies, *Statistiques du commerce des colonies françaises pour l'année 1912* (Paris, 1913), I:472.
19. France, Agence générale des Colonies, *Statistique du commerce des colonies françaises pour l'année 1907* (Paris, 1908), I:151.
20. See Appendix 4 on the estimation of cask prices and quantities.
21. The two figures cited, when summed, give the calculated R^2 of 0.7 or 70%. Domestic maize output, which diverged somewhat from maize exports, may have accounted for an additional portion of the variance in jute sack imports.
22. I calculated regressions, without significant results, comparing thread and cord imports with prices of textile imports, the quantity of domestically-produced textile exports, and the quantity of fish exports.

307

23. In addition to the wood imports shown in Figure 5.13, canoes and surf-boats were imported each year from Lagos, Togo and Europe.
24. See above, pp. 83–4, 111–12.
25. Marvin P. Miracle and Bruce Fetter, 'Backward-Sloping Labor Supply Functions and African Economic Behavior,' *Economic Development and Cultural Change 18* (1970), 240–51.

6 Exchange, 1890–1914

1. I. A. Asiwaju, 'The Alaketu of Ketu and the Onimeko of Meko: the Changing Status of Two Yoruba Rulers Under French and British Rule,' in Michael Crowder and Obaro Ikime, eds., *West African Chiefs* (New York, 1970), 141–4; Palau Marti, *Le Roi–dieu*, 47; Archives nationales du Bénin, 2-D-95 (Zagnanado, Aug. 1914).
2. The revolt was repressed by 40 soldiers and 16 police; most of the leaders were imprisoned and some were exiled to Mauritania. Archives nationales du Bénin, 2-D-10 (Allada, May 1909), 2-D-11 (Allada, Sept.–Nov. 1914, Rapport annuel 1914).
3. The Hueda fled and would only return under protection of a French administrator; the Aja then refused to deliver palm products to market. Archives nationales du Bénin 2-D-54 (Mono, Feb. 1905).
4. Archives nationales du Bénin, 2-D-94 (Zagnanado, Dec. 1912).
5. Tardits, 'Enquête sociologique,' 12, 50–1; Claude and Claudine Tardits, 'Market Economy,' 94–5; Herskovits, *Dahomey*, 1 : 54, 57–60.
6. Pierre B. Bouche, *Sept ans*, 292; Les Officiers, *Notice*, 36; d'Albéca, *Les Etablissements*, 61–2.
7. See pp. 149–51.
8. Archives nationales du Bénin, 2-D-2 (Abomey, Nov. 1909), 2-D-3 (Abomey, Sept. 1911). In Herskovits' time the markets and their days were as follows: *Mionhi* – Cana, Abomey, Ounbégamé, Djidja; *Adokwi* – Savako, Idjesi, Ekpota; *Zogodu* – Bohicon, Tindji, Bolizo, Damoshi, Mochi, Aodo; *Adjahi* – Koulikamé, Okonsa. Other sources give less complete but slightly varying versions of Fon markets and market days. Herskovits, *Dahomey*, I : 52; d'Albéca, *La France au Dahomey*, 104; Quénum, *Au pays des Fons* 135; Brasseur, *La Palmeraie*, 111, 113; Tidjani, 'Calendrier,' II: 291. See also B. W. Hodder and U. I. Ukwu, *Markets in West Africa* (Ibadan, 1969).
9. Foà, *Le Dahomey*, 144; Brasseur, *La Palmeraie*, 111, 113; Archives nationales du Bénin, 2-D-11 (Allada, Aug. 1913, Oct. 1913, Feb. 1914, Apr. 1914), 2-D-92 (Zagnanado, Aug. 1905).
10. Archives nationales du Bénin, 2-D-92 (Zagnanado, Jan. 1908). On the restriction of sales outside markets, see Brasseur, *La Palmeraie*, 114, and Bastide and Verger, 'Etude sociologique,' 53, 62–3.
11. The institutions of West African caravan trade – landlords, brokers, credit, etc – have not, unfortunately, been well described in the sources on Dahomey. See Claude Meillassoux, ed., *The Development of Indigenous Trade and Markets in West Africa* (London, 1971).

12. Skertchly, *Dahomey*, 346; Marty, *Islam*, 15–19, 75, 113–22, 151; Turner, 'Les Bresiliens.'

13. For lively descriptions of the work of regional merchants near the coast, see Fonssagrives, *Notice*, 368–70, and G. François, *Notre colonie du Dahomey* (Paris, 1906), 147.

14. Archives nationales du Bénin, 2-D-83 (Savalou, Jan.–Dec. 1912, June 1913, Jan. 1914, June 1914).

15. Archives nationales du Bénin, 2-D-94 (Zagnando, Jan.–July 1912, Nov.–Dec. 1913).

16. Commercial houses paid wages both higher and lower than those paid by the state. Porters refused to carry loads of as much as 45 kg when working on salary, but were sometimes reported to carry heavier loads when working on their own account. Fonssagrives, *Notice*, 384–6; A. Couchard, *Au Moyen-Dahomey: notes sur le cercle de Savè* (Bordeaux, 1911), 56; Archives nationales du Bénin, 2-D-11 (Grand Popo, July 1910).

17. Foà, *Le Dahomey*, 142, 306; d'Albéca, *Les Etablissements*, 57; Fonssagrives, *Notice*, 382; Savariau, *L'Agriculture*, 27; Henry and Amman, *Maïs, igname et patate*, 40–1.

18. D'Albéca, *Les Etablissements*, 49; d'Albéca, *La France*, 10; Foà, *Le Dahomey*, 70.

19. Hopkins, *Economic History*, 149–51; François, *Notre colonie*, 156, 171–2; d'Albéca, *Les Etablissements*, 60; Newbury, *Western Slave Coast*, 125–6.

20. This firm, in turn, had acted as an agent for Victor Régis. For an analysis of the financing of the railroad, see Chapter 7.

21. R. Godferneaux, *Les Chemins de fer coloniaux français* (Paris, 1911), 233–57, 430–2; Newbury, *Western Slave Coast*, 143–4. A line from Lomé northwest to Palimé was completed in 1907.

22. Archives nationales du Bénin, 1-Q (Mouvement caravanier, 1909), 1-E-42 (Dossier Pohizoun, 1912): Les Officiers, *Notice*, 42.

23. Archives nationales du Bénin, 2-D-54 (Mono, Jan. 1905); Marty, *Islam*, 116–22.

24. Archives nationales du Bénin, 2-D-82 (Savalou, July 1907, Nov. 1907). The *gambari* population of Savalou and Paouignan continued modest growth. Archives nationales du Bénin, 2-D-83 (Savalou, Sept. 1912).

25. Archives nationales du Bénin, 5-E (Mono (frontières), 1885–1907); Newbury, *Western Slave Coast*, 169. The town and market of Togodo have all but ceased to exist.

26. On eighteenth- and nineteenth-century routes see pp. 36–47; see also Lombard, *Structures*, 82, and Archives nationales du Bénin, 1-Q (Mouvement caravanier, 1909).

27. Archives nationales du Bénin, 2-D-88 (Savè, Jan. 1910, June 1910), 2-D-89 (Savè, May 1914).

28. Archives nationales du Bénin, 2-D-55 (Mono, Apr. 1909), 2-D-92 (Zagnanado, Rapport annuel 1905).

29. Archives nationales du Bénin, 2-D-55 (Mono, Mar. 1909, Sept. 1908, Feb. 1909). See below pp. 207–9.

30. This, however, would change with time: private merchants would buy trucks, and merchants and villagers would cut roads regardless of the state. On road construction, see pp. 181–2, 207–9.
31. Rates were calculated or listed as follows. *By head* – 1.25 francs per day, a load of 40 kg, and a distance of 30 km per day. Variations in these assumptions could yield costs as low as 0.35 francs per ton-km (0.75 francs per day, 70 kg, 30 km), or as high as 2.0 francs per ton-km (1.5 francs per day, 25 kg, 30 km). *By canoe*: rates ranged from 0.12 to 0.25 francs per ton-km. See note 17, p. 309. *By railroad*: Henry and Amman, *Maïs igname et patate*, 40. *Pier*: Chevalier, 272. *Shipping to Europe*: Chevalier, 'Maïs,' 272. Since the distance is roughly 7500 km, the cost per ton-km was under 0.005 franc.
32. For palm oil, we have an estimated labor cost of 315 work days per ton, and for palm kernels, 167 work days per ton. (See p. 99.) Assuming wages of 1.0 franc per day, this would amount to 315 francs per ton of oil and 167 francs per ton of kernels, or two-thirds of the export price in each case. Application of this rule of thumb to all exports must, however, be regarded as a crude approximation only.
33. The line for maize is drawn at a distance which would consume 20 francs in transport cost, using the lowest cost transport as indicated in Table 6.1, and the line for palm kernels is drawn at a distance which would consume 165 francs in transport cost.
34. See Map 3 for the location of oil palm groves.
35. The regulations for concessions, the granting and retraction of concessions are listed in the *Journal officiel du Dahomey*.
36. A few larger concessions were granted for agricultural purposes: see pp. 174–5.
37. Archives nationales du Bénin, 2-D-65 (Ouidah, Jan.-Mar. 1905), 2-D-75 (Porto-Novo, Oct. 1908), 2-D-41 (Grand Popo, May 1910). The number of merchants registered in Abomey *cercle* is illustrative of the trend:

Year	European merchants	Dahomean merchants
1908	15	14
1909	18	18
1910	26	18
1911	29	20
1912	31	19

The four largest firms were European-owned. Archives nationales du Bénin, 2-D-3 (Abomey, Rapport annuel 1912).

38. See Appendix 5 for definitions and calculations.
39. This distinction, which corresponds to that between subsistence and satisfaction targets discussed in Chapter 5, is seen even more clearly later in the colonial period.

40. Palm oil production was of greater value than palm kernel production, and was concentrated in a shorter period of time.
41. See Figures 2.4 and 6.2 for the cyclical fluctuations in export volume.
42. Cowrie imports continued until the 1890s, however: over 1 million francs' worth of cowries were imported to Porto-Novo from Lagos between 1878 and 1891. See also A. G. Hopkins, 'The Currency Revolution in South-West Nigeria in the Late Nineteenth Century,' *Journal of the Historical Society of Nigeria 3*, 3 (1966), 471–83.
43. France, Archives nationales, Section Outre-mer, Dahomey IX-3, 'Rapport sur la situation douanière du Bénin,' 9 Nov. 1891, Ehrmann; Archives nationales du Bénin, Q (Alby to Ouidah, 30 Apr. 1895 and 3 June 1895).
44. Baillaud, *Situation économique*, 69–77; François, *Notre colonie*, 135; *Journal officiel du Dahomey*, 12 Dec. 1907, 337.
45. Archives nationales du Bénin, 2-D-92 (Zagnanado, Rapport annuel 1905, Sept. 1908), 2-D-93 (Zagnanado, June 1911), 2-D-82 (Savalou, July 1907), 2-D-55 (Mono, June 1908), 2-D-2 (Abomey, Aug. 1909).
46. In the eighteenth century, cowrie imports ranged up to one-third of the value of exports. See p. 44.
47. On the other hand, the value of cowries fell through inflation, cowries are perishable to a degree, and they were demonetized or destroyed by the French to a significant degree. *Journal officiel du Dahomey*, 1 Feb., 1907, 43.
48. This can be seen in the detailed breakdown of the official estimate for 1909, where currency in the hands of the general population is projected to be less than half the currency in circulation:

	Treasury	Banks	Other administrative	Commerce	Individuals	Total
Paper money	100,000	757,840	—	1,369,200	200,000	2,427,040
French coin	629,925	518,737	82,067	1,480,300	3,700,000	6,411,029
British coin	263	15,258	—	112,500	612,500	740,521
Total	730,188	1,291,835	82,067	2,962,000	4,512,500	9,578,590

49. Net recorded imports for 1901–9 (the years in which francs predominated) totalled 5.4 million francs, while the official estimate of French currency holdings was 6.4 million francs in coin, plus 2.4 million francs in paper. Since the latter exceed the former, this gives me further confidence that net imports are an adequate measure of the money supply.
50. See p. 44.
51. French coin in the hands of the general public, according to the official estimate of 1909, was broken down as follows:

		francs
Silver:	crowns	900,000
	2-franc pieces	100,000

311

1-franc pieces	1,100,000
0.5-franc pieces	1,100,000
Copper and lead:	
10- and 5-centime pieces	500,000

52. Archives nationales du Bénin, 2-D-2 (Abomey, Aug. 1910), 2-D-3 (Abomey, June 1912, Sept. 1912), 2-D-66 (Ouidah, Mar. 1911, May 1911), 2-D-67 (Ouidah, Nov. 1912, Apr. 1913), 2-D-93 (Zagnanado, Aug. 1911, Nov. 1911), 2-D-41 (Grand Popo, May 1910), 2-D-11 (Allada, July 1913). In collecting the *impôt* among the Holli in 1912, a year of low cash reserves, the government collected and retired 287 francs worth of 5- and 10-centime pieces dated 1855 and 1857, struck with the image of Napoleon III. Archives nationales du Bénin, 2-D-94 (Zagnanado, Dec. 1912).
53. Archives nationales du Bénin, 2-D-2 (Abomey, Aug. 1910), 2-D-3 (Abomey, Apr.-May 1912), 2-D-66 (Ouidah, May 1911).
54. On the BAO, see Michel Leduc, *Les Institutions monétaires africaines, pays francophones* (Paris, 1965).

7. The alien state, 1890–1914

1. Newbury, *Western Slave Coast,* 115, 169; d'Albéca, *Les Etablissements,* 34–40. On the early years of French administration see Koovi Pierre Agossou, 'L'Installation de l'administration française dans le sud du Dahomey de 1880 à 1894' (unpublished mémoire de maîtrise, University of Dakar, 1970).
2. Observers on the coast claimed that the commerce of Ouidah came to a complete halt for six months during both the wars of 1890 and 1892, and that the wars seriously depressed the commerce of Porto-Novo, Cotonou and other ports. While this was doubtless true in absolute terms, the available commercial statistics are insufficient to confirm that 1890, 1892 or 1893 were years of extraordinary declines in commerce. See Appendix 4; Foà, *Le Dahomey,* 309–10; Djivo, 'Gbehanzin et Ago-Li-Agbo,' 589–95.
3. Those who have analyzed Dahomey's more recent politics in terms of 'regionalism' have missed this point, by attributing to the Fon 'region' more solidarity than it had in fact. Justin Ahomadegbé was able to achieve majority support within the Fon areas, but did not gain support from the *chefs de canton*; if the people of Danhomé been fully united they could easily have dominated the politics of Dahomey. See Glélé, *Le Danxomę,* 251–2; for regionalist views see Ronen, *Dahomey,* 87–8; Martin Staniland, 'The Three-Party System in Dahomey. I: 1946–56,' *Journal of African History 14,* 2 (1973), 291–312.
4. Cornevin, *Histoire du Dahomey,* 352–9, 410–11; Archives nationales du Bénin, 1-E-42 (Dossier Pohizoun, 1912).
5. Asiwaju, 'Alaketu,' 141.
6. Archives nationales du Bénin, 2-D-75 (Porto-Novo, Feb. 1908), 2-D-10 (Allada, July 1909, Sept. 1909); Asiwaju, 'Alaketu,' 143; Glélé, *Le Danxomę,* 24. Some *chefs de canton* have claimed to be heir to the throne of

Abomey: Justin Aho, for example, convinced I.A. Akinjogbin of his claim. See Akinjogbin, *Dahomey,* 6.

7. Archives nationales du Bénin, 2-D-74 (Porto-Novo, Mar. 1905), 2-D-95 (Zagnanado, Jan.–May 1914); Luc Garcia, 'Les Mouvements de résistance au Dahomey (1914–1917),' *Cahiers d'Etudes africaines 10,* 37 (1970), 144–78; Hélène d'Almeida-Topor, 'Les Populations dahoméennes et le recrutement militaire pendant la première guerre mondiale,' *Revue française d'Histoire d'Outre-mer 60,* 219 (1973), 196–241; John A. Ballard, 'The Porto-Novo Incidents of 1923: Politics in the Colonial Era,' *Odu 2,* 1 (1965), 52–75.

8. The 'crise de la chefferie' existed in fact from the turn of the century, but gained its name in later years. See Reste, *Le Dahomey;* R. Grivot, *Réactions dahoméennes* (Paris, 1954), 95–104.

9. See p. 91.

10. Archives nationales du Bénin, 2-D-41 (Grand Popo, Feb., May-June 1910), 2-D-88 (Savè, Dec. 1909, June 1910).

11. Archives nationales du Bénin, 5-E (Mono (frontières), 1885–1907), 1-E-42 (Dossier Pohizoun, 1912); Luc Garcia, 'La Genèse de l'administration française au Dahomey, 1894–1920' (unpublished doctoral thesis, University of Paris, 1969), 36–44.

12. Figure 7.1 includes taxes collected from all Dahomeans, north and south; in fact the great majority (perhaps ninety percent) of taxes in these years were paid by those in the south. Figure 7.2 includes all expenditures of the governments of Dahomey and AOF in Dahomey; it neglects the export of revenue in the form of travel expenses and salary remittances.

13. Cornevin, *Histoire du Dahomey,* 305–6.

14. The 1892 grant was spent directly by the military, while the 1894 grant was paid to the colonial government.

15. *Journal officiel du Dahomey,* 1 July 1899, 2; see also p. 122 above.

16. Dahomey was formally attached to the Government General by decree on October 17, 1899. Colonie du Dahomey, *Rapport d'ensemble sur la situation générale de la colonie, 1899* (Porto-Novo, 1900), 73. In 1905 customs duties were increased again and were made uniform throughout AOF, except for the requirements of the convention in Dahomey and Ivory Coast.

17. France, Ministère des Colonies, Office Colonial, *Statistiques des finances des colonies françaises pour les années 1902–1911* (Melun, 1912), 446; Afrique Occidentale Française, Gouvernement Général, *Situation générale de l'année 1908* (Gorée, 1909).

18. See Appendix 7.

19. Remittances to France, as shown in Figure 7.3, were estimated from Colonie du Dahomey, *Compte définitif des recettes et des dépenses du budget local du Dahomey 1904* (Portò-Novo, 1905); Banque de l'Afrique Occidentale, *Rapport* (Dakar, 1904–14). Such remittances of salaries have also been of concern to development economists investigating post-independence West Africa: see International Monetary Fund, *Surveys of African Economies, vol. 3* (Washington, DC, 1970), 92, 120, 216.

20. Other AOF payments dealing with Dahomey did not constitute revenue imports to Dahomey: purchase of the railroad company, purchase of the pier company, the annual subsidy covering the losses of the railroad company, and debt service on the AOF bonds. Even if all these were included as revenue imports, however, Dahomey would still show a large revenue outflow for the years 1905–14.
21. Or, neglecting the remittances to France, a net revenue inflow of 120,000 francs.
22. Neglecting remittances to France, Dahomey had a modest revenue inflow.
23. *Journal officiel du Dahomey*, 1 June 1898, 1–2; 15 Apr. 1900, 1–3.
24. Archives nationales du Bénin, 2-D-92 (Zagnanado, Jan. 1905); Reste, *Le Dahomey*, 164–5; Godferneaux, *Chemins de fer*, 236, 239–40; René Le Herissé, *Voyage au Dahomey et en Côte d'Ivoire* (Paris, 1903), 107–16.
25. Elisabeth Rabut, 'Le Mythe parisien de la mise en valeur des colonies françaises à l'aube du XXe siècle: la commission des concessions coloniales 1898–1912,' *Journal of African History 20*, 2 (1989), 275, 278. On concessions of commercial lots, see pp. 151–2; on land disputes see pp. 198–203. For the definitive study on concessions in French Equatorial Africa, see Catherine Coquery-Vidrovitch, *Le Congo au temps des grandes compagnies concessionnaires, 1898–1930* (Paris, 1972).
26. Adam, *Palmier*, 231–9; *Journal officiel du Dahomey*, 9 Feb. 1907, 73–4; 6 Sept. 1912, 313; 1 Mar. 1914, 117, 124.
27. Laffitte, *Le Dahomé*, 143.
28. 16,000 francs was 0.4% of the budget in 1902; by 1913 the two services had achieved an allocation of 76,000 francs or 1.6% of the budget.
29. Archives nationales du Bénin, 2-D-1 (Abomey, Mar.–June 1907), 2-D-9 (Allada, Sept. 1907). When the people of Sinhoué objected to the expropriation of their palms for the agricultural station without compensation, the agricultural service relented, and later built a station at Boguila instead.
30. Savariau died in Porto-Novo in 1909, at the age of 29. Archives nationales du Bénin, 2-D-75 (Porto-Novo, June 1909). He wrote *L'Agriculture au Dahomey* and several articles. Chevalier went on to become one of the leading figures in tropical agriculture. Several works by Chevalier, Adam and Henry are listed in the Bibliography.
31. Chevalier, *Caoutchouc*, 7–8; Chevalier, 'Maïs,' 271; Afrique Occidentale Française, Gouvernement Général, *Rapport d'ensemble annuel, 1910* (Gorée, 1911), 204; Yves Henry, *Matières premières africaines, vol. 1* (Paris, 1918), 75–6.
32. Archives nationales du Bénin, 2-D-1 (Abomey, Feb. 1906), 2-D-9 (Allada, Apr. 1906), 2-D-54 (Mono, May 1906), 2-D-65 (Ouidah, Oct. 1907), 2-D-82 (Savalou, Dec. 1907), 2-D-92 (Zagnanado, July 1905, May 1907).
33. Archives nationales du Bénin, 2-D-88 (Savé, July 1910, June 1911), 2-D-95 (Zagnanado, July 1914). The initiation of cottonseed exports followed the construction of cotton gins.
34. Chevalier, *Caoutchouc*, 7–8; Archives nationales du Bénin, 2-D-9 (Allada, Aug. 1906), 2-D-92 (Zagnanado, Sept. 1906).
35. Adam, *Cocotier*, 22–5.

36. Archives nationales du Bénin, 2-D-74 (Porto-Novo, May 1907, Sept. 1907); Savariau, 'Kolatier'; Chevalier, *Kolatiers*; Archives nationales du Bénin, 2-D-11 (Allada, Rapport annuel 1914).
37. Archives nationales du Bénin, 2-D-2 (Abomey, May–Aug. 1909).
38. The first concession was to Edouard Viard for the pier in 1891. It opened in 1893 but then passed to three separate companies before being purchased by AOF in 1908. Afrique Occidentale Française, Gouvernement Général, *Rapport d'ensemble annuel, 1910* (Gorée, 1910), 27. For Viard's earlier career in West Africa, see Cornevin, *Histoire du Dahomey*, 307–8.
39. Colonie du Dahomey, *Rapport d'ensemble sur la situation générale de la colonie, 1900–02* (Porto-Novo, 1903), 58–62. The colony is listed in a summary publication as having paid over 300,000 francs each for debt service in 1903 and 1904, though the reason is not clear. France, *Statistiques des finances des colonies françaises*, 106.
40. To estimate the order of magnitude of labor input: 4,000 men working 250 days per year for 5 years at 1 franc per day would receive 5 million francs. Garcia is of the opinion that pay was much worse in the years after 1905. Garcia, 'La Genèse,' 336.
41. Subsidies from AOF to the company, in thousands of francs, were as follows: 1905–240; 1906–390; 1907–360; 1908–630; 1909–310; 1910–n.a.; 1911–90; 1912–100; 1913–110; 1914–230. Afrique Occidentale Française, Direction des Finances et de la Comptabilité, *Comptes définitifs des recettes et des dépenses du budget général*, 1905–1914 (Gorée, 1906–15). See Also Afrique Occidentale Française, Gouvernement Général, *Rapport d'ensemble annuel, 1909* (Gorée, 1910), 27; Dahomey, *Rapport d'ensemble, 1904* (Porto-Novo, 1906).
42. Afrique Occidentale Française, Gouvernement Général, *Rapport d'ensemble annuel, 1909* (Gorée, 1910), 27. In a later acquisition, AOF bought the pier company in 1908, but purchased it with an annual payment of 73,000 francs for thirty years.
43. Archives nationales du Bénin, 2-D-54 (Mono, Jan. 1905), 2-D-1 (Abomey, Nov. 1905, Nov. 1906), 2-D-2 (Abomey, Aug.–Dec. 1910), 2-D-3 (Abomey, Rapport annuel 1912), 2-D-56 (Mono, Oct. 1912), 2-D-11 (Allada, Aug. 1914), 2-D-67 (Ouidah, Rapport annuel 1914). The wells were built with structural steel and concrete.
44. Administrative reports are generally vague on the sex of the road workers. Most were men, but it is unlikely that women were excluded from road work. For female forced labor in a later period, see A. I. Asiwaju, *Western Yorubaland under European Rule, 1889–1945* (London, 1976), 118.
45. Archives nationales du Bénin, 2-D-9 (Allada, Nov. 1907). Level tracks were important to the rollers of puncheons. Archives nationales du Bénin, 2-D-65 (Ouidah, July–Aug. 1905).
46. Archives nationales du Bénin, 2-D-55 (Mono, Nov. 1907, Feb. 1908), 2-D-66 (Ouidah, May 1908), 2-D-75 (Porto-Novo, May 1908), 2-D-82 (Savalou, June 1907); 2-D-55 (Mono, Mar. 1908). See also Archives nationales du Sénégal, P 98 through P 109 (Dahomey, Travaux publics).
47. This estimate is calculated by assuming 5 days of forced labor per adult for

300,000 adults, at a rate of 1 franc per day: the resultant 1.5 million francs is roughly 20% of the average tax collection for 1908–14.

48. Surplus accumulated by the state is assumed to be the value of taxes collected each year multiplied by 1.2 (see n. 47 above). Gross domestic product is assumed to be the value of exports divided by 0.15 (see p. 4). The ratio of the two figures rose from 2% in 1893 to 9% in 1903. Taxes collected rose as a proportion of export value in bad years, and fell in good years.

An independent estimate of GDP helps to confirm the magnitude and internal consistency of these figures. GDP calculated by the method above for 1911, a prosperous year, is 147 million francs. Assuming a workforce of half the population (300,000), 250 work days per year and 1 franc earnings per day, GDP is estimated at 75 million francs. The two figures are, encouragingly, of the same order of magnitude; further, since 1 franc per day is taken as a minimum wage, it is reasonable that the latter estimate of GDP should be lower than the former.

49. Surplus in the capitalist sector is defined narrowly as the firm's profit or broadly as surplus value of revenue over wages, variable capital and fixed capital.

8 Social struggles for economic ends, 1890–1914

1. Archives nationales du Bénin, 2-D-2 (Abomey, May 1910). Three months later, Giscard's reports were as terse as ever.
2. Archives nationales du Bénin, 2-D-3 (Abomey, July 1913). Adohé, an elder who called himself king of Adonpodji, led this movement against the chief of Adonpodji *quartier* in Abomey; the 'students' were children of the families of the quarter, attending mission or lay school.
3. A. G. Hopkins, 'Imperial Connections,' in Clive Dewey and A. G. Hopkins, eds., *The Imperial Impact: Studies in the Economic History of Africa and Asia* (London, 1978), 12. The approach to socio-economic conflict I have adopted in this chapter owes much to the example of E. P. Thompson's work on England, and to the cross-cultural insights of Marjorie Murphy. E. P. Thompson, *The Making of the English Working Class* (Harmondsworth, 1965).
4. The *indigénat* was promulgated by the Government General in the 'décret du 21 novembre 1904 relatif à l'internement des indigènes non justiciables des tribunaux français.' Further details were spelled out in an *arrêté* of September 14, 1907. For a critical assessment of the *indigénat* in the 1920s, see Raymond Leslie Buell, *The Native Problem in Africa* (2 vols., New York, 1928), I:1016–20.
5. This investigation is based primarily on the Rapports mensuels des cercles, 1905–1914 (Archives nationales du Bénin, 2-D). Further information on such conflicts awaits the investigator of records of courts, prisons, chambers of commerce and the Conseil général; the latter in particular may provide more documentation on merchants and government employees.
6. Foà, *Le Dahomey*, 211–12; Auguste Le Herissé, *L'Ancien Royaume*, 50–5; Laffitte, *Le Dahomè*, 125.

316

7. Archives nationales du Sénégal, K22 (Enquête sur la captivité au Dahomey, 1904). This includes reports from twelve *cercles* and the governor's summary. The governor's summary is published in C. W. Newbury, 'An Early Inquiry into Slavery and Captivity in Dahomey,' *Zaire 14*, 1 (1960), 53–67; the report from Allada *cercle* is published in Patrick Manning, 'Un Document sur la fin de l'esclavage au Dahomey,' *Notes africaines*, 147 (1975), 88–92.
8. G. Toutée, *Dahomé, Niger, Touareg* (Paris, 1897), 73.
9. According to contemporary observers, the result of the flight of slaves and the new terms achieved by slaves who did not flee was that field work and agricultural output declined, particularly in the Fon kingdom. Archives nationales du Sénégal, K22, no. 9 (Ouidah). For a similar assertion further east, see Agiri, 'Kola,' 46.
10. Herskovits, *Dahomey*, I:103–4.
11. Slaves in the Abomey region were listed in 1904 as Aja, Mahi, Itsha and Bariba in origin. The absence of Yoruba slaves from this list is logical only if they had selectively departed.
12. The administrator of the protectorate of Porto-Novo reported an estimate of 2,500 slaves within its boundaries in 1904, while acting-Lieutenant-Governor Penel, also stationed in Porto-Novo, estimated 48,000 Yoruba slaves out of 154,000 inhabitants in the protectorate. It is not clear how to resolve this discrepancy.
13. In Northern Nigeria, by contrast, Lord Lugard's policy was to restrict the liberation of slaves to a minimum in order to maintain an alliance with their owners. Frederick D. Lugard, *The Dual Mandate in British Tropical Africa* (London, 1922), 372–6.
14. The price of an adult slave had been roughly ten pounds sterling, or 250 francs.
15. R. Mansell Prothero, 'A Typology of African Mobility' (unpublished paper, 1968); Montserrat Palau Marti, 'Notes sur les rois de Daṣa (Dahomey),' *Journal de la Société des Africanistes 27*, 2 (1957), 201; R. Grivot, 'La Pêche chez les Pédah du Lac Ahémé, *Bulletin de l'IFAN 11* (1949), 124.
16. Pélissier, *Bas-Ouémé*, 53–4.
17. Tardits, 'Régime d'appropriation,' 304–6; Tardits, 'Enquête sociologique,' 9–58; Pélissier, *Bas-Ouémé*; Hurault and Vallet, *Structures agraires*.
18. See Hopkins, *Economic History* 37–9.
19. Auguste Le Herissé, *L'Ancien Royaume*, 243–6; Archives nationales du Bénin, 2-D-1 (Abomey, June 1907).
20. Afrique Occidentale Française, Gouvernement Général, *Rapport d'ensemble annuel, 1909* (Gorée, 1909), 146.
21. Archives nationales du Bénin 2-D-28 (Cotonou, Mar. 1908- to Aug. 1910; Rapport spécial no. 25, 8 Feb. 1909). See also le Dr. Gaillard, 'Etudes sur les lacustres du Bas-Dahomey,' *L'Anthropologie, Paris 17* (1907), 113–16; Bourgoignie, *Les Hommes de l'eau*, 66–70.
22. Chief Hounkarin was apparently not related to teacher and political activist Louis Hunkanrin, who was from Porto-Novo. Archives nationales du Bénin 2-D-28 (Cotonou, Aug. 1908, Nov. 1908, Jan. 1909, Rapport spécial no. 25, 8 Feb. 1909).

317

23. Archives nationales du Bénin 2-D-28 (Cotonou, Sept. 1910); Bourgoignie, *Les Hommes de l'eau*, 69–70.
24. They wished to set aside a time when there would be no fishing, and were apparently asking the French administration to help them enforce it.
25. Archives nationales du Bénin, 2-D-42 (Grand Popo, Apr. 1913, Sept.-Nov. 1913), 2-D-67 (Ouidah, Aug. 1913).
26. Archives nationales du Bénin, 2-D-1 (Abomey, Jan. 1905, June 1907).
27. Archives nationales du Bénin, 2-D-1 (Abomey, Dec. 1906, Feb.-Mar. 1907).
28. Forbes visited, in 1849, the plantation of Azammado Houénou, father and predecessor of Kpadonou; Skertchly met Kpadonou in 1871. (The Fon name Houénou became Quénum in Portuguese and French.) Forbes, *Dahomey and the Dahomans*, I:112–13; Skertchly, *Dahomey*, 7, 32–3, 45.
29. Archives nationales du Bénin, 2-D-23 (Tovalou Quénum, 15 July 1906).
30. Archives nationales du Bénin, 2-D-23 (Tovalou Quénum, 15 July 1906); 2-D-65 (Ouidah, Oct. 1905). The question of why the full family should agree to put everything in Tovalou's name in 1896 is intriguing. One possibility is that all family leaders saw that such unity would prevent their slaves from claiming the land. Once the slaves had been excluded from such claims, it was safe to resume disputes within the family.
31. Archives nationales du Sénégal 8G12 (Affaire Adjovi–Kenney); Archives nationales du Bénin, 2-D-27 (Cotonou, Apr.-May 1906, Dec. 1906), 2-D-65 (Ouidah, Dec. 1905, Mar.–Apr. 1906).

    The customary courts, or *tribunaux de province* and *tribunaux de cercle*, were established by decree in November 1903. Afrique Occidentale Française, Gouvernement Général, *Rapport d'ensemble annuel, 1909* (Gorée, 1909), 146.
32. Crespin's client was Alihonou, brother of Houssinou. Their opponent in court was Fakon Kakarakou, chief of Zombodji. Archives nationales du Bénin, 1-E-1 (Affaire Alihonou–Kakarakou, 1908).
33. Archives nationales du Bénin, 2-E-23 (Crespin to governor, 14 Jan. 1909); Archives nationales du Sénégal 8G12 (Affaire Adjovi–Kenney).
34. Archives nationales du Bénin, 2-D-66 (Ouidah, Dec. 1908), 2-E-23 (Crespin to governor, 14 Jan. 1909; Cuvillier to governor, 27 Jan. 1909; Possy Berry and others to governor, 26 Jan. 1909; Dagba and others to governor, 28 Jan. 1909). The long lists of signatures on the latter two letters may permit a detailed reconstruction of the factions.
35. Archives nationales du Bénin, 2-D-66 (Ouidah, Mar.-Apr. 1909).
36. Archives nationales du Bénin, 2-E-23 (administrator-adjoint to governor, 8 Nov. 1909), 2-D-66 (Ouidah, Nov. 1909, Apr. 1910).
37. Casimir Agbo, *Histoire de Ouidah du XVIe au XXe siècle* (Avignon, 1959), 221; Archives nationales du Bénin, 2-D-66 (Ouidah, July 1910). The two branches of the family were henceforth known as Tovalou Quénum and Bhêly-Quénum. The noted writer Olympe Bhêly-Quénum is a member of the latter.
38. Archives nationales du Bénin, 2-D-67 (Ouidah, Nov. 1913, Apr.-May 1914).
39. See Michael Crowder, *Senegal, A Study in French Assimilation Policy* (New York, 1962).

318

40. Archives nationales du Bénin, 2-E-23 (Ouidah, Litiges à propos terrains).
41. Archives nationales du Bénin, 2-D-76 (Porto-Novo, July 1912, Sept. 1912, May 1913, Oct. 1913), 19-E (also labelled 4-E) (Islam 1906–23, memo by Le Herissé 15 Feb. 1914).
42. Archives nationales du Bénin, 2-D-3 (Abomey, Apr.-May 1911, Nov. 1911).
43. Archives nationales du Bénin, 2-D-93 (Zagnanado, Aug.-Sept. 1911).
44. Archives nationales du Bénin, 2-D-41 (Grand Popo, May 1910–Dec. 1911). See also pp. 207–9.
45. Adam, *Palmier*, 227; see also pp. 000–00.
46. The merchant who was assailed at Sô–Awa had also carried off a woman from the village. Archives nationales du Bénin, 2-D-74 (Porto-Novo, May 1905). That the aging Toffa should support a boycott against the French indicates how little remained of the former alliance. Archives nationales du Bénin, 2-D-74 (Porto-Novo, July-Sept. 1905).
47. Archives nationales du Bénin, 2-D-9 (Allada, Aug. 1906, Mar. 1907), 2-D-65 (Ouidah, Nov. 1906), 2-D-41 (Grand Popo, Feb. 1910), 2-D-88 (Savè, June 1910); Asiwaju, *Western Yorubaland*, 141–4.
48. Archives nationales du Bénin, 2-D-82 (Savalou, Dec. 1905, May 1906, June 1907).
49. Archives nationales du Bénin, 2-D-88 (Savè, Oct. 1910–Feb. 1911, Mar. 1912).
50. Archives nationales du Bénin, 2-D-82 (Savalou, Apr. 1907), 2-D-72 (Affaire Rouhaud). Rouhaud, for all his similarity to a Joseph Conrad character, was real; he was born in 1864 and entered the colonial service in 1885. Afrique Occidentale Française, Gouvernement Général, *Annuaire du Gouvernement Général de l'AOF, 1905* (Paris, 1906), 92–3.
51. Archives nationales du Bénin, 2-D-41 (Grand Popo, Aug. 1909–Dec. 1911); see also p. 204.
52. In 1917 the administration declared the Grand Popo to Lokossa road to be in bad repair and seemed ready to go through with the whole affair again. The 1917 revolt in the Mono is not entirely unrelated. Archives nationales du Bénin, K (Mono 1917, Route Grand Popo–Lokossa). For additional information on the Rouhaud affair and on the subsequent Mono revolt, see Sylvain C. Anignikin, 'Les Origines du mouvement national au Dahomey, 1900–1939' (unpublished thèse de 3e cycle, University of Paris VII, 1980), 90–2, 180–96.
53. Archives nationales du Bénin, 2-D-93 (Zagnanado, Nov. 1910–June 1911); Asiwaju, 'Alaketu,' 143–5.
54. Archives nationales du Bénin, 2-D-3 (Abomey, Oct. 1911).
55. Rousseau's characterization of the approach of the conqueror seems apt: 'I hereby make a covenant with you which is wholly at your expense and wholly to my advantage; I will respect it so long as I please and you shall respect it so long as I wish.' J. J. Rousseau, *The Social Contract* (London, 1968), 58.
56. Turner, 'Les Brésiliens,' 156–63, 199–203.
57. Denise Bouche, *L'Enseignement dans les territoires français de l'Afrique occidentale de 1817 à 1920* (2 vols., Paris, 1975), II:468–73, 684–5; Cornevin, *Histoire du Dahomey*, 434–6; Ronen, *Dahomey*, 64.

319

58. Clément Koudessa Lokossou, 'La Presse au Dahomey, 1894–1960': évolution et réaction face à l'Administration coloniale' (unpublished doctoral thesis, University of Paris, 1976), 62–70, 82; Archives nationales du Bénin, 2-D-9 (Allada, Sept.-Nov. 1906). Bada had running disputes with Silibo Klouna and the Alapini family, both prominent in the area, and a dispute of some years with the village of Hevié. In 1907 his compound was set afire by arsonists.

    L'Echo du Dahomey died as Cressent's business failed and he returned to France. Independent journalism in Dahomey lapsed until World War I when Louis Hunkanrin wrote the clandestine *Le Récadère de Béhanzin*.

59. *Journal officiel du Dahomey*, 15 Aug. 1914, 1–2; Lokossou, 'La Presse,' 75–6.

60. See Ronen, *Dahomey;* also Virginia Thompson, 'Dahomey,' in Gwendolyn M. Carter, ed., *Five African States: Responses to Diversity* (Ithaca, 1963), 161–262.

61. Archives nationales du Bénin, 2-D-66 (Ouidah, Rapport annuel 1911), 2-D-76 (Porto-Novo, May 1913).

62. Archives nationales du Bénin, 2-D-82 (Savalou, Sept. 1905).

63. Archives nationales du Bénin, 2-D-89 (Savè, March 1914). See the song about Adido and World War I in Asiwaju, *Western Yorubaland*, p. 274.

64. Archives nationales du Bénin, 2-D-92 (Zagnanado, Rapport annuel 1905).

65. Archives nationales du Bénin, 2-D-88 (Savè, July 1911).

66. Archives nationales du Bénin, 2-D-93 (Zagnanado, Oct. 1911).

9 The mechanism of accumulation

1. Compare Laffitte, *Le Dahomé* 136–53; Colonie du Dahomey, *Notice*.

2. I have used the term 'accumulation' to refer to the concentration of surplus in several modes of production. This usage of the term is broader than is usual in the Marxian literature, where it is generally restricted to the accumulation of capital within the capitalist mode of production. 'Primitive accumulation,' in Marx's terminology, corresponds to the expropriation of independent producers, 'the historical process of divorcing the producer from the means of production,' thus creating a wage-labor force. See Marx, *Capital*, I:543–46, 667–70. For applications of the notion of primitive accumulation to colonial Africa, see Bogumil Jewsiewicki, 'The Great Depression and the Making of the Colonial Economic System in the Belgian Congo,' *African Economic History*, 4 (1977), 153–76; Bogumil Jewsiewicki, 'Introduction' to special issue of *African Economic History*, 7 (1979), 2–8.

3. The estimated rates of population change were established in part from occasional published population estimates, but mostly from reported annual *impôt* collections by *cercle*, which were divided by the relevant tax rate to obtain population estimates.

4. The *akadja* or fish sanctuary technique may have been developed in this period (see pp. 72, 104–7).

5. Examples include Xavier and Achille Béraud, who began as translators in the

1880s and rose to hold key administrative posts; Lawani Kossoko, son of the deposed king of Lagos, who became a chief east of Cotonou; and the embattled Bada, appointed chief of Abomey-Calavi.

6. See pp. 141–53.
7. Growth rates of imports and exports are calculated from Appendixes 4 and 5. A correlation in growth rates for exports and domestic product is less to be expected in the short run than in the long run, and such a correlation is asserted here only on the basis of the argument which follows.
8. For the case of slavery in the United States, Conrad and Meyer defined the analogous issues as the questions of the profitability and the viability of slavery, and spawned a huge literature. See Alfred H. Conrad and John R. Meyer, 'The Economics of Slavery in the Ante Bellum South,' *Journal of Political Economy* 66 (1958), 95–130; Robert W. Fogel and Stanley L. Engerman, *Time on the Cross* (2 vols., Boston, 1974).
9. This formulation assumes that current reductions in consumption and investment spending (because of revenue exports) led to equivalent reductions in consumption and investment in the next period, and so forth. A Keynesian model assuming a multiplier effect and the possibility of unemployment would project an even larger divergence of actual and potential GDP as a result of such revenue exports.
10. The minimum figure is the export of one or two years' revenue surplus, reducing current GDP regardless of its impact on growth.
11. Maize requires more labor per ton than yams, so the adoption of maize in the sixteenth century may have led to an increase in satisfaction without bringing an improvement in physical productivity.
12. Based on a backward extrapolation of data shown on pp. 3–5.
13. Dalzel, *History of Dahomy*; Fonssagrives, *Notice*, 405–6.
14. Akinjogbin, *Dahomey*; Jean Suret-Canale, *Afrique noire occidentale et centrale. Vol. 2: l'Ere coloniale, 1900–1945* (Paris, 1964), 203–78; Samir Amin, *L'Afrique de l'Ouest bloquée* (Paris, 1971), 134–50, 235–47; Catherine Coquery-Vidrovitch, 'Mutation de l'impérialisme colonial français dans les années 30,' *African Economic History*, 4 (1977), 103–52.
15. For an authoritative introduction to the use of counterfactuals, see Robert W. Fogel, 'The New Economic History: its Findings and its Methods,' *Economic History Review 19*, 3 (1966), 642–56. For a discussion of counterfactuals in an African context, see Patrick Manning, 'Notes toward a Theory of Ideology in Historical Writing on Modern Africa,' *Canadian Journal of African Studies 8*, 2, (1974), 235–53.
16. Senegambia, Sierra Leone and the kingdom of Benin exported relatively few slaves; the Bight of Biafra began serious exports only in the 1730s, and the Yoruba exported few slaves before the 1760s. Curtin, *Slave Trade*, 224–5.
17. In contrast, another counterfactual – that of strict autarky – could be used to test the benefits of outside economic contacts in general rather than slave trade in particular.
18. These questions are too often restricted to whether blame for slave trade lay

mostly with Europeans or Africans. Analysis of the slave trade may, instead, prove relevant to current economic issues: Africa, which was faced in its past with burdensome economic pressures in the era of the slave trade, is faced today with equally weighty pressures from multinational corporations, from former colonial masters, and from the Cold War. African leaders, in understanding the continent's responses to the slave trade, may be able to accommodate more successfully to current pressures.

19. Another useful counterfactual is the absence of a slave-labor mode of production: it differs from the counterfactual of 'no slavery' in that it allows for slaves in the familial and commodity exchange modes of production and in the mercantile system, but without large-scale slave production. It is more realistic and more relevant than 'no slavery', but is somewhat more complex to discuss.

20. Gemery and Hogendorn argue that technology in West Indian sugar was static, but that the technology of African slave supply improved steadily. The technology of African slave production is yet another matter. Gemery and Hogendorn, 'Technological Change,' 243–58.

21. It is remarkable that Africanists have not put more effort into comparisons of African slavery with slavery in such other Old World areas as the Mediterranean, India and China.

22. A. I. Asiwaju, in his detailed study, in effect paints British Nigeria as 'benign' in comparison with French Dahomey. C. W. Newbury compares British, French and German regimes in adjoining territories, though with less explicit commentary. Asiwaju, *Western Yorubaland;* Newbury, *Western Slave Coast* 141–204.

23. The transfer of funds from Dahomey to other AOF territories does not necessarily mean that the other territories experienced a net inflow of public funds.

24. Anglo-American investment in the Transvaal goldfields, for example, preceded British conquest of the region. Gann and Duignan have compared Ethiopia with Southern Rhodesia to argue that the balance sheet of colonialism was positive; I believe they erred and attributed the presence of the mines to the Europeans rather than the reverse. Lewis Gann and Peter Duignan, *Burden of Empire* (New York, 1967), 366–7.

25. During the 1920s the League of Nations investigated reports of slavery in Liberia, Saudi Arabia and Ethiopia in preference to similar investigations for European colonies.

10 Capitalism and colonialism, 1915–60

1. On export and import statistics, see the discussion in Appendix 4.

2. Table A5.4. For a view treating high export volume as a compensation for low prices, see Coquery-Vidrovitch, 'Mutation,' 113, 123.

3. Benoit Antheaume, 'La Palmeraie du Mono: approche géographique,' *Cahiers d'Etudes africaines 12*, 47 (1972), 472; Rancoule, *Palmier*; Machioudi Dissou, 'Développement et mise en valeur des plantations de palmier à huile au Dahomey,' *Cahiers d'Etudes africaines 12*, 47 (1972), 488–9.

4. All export volumes declined after the war: the greatest declines were the halt in

maize exports after 1945, the sharp drop of palm oil exports in 1946 and 1947, and the decline in coffee exports for 1947; lesser declines were recorded for palm kernels in 1946, castor beans and cotton in 1947, and copra in 1950. The 1947–8 railroad strike virtually halted exports for months. See Table A4.6; also Grivot, *Reactions*, 45.

5. Jesel, 'Le Maïs au Dahomey,' *Etudes dahomèennes*, 8 (1952), 16; Abdoulaye Wade, *Economie de l'Ouest africain* (Paris, 1959).

6. A smaller amount of cotton was grown in the North, especially beginning in the thirties; peanut-shelling plants had been established by the forties in Abomey, but hand shelling continued in the North. H. Desanti, *Du Danhomé au Bénin–Niger* (Paris, 1945), 167, 213–14, 250–1; Lombard, *Structures*, 425–6.

7. Adam, *Cocotier*; Christophe Batsch, 'Le Togo et la crise: contrastes régionaux et dépendance accrue,' *Revue française d'Histoire d'Outre-mer 63*, 232–3 (1976), 591; Desanti, *Bénin–Niger*, 157–8; Reste, *Le Dahomey*, 105–7; Archives nationales du Bénin, R (unclassified), 'Sommaire administratif du Service local de l'Agriculture,' 31 Dec. 1936.

8. Alfred Mondjannagni, 'Quelques aspects historiques, économiques et politiques de la frontière Dahomey–Nigéria,' *Etudes dahomèennes*, n.s. 1 (1963), 48.

9. Raphia cloth (*botoyi*) was woven as a substitute. Maurice A. Glélé, *Naissance d'un état noir: l'évolution politique et constitutionnelle du Dahomey, de la colonisation à nos jours* (Paris, 1969), 65.

10. An Athiémé producer of *sodabi* in the thirties bottled and sold it as 'Royal Gin Dahomey.' Antheaume, 'La Palmeraie du Mono,' 472; Segurola, *Dictionnaire*, II: 483.

11. Grivot, *Réactions*, 47–8; interview with Valentin Djibodé Aplogan, January 1967.

12. Published trade statistics, however, give uneven information after 1914 on commerce in foodstuffs with Togo and Nigeria. Dahomey was clearly a net exporter of food during the World War II years of maize exports.

13. See pp. 102, 127.

14. The totals of the three in percentage of current import value, as shown in Table 10.2, were 12.2% for 1906–8, 14.5% for 1927–9, and 14.8% for 1952–4. These figures tend to underestimate the growth of metallic and mechanical imports, however, since some goods such as motor vehicles were not included in them.

15. See Appendix 5 for details. Terms of trade calculated for AOF as a whole and for Nigeria and Ghana show similar results. Jean-Jacques Poquin, *Les Relations économiques extérieures des pays d'Afrique noire de l'union française. 1925–1955* (Paris, 1955), 122–3, 134–5; Hopkins, *Economic History*, 180–1; G.K. Helleiner, *Peasant Agriculture, Government, and Economic Development in Nigeria, 1900–1960* (Homewood, Ill., 1966), 500.

16. The reported values of imports, after roughly 1905, are exclusive of customs duties. While the balance of trade as shown is appropriate from the viewpoint of the state, from the viewpoint of private citizens the amount of customs duties paid each year should be subtracted from the amounts shown.

17. Two meanings of the term 'surplus' are relevant here, and the analysis

addresses both of them. In Marxian terms, all domestic revenue of the state may be seen as surplus extracted from the domestic economy: in the text I refer to the 'size of the state' (i.e., the level of state revenue and, to a lesser degree, expenditure) to indicate this sort of surplus. The term 'fiscal surplus' is used in the text in its accounting sense, as state revenue less expenditure. See also pp. 167–74.

18. See Appendix 7 for details.

19. Published budgets for Dahomey in 1932 and 1933, in contrast to all other years, show deficits of 10 million francs each and no means of financing the deficits. These are certainly errors: most likely, they represent expenditures of moneys which, while listed as AOF expenditure in Dahomey, were actually AOF grants to Dahomey in earlier years. See Table A7.2, columns 2, 4, 7 and 8.

20. FIDES is the acronym for Fonds d'Investissement pour le Développement économique et social. Virginia Thompson and Richard Adloff, *French West Africa* (Stanford, 1958), 253–65, 270–1; Jean Suret-Canale, *Afrique noire, occidentale et centrale. Vol. 3, Pt. 1: De la colonisation aux indépendances, 1945–1960* (Paris, 1977), 103–11.

21. Thompson and Adloff, *French West Africa*, 258, 264; Wade, *Economie de l'Ouest africian*, 277; Marcel Capet, *Traité d'économie tropicale: les économies d'AOF?* (Paris, 1958), 198–9; William J. Foltz, *From French West Africa to the Mali Federation* (New Haven, 1965), 27.

22. This was the period in which African civil servants were raised to the same salary schedule as French citizens.

23. Reports for the Caisse de Réserve du Dahomey and the Caisse de Réserve de l'AOF were published annually as appendixes to the *Compte définitif* of each. Annual balances for each are shown in Table A7.2.

24. The BAO was chartered in 1901 as a private bank with rights to circulate bank notes, in effect according to a gold exchange standard. In 1929 its charter was revised to make it a *société mixte*, with AOF ownership of part of its stock. In 1955 it was replaced by the Institut d'Emission de l'AOF et du Togo, which in 1959 became the Banque centrale des Etats de l'Afrique de l'Ouest. Until 1955 the Cotonou office emitted currency for both Dahomey and Niger, most of which remained in Dahomey; in 1955 an office opened in Niamey. Actual money supply figures for Dahomey were not published until 1964. Leduc, *Les Institutions monétaires*, 22–38; Lionel Zinsou-Derlin, 'La Banque de l'Afrique Occidentale dans la crise,' *Revue française d'Histoire d'Outre-mer 63*, 232–3 (1976), 509–12.

25. A busy Dahomean money market not only discounted bank notes against coin, but speculated actively on varying values of coins, thus leading to ceaseless administrative consternation. For a lively if negative account, see Desanti, *Bénin–Niger*, 234–8; see also Glélé, *Naissance*, 56.

   The circulation of bank notes varied considerably within each year, leading in effect to an inflation during harvests and a deflation in between: monthly figures for 1925, in millions of francs, are typical.

Jan.	*Feb.*	*Mar.*	*Apr.*	*May*	*June*	*July*	*Aug.*	*Sept.*	*Oct.*	*Nov.*	*Dec.*
50	56	49	53	45	49	46	46	45	45	47	48

26. The development of commercial and personal checking accounts as a large portion of the money supply took place after 1960.

27. Poquin, in a book which is otherwise responsible, though overly defensive of French policy, is guilty of both error and rhetorical excess when he concludes, referring to the decline in AOF exports during 1940–2, 'This shows that the Black lives from day to day, that his economic education is still rudimentary and that he does not know how to save.' Poquin, *Les Relations économiques*, 36. In fact the level of savings went to a remarkably high level.

28. Desanti, *Bénin–Niger*, 211; Reste, *Le Dahomey*, 107, 165–6; Cornevin, *Histoire du Dahomey*, 474. Germain Crespin was a leading figure in the development of the coçonut plantations.

29. Reste, *Le Dahomey*, 167–8; Desanti, *Bénin–Niger*, 201.

30. The proportions of imports originating in France were 17% in 1909 and 30% in 1934. For an excellent study of the French firms, see Catherine Coquery-Vidrovitch, 'L'Impact des intérêts coloniaux: SCOA et CFAO dans l'Ouest africain , 1910–65,' *Journal of African History 16*, 4 (1975), 595–621.

31. Zinsou-Derlin, 'La Banque,' 509; Katharine Payne Moseley, 'Indigenous and External Factors in Colonial Politics: Southern Dahomey to 1939' (unpublished PhD dissertation, Columbia University, 1975), 418.

32. Dissou, 'Plantations de palmier à huile,' 488–9, 496–7.

33. The expansion of motor transport tended to accentuate the independence of women, who might now be absent on market business for weeks. The fragmentation in land holdings which Tardits documented may be exaggerated to the extent that he underestimated the level of individual land holding in precolonial years, Tardits, 'Enquête sur le droit foncier,' 59–71; Tardits, 'Régime d'appropriation,' 304–6; Bastide and Verger, 'Etude sociologique,' 62–3.

34. In 1945 1 CFA franc was set at 1.7 metropolitan franc; at the end of 1948 the rate was changed to 1 FCFA = 2 FF. Leduc, *Les Institutions monétaires*, 36, 38, 53–4, 61–4.

35. Capet, *Traité*, 204; Elliot J. Berg, 'The Economic Basis of Political Choice in French West Africa,' *American Political Science Review 54*, 2 (1960), 396, 400.

36. The CFAO palm oil mill at Avrankou in 1929 failed for lack of sufficient transport – a problem in levels of income and investment, not technology. Desanti, *Bénin–Niger*, 155–6.

37. Wade, *Economie de l'Ouest africain,* 188–91; Coquery-Vidrovitch, 'CFAO et SCOA.'

38. Moise Mensah, 'Problèmes du développement de l'agriculture dahoméenne,' *Etudes dahoméennes*, n.s. 1 (1963), 62.

39. Jacques Lombard, 'Cotonou, ville africaine,' *Bulletin de l'IFAN 16* (1954), 351–3.

40. White-collar employees were members of the Union des Syndicats libres du Dahomey (USLD), affiliated with the French Catholic central Confédération française des Travailleurs chrétiens (CFTC). Transport, industrial and commercial workers were members of the Union des Syndicats confédérés du Dahomey (USCD), affiliated after the 1947 railroad strike with the French

Confédération générale du Travail (CGT). The differences between the two were more than ideological: the USLD emphasized parity in African and European conditions as its main bargaining objective, while USCD, lacking an equivalent comparison, gave primacy to wage demands. Virtually all Dahomean unions joined the territorial branch of the Union générale des Travailleurs d'Afrique noire (UGTAN) at the time of its foundation in 1957; this was formalized in 1958 as the Union des Syndicats des Travailleurs du Dahomey. Claude Tardits, *Porto-Novo; les nouvelles générations africaines entre leurs traditions et l'occident* (Paris, 1958), 87–91; Virginia Thompson, 'Dahomey,' in Gwendolen M. Carter, ed., *Five African States: Responses to Diversity* (Ithaca, 1963), 213, 217–18.

41. Herschelle Sandra Challenor, 'French Speaking West Africa's Dahomeyan Strangers in Colonization and Decolonization' (unpublished PhD dissertation, Columbia University, 1970).

11 The Dahomean national movement

1. Jean Suret-Canale, 'Un Pionnier méconnu du mouvement démocratique et national en Afrique,' *Etudes dahoméennes*, n.s. 3 (1964), 16.
2. Hunkanrin and Hazoumé were from Porto-Novo and of the Gun people, Adjovi was from Ouidah and of Fon and Hueda ancestry, and Johnson was of Gen (Mina) origin from Athiémé.
3. Suret-Canale, 'Un Pionnier,' 11–12; Ballard, 'Porto-Novo Incidents,' 64–5; James S. Spiegler, 'Aspects of Nationalist Thought Among French-Speaking West Africans, 1921–1939' (unpublished PhD dissertation, Nuffield College, University of Oxford, 1968), 17–49; Moseley, 'Colonial Politics,' 333. On Blaise Diagne see G. Wesley Johnson, *The Emergence of Black Politics in Senegal* (Stanford, 1971).
4. Lokossou, 'La Presse,' 82–7.
5. For a clear and detailed study of the impact of recruitment, see d'Almeida-Topor, 'Recrutement,' 196–241. On the revolts, see Garcia, 'Les Mouvements de résistance,' 144–78; Lombard, *Structures*, 416–18; Paul Mercier, *Tradition, changement, histoire: les 'Somba' du Dahomey septentrional* (Paris, 1968), 435–40. The most complete treatment of the revolts is in Anignikin, 'Mouvement national,' 83–207.
6. One of the two administrators, Combe, was dismissed on charges stemming from his repression of the 1914 rising in Yévié. See p. 137.
7. Archives nationales du Sénégal, 8G12 (Affaire Adjovi–Kenney). For an authoritative review of French conscription, see Myron J. Echenberg, 'Paying the Blood Tax: Military Conscription in French West Africa,' *Canadian Journal of African Studies 9*, 2 (1975), 171–92.
8. Jean Suret-Canale, 'L'Internationale communiste et la lutte contre le colonialisme,' *Cahiers de l'Institut Maurice Thorez*, 13 (1969). Another major Dahomean contributor to radical and Pan-African politics was Marc Tovalou Quénum (or Kojo Marc Tovalou-Houénou), doctor, lawyer, and brother of

Georges Tovalou Quénum. On his life and work see Spiegler, 'Aspects of Nationalist Thought,' 50–80. On Pan-Africanism more generally, see J. Ayodele Langley, *Pan-Africanism and Nationalism in West Africa, 1900–1945* (Oxford, 1973).

9. Moseley, 'Colonial Politics,' 373–4, 395. This study establishes the chronology of interwar Dahomean electoral politics and their ties to economic affairs and international politics.
10. Councils of chiefs were also established in the twenties. Buell, *Native Problem*, I:981–2.
11. D'Almeida-Topor, 'Recrutement,' 210.
12. Ballard, 'Porto-Novo Incidents,' 57. This pioneering study, giving many details on the background and the 1923 incidents themselves, has pointed the way for several subsequent studies.
13. On the earlier destruction of Awansouri, see p. 197.
14. Among the others sentenced were Oni Bello, Aminu Balogun, El-Hadj Mouteiro Soulé, and chief Gandonou Kri. For an insightful analysis of the impact of the administration's repression of this movement, see Anignikin, 'Mouvement national,' 278–303.
15. Buell, *Native Problem*, I:1017–19; Moseley, 'Colonial Politics,' 377, 380, 385.
16. Aupiais was appointed Provincial of the SMA Fathers in 1928. Georges Hardy, *Un Apôtre d'aujourd'hui: le révérend Père Aupiais* (Paris, 1949); Jerôme Comlan Alladaye, 'Les Missionnaires catholiques du Dahomey à l'époque coloniale: 1905–1957' (unpublished thèse de 3ᵉ cycle, University of Paris VII, 1978).
17. Bellarmin Cofi Codo, 'La Presse dahoméenne face aux aspirations des "évolués": "La Voix du Dahomey" (1927–1957)' (unpublished thèse de 3ᵉ cycle, University of Paris VII, 1978).
18. Moseley, 'Colonial Politics,' 471, 480; Fr Francis Aupiais, 'Le Travail forcé,' *Revue apologétique* (Aug. 1929); Hardy, *Un Apôtre*, 262–8.
19. Sant'Anna's death was reported without comment by *La Voix*. Thirty-five years later Michael Turner, interviewing Brazilian families, pieced together the story of the murder that had never been investigated. Turner, 'Les Bresiliens,' 378–9. For Sant'Anna's candidacy and subsequent developments, see *La Voix du Dahomey*, nos. 31–7 (1929).
20. See Reste, *Le Dahomey*. He acted, in effect, to implement the doctrines laid out at the end of World War I by Albert Sarraut, *La Mise en valeur des colonies françaises* (Paris, 1923), and Henri Cosnier, *L'Ouest africain français, ses ressources agricoles, son organisation économique* (Paris, 1921). See also pp. 254–60.
21. In 1931, 315,000 francs went to village chiefs, in proportion to the *impôt* they brought in. The 150 canton chiefs received 180,000 francs in salaries and 315,000 francs in merit pay. By 1941, village chiefs received 582,000 francs, while canton chiefs received 784,000 francs in salaries and 200,000 francs in merit pay ('remise de rendement'). Reste, *Le Dahomey*, 58–64; Desanti, *Bénin–Niger*, 88; Glélé, *Le Danxomę*, 240–2.

22. On Justin Aho, see Reste, *Le Dahomey*, 64; Moseley, 'Colonial Politics,' 425, 433, 508–9; Glélé, *Le Danxomę*, 237–8. His brother René Aho, who also served in the military and held substantial properties, acted as chief informant to the anthropologist Melville J. Herskovits in 1931; Maurice Glélé has accused him of distorting the history of the Fon kingdom to reinforce the current position of himself and his family. Glélé, *Le Danxomę*, 25, 83.

23. Jean-Claude Pauvert, 'L'Evolution politique des Ewé,' *Cahiers d'Etudes africaines 1*, 2 (1960), 177–8. In 1932, 3.5 million francs of *impôt* payments assessed remained uncollected. It took until 1935 before the government could again collect the full assessment. Moseley, 'Colonial Politics,' 407–13, 420, 428–30.

24. A 1933 document lists 25 episodes of locust flights, each lasting from one to eighteen days, in various parts of Dahomey from December 1929 to May 1932. Archives Nationales, de Bénin, R, 'Tableau de vols de sauterelles,' July 1933.

25. Reported unemployment for Dahomey was 1,700 persons at the end of 1933, 800 at the end of 1934, and 300 each at the end of 1935 and 1936. The reported workforce for Dahomey in 1935 consisted of 3,100 persons in the private sector and 2,400 in the public, sector, for a total of 5,500. These figures would imply an unemployment rate of from 30% to 50% in 1933. Hélène d'Almeida-Topor, 'Recherches sur l'évolution du travail salarié en AOF pendant la crise économique, 1930–36,' *Cahiers d'Etudes africaines 16*, 61–2 (1976), 110; Afrique Occidentale Française, Gouvernement Général, *Annuaire statistique de l'AOF, vol. 2 (1934–6)*.

26. Lists of Dahomean newspapers during the colonial era are given in Guy Landry Hazoumé, *Idéologies tribalistes et nation en Afrique: le cas dahoméen* (Paris, 1972), 218–20; and Dov Ronen, 'The Colonial Elite in Dahomey,' *African Studies Review 17*, 1 (1974), 71–4.

27. These characterizations appeared in the *Presse Porto-Novienne*, edited by V. M. Pinto, and were directed particularly at Casimir d'Almeida. Moseley, 'Colonial Politics,' 444–6.

28. Glélé, *Naissance*, 59–62. Dorothée Lima replaced Adjovi as editor when *La Voix* returned to publication. For the best study of the prosecution of *La Voix* and of the role of Hunkanrin in it, see Codo, 'La Presse dahoméenne.'

29. It was in this political situation that Hazoumé completed his novel *Doguicimi*, which provides a detailed description of the court of Abomey in the nineteenth century, but also justifies the French conquest of the Fon.

30. Administrator Bernard Maupoil of Athiémé *cercle* was charged by Kuassi of beating prisoners to extract false testimony. Maupoil was later author of *La Géomancie à l'ancien Côte des Esclaves*.

31. Glélé, *Naissance*, 61–3; Moseley, 'Colonial Politics,' 497–508.

32. Desanti, *Bénin–Niger*, 242–3; Moseley, 'Colonial Politics,' 515–19.

33. Glélé, *Naissance*, 63, 65; Moseley, 'Colonial Politics,' 508–10; Glélé, *Le Danxomę*, 243–4.

34. After an initial annoucement that forced labor had been abolished, the administration soon issued clarifications emphasizing that clearing of roads

and markets was to be continued. Archives nationales du Bénin, R, com-
mandant Porto-Novo to lieutenant-governor, 7 June 1939.

35. Moseley, 'Colonial Politics,' 534–5; Glélé, *Naissance*, 65; Suret-Canale, 'Un
Pionnier,' 27–8. Some twenty other Dahomeans, mostly from Porto-Novo,
were interned in the North.

36. Albert Tevoedjre, who was a schoolboy outside Porto-Novo during the war,
punctuates his emphasis on the African contribution to the war effort with an
ironic quotation, in French and Gun, of one of the songs he heard on the radio
and sang at school:

    Marshall Pétain, we the scholars of Dahomey
    We salute you, salute you again
    For the great work you have achieved
    In our behalf, in this world!

    Albert Tevoedjre, *L'Afrique révoltée* (Paris, 1958), 35. On the impact of Vichy
in Africa, see Suret-Canale, *Afrique noire, Vol. 2*, 568–87.

37. Both the *Voix* group and the *Phare* group were represented on the founding
committee; Augustin Azango, a 'neutral,' was selected president. The executive
committee, while it included Santos, was dominated by the *Phare* group. Glélé,
Naissance, 78–80. Glélé is the most knowledgeable of the writers on postwar
Dahomean politics.

38. The Mouvement républicain populaire (MRP) was the liberal party which,
with the Socialists and Communists, dominated the Constituent Assembly. For
the best review of the changing complexion of politics in immediate postwar
France and her African colonies, see Suret-Canale, *Afrique noire, Vol. 3, Pt. 1.*

39. After the first Constituent Assembly, Apithy was elected to the second
Constituent Assembly (June 1946) with Fr Jacques Bertho and to the National
Assembly in November 1946. Glélé, *Naissance*, 87; Ronen, *Dahomey*, 77;
Lombard, *Structures*, 505.

40. The Territorial Council replaced the Administrative Council of interwar years:
UPD won 5 of 12 citizen seats and 16 of 18 subject seats. The UPD took as its
official organs Nicoué's *Le Phare* and E. D. Zinsou's *Le Progressiste*; *La Voix*
ceased publication in 1948.

41. Ahomadegbé was a physician residing in Porto-Novo though born in Abomey;
Poisson was the son of Eugène Poisson, representative of the Association
cotonnière. On the RDA (Rassemblement démocratique africain), see Ruth
Schacter Morgenthau, *Political Parties in French-Speaking West Africa*
(Oxford, 1964), 56, 88–90, 301–5; Foltz, *From French West Africa to the Mali
Federation*, 54–5.

42. Citizens and subjects were now combined in a much enlarged electorate of
335,000. Ronen, *Dahomey*, 93; Morgenthau, *Political Parties*, 102–3;
Staniland, 'Three-Party System: I,' 297–303. More generally, Ronen argues
that the regionalization of Dahomean politics came from the inability of a
traditional society to adjust to modern institutions. Rather than reify the
concepts of 'tradition' and 'modernity,' it is surely wiser to give attention to the
specific content of the modern institutions offered, which in this case made a

breakdown of national unity almost unavoidable. Staniland, too, would have benefitted from a better understanding of prewar politics.

43. Apithy's party was the PRD (Parti républicain du Dahomey), strongest in Porto-Novo and the southeast; Maga's party was the MDD (Mouvement démocratique dahoméen). The UPD had already lost its newspapers, as *Le Phare* passed out of existence in 1949, a year after *Le Progressiste*.

44. Poquin, *Les Relations économiques*; Capet, *Traité*; Wade, *Economie de l'Ouest africain*; Berg, 'Political Choice.' By and large, these studies served as apologetics for France and AOF.

45. On Houphouët-Boigny, see Aristide Zolberg, *One-Party Government in the Ivory Coast* (Princeton, 1964).

46. Glélé, *Naissance*, 136–44; Glélé, *Le Danxome*, 251–4.

47. In the 1957 Territorial Assembly elections PRD, UDD and the parties of the North divided the popular vote in thirds, but PRD won 35 seats, UDD 7 seats, MDD 6 seats, and independents in the North won 12 seats: Apithy became head of the first territorial government. The governor had actually settled the strike by the end of January, but Apithy resigned February 2. Glélé, *Naissance*, 148–9; Virginia Thompson, 'Dahomey,' 213–15.

48. Among the major decisions were the balkanization of AOF in 1956–7, the ratification of the Fifth Republic constitution in 1958, the establishment and subsequent collapse of the Mali Federation in 1959, the establishment of the Council of the Entente in 1959, and independence in August 1960. Hubert Maga became prime minister in 1959, and headed the government until 1963.

49. Some 12,000 Dahomeans were expelled. In later years, a similar number would be expelled from Niger, and smaller numbers from Gabon and other countries. Ronen, *Dahomey,* 112; Herschelle S. Challenor, 'Strangers as Colonial Intermediaries: the Dahomeyans in Francophone Africa,' in William A. Shack and Elliott P. Skinner, eds., *Strangers in African Societies* (Berkeley, 1979).

12 Epilogue

1. See pp. 109 and 253.

2. Samir Amin, in an analysis of the 1960s, accurately labels the colonization of Dahomey as 'devastating.' But his case would have been stronger if he had emphasized that Dahomey's fiscal deficit and receipt of subsidies had begun in the last years of colonial rule. Amin, *L'Afrique de l'Ouest bloquée*.

3. Société nationale du Développement rural.

4. In an ironic twist, many of the places vacated by Dahomean civil servants in Niger and Ivory Coast were filled by French expatriates. Challenor, 'Strangers,' 83. I am reminded of the charming gentleman I met in Porto-Novo in 1966, who introduced himself as 'le Ministre de Chômage.'

Appendixes

Export revenue from Dahomey, 1640s–1950s

Table A1.1. *Export revenue from Dahomey, 1640s–1950s*

1 Decade	2 Slave exports per decade	3 Slave prices (£ per slave)	4 Palm oil exports (tons/yr)	5 Palm oil prices (£/ton)	6 Palm kernel exports (tons/yr)	7 Palm kernel prices (£/ton)
1640s	12,000	7.3				
1650s	9,000	7.9				
1660s	17,000	4.4				
1670s	32,000	3.5				
1680s	55,200	4.9				
1690s	104,900	5.8				
1700s	161,300	12.7				
1710s	153,400	16.2				
1720s	120,200	17.0				
1730s	118,000	23.0				
1740s	70,100	18.9				
1750s	70,500	18.2				
1760s	102,700	22.1				
1770s	90,700	22.6				
1780s	102,000	24.0				
1790s	49,000	28.5				
1800s	41,000	28.5				
1810s	42,000	22.2				
1820s	39,000	18.0				
1830s	35,000	15.5				
1840s	41,000	14.4	1,900	25		
1850s	48,200	13.0	4,700	25		
1860s	24,100	12.0	5,400	28	4,100	12
1870s			5,200	30	7,600	12
1880s			5,100	23	14,200	9
1890s			7,300	23	20,000	9
1900s						
1910s						
1920s						
1930s						
1940s						
1950s						

Table A1.1 (*cont.*)

8 Current export revenue (£/yr)	9 British wholesale prices (1913 = 100)	10 Export revenue (1913 £/yr)	11 Estimated population	12 Per capita export revenue (1913 £/yr)
8,800			449,000	
7,100			472,000	
7,500	110	6,800	496,000	0.014
11,000	95	11,600	522,000	0.02
27,000	85	32,000	524,000	0.06
61,000	95	64,000	502,000	0.13
205,000	95	216,000	460,000	0.47
249,000	95	262,000	422,000	0.62
204,000	90	227,000	388,000	0.59
271,000	80	339,000	358,000	0.95
132,000	80	165,000	361,000	0.46
128,000	85	151,000	363,000	0.42
227,000	92	247,000	351,000	0.70
205,000	95	216,000	354,000	0.61
245,000	105	233,000	329,000	0.71
140,000	135	104,000	332,000	0.31
117,000	170	69,000	336,000	0.21
93,000	155	60,000	339,000	0.18
70,000	115	61,000	356,000	0.17
54,000	110	49,000	375,000	0.13
106,000	100	106,000	394,000	0.27
180,000	105	171,000	414,000	0.41
229,000	110	208,000	435,000	0.48
247,000	110	225,000	457,000	0.49
245,000	85	288,000	506,000	0.57
348,000	75	464,000	559,000	0.83
472,000	85	555,000	618,000	0.90
848,000	130	652,000	682,000	0.96
1,734,000	190	913,000	755,000	1.21
1,932,000	170	1,136,000	836,000	1.36
2,606,000	260	1,002,000	1,019,000	0.98
4,746,000	410	1,158,000	1,242,000	0.93

Exported revenue from Dahomey, 1640s–1950s

Notes to columns

1. Decades run 1641–50, 1651–60, etc., according to the convention followed by Curtin.
2. These are slave exports for Dahomey only (i.e., the coast from Little Popo to Porto-Novo). These are assumed to be the same as the total of slave exports from the entire Bight of Benin, except for the 1780s through the 1840s, when I have used speculative estimates to allocate slave exports between Dahomey and Nigeria (i.e., Badagry and Lagos) as follows:

Decade	Total slave exports	Dahomey		Nigeria	
		% Total	Quantity	% Total	Quantity
1780s	153,100	67	102,000	33	51,000
1790s	74,000	67	49,000	33	25,000
1800s	81,800	50	41,000	50	42,000
1810s	83,800	50	42,000	50	42,000
1820s	77,500	50	39,000	50	39,000
1830s	105,700	33	35,000	67	71,000
1840s	81,000	50	41,000	50	40,000

3. For the 1640s–1770s, prices from Richard Nelson Bean, *The British Trans-Atlantic Slave Trade, 1650–1775* (New York, 1975), 158–9. For the 1780s–1860s, prices from E. Phillip LeVeen, *British Slave Trade Suppression Policies 1821–65* (New York, 1977), 8, 113. Prices taken from LeVeen have been multiplied by 5 to convert from dollars to pounds; prices taken from Bean were divided by 1.1 to convert from prices of prime male slaves to average prices. These figures, which are FOB for European goods exchanged for slaves, were multiplied by 1.5 for the period through the 1810s and by 1.25 thereafter. The result gives estimates of CIF prices, in current pounds, for goods exchanged for slaves; these are also, therefore, the FOB prices of slaves exported. I am indebted to Richard Bean and Henry Gemery for advice on these calculations.
4. From Figure 2.4 . Exports from Lagos not included.
5. Prices from Lagos Blue Books 1860s–1880s, by extrapolation 1840s–50s, and from published returns for Dahomey 1890s.
6. From Figure 2.4. Exports from Lagos not included.
7. Prices as in column 5.
8. This is Time Series I in Figure 1.1. It is the sum of columns 1 × 2, 3 × 4, and 5 × 6 through the 1890s. From the 1900s through the 1950s it is taken from published trade statistics, with the following conversions: figures in current francs were deflated to 1908 francs using an index of export prices (Appendix 6); these values were then converted into 1908 pounds sterling at 25 francs per pound, and were finally inflated into current pounds using the index of British wholesale prices shown in column 9. The figures shown are FOB value of exports.
9. Phyllis Deane and W. A. Cole, *British Economic Growth, 1688–1959* (Cambridge, 1964), endpapers.
10. This is Time Series II in Figure 1.1. It is column 8 divided by column 9 × 100.
11. Calculated as Aja population plus 5% of Yoruba population for each decade (see Tables A3.1 and A3.3). This population refers to the area of modern southern Bénin. A population calculated as Aja population plus 10% of Yoruba population would begin 6% higher than this series, would rise to 20% greater than this series in the 1790s, and would remain stable at that level.
12. This is Time Series III in Figure 1.1. It is column 10 divided by column 11.

APPENDIX 2

Slave exports by ethnic origin

The detailed estimates are shown first, followed by the method and sources used for their calculation.

Table A2.1. *Slave exports by ethnic origin.*

Decade	Total slave exports	Slave exports by ethnic origin: number (percent)				
		Aja	Yoruba	Voltaic	Nupe	Hausa
1640s	12,000	10,400(90)	1,200(10)			
1650s	9,000	8,100(90)	900(10)			
1660s	17,000	15,300(90)	1,700(10)			
1670s	32,000	28,800(90)	3,200(10)			
1680s	55,200	53,500(97)	1,700(3)			
1690s	104,900	101,800(97)	3,100(3)			
1700s	161,300	154,800(96)		6,500(4)		
1710s	153,400	142,700(93)	3,100(2)	7,700(5)		
1720s	120,200	108,200(90)	4,800(4)	7,200(6)		
1730s	118,000	103,800(88)	7,100(6)	7,100(6)		
1740s	70,100	57,500(82)	7,000(10)	4,900(7)	700(1)	
1750s	70,500	50,100(71)	11,300(16)	8,500(12)	700(1)	
1760s	102,700	63,700(62)	22,600(22)	15,400(15)	1,000(1)	
1770s	90,700	57,100(63)	20,000(22)	13,600(15)	900(1)	
1780s	153,100	94,900(62)	36,700(24)	15,300(10)	3,100(2)	3,100(2)
1790s	74,000	40,700(55)	14,800(20)	9,600(13)	1,500(2)	7,400(10)
1800s	81,800	40,100(49)	15,500(19)	8,200(10)	1,600(2)	16,400(20)
1810s	83,800	30,200(36)	30,200(36)	800(1)	6,700(8)	15,900(19)
1820s	77,500	22,500(29)	41,100(53)	800(1)	2,400(3)	10,900(14)
1830s	105,700	7,400(7)	89,800(85)		2,100(2)	6,300(6)
1840s	81,000	9,700(12)	64,000(79)		800(1)	5,700(7)
1850s	48,200	5,800(12)	38,100(79)		500(1)	3,400(7)
1860s	24,100	2,900(12)	19,000(79)		200(1)	1,700(7)

Sources: Percentages are taken from Table A2.2; slave export quantities are taken from Patrick Manning, 'The Slave Trade in the Bight of Benin 1640–1890,' in Henry Gemery and Jan Hogendorn, eds., *The Uncommon Market: Essays in the Economic History of the Atlantic Slave Trade* (New York, 1979), 117.

Appendix 2

The method utilized was to collect New World samples of slaves listing ethnic origins of slaves from the Bight of Benin (summarized in Table A2.3), assume that they reflected slave exports in current or prior decades, and combine them to get a mean proportion of slave exports by decade (calculated in Table A2.2), which was then applied to total slave exports to get slave exports by ethnic origin (calculated in Table A2.1). Only slaves whose ethnic identity was clearly specified were included in the samples – for example, those labelled with the general term 'Mina' were usually excluded, unless the context indicated a specific reference to the Gen or Mina group of the Aja peoples. It is surely true that the tendency to label slaves by port of departure (as well as by ethnic group) biases the percentage of Aja and even Yoruba slaves upward. I believe, however, that the magnitude of this effect is not sufficient to bring great change to the figures presented here.

The longevity of slaves in the New World is a key factor in determining whether a New World slave census in a given year best reflects African slave exports for that year, the previous year, or as much as two decades earlier. Many New World slaves died quite rapidly, while others lived very long. I have assumed a fairly high level of mortality, so that a New World slave census is generally applied to African exports for the period from five to ten years previous. In attempt to stretch scarce data for the important early eighteenth century, however, I have taken the sample labelled 'Debien 1760s' and applied it not only to exports for the 1750s, but with diminished weight as far back as the 1710s. Similarly, the 'Schwartz' sample, drawn from 1684 to 1745 but mostly in the 1720s and 1730s, is applied to the first four decades of the eighteenth century. Then, in a concession to strong statements in the qualitative literature, I have assumed that Yoruba slaves amounted to ten percent of exports from the 1640s through the 1670s, even though no quantitative confirmation could be found.

Table A2.2. *Estimated ethnic distribution of slave exports, by decade*

Decade	Sample	Percentage of decennial slave exports				
		Aja	Yoruba	Voltaic	Nupe	Hausa
1640s–						
1670s	*Dapper-Bosman (0)*	90	10			
1680s	*Debien 1690s (33)*	97	3			
1690s	*Debien 1690s (33)*	97	3			
1700s	Schwartz (15)	93		7		
	Verger 1730s (1)	100				
	Mean	96		4		
1710s	Schwartz (15)	93		7		
	Verger 1730s (1)	100				
	Debien 1760s (52)	60	23	15	2	
	Mean (Debien weighted 1/5)	93	2	5		
1720s	Schwartz (15)	93		7		
	Verger 1730s (1)	100				
	Debien 1760s (52)	60	23	15	2	
	Mean (Debien weighted 2/5)	90	4	6		

336

Table A2.2 (*cont.*)

1730s	Schwartz (15)	93		7		
	Verger 1730s (1)	100				
	Debien 1760s (52)	60	23	15	2	
	Mean (Debien weighted 3/5)	*88*	*6*	*6*		
1740s	Verger 1740s (7)	100				
	Debien 1760s (52)	60	23	15	2	
	Mean (Debien weighted 4/5)	*82*	*10*	*7*	*1*	
1750s	Verger 1750s (12)	83	8	8		
	Debien 1760s (52)	60	23	15	2	
	Mean	*71*	*16*	*12*	*1*	
1760s	Verger 1760s (38)	92	8			
	Debien 1760s (52)	60	23	15	2	
	Debien 1770s (73)	35	36	29		
	Mean	*62*	*22*	*15*	*1*	
1770s	Verger 1770s (64)	91	9			
	Debien 1770s (73)	35	36	29		
	Debien 1780s (196)	62	21	15	2	
	Mean	*63*	*22*	*15*	*1*	
1780s	Verger 1780s (10)	80	20			
	Debien 1780s (196)	62	21	15	2	
	Debien 1790s (175)	44	30	16	4	6
	Mean	*62*	*24*	*10*	*2*	*2*
1790s	Verger 1790s (29)	86	10	4		
	Debien 1790s (175)	44	30	16	4	6
	Mattoso 1805–6 (52)	38	35	2	2	23
	Higman 1811 (926)	54	4	30		12
	Mean	*55*	*20*	*13*	*2*	*10*
1800s	Verger 1800s (15)	60	7	7		26
	Mattoso 1805–6 (52)	38	35	2	2	23
	Mattoso 1810–11 (73)	45	30		6	19
	Higman 1811 (926)	54	4	30		12
	Mean	*49*	*19*	*10*	*2*	*20*
1810s	Verger 1810s (30)	27	37		10	27
	Reis 1812–25 (287)	47	35	1	5	12
	Mean	*36*	*36*	*1*	*8*	*19*
1820s	Verger 1820s (176)	12	70	2	1	16
	Reis 1812–25 (287)	47	35	1	5	12
	Mean	*29*	*53*	*1*	*3*	*14*
1830s	Verger 1830s (171)	1	92		2	5
	Sierra Leone 1848 (9009)	12	79		1	7
	Mean	*7*	*85*		*2*	*6*
1840s– 1860s	Sierra Leone 1848 (9009)	12	79		1	7

Note: Figures in italics for each decade are those used in Table A2.1. Figures in parentheses after each sample name indicate sample size.
Source: Table A2.3.

Table A2.3. *Slave samples giving ethnic identity*

Sample	Description and source
Dapper-Bosman	These sources indicate large numbers of Yoruba slave exports in the seventeenth century, though no New World sources yet confirm this. See p. 289, n. 20, and p. 290, n. 28, above.
Schwartz (15)	Records of manumitted slaves in Bahia; of 112 'Mina,' 30 were noted before 1725 and 82 between 1726 and 1745. Of 15 slaves more specifically designated, 10 were 'Arda' and 4 were 'Gege' (Aja); one was 'Samba' (Voltaic). Stuart B. Schwartz, 'The Manumission of Slaves in Colonial Brazil: Bahia, 1684–1745,' *Hispanic American Historical Review 54*, 4 (1974), 613.
Mattoso 1805–6, Mattoso 1810–11	Slaves listed in inheritance records in Bahia. 1805–6: 20 Gege, 18 Nago, 1 Barba, 1 Tapa, 12 Aussa, 28 Mina. 1810–11: 33 Gege, 22 Nago, 4 Tapa, 14 Aussa, 9 Mina. (Mina were not counted in either case.) Katia M. de Queirós Mattoso, 'Os Excravos na Bahia no Alvorecer do Século XIX (Estude de un Grupo Social),' *Revista de História 47*, 97 (1974), 117.
Reis 1812–25	Inheritance records in Bahia, 1812–25: 135 Gege, 101 Nago, 3 Barba, 14 Tapa, 34 Ausa. Twenty-five 'Mina' were included with the Gege or Aja. João José Reis, personal communication.
Higman 1811	Results of a careful census of slaves in Trinidad, for 926 of the 1075 slaves listed as from the Bight of Benin (largest exclusion is 99 'Ada'). Names are quite detailed and specific: Higman lists 283 'Mine' and 'Minre' with the Gold Coast and 33 'Mina' and 'Minna' with the Bight of Benin, and I have followed him, and have included the latter with the Aja. The sample included 504 Aja, 35 Yoruba, 278 Voltaic, and 109 Hausa. B. W. Higman, 'African and Creole Family Patterns in Trinidad,' *Journal of Family History 3* (1978), 178–180.
Sierra Leone 1848	Census of recaptives in Sierra Leone, with only general description of ethnic origin: 1075 Aja, 7114 Yoruba, 163 Nupe, 657 Hausa. Philip D. Curtin and Jan Vansina, 'Sources of the Nineteenth-Century Atlantic Slave Trade,' *Journal of African History 5*, 2 (1964), 207–8.
Debien	For 1690s, census of a sugar plantation in French Guiana; otherwise records from plantations in Saint-Domingue, collected by Debien and his associates and summarized by Curtin. Almost all these slaves have clear ethnic identities:

	Aja	Yoruba	Voltaic	Nupe	Hausa	Total
1690s	32	1				33
1760s	31	12	8	1		52
1770s	26	26	21			73
1780s	122	41	29	4		196
1790s	77	53	28	7	10	175

Philip D. Curtin, *The Atlantic Slave Trade: a Census* (Madison, 1969), 189, 192–7.

Verger	Inventory of slaves in the town of São Francisco do Conde, near Bahia, upon the heritage of minors. Those classified as Aja include 'Gege,' 'Mondobi,' 'Lada,' 'Maquim,' and 'Savaru.' Also listed are 'Nago,' 'Barba,' 'Tapa' and 'Aussa.' Those classified either as 'Mina' or 'Guiné' were left out of the samples – these came to 32 out of 591 persons listed.

Table A2.3 (*cont.*)

Note that I have used a five-year lag in setting up the samples: thus
'Verger 1780s' includes slaves noted between 1786 and 1795.

	Aja	Yoruba	Voltaic	Nupe	Hausa	Total
1730s	1					1
1740s	7					7
1750s	10	1	1			12
1760s	35	3				38
1770s	58	6				64
1780s	8	2				10
1790s	25	3	1			29
1800s	9	1		1	4	15
1810s	8	11		3	8	30
1820s	25	124	3	2	28	176
1830s	1	158		4	8	171

Pierre Verger, *Flux et reflux de la traite des Nègres entre le golfe du Bénin et Bahia de Todos os Santos du 17ᵉ et 18ᵉ siècles* (The Hague, 1968), 672–80.

APPENDIX 3

Population loss due to slave exports

The estimation of decennial rates of population loss requires two sorts of data: population by ethnic origin in each decade, and numbers of slaves exported. The latter are taken from Table A2.1. The former are based on retrospective projections of population growth from base populations of the 1930s, using growth rates selected on an *a priori* basis. Base populations are taken from the *Annuaire Statistique de l'AOF* and from Kuczynski's survey of the demography of British colonies.[1] Base populations for the 1930s are as follows:

Aja – 656,000 (all in Dahomey)
Yoruba – 3,550,000 (3,400,000 in Nigeria, 150,000 in Dahomey)
Voltaic – 610,000 (420,000 in Dahomey, 190,000 in Nigeria)
Nupe – 470,000 (all in Nigeria)
Hausa – 5,570,000 (all in Nigeria)

No population from Togo was included in the base population, but the inclusion of all Yoruba and Voltaic peoples of Nigeria is a compensating addition. In any case, modern Togo was not as heavily involved in slave trade as surrounding regions.

For the Yoruba, Voltaic, Nupe and Hausa populations, common growth rates were assumed: 1.0% per year from the 1870s to the 1930s, and 0.5% per year before the 1870s. Population growth rates in West Africa seem commonly to have been of the order of one percent in the early colonial years, and this growth rate probably preceded the colonial era by some decades. I have assumed a smaller growth rate for earlier years because it is more in line with growth rates known for other areas of the world. Professor Fage has assumed slower growth rates for African population.[2] Perhaps some empirical tests can be devised to estimate African population growth. But if, in the extreme, one assumed no African population growth before the twentieth century, this would imply a seventeenth-century West African population denser than that of Europe.

For the Aja population, I have used the same assumptions as above, except for the years before the 1820s where slave exports far exceeded population growth. For these earlier years I adopted the following rules of thumb: (1) if the estimated loss rate due to slave exports is over 1.0% of population, then the estimated population growth rate is reduced from 0.5% to zero; (2) if the estimated loss rate is over 2.0%, then the estimated rate of population change is reduced to -0.5%; (3) if the

340

estimated loss rate is over 3.0%, then the estimated rate of population change is − 1.0%. On this basis, the population for each decade is recalculated.[3] These assumptions are intended to understate the negative influence of slave exports on population. Women of childbearing age were perhaps one-fourth of all exports, and as more women were exported, the effect on population became more severe. The depopulation of the Aja peoples is shown to have been extreme, with population falling from an estimated 486,000 in the 1690s to an estimated 267,000 a century later.

These estimates, while obviously speculative, are nonetheless robust. Assuming the quantities of slave exports to be roughly correct, the Aja would be seen to have suffered depopulation even if a zero rate of growth were projected back from the 1930s. For the Voltaic peoples, and to a lesser degree for the Yoruba, slight variations in assumptions on populations growth rate and the impact of slave exports would indicate depopulation in the eighteenth century for the Voltaic peoples, and in the nineteenth century for the Yoruba. Further, it is more likely that the estimated quantities of slave exports are too low than that they are too high.[4]

Table A3.1. *Yoruba and Voltaic loss rates due to slave exports*

Decade	Yoruba			Voltaic		
	Estimated population	Slave exports	Loss rate, percent	Estimated population	Slave exports	Loss rate, percent
1930s	3,550,000			610,000		
1920s	3,212,000			552,000		
1910s	2,906,000			499,000		
1900s	2,630,000			452,000		
1890s	2,380,000			409,000		
1880s	2,153,000			370,000		
1870s	1,948,000			335,000		
1860s	1,853,000	19,300	0.10	318,000		
1850s	1,763,000	38,600	0.22	303,000		
1840s	1,677,000	64,000	0.38	288,000		
1830s	1,595,000	89,800	0.56	274,000		
1820s	1,517,000	41,100	0.27	261,000	800	0.03
1810s	1,443,000	30,200	0.21	248,000	800	0.03
1800s	1,373,000	15,500	0.11	236,000	8,200	0.35
1790s	1,306,000	14,800	0.11	224,000	9,600	0.43
1780s	1,242,000	36,700	0.30	213,000	15,300	0.72
1770s	1,182,000	20,000	0.16	203,000	13,600	0.67
1760s	1,124,000	22,600	0.20	193,000	15,400	0.80
1750s	1,069,000	11,300	0.10	184,000	8,500	0.46
1740s	1,017,000	7,000	0.06	175,000	4,900	0.28
1730s	967,000	7,100	0.07	166,000	7,100	0.43
1720s	920,000	4,800	0.05	158,000	7,200	0.46
1710s	875,000	3,100	0.03	150,000	7,700	0.51
1700s	833,000			143,000	6,500	0.45
1690s	792,000	3,100	0.04	136,000		
1680s	753,000	1,700	0.02	129,000		

Appendix 3

Table A3.1. (*cont.*)

	Yoruba			Voltaic		
Decade	Estimated population	Slave exports	Loss rate, percent	Estimated population	Slave exports	Loss rate, percent
1670s	717,000	3,200	0.04	123,000		
1660s	682,000	1,700	0.02	117,000		
1650s	649,000	900	0.01	111,000		
1640s	617,000	1,200	0.02	106,000		

Table A3.2. *Nupe and Hausa loss rates due to slave exports*

	Nupe			Hausa		
Decade	Estimated population	Slave exports	Loss rate, percent	Estimated population	Slave exports	Loss rate, percent
1930s	470,000			5,569,000		
1920s	425,000			5,039,000		
1910s	385,000			4,560,000		
1900s	348,000			4,126,000		
1890s	315,000			3,733,000		
1880s	285,000			3,378,000		
1870s	258,000			3,056,000		
1860s	245,000	200	0.01	2,907,000	1,700	0.01
1850s	233,000	500	0.02	2,765,000	3,400	0.01
1840s	222,000	800	0.04	2,631,000	5,700	0.02
1830s	211,000	2,100	0.10	2,502,000	6,300	0.03
1820s	201,000	2,400	0.12	2,380,000	10,900	0.05
1810s	191,000	6,700	0.35	2,264,000	15,900	0.07
1800s	182,000	1,600	0.09	2,154,000	16,400	0.08
1790s	173,000	1,500	0.09	2,049,000	7,400	0.04
1780s	164,000	3,100	0.19	1,949,000	3,100	0.02
1770s	156,000	900	0.06	1,854,000		
1760s	149,000	1,000	0.07			
1750s	142,000	700	0.05			
1740s	135,000	700	0.05			
1730s	128,000					
1720s	122,000					
1710s	116,000					
1700s	110,000					
1690s	105,000					
1680s	100,000					
1670s	95,000					
1660s	90,000					
1650s	86,000					
1640s	82,000					

Table A3.3. *Aja loss rates due to slave exports*

Decade	Estimated population	Slave exports	Estimated loss rate, percent	Adjusted growth rate, percent	Adjusted population	Adjusted loss rate
1930s	656,000					
1920s	594,000					
1910s	537,000					
1900s	486,000					
1890s	440,000					
1880s	398,000					
1870s	360,000					
1860s	342,000	4,800	0.14			
1850s	326,000	9,600	0.29			
1840s	310,000	9,700	0.31			
1830s	295,000	7,400	0.25			
1820s	280,000	22,500	0.80			
1810s	267,000	30,200	1.13	0	280,000	1.08
1800s	267,000	40,100	1.50	0	280,000	1.43
1790s	267,000	40,700	1.52	0	280,000	1.45
1780s	267,000	94,900	3.55	− 1.0	310,000	3.06
1770s	295,000	57,100	1.94	0	310,000	1.84
1760s	295,000	63,700	2.16	− 0.5	326,000	1.96
1750s	310,000	50,100	1.61	0	326,000	1.54
1740s	310,000	57,500	1.85	0	326,000	1.77
1730s	310,000	103,800	3.34	− 1.0	360,000	2.89
1720s	342,000	108,200	3.15	− 1.0	398,000	2.72
1710s	378,000	142,700	3.77	− 1.0	440,000	3.25
1700s	418,000	154,800	3.70	− 1.0	486,000	3.19
1690s	462,000	101,800	2.20	− 0.5	511,000	1.99
1680s	486,000	53,500	1.10	0	511,000	1.05
1670s	486,000	28,800	0.59			
1660s	462,000	15,300	0.33			
1650s	440,000	8,100	0.18			
1640s	418,000	10,400	0.24			

Notes to appendix 3

1. Afrique Occidental Française, Gouvernement Général, *Annuaire statistique de l'AOF, vol. 1 (1933–4)*; Robert Rene Kuczynski, *Demographic Survey of the British Colonial Empire* (3 vols., London, 1948), I:585, 594.
2. J. D. Fage, *A History of West Africa*, 4th edn (Cambridge, 1969), 85–6.
3. Note that in Table A3.3 the 'estimated loss rate' (based on population remaining at the end of the decade) rather than 'adjusted loss rate' (based on the whole population at risk) is taken as the reported rate of loss.
4. Note that loss rates in the tables below are calculated per year rather than per decade.

APPENDIX 4

Foreign trade of Dahomey

The seven tables in this appendix provide a comprehensive summary of the recorded foreign trade of the area of modern Bénin from 1863 to 1960. The tables have been set up to display a wide range of goods and to facilitate comparisons over time.

Table A4.1: Lagos exports to Porto-Novo, 1863–1896. Although no records were kept at Porto-Novo until 1884, most of Porto-Novo's trade went through Lagos, where the Blue Books list commercial returns beginning in 1863. In fact, only imports to Porto-Novo from Lagos were recorded in detail, as shown in this table. (For purposes of conversion between this and subsequent tables, £1 sterling was the equivalent of 25 francs until 1914.) Exports of palm products from Porto-Novo via Lagos were reported as Lagos exports: Porto-Novo exports comprised from ten to twenty percent of the reported Lagos total until the end of the century, when Cotonou gained dominance in Porto-Novo's trade. Consular reports, both British and French, contain further data on Bight of Benin trade before 1890.

Table A4.2: Exports by port, 1884–1895. For 1884 and 1887, though not for other years, commercial returns were listed for portions of the Bight of Benin in *Statistiques coloniales*, published annually by the French Ministry of Colonies. For 1889 through 1895, export statistics listed by port and by quarter are held in Paris at the Archives nationales, Section Outre-mer (Dahomey IX-7), and are also to be found in a bound volume in the Archives nationales du Bénin. I have used both sets (there are some discrepancies) to compile the totals by port and by year.

Table A4.3: Imports by port, 1884–1895. These figures are drawn from the same sources as exports, discussed above. The presentation, however is more complex. For alcoholic beverages, I have conserved the terms listed in the source, setting them inside quotes, rather than relabel them in English, because the products imported and the terms used varied greatly from year to year. Customs duties were included in the values of goods, and money imports were included in the value of imports. Many imports, especially from Lagos and Togo, went unrecorded. The large category of 'unenumerated' goods is a clear weakness in these returns: goods recorded specifically in one port might be unenumerated in another, making it appear, for instance, that only Porto-Novo imported matches when in fact all ports did.

Table A4.4: Exports, 1889–1914. Figures for 1889–1895 are taken from

344

Table A4.2; those for 1896–1914 are taken from *Statistiques du commerce des colonies françaises*, published annually by the Agence générale des Colonies. Records are incomplete for many of the minor exports, and many value figures were arbitrarily rounded off. Commissions of administrators and merchants established *mercuriales* or accounting prices for trade records. *Mercuriales* for exports were based on the price at the coast, but they were rounded off to nice even numbers for ease of calculation, they tended to be set at the beginning of the year, and they were often left unchanged for suspiciously long periods of time – the *mercuriale* for sheep was 15 francs a head from 1901 to 1914. After the formation of AOF, local differences in *mercuriales* tended to be reduced or even abolished by the Government General.

Table A4.5: Imports, 1889–1914. Sources on imports are Table A4.3 up to 1895 and *Statistiques du commerce* from 1896 to 1914. Again, there are substantial gaps in recording for minor goods and for West African commerce. The most serious problem, however, was the handling of customs duties. In the 1890s, customs officials added customs duties to the landed price of imports plus 25%, and rounded off to get a *mercuriale* which was an approximation to the selling price in Dahomey. In 1902, however, customs duties suddenly ceased to be counted as part of the unit value of alcoholic beverages, tobacco, and gunpowder: as a result, the reported value of liquor imports fell by two-thirds, and that of tobacco imports fell by one-fourth. Import duties were dropped from the *mercuriales* for textiles in 1904. (These changes can only be determined through variations in the implicit unit values in reported imports.) The value of imports reported in 1902 was 10–20% lower because of the new system; the relative value of liquor, tobacco and gunpowder imports appeared to fall, and all others appeared to rise.

By 1893, officials recorded virtually all trans-Atlantic trade, but they recorded only the most obvious aspects of the lagoon trade to Nigeria and Togo until about 1897. The foreign trade of northern Dahomey did not enter significantly into the trade statistics.

The irony of Cartesian logic is that pursuit of rationality leads to constant reorganization: the structure for reporting imports changed repeatedly so that statistics for many goods are not strictly comparable from one year to the next. The imports which I have listed as 'trade alcohol' are presented in the published returns as 'alcools et eaux-de-vie, de 81° à 100°' from 1898 to 1907, as 'alcools et esprits à dédoubler' in 1908 and 1909, and as 'alcools de traite' from 1910 to 1914. Similarly, the category I have presented as 'gin, geneva and rum' was given in the returns as 'alcools et eaux-de-vie, de 51° à 80°' from 1898 to 1907, then separately as 'genièvre' and 'rhum' from 1908. Reported categories of imported metals, metallic goods and machinery were even more ill-defined and oft-revised. Rails, for example, were reported (without being enumerated specifically) as part of 'mécanique générale' until 1907. after which they were listed as part of 'métaux.' In Table A4.5 I have included rails as part of 'machinery': rails comprised roughly 30% of total machinery imports between 1902 and 1912.

Imports and exports of money are included as commodities in the foreign trade statistics in the years before 1903 – a large portion of the value of imports not accounted for in those years was simply imports of money (see Table A8.1). From 1903 to 1911, commercial returns gave no indication on money flows; beginning in 1912 money flows were again published, but they were not included in the value of trade.

Also shown in Table A4.5, for several imports, are estimated or proxy prices which are used in the regression calculations of Chapter 5. Recorded import values (and hence prices) could not be depended upon because of the *mercuriale* system. The most consistent and readily available alternative set of prices for these goods was that published annually for British foreign trade, as given in the Statistical Abstract for the United Kingdom and the monthly Accounts of Trade and Navigation, published annually in the British Parliamentary Papers. It was assumed that the fluctuations in these prices paralleled the fluctuations of prices in Dahomey. It was often necessary to apply a scaling factor to the British prices to make them the same order of magnitude as the Dahomean prices; then the amount of the Dahomean customs duty (Table 7.1) was added to the price for each good in each year. These adjusted prices were used in the linear regressions. For certain imports (casks and thread) I constructed series for import volume by dividing these proxy prices into reported import values.

Table A4.6: Exports, 1915–60. Export quantities (but not values) were published for 1915 to 1917 in France, Agence générale des Colonies, *Renseignements généraux sur le commerce des colonies françaises, 1914–17* (Paris, 1918). From 1918 to 1928, major exports are listed in similar annual publications. But the best source for export statistics from 1915 to 1938 is Afrique Occidentale Française, Agence économique, *Bulletin mensuel,* beginning in 1923. (Figures for the years 1915–22 are scattered through the 1923–4 issues of the *Bulletin mensuel.*) For 1939 to 1955, export figures are most readily available in the *Annuaire statistique de l'AOF*: 1939–49 are contained in vol. 4, no. 1 (1949); 1949 is given in vol. 4, no. 2 (1951); 1950–4 are given in vol. 5 (1955); 1955 is given in vol. 6 (1957). A far more detailed set of export returns for 1939–55 is given in Afrique Occidentale Française, Direction de Mécanographie et de la Statistique, *Le Commerce extérieur de l'AOF* (Dakar). After 1955, exports are taken from occasional summaries in République du Dahomey, *Bulletin du statistique,* and in Banque Centrale des Etats de l'Afrique de l'Ouest, *Notes d'information et statistiques.* I wish to express special thanks to Hélène d'Almeida-Topor who, with her unexcelled knowledge of French colonial statistical publications, brought to my attention certain of the above returns, especially for the two World Wars.

Table A4.7: Imports, 1915–1960. Sources are as in Table A4.6. The AOF *Bulletin mensuel* reports 'principal imports' for the years 1915–39: these were imports of particular interest to the colonial ministry, and did not necessarily include all of Dahomey's principal imports. Imports from neighboring African territories tended to be neglected in this period. The categorization of imports changed from time to time, and import value figures were subject to the same problems as in earlier years – all the more so because of the severity of inflation. Customs duties were excluded from all import values: thus, textile imports appear to have been far greater in value than beverage imports. In terms of the prices paid by consumers, however, the reverse was often the case.

Table A4.1. *Lagos exports to Porto-Novo, 1863–96 (values in pounds)*

Year	Total Lagos import value	Lagos imports from Porto-Novo	Total Lagos export value	Lagos exports to Porto-Novo	Lagos exports to Porto-Novo accounted for (d)
1863	59,038	657	64,226	2,416	1,171
1864	*a*	*a*	*a*	*a*	*a*
1865	114,284	3,333	175,636	19,682	15,798
1866	220,766	4,312	262,699	9,810	9,429
1867	321,978	9,430	513,158	11,197	10,990
1868	340,815	7,872	517,254	9,758	8,401
1869	416,895	3,748	669,598	6,545c	8,434c
1870	400,558	3,638	515,365	20,823	19,789
1871	391,653	3,931	589,262	23,734	23,304
1872	366,256	7,050	444,849	39,794	38,084
1873	258,883	3,005	406,986	44,258	b
1874	348,636	2,490	486,328	37,192	b
1875	459,736	2,983	517,535	43,776	b
1876	476,813	776	619,260	74,365	b
1877	614,359	1,245	734,708	118,173e	b
1878	483,623	1,690	577,336	103,649	110,137
1879	527,872	2,904	654,380	115,545	113,252
1880	407,369	1,378	576,510	72,356	70,406
1881	339,659	642	460,007	64,040c	64,100c
1882	428,883	1,165	581,064	65,510	63,285
1883	515,393	1,432	594,136	60,592	59,452
1884	538,221	988	672,414	81,410	76,795
1885	542,564	1,813	642,181	82,689	78,181
1886	357,831	1,779	538,990	37,954	35,508
1887	415,343	1,440	491,468	52,532	50,308
1888	442,062	2,177	508,237	45,829	43,717
1889	464,259	7,106	457,649	51,497	48,808
1890	500,828	7,874	595,193	47,599	42,356
1891	607,719	5,999	717,642	83,740	77,654
1892	522,040	11,633	577,083	118,873	86,740
1893	749,027	3,903	836,295	115,679	81,747
1894	744,561	5,321	821,682	128,118	93,770
1895	815,815	2,081	985,595	108,728	82,103
1896	901,474	4,798	975,263	54,936	35,994

Table A4.1 (*cont.*)

Year	Cotton goods		Gin and geneva		Rum		Wine	
	Packages	Value	Gallons	Value	Gallons	Value	Gallons	Value
1863	3	35	300	45	600	60	40	36
1864	*a*	*a*	*a*	*a*	*a*	*a*	*a*	*a*
1865	2	5	*f*	*f*	91,109	9,236	135	77
1866	124	1,226	980	178	41,191	4,340	*f*	*f*
1867	305	6,605	200	25	20,921	2,204	44	36
1868	321	5,793	1,000	111	386	35	*f*	*f*
1869	122	2,440	850	110	33,751	2,890	192	19
1870	459	6,631	6,085	616	45,798	3,540	20	4
1871	329	3,623	5,019	644	74,750	7,191	*f*	*f*
1872	1039	16,450	14,218	2,130	7,803	1,629	251	73
1873	*b*	*b*	*b*	*b*	*b*	*b*	*b*	*b*
1874	*b*	*b*	*b*	*b*	*b*	*b*	*b*	*b*
1875	*b*	*b*	*b*	*b*	*b*	*b*	*b*	*b*
1876	*b*	*b*	*b*	*b*	*b*	*b*	*b*	*b*
1877	*b*	*b*	*b*	*b*	*b*	*b*	*b*	*b*
1878	1394	23,592	110,581	16,713	321,140	29,522	1,005*h*	682
1879	1039	20,549	213,018	24,054	678,721	41,046	6,428*h*	1,845
1880	1304	26,310	113,027	11,173	125,114	9,655	260*h*	292
1881	904	16,524	97,945	14,092	260,420	16,939	586*h*	305
1882	1544	24,142	112,465*g*	14,078	118,736	7,108	647*h*	301
1883	1106	17,380	220,681	20,258	152,967	6,139	293*h*	116
1884	1459	19,940	317,530	30,801	151,719	8,710	1,539	340
1885	1175	16,543	347,397	33,059	184,640	9,802	1,796	401
1886	708	8,715	95,892	8,860	57,109	2,827	2,003	308
1887	1203	16,999	146,777	13,919	102,321	4,937	474	189
1888	950	12,630	170,773	14,315	136,369	5,594	669	133
1889	1196	16,409	144,817	13,469	130,610	5,335	868	241
1890	980	15,966	38,403	3,524	143,696	5,418	768	289
1891	1484	25,044	112,033	12,047	190,018	11,047	1,880	313
1892	1105	20,639	266,612	24,187	163,429	8,544	*i*	*i*
1893	1077	20,831	82,520	6,424	277,188	14,930	*i*	*i*
1894	1994	33,290	30,625	2,155	208,725	8,676	*i*	*i*
1895	1049	28,685	6,148	484	146,701	6,474	*i*	*i*
1896	1086	15,262	1,364	100	14,048	1,368	*i*	*i*

Table A4.1 (*cont.*)

Year	Tobacco		Cowries		Specie		Shooks	
	Tons	Value	Tons	Value	Packages	Value	Packages	Value
1863	10	896					30	40
1864	a	a					a	a
1865	123	5,872					382	336,
1866	52	1,952	6	622			610	605
1867	35	1,601	f	f			277	332
1868	39	1,980	4	150			f	f
1869	31	2,821	f	f			f	f
1870	123	8,461	f	f			f	f
1871	184	9,472	213	1,690			209	220
1872	73	13,282	175	2,253	1	50	747	1,126
1873	b	b	b	b	b	b	b	b
1874	b	b	b	b	b	b	b	b
1875	b	b	b	b	b	b	b	b
1876	b	b	b	b	b	b	b	b
1877	b	b	b	b	b	b	b	b
1878	j	16,938	1017	11,349	f	f	70	83
1879	302	13,410	1080	10,055	f	f	f	f
1880	275	11,990	736	8,026	1	625	499	513
1881	241	10,938	264	2,946	f	f	188	267
1882	217	10,423	245	3,180	f	f	f	f
1883	213	10,006	428	2,690	f	f	f	f
1884	268	12,339	95	942	f	f	260	180
1885	260	12,423	61	558	f	f	280	313
1886	229	11,616	20	187	8	1,025	679	756
1887	203	9,896	59	613	4	770	629	484
1888	140	7,301	32	229	3	300	780	730
1889	204	9,185	1	41	f	1,250	352	350
1890	188	8,989	f	f	f	4,295		1,777
1891	175	7,841	125	1,072	f	13,498	2,661	2,882
1892	147	6,700	i	i	132	26,670	i	i
1893	148	7,032	i	i	160	32,530	i	i
1894	156	7,614	i	i	99	42,035	i	i
1895	162	6,760	i	i	106	39,700	i	i
1896	63	2,982	i	i	44	16,282	i	i

Table A4.1 (*cont.*)

Year	Hoop Iron		Salt		Guns		Gunpowder	
	Packages	Value	Tons	Value	Pieces	Value	Barrels	Value
1863	18	9						
1864	*d*	*a*						
1865	625	272						
1866	181	51			499	272	57	153
1867	80	25			180	82	45	80
1868	*f*	*f*			535	291	25	41
1869	*f*	*f*			9	4	54	150
1870	*f*	*f*			1,405	447	75	17
1871	200	66			525	267	50	97
1872	347	139	37	108	562	408	181	348
1873	*b*	*b*	*b*	*b*	*b*	*b*	*b*	*b*
1874	*b*	*b*	*b*	*b*	*b*	*b*	*b*	*b*
1875	*b*	*b*	*b*	*b*	*b*	*b*	*b*	*b*
1876	*b*	*b*	*b*	*b*	*b*	*b*	*b*	*b*
1877	*b*	*b*	*b*	*b*	*b*	*b*	*b*	*b*
1878	*f*	*f*	292	342	*b*	*b*	3,225*h*	809
1879	*f*	*f*	150	225	95*h*	672	2,281*h*	329
1880	1018	262	*f*	*f*	159*h*	1,216	418*h*	120
1881	*f*	*f*	465	942	70*h*	606	3,447*h*	353
1882	*f*	*f*	805	2,340	45*h*	300	43,163*h*	1,178
1883	*f*	*f*	456	1,548	48*h*	321	272	371
1884	*f*	*f*	680	1,636	*f*	*f*	396	764
1885	*f*	*f*	1701	1,680	2,112	1,356	170	243
1886	*f*	*f*	*f*	*f*	1,061	424	160	226
1887	505	266	314	1,101	543	252	*f*	*f*
1888	264	150	394	1,087	1,220	449	100	115
1889	*f*	*f*	272	864	1,880	712	69	100
1890	400	134	184	279	20	6	*f*	*f*
1891	*f*	*f*	744	1,167	120	46	235	320
1892	*i*	*i*	*i*	*i*	*i*	*i*	*i*	*i*
1893	*i*	*i*	*i*	*i*	*i*	*i*	*i*	*i*
1894	*i*	*i*	*i*	*i*	*i*	*i*	*i*	*i*
1895	*i*	*i*	*i*	*i*	*i*	*i*	*i*	*i*
1896	*i*	*i*	*i*	*i*	*i*	*i*	*i*	*i*

Table A4.1 (*cont.*)

Year	Pottery Packages	Pottery Value	Matchets Packages	Matchets Value	Matches Packages	Matches Value	Rice Tons	Rice Value
1863	8	50						
1864	*a*	*a*						
1865	*f*	*f*						
1866	*f*	*f*	6	30				
1867	*f*	*f*	*f*	*f*				
1868	*f*	*f*	*f*	*f*				
1869	*f*	*f*	*f*	*f*				
1870	9	36	5	37				
1871	6	30	*f*	*f*			6*k*	4
1872	1	5	10	83			*f*	*f*
1873	*b*	*b*	*b*	*b*			*b*	*b*
1874	*b*	*b*	*b*	*b*			*b*	*b*
1875	*b*	*b*	*b*	*b*			*b*	*b*
1876	*b*	*b*	*b*	*b*			*b*	*b*
1877	*b*	*b*	*b*	*b*			*b*	*b*
1878	2	55	6	20	4	18	11*h*	14
1879	504	710	*f*	*f*	*f*	*f*	304*h*	357
1880	118	133	*f*	*f*	*f*	*f*	24*h*	91
1881	143	152	*f*	*f*	10	36	*f*	*f*
1882	179	183	*f*	*f*	15	52	*f*	*f*
1883	62	141	299	416	4	22	100*h*	44
1884	195	347	343	623	18	91	122*h*	82
1885	379	1,238	291	610	*f*	45	*f*	*f*
1886	188	312	64	149	11	31	9	72
1887	159	420	164	242	33	128	12	92
1888	62	237	*f*	*f*	67	301	18	146
1889	142	194	32	66	93	371	27	221
1890	137	472	71	151	174	644	45	412
1891	355	716	60	103	210	872	24	236
1892	*i*	*i*	*i*	*i*	*i*	*i*	*i*	*i*
1893	*i*	*i*	*i*	*i*	*i*	*i*	*i*	*i*
1894	*i*	*i*	*i*	*i*	*i*	*i*	*i*	*i*
1895	*i*	*i*	*i*	*i*	*i*	*i*	*i*	*i*
1896	*i*	*i*	*i*	*i*	*i*	*i*	*i*	*i*

Notes:

a No Lagos Blue Book for 1864.
b Not available: Blue Books do not give details, 1873–1878.
c Addition error in official Lagos exports to Porto-Novo makes it smaller than the sum of values of exports accounted for.
d Sum of values of exports shown.
e 'British foreign and native manufactures exported.'
f Not listed in Blue Book.
g Correction of typographical error in Blue Book.
h Packages.
i Listed in Blue Book but not shown here.
j 16,050 rolls of tobacco, plus 16 tons of tobacco leaves.
k Hundredweight.

Table A4.2. *Exports by port, 1884–95 (values in thousands of francs)*

Year	Item	Porto-Novo		Cotonou		Ouidah		Grand Popo–Agoué		Total	
		Tons	Value	Tons	Value	Tons	Value	Tons	Value	Tons	Value
1884	Palm kernels	11,436	2,859		b		b		b	11,436	2,859
	Palm oil	4,699a	2,196		b		b		b	4,699	2,196
	Total		5,055								5,055
1885 b			b		b		b		b		b
1886 b			b		b		b		b		b
1887c	Palm kernels	10,420	1,486		d		b	6,579	1,480	16,999	2,966
	Palm oil	2,598a	1,142		d		b	1,992e	796	4,590	1,936
	Total		2,629						2,276		4,904
1888 b			b		b		b		b		b
1889c	Palm kernels	7,441	1,860		d		b	2,856	714	10,298	2,574
	Palm oil	2,951	1,476		d		b	715	358	3,666	1,834
	Maize							22	4	22	4
	Re-exports								23		23
	Other								2f		2
	Total		3,336						1,101		4,436
1890	Palm kernels	6,149	1,457	2,770	693		b	4,260	1,067	13,179	3,217
	Palm oil	2,683	1,341	1,599	799		b	525	263	4,807	2,403
	Maize							84	16	84	16
	Coconuts							42g	3	42g	3
	Copra	5							1		6
	Re-exports		128		28				32		188
	Other				4h				i		4
	Total		2,931		1,524				1,382		5,838

352

1891								
Palm kernels	5,846	4,896	1,224	b	5,512	1,347	16,254	3,811
Palm oil	3,756	1,751	876	b	1,109	554	6,616	3,308
Maize	24g				17	2	17	2
Coconuts					45g	2	69g	3
Copra						1		1
Kola	6						6	9
Cattle	707j						707j	35
Sheep and goats	158j						158j	2
Pigs								14
Poultry								14
Re-exports	304k		168			11		483
Other	1					1m		2
Total	3,498		2,268			1,918		7,684

1892								
Palm kernels	8,090	3,707	927	b	3,801	942	15,598	3,891
Palm oil	3,803	475	237	b	767	381	5,045	2,520
Coconuts	54g				3g		57g	3
Kola	97						97	156
Livestock	114n							114
Re-exports	567k					16		655
Other	3p					1q		4
Total	4,767		1,236			1,340		7,343

1893									
Palm kernels	8,836	2,638	615	2,656	673	6,525	1,493	20,656	4,593
Palm oil	3,439	1,563	672	968	444	1,475	765	7,445	3,522
Coconuts	745g							745g	45
Kola	62							62	93
Re-exports	264k						91		355
Other	2r				1s		1i		3
Total	3,857		1,287		1,118		2,349		8,611

Table A4.2 (*cont.*)

Year	Item	Porto-Novo		Cotonou		Ouidah		Grand Popo–Agoué		Total	
		Tons	Value	Tons	Value	Tons	Value	Tons	Value	Tons	Value
1894[t]	Palm kernels	9,968	2,243	4,782	1,081	2,196	491	7,116	1,709	24,062	5,524
	Palm oil	3,058	1,407	2,339	1,076	823	369	2,198	1,013	8,418	3,865
	Coconuts	641g	34					2g	u	643g	34
	Kola	103	154							103	154
	Re-exports		311k		8				77		396
	Other		1h								1
	Total		4,150		2,165		860		2,799		9,974
1895[v]	Palm kernels	6,975	1,569	4,746	980	2,894	651	7,317	1,646	21,932	4,846
	Palm oil	5,363	2,467	3,243	1,490	901	415	2,176	1,000	11,683	5,372
	Coconuts	245g	15					11g	1	256g	16
	Kola	20	31	1	2	1	2			22	35
	Re-exports		196		7		9		51		263
	Other		126w		2x		y		z		128
	Total		4,404		2,481		1,077		2,698		10,660

Notes:

a Converted from gallons of 3.75 liters at 300 gallons per ton.
b Not available.
c Porto-Novo and Cotonou combined and listed under Porto-Novo.
d Included with Porto-Novo.
e Tons, although erroneously listed as gallons in published returns.
f Ivory, chalk, bricks, castor beans, cattle hides.
g Thousands of coconuts.
h Hides.
i Trace of ivory.
j Head.
k Including exports of unenumerated goods.
m Ivory and kola.
n Cattle, sheep, goats, pigs, poultry.
p Cattle hides and ivory.
q Copra, coconuts, cattle hides and rubber.
r Cattle and sheep hides.
s Textiles.
t Cotonou includes Godomey, Ouidah includes Avrékété, Grand Popo–Agoué includes Hilacondji.
u 144 Francs.
v Ouidah includes Avrékété, Grand Popo–Agoué includes Hilacondji.
w Unenumerated goods.
x Jewelry and unenumerated goods.
y Goats and poultry.
z Rubber and kola.

355

Table A4.3. *Imports by port, 1884–95 (values in thousands of francs)*

Year	Item	Porto-Novo		Cotonou		Ouidah		Grand Popo–Agoué		Total	
		Tons	Value	Tons	Value	Tons	Value	Tons	Value	Tons	Value
1884	'Tafia'	3,075a	1,687							3,075a	1,687
	'Genièvre'	6,327a	1,694							6,327a	1,694
	'Anisado'	32a	68							32a	68
	'Muscat'	103a	103							103a	103
	'Liqueurs'	19a	21							19a	21
	Beverages	9,556a	3,573		b		b		b	9,556a	3,573
	Tobacco	77	127							77	127
	Textiles	10,800c	102							10,800c	102
	Salt	246	16							246	16
	Guns	400c	2							400	2
	Powder	16	112							16	112
	Hardware	290d	6							290d	6
	Notions	2,746d	7							2,746d	7
	Shoes	590e	7							590e	7
	Foodstuffs	1,075d	15							1,076d	15
	Glassware	9,369d	3							9,369d	3
	Total		3,970								3,970
1885	b		b		b		b		b		b
1886	b		b		b		b		b		b

356

Table (page rotated). Data for 1887f, 1888, and 1889f. Footnote letters (a, c, h, i) are printed as superscripts on the figures; isolated italic letters b and g are footnote markers.

1887f

	1	2	3	4	5	6
'Tafia et alcool'	950	2,939a	1,523a	384	4,462a	1,334
'Geniévre'	589	1,069a	243a	127	1,312a	716
'Liqueurs'	121	124a	18a	21	142a	142
Beverages	1,600	4,132a	1,784a	532	5,916a	2,192
Tobacco	188	63	165	261	228	449
Textiles	496	1,066h	568h	219	1,634h	715
Salt	39	417	244	117	661	156
Guns	26	844c	3,170c	36	4,014c	62
Powder	45	46	71	98	117	143
Crockery	28	209i		40		68
Hardware	5	416i			416i	5
Notions	15	500i			500i	15
Shoes	2					2
Foodstuffs		106i			106i	11
Unenumerated	11			175		175
Total	2,515			1,478		3,993

Footnote markers: Beverages — g; Total — g, b. 1888 — b.

1889f

	1	2	3	4	5	6
'Rhum'	569	5,692a	2,229a	229	7,921a	798
'Geniévre'	141	1,131a	931a	116	2,062a	258
'Liqueurs'	25	151a	167a	28	318a	53
'Vins et bières'	23	46a	34a	17	79a	40
Beverages	758	7,020a	3,361a	390	10,380a	1,149
Tobacco	267	152	173	311	325	578
Textiles	867	1,869h		266		1,133
Salt	15	51	86	26	137	41
Guns	7	1,440c	11,968c	60	13,408c	67
Powder	94	94		74		167
Unenumerated	353			196		548
Total	2,361			1,323		3,684

Footnote markers: Beverages — g; Total — g, b.

Table A4.3 (*cont.*)

Year	Item	Porto-Novo		Cotonou		Ouidah		Grand Popo–Agoué		Total	
		Tons	Value	Tons	Value	Tons	Value	Tons	Value	Tons	Value
1890	'Rhums'	373a	40	3,495a	419			1,511a	149	5,379a	608
	'Genièvres'	370a	138	147a	43			67a	27	584a	208
	'Alcools anisés'			123a	20			3a	1	126a	22
	'Muscats'			67a	11					67a	11
	'Absinthes'			11a	4			2a	2	13a	6
	'Vins en fûts'			52j	7			15j	2	67j	9
	Other		33		45				14		92
	Beverages	743a	211	3,856a	549		b	1,587a	195	6,186a	956
	Tobacco	169	222	42	59			123	293	298	574
	Cigars								1		1
	Textiles		448	270h	116				268		832
	Thread		6						2		8
	Salt	176	19	4	1			226	68	406	88
	Guns	1,100c	2					500c	7	1,600c	9
	Powder	2	2					3	3	5	5
	Matches		25								25
	Sugar	6	4	12	6			9	6	27	16
	Flour and hard-tack		19								20
	Rice	30	10	2	2			11	6	48	18
	Wood	175k	17	7	2			63k	7	260k	26
	Iron and zinc		18	22k	2						20
	Building materials			4	6						6
	Casks		2								2
	Other		25		16				5		46
	Unenumerated		285		148				41		474
	Money		373						12		385
	Total		1,688		908		b		914		3,511

Rotated table (read with the page turned clockwise). Row categories run down the left; the eight numeric columns are four quantity/value pairs.

1891								
'Rhums'	645a	158	1,668a	427	920a	233	3,233a	818
'Genièvres'	545a	299	175a	72	29a	14	749a	384
'Alcools anisés'			268a	190			268a	191
'Absinthes'			12a	25	1a	4	14a	29
'Vins en fûts'			96j	12	27j	3	123j	15
Other		16		90		38		144
Beverages	1,190a	473	2,147a	816	957a	292	4,295a	1,581
Tobacco	190	317	12	15	191	336	394	668
Cigars				2		1		3
Textiles		988		7		483		1,478
Thread		36				27		63
Salt	843	75	48	10	828	55	1,719	140
Guns	106c	1				2		3
Powder	11	11	21	21	33	33	66	66
Matches		17						17
Sugar	8	5			12	9	21	14
Flour and hard-tack				1				1
Rice		10		11		4		25
Potash	32	13	40		14		86	13
Wood			11k	1	84k	8	95k	9
Iron	9	6					9	6
Metallic goods		25	5	5				30
Casks		120						120
Other		12		15		9		36
Unenumerated		300		113		189		602
Money		783						783
Total		3,192		1,017	b	1,448		5,658

(Footnote markers b appear beside the 'Beverages' and 'Total' entries of the 957a column.)

Table A4.3 (cont.)

Year	Item	Porto-Novo Tons	Porto-Novo Value	Cotonou Tons	Cotonou Value	Ouidah Tons	Ouidah Value	Grand Popo–Agoué Tons	Grand Popo–Agoué Value	Total Tons	Total Value
1892	'Rhums'	523a	180	1,432a	425			730a	214	2,685a	820
	'Genièvres'	1,188a	792	133a	83			45a	31	1,366a	906
	'Alcools anisés'			267a	222			20a	17	287a	239
	'Muscats'				42						42
	'Absinthes'			10a	27			2a	5	12a	32
	'Vins en fûts'			225j	30			29j	5	254j	35
	Other	11a	16		61				39		116
	Beverages	1,722a	988	1,898a	890		b	804a	311	4,413a	2,190
	Tobacco	154	266	29	76			84	147	267	490
	Textiles		813		173				421		1,407
	Thread		20						26		46
	Salt	357	30	76	15			947	63	1,380	108
	Guns	17c	–					2,259c	28	2,276c	28
	Powder	3	3	41	41			21	21	65	65
	Matches		13								13
	Sugar	5	4					15	10	20	14
	Flour and hard-tack	42	21	7	3					49	24
	Rice	140	47	15	4			11	4	166	55
	Potash		18								18
	Wood			321k	32			88k	9	409k	41
	Iron and zinc			3	2			13	6	16	8
	Metallic goods		120	93	165			1	1		286
	Building materials	28	6	34	5					62	11
	Casks		151								151
	Other		42		18				13		73
	Unenumerated		407		142				106		655
	Money		824								824
	Total		3,773		1,566		b		1,166		6,507

1893m										
'Rhums'	359a	113	49a	16	282a	89	122a	37	812a	255
'Alcools et spiritueux'	682a	365	1,407a	806	99a	106	1,187a	649	3,375a	1,926
'Genièvres'	351a	281	93a	70	17a	12	89a	69	550a	432
'Alcools anisés'			33a	28					33a	28
'Bière'	2a	3		110	14a	31				145
'Vins en fûts'			592j	81	123j	16			715j	96
Other				182		16		30		229
Beverages	1,394a	762	1,730a	1,293	443a	270	1,398a	785	4,948a	3,111
Tobacco	170	291	76	144	21	32	157	263	424	731
Cigars					1	8			1	8
Textiles		973	25	26	28	126		517		1,641
Thread		34				1		109		144
Salt	574	36	81	8		2	1,754	127	2,438	174
Guns				1			2,840c	26	2,480c	27
Powder							26	26	26	26
Matches		28								28
Sugar			17	12	14	9	19	13	50	35
Rice	147	48	44	11	2		28	7	221	66
Potash		6								6
Wood	560k	63	2,300k	253	626k	18	15	11	3,486k	335
Zinc	160	113	65	78	4	4	23	34	180	128
Metallic goods	214	75				16			214	204
Cement		31								31
Casks		87								87
Coal				61						61
Other		211	1,526	176		86		26	1,526	499
Unenumerated		916		446		230		394		1,986
Cowries		1,264	98	27					98	27
Money								13		1,277
Total		4,938		2,536		802		2,351		10,632

Table A4.2 (cont.)

Year	Item	Porto-Novo		Cotonou		Ouidah		Grand Popo–Agoué		Total	
		Tons	Value	Tons	Value	Tons	Value	Tons	Value	Tons	Value
1894m	'Rhums'	162a	91	489a	221	169a	72	711a	295	1,531a	679
	'Alcools'	546a	372	793a	364	282a	123	575a	276	2,197a	1,135
	'Spiritueux'	23a	9	14a	19	3a	5	41a	16	81a	49
	'Genièvres'	146a	108	68a	51	29a	21	70a	59	313a	240
	'Alcools anisés'	56a	50	825a	725	45a	38	20a	13	946a	826
	'Bière'	4a	6			4a	6			8a	13
	'Vins en fûts'			489j	64	46j	6			535j	70
	Other		4		67		9		26		107
	Beverages	937a	640	2,311a	1,511	543a	280	1,417a	685	5,209a	3,119
	Tobacco	162	280	115	205	24	38	94	150	396	674
	Textiles		1,054		68		91		436		1,649
	Thread		54				2		39		94
	Salt	764	57	148	16	186	15	1,520	127	2,618	215
	Guns							1,640c	17	1,640	17
	Powder			15	15	10	10	27	27	51	52
	Matches										5
	Sugar	45	23	26	18	19	13	10	15	55	46
	Flour		30	17	8					63	30
	Rice	115		120	31	38	10	26	7	300	78
	Potash		9								9
	Wood	589k	54	105k	111	64k	6	426k	41	1,184k	212
	Zinc	4	3							4	3
	Metallic goods		18		78						96
	Casks		155								155
	Other		313		120		29		28		490
	Unenumerated		1,040		509		139		356		2,044
	Money		1,594				18		164		1,777
	Total		5,324		2,690		656		2,092		10,765

1895n

'Rhums'	166a	126	1,347a	596	200a	80	851a	340	2,565a	1,142
'Alcools'	302a	224	602a	428	252a	144	558a	224	1,714a	1,020
'Spiritueux'	52a	71		9	12a	9	21a	14	73a	94
'Genièvres'	7a	7	70a	53	52a	44	24a	18	113a	87
'Alcools anisés'	25a	21	851a	709	3a	4	24a	20	952a	794
'Bières'						5	5a	8	8a	12
'Vins en fûts'			233j	31	22j	7	54j	8	309j	44
Other				93				10		110
Beverages	552a	449	2,928a	1,919	524a	293	1,496a	642	5,502a	3,303
Tobacco	150	277	115	226	43	74	125	211	432	788
Textiles		935		253		146		647		1,981
Thread		43				15		48		105
Salt	837	71	158	21	49	4	1,931	94	2,975	190
Guns			24c	–	44c	–	2,440c	19	2,508c	20
Powder			9	9			64	64	73	73
Matches		24								24
Sugar			16	11	10	7	15	10	40	28
Rice	54	22	5	1	6	2	12	3	78	28
Manioc and yams		42								42
Maize	63	11							63	11
Potash		14								14
Wood	260k	23	193k	30	43k	5	198k	19	694k	76
Metallic goods		34	40	36	5	7	14	12		89
Casks		138				13	5	1	5	151
Kerosene								2		2
Coal			1,008	40					1,008	40
Other		187		76		35		40		338
Unenumerated		916		495		192		491		2,095
Money		1,065						79		1,144
Total		4,251		3,117		793		2,382		10,542

Appendix 4

Notes:

a Thousands of liters.
b Not available.
c Pieces.
d Packages.
e Pairs.
f Porto-Novo and Cotonou combined and listed under Porto-Novo.
g Included with Porto-Novo.
h Bales.
i Kilograms.
j Barrels, of approximately 250 liters.
k Cubic meters.
m Cotonou includes Godomey, Ouidah includes Avrékété, Grand Popo–Agoué includes Hilacondji.
n Ouidah includes Avrékété, Grand Popo–Agoué includes Hilacondji.

Table A4.4. *Exports, 1889–1914 (values in thousands of francs)*

Year	Total export value	Export value[a] accounted for	Palm kernels Tons	Value	Palm oil Tons	Value
1889	4,974	4,949	11,637*b*	2,909*b*	4,069*c*	2,036*c*
1890	6,519	6,327	14,892*b*	3,635*b*	5,336*c*	2,667*c*
1891	8,543	8,058	18,367*b*	4,306*b*	7,344*c*	3,672*c*
1892	8,126	7,353	17,626*b*	4,397*b*	5,600*c*	2,797*c*
1893	8,611	8,253	20,213	4,593	6,427	3,522
1894	9,974	9,577	23,702	5,524	8,418	3,865
1895	10,660	10,394	21,883	4,846	11,683	5,372
1896	9,224	9,033	25,152	5,656	5,525	2,864
1897	5,779	5,084	12,875	3,015	4,077	1,737
1898	7,539	7,344	18,091	4,251	6,060	2,727
1899	12,719	12,472	21,851	6,755	9,650	5,066
1900	12,756	12,572	21,986	6,596	8,920	5,352
1901	10,479	9,870	24,212	4,482	11,291	4,742
1902	13,669	13,423	29,778	7,444	12,676	5,324
1903	9,540	9,319	21,685	5,421	6,964	2,925
1904	11,156	10,687	25,997	5,459	8,368	3,766
1905	7,634	7,422	17,480	3,933	5,637	2,396
1906	8,506	8,331	18,835	4,238	6,378	2,716
1907	9,671	9,393	18,811	4,673	7,835	3,427
1908	12,180	11,978	23,036	5,558	9,521	4,596
1909	16,351	16,055	33,224	8,123	15,016	6,448
1910	17,886	17,648	34,784	9,980	14,628	6,354
1911	21,958	21,736	39,346	12,577	15,252	8,088
1912	21,451	21,201	37,296	13,398	11,917	6,361
1913	16,477	15,942	26,371	10,104	7,971	3,887
1914	14,953*d*	14,609	21,238	7,655	6,622	5,593

Table A4.4 (*cont.*)

Year	Maize Tons	Maize Value	Fish Tons	Fish Value	Shrimp Tons	Shrimp Value	Poultry Tons	Poultry Value
1889	22	4						
1890	84	16						
1891	17	2						14
1892								
1893								
1894								
1895				126				
1896				382				
1897				207				10
1898	213	75		113				15
1899	1	3		267				22
1900	56	22		232				20
1901	2	e		290				31
1902	2	e		329				61
1903	24	5		599				77
1904	207	41		696				299
1905	2,059	111		462				74
1906	7,282	364		447				129
1907	7,840	392	766	383				107
1908	19,974	1,198	418	209	35	29	86	69
1909	9,334	700	397	261	53	65	177	108
1910	2,055	172	802	441	80	105	219	123
1911	65	5	803	441	88	94	96	97
1912	4,063	325	554	305	321	299	66	70
1913	13,256	1,060	308	170	44	52	51	52
1914	4,763	381	278	153	75	90	72	80

Table A4.4 (*cont.*)

Year	Cattle		Pigs		Sheeps and goats		Kola	
	Head	Value	Head	Value	Head	Value	Tons	Value
1889								
1890								
1891	707	35		14	158	2	6	9
1892							97	156
1893							62	93
1894							103	154
1895							22	35
1896							32	48
1897		37				*e*	24	32
1898	718	36		5	260	4	30	45
1899	1,937	97		16	1,656	25	43	87
1900	1,168	58		31	550	11	40	80
1901	1,303	65	3,423	43	692	10	26	130
1902	921	69	3,629	44	328	5	10	49
1903	1,217	91	3,849	46	535	8	13	66
1904	1,752	131	5,603	67	675	10	23	117
1905	1,990	148	4,322	65	1,380	21	24	119
1906	2,416	109	6,002	60	2,011	30	28	70
1907	964	52	4,853	53	1,283	19	19	44
1908	442	27	2,666	32	483	7	33	65
1909	285	17	927	15	414	6	30	59
1910	243	29	1,129	31	499	7	35	70
1911	298	36	1,184	36	498	7	23	46
1912	363	44	1,106	33	263	4	24	48
1913	567	68	741	22	147	3	12	24
1914	774	92	1,189	36	2,967	40	12	23

Table A4.4 (*cont.*)

Year	Coconuts		Copra		Cotton		Peanuts	
	Thou-sands*f*	Value	Tons	Value	Tons	Value	Tons	Value
1889								
1890	42	3		6				
1891	69	3		1				
1892	57	3						
1893	745	45						
1894	643	34						
1895	256	16						
1896	394	78						
1897	494	33					13*g*	5
1898	248	17					63*h*	18
1899	456*d*	32*d*	143*d*	29*d*			53*h*	16
1900	199	14	221	44			50*h*	13
1901	132	9	185	37			7*h*	2
1902	44	3	352	88			8*h*	2
1903	94	7	257	64			16*h*	4
1904	23	1	227	57	63	15	35*h*	9
1905	8	*e*	261	65		10	21*h*	5
1906	13	1	206	51		55	206*h*	52
1907	9	*e*	337	104	93	80	464*h*	47
1908	10	1	288	81	74	69	163*h*	16
1909			378	99	130	130	38*h, i*	4
1910			467	149	120	140	16*h*	2
1911			350	105	132	165	21*h*	2
1912			301	105	123	154	*j*	*e*
1913			236*d*	83	171	214	1	*e*
1914			199	75	135	168		

Table A4.4 (*cont.*)

Year	Rubber		Shea butter		Textiles	
	Tons	Value	Tons	Value	Tons	Value
1889						
1890						
1891						
1892	*j*					
1893						
1894						
1895	*j*	*e*				
1896	2	5				
1897	3	8				
1898	14	38				
1899	14	57				
1900	20	99				
1901	6	29				
1902	2	5				
1903	2	6				
1904	4	19				
1905	4	13				
1906	2	6		3		
1907	2	5	*j*	*e*		7
1908	1	4	*j*	*e*	3	17
1909			4	1	4	19
1910	1	4	37	19	7	22
1911	6	19	16	7	2	11
1912	7	25	2	1	6	29
1913	5	17	170	76	21	110
1914	1	2	78*k*	35*k*	22	108

Notes:

a Sum of values of exports shown.
b Figures from Table A5.2 increased by 13% to estimate total including Ouidah.
c Figures from Table A5.2 increased by 11% to estimate total including Ouidah.
d Correction of typographical error in source.
e Less than five hundred francs.
f Thousands of coconuts.
g Shelled.
h Unshelled.
i Plus exports of 46 tons of shelled peanuts valued at seven thousand francs.
j Less than one half ton.
k Plus exports of 340 tons of shea nuts, valued at 78 thousand francs.

Table A4.5. *Imports, 1889–1914 (values in thousands of francs)*

Year	Total import value	Import value[a] accounted for	Beverages Value	Trade alcohol Liters	Value	Estimated price[c]
1889	3,684*b*	3,135*b*	1,148			
1890	3,465*b*	2,525*b*	961			
1891	5,656*b*	4,224*b*	1,582			
1892	6,506*b*	4,913*b*	2,149			
1893	10,411	6,666	2,896		1,726	
1894	10,767	6,486	3,119	2,278,031	1,184	
1895	10,542	7,270	3,302	1,713,956	1,020	
1896	9,729	8,074	4,306	4,133,205	2,680	0.855
1897	8,243	7,300	3,677	3,126,881	2,541	0.868
1898	9,995	8,548	4,117	3,586,309	2,869	0.870
1899	12,349	9,567	4,554	1,171,249	1,171	1.33
1900	15,221	11,619	4,324	1,249,029	1,709	1.34
1901	15,753	12,632	4,927	1,830,455	2,831	1.35
1902	17,090	13,796	1,885	2,272,835	1,023	1.36
1903	11,264	9,659	1,510	1,965,125	884	1.35
1904	10,681	9,197	1,589	2,234,827	1,006	1.33
1905	10,733	9,411	1,114	1,319,652	660	1.38
1906	10,514	9,124	1,196	1,456,125	728	1.39
1907	11,655	9,909	1,514	1,666,912	893	1.38
1908	10,737	9,694	907	1,039,266	503	1.59
1909	14,216	13,376	1,491	1,547,877	763	1.62
1910	17,839	15,472	2,180	2,161,378	933	1.57
1911	19,674	17,080	2,218	1,780,909	713	1.60
1912	20,310	17,003	2,483	2,112,404	847	1.64
1913	15,152	23,367	1,986	1,655,191	664	1.64
1914	11,880	9,520	1,100	775,008	349	1.62

Table A4.5 (*cont.*)

	Rum			Gin and geneva		
Year	Liters	Value	Estimated price[d]	Liters	Value	Estimated price[f]
1889	7,921,181	798e		2,062,632	257	
1890	5,377,923	611e		1,340,176	208	
1891	3,232,556	818e		750,488	384	
1892	2,684,690	820e		1,366,328	906	
1893	812,241	241		551,368	433	
1894	1,386,594	679		312,720	240	
1895	2,564,594	1,142		113,640	87	
1896			0.741			
1897			0.751			
1898			0.735			
1899			0.748			
1900			1.13			
1901			1.12			
1902			1.06			
1903			1.25			
1904			1.25			1.26
1905			1.77			1.41
1906			1.77			1.31
1907			1.79			1.34
1908	85,036	30	2.01	262,092	115	1.70
1909	247,613	99	2.13	687,240	298	1.56
1910	310,783	158	2.04	1,282,541	642	1.51
1911	242,162	126	1.91	1,767,184	886	1.55
1912	211,586	111	1.96	1,556,704	803	1.62
1913	230,911	116	2.00	1,103,633	607	1.67
1914	74,147	37	2.01	563,699	322	1.66

Table A4.5 (*cont.*)

Year	Gin, geneva and rum			Bulk wine		Beer	
	Liters[g]	Value[h]	Estimated price[d]	Barrels	Value	Liters	Value
1889							
1890					11		
1891				96	12		
1892				254	35		
1893				592	81		145
1894				535	70	8,422	13
1895				309	44	7,950	12
1896			0.741			36,776	61
1897	324,165	524	0.751	582	110	26,846	27
1898	768,598	692	0.735		90	23,405	23
1899	2,904,983	2,593	0.748	607	87	18,060	18
1900	1,092,319	1,256	1.13	708	135	39,618	40
1901	1,132,626	1,416	1.12	609	104	51,538	52
1902	923,748	277	1.06	1,037	104	56,201	56
1903	619,993	186	1.25	1,024	102	54,768	55
1904	593,361	208	1.25	561	67	40,734	41
1905	328,634	131	1.77	724	72	43,583	41
1906	277,038	111	1.77	796	71	47,636	33
1907	242,555	97	1.79	768	69	57,548	40
1908	347,128	145	2.01	960	86	47,792	33
1909	687,240	298	2.13	880	79	68,141	48
1910	1,593,324	800	2.04	216,771*i*	82	102,562	72
1911	2,019,346	1,012	1.91	183,645*i*	108	98,091	69
1912	1,768,290	914	1.96	273,496*i*	152	155,090	113
1913	1,334,544	723	2.00			85,231	65
1914	637,846	359	2.01			53,895	42

Table A4.5 (*cont.*)

Year	Cotton textiles Value	Dyed and printed cottons			Bleached cottons		
		Tons	Value	Estimated price^k	Tons	Value	Estimated price^n
1889	1,133						
1890	830						
1891	1,478						
1892	1,407						
1893	1,641						
1894	1,649						
1895	1,981						
1896	1,604		988			245	
1897	1,095	188*j*	757	3.86	71*m*	184	2.26
1898	1,873	250*j*	1,008	3.65	89*m*	222	2.20
1899	1,678	205*j*	837	3.63	77*m*	263	2.21
1900	2,991	367*j*	1,842	4.00	115*m*	469	2.43
1901	2,895	351	1,754	4.03	76	303	2.46
1902	4,753	630	3,148	3.93	120	480	2.46
1903	3,272	446	2,232	4.00	64	254	2.54
1904	2,551	270	1,620	4.30	26	130	2.63
1905	3,425	312	2,561	4.24	75	271	2.67
1906	2,838		1,798			458	
1907	3,014	358	1,655	4.81	138	538	2.89
1908	3,546	354	1,685	4.73	157*p*	676*p*	2.91
1909	5,855	667	3,102	4.56	242*p*	673*p*	2.79
1910	5,696	757	3,299	4.83	129	536	2.96
1911	6,017	730	3,203	4.92	118	535	3.11
1912	5,424	694	3,474	4.90	123	493	3.04
1913	3,469	456	2,218	4.99	101	364	3.17
1914	2,665	396	1,770	5.22	77	299	3.17

Table A4.5 (*cont.*)

	Unbleached cottons			Velvet			Pipe tobacco		
Year	Tons	Value	Estimat-ed price^q	Tons	Value	Estimat-ed price^s	Tons	Value	Estimat-ed price^u
1889							325	578	
1890							298	484	
1891							394	667	
1892							267	490	
1893							424	731	
1894							396	674	
1895							432	788	
1896		36			79		376	669	1.88
1897	16r	39	1.85	6t	58	9.5	448	1,009	1.89
1898	107r	256	1.78	14t	138	9.9	419	970	1.97
1899	85r	205	1.81	39t	265	6.8	402	914	2.08
1900	42r	125	2.02	40t	469	11.7	511	1,036	2.08
1901	84	252	2.09	28	343	12.0	387	783	2.17
1902	148	443	2.01	43	514	11.9	555	840	2.13
1903	73	218	2.03	29	364	12.8	492	732	2.08
1904	89	313	2.23	24	343	14.3	574	858	1.96
1905	130	325	2.25	16	105	6.5	526	634	1.92
1906		390			152		549	661	1.91
1907	109	436	2.52	35	300	8.5	559	744	2.15
1908	157p	676p	2.51	34	364	10.7	504	756	2.22
1909	242p	673p	2.32	54	475	8.8	751	1,127	2.06
1910	106	273	2.56	95	941	9.9	477	716	2.13
1911	145	386	2.73	149	1,270	8.6	859	1,289	2.29
1912	63	163	2.63	88	793	9.0	622	933	2.48
1913	51	105	2.79	39	296	7.6	596	894	2.69
1914	36	110	2.73	16	124	9.0	488	748	2.65

Table A4.5 (*cont.*)

Year	Kerosene		Matches		Staple foods		Rice	
	Tons	Value	Tons	Value	Tons^v	Value^v	Tons	Value
1889								
1890				25		38		18
1891				17		26		25
1892				13	215	79	166	55
1893				28		77	221	68
1894				5	388	119	300	78
1895	5	2		24		180	78	28
1896	38	14		81		247	117	54
1897	42	19		64	613	272	181	76
1898	48	22		67	327	166	124	52
1899	53	40		118	537	215	132	56
1900	117	59		99	832	320	149	63
1901	213	107		146	1,339	443	156	66
1902	203	61		221	967	332	290	122
1903	359	108		119	2,965	643	272	114
1904	565	155		144	1,126	288	155	65
1905	678	203	69	102	1,941	345	185	41
1906	918	276	76	114	819	166	168	37
1907	1,256	377	66	98	1,353	227	146	35
1908	1,529	462	122	183	807	178	155	38
1909	1,272	381	94	142	1,056	252	182	46
1910	1,919	528	190	193	2,247	571	506	128
1911	2,318	695	224	240	4,188	724	590	155
1912	2,590	777	276	200	5,299	1,127	858	277
1913	2,356	716	303	306	2,868	763	280	94
1914	1,643	493	185	198	3,758	767	308	87

Appendix 4

Table A4.5 (*cont.*)

Year	Wheat flour		Hard-tack		Maize		Manioc		Yams	
	Tons	Value	Tons	Value	Tons	Value	Tons	Value	Tons	Value
1889										
1890		20w								
1891		1w								
1892	49	24w								
1893						9				
1894	63	30								
1895					63	11		42x		
1896	40	19			175	32		31		
1897	74	44	36	25	113	47		19		17
1898	43	26	60	42	19	7		7		7
1899	51	36	24	17	69	24		27		18
1900	98	69	52	37	23	68		40		41
1901	122	86	127	51	107	21		68		77
1902	152	69	159	48	57	11		36		15
1903	114	51	328	99	20	4		307		47
1904	134	60	80	40	129	26		65		41
1905	103	33	68	24	348	32		175		20
1906	123	37	35	12	176	9		31		23
1907	157	48	83	25	546	27	261	40		32
1908	127	46	36	13	192	12	176y	25	121	23
1909	199	76	57	23	163	12	272	31	183	18
1910	352	134	353	145	478	39	358	29	200	12
1911	437	153	328	145	1,194	96	1,370	125	269	16
1912	940	303	500	217	1,895	152	735	60	372	30
1913	370	130	157	72	719	57	1,343	339		
1914	290	102	71	36	1,180	142	1,908	344		

376

Table A4.5 (*cont.*)

Year	Kola		Guns			Gunpowder		
	Tons	Value	Pieces	Value	Estimat-ed price[z]	Tons	Value	Estimat-ed price[aa]
1889			11,968	67			168	
1890				9			5	
1891				3		66	66	
1892			2,276	28		65	65	
1893				27		26	26	
1894			1,640	17		51	52	
1895			2,508	20		73	73	
1896	7	4		21		37	37	
1897	9	14		19		100y	198	
1898	5	8		41		71	135	
1899	18	37	3,751	57	11.1	142	281	1.70
1900	48	96	6,432	96	11.8	169	339	1.69
1901	39	197	9,895	198	15.6	115	231	1.82
1902	17	87	14,332	172	14.1	236	354	1.75
1903	8	41	10,237	123	15.7	196	294	1.76
1904	24	119	7,194	108	15.2	104	156	1.73
1905	21	103	3,271	49	15.2	169	169	1.62
1906	27	68	3,012	30	14.3	159	159	1.78
1907	77	171	5,034	53	12.9	201	201	1.71
1908	57	115	7,480	75	16.2	204	204	1.57
1909	77	154	10,546	120	14.7	163	163	1.65
1910	89	177	20,152	225	13.4	360	360	1.66
1911	66	132	23,615	262	15.3	165	165	1.65
1912	103	205	17,237	194	16.1	212	212	1.62
1913	90	180	14,746	166	15.6	182	182	1.70
1914	302	605	2,337	27	17.3	63	63	1.65

Table A4.5 (*cont.*)

Year	Soaps Tons	Soaps Value	Pottery Value	Salt Tons	Salt Value	Salt Estimated price[bb]	Sugar Tons	Sugar Value
1889					41			
1890		7			88			16
1891		3			140		21	14
1892		1		1,380	108		20	14
1893		5		2,438	174		49	35
1894	15	7	23	2,618	215		55	46
1895	177	89	120	2,975	190		40	28
1896	27	22	137	1,887	177	14.2	74	54
1897	47	23	56	2,013	193	14.0	69	65
1898	59	29	115	2,211	211	13.4	68	63
1899	52	39	133	1,887	470	14.2	64	64
1900	69	48	168	3,029	361	16.7	153	153
1901	108	54	198	2,497	270	16.5	183	183
1902	118	47	209	2,562	278	16.5	450	180
1903	58	23	132	2,512	165	16.2	372	153
1904	104	38	143	3,257	350	16.4	283	117
1905	99	32	114	1,966	110	15.0	141	64
1906	142	46	69	3,267	187	14.2	340	119
1907	161	54	150	2,493	144	15.2	278	99
1908	196	76	122	2,959	166	16.1	275	104
1909	100	38	124	3,981	224	16.9	426	187
1910	216	75	206	3,340	188	16.5	448	202
1911	329	137	160	3,176	187	16.1	602	286
1912	260	124	140	3,274	201	16.6	624	300
1913	324	154	100	3,843	214	17.7	635	314
1914	226	99	56	2,238	131	18.5	307	138

Table A4.5 (*cont.*)

Year	Metals Value[cc]	Metallic goods Value[dd]	Machi- nery Value[ee]	Casks Tons	Casks Value	Casks Esti- mated price[ff]	Jute sacks Thou- sands[gg]	Jute sacks Value	Jute sacks Esti- mated price[hh]
1889									
1890	20				2				
1891	36				120				
1892	44		250		151				
1893	83		250		87				
1894	99				155				
1895	90				152				
1896	90		78		170	4.74	149	88	2.12
1897	76	77			27	4.49	133	63	2.16
1898	105	84	11		71	4.64	196	98	2.04
1899	74	103	9		247	5.22	292	146	2.14
1900	145	309			328	4.97	316	158	2.59
1901	218	346			407	5.22	272	223	2.39
1902	371	282	1,950		589	5.57	507	304	2.34
1903	153	382	848		292	4.40	265	159	2.32
1904	280	345	730		246	3.99	367	220	2.38
1905	208	796	789		202	4.64	233	117	2.79
1906	80	387	1,387		226	4.55	385	190	3.42
1907	142	547	1,031		319	4.29	388	214	3.68
1908	187	480	395	1,308	337	4.64	671	391	2.91
1909	235	461	384	2,779	754	4.32	738	443	2.69
1910	331	938	616	3,637	1,109	4.15	464	244	2.81
1911	361	1,574	575	2,062	678	4.85	606	303	3.28
1912	337	958	1,169	2,391	706	5.68	575	320	3.62
1913	397	518	401	1,060	271	5.49	451	301	4.24
1914	337	317	581	714	179	5.95	290	181	4.55

Appendix 4

Table A4.5 (*cont.*)

Year	Thread and cord Value	Estimated price[ii]	Wood Value	Cement Tons	Cement Value	Coal Tons	Coal Value	Paper Value
1889								
1890	8		26		6jj			
1891	63		9					
1892	62		41		11jj			
1893	179		335	214	31	1,526	61	
1894	94		212					
1895	110		76			1,008	40	5
1896	132		98	145	21	35	9	15
1897	174	3.33	124	204	43	1	1	11
1898	143	3.33	175	144	30	28	2	12
1899	170	3.18	151	244	50	25	2	15
1900	332	3.01	189	165	35	5	5	28
1901	410	3.06	239	589	88	215	21	44
1902	341	2.96	253	1,059	127	1,319	106	54
1903	184	3.08	109	1,083	130	450	36	51
1904	234	3.71	115	1,321	132	1,310	97	45
1905	247	3.82	102	3,930	275	2,420	163	48
1906	249		293	2,402	162	3,663	165	56
1907	265	4.12	103	1,103	77	5,752	285	80
1908	354	4.13	105	1,684	118	5,153	251	82
1909	425	4.21	130	1,038	67	3,539	133	86
1910	322	4.54	221	2,048	143	3,580	123	108
1911	380	4.57	264	2,494	175	3,673	142	116
1912	426	4.58	252	3,401	238	3,485	149	128
1913	293	4.41	192	2,676	187	5,609	218	145
1914	188	4.45	90	2,630	184	4,228	259	114

380

Notes:

a Sum of values shown.

b Excluding Ouidah.

c Prices for British exports of spirits, scaled and adjusted for customs duties.

d Prices for British imports of rum, scaled and adjusted for customs duties.

e Including trade alcohol.

f Prices for British imports of geneva and other spirits, scaled and adjusted for customs duties.

g Reported as 'alcools et eaux-de-vie, de 51° à 80°' from 1897 to 1907; sum of gin and rum from 1908 to 1914.

h See *g* above.

i Liters.

j Converted from meters at 9 meters per yard.

k Prices for British exports of dyed cottons, in pence per yard, adjusted for customs duties.

m Converted from meters at 5 meters per yard.

n Prices for British exports of bleached cottons, in pence per yard, adjusted for customs duties.

p Bleached and unbleached cottons.

q Prices for British exports of unbleached cottons, in pence per yard, adjusted for customs duties.

r Converted from meters at 6 meters per yard.

s Prices calculated from reported quantity and value.

t Converted from meters at 4.5 meters per yard.

u Prices for British imports of unmanufactured tobacco, scaled and adjusted for customs duties.

v Sum of reported imports for rice, wheat flour, hard-tack, maize, manioc, and yams.

w Including hard-tack.

x Including yams.

y Correction of typographical error in published return.

z Prices for British exports of fire arms, scaled and adjusted for customs duties.

aa Prices for British exports of gunpowder, scaled and adjusted for customs duties.

bb Prices for British exports of salt, in shillings per ton.

cc Imports of metals, less rails 1908–1914, and less estimated state imports of metals and machinery 1892, 1893 and 1896. Includes metallic goods for years before 1897.

dd Imports of metallic goods after 1896, excluding machinery.

ee Estimated state and capitalist imports of metals and machinery.
  For 1908–1914, it includes rails, machinery, automobiles, bicycles, railroad cars and boats.
  For 1896–1907, it includes machinery and steam engines. In addition, state imports of metals and machinery were estimated at 250 thousand francs each in 1892 and 1893, and at 50 thousand francs in 1896.

ff British imports of staves, in pounds per load.

gg Thousands of sacks.

hh Prices of British exports of jute manufactures, in pence per yard.

ii Prices of British thread exports, scaled and adjusted for customs duties.

jj Building materials.

Table A4.6. *Exports, 1915–60 (values in thousands of francs)*

Year	Total export value	Export value[a] accounted for	Palm kernels Tons	Value	Palm oil Tons	Value
1915	13,164	10,846	23,224	5,688	9,597	4,835
1916	18,881	15,902	28,477	8,642	12,633	6,800
1917	19,545	16,403	17,013	5,981	11,865	9,432
1918	29,987	27,465	26,250	12,189	7,637	13,690
1919	70,105	66,939	68,982	45,189	22,512	20,260
1920	63,651	58,275	29,342	41,482	11,411	14,567
1921	35,538	31,766	25,444	20,273	4,862	6,512
1922	41,894	38,793	34,726	23,140	11,646	13,113
1923	56,207	53,193	36,967	32,295	13,701	18,528
1924	100,376	98,074	45,654	63,777	17,195	31,543
1925	125,561	123,369	45,228	74,778	16,852	41,911
1926	181,704	175,214	42,066	95,830	17,909	68,892
1927	135,517	131,865	48,250	82,026	16,375	41,511
1928	97,773	92,122	31,606	59,878	9,759	23,598
1929	120,692	113,777	36,046	60,002	15,328	37,528
1930	125,647	121,687	51,701	64,527	21,587	41,101
1931	67,606	66,346	46,953	37,292	15,934	21,007
1932	43,373	41,517	49,915	28,748	11,070	9,097
1933	27,652	25,800	38,125	15,930	8,564	4,803
1934	34,218	31,417	57,989	18,873	13,697	6,207
1935	56,364	54,546	61,123	27,884	23,905	16,970
1936	90,385	88,816	74,743	47,843	24,956	26,276
1937	121,882	120,219	47,201	51,565	15,068	28,832
1938	114,180c	129,538c	38,887	58,000	8,961	15,583
1939	92,854	90,798	30,205	27,276	9,475	14,457
1940	71,072	69,390	36,213	37,243	9,443	17,418
1941	115,930	110,345	39,018	39,614	14,494	28,587
1942	133,810	125,581	34,798	65,688	6,059	20,467
1943	119,366c	120,076c	38,564	84,349	4,861	20,049
1944	162,643c	167,869c	38,061	85,507	8,006	33,056
1945	147,795c	220,724c	32,120	79,780	3,215	13,495
1946	172,511	150,661	22,046	98,959	570	2,391
1947	339,460	309,966	25,713	204,128	711	9,294
1948	1,515,124	1,323,763	38,572	585,917	9,959	328,802
1949	1,881,000	1,712,579	44,204	916,626	6,864	272,000
1950	2,233,000c	2,525,936c	46,140	1,238,000	10,125	401,000
1951	2,810,000	2,469,053	32,334	1,198,000	13,263	853,000
1952	1,939,000	1,849,237	38,313	947,000	7,694	294,000
1953	2,606,000	2,530,552	47,584	1,376,000	15,111	557,000
1954	2,509,000	2,420,987	47,800	1,249,000	12,914	549,000
1955	2,743,447	2,663,501	50,634	1,165,000	16,427	663,800
1956	2,629,183	2,543,798	49,910	1,107,000	16,185	678,000
1957	2,447,168	2,352,387	44,667	1,054,921	10,399	426,000
1958	3,371,000	3,250,000	61,009	1,665,000	12,350	606,000
1959	2,833,000	2,280,000	50,372	1,475,000	5,943	262,000
1960	4,067,000	3,879,000	61,274	2,177,000	10,727	538,000

Table A4.6 (*cont.*)

Year	Maize		Cotton		Peanuts	
	Tons	Value	Tons	Value	Tons	Value
1915	5,385	*b*	68	85	*g*	*g*
1916	4,459	*b*	99	126	12	2
1917	1,923	*b*	102	128	*g*	*g*
1918	*b*	*b*	267	221	1	*g*
1919	28	10	134	381	1	*g*
1920	29	9	122	1,271	*g*	*g*
1921	1,984	1,360	422	1,670	12*f*	11*f*
1922	415	61	276	951	1*f*	1*f*
1923	464	185	314	1,098	2	3
1924	24	8	321	1,929	2	3
1925	74	33	681	4,764	20*f*	24*f*
1926	12	15	1,024	9,598	135*f*	204*f*
1927	2	*b*	727	5,999	1	1
1928	57	*b*	697	4,896	202	307
1929	23	*b*	1,131	8,528	375	554
1930	5	*b*	1,069	8,588	111	146
1931	11	*b*	682	4,930	2	2
1932	20	14	449	1,572		
1933	18	*b*	446	1,630	35	*b*
1934	7,242	*b*	888	3,091	111	48
1935	1,640	522	1,140	3,714	2,020	2,461
1936	2,781	1,445	947	2,128	3,971	5,282
1937	18,327	10,194	1,071	6,134	8,949	10,788
1938	34,104	22,228	1,202	5,740	8,322	11,875
1939	45,925	24,187	1,158	5,371	6,815	8,722
1940	2,458	1,160*d*	121	607	3,699	5,238
1941	14,454	7,940*d*	2,538	25,280	2,133	4,238
1942	14,268	7,000*d*	1,888	25,114	404	1,035
1943	9,026	10,650*d*			208	544
1944	10,358	12,820*d*	1,690	29,675	1,064	2,986
1945	77,495	70,000*d*	1,519	22,453	472	1,933
1946	30	62	1,207	16,381	2,387	11,223
1947	*g*	3	719	25,835	1,352	13,033
1948			748	57,014	6,552	127,317
1949			2,116	176,928	6,861	189,454
1950			3,170*e*	421,000	9,746	285,000
1951			1,089	195,000	2,891	148,000
1952			1,036	149,000	6,717	284,000
1953	10	139	750	95,000	4,409	189,000
1954	104	1,610	621	74,000	7,504	307,000
1955	19	420	756	93,064	10,964	470,000
1956			514	53,115	12,028	500,000
1957	20	228	720	89,919	14,306	569,000
1958			893	107,000	13,493	616,000
1959			808	64,000	2,062	129,000
1960			911	108,000	15,406	681,000

Table A4.6 (*cont.*)

Year	Coffee Tons	Coffee Value	Fish Tons	Fish Value	Shea butter Tons	Shea butter Value	Shea nuts Tons	Shea nuts Value
1915	13	b	429	235	9	3		
1916	g	g	595	327	15	5		
1917	g	g	1,566	861	2	1		
1918	g	g	1,802	1,278	g	g		
1919	g	g	798	1,040	g	g		
1920	g	g	783	719	3	5		
1921	g	g	1,802	1,856	17	32		
1922	g	g	1,400	1,437	16	29		
1923	19	44	949	949	8	12		
1924	47	105	420	420	18	b	24	5
1925	22	53	570	1,140			251	50
1926	g	g	g	1			637	363
1927	3	48	1	1			413	299
1928	22	160	54	140			1,336	1,191
1929			370	1,291	186	641	3,096	2,786
1930	g	1	741	2,601	219	658	1,291	1,161
1931	g	g	393	1,379	91	232	857	662
1932	32	148	79	265	137	289	1,425	1,004
1933	42	209	164	491	110	191	2,158	1,511
1934	71	352	278	869	146	221	916	264
1935	56	272	276	543	355	436	593	237
1936	180	711	293	575	581	615	5,387	2,585
1937	183	870	1,527	4,187	638	1,103	7,123	4,480
1938	124	659	2,788	11,136	160	352	2,355	1,724
1939	201	1,191	657	2,888	93	156	5,256	5,148
1940	476	2,927	235	929	215	503	1,651	1,667
1941	212	1,609	68	268	62	153	3,734	3,476
1942	153	1,510	58	527	453	1,734	1,734	181
1943	22	275	3	44	11	64		
1944	46	656	18	249	45	242		
1945	516	5,826	131	1,558	1,178	13,508	939	2,652
1946	30	580	240	4,979	255	3,297	1,439	6,400
1947	8	158	295	8,736	91	1,596	4,535	29,438
1948	76	3,287	274	7,360	241	11,958	10,214	155,221
1949	404	27,456	156	6,815	108	6,149	1,997	39,936
1950	294	39,000	192	9,178	10	254	4,231	96,811
1951	764	125,000	106	5,000	231	19,000	6,032	128,053
1952	356	58,000	734	16,000	1	50	2,755	44,187
1953	756	130,000	664	33,000	23	963	4,635	65,450
1954	544	97,000	802	41,000	15	1,000	2,848	42,377
1955	934	135,000	652	39,000	75	3,000	3,742	53,236
1956	1,285	143,000	78	4,000	15	1,000	1,196	15,427
1957	934	127,000	219	14,000	79	4,000	1,983	30,946
1958	462	79,000	1,433	94,000	78	6,000	2,267	35,000
1959	1,373	187,000	1,519	124,000	30	2,000	1,919	35,000
1960	880	125,000	2,194	210,000	16	1,000	813	16,000

Notes:

a Sum of the values of exports listed.

b Not available.

c Sum of the values of exports listed exceeds reported total value of exports, because of error in returns. For 1943–5 the reason is that obligatory maize deliveries, sent from Dahomey to Senegal and beyond as part of the war effort, were not counted as exports in official returns.

Table A4.6 (*cont.*)

Year	Castor beans		Copra		Kapok	
	Tons	Value	Tons	Value	Tons	Value
1915			214	*b*		
1916			225	*b*		
1917			246	*b*		
1918			123	87		
1919	69	*b*	53	29	36	30
1920	162	*b*	102	222		
1921	83	*b*	41	52		
1922	65	*b*	61	61	*g*	*g*
1923	67	*b*	74	79		
1924	137	189	55	85	6	15
1925	180	246	145	221	40	199
1926	403	678	80	223	78	452
1927	498	508	84	200	321	1,272
1928	473	722	112	267	130	963
1929	965	1,360	94	188	134	899
1930	1,284	1,529	89	133	197	1,243
1931	426	307	104	127	59	408
1932	228	172	178	155	14	53
1933	940	765	134	73	37	197
1934	1,717	900	281	159	102	433
1935	1,395	877	332	273	163	357
1936	915	617	348	345	187	394
1937	935	832	329	548	252	686
1938	1,493	1,291	389	555	131	395
1939	715	629	305ᵉ	467	92	306
1940	483	495	629	1,000	70	203
1941	561	615			239	1,565
1942	2	4	214	1,340*d*	74	981
1943	306	1,414	692	2,645	4	42
1944	28	126	676	2,552		
1945	1,810	6,962	674	2,557		
1946	816	3,499	19	143	193	2,747
1947	365	2,602	375	4,049	329	11,094
1948	1,040	17,606	754	20,094	224	9,237
1949	2,284	47,909	329	9,550	240	19,756
1950	612	13,000	163	5,693	181	17,000
1951	777	41,000	253	10,000	113	17,000
1952	778	32,000	359	12,000	123	13,000
1953	750	24,000	1,039	37,000	211	23,000
1954	782	18,000	930	32,000	74	9,000
1955	800	16,981	450	14,000	82	10,000
1956	492	12,256	506	16,000	125	14,000
1957	520	15,373	207	7,000	120	14,000
1958	534	17,000	255	11,000	154	14,000
1959	646	*b*	244	*b*	22	2,000
1960	988	*b*			38	3,000

d Estimated on the basis of unit value for exports from all of AOF
e Correction of typographical error in published source.
f Including some unshelled peanuts.
g Exports recorded, but of less than one of the units shown.

Appendix 4

Table A4.7. *Imports, 1915–60 (values in thousands of francs)*

Year	Total import value	Import value[a] accounted for	1. Cotton fabric		2. Beverages	
			Tons	Value	Liters	Value
1915	10,631	6,366	728	3,112	695,194	523
1916	17,389	10,806	1,057	5,478	1,326,167	1,956
1917	18,626	11,661	920	6,455	1,540,884	1,369
1918	28,347	14,897	719	8,193	912,436	2,332
1919	44,385	23,695	563	9,009	1,574,416	5,013
1920	93,656	63,298	745	27,410	2,110,835	9,776
1921	39,256	29,276	315	11,545	809,551	5,245
1922	42,799	30,279	758	14,949	525,278	1,938
1923	62,231	42,278	839	20,091	1,764,377	5,580
1924	83,138	54,555	744	24,083	2,278,719	7,623
1925	111,601	73,121	940	37,483	2,459,220	9,532
1926	186,538	120,441	1,086	58,687	4,378,620	17,793
1927	159,024	98,254	903	41,555	2,504,942	12,130
1928	134,349	88,019	772	32,587	1,884,864	11,561
1929	147,647	103,371	985	33,820	2,511,200	10,993
1930	155,960	111,848	864	30,700	3,108,000	13,630
1931	102,815	69,241	474	11,223	2,609,000	10,174
1932	61,415	44,435	891	16,194	2,688,700	8,776
1933	42,945	29,615	701	9,970	1,186,797	4,316
1934	44,312	31,788	1,281	13,243	771,021	3,138
1935	55,500	40,593	1,074	14,904	916,600	2,882
1936	86,939	66,808	2,029	32,127	1,257,300	3,002
1937	107,048	72,093	716	21,311	1,349,800	5,335
1938	108,076	67,772	338	14,500	959,400	4,320
1939	140,540	100,451	2,281	35,647	1,759,000	7,964
1940	76,663	62,258	1,057	27,961	882,000	4,185
1941	48,747	30,133	183	9,895	862,000	5,362
1942	70,597	40,202	130	8,609	602,000	6,781
1943	95,212	89,219	953	52,862	898,000	8,466
1944	50,043	39,178	177	10,201	543,000	6,381
1945	97,084	47,903	144	2,961	863,000	15,784
1946	265,931	209,181	359	72,173	742,000	29,650
1947	603,618	470,092	900	223,421	1,510,000	56,568
1948	1,162,284	892,613	1,543	289,305	1,791,000	95,837
1949	2,242,000	1,543,891	568	283,682	3,821,000	203,623
1950	2,137,000	1,402,625	337	174,000	4,340,000	241,285
1951	3,564,000	2,224,129	550	303,000	6,258,000	369,129
1952	3,775,000	2,438,049	569	306,000	4,232,000	416,049
1953	2,874,000	1,877,192	810	309,000	7,040,000	276,192
1954	3,970,000	2,638,271	1,585	451,000	11,704,900	398,271
1955	4,177,000	2,210,368	1,377	288,000	8,643,400	288,768
1956	3,718,000	2,258,698	556	197,000	6,646,700	252,098
1957	4,269,296	2,719,000	850	250,000	4,477,000	215,000
1958	4,329,000	2,987,000	661	231,000	2,976,000	186,000
1959	4,335,000	3,016,000	624	226,000	2,620,000	172,000
1960	6,630,000	4,657,000	899	479,000	3,077,000	229,000

Table A4.7 (*cont.*)

Year	2A Beers		2B Wines		2C Distilled beverages	
	Liters	Value	Liters	Value	Liters	Value
1915	*b*	*b*	150,659	120	544,535	403
1916	*b*	*b*	251,631	348	1,974,536	1,608
1917	*b*	*b*	160,731	296	1,380,153	1,073
1918	*b*	*b*	223,253	578	689.183	1,754
1919	37,115	88	214,113	890	1,323,188	4,035
1920	55,515	131	699,359	2,390	1,355,961	7,255
1921	20,053	98	344,624	1,457	435,874	3,690
1922	34,717	84	300,451	1,011	190,110	843
1923	63,846	144	751,468	2,159	949,063	3,277
1924	110,678	274	745,321	2,617	1,422,720	4,732
1925	120,691	347	920,896	2,763	1,417,633	6,422
1926	199,975	650	2,760,245	7,181	1,418,400	9,962
1927	178,014	616	1,348,028	4,983	978,900	6,530
1928	184,189	691	819,075	3,404	931,600	7,466
1929	261,600*c*	1,001	1,768,400	6,378	481,200	3,614
1930	266,500	1,063	2,344,400	9,022	497,100	3,545
1931	233,000*d*	973	2,235,000	7,582	141,000	1,618
1932	223,200	891	2,351,200	6,809	114,300	1,076
1933	182,304*c*	678	960,432	3,097	44,061	541
1934	232,300	805	496,400	1,561	42,321	771
1935	306,600*c*	902	581,900	1,473	28,100	507
1936	460,100	1,031	789,900	1,568	7,300	404
1937	607,700	2,148	684,800	2,193	57,300	994
1938	341,400	1,701	533,300	1,516	84,700	1,103
1939	383,500	2,074	1,166,500	3,853	103,100	1,602
1940	87,900	487	627,100	2,194	93,400	1,199
1941	5	34	728,700	3,823	57,600	1,182
1942	*e*	3	449,900	4,713	47,600	1,820
1943			856,700	6,427	21,400	1,927
1944	*e*	3	510,100	3,964	30,700	2,400
1945	*e*	8	787,100	9,587	47,100	5,828
1946	1	17	496,700	11,809	172,300	16,685
1947	7,000	190	1,461,700	30,351	193,800	24,383
1948	315,000	9,477	1,002,300	43,802	356,800	17,644
1949	1,334,000	45,330	1,285,000	67,463	330,200	82,062
1950	1,644,000	73,574	1,188,000	64,782	370,000	89,530
1951	2,037,000	98,753	2,185,000	112,096	498,500	127,756
1952	1,860,000	103,310	2,187,000	83,251	185,400	58,407
1953	2,067,000	108,436	4,235,000	109,685	79,700	20,386
1954	3,233,000	157,857	8,402,000	214,193	69,900	26,221
1955	3,152,000	148,967	5,469,000	128,913	22,400	10,888
1956	2,921,000	134,491	3,488,000	101,707	38,700	15,900
1957	2,059,000	92,399	1,932,000	88,530	22,700	12,400
1958	1,950,000	99,000	1,909,000	53,000	*b*	*b*
1959	1,438,000	77,000	1,065,000	62,000	*b*	*b*
1960	845,000	57,000	1,913,000	91,000	87.000	78,000

Table A4.7 (*cont.*)

Year	3. Tobacco		3A. Pipe tobacco		3B. Cigarettes	
	Tons	Value	Tons	Value	Tons	Value
1915	648	1,137	*b*	*b*	*b*	*b*
1916	802	1,541	*b*	*b*	*b*	*b*
1917	525	1,167	*b*	*b*	*b*	*b*
1918	393	1,601	*b*	*b*	*b*	*b*
1919	1,017	5,669	1,007	5,451	10	202
1920	768	9,710	753	9,233	15	433
1921	165	2,407	159	2,147	6	220
1922	569	5,118	558	4,774	11	340
1923	569	6,375	559	6,126	9	232
1924	727	9,219	719	8,961	8	245
1925	700	8,482	683	7,903	16	552
1926	627	11,951	599	10,519	27	1,242
1927	748	11,189	713	9,601	35	1,563
1928	745	11,400	710	9,434	34	1,942
1929	894	13,710	838	10,689	57	3,071
1930	680	8,680	634	6,702	46	1,978
1931	519	5,956	487	4,861	32	1,095
1932	440	4,869	414	4,337	26	532
1933	375	3,221	340	2,714	17	322
1934	391	2,624	368	2,079	23	546
1935	445	3,666	423	3,105	22	561
1936	529	3,893	502	3,234	27	659
1937	561	6,343	521	5,149	40	1,194
1938	545	9,000	495	7,809	50	1,191
1939	536	10,021	481	8,738	55	1,283
1940	424	7,222	280	6,012	44	1,210
1941	103	3,293	3	88	100	3,205
1942	75	3,285	7	255	68	3,030
1943	65	3,694	11	362	54	3,332
1944	30	1,796	11	276	19	1,520
1945	33	2,277	14	446	19	1,831
1946	125	8,753	32	2,172	93	6,581
1947	130	11,745	58	4,647	72	7,098
1948	132	18,911	39	3,291	93	15,620
1949	299	30,847	139	9,476	160	21,371
1950	222	35,762	104	7,154	118	28,608
1951	281	63,000	120	18,000	160	45,000
1952	243	64,000	87	10,000	156	54,000
1953	436	96,000	245	30,000	191	66,000
1954	383	103,000	131	18,000	252	85,000
1955	458	127,600	179	32,400	278	95,300
1956	370	87,600	149	25,600	307	94,000
1957	492	125,000	257	30,000	306	103,000
1958	257	91,000	104	26,000	153	66,000
1959	269	*b*	110	24,000	159	*b*
1960	480	195,000	137	33,000	343	162,000

Table A4.7 (*cont.*)

Year	4. Sugar		5A. Wheat flour		5B. Rice		6. Jute sacks	
	Tons	Value	Tons	Value	Tons	Value	Tons	Value
1915	50	32	110	51	110	32	*b*	*b*
1916	134	131	223	125	163	68	*b*	*b*
1917	63	73	110	69	110	61	*b*	*b*
1918	73	133	65	65	14	19	*b*	*b*
1919	132	209	270	366	129	203	*b*	*b*
1920	132	209	429	632	186	373	845	3,478
1921	303	1,786	173	314	145	158	242	586
1922	305	605	312	385	267	281	463	878
1923	500	1,332	564	678	492	476	628	1,906
1924	487	1,436	780	982	527	612	772	3,061
1925	537	1,290	587	1,067	829	516	836	4,680
1926	1,429	4,707	474	1,072	745	1,310	791	6,558
1927	980	2,434	602	1,636	499	911	728	4,886
1928	884	2,790	507	1,164	454	662	567	3,796
1929	993	2,340	631	1,289	446	644	*b*	*b*
1930	748	1,883	698	1,226	769	1,232	872	3,955
1931	567	1,219	1,302	933	687	945	666	2,599
1932	435	685	384	449	479	456	515	1,607
1933	56	127	459	422	635	515	615	1,549
1934	427	466	470	319	965	555	1,070	2,292
1935	569	556	646	553	1,055	618	1,469	3,060
1936	1,299	1,455	991	811	2,455	1,525	1,469	3,061
1937	1,282	2,141	856	1,765	1,226	1,374	1,280	3,635
1938	899	1,896	615	1,536	1,183	1,669	1,208	4,863
1939	796	1,915	633	1,628	1,146	1,467	1,130	5,439
1940	510	2,146	779	2,490	699	1,018	459	3,397
1941	288	1,457	122	515	*e*	2	28	372
1942	249	1,886	64	388			55	1,848
1943	30	240	106	784	2	21	602	9,756
1944			1	7	3	40	112	1,864
1945	*e*	1	*e*	1	2	21	14	259
1946	*e*	7	1	7	*e*	5	*e*	4
1947	748	11,491	1	11	3	46	11	324
1948	1,194	42,858	915	13,977	*e*	28	757	24,545
1949	1,438	74,247	1,240	35,547	*e*	7	292	25,866
1950	1,402	71,977	835	18,877	1	45	357	24,594
1951	2,049	102,000	2,153	64,000	2,021	67,000	125	13,000
1952	1,687	93,000	1,336	43,000	526	22,000	1,020	90,000
1953	2,622	136,000	1,552	49,000	499	21,000	528	27,000
1954	2,808	142,000	2,828	75,000	1,367	43,000	1,336	72,000
1955	2,665	127,000	1,910	55,000	2,186	67,000	1,033	59,000
1956	2,707	129,000	1,552	41,000	3,054	89,000	917	57,000
1957	4,155	191,000	1,112	29,000	2,008	59,000	1,010	51,000
1958	5,164	255,000	1,456	41,000	3,297	109,000	1,819	107,000
1959	5,901	316,000	2,040	57,000	2,582	97,000	495	28,000
1960	6,143	329,000	2,889	73,000	5,952	168,000	952	75,000

Table A4.7 (*cont.*)

Year	7. Motor vehicles		7A. Trucks		7B. Automobiles		8. Paper goods	
	No.	Value	No.	Value	No.	Value	Tons	Value
1915	b	b	b	b	b	b	b	b
1916	b	b	b	b	b	b	b	b
1917	b	b	b	b	b	b	b	b
1918	b	b	b	b	b	b	b	202
1919	b	b	b	b	b	b	b	b
1920	b	b	b	b	b	b	b	b
1921	b	b	b	b	b	b	b	b
1922	b	b	b	b	b	b	b	b
1923	8	220	b	b	b	b	b	b
1924	25	417	b	b	b	b	b	b
1925	113	1,788	b	b	b	b	b	b
1926	109	2,125	61	1,322	48	803	b	b
1927	121	3,338	81	2,421	40	918	b	b
1928	72	1,952	38	1,224	34	728	b	b
1929	119	3,004	b	b	b	b	b	b
1930	121	3,353	b	b	b	b	b	b
1931	58	1,303	b	b	b	b	b	b
1932	32	526	b	b	b	b	b	b
1933	54	774	b	b	b	b	b	b
1934	79	973	b	b	b	b	b	b
1935	165	1,807	b	b	b	b	b	b
1936	271	4,681	b	b	b	b	b	b
1937	169	3,821	b	b	b	b	b	b
1938	148	5,105	b	b	b	b	b	b
1939	275	3,148	205	1,278	70	1,870	134	1,648
1940	42	1,270	31	929	11	341	75	874
1941	2	382	2	382			62	1,401
1942	6	1,441	6	1,441			76	2,076
1943							14	608
1944	3	163	2	100	1	63	1	47
1945	28	1,802	28	1,802			29	1,571
1946	179	22,760	158	21,141	21	1,619	101	8,780
1947	285	49,995	208	39,624	77	10,371	132	9,659
1948	329	90,150	163	51,568	166	38,582	179	19,435
1949	706	261,390	537	207,562	169	53,828	231	52,864
1950	506	176,000	380	142,000	126	34,000	176	30,000
1951	571	227,000	363	168,000	208	59,000	443	60,000
1952	443	232,000	269	171,000	174	61,000	384	63,000
1953	398	164,000	216	107,000	182	57,000	258	46,000
1954	425	452,000	213	395,000	212	57,000	336	48,000
1955	937	417,000	530	291,000	407	126,000	269	33,000
1956	675	287,000	341	174,000	334	112,000	348	59,000
1957	1,003	424,000	447	234,000	556	190,000	546	76,000
1958	909	612,000	371	219,000	538	192,000	437	76,000
1959	b	779,000	287	b	b	b	542	85,000
1960	1,105	738,000	382	b	723	b	790	133,000

Table A4.7 (*cont.*)

Year	9. Matches		10. Petroleum		10A. Kerosene	
	Tons	Value	Tons	Value	Tons	Value
1915	*b*	*b*	2,518	1,003	*b*	*b*
1916	*b*	*b*	1,592	651	*b*	*b*
1917	*b*	*b*	1,715	811	*b*	*b*
1918	*b*	*b*	736	266	*b*	*b*
1919	*b*	*b*	942	352	*b*	*b*
1920	*b*	*b*	1,752	2,198	*b*	1,617
1921	*b*	*b*	953	1,340	*b*	*b*
1922	210*f*	1,047	779	726	*b*	*b*
1923	245*f*	907	2,008	1,542	*b*	*b*
1924	385*f*	1,742	2,523	2,497	*b*	*b*
1925	210*f*	974	3,022	2,963	*b*	*b*
1926	368*f*	2,039	3,247	5,880	4,073	2,503
1927	*b*	*b*	3,411	5,613	2,769	4,255
1928	*b*	*b*	4,974	8,106	3,651	5,046
1929	315*f*	1,863	4,407	6,719	*b*	*b*
1930	210*f*	2,160	4,471	6,091	3,257	4,044
1931	*b*	*b*	3,098	3,457	1,874	1,718
1932	228*f*	1,104	2,083	2,239	1,038	1,006
1933	180*f*	517	1,459	1,424	*b*	*b*
1934	210*f*	751	1,623	886	473	260
1935	140	615	2,298	1,259	*b*	*b*
1936	*b*	*b*	3,780	1,890	1,714	669
1937	*b*	*b*	4,400	3,860	2,069	1,558
1938	*b*	*b*	4,142	5,113	1,829	1,956
1939	181	1,995	5,236	6,018	1,281	648
1940	58	823	2,053	3,067	305	291
1941	5	145	142	318	*e*	1
1942	5	799	38	92		
1943	8	351	1,788	3,618	411	548
1944			2,681	4,944	1,092	1,465
1945			2,879	6,445	1,070	2,046
1946	47	2,407	4,100	16,729	1,198	5,172
1947	109	5,398	7,744	24,937	3,703	5,931
1948	159	10,535	9,689	76,329	1,419	9,682
1949	91	9,059	11,328	96,059	2,508	19,775
1950	126	13,000	15,100	110,000	4,200	28,000
1951	208	22,000	17,954	178,000	4,200	33,000
1952	179	24,000	27,100	226,000	7,100	51,000
1953	24	2,000	19,773	213,000	6,500	51,000
1954	79	9,000	28,400	206,000	10,400	75,000
1955	52	7,000	25,940	219,000	10,600	85,000
1956	*b*	*b*	38,493	355,000	11,500	93,000
1957	*b*	*b*	42,564	446,000	13,200	113,000
1958	*b*	*b*	42,620	468,000	*b*	*b*
1959	*b*	*b*	35,710	422,000	*b*	*b*
1960	*b*	*b*	55,047	734,000	*b*	*b*

Table A4.7 (*cont.*)

Year	10B. Gasoline		11. Coal		12. Cement	
	Tons	Value	Tons	Value	Tons	Value
1915	*b*	*b*	493	54	278*g*	19*g*
1916	*b*	*b*	173	219	640*g*	56*g*
1917	*b*	*b*	4,171	541	1,112*g*	103*g*
1918	*b*	*b*	2,271	372	1,234*g*	159*g*
1919	*b*	*b*	*b*	*b*	1,469*g*	281*g*
1920	*b*	*b*	2,974	1,098	2,165*g*	698*g*
1921	*b*	*b*	1,307	245	926*g*	309*g*
1922	*b*	*b*	1,627	245	2,143*g*	506*g*
1923	*b*	*b*	2,793	465	2,374*g*	479*g*
1924	*b*	*b*	3,037	579	2,549*g*	347*g*
1925	*b*	*b*	2,337	215	4,044*g*	969*g*
1926	745	1,807	3,371	496	5,295*g*	1,758*g*
1927	641	1,358	5,882	2,140	4,883*g*	1,527*g*
1928	1,084	2,370	4,938	1,511	5,727*g*	1,432*g*
1929	*b*	*b*	5,054	1,478	7,596	2,877
1930	1,214	2,048	3,759	1,104	9,273	3,229
1931	1,224	1,740	4,260	1,763	5,235	1,635
1932	1,045	1,233	3,944	752	3,686	803
1933	*b*	*b*	4,916	1,563	2,854*g*	617*g*
1934	998	581	2,103	224	4,495	866
1935	*b*	*b*	4,247	441	5,140*g*	798*g*
1936	2,066	1,221	6,806	915	8,528	952
1937	2,331	2,302	12,100*d*	1,600	8,670	1,766
1938	2,313	3,157	5,763	1,260	8,785	2,440
1939	2,588	2,702	9,583	2,436	11,272	3,331
1940	1,298	1,758			2,011	607
1941	142	317	75	55	2,784	988
1942	38	92	1,363	1,675	2,367	1,389
1943	1,033	1,998	1,529	2,868	340	175
1944	911	1,857	2,103	2,264	3,493	3,600
1945	1,422	3,364	2,315	2,564	1,153	811
1946	1,820	6,848	12,147	16,750	2,634	3,350
1947	2,638	9,438	1,371	1,923	3,387	6,081
1948	6,356	47,196	2,837	11,869	7,186	22,610
1949	6,154	51,474	9,163	28,802	20,032	83,815
1950	10,900	91,000	3,056	8,158	15,815	66,927
1951	13,100	115,000	15,024	45,000	29,289	162,000
1952	20,000	175,000	5,229	28,000	26,429	182,000
1953	9,103	95,000	337	1,000	24,914	111,000
1954	18,000	131,000	3,257	10,000	29,429	127,000
1955	15,297	134,000	25,153	28,000	27,327	117,000
1956	16,547	148,000	1,100	7,000	29,995	134,000
1957	17,954	170,000	91	2,000	38,195	192,000
1958	*b*	*b*	79	2,000	39,339	191,000
1959	*b*	*b*	4,000	*b*	49,240*g*	258,000*g*
1960	*b*	*b*	1,000	*b*	65,689*g*	341,000*g*

Notes:
a Sum of the values of imports listed.
b Not available.
c Including lemonade.
d Correction of typographical error in published source.

Table A4.7 (*cont.*)

	13. Iron/steel		14. Metal goods		15. Machinery	
Year	Tons	Value	Tons	Value	Tons	Value
1915	279*h*	132*h*	*b*	271	*b*	*b*
1916	124*h*	127*h*	225	454	*b*	*b*
1917	104*h*	108*h*	*b*	904	*b*	*b*
1918	195*h*	330*h*	*b*	1,225	*b*	*b*
1919	606*h*	1,099*h*	*b*	1,494	*b*	*b*
1920	1,308*h*	2,336*h*	*b*	5,389	*b*	*b*
1921	949*h*	2,329*h*	*b*	3,012	*b*	*b*
1922	471*h*	625	*b*	2,428	86	548
1923	475	892	*b*	*b*	135	1,335
1924	583	1,110	*b*	*b*	105	847
1925	760	1,748	*b*	*b*	49	1,414
1926	1,484	3,367	*b*	*b*	253	2,698
1927	5,821	7,769	*b*	*b*	228	3,126
1928	5,853	7,689	*b*	*b*	358	3,369
1929	4,486	7,532	*b*	13,367	287	3,735
1930	13,544	16,567	3,289	12,407	330	5,561
1931	10,300	13,255	7,398	13,164	142	1,615
1932	269	808	1,858	4,089	108	1,078
1933	554	750	1,023	2,661	119	1,189
1934	605	766	1,125	3,466	138	1,219
1935	937	1,108	2,338	6,319	218	2,007
1936	1,981	2,047	2,651	8,287	283	2,162
1937	1,963	3,556	3,060	11,344	244	4,242
1938	1,085	2,340	1,923	10,482	158	3,248
1939	991	2,586	2,196	15,208	*i*	*i*
1940	437	1,323	730	5,875	*i*	*i*
1941	134	633	447	5,315	*i*	*i*
1942	60	272	493	9,661	*i*	*i*
1943	12	53	550	5,723	*i*	*i*
1944	*e*	1	932	7,870	*i*	*i*
1945	5	77	1,156	13,329	*i*	*i*
1946	44	437	1,233	27,369	*i*	*i*
1947	274	4,717	3,042	63,776	*i*	*i*
1948	1,037	16,284	4,574	159,940	*i*	*i*
1949	1,167	36,718	2,380	171,365	930	150,000
1950	3,491	80,000	2,487	113,000	1,186	230,000
1951	3,693	120,000	4,160	205,000	926	224,000
1952	6,312	192,000	4,017	244,000	758	213,000
1953	3,250	111,000	2,423	145,000	421	170,000
1954	4,311	173,000	1,360	115,000	655	214,000
1955	6,117	216,000	2,764	161,000	*b*	*b*
1956	5,896	234,000	1,472	99,000	757	231,000
1957	7,720	301,000	1,330	106,000	753	252,000
1958	6,081	307,000	1,184	98,000	464	213,000
1959	5,913	338,000	*b*	*b*	443	214,000
1960	13,702	802,000	*b*	*b*	763	361,000

e Imports recorded, but of less than one of the units shown.
f Assuming 55,000 boxes of matches per ton.
g Estimate based on 90% of reported building materials.
h Metals.
i Not specified, or reported as part of metal goods.

APPENDIX 5

Foreign trade indices

The export price index shown in Table A5.2 is calculated very simply: it is based entirely on the export of palm oil and palm kernels, which accounted for seventy to ninety-five percent of export values in each year. Quantities and values are taken from Tables A4.4 and A4.6; the base year is 1908, the price index is current-weighted and the quantity index is base-weighted.

Import indices are more complex because of the composition of imports and the problem of customs duties. The import indices in Table A5.1, for the years 1889–1914, were calculated as follows: proxy prices were estimated for the major import goods, since reported unit values were not dependable, as noted in Appendix 4. The proxy prices were taken from the Annual Statements of Trade in the British Parliamentary Papers, were scaled to the appropriate magnitude, and then the amount of customs duties was added to them for each year: these 'estimated prices' are listed in Table A4.5. They were used to calculate several import price indices. For the years 1897–1914 a narrow and dependable Index 1 was calculated for trade alcohol, gin and rum, cotton print and pipe tobacco, with a base year of 1908. Then two more indices were calculated (Index 2 with base year 1908, Index 3 with base year 1896) for the more heterogeneous but more frequently reported categories of beverages, textiles and pipe tobacco. Index 2 paralleled Index 1 from 1905 to 1914; Index 3 paralleled Index 1 from 1897 to 1904. Index 4, which is reported in Table A5.1, therefore consists of Index 2 for 1905–14, and Index 3 for 1889–1904 (scaled so that 1908 = 100). The reason two different base periods must be used is that the sharp increase in customs duties on alcoholic beverages from 1899 to 1904 changed the composition of imports. The resultant import indices cover the majority of the value of imports (if intermediate-good imports were added to the calculations, they would tend to bring the import price index downward and the import quantity index upward with the passage of time). By including customs duties, the price index in Table A5.1 gives the prices relevant to the Dahomean purchasers.

Table A5.2 gives import indices neglecting customs duties. For the period up to 1914 it is based on reported quantities of beverages, textiles and pipe tobacco (Table A4.5), using prices for rum, cotton print and pipe tobacco from the Annual Statements of Trade (converted to francs but without addition of customs duties), and a 1908 base year.

394

Table A5.3 gives terms of trade from the producers' viewpoint: net barter terms of trade are export prices (Table A5.2) divided by import prices (Table A5.1); income terms of trade are export values (Table A5.2) divided by import prices (Table A5.1). Table A5.4 gives terms of trade from the viewpoint of the state in Dahomey, with all figures taken from Table A5.2: net barter terms of trade are export prices divided by import prices; income terms of trade are export values divided by import prices.

The export indices for the whole period, along with the import indices in Tables A5.1 and A5.2 for the years 1889–1914, may be assumed to be fairly precise. The difference between the two import indices, for example, reflects a difference in viewpoint rather than a lack of precision in calculation. But all pretense to precision must be abandoned for the import indices after 1914, which are shown in Table A5.2: they must be seen as no more than an indication of general trends.

The factors which make these post-1914 import calculations less dependable are the pervasiveness of inflation, the inconsistency of commercial statistics, changes in the burden of customs duties, and changes in the composition and quality of imports. All import indices after 1914 were calculated with a base year of 1927, and were scaled so as to make $1908 = 1.0$. Quantities and values of imports in the calculations are those given in Table A4.7. For the years 1915–19, indices were based on imports of beverages, cotton textiles, tobacco and petroleum; jute sacks were added to the indices beginning in 1919, and automobiles were added in 1924. The resultant import indices cover just over half the value of imports from the twenties through the forties, and cover slightly less than forty percent of imports in the fifties.

The most important changes in composition within import categories (each assumed to be homogenous for purposes of the calculations!) were in beverages, where wines and beers displaced the more expensive distilled liquors after World War II, and in tobacco, where cigarettes displaced the cheaper pipe tobacco at the same time – the two changes thus cancel each other to a degree. Changes in composition of textile and automobile imports were also important, though they were cyclical in part.

Terms of trade figures calculated for the years after 1914 are based, therefore, on export indices which are rather dependable, and on import indices which are vaguely approximative. The AOF government calculated some import price indices for interwar and postwar years; Poquin and others have used them or followed their approach to calculate terms of trade for AOF, as I have done for Dahomey in Table A5.4. In each case, the calculations neglect the effect of customs duties. The impact of customs duties, however, continued to be significant and variable. Accounting in detail for this factor is not feasible, given the state of available data, but a few figures are indicative of its importance: customs duties (see Tables A7.1 and A7.2, 'Taxes to AOF') were 30% of the value of imports after 1900, fell to 20% of imports in the twenties, rose steadily to 50% of import value in 1945, and then declined slightly.

Appendix 5

Table A5.1. *Import indices, including customs duties*

Year	Price index	Quantity index	Value index
1889	0.47	0.64	0.30
1890	0.52	0.46	0.24
1891	0.55	0.71	0.39
1892	0.50	0.85	0.42
1893	0.53	1.03	0.55
1894	0.60	0.95	0.57
1895	0.59	1.09	0.65
1896	0.60	1.19	0.71
1897	0.61	0.98	0.60
1898	0.60	1.20	0.72
1899	0.61	1.25	0.76
1900	0.76	1.18	0.90
1901	0.78	1.20	0.94
1902	0.72	1.77	1.27
1903	0.83	1.38	1.15
1904	0.85	1.35	1.15
1905	0.88	1.33	1.18
1906	0.90	1.29	1.16
1907	0.93	1.45	1.35
1908	1.00	1.00	1.00
1909	1.00	1.44	1.44
1910	1.01	1.87	1.89
1911	0.98	2.45	2.41
1912	1.00	2.26	2.27
1913	1.03	1.64	1.68
1914	1.06	0.96	1.01

Table A5.2. *Foreign trade indices, neglecting customs duties*

Year	Export indices			Import indices		
	Price index	Quantity index	Value index	Price index	Quantity index	Value index
1889	1.04	0.42	0.43	0.89	0.56	0.50
1890	1.04	0.54	0.56	0.95	0.40	0.38
1891	0.95	0.70	0.66	0.99	0.63	0.62
1892	1.04	0.61	0.63	0.97	0.70	0.68
1893	0.93	0.86	0.80	0.86	0.85	0.73
1894	0.94	0.98	0.92	0.85	0.80	0.67
1895	0.95	1.08	1.03	0.80	0.93	0.74
1896	0.98	0.86	0.84	0.81	0.95	0.77
1897	0.94	0.50	0.47	0.84	0.76	0.64
1898	0.96	0.72	0.69	0.83	0.98	0.80
1899	1.19	0.98	1.16	0.81	1.00	0.81
1900	1.24	0.95	1.18	0.89	1.09	0.96
1901	0.79	1.11	0.88	0.89	1.08	0.96
1902	0.96	1.31	1.26	0.83	1.65	1.37
1903	0.97	0.85	0.82	0.80	1.23	0.98
1904	0.90	1.02	0.91	0.81	1.14	0.93
1905	0.91	0.68	0.62	0.86	1.21	1.03
1906	0.91	0.75	0.69	0.89	1.09	0.96
1907	0.97	0.82	0.80	0.96	1.15	1.10
1908	1.00	1.00	1.00	1.00	1.00	1.00
1909	0.96	1.50	1.44	1.00	1.53	1.52
1910	1.06	1.52	1.61	1.03	1.67	1.72
1911	1.23	1.66	2.03	0.96	1.96	1.93
1912	1.34	1.45	1.95	1.01	1.81	1.82
1913	1.37	1.01	1.38	1.07	1.29	1.38
1914	1.59	0.82	1.31	1.11	0.87	0.97
1915	1.03	1.01	1.04	1.20	0.74	0.88
1916	1.19	1.28	1.52	1.45	1.01	1.47
1917	1.57	0.97	1.52	1.70	0.88	1.50
1918	2.58	0.99	2.55	2.92	0.65	1.89
1919	2.38	2.71	6.45	4.18	0.73	3.06
1920	4.45	1.24	5.52	8.54	0.94	8.02
1921	3.16	0.84	2.64	9.21	0.35	3.22
1922	2.59	1.38	3.57	4.92	0.73	3.60
1923	3.27	1.53	5.01	5.91	0.92	5.45
1924	4.94	1.90	9.39	7.44	0.96	7.15

Table A5.2 (*cont.*)

Year	Export indices			Import indices		
	Price index	Quantity index	Value index	Price index	Quantity index	Value index
1925	6.13	1.88	11.5	8.59	1.15	9.9
1926	8.77	1.85	16.2	11.5	1.37	15.7
1927	6.32	1.93	12.2	10.5	1.14	12.0
1928	6.77	1.22	8.2	10.4	1.01	10.6
1929	6.12	1.59	9.7	8.8	1.26	11.1
1930	4.62	2.25	10.4	8.6	1.19	10.1
1931	3.07	1.87	5.7	6.9	0.81	5.5
1932	2.18	1.71	3.7	5.3	0.99	5.2
1933	1.56	1.31	2.0	4.3	0.75	3.2
1934	1.24	2.00	2.5	3.0	1.17	3.5
1935	1.71	2.59	4.4	3.7	1.14	4.2
1936	2.47	2.96	7.3	3.9	1.90	7.4
1937	4.31	1.84	7.9	6.8	0.99	6.8
1938	5.41	1.34	7.2	9.5	0.69	6.5
1939	3.52	1.17	4.1	4.9	2.11	10.4
1940	4.11	1.31	5.4	7.4	0.97	7.2
1941	4.16	1.62	6.7	14.1	0.21	3.0
1942	7.61	1.11	8.5	21.8	0.15	3.4
1943	8.96	1.15	10.3	14.7	0.82	12.0
1944	9.09	1.28	11.7	16.2	0.24	3.9
1945	10.0	0.92	9.2	18.3	0.25	4.5
1946	18.1	0.55	10.0	46.8	0.49	22.9
1947	32.6	0.64	21.0	43.4	1.29	56.0
1948	72.5	1.24	90.1	55.9	1.62	90.8
1949	78.7	1.49	117	106	1.29	138
1950	102	1.58	161	100	1.18	118
1951	144	1.40	202	114	1.54	176
1952	96	1.28	122	131	1.56	204
1953	103	1.85	190	91.2	1.82	166
1954	101	1.75	177	87.2	2.95	257
1955	90.7	1.98	180	78.4	2.73	214
1956	89.9	1.96	176	86.2	2.19	188
1957	93.8	1.56	146	91.9	2.51	231
1958	110	2.04	224	114	2.27	259
1959	116	1.48	171	130	2.03	264
1960	137	1.97	269	135	2.78	374

Table A5.3. *Terms of trade, including customs duties*

Year	Net barter terms of trade	Income terms of trade
1889	2.21	0.91
1890	2.00	1.08
1891	1.72	1.20
1892	2.08	1.26
1893	1.75	1.51
1894	1.57	1.53
1895	1.61	1.75
1896	1.63	1.40
1897	1.54	0.77
1898	1.60	1.15
1899	1.95	1.90
1900	1.63	1.55
1901	1.01	1.13
1902	1.33	1.75
1903	1.17	0.99
1904	1.06	1.07
1905	1.03	0.70
1906	1.01	0.77
1907	1.04	0.86
1908	1.00	1.00
1909	0.96	1.44
1910	1.05	1.59
1911	1.26	2.07
1912	1.34	1.95
1913	1.33	1.34
1914	1.50	1.24

Appendix 5

Table A5.4. *Terms of trade, neglecting customs duties*

Year	Net barter terms of trade	Income terms of trade
1889	1.17	0.48
1890	1.09	0.59
1891	0.96	0.67
1892	1.07	0.65
1893	1.08	0.93
1894	1.11	1.08
1895	1.19	1.29
1896	1.21	1.04
1897	1.12	0.56
1898	1.16	0.83
1899	1.47	1.43
1900	1.39	1.33
1901	0.89	0.99
1902	1.16	1.52
1903	1.21	1.03
1904	1.11	1.12
1905	1.06	0.72
1906	1.02	0.78
1907	1.01	0.83
1908	1.00	1.00
1909	0.96	1.44
1910	1.03	1.56
1911	1.28	2.11
1912	1.33	1.93
1913	1.28	1.29
1914	1.43	1.18
1915	0.86	0.87
1916	0.82	1.05
1917	0.92	0.89
1918	0.88	0.87
1919	0.57	1.54
1920	0.52	0.65
1921	0.34	0.29
1922	0.53	0.73
1923	0.55	0.85
1924	0.66	1.26

Table A5.4 (*cont.*)

Year	Net barter terms of trade	Income terms of trade
1925	0.71	1.34
1926	0.76	1.41
1927	0.60	1.16
1928	0.65	0.79
1929	0.70	1.10
1930	0.54	1.21
1931	0.44	0.83
1932	0.41	0.70
1933	0.36	0.47
1934	0.41	0.83
1935	0.46	1.19
1936	0.63	1.87
1937	0.63	1.16
1938	0.57	0.76
1939	0.72	0.84
1940	0.56	0.73
1941	0.30	0.48
1942	0.35	0.39
1943	0.61	0.70
1944	0.56	0.72
1945	0.55	0.50
1946	0.39	0.21
1947	0.75	0.48
1948	1.30	1.61
1949	0.74	1.10
1950	1.02	1.61
1951	1.26	1.77
1952	0.73	0.93
1953	1.13	2.08
1954	1.16	2.03
1955	1.16	2.30
1956	1.04	2.04
1957	1.02	1.62
1958	0.96	1.96
1959	0.89	1.32
1960	1.01	1.99

Rainfall

Monthly rainfall, as recorded in Porto-Novo up to 1911, and in Cotonou thereafter, in millimeters.

Table A6.1. *Rainfall, 1897–1914*

	1897	1898	1899	1900	1901	1902	1903	1904	1905
Jan.	0	26	19	16	9	6	0	0	0
Feb.	52	1	10	1	18	34	134	9	0
Mar.	76	57	17	81	114	104	41	28	41
Apr.	73	148	69	132	33	162	102	58	100
May	257	321	94	439	177	50	97	208	125
June	50	382	179	250	302	183	268	404	283
July	30	214	131	407	381	114	30	183	290
Aug.	0	26	115	78	24	6	16	2	0
Sept.	22	153	48	84	416	20	62	42	4
Oct.	139	160	173	130	262	43	127	162	238
Nov.	63	48	43	16	27	14	71	160	73
Dec.	0	6	20	5	4	64	29	1	30
Total	762	1542	918	1639	1767	800	977	1257	1184
$R1^a$	710	1483	754	1539	1712	690	798	1245	1154
$R2^b$	0	32	135	83	28	70	45	3	30
$R3^c$		1346	851	1573	1237	1318	615	1141	1203
$R4^d$		26	121	98	29	10	80	31	1

402

Table A6.1 (*cont.*)

	1906	1907	1908	1909	1910	1911	1912^g	1913^h	1914^g
Jan.	10	23	36	124	10	10	90		90
Feb.	41	14	3	124	36	20	10		100
Mar.	6	10	94	114	49	72^e	40		160
Apr.	153	286	270	328	71	151^f	270		150
May	359	168	169	101	154	122^e	195^f		210
June	289	572	253	230	388	560	790		600
July	205	560	70	205	422	590	210		110
Aug.	4	0	9	23	168	170	10		70
Sept.	17	231	231	64	15	220	40		20
Oct.	218	215	247	285	187	330	60		60
Nov.	135	51	134	109	313	240	80		80
Dec.	86	0	12	18	14	40	0		20
Total	1523	2131	1528	1725	1827	2525	1795		1670
$R1^a$	1382	2094	1468	1436	1599	2285	1685		1390
$R2^b$	90	0	21	41	182	210	10		90
$R3^c$	1327	1967	1353	1590	1542	2010	2295		
$R4^d$	34	86	9	35	186	184	50		

Notes:

a R1 is the sum of rains for the current March through July and September through November; it is a measure of growing-season rains.

b R2 is the sum of rains for the current August and December; it is a measure of harvest-season rains.

c R3 is the sum of rains for the current March through July and the prior year's September through November; it is a measure of growing-season rains.

d R4 is the sum of rains for the current August and the prior year's December; it is a measure of harvest-season rains.

e Correction of decimal placement in published source.

f Replacement of missing data with the average rainfall for that month.

g Cotonou.

h Not available.

Sources: Colonie du Dahomey, *Rapport d'Ensemble sur la situation générale de la colonie* (Porto-Novo, 1899–1906); Afrique Occidentale Française, *Rapport d'Ensemble annuel* (Gorée, 1909–10); Afrique Occidentale Française, Gouvernement Général, *Situation générale de l'année 1908* (Gorée); Jean Adam, *Le Palmier à huile* (Paris, 1910), 63–4; Afrique Occidentale Française, Service météorologique, *Résumé des observations météorologiques faites en AOF jusqu'à 31 décembre 1921* (Paris, 1923).

APPENDIX 7

Fiscal flows

Dahomey and AOF each published budgets for every fiscal year. The relevant documents for this analysis, however, are the financial reports: Afrique Occidentale Française, Direction des Finances et de la Comptabilité, *Compte définitif des recettes et des dépenses du budget général*; Colonie du Dahomey, *Compte définitif des recettes et des dépenses du budget local du Dahomey*. At the beginning and the end of the colonial period when these were unavailable or inadequate, figures were drawn from Colonie du Dahomey, *Rapport d'Ensemble*; Afrique Occidentale Française, Gouvernement Général, *Annuaire statistique de L'AOF*, and République du Dahomey, *Bulletin du statistique*. Comparison of all available documents helps to compensate for insufficient reporting on flows of funds between AOF and Dahomey. The format of financial reports changed frequently, making time-series comparisons difficult, especially for expenditures, Successive deposits and withdrawals from reserves artificially inflated reported budget totals; I have reduced published totals to show net movements of reserves only.

Catherine Coquery-Vidrovitch generously made available to me the figures on public finance in Dahomey and AOF compiled as part of a broad and important study which is being completed under her leadership: Recherche Coopérative du Programme 326, CNRS, 'Commerce, investissements et profits dans l'Outre-mer français.' These figures confirm those shown in Tables A7.1 and A7.2, except for small differences. For instance, I included railroads as part of the revenues and expenditures of Dahomey, 1920–34, while Coquery-Vidrovitch's group left them out.

For the era of price stability up to 1914, I included estimates of the payments of AOF salaries in Dahomey and of salary remittances from Dahomey to France; the latter was larger than the former. I did not attempt equivalent estimates for the more complex inflationary period which followed.

Indications of the relative importance of the revenue export from Dahomey are given, for the years after 1914, in columns 14 and 17 of Table A7.2. Earlier, in individual years from 1906 to 1914, the revenue outflow ranged from 8% to 26% of export values, neglecting remittances to France, and averaged over 16%. Assuming the value of exports to have been 15% of GDP, the revenue outflow would then have been 2.4% per year. Calculations of longer-term rates of revenue export range as follows: for the whole period 1890–1914, neglecting remittances to France, 80 million francs were spent, but 105 million francs were collected, yielding a 25% rate of revenue export. For the years 1905–14, and including remittances to France, 42 million francs were spent in Dahomey out of 68 million collected, yielding a 40% rate of revenue export.

404

Table A7.1. *Fiscal flows, 1890–1914 (figures in thousands of francs)*

| | | | | | | | | | | | | | Measures of revenue exports | | | |
Year	1 Customs duties	2 Impôt	3 Other local revenue	4 Grants	5 From reserves	6 Total local revenue	7 Taxes to AOF	8 Taxes collected in Dahomey	9 Remittances Dahomey to France	10 Local government expenditure	11 AOF expenditure in Dahomey	12 Local reserve level	13	14	15	16
1890	203		122			325		325		325*						
1891	411		49			461		461		461*						
1892	607		32			639		639		639*						50
1893	1,002		44			1,046		1,046	50	1,046*				50		100
1894	1,281		240	500		1,521		1,521	100	1,821*		200*	(500)	(400)	(300)	(200)
1895	1,627		68			1,695		1,695	150	1,448*		448*		150	248	398
1896	1,527		39		560	1,565		1,565	150	1,453		560		150	112	262
1897	1,329		134			1,463		1,463	200	2,022		0		200	560	(360)
1898	1,565		105	740		1,670		1,670	200	2,419		0	(740)	(540)	(740)	(540)
1899	2,318	266	125			2,710		2,710	250	2,321		388		250	388	638
1900	2,648	557	209			3,414		3,414	250	2,992		811		250	423	673
1901	3,580	713	221			4,514		4,514	300	3,621		1,703		300	892	1,192
1902	4,427	633	433			5,492		5,492	350	4,543		2,652		350	949	1,299
1903	3,539	664	367			4,571		4,571	400	4,491		2,732		400	80	480
1904	3,753	699	397			4,848		4,848	400	4,556		3,025		400	293	693
1905		696	262	2,170	1,362	3,128	3,168	4,126	400	2,950	1,078	3,202	(80)	320	98	498
1906		780	310	1,886	190	4,339	3,657	4,747	400	4,339	869	1,840	902	1,302	(460)	(60)
1907		1,067	540	1,675		3,471	4,489	6,095	400	3,403	602	1,650	2,212	2,611	2,021	2,421
1908		1,105	525	1,500		3,130	3,145	4,776	400	3,070	298	1,722	1,347	1,747	1,407	1,807
1909		1,247	578	1,480	165	3,470	4,954	6,778	400	3,468	246	1,558	3,228	3,627	3,064	3,463
1910		1,257	802	1,540		3,600	6,687	8,747	450	3,435	511	1,722	4,636	5,086	4,801	5,251
1911		1,281	882	1,700		3,863	7,184	9,347	450	3,582	1,888	2,005	3,596	4,046	3,877	4,327
1912		1,265	942	1,825		4,032	7,170	9,377	500	3,893	1,970	2,144	3,375	3,875	3,514	4,014
1913		1,300	1,118	2,000	124	4,542	5,845	8,263	500	4,542	795	2,021	3,050	3,549	2,926	3,425
1914		1,332	1,086	2,200	346	4,964	3,900	6,317	500	4,937	576	1,674	1,124	1,623	778	1,277

Appendix 7

* Estimate.

1. Customs duties collected by Dahomey.
2. Head tax or *impôt* revenue.
3. Including postal revenues, patents and licenses, railroad revenue and market duties.
4. Grants from France 1894 and 1898; otherwise from AOF.
5. Withdrawals from the Caisse de Réserve of Dahomey.
6. Sum of columns 1 through 5.
7. Customs duties collected by AOF in Dahomey.
8. Sum of columns 1, 2, 3 and 7.
9. Estimated from reports of the Banque de l'Afrique Occidentale, from the level of government expenditure and from European population.
10. From *Comptes définitifs*, 1896–1914. Assumed to be equal to revenue 1890–3, then allowing for build-up of 448 thousand francs in reserves in 1894–5.
11. Recorded AOF expenditure on construction in Dahomey, plus 200 thousand francs per year for Dahomean and European salaries paid in Dahomey.
12. Level of reserves at the conclusion of each fiscal year.
13. Net revenue export, measured as column 7 less column 4 less column 11. This corresponds to tax exports less grants less AOF expenditures.
14. Net revenue export, measured as column 7 plus column 9 less column 4 less column 11. This corresponds to tax and other remittances less grants less AOF expenditures.
15. Net revenue export, measured as column 7 plus the change in column 12 less column 4 less column 11. This corresponds to reserve growth and tax remittances less grants less AOF expenditures.
16. Net revenue export, measured as column 7 plus column 9 plus the change in column 12 less column 4 less column 11. This corresponds to reserve growth, tax and other remittances less grants less AOF expenditures.

Table A7.2. *Fiscal flows, 1915–60 (figures in millions of francs)*

Year	1 Local taxes	2 Grants to Dahomey	3 From local reserves	4 Total local revenue	5 Taxes to AOF	6 Taxes collected in Dahomey
1915	3.4	0.7		4.1	2.7	6.1
1916	4.1	0.7		4.8	4.0	8.1
1917	4.5			4.5	4.2	8.7
1918	5.3			5.3	4.1	9.4
1919	6.1			6.1	6.8	12.9
1920	7.7	1.0		8.7	11.2	18.9
1921	8.1		0.7	8.8	8.7	16.8
1922	10.0			10.0	10.0	20.0
1923	11.1	0.6		11.7	15.6	26.7
1924	14.0			14.0	25.0	39.0
1925	17.0	0.1		17.1	26.1	43.1
1926	26.5			26.5	34.9	61.4
1927	38.0			38.0	35.2	73.2
1928	35.1		0.4	35.5	44.2	79.3
1929	35.5	0.7	6.1	42.3	39.5	75.0
1930	51.6	1.0	0.4	53.0	40.0	91.6
1931	39.7	0.5	3.1	43.3	26.7	66.4
1932	30.8	0.4		31.2	20.4	51.2
1933	25.1	0.1		25.2	15.9	41.0
1934	27.9	2.7	5.4	36.0	14.4	42.3
1935	25.6	7.5		33.1	16.7	42.3
1936	28.1	8.2		36.3	24.8	52.9
1937	34.5	9.1		43.6	35.9	70.4
1938	41.9	8.7	2.6	53.2	31.1	73.0
1939	56.4	6.2		62.6	36.5	92.9
1940	54.0	0.3		54.3	25.3	79.3
1941	48.2	1.6	8.2	58.0	23.6	71.8
1942	60	24		84	39	99
1943	80			80	48	128
1944	92			92	47	139
1945	81	46	5	132	44	125
1946	120	84	4	208	117	237
1947	151	100	17	268	233	384
1948	257	306		563	447	704
1949	387	593	4	984	722	1109
1950	538	493		1036	812	1350
1951	562	870	28	1460	1167	1729
1952	1078	757		1835	1049	2127
1953	1180	802	23	2005	1189	2369
1954	1311	830		2141	1581	2892
1955	1375	909	99	2383	1685	3060
1956		1086			2138	
1957	1333	1634		2967	2200	3533
1958	1572*	2087		3659		
1959	3483*	1718		5201		
1960	4224*	1056		5280	4224	5550

407

Appendix 7

Table A7.2 (*cont.*)

Year	7 Local government expenditure	8 AOF expenditure in Dahomey	9 Dahomey reserves	10 AOF reserves	11 Revenue export to AOF
1915	3.8		1.2	2.6	2.0
1916	3.9		1.7	2.6	3.3
1917	4.2		1.7	4.2	4.2
1918	4.6		2.7	4.3	4.1
1919	6.1		2.7	4.3	6.8
1920	8.7		2.8	10.8	10.2
1921	9.4		2.1	24.6	8.7
1922	10.7		2.1	37.8	10.0
1923	10.4		4.0	44.6	15.0
1924	11.8	0.4	5.3	71.8	24.6
1925	14.8		7.8		26.0
1926	19.6	2.6	13.7	142.7	32.3
1927	31.2	8.3	15.7	94.0	26.9
1928	32.1	12.6	15.3	84.2	31.6
1929	39.7	13.5	9.2	112.4	25.3
1930	45.8	23.1	8.8	77.6	16.9
1931	42.1	18.1	5.7	26.6	8.1
1932	39.8	0.7	6.3	10.6	19.3
1933	33.8		6.3	48.4	15.8
1934	33.8	4.5	0.9	19.3	7.2
1935	32.3		2.0	44.6	9.2
1936	32.9		3.0	7.7	16.6
1937	37.2		6.8	44.1	26.1
1938	51.0		4.2	116.8	22.4
1939	57.4		11.4	218	30.3
1940	53.8		14.1	175	25.0
1941	60.0		5.9	161	22.0
1942	76		10.0	249	15.0
1943	67		15.0	236	47.7
1944	72	2.2	29.6	279	44.9
1945	131		24.6	678	(2.0)
1946	208		20.6	476	33
1947	268		3.5	1394	133
1948	562		4.3	2528	141
1949	984		0.2	3867	129
1950	987		50	4771	314
1951	1441		22	8568	297
1952	1787		71	4660	292
1953	1981		48	2713	387
1954	2042		110	8902	751
1955	2301		11	7373	776
1956				6532	
1957	3533			8227	
1958					
1959	5550				(1326)
1960					

408

12 Revenue in 1908 francs	13 Expenditure in 1908 francs	14 Revenue export in 1908 francs	15 Revenue as percent of exports	16 Expenditure as percent of exports	17 Revenue export as percent of exports
5.9	3.7	1.9	46	29	15
6.8	3.3	2.8	42	21	17
5.5	2.7	2.7	45	22	22
3.6	1.8	1.6	31	15	14
5.4	2.6	2.9	18	9	10
4.2	2.0	2.3	30	14	16
5.3	3.0	2.8	46	26	24
7.7	4.1	3.9	48	26	24
8.2	3.2	4.6	48	19	27
7.9	2.5	5.0	39	12	24
7.0	2.4	4.2	34	12	21
7.0	2.5	3.7	34	12	18
11.6	6.3	4.3	54	29	20
11.7	6.6	4.7	81	46	32
12.3	8.7	4.1	62	44	21
19.8	14.9	3.7	73	55	13
21.6	19.6	2.6	98	89	12
23.5	18.6	8.9	118	93	44
26.3	21.7	10.1	148	122	57
34.1	30.9	5.8	124	112	21
24.7	18.9	5.4	75	57	16
21.4	13.3	6.7	59	36	18
16.3	8.6	6.1	58	30	21
13.5	9.4	4.4	64	45	20
26.4	16.3	8.6	100	62	33
19.3	13.1	6.1	112	76	35
17.3	14.4	5.3	63	53	19
13.0	10.0	2.0	74	57	11
14.3	7.5	5.3	108	56	40
15.3	7.9	4.9	86	45	28
12.5	13.1	(0.2)	84	89	(1)
13.1	11.5	1.8	137	120	19
11.8	8.2	4.1	113	79	40
9.7	7.8	2.0	46	37	9
14.1	12.5	1.6	59	54	7
13.2	9.7	3.1	60	44	14
12.0	10.0	2.1	62	51	11
22.1	18.6	3.0	110	92	15
23.0	19.2	3.8	91	76	15
28.6	20.2	7.4	115	81	30
33.6	25.3	8.5	112	84	28
37.6	36.4		114	144	
40.5	40.5	(9.7)	103	136	(33)

Appendix 7

Notes to columns

* Includes 385 million francs in customs duties for 1958, 1,914 million francs for 1959, and 2,529 million francs for 1960.
1. *Impôt* and other revenue collected by the government of Dahomey.
2. Grants from AOF and from France.
3. Net withdrawals from reserves, estimated as the amounts of any decline in local reserves (column 9).
4. Sum of columns 1, 2 and 3.
5. Customs duties collected by AOF in Dahomey.
6. Sum of columns 1 and 5.
7. Local government expenditure for all purposes except reserves.
8. AOF expenditures for construction in Dahomey. Salaries to AOF employees working in Dahomey are neglected.
9. Level of reserves at the conclusion of each fiscal year.
10. Level of AOF reserves at the conclusion of each fiscal year.
11. Column 5 less column 2 less column 8. This corresponds to column 13 in Table A7.1.
12. Column 6 deflated by the export price index in Table A5.2.
13. The sum of columns 7 and 8 deflated by the export price index.
14. Column 11 deflated by the export price index.
15. Column 6 as a percentage of current total export value (Table A4.6).
16. The sum of columns 7 and 8 as a percentage of current export value.
17. Column 11 as a percentage of current export value.

410

APPENDIX 8

Money supply of colonial Dahomey

Table A8.1 provides an estimate of the money supply, calculated as the sum of net money imports. Imports and exports of money are listed in Table A4.3, France, Agence générale des Colonics, *Statistiques du commerce des colonies françaises*, and Afrique Occidentale Française, Gouvernement Général, *Situation générale*. Money imports show a strong correlation with export values, and money exports show an inverse correlation with export values: estimates for missing data (especially for money exports) were constructed based on this correlation. The result, the sum of net imports, may be taken as a proxy for the money supply after 1900.

Sources for Table A8.2 are Banque de l'Afrique Occidentale, *Rapport* (for the years up to 1938); Afrique Occidentale Française, Gouvernement Général, *Annuaire statistique* (for subsequent years); and Tables A4.4, A4.6, and A5.2.

Table A8.1. *Money imports and exports, 1890–1914 (in millions of francs)*

Year	1 Money imports	2 Money exports	3 Net imports	4 Estimated money supply
1889				
1890	0.37	0.05	0.32	0.32
1891	0.79	0.05	0.74	1.06
1892	0.83	0.06	0.77	1.83
1893	1.30	0.06	1.24	3.07
1894	1.71	0.04	1.67	4.74
1895	1.19	0.03	1.16	5.90
1896	0.60	0.09	0.51	6.41
1897	0.51	0.11	0.40	6.81
1898	0.73	0.10	0.63	7.44
1899	1.75	0.02	1.73	9.17
1900	1.88	0.03	1.84	11.01
1901	1.15	0.10	1.05	12.06
1902	1.36	0.11	1.25	13.31
1903	0.78	0.13	0.65	13.96
1904	1.20	0.11	1.09	15.05
1905	0.50	0.13	0.37	15.42
1906	0.37	0.20	0.17	15.59
1907	1.06	0.13	0.93	16.52
1908	0.22	0.33	(0.11)	16.41
1909	1.30	0.27	1.03	17.44
1910	1.40	0.22	1.18	18.62
1911	1.80	0.17	1.63	20.25
1912	1.80	0.10	1.70	21.95
1913	0.22	0.18	0.04	21.99
1914	0.12	0.17	(0.05)	21.94

Notes to columns

1. Recorded and estimated imports of sterling and francs.
2. Recorded and estimated exports of sterling and francs.
3. Column 1 less column 2.
4. Sum of net imports for all preceding years, beginning with 1890. After 1900 this can be taken as an estimate of the value of the money supply in southern Dahomey.

Table A8.2. *BAO notes in circulation, 1903–60 (in millions of francs)*

Year	1 BAO notes in circulation	2 Percent current export value	3 BAO notes in 1908 francs
1903	0.16	1.7	0.16
1904	0.44	4.0	0.49
1905	0.65	8.5	0.71
1906	0.68	8.0	0.74
1907	0.78	8.0	0.80
1908	1.27	10.5	1.3
1909	1.16	7.1	1.2
1910	1.14	6.3	1.1
1911	2.15	9.8	1.7
1912	1.63	7.6	1.2
1913	1.87	11.4	1.4
1914	2.02	15.6	1.3
1915	1.89	14.4	1.8
1916	3.1	16.5	2.6
1917	5.1	26	3.2
1918	7.1	24	2.7
1919	14.2	20	6.0
1920	24.4	38	5.5
1921	15.3	42	4.9
1922	23.0	55	8.9
1923	31	56	9.6
1924	43	43	8.8
1925	49	39	8.0
1926	64	35	7.3
1927	69	51	10.9
1928	77	79	11.3
1929	86	71	14.0
1930	39	31	8.6
1931	29	44	9.6
1932	31	71	14.2
1933	5.7	21	3.7
1934	5.3	16	4.3
1935	5.3	9.5	3.1
1936	13.2	15	5.4
1937	43	35	9.9
1938	48	42	8.9
1939	62	67	17
1940	88	124	21
1941	137	118	33
1942	321	240	42
1943	525	440	58
1944	492	302	52
1945	129	87	13.5
1946	202	117	11.8
1947	384	113	11.1
1948	998	66	14.1

Table A8.2 (*cont.*)

Year	1 BAO notes in circulation	2 Percent current export value	3 BAO notes in 1908 francs
1949	1,856	99	22
1950	1,987	89	19
1951	2,777	99	19
1952	3,697	191	39
1953	4,559	175	44
1954	4,924	196	49
1955	4,850	177	54

Notes to columns

1. BAO notes in circulation at end of fiscal year indicated.
2. BAO notes in circulation as a percent of the value of current exports.
3. Deflating with the export price index shown in Table A5.2.

Bibliography

I. Archives

Bénin. Archives nationales, Porto-Novo.
    Registres de correspondance, 1889–95 (bound volumes).
    Mouvement commerciel, 1889–95 (bound volume).
    2-D. Rapports mensuels des cercles, 1905–14.
    2-D-72. Affaire Rouhaud, 1912.
    1-E-1. Affaire Alihonou–Kakarakou, 1908.
    1-E-42. Dossier Pohizoun, 1912.
    2-E-23. Cercle de Ouidah, politique, 1910–38.
    2-E-26. Porto-Novo et banlieue, 1908–14.
    5-E. Mono (frontières), 1885–1907.
    19-E. Islam, 1906–23.
    K. Mono, 1917.
    1-Q. Mouvement caravanier, 1909.
    Q. Douanes (not classified).
    R. Agriculture (not classified).
Senegal. Archives nationales, Dakar.
    8G12. Affaire Adjovi–Kenney, 1904–18.
    K22. Enquête sur la captivité au Dahomey, 1904.
    P98 through P109. Dahomey, Travaux publics, 1900–20.
France, Archives nationales, Section Outre-mer, Paris.
    Dahomey IX-3. Régime douanier, 1889–91.
    Dahomey IX-7. Douanes, 1890–5.
Great Britain. Public Record Office, Kew.
    C. O. 151. Blue Books for Lagos Colony, 1863–95.
S.M.A. Fathers Archives, Tenafly, New Jersey, USA.
    Fr A. Guilcher, 'Dahomey' (typescript).

II. Official publications

Afrique Occidentale Française, Gouvernement Général. *Annuaire du Gouvernement General de l'AOF.* Paris, 1900, 1903–21.
    Annuaire statistique de l'AOF. Vol. 1, 1933–4; Vol. 2, 1934–6; Vol. 3, 1936–8; Vol. 4, 1939–49; Vol. 5, 1950–4; Vol. 6, 1955–7.
    Direction des Finances et de la Comptabilité. *Compte définitif des recettes et des*

415

dépenses du budget général. Gorée, 1905–57.

Direction de Mécanographic et de la Statistique. *Le Commerce extérieur de l'AOF.* Dakar, 1939–55.

Le Dahomey. Corbeil, 1906.

Le Dahomey. Paris, 1931.

Rapport d'Ensemble annuel. Gorée, 1909, 1910, 1913.

Situation générale (also titled *Statistiques générales*) Gorée, 1907–9.

Statistiques du commerce extérieur de l'AOF. Gorée, 1939–51.

Agence économique. *Bulletin mensuel.* Gorée, 1921–3, 1929–39.

Service météorologique. *Résumé des observations météorologiques faits en AOF jusqu'à 31 décembre 1921.* Paris, 1923.

Banque de l'Afrique Occidentale. *Rapport.* Dakar, 1904–35, 1939.

Banque Centrale des Etats de l'Afrique de l'Ouest. *Notes d'informations et statistiques.* Dakar, 1959–64.

Dahomey, Colonie du. *Compte définitif des recettes et des dépenses du budget local du Dahomey.* Porto-Novo, 1897–1957.

Journal officiel du Dahomey. Porto-Novo, 1889–1934.

Notice sur l'agriculture au Dahomey. Porto-Novo, 1917.

Rapport d'Ensemble sur la situation générale de la colonie. Porto-Novo, 1898–1902, 1904–6.

Dahomey, République du. *Bulletin du statistique.* Cotonou, 1963, 1968, 1973.

Etude sur la pêche lagunaire, 1962–1965. Nogent-sur-Marne, 1965.

Etude de la pêche maritime et de ses possibilités de développement au Dahomey. Cotonou, 1962.

France. Agence générale des Colonies. *Renseignements généraux sur le commerce des colonies françaises, 1914–1917.* Paris, 1918.

Renseignements généraux sur le commerce des colonies françaises et la navigation. Paris, 1918–28.

Statistiques des chemins de fer des colonies françaises jusqu'à 1910. Paris, 1911.

Statistiques des finances des colonies françaises pour les années 1902–1911. Melun, 1912.

Statistiques du commerce des colonies françaises. Paris, 1897–1914.

France. Ministère des Colonies. *Statistiques coloniales.* Paris, 1882–96.

France. Secrétariat d'Etat aux Colonies. *Les Exportations agricoles des Cercles de l'AOF et du Togo français.* Paris, 1944.

United Kingdom. House of Commons Sessional Papers (Parliamentary Papers). Statistical Abstracts for Lagos Colony, 1867–99.

Accounts of Trade and Navigation, 1891–1915.

Annual Statements of Trade, 1891–1915.

United States Bureau of the Census. *Historical Statistics of the United States, Colonial Times to 1957. Washington,* 1961.

III. Books and Articles

Adam, Jean. *Le Palmier à huile.* Paris, 1910.

Le Cocotier. Paris, 1915.

Adams, Capt. John. *Remarks on the Country Extending from Cape Palmas to the River Congo.* London, 1966. (First published 1823.)

Adandé, Alexandre. 'Regard rétrospectif sur l'économie africaine et perspective de développement agricole au Dahomey.' *Etudes dahoméennes*, n.s. 1 (1963), 7–16.

Afana, Osendé. *L'Economie de l'Ouest africain: perspectives de développement.* Paris, 1977.

Agbo, Casimir. *Histoire de Ouidah du XVIᵉ au XXᵉ siècle.* Avignon, 1959.

Aguessy, Cyrille. 'Esclavage, colonisation et traditions au Dahomey (sud).' *Présence africaine*, n.s. 6 (1956), 58–67.

Aguessy, Honorat. 'Le Dan-Homê du XIXᵉ siécle était-il une société esclavagiste?' *Revue française d'Etudes politiques africaines*, 50 (1970), 71–91.

Ajayi, J. F. A. 'Colonialism: an Episode in African History.' In L. H. Gann and Peter Duignan, eds., *Colonialism in Africa*, 5 vols. (Cambridge, 1969), I: 497–508.

Akindélé, Adolphe, and Cyrille Aguessy. *Contribution à l'étude de l'histoire de l'ancien royaume de Porto-Novo.* Dakar, 1953.

Akinjogbin, I. A. 'Archibald Dalzel: Slave Trader and Historian of Dahomey.' *Journal of African History 7*, 1 (1966), 67–78.

Dahomey and its Neighbours, 1708–1818. Cambridge, 1967.

'The Expansion of Oyo and the Rise of Dahomey, 1600–1800.' In J. F. A. Ajayi and Michael Crowder, eds., *History of West Africa*, 2 vols. (London, 1971), I: 304–43.

Alapini, Julien. *Le petit dahoméen: grammaire, vocabulaire, lexique en langue de Dahomey.* Paris, 1950.

Les Noix sacrées. Monte Carlo, c. 1950.

Albéca, Alexandre d'. *Les Etablissements français du golfe du Bénin.* Paris, 1889.

La France au Dahomey. Paris, 1895.

Almeida Prato, J. F. de. 'Les Relations de Bahia avec le Dahomey.' *Revue d'Histoire des Colonies* (1954), 167–226.

Almeida-Topor, Hélène d'. 'Les Populations dahoméennes et le recrutement militaire pendant la première guerre mondiale.' *Revue française d'Histoire d'Outre-mer 60*, 219 (1973), 196–241.

'Recherches sur l'évolution du travail salarié en AOF pendant la crise économique, 1930–36.' *Cahiers d'Etudes africaines 16*, 61–2 (1976), 103–18.

Amin, Samir. *L'Afrique de l'Ouest bloquée.* Paris, 1971.

Le Développement inégal. Paris, 1973.

Anstey, Roger. *The Atlantic Slave Trade and British Abolition, 1760–1810.* Cambridge, 1975.

'The Historical Debate on the Abolition of the British Slave Trade.' In Roger Anstey and P. E. H. Hair, eds., *Liverpool, the African Slave Trade, and Abolition* (Bristol, 1976), 157–66.

Antheaume, Benoit. 'La Palmeraie du Mono: approche géographique.' *Cahiers d'Etudes africaines 12*, 47 (1972), 458–84.

Argyle, W. J. *The Fon of Dahomey.* Oxford, 1966.

Armstrong, Robert G. *The Study of West African Languages.* Ibadan, 1964.

417

Bibliography

Arnold, Rosemary. 'A Port of Trade: Whydah on the Guinea Coast.' In Karl Polanyi and others, eds., *Trade and Market in the Early Empires* (Glencoe, Ill., 1957), 154–76.

'Separation of Trade and Market: Great Market of Whydah.' In Karl Polanyi and others, eds., *Trade and Market in the Early Empires* (Glencoe, Ill., 1957), 177–87.

Asiwaju, I. A. 'The Alaketu of Ketu and the Onimẹkọ of Mẹkọ: the Changing Status of Two Yoruba Rulers under French and British Rule.' In Michael Crowder and Obaro Ikimẹ, eds., *West African Chiefs* (New York, 1970), 134–60.

Western Yorubaland under European Rule, 1889–1945. London, 1976.

Atanda, J. A. *The New Oyo Empire.* London, 1973.

Atkins, John. *A Voyage to Guinea, Brasil, and the West-Indies.* London, 1737.

Aubréville. A. 'Les Forêts du Dahomey et du Togo.' *Bulletin du Comité d'Etudes historiques et scientifiques de l'AOF 20*, 1 (1937), 1–112.

Aupiais, Fr Francis. 'Le Travail forcé.' *Revue apologétique* (Aug. 1929). (As cited in Hardy, Georges, *Un Apôtre d'aujourd'hui: le révérend Père Aupiais*, Paris, 1949.)

Baillaud, Emile. *La Situation économique de l'Afrique occidentale anglaise et française.* Paris, 1907.

Ballard, John A. 'The Porto-Novo Incidents of 1923: Politics in the Colonial Era.' *Odu 2*, 1 (1965), 52–75.

Barbot, John. *A Description of the Coasts of North and South Guinea.* In A. Churchill, ed., *A Collection of Voyages and Travels* (London, 1732), V.

Bastide, Roger, and Pierre Verger. 'Contribution à l'étude sociologique des marchés nagô du Bas-Dahomey.' *Humanités 1*, 95 (1959), 33–65.

Batsch, Christophe. 'Le Togo et la crise: contrasts régionaux et dépendance accrue.' *Revue française d'Histoire d'Outre-mer 63*, 232–3 (1976), 590–600.

Bay, Edna. 'On the Trail of the Bush King: a Dahomean lesson in the use of evidence.' *History in Africa 6* (1979), 1–15.

Bean, Richard Nelson. 'A Note on the Relative Importance of Slaves and Gold in West African Exports.' *Journal of African History 15*, 3 (1974), 351–6.

The British Trans-Atlantic Slave Trade, 1650–1775. New York, 1975.

Berbain, Simone. *Le Comptoir français de Juda au XVIIIᵉ siècle.* Paris, 1942.

Berg, Elliot J. 'The Economic Basis of Political Choice in French West Africa.' *American Political Science Review 54*, 2 (1960), 391–405.

Bernard, M. 'Le Cocotier dans le golfe du Bénin.' *Etudes dahoméennes*, 1 (1948), 20–46.

Berry, Sara S. *Cocoa, Custom and Socio-Economic Change in Rural Western Nigeria.* Oxford, 1975.

Bertho, Jacques. 'La Parenté des Yorouba aux peuplades de Dahomey et de Togo.' *Africa 19*, 2 (1949), 121–32.

Biobaku, Saburi O. *The Egba and their Neighbours, 1842–1872.* Oxford, 1957.

Birmingham, David. *Trade and Conflict in Angola.* Oxford, 1966.

Blake, John W. *West Africa: Quest for God and Gold, 1454–1578*, 2nd edn. London, 1977.

418

Blanchard, M. 'Administrateurs en Afrique noire.' *Revue d'Histoire des Colonies 9*, 40 (1953), 377–430.

Bobrie, François. 'L'Investissement public en Afrique noire française entre 1924 et 1938: contribution méthodologique.' *Revue française d'Histoire d'Outre-mer 63*, 232–3 (1976), 459–76.

Boeke, J. H. *Economics and Economic Policy of Dual Societies.* New York, 1953.

Bosman, William. *A New and Accurate Description of the Coast of Guinea.* London, 1967. (First published in 1705.)

Bouche, Denise. *Les Villages de liberté en Afrique noire française, 1887–1910.* Paris, 1968.

  L'Enseignement dans les territoires françaises de l'Afrique occidentale de 1817 à 1920, 2 vols. Paris, 1975.

Bouche, Pierre B. *Sept ans en Afrique occidentale: la Côte des Esclaves: le Dahomey.* Paris, 1885.

Bourgoignie, Georges Edouard. *Les Hommes de l'eau: ethno-écologie du Dahomey lacustre.* Paris, 1972.

Bowser, Frederick. *The African Slave in Colonial Peru, 1524–1650.* Stanford, 1974.

Boxer, C. R. *The Dutch in Brazil, 1624–54.* Oxford, 1957.

Brasseur, Georges. *La Palmeraie de Porto-Novo.* Dakar, 1953.

Brasseur-Marion, Paule. *Porto-Novo et sa palmeraie.* Dakar, 1953.

  'Cotonou, Porte de Dahomey.' *Cahiers d'Outre-mer 24*, 6 (1953), 364–78.

Brooks, George E., Jr. *Yankee Traders, Old Coasters and African Middlemen.* Boston, 1970.

Brunet, L., and Louis Giethlen. *Dahomey et dépendances.* Paris, 1900.

Brunschwig, Henri. *L'Expansion allemande outre-mer.* Paris, 1957.

Buell, Raymond Leslie. *The Native Problem in Africa*, 2 vols. New York, 1928.

Buffe, J. 'Les Pêcheries en branchage "acadja" des lagunes du Bas-Dahomey.' *Bois et Forêts des Tropiques* (July–Aug. 1958), 19–24.

Burton, Richard. *A Mission to Gelele, King of Dahome*, 2 vols. London, 1864.

Caldwell, J. C. 'Major Questions in African Demographic History.' In University of Edinburgh, Centre of African Studies, *African Historical Demography* (Edinburgh, 1977), 7–22.

Capet, Marcel. *Traité d'économie tropicale: les économies d'AOF?* Paris, 1958.

Challenor, Herschelle S. 'Strangers as Colonial Intermediaries: the Dahomeyans in Francophone Africa.' In William S. Shack and Elliott P. Skinner, eds., *Strangers in African Societies* (Berkeley, 1979), 67–83.

Chenery, Hollis B., and Paul G. Clark. *Interindustry Economics.* New York, 1959.

Chevalier, Auguste. *Les Kolatiers et les noix de kola.* Paris, 1909.

  L'Exploitation du caoutchouc et la culture des plantes productrices au Dahomey. Paris, 1910.

  'La Culture du maïs en Afrique occidentale et spécialement au Dahomey.' *Journal d'Agriculture tropicale*, 111 (1910), 269–73.

Clapperton, Hugh. *Journal of a Second Expedition into the Interior of Africa from the Bight of Benin to Soccatoo.* London, 1829.

419

Bibliography

Clemens, Ursula, Wolfgang Hildebrand and Thomas Kessler. *Dahomey und seine wirtschaftsräumliche Gliederung*. Hamburg, 1970.

Clerc, J., P. Adam and C. Tardits. *Société paysanne et problèmes fonciers de la palmeraie dahoméenne*. Paris, 1956.

Coatsworth, John J. 'Obstacles to Economic Growth in Nineteenth-Century Mexico.' *American Historical Review 83*, 1 (1978), 80–100.

Conrad, Alfred H., and John R. Meyer. 'The Economics of Slavery in the Ante Bellum South.' *Journal of Political Economy 66* (1958), 95–130.

Coquery, Catherine. 'Le Blocus de Whydah (1876–77) et la rivalité franco-anglaise au Dahomey.' *Cahiers d'Etudes africaines 2*, 7 (1962), 373–419.

Coquery-Vidrovitch, Catherine. 'La Fête des coutumes au Dahomey: historique et essai d'interprétation.' *Annales – Economies, Sociétés, Civilisations 19*, 4 (1964), 696–714.

'Recherches sur un mode de production africain.' *La Pensée*, 144 (1969), 61–78.

'De la traite des esclaves à l'exportation de l'huile de palme et des palmistes au Dahomey au XIXe siécle.' In Claude Meillassoux, ed., *The Development of Indigenous Trade and Markets in West Africa* (London, 1971), 107–23.

Le Congo au temps des grandes compagnies concessionnaires, 1898–1930. Paris, 1972.

'L'Impact des intérêts coloniaux: SCOA et CFAO dans l'Ouest africain, 1910–65.' *Journal of African History 16*, 4 (1975), 595–621.

'La Mise en dépendance de l'Afrique noire: essai de périodisation, 1800–1970.' *Cahiers d'Etudes africaines 16*, 61–2 (1976), 7–57.

'L'Afrique coloniale française et la crise de 1930: crise structurelle et genèse du sous-développement: rapport d'ensemble.' *Revue française d'Histoire d'Outre-mer 63*, 232–3 (1976), 386–424.

'Mutation de l'impérialisme colonial français dans les années 30.' *African Economic History*, 4 (1977), 103–52.

Cornevin, Robert. *Histoire du Dahomey*. Paris, 1962.

Cosnier, Henri. *L'Ouest africain français, ses ressources agricoles, son organisation économique*. Paris, 1921.

Couchard, A. *Au Moyen-Dahomey: notes sur le cercle de Savé*. Bordeaux, 1911.

Courdioux, E. 'La Côte des Esclaves: XXVI: monnaies.' *Les Missions catholiques 10* (1878), 538–9.

Coursey, D. G. *The Yam*. London, 1967.

'The Origins and Domestication of Yams in West Africa.' In Jack R. Harlan, Jan M. J. de Wet and Ann B. L. Stemler, eds., *Origins of African Plant Domestication* (The Hague, 1976), 383–408.

Crowder, Michael. *Senegal: A Study in French Assimilation Policy*. New York, 1962.

Crozon, H. 'Le Tabac au Dahomey: historique et culture actuelle.' *Etudes dahoméennes*, 4 (1950), 23–7.

Curtin, Philip D. *The Atlantic Slave Trade: a Census*. Madison, 1969.

Economic Change in Precolonial Africa: Senegambia in the Era of the Slave Trade, 2 vols. Madison, 1975.

'Measuring the Atlantic Slave Trade.' In Stanley L. Engerman and Eugene D. Genovese, eds., *Race and Slavery in the Western Hemisphere: Quantitative Studies* (Princeton, 1975), 107–28.

'Measuring the Atlantic Slave Trade once again.' *Journal of African History 17*, 4 (1976), 595–606.

Curtin, Philip D., and Jan Vansina. 'Sources of the Nineteenth-Century Atlantic Slave Trade.' *Journal of African History 5*, 2 (1964), 185–208.

Da Cruz, Clément. 'Les Bois de construction dans le cercle de Porto-Novo.' *Etudes dahoméennes*, 8 (1952), 25–56.

Dalzel, Archibald. *The History of Dahomy, an Inland Kingdom of Africa*. London, 1967. (First published 1793.)

Dalziel, J. M. *The Useful Plants of West Tropical Africa*. London, 1948.

Dapper, O. *Description de l'Afrique*. Amsterdam, 1686.

Davidson, Basil. *Black Mother: the Years of the African Slave Trade*. London, 1961.

Davies, K. G. *The Royal African Company*. London, 1957.

Davis, David Brion. *The Problem of Slavery in the Age of Revolution*. New York, 1975.

Deane, Phyllis, and W. A. Cole. *British Economic Growth, 1688–1959*. Cambridge, 1964.

Debien, G., and others. 'Les Origines des esclaves des Antilles.' *Bulletin de l'IFAN 23* (1961), 363–87; *25* (1963), 1–41, 215–66; *26* (1964), 166–211, 601–75; *27* (1965), 319–71, 755–90; *29* (1967), 536–58.

Decalo, Samuel. *Historical Dictionary of Dahomey*. Metuchen, N.J., 1976.

Delafosse, Maurice. *Manuel dahoméen*. Paris, 1894.

Desanti, H. *Du Danhomé au Bénin–Niger*. Paris, 1945.

Dissou, Machioudi. 'Développement et mise en valeur des plantations de palmier à huile au Dahomey.' *Cahiers d'Etudes africaines 12*, 47 (1972), 485–99.

Duncan, John. *Travels in Western Africa in 1845 and 1846*, 2 vols. London, 1847.

Dunglas, Edouard. 'La Pêche dans le Bas-Ouémé.' *Bulletin du Comité d'Etudes historiques et scientifiques de l'AOF 20*, 3 (1937), 350–9.

'Contribution à l'histoire du Moyen-Dahomey.' *Etudes dahoméennes*, 19 and 20 (1957).

'Adjohon: étude historique.' *Etudes dahoméennes* n.s. 8 (1966), 57–74.

Dupré, Georges, and Pierre-Philippe Rey. 'Reflections on the Pertinence of a Theory of the History of Exchange.' *Economy and Society 2*, 2 (1973), 131–63.

Echenberg, Myron. 'Paying the Blood Tax: Military Conscription in French West Africa.' *Canadian Journal of African Studies 9*, 2 (1975), 171–92.

Edinburgh, University of, Centre of African Studies. *African Historical Demography*. Edinburgh, 1977.

Ekundare, R. O. *An Economic History of Nigeria, 1860–1960*. London, 1973.

Elbée, Sieur d'. 'Journal du voyage du Sieur d'Elbée . . . en l'année 1669.' In Clodoré, J., ed., *Relation de ce qui s'est passé dans les isles et terre-firme de l'Amérique . . .*, 2 vols. (Paris, 1671), II:347–558.

Abridged version of the above in Jean-Baptiste Labat, *Voyage du Chevalier des Marchais*, 4 vols. (Paris, 1730), II:286–364.

421

Bibliography

Ellingworth, Paul. 'Christianity and Politics in Dahomey, 1843–1867.' *Journal of African History 5*, 2 (1964), 209–20.

Ellis, Alfred B. *The Ewe-Speaking Peoples of the Slave-Coast of West Africa.* London, 1890.

Elwert, Georg. *Wirtschaft und Herrchaft von 'Dāxome' (Dahomey) im 18. Jahrhundert: Ökonomie des Sklavenraubs und Gesellschaftsstruktur 1724 bis 1818.* Munich, 1973.

Engerman, Stanley L., and Eugene D. Genovese, eds. *Race and Slavery in the Western Hemisphere: Quantitative Studies.* Princeton, 1975.

Fage, J. D. 'Slavery and the Slave Trade in the Context of West African History.' *Journal of African History 10*, 3 (1969), 393–404.

    A History of West Africa, 4th edn. Cambridge, 1969.

    'The Effect of the Export Slave Trade on African Populations.' In R. P. Moss and R. J. A. Rathbone, eds., *The Population Factor in African Studies* (London, 1975), 15–23.

Fallers, Lloyd A. 'Are African Cultivators to be Called "Peasants"?' *Current Anthropology 2* (1961), 108–11.

Foà, Edouard. *Le Dahomey.* Paris, 1895.

Fogel, Robert W. 'The New Economic History: its Findings and its Methods.' *Economic History Review 19* (1966), 642–56.

Fogel, Robert W., and Stanley L. Engerman. *Time on the Cross*, 2 vols. Boston, 1974.

Foltz, William J. *From French West Africa to the Mali Federation.* New Haven, 1965.

Fonssagrives, Jean Baptiste. *Notice sur le Dahomey.* Paris, 1900.

Forbes, Capt. Frederick E. *Dahomey and the Dahomans*, 2 vols. London, 1851.

Forde, Daryll. *The Yoruba-Speaking Peoples of South-Western Nigeria.* London, 1951.

François, G. *Notre colonie du Dahomey.* Paris, 1906.

Freeman, Thomas B. *Journal of Various Visits to the Kingdoms of Ashanti, Kaku and Dahomi, in Western Africa.* London, 1844.

Fugelstad, Finn. 'Quelques reflexions sur l'histoire et les institutions de l'ancien royaume du Dahomey et de ses voisins.' *Bulletin de l'IFAN 39* (1977), 493–517.

Gaillard, le Dr. 'Etude sur les lacustres du Bas-Dahomey.' *L'Anthropologie' Paris 17* (1907), 99–125.

Gann, L. H., and Peter Duignan. *Burden of Empire.* New York, 1967. —— ——

    ,eds. *Colonialism in Africa: Vol. I, The History and Politics of Colonialism, 1870–1914.* Cambridge, 1969.

Garcia, Luc. 'Les Mouvements de résistance au Dahomey (1914–1917).' *Cahiers d'Etudes africaines 10*, 37 (1970), 144–78.

    'L'Organisation de l'instruction publique au Dahomey, 1894–1920.' *Cahiers d'Etudes africaines 11*, 41 (1971), 59–100.

    'Archives et tradition orale: à propos d'une enquête sur la politique du royaume du Danhomé à la fin du 19ᵉ siècle.' *Cahiers d'Etudes africaines 16*, 61–2 (1976), 189–206.

Gavoy, l'Administrateur. 'Note historique sur Ouidah.' *Etudes dahoméennes*, 13 (1955), 47–70.

Gemery, Henry A., and Jan S. Hogendorn. 'The Atlantic Slave Trade: a Tentative Economic Model.' *Journal of African History 15*, 2 (1974), 223–46.

'Technological Change, Slavery and the Slave Trade.' In Clive Dewey and A. G. Hopkins, eds., *The Imperial Impact* (London, 1978), 243–58.

, eds. *The Uncommon Market: Essays on the Economic History of the Atlantic Slave Trade*. New York, 1979.

'The Economic Costs of West African Participation in the Atlantic Slave Trade: a Preliminary Sampling for the Eighteenth Century.' In Henry A. Gemery and Jan S. Hogendorn, eds., *The Uncommon Market: Essays on the Economic History of the Atlantic Slave Trade* (New York, 1979), 143–62.

Gleason, Judith. *Agotime*. New York, 1969.

Glélé, Maurice A. *Naissance d'un état noir: l'évolution politique et constitutionnelle du Dahomey, de la colonisation à nos jours*. Paris, 1969.

Le Danxomẹ, du pouvoir aja à la nation fon. Paris, 1974.

Godelier, Maurice. *La Notion de mode de production asiatique et les schémas marxistes d'évolution des sociétés*. Paris, 1963.

Godfernaux, R. *Les Chemins de fer coloniaux français*, Paris, 1911.

Gosselin, G. *L'Afrique désenchantée: société et stratégie de transition en Afrique tropicale*. Paris, 1978.

Greenberg, Joseph. *The Languages of Africa*. Bloomington. 1966.

Grivot, R. 'L'Industrie du sel dans la subdivision de Grand-Popo.' *Notes africaines*, 21 (1944), 23–24.

'La Pêche chez les Pédah du Lac Ahémé.' *Bulletin de l'IFAN 11* (1949), 106–28.

Réactions dahoméennes. Paris, 1954.

Gruvel, A. *L'Industrie des pêches sur la côte occidentale d'Afrique*. Paris, 1913.

Guilcher, A. 'La Région côtière du Bas-Dahomey occidental.' *Bulletin de l'IFAN 21* (1959), 357–424.

Hair, P. E. H. 'The Enslavement of Koelle's Informants.' *Journal of African History 6*, 2 (1965), 193–203.

'Ethnolinguistic Continuity on the Guinea Coast.' *Journal of African History 8*, 2 (1967), 247–68.

The Atlantic Slave Trade and Black Africa. London, 1978.

Hardy, Georges, *Un Apôtre d'aujourd' hui: le révérend Père Aupiais*. Paris, 1949.

Hargreaves, John D. *Prelude to the Partition of West Africa*. London, 1963.

West Africa Partitioned. Madison, 1974.

Hazoumé, Guy Landry. *Idéologies tribalistes et nation en Afrique: le cas dahoméen*. Paris, 1972.

, and others. *La Vie et l'oeuvre de Louis Hunkanrin*. Cotonou, 1976.

Hazoumé, Paul. *Le Pacte de sang au Dahomey*. Paris, 1937.

Doguicimi. Paris, 1938.

Helleiner, G. K. *Peasant Agriculture, Government, and Economic Development in Nigeria, 1900–1960*. Homewood, Ill, 1966.

Henige, David, and Marion Johnson. 'Agaja and the Slave Trade: another Look at the Evidence.' *History in Africa 3* (1976), 57–68.

Henry, Yves. *Le Coton dans l'Afrique Occidentale Française*. Paris, 1906.

Le Caoutchouc dans l'Afrique Occidentale Française. Paris, 1907.

Le Maïs africain, culture et production au Dahomey. Paris, 1912.

Matières prémières africaines, vol. 1. Paris, 1918.

Henry, Yves, and Paul Amman. *Maïs, igname et patate*. Paris, 1913.

Herskovits, Melville J. *Dahomey: an Ancient West African Kingdom*, 2 vols. New York, 1938.

Herskovits, Melville J., and Frances S. Herskovits. *Dahomean Narrative*. Evanston, 1958.

Hervet, G. *Le Commerce extérieur de l'Afrique Occidentale Française*. Paris, 1911.

Heudebert, Lucien. *Promenades au Dahomey*. Paris, 1902.

Hiecke, E. *Zur Geschichte des deutschen Handels mit Ostafrika: Wm. O'Swald & Co., 1831–1870*. Hamburg, 1939.

G. L. Gaiser: Hamburg, Westafrika. Hamburg, 1958.

Higgins, Benjamin. *Economic Development*. New York, 1959.

Higman, B. W. 'African and Creole Family Patterns in Trinidad.' *Journal of Family History 3* (1978), 163–80.

Hill, Frances. 'Experiments with a Public Sector Peasantry: Agricultural Schemes and Class Formation in Africa.' *African Studies Review 20*, 3 (1977), 25–41.

Hill, Polly. Review of R. Szereszewski, *Structural Changes in the Economy of Ghana. Economic Development and Cultural Change 16*, 1 (1967), 131–7.

Studies in Rural Capitalism in West Africa. Cambridge 1970.

Hodder, B. W., and U. I. Ukwu. *Markets in West Africa*. Ibadan, 1969.

Hogendorn, Jan S. 'The Economics of Slave Use on Two "Plantations" in the Zaria Emirate of the Sokoto Caliphate.' *International Journal of African Historical Studies 10*, 3 (1977), 369–83.

Nigerian Groundnut Exports: Origins and Early Development. Oxford, 1977.

Hopkins, A. G. 'The Currency Revolution in South-West Nigeria in the Late Nineteenth Century.' *Journal of the Historical Society of Nigeria 3*, 3 (1966), 471–83.

'Economic Imperialism in West Africa: Lagos, 1880–92.' *Economic History Review 21* (1968), 580–606.

An Economic History of West Africa. London, 1973.

'Imperial Connections.' In Clive Dewey and A. G. Hopkins, eds., *The Imperial Impact: Studies in the Economic History of Africa and Asia* (London, 1978), 1–19.

Hubert, Henry. *Contribution à l'étude de la géographie physique du Dahomey*. Paris, 1908.

Huggins, Nathan I., Martin Kilson and Daniel M. Fox, eds. *Key Issues in the Afro-American Experience*. New York, 1971.

Hurault, Jean, and Jacques Vallet. *Mission d'étude des structures agraires dans le Sud-Dahomey*. Paris, 1963.

Inikori, J. E. 'Measuring the Atlantic Slave Trade: an Assessment of Curtin and Anstey.' *Journal of African History 17*, 2 (1976), 197–223.

'Measuring the Atlantic Slave Trade: a Rejoinder.' *Journal of African History 17*, 4 (1976), 607–27.

Institut de Recherches Appliquées du Dahomey. *Dictionnaire bio-bibliographique du Dahomey*. Porto-Novo, 1969.

International Bank for Reconstruction and Development. *World Bank Atlas*, 11th edn. Washington, 1976.

International Monetary Fund. *Surveys of African Economies, vol. 3.* Washington, 1970.

Jahn, Jahnheinz. *Muntu, an Outline of the New African Culture.* New York, 1961.

Jesel. 'Le Maïs au Dahomey.' *Etudes dahoméennes*, 8 (1952); 5–18.

Jewsiewicki, Bogumil. 'The Great Depression and the Making of the Colonial Economic System in the Belgian Congo.' *African Economic History*, 4 (1977), 153–76.

'Introduction.' Special issue of *African Economic History*, 7 (1979), 2–8.

Johnson, G. Wesley. *The Emergence of Black Politics in Senegal.* Stanford, 1971.

Johnson, Marion. 'The Ounce in Eighteenth-Century West African Trade.' *Journal of African History 7*, 2 (1966), 197–214.

'The Cowrie Currencies of West Africa, Part I.' *Journal of African History 11*, 1 (1970), 17–49.

'The Cowrie Currencies of West Africa, Part II.' *Journal of African History 11*, 2 (1970), 331–53.

'The Atlantic Slave Trade and the Economy of West Africa.' In Roger Anstey and P. E. H. Hair, eds., *Liverpool, the African Slave Trade, and Abolition* (Bristol, 1976), 14–38.

'Technology, Competition, and African Crafts.' In Clive Dewey and A. G. Hopkins, eds., *The Imperial Impact: Studies in the Economic History of Africa and India* (London, 1978), 259–69.

Johnson, Samuel. *The History of the Yorubas.* Lagos, 1937.

Johnston, Bruce F. *The Staple Food Economies of Western Tropical Africa.* Stanford, 1958.

Jones, William O. *Manioc in Africa.* Stanford, 1959.

Karl, Emmanuel. *Traditions orales au Dahomey–Bénin.* Niamey, 1974.

Kea, R. A. 'Firearms and Warfare on the Gold and Slave Coasts from the Sixteenth to the Nineteenth Centuries.' *Journal of African History 12*, 2 (1971), 185–213.

Ki Zerbo, J. 'L'Economie de traite en Afrique noire ou le pillage organisé (XVᵉ au XXᵉ siècle).' *Présence africaine*, 11 (1956–7), 7–31.

Kilson, Marion D. de B. 'West African Society and the Atlantic Slave Trade, 1441–1865.' In Nathan I. Huggins, Martin Kilson and Daniel M. Fox, eds., *Key Issues in the Afro-American Experience* (New York, 1971), 39–53.

Klein, Herbert S. *The Middle Passage.* Princeton, 1978.

Kopytoff, Jean Herskovits. *A Preface to Modern Nigeria: the 'Sierra Leonians' in Yoruba, 1830–1890.* Madison, 1965.

Kuczynski, Robert Rene. *Demographic Survey of the British Colonial Empire*, 3 vols. London, 1948.

Labat, Jean Baptiste. *Voyage du Chevalier des Marchais en Guinée, isles voisines, et à Cayenne fait en 1725, 1726 et 1727*, 4 vols. Paris, 1730.

Labouret, Henri, and Paul Rivet. *Le Royaume d'Arda et son évangélisation au XVIIᵉ siècle.* Paris, 1929.

Laffitte, l'Abbé J. *Le Dahomé: souvenirs de voyage et de mission.* Tours, 1873.

Bibliography

Lambinet, Col. E. *Notice géographique, topographique et statistique sur le Dahomey.* Paris, 1893.

Langley, J. Ayodele. *Pan-Africanism and Nationalism in West Africa, 1900–1945.* Oxford, 1973.

Latham, A. J. H. *Old Calabar, 1600–1891.* Oxford, 1973.
  'Price Fluctuations in the Early Palm Oil Trade.' *Journal of African History 19*, 2 (1978), 213–18.

Law, Robin. *The Oyo Empire, c. 1600–c. 1836.* Oxford, 1977.
  'Royal Monopoly and Private Enterprise in the Atlantic Trade: the Case of Dahomey.' *Journal of African History 18*, 4 (1977), 555–77.

Le Herissé, Auguste. *L'Ancien Royaume du Dahomey.* Paris, 1911.

Le Herissé, René. *Voyage au Dahomey et en Côte d'Ivoire.* Paris, 1903.

Leduc, Michel. *Les Institutions monétaires africaines, pays francophones.* Paris, 1965.

LeVeen, E. Phillip. *British Slave Trade Suppression Policies 1821–65.* New York, 1977.

Lloyd, Christopher. *The Navy and the Slave Trade.* London, 1968.

Lombard, Jacques. 'Cotonou, ville africaine.' *Bulletin de l'IFAN 16* (1954), 341–77.
  'Les Moyens de contrôle social dans l'ancien Dahomey: survivances actuelles et formes nouvelles.' *Le Monde non chrétien 38* (1956), 145–57.
  Structures de type 'féodal' en Afrique noire. Paris, 1965.
  Autorités traditionnelles et pouvoirs européens en Afrique noire. Paris, 1967.
  'Contribution à l'histoire d'une ancienne société politique au Dahomey: la royauté d'Allada.' *Bulletin de l'IFAN 29* (1967), 40–66.
  'The Kingdom of Dahomey.' In Daryll Forde and Phyllis M. Kaberry, eds., *West African Kingdoms in the Nineteenth Century* (London, 1967), 70–92.

Lovejoy, Paul E. 'Interregional Monetary Flows in the Precolonial Trade of Nigeria.' *Journal of African History 15*, 4 (1974), 563–86.
  'Plantations in the Economy of the Sokoto Caliphate.' *Journal of African History 19*, 3 (1978), 341–68.
  'The Economy of the Sokoto Caliphate.' *American Historical Review 84*, 5 (1979), 1267–92.

Lugard, Frederick D. *The Dual Mandate in British Tropical Africa.* London, 1922.

McPhee, Allan, *The Economic Revolution in British West Africa.* London, 1926.

Maldant, B., and M. Haubert. *Croissance et conjoncture dans l'économie de l'Ouest africain.* Paris, 1973.

Manning, Patrick. 'Some Export Statistics for Nigeria, 1880–1905.' *Nigerian Journal of Economic and Social Studies 9*, 2 (1967), 229–34.
  'Slaves, Palm Oil, and Political Power on the West African Coast.' *African Historical Studies 2*, 2 (1969), 279–88.
  'Notes toward a Theory of Ideology in Historical Writing on Modern Africa.' *Canadian Journal of African Studies 8*, 2 (1974), 235–53.
  'Un Document sur la fin de l'esclavage au Dahomey.' *Notes africaines, 147* (1975), 88–92.
  'The Economy of Early Colonial Dahomey.' In Joseph Smaldone, ed., *Explorations in Quantitative African History* (Syracuse, 1978), 25–52.

426

'The Slave Trade in the Bight of Benin, 1640–1890.' In Henry A. Gemery and Jan S. Hogendorn, eds., *The Uncommon Market: Essays on the Economic History of the Atlantic Slave Trade* (New York, 1979), 107–41.

'The Technology of Production in Southern Dahomey, c. 1900.' *African Economic History*, 9 (1980), 49–67.

Marty, Paul. *Etudes sur l'Islam au Dahomey.* Paris, 1926.

Marx, Karl. *Capital*, 3 vols. Moscow, 1971. (German edn first published 1867, English edn first published 1887.)

Mason, Michael. 'Captive and Client Labour and the Economy of the Bida Emirate, 1857–1901.' *Journal of African History 14*, 3 (1973), 453–72.

Mattoso, Katia M. De Queirós. 'Os Escravos na Bahia no Alvorecer do Século XIX (Estudo de un Grupo Social).' *Revista de História 47*, 97 (1974), 109–35.

Maupoil, Bernard. *La Géomancie à l'ancienne Côte des Esclaves.* Paris, 1943.

Meillassoux, Claude. 'Essai d'interpretation du phénomène économique dans les sociétés traditionnelles d'auto-subsistance.' *Cahiers d'Etudes africaines 1*, 4 (1960), 38–67.

——, ed. *The Development of Indigenous Trade and Markets in West Africa.* London, 1971.

Mensah, Moise. 'Problèmes du développement de l'agriculture dahoméenne.' *Etudes dahoméennes*, n.s. 1 (1963), 59–78.

Mercier, Paul. 'Notice sur le peuplement yorouba au Dahomey–Togo.' *Etudes dahoméennes*, 4 (1950), 29–40.

'Travail et service public dans l'ancien Dahomey.' *Présence africaine*, 13 (1952), 84–91.

Cartes ethno-démographiques de l'Ouest africain, Feuilles n° 5. Dakar, 1954.

'The Fon of Dahomey.' In Daryll Forde, ed., *African Worlds* (London, 1954), 210–34.

Tradition, changement, histoire: les 'Somba' du Dahomey septentrional. Paris, 1968.

Mettas, Jean. *Répertoire des expéditions négrières françaises au XVIIIe siècle*, edited by Serge Daget. Paris, 1979.

Meyerowitz, Eva. *The Early History of the Akan States of Ghana.* London, 1974.

Miller, Joseph C. 'Legal Portuguese Slaving from Angola: some Preliminary Indications of Volume and Direction.' *Revue française d'Histoire d'Outre-mer 62*, 226–7 (1975), 135–76.

Miracle, Marvin P. *Maize in Tropical Africa.* Madison, 1966.

Miracle, Marvin P., and Bruce Fetter. 'Backward-Sloping Labor Supply Functions and African Economic Behavior.' *Economic Development and Cultural Change 18* (1970), 240–51.

Mondjannagni, Alfred. 'Quelques aspects historiques, économiques et politiques de la frontière Dahomey–Nigéria.' *Etudes dahoméennes* n.s. 1 (1963), 17–57.

Campagnes et villes au sud de la République Populaire du Bénin. Paris, 1977.

Morel, Alain. 'Un Exemple d'urbanisation en Afrique occidentale: Dassa Zoumé (Dahomey).' *Cahiers d'Etudes africaines 14*, 56 (1974), 727–48.

Morgenthau, Ruth Schacter. *Political Parties in French-Speaking West Africa.* Oxford, 1964.

Morton-Williams, Peter. 'The Oyo Yoruba and the Atlantic Trade, 1670–1830.' *Journal of the Historical Society of Nigeria 3*, 1 (1964), 25–46.

Moseley, Katharine P. 'The Political Economy of Dahomey.' *Research in Economic Anthropology 2* (1979), 69–90.

Mouléro, Th. 'Histoire des Wémènous ou Dékammènous.' *Etudes dahoméennes*, n.s. 3 (1964), 51–76.

'Histoire et légendes des Djèkens.' *Etudes dahoméennes*, n.s. 8 (1966), 39–56.

Murdock, G. P. *Africa, its Peoples and their Culture History.* New York, 1959.

Nardin, Jean-Claude. 'La Reprise des relations franco-dahoméennes au XIXᵉ siècle: la mission d'Auguste Bouët à la cour d'Abomey (1851).' *Cahiers d'Etudes africaines 7*, 25 (1967), 59–126.

Newbury, C. W. 'A Note on the Abomey Protectorate.' *Africa 29*, 2 (1959), 146–55.

'An Early Inquiry into Slavery and Captivity in Dahomey.' *Zaire 14*, 1 (1960), 53–67.

'The Formation of the Government General of French West Africa.' *Journal of African History 1*, 1 (1960), 111–28.

The Western Slave Coast and its Rulers. Oxford, 1961.

'Trade and Authority in West Africa from 1850 to 1880.' In L. H. Gann and Peter Duignan, eds., *Colonialism in Africa, vol. 1* (Cambridge, 1969), 66–99.

'Prices and Profitability in Early Nineteenth-Century West African Trade.' In Claude Meillassoux, ed., *The Development of Indigenous Trade and Markets in West Africa* (London, 1971), 91–106.

'Credit in Early Nineteenth-Century West African Trade.' *Journal of African History 13*, 1 (1972), 81–95.

Norris, Robert. *Memoirs of the Reign of Bossa Ahádee, King of Dahomy.* London, 1968. (First published 1789.)

Northrup, David. *Trade Without Rulers: Pre-Colonial Economic Development in South-Eastern Nigeria.* Oxford, 1978.

Obichere, Boniface I. *West African States and European Expansion: the Dahomey–Niger Hinterland, 1885–1898.* New Haven, 1971.

'Women and Slavery in the Kingdom of Dahomey.' *Revue française d'Histoire d'Outre-mer 64*, 238 (1978), 5–20.

Officiers de l'Etat-Major du Corps expéditionnaire du Bénin, les. *Notice géographique, topographique et statistique sur le Dahomey.* Paris, 1894.

Palau Marti, Montserrat. 'Notes sur les Rois de Dasa (Dahomey).' *Journal de la Société des Africanistes 27*, 2 (1957), 197–209.

Le Roi–dieu au Bénin. Paris, 1964.

Parrinder, Geoffrey. 'Yoruba-speaking Peoples in Dahomey.' *Africa 17*, 2 (1947), 122–9.

The Story of Ketu, an Ancient Yoruba Kingdom. Ibadan, 1956.

Patterson, K. David. 'A Note on Slave Exports from the Costa da Mina, 1760–1770.' *Bulletin de l'IFAN 33* (1971), 249–56.

Pauvert, Jean-Claude. 'L'Evolution politique des Ewé.' *Cahiers d'Etudes africaines 1*, 2 (1960), 161–92.

Pécaud, G. *L'Elévage et les animaux domestiques au Dahomey.* Gorée, 1912.

Pélissier, Paul. *Les Pays du Bas-Ouémé, un région témoin du Dahomey méridional.* Dakar, 1963.

Person, Yves. 'Dauma et Danhomè.' *Journal of African History 15,* 4 (1974), 547–61.

'Chronologie du royaume gun de Hogbonou (Porto-Novo).' *Cahiers d'Etudes africaines 15,* 58 (1975), 217–38.

'La Toponymie ancienne de la côte entre la Volta et Lagos.' *Cahiers d'Etudes africaines 15,* 60 (1975), 715–22.

Peukert, Werner. *Der Atlantische Sklavenhandel von Dahomey, 1740–1797.* Wiesbaden, 1978.

Pires, Vicente Ferreira. *Crônica de uma Embaixada luso-brasileira à Costa d'Africa em Fins do Século XVIII, incluindo o Texto da Viagem de Africa em o Reino de Dahomé.* São Paulo, 1957.

Polanyi, Karl. 'Sortings and "ounce trade" in the West African Slave Trade.' *Journal of African History 5,* 3 (1964), 381–94.

Polanyi, Karl, with Abraham Rotstein. *Dahomey and the Slave Trade, an Analysis of an Archaic Economy.* Seattle, 1966.

Polanyi, Karl, Conrad M. Arensberg and Harry W. Pearson. *Trade and Market in the Early Empires.* New York, 1957.

Poquin, Jean-Jacques. *Les Relations économiques extérieures des pays d'Afrique noire de l'union française, 1925–1955.* Paris, 1957.

Postma, Johannes. 'The Dimension of the Dutch Slave Trade from Western Africa.' *Journal of African History 13,* 2 (1972), 237–48.

Pryor, Frederic. *The Origins of the Economy.* New York, 1977.

Quénum, Maximilien. *Au pays des Fons.* Paris, 1938.

Rabut, Elisabeth. 'Le Mythe parisien de la mise en valeur des colonies françaises à l'aube du XXe siècle: la commission des concessions coloniales 1898–1902.' *Journal of African History 20,* (1979), 271–87.

Rancoule, A. *Le Palmier à huile au Dahomey.* Porto-Novo, 1943.

Randles, W. G. L. 'La Civilisation bantou, son essor et son declin.' *Annales – Economies, Sociétés, Civilisations 29,* 2 (1974), 267–81.

Reefe, Thomas Q. 'Traditions of Genesis and the Luba Diaspora.' *History in Africa 4* (1977), 183–206.

Régis, Jean-F. *Les Régis au Dahomey, un centenaire familial.* Marseille, 1941.

Reste, J.-F. *Le Dahomey, réalisations et perspectives d'avenir.* Paris, 1934.

Rey, Pierre-Philippe. *Colonialisme, néo-colonialisme et transition au capitalisme: exemple de la 'Comilog' au Congo–Brazzaville.* Paris, 1971.

Les Alliances des classes. Paris, 1973.

Reynolds, Edward. *Trade and Economic Change on the Gold Coast, 1807–1874.* London, 1974.

Rodney, Walter. 'African Slavery and Other Forms of Social Oppression on the Upper Guinea Coast.' *Journal of African History 7,* 3 (1966), 431–43.

How Europe Underdeveloped Africa. London, 1972.

Ronen, Dov. 'On the African Role in the Trans-Atlantic Slave Trade in Dahomey.' *Cahiers d'Etudes africaines 11,* 41 (1971), 5–13.

'The Colonial Elite in Dahomey.' *African Studies Review 17*, 1 (1974), 55–76.
Dahomey: between Tradition and Modernity. Ithaca, 1975.

Ross, David A. 'The Career of Domingo Martinez in the Bight of Benin, 1833–1864.' *Journal of African History 6*, 1 (1965), 79–90.

'Dahomey.' In Michael Crowder, ed., *West African Resistance* (London, 1971), 144–69.

Rousseau, J.-J. *The Social Contract*. London, 1968. (First published 1762.)

Roussier, Paul. *L'Etablissement d'Issiny, 1687–1702*. Paris, 1935.

Russell-Wood, A. J. R. 'Technology and Society: the Impact of Gold Mining on the Institution of Slavery in Portuguese America.' *Journal of Economic History 37*, 1 (1977), 59–83.

Ryder, A. F. C. 'The Re-establishment of Portuguese Factories on the Costa da Mina to the Mid-Eighteenth Century.' *Journal of the Historical Society of Nigeria 1*, 3 (1958), 157–83.

'Dutch Trade on the Nigerian Coast During the Seventeenth Century.' *Journal of the Historical Society of Nigeria 3*, 2 (1965), 195–210.

Benin and the Europeans, 1485–1897. London, 1969.

Sarraut, Albert. *La Mise en valeur des colonies françaises*. Paris, 1923.

Savariau, N. *L'Agriculture au Dahomey*. Paris, 1906.

'Le Kolatier au Dahomey.' *Journal officiel du Dahomey 15* (1906), 346–50.

Schnapper, Bernard. *La Politique et le commerce français dans le golfe de Guinée de 1838 à 1871*. Paris, 1961.

Schwartz, Stuart B. 'The Manumission of Slaves in Colonial Brazil: Bahia, 1684–1745.' *Hispanic American Historical Review 54*, 4 (1974), 603–35.

Segurola, B. *Dictionnaire fõ-français*, 2 vols. Cotonou, 1963.

Shòn, J. F., and Samuel Crowther. *Journals of the Rev. James Frederick Shön and Mr. Samuel Crowther*, 2nd edn. London, 1970.

Skertchly, J. A. *Dahomey as it is*. London, 1874.

Smith, Alan K., and Claude E. Welch, Jr., eds. 'Peasants in Africa.' Special issue of *African Studies Review 20*, 3 (1977).

Smith, Robert. *Kingdoms of the Yoruba*, 2nd edn. London, 1976.

Smith, William. *A New Voyage to Guinea*. London, 1745.

Snelgrave, Capt. William. *A New Account of Guinea and the Slave-Trade*. London, 1754.

Southworth, Constant. *The French Colonial Venture*. London, 1931.

Staniland, Martin. 'The Three-Party System in Dahomey. I:1946–56.' *Journal of African History 14*, 2 (1973), 291–312.

'The Three-Party System in Dahomey. II:1956–57.' *Journal of African History 14*, 3 (1973), 491–504.

Stein, Robert Louis. *The French Slave Trade in the Eighteenth Century: an Old Regime Business*. Madison, 1979.

Suret-Canale, Jean. *Afrique Noire, équatoriale et centrale. Vol. 2: L'Ere coloniale, 1900–1945* (Paris, 1964).

'Un Pionnier méconnu du mouvement démocratique et national en Afrique.' *Etudes dahoméennes*, n.s. 3 (1964), 5–30.

430

'Les Sociétés traditionnelles en Afrique noire et le concept du mode de production asiatique.' *La Pensée*, 177 (1964), 19–42.

'L'Internationale communiste et la lutte contre le colonialisme.' *Cahiers de l'Institut Maurice Thorez* 13 (1969). 65–77.

Afrique Noire, équatoriale et centrale. Vol. 3, Part 1: De la colonisation aux indépendances, 1945–1960. Paris, 1977.

'La Grève des cheminots africains d'AOF (1947–1948).' *Cahiers d'Histoire de l'Institut Maurice Thorez*, 28 (1978), 82–122.

Szereszewski, R. *Structural Changes in the Economy of Ghana, 1891–1911.* London, 1965.

Tambo, David C. 'The Sokoto Caliphate Slave Trade in the Nineteenth Century.' *International Journal of African Historical Studies 9*, 2 (1976), 187–217.

Tardits, Claude. 'Enquête sociologique sur la Population de la Palmeraie.' In Joseph Clerc, P. Adam and C. Tardits, eds., *Société paysanne et problèmes fonciers de la palmeraie dahoméenne* (Paris, 1956), 9–58.

'Enquête sur le droit foncier des pays gun et fon.' In Joseph Clerc, P. Adam and C. Tardits, eds., *Société paysanne et problèmes fonciers de la palmeraie dahoméenne* (Paris, 1956), 59–71.

Porto-Novo: les nouvelles générations africaines entre leurs traditions et l'occident. Paris, 1958.

'Développement du régime d'appropriation privée des terres de la palmeraie du Sud-Dahomey.' In Daniel Biebuyck, ed., *African Agrarian Systems* (London, 1963), 297–313.

'Parenté et classe sociale à Porto-Novo, Dahomey.' In P. C. Lloyd, ed., *The New Elites of Tropical Africa* (London, 1978), 184–98.

Tardits, Claude, and Claudine Tardits. 'Traditional Market Economy in South Dahomey.' In Paul Bohannan and George Dalton, eds., *Markets in Africa* (Evanston, 1962), 89–102.

Taylor, John G. *From Modernization to Modes of Production.* London, 1979.

Tereau, Lt.-Col. Médecin, and Dr. Huttel. 'Monographie du Hollidgé.' *Etudes dahoméennes*, 2 (1949), 59–72; 3 (1950), 7–37.

Terray, Emmanuel. *Le Marxisme devant les sociétés 'primitives.'* Paris, 1968.

Tevoedjre, Albert. *L'Afrique révoltée.* Paris, 1958.

Thomas, Robert Paul, and Richard Nelson Bean. 'The Fishers of Men: the Profits of the Slave Trade.' *Journal of Economic History 34*, 4 (1974), 885–914.

Thompson, E. P. *The Making of the English Working Class.* Harmondsworth. 1965.

Thompson, Virginia. 'Dahomey.' In Gwendolen M. Carter, ed., *Five African States: Responses to Diversity* (Ithaca, 1963), 161–262.

Thompson, Virginia, and Richard Adloff. *French West Africa.* Stanford, 1967.

Tidjani, A. Serpos. 'Calendrier agraire et réligieux au Bas-Dahomey.' *Première Conférence internationale des Africanistes de l'Ouest, Comptes rendus* (Dakar, 1951) II:290–8.

Toutée, Comdt. *Dahomey, Niger, Touareg.* Paris, 1897.

Du Dahomey au Sahara. Paris, 1899.

Bibliography

Trautmann, René. *La Divination à la Côte des Esclaves et à Madagascar*. Paris, 1940.
  La Littérature populaire à la Côte des Esclaves. Paris, 1927.
Uzoigwe, G. N. 'The Slave Trade and African Societies.' *Transactions of the Historical Society of Ghana 14*, 2 (1973), 187–212.
van Dantzig, Albert. 'Effects of the Atlantic Slave Trade on some West African Societies.' *Revue française d'Histoire d'Outre-mer 62*, 226–7 (1975), 252–69.
Vansina, Jan. 'Traditions of Genesis.' *Journal of African History 15*, 2 (1974).
Vengroff, Richard. 'Population Density and State Formation in Africa.' *African Studies Review 19*, 1 (1976), 67–74.
Verger, Pierre. 'Influence du Brésil au golfe du Bénin.' In Théodore Monod, ed., *Les Afro-américains* (Dakar, 1953), 11–101.
  'Le Culte des Vodoun d'Abomey aurait-il été apporté à St.-Louis de Maranhon par la mère du roi Ghézo? *Etudes dahoméennes*, 8 (1952), 19–24.
  Dieux d'Afrique. Paris, 1954.
  Notes sur le culte des Orisa et Vodun. Dakar, 1957.
  'Rôle joué par le tabac de Bahia dans la traite des esclaves au golfe du Bénin.' *Cahiers d'Etudes africaines 4*, 15 (1964), 349–69.
  'Le Fort portugais de Ouidah (première partie).' *Etudes dahoméennes*, n.s. 4 (1965), 5–50.
  'Le Fort portugais de Ouidah (seconde partie).' *Etudes dahoméennes*, n.s. 5 (1965), 5–50.
  'Le fort portugais de Ouidah (troisième partie).' *Etudes dahoméennes*, n.s. 6–7 (1966), 5–46.
  'Retour des "brésiliens" au golfe du Bénin au XIXe siècle.' *Etudes dahoméennes*, n.s. 8 (1966), 5–28.
  'Mouvement de navires entre Bahia et le golfe de Bénin (XVII–XIX siècles).' *Revue française d'Histoire d'Outre-mer 55* (1968), 1–36.
  Flux et reflux de la traite des nègres entre le golfe du Bénin et Bahia de Todos os Santos du 17e et 18e siècles. The Hague, 1968.
  'Les Côtes d'Afrique occidentale entre Rio Volta et Rio Lagos, 1535–1773.' *Journal de la Société des Africanistes 38*, 1 (1968), 35–58.
Viard, *Histoire du Wharf de Cotonou*. Paris, 1893.
Wade, Abdoulaye. *Economie de l'Ouest africain*. Paris, 1959.
Waldman, Loren K. 'An Unnoticed Aspect of Archibald Dalzel's *The History of Dahomey* [sic].' *Journal of African History 6*, 2 (1965), 185–92.
Wallerstein, Immanuel. *The Modern World-System: Capitalist Agriculture and the Origins of the European World-Economy in the Sixteenth Century*. New York, 1974.
Walras, Léon. *Eléments d'économie politique pure*. Paris, 1977.
Wilks, Ivor. 'The Mossi and Akan States, 1500–1800.' In J. F. A. Ajayi and M. Crowder, eds., *History of West Africa* (London, 1971), 1:344–86.
Williams, Eric. *Capitalism and Slavery*. London, 1944.
Wolf, Eric. *Peasants*. Englewood Cliffs, N. J., 1966.
Wrigley, C. C. 'Historicism in Africa: Slavery and State Formation.' *African Affairs 80*, 279 (1971), 113–24.
Wrigley, E. H. *Population and History*. New York, 1969.

432

Yoder, John C. 'Fly and Elephant Parties: Political Polarization in Dahomey, 1840–70.' *Journal of African History 15*, 3 (1974), 417–32.
Zimmer, Balduin. *Dahomey*. Bonn, 1969.
Zinsou-Derlin, Lionel. 'La Banque de l'Afrique Occidentale dans la crise.' *Revue française d'Histoire d'Outre-mer 63*, 232–3 (1976), 506–18.
Zolberg, Aristide. *One-Party government in the Ivory Coast*. Princeton, 1964.

IV. Unpublished theses and dissertations

Agiri, Babatunde Aremu. 'Kola in Western Nigeria, 1850–1950.' PhD dissertation, University of Wisconsin-Madison, 1972.
Agossou, Koovi Pierre. 'L'Installation de l'administration française dans le Sud du Dahomey de 1880 à 1894.' Mémoire de maîtrise, University of Dakar, 1970.
Alladaye, Jerôme Comlan. 'Les Missionaires catholiques du Dahomey à l'époque coloniale: 1905–1957.' Thèse de 3ᵉ cycle, University of Paris VII, 1978.
Allioza, Lin Richard. 'Le Commerce entre Marseille et le Dahomey de 1866 à 1900.' Mémoire, University of Aix-en-Provence, 1970.
Almeida, Damien d'. 'Fonctionnaires et autres salariés dahoméens hors du Dahomey: un malaise social. Le cas ivoirien, 1945–1958.' Thèse de doctorat d'université, University of Paris I, 1974.
Almeida-Topor, Hélène d'. 'Histoire économique du Dahomey, 1890–1920.' Thèse d'état, University of Paris IV, 1981.
Amoussou, Cocou. 'Les Travailleurs de chemin de fer au Dahomey sous la colonisation des origines à 1952.' Thèse de 3ᵉ cycle, University of Paris VII, 1977.
Anignikin, Sylvain C. 'Les Origines du mouvement national au Dahomey, 1900–1939.' Thèse de 3ᵉ cycle, University of Paris VII, 1980.
Bay, Edna G. 'The Royal Women of Abomey.' PhD dissertation, Boston University, 1977.
Buhler, Peter. 'The Volta Region of Ghana: Economic Change in Togoland, 1850–1914.' PhD dissertation, University of California, San Diego, 1975.
Challenor, Herschelle Sandra. 'French Speaking West Africa's Dahomeyan Strangers in Colonization and Decolonization.' PhD dissertation, Columbia University, 1970.
Codo, Bellarmin Cofi. 'La Presse dahoméenne face aux aspirations des "évolués": "La Voix du Dahomey" (1927–57).' Thèse de 3ᵉ cycle, University of Paris VII, 1978.
Diamond, Stanley. 'Dahomey: A Proto-state in West Africa.' PhD dissertation, Columbia University, 1951.
Djivo, Joseph Adrien. 'Gbehanzin et Ago-Li-Agbo, le refus de la colonisation dans l'ancien Royaume de Danxome: 1875–1900 (fin de la monarchie).' Thèse d'état, University of Paris I, 1979.
Garcia, Luc. 'La Genèse de l'administration française au Dahomey, 1894–1920.' Thèse de 3ᵉ cycle, University of Paris, 1969.
Goerg Odile. 'Le Dahomey, 1918–1938: de la convention du Niger à l'assimilation douanière.' Mémoire de maîtrise, University of Paris I, 1976.

Hopkins, A. G. 'An Economic History of Lagos, 1880–1914.' PhD dissertation, University of London, 1964.

Huannou, Adrien. 'Histoire de la littérature écrite de langue française dans l'ex-Dahomey (des origines à 1972).' Thèse d'état, University of Paris XIII, 1979.

Katz, Naomi. 'The Kingdom of Dahomey: Political Organization and Ecological Relations in a Slave-Trading State.' PhD dissertation, University of California, Los Angeles, 1967.

La Torre, Joseph R. 'Wealth Surpasses Everything: an Economic History of Asante, 1750–1874.' PhD dissertation, University of California, Berkeley, 1978.

Lokossou, Clément Koudessa. 'La Presse au Dahomey, 1894–1960: évolution et réaction face à l'administration coloniale.' Thèse de 3e cycle, University of Paris, 1976.

Maroukis, Thomas C. 'Warfare and Society in the Kingdom of Dahomey, 1818–1894.' PhD dissertation, Boston University, 1974.

Moseley, Katharine Payne. 'Indigenous and External Factors in Colonial Politics: Southern Dahomey to 1939.' PhD dissertation, Columbia University, 1975.

Pinçon, René Georges. 'L'Intégration du protectorat de Porto-Novo à la colonie du Dahomey, 1880–1914.' Thèse de 3e cycle. University of Paris VII, 1978.

Ross, David A. 'The Autonomous Kingdom of Dahomey, 1818–94.' PhD dissertation, University of London, 1967.

Ryan, T. C. I. 'The Economics of Trading in Slaves.' PhD dissertation, Massachusetts Institute of Technology, 1975.

Senkomango, N. S. 'The Kingdom of Porto-Novo, with Special Reference to its External Relations, 1862–1908.' PhD dissertation, University of Aberdeen, 1978.

Spiegler, James S. 'Aspects of Nationalist Thought Among French-Speaking West Africans, 1921–1939.' PhD dissertation, Nuffield College, Oxford University, 1968.

Turner, J. Michael. 'Les Bresiliens: the Impact of former Brazilian Slaves upon Dahomey.' PhD dissertation, Boston University, 1975.

Index

442